FOURTH EDITION

A BRIEF HISTORY OF WESTERN CIVILIZATION

THE UNFINISHED LEGACY

VOLUME II: SINCE 1555

MARK KISHLANSKY
Harvard University

PATRICK GEARY
University of California, Los Angeles

PATRICIA O'BRIEN
University of California, Riverside

New York San Francisco Boston
London Toronto Sydney Tokyo Singapore Madrid
Mexico City Munich Paris Cape Town Hong Kong Montreal

Vice President and Publisher: Priscilla McGeehon
Acquisitions Editor: Erika Gutierrez
Development Manager: Lisa Pinto
Development Editor: Nancy Crochiere
Executive Marketing Manager: Sue Westmoreland
Supplements Editor: Kristi Olson
Media Editor: Patrick McCarthy
Production Manager: Donna DeBenedictis
Project Coordination, Text Design, and Electronic Page Makeup: Elm Street Publishing Services, Inc.
Cover Design Manager: Wendy Ann Fredericks
Cover Designer: Joel Zimmerman
Cover Image: Detail from *Christmas Shopping*, by Eugene Laloue (1854–1941). Collection of Adam Levene, Albourne, Great Britain/Fine Art Photographic Library, London/Art Resource, NY.
Photo Researcher: Photosearch, Inc.
Manufacturing Buyer: Lucy Hebard
Printer and Binder: Quebecor World Dubuque
Cover Printer: Coral Graphic Services, Inc.

For permission to use copyrighted material, grateful acknowledgment is made to the copyright holders on pp. C-1–C-2, which are hereby made part of this copyright page.

Library of Congress Cataloging-in-Publication Data
Kishlansky, Mark A.
A brief history of Western civilization: the unfinished legacy / Mark Kishlansky, Patrick Geary, Patricia O'Brien.—4th ed.
p. cm.
Includes bibliographical references and index.
ISBN 0-321-19675-9 (complete ed.)—ISBN 0-321-19676-7 (v. 1)—ISBN 0-321-19677-5 (v. 2)
1. Civilization, Western—History. I. Geary, Patrick J., 1948– II. O'Brien, Patricia, 1945– III. Title.

CB245.C545 2005
909' .09821—dc22 2003022063

Please visit our website at http://www.ablongman.com/kishlansky

ISBN 0-321-19675-9 (Complete Edition)
ISBN 0-321-19676-7 (Volume I)
ISBN 0-321-19677-5 (Volume II)

1 2 3 4 5 6 7 8 9 10—QWD—07 06 05 04

BRIEF CONTENTS

DETAILED CONTENTS

CHAPTER 21
INDUSTRIAL EUROPE 420

CHAPTER 22
POLITICAL UPHEAVALS AND SOCIAL TRANSFORMATIONS, 1815–1850 440

CHAPTER 23
STATE BUILDING AND SOCIAL CHANGE IN EUROPE, 1850–1871 464

CHAPTER 24
THE CRISIS OF EUROPEAN CULTURE, 1871–1914 480

MAPS AND GEOGRAPHICAL TOURS

CHRONOLOGIES, GENEALOGIES, AND FIGURES

DOCUMENTS

PREFACE

When we set out to write *Civilization in the West,* we tried to write, first of all, a book that students would *want* to read. Throughout many years of planning, writing, revising, rewriting, and numerous meetings together, this was our constant overriding concern. Would the text work across the variety of Western civilization courses, with the different levels and formats that make up this fundamental course? We also solicited the reactions of scores of reviewers to this single question: "Would students *want* to read these chapters?" Whenever we received a resounding "No!" we began again—not just rewriting, but rethinking how to present material that might be complex in argument or detail or that might simply seem too remote to engage the contemporary student. Though all three of us were putting in long hours in front of word processors, we quickly learned that we were engaged in a teaching rather than a writing exercise. And though the work was demanding, it was not unrewarding. We enjoyed writing this book, and we wanted students to enjoy reading it. We have been gratified to learn that our book successfully accomplished our objectives. It stimulated student interest and motivated students to want to learn about European history. *Civilization in the West* was successful beyond our expectations.

The text has been so well received, in fact, that we decided to publish this alternative, brief version: *A Brief History of Western Civilization: The Unfinished Legacy.* In an era of rapidly changing educational materials, alternative formats and models should be available. We believe that students and general readers alike will enjoy a conveniently sized book that offers them a coherent, well-told story. In this edition of the brief text, we have increased the size of many of the full-color maps and photographs so that they are easier to see and use. We have also added 10 new excerpts from primary source documents to give students a feel for the concreteness of the past, and we have replaced several of the chapter-opening "Visual Record" narratives.

APPROACH

The approach used in *A Brief History of Western Civilization: The Unfinished Legacy,* Fourth Edition, upholds and confirms a number of decisions made early in the writing of *Civilization in the West.* First, this brief, alternative version is, like the full-length text, a mainstream text in which most energies have been placed in developing a solid, readable narrative of Western civilization that integrates coverage of women and minorities into the discussion. We highlight personalities while identifying trends. We spotlight social history, both in sections of chapters and in separate chapters, while maintaining a firm grip on political developments.

Neither *A Brief History of Western Civilization: The Unfinished Legacy* nor *Civilization in the West* is meant to be an encyclopedia of Western civilization. Information is not included in a chapter unless it fits within the themes of that chapter. In both the full-length and brief versions of this text, we are committed to integrating the history of ordinary men and women into our narrative. We believe that isolated sections placed at the end of chapters that deal with the experiences of women or minority groups in a particular era profoundly distort historical experience. We call this technique "cabоosing," and whenever we found ourselves segregating women or families or the masses, we stepped back and asked how we might recast our treatment of historical events to account for a diversity of actors. How did ordinary men, women, and children affect the course of world historical events? How did world historical events affect the fabric of daily life for men, women, and children from all walks of life? We tried to rethink critical historical problems of civilization as gendered phenomena.

CHAPTER 21

INDUSTRIAL EUROPE

- THE VISUAL RECORD: An Iron Forge
- THE TRADITIONAL ECONOMY
- THE INDUSTRIAL REVOLUTION IN BRITAIN
- THE INDUSTRIALIZATION OF THE CONTINENT

THE VISUAL RECORD

AN IRON FORGE

THE KEY TO INDUSTRIALIZATION was the replacement of muscle with machine. This demanded ingenuity on the part of inventors, capital on the part of investors, and adaptability on the part of workers.

that almost resembles a nativity scene except that the birth being celebrated is the machine forging of iron, the miracle product of the age.

Joseph Wright of Derby was born and bred in the English Midlands where the Industrial Revolution first began. He was fascinated by the scientific developments of his age and specialized in paintings that were technically accurate. *An Iron Forge* was one of a number of industrial scenes that Wright painted in the 1770s when advances in technology were changing the face of rural

had previously been associated with smithing. Indeed, of the three workmen in the picture, only one is actually laboring and he is simply holding the tongs which keeps the iron in place. It is the machine that labors—the drum turning, the cam lifting, the hammer falling—and the people who benefit—proud parents, healthy and happy children. All are the product, the artist seems to be saying, of the new industrialization.

LOOKING AHEAD

As this chapter will discuss, industrialization began in Great Britain around forges like the one portrayed by Joseph Wright. It was the result of changes in agricultural practices that allowed for a larger population to be supported by fewer farmers. It was powered first by coal and its use in the production of iron

We take the same approach to the coverage of central and eastern Europe that we did to women and minorities. Even before the epochal events of the late 1980s and early 1990s that returned this region to the forefront of international attention, we realized that many textbooks treated the Slavic world as marginal to the history of Western civilization. Therefore, we worked to integrate more of the history of eastern Europe into our text than is found in most others and to do so in a way that presented these regions, their cultures, and their institutions as integral rather than peripheral to Western civilization.

FEATURES

In *A Brief History of Western Civilization: The Unfinished Legacy*, we wanted to reuse the features that had the most immediate and positive impact on our readers and fulfill our goal of involving students in learning. Therefore, this edition features the following:

The Visual Record: Pictorial Chapter Openers

In these pictorial chapter openers, an illustration—a painting, a photograph, an artifact, or an edifice—appears at the beginning of each chapter, accompanied by text through which we explore the picture, guiding students across a canvas or helping them to see in an artifact or a piece of architecture details that are not immediately apparent. It is the direct combination of text and image that allows us to achieve this effect, to "unfold" both an illustration and a theme. All of the opening images have been chosen to illustrate a dominant theme within the chapter, and the dramatic and lingering impression they make helps to reinforce that theme. A new section at the end of each essay called *Looking Ahead* provides a brief overview of chapter coverage and further strengthens the connection between the subject of the opener and the major topics and themes of the chapter.

Geographical Tours of Europe

A Brief History of Western Civilization: The Unfinished Legacy continues the image-based approach to the presentation of geography used in *Civilization in the West.* When teachers of Western civilization courses are surveyed, no single area of need is cited more often than geographical knowledge. Many American students have no mental image of Europe, no familiarity with those geophysical features that are a fundamental

Christian Institutions. As the number of Christians increased in the face of persecution, the organization and teaching of this new faith began to evolve. A hierarchy developed within the various communities that Paul and the other apostles established. The leader of each community was the bishop, an office derived from the priestly leader of the Jewish synagogue, who was responsible for both charity and the Torah. Assisted by *presbyters* (priests), deacons, and deaconesses, bishops assumed growing responsibilities as expectations for the second coming receded. These respon-

damental role in the transformation of the Roman world would not become clear until the third and fourth centuries.

GEOGRAPHICAL TOUR

A Tour of the Empire

Each town in the sprawling empire, from York in the north of Britain to Dura Europus on the Euphrates, was a center

▼ Map A. The Roman Empire at the Time of Hadrian. Hadrian's empire was a well-ordered world of provinces governed by a vast bureaucracy and held together by a common culture and the power of the imperial army.

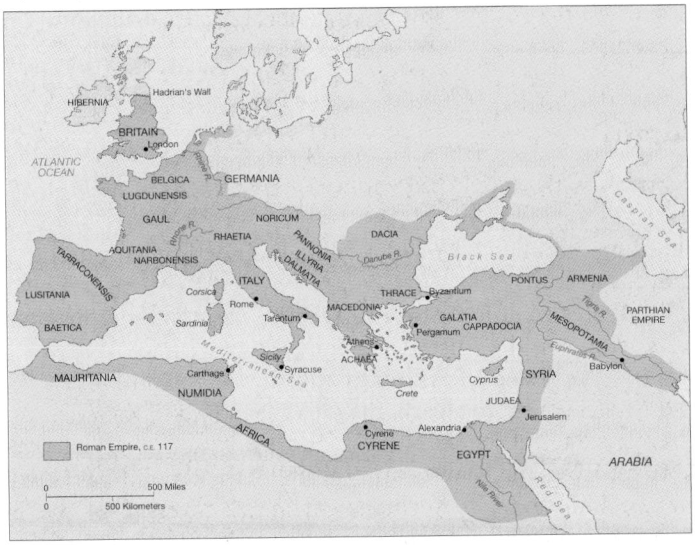

part of the geopolitical realities of Western history. Maps, carefully planned and skillfully executed, are an important component of our text.

To complement the standard map program of the text, we have added a special geographical feature, the "Geographical Tour of Europe." Six times throughout the book, we pause in the narrative to take a tour of Europe. Sometimes we follow an emperor as he tours his realm; sometimes we examine the impact of a peace treaty; sometimes we follow the travels of a merchant. Whatever the thematic occasion, our intention is to guide students around the changing contours of the geography of Western history. In order to do this effectively, we include several small, detailed maps to complement the overview map that appears at the beginning of each tour section. Using small maps allows us to integrate maps directly into the relevant text so that they are easy to locate and immediately available as the students follow the "tour." In addition, in this fourth edition, we have added specific in-text references to direct students to the corresponding map at key points in the narrative. The number of maps throughout the text, the specially designed tour-of-Europe geographical feature, and the ancillary program of map transparencies and workbook exercises combine to provide the strongest possible program for teaching historical geography.

DISCOVERING WESTERN CIVILIZATION ONLINE

You can obtain more information about Europe and the world between 1870 and 1914 at the websites listed below. See also the companion website that accompanies this text: www.ablongman.com/kishlansky, which contains an online study guide and additional resources.

The European Balance of Power, 1870–1914

www.fordham.edu/halsall/mod/modsbook38.html
This site is part of a larger site on World War I primary and secondary sources, but it contains a section on the developments among the great powers from the 1870s to 1914.

The New Imperialism

www.fordham.edu/halsall/mod/modsbook34.html
A comprehensive site of links arranged by continent to primary source materials and bibliographies on imperialism.

The European Search for Territory and Markets

www.hum.port.ac.uk/slas/francophone/bibliographies.htm
A collection of bibliographies on the partition of Africa and the impact of colonization in Africa.

www.geocities.com/Vienna/5048/TREATY01.html
This site is devoted to the treaties that gave foreign governments access to political and commercial power in China.

www.chinaexhibit.org
A virtual museum exhibit of photographs taken in 1903 of the Chinese countryside after the Boxer Rebellion.

Discovering Western Civilization Online

Discovering Western Civilization Online encourages students to explore the study of Western civilization beyond the confines of a textbook. These end-of-chapter website resources link students to enriching documents, images, and cultural sites. They have been thoroughly updated for this fourth edition.

A WOMAN REPORTER BEHIND THE LINES OF THE WAR IN CHECHNYA

Anne Nivat was the Moscow correspondent for the French daily newspaper Libération in October 2000 when she interviewed the rebel president of Chechnya. Fluent in Russian and holding a doctorate in political science, Nivat traveled to southern Russia disguised as a Chechen woman to cover the war from the Chechen side. Her newspaper reports led to antiwar protests in Paris.

FOCUS QUESTIONS

What indications does the Chechen rebel leader give that he sees guerrilla warfare within Chechnya as the best means of defeating Russia? What are his motives for opposition to the presence of Russian troops in Chechnya?

I FINALLY FIND MASKHADOV. He is wearing a military uniform with a pistol in his belt and appears to be in perfect health. Seated on a comfortable sofa in a "safe house," he seems relaxed and eager to share his thoughts on the situation in Chechnya. Outside, Russian armored vehicles pass through the autumn mist. Since he left Grozny the previous winter, the rebel president hasn't spent more than two consecutive days in any one spot. He usually communicates with his men and with the outside world by means of audiotapes. Few journalists take the

our territory—that is, while they remain inactive—their forces grow weaker, while ours get stronger. Our men are everywhere. The Russians know it, and yet they never mount an offensive. Their army is demoralized." . . .

Maskhadov is silent for a moment. He lets out a deep sigh. The Chechens, he admits, are tired of this war. "I recognize that the situation is difficult for the civilian population, which has become the target of the Russian army. I also regret that thousands of my countrymen have had to leave for Ingushetia or elsewhere. But each time I send out my representatives, they come back with the same message: 'Continue the fight. We're with you.' We can't afford to lose face, and the population knows it as well as I do. One way or another, the Russians will be forced to come to the negotiating table. I am constantly reminding Putin that he will be better off negotiating with me, as long as I am alive. It will be worse without me. And the Russians will leave in the end. Last time they led us to believe that they would never leave and then they disappeared. The worse

Primary Sources

A Brief History of Western Civilization: The Unfinished Legacy contains selections from primary sources in order to stimulate students' interest in history by allowing them to hear the past speak in its own voice. The extracts relate directly to discussion within the chapter, thus providing students with a fuller understanding of a significant thinker or event. Each selection is accompanied by an explanatory headnote that identifies the author and work and provides the necessary historical context. New to this edition are Focus Questions following the headnote; these questions guide students' reading and spark critical thinking about the document.

CHANGES IN THE NEW EDITION

In the fourth edition of *A Brief History of Western Civilization: The Unfinished Legacy*, we have made several changes to the book's coverage.

Chapter Content

- The text now opens with a two-page introductory essay: *The Idea of Western Civilization*.
- Chapter 9: The High Middle Ages, 900–1300 includes more on the status of women in medieval society.
- In Chapter 10: The Later Middle Ages, 1300–1500, there is more extensive treatment of the multiethnic world of medieval Spain.
- Parts of Chapter 20: The French Revolution and the Napoleonic Era, 1789–1815 were reorganized to present more clearly the factors leading to the crisis of the Old Regime and the early stages of the revolution.
- Chapter 30: The West Faces the New Century, 1989 to the Present has been updated through the War in Iraq and also includes expanded coverage of the European Union, the women's movement, and terrorism in the early twenty-first century.

New Pictorial Essays

Several new *The Visual Record* pictorial essays were added to the fourth edition as well.

- Chapter 1: The First Civilizations opens with a pictorial essay on the discovery of the ancient iceman Ötzi.
- Chapter 5: Imperial Rome, 146 B.C.E.–192 C.E. examines the Augustan Altar of Peace.
- Chapter 18: The Balance of Power in Eighteenth-Century Europe explores the rise of militarism through an examination of military portraiture.
- Chapter 21: Industrial Europe considers imagery of technology in the early industrial period.
- Chapter 28: Global Conflagration: Hot and Cold War opens with Hitler's entry into Austria in 1938.
- Chapter 29: Postwar Recovery and the New Europe to 1989 illustrates the devastation of postwar Europe in Warsaw, 1946.

We believe that each of these new pictorial essays will help students in understanding the dominant themes of their respective chapters.

New Primary Source Documents

To freshen the fourth edition, new primary source documents replace the previous documents in many chapters.

- Chapter 4 has a document from Greek historian Polybius describing the siege of New Carthage.
- Chapter 9 includes the appeal from Pope Urban II that launched the First Crusade.
- Chapter 10 includes a new document on religious intolerance in medieval Spain.
- Chapter 15 includes an excerpt from a document explaining how to root out witches.
- Chapter 17 has a first-hand account of encountering pirates while at sea.

- Chapter 19 includes an excerpt on love and marriage from an eighteenth-century periodical.
- Chapter 23 contains a document from a member of the Paris Commune.
- Chapter 24 includes an account of the abuse endured by a British suffragette.
- Chapter 28 has the text of FDR's request for a declaration of war against Japan.
- Chapter 30 contains a reporter's insight on the war in Chechnya.

Expanded Heading Structure

Finally, to make the book more accessible to students, additional headings have been incorporated to allow easier comprehension and mastery of a chapter's main ideas. These headings break the text into smaller segments, aiding students in identifying and retaining key information.

* * *

There are many new features in our text and much that is out of the ordinary. But there are important traditional aspects of the narrative itself that also deserve mention. *A Brief History of Western Civilization: The Unfinished Legacy* is a mainstream text in which most of our energies have been placed in developing a solid, readable narrative of Western civilization that integrates coverage of women and minorities into the discussion. We have highlighted personalities while identifying trends. We have spotlighted social history, both in sections of chapters and in separate chapters, while maintaining a firm grip on political developments. We hope that there are many things in this book that teachers of Western civilization will find valuable. But we also hope that there are things here with which you will disagree, themes that you can develop better, arguments and ideas that will stimulate you. A textbook is only one part of a course, and it is always less important than a teacher. What we hope is that by having done our job successfully, we will have made the teacher's job easier and the student's job more enjoyable.

ACKNOWLEDGMENTS

We want to thank the many conscientious historians who gave generously of their time and knowledge to review our manuscript. We would like to thank the reviewers of the first three editions as well as those of the current edition. Their valuable critiques and suggestions have contributed greatly to the final product. We are grateful to the following:

Daniel F. Callahan, *University of Delaware;* Gary P. Cox, *Gordon College;* Peter L. de Rosa, *Bridgewater State College;* Frank Lee Earley, *Arapahoe Community College;* Patrick Foley, *Tarrant County College;* Charlotte M. Gradie, *Sacred Heart University;* Richard Grossman, *Northeastern Illinois University;* Gary L. Johnson, *University of Southern Maine;* Oscar Lansen, *University of North Carolina at Charlotte;* Michael R. Lynn, *Agnes Scott College;* John M. McCulloh, *Kansas State University;* Martha G. Newman, *University of Texas at Austin;* Lisa Pace-Hardy, *Jefferson Davis Community College;* Marlette Rebhorn, *Austin Community College;* Steven G. Reinhardt, *University of Texas at Arlington;* Robert Rockwell, *Mt. San Jacinto College;* Maryloy Ruud, *University of West Florida;* Jose M. Sanchez, *St. Louis University;* Erwin Sicher, *Southwestern Adventist College;* and John E. Weakland, *Ball State University.*

Our special thanks go to our colleagues at Marquette University for their longstanding support, valuable comments, and assistance on this edition with the design of the book: Lance Grahn, Lezlie Knox, Timothy G. McMahon, and Alan P. Singer.

We also acknowledge the assistance of the many reviewers of *Civilization in the West* whose comments have been invaluable in the development of *A Brief History of Western Civilization: The Unfinished Legacy:*

Achilles Aavraamides, *Iowa State University;* Meredith L. Adams, *Southwest Missouri State University;* Arthur H. Auten, *University of Hartford;* Suzanne Balch-Lindsay, *Eastern New Mexico University;* Sharon Bannister, *University of Findlay;* John W. Barker, *University of Wisconsin;* Patrick Bass, *Mount Union College;* William H. Beik, *Northern Illinois University;* Patrice Berger, *University of Nebraska;* Lenard R. Berlanstein, *University of Virginia;* Raymond Birn, *University of Oregon;* Donna Bohanan, *Auburn University;* Werner Braatz, *University of Wisconsin, Oshkosh;* Thomas A. Brady, Jr., *University of Oregon;* Anthony M. Brescia, *Nassau Community College;* Elaine G. Breslaw, *Morgan State University;* Ronald S. Brockway, *Regis University;* April Brooks, *South Dakota State University;* Daniel Patrick Brown, *Moorpark College;* Ronald A. Brown, *Charles County Community College;* Blaine T. Browne, *Broward Community College;* Kathleen S. Carter, *High Point University;* Robert Carver, *University of Missouri, Rolla;* Edward J. Champlin, *Princeton University;* Stephanie Evans Christelow, *Western Washington University;* Sister Dorita Clifford, BVM, *University of San Francisco;* Gary B. Cohen, *University of Oklahoma;* Jan M. Copes, *Cleveland State University;* John J. Contreni, *Purdue University;* Tim Crain, *University of Wisconsin, Stout;* Norman Delaney, *Del Mar College;* Samuel E. Dicks, *Emporia State University;* Frederick Dumin, *Washington State University;* Laird Easton, *California State University, Chico;* Dianne E. Farrell, *Moorhead State University;* Margot C. Finn, *Emory University;* Allan W. Fletcher, *Boise State University;* Luci Fortunato De Lisle, *Bridgewater State College;* Elizabeth L. Furdell, *University of North Florida;* Thomas W. Gallant, *University of Florida;* Frank Garosi, *California State University, Sacramento;* Lorne E. Glaim, *Pacific Union College;* Joseph J. Godson, *Hudson Valley Community College;* Sue Helder Goliber, *Mount St. Mary's College;* Manuel G. Gonzales, *Diablo Valley College;* Louis Haas, *Duquesne University;* Eric Haines, *Bellevue Community College;* Paul Halliday, *University of Virginia;* Margaretta S. Handke, *Mankato State University;* David A. Harnett, *University of San Francisco;* Paul B. Harvey, Jr., *Pennsylvania State University;* Neil Heyman, *San Diego State University;* Daniel W. Hollis, *Jacksonville State University;* Kenneth G. Holum, *University of Maryland;* Patricia Howe, *University of St. Thomas;* David Hudson, *California State University, Fresno;* Charles Ingrao, *Purdue University;* George F. Jewsbury, *Oklahoma State University;* Donald G. Jones, *University of Central Arkansas;* William R. Jones, *University of New Hampshire;* Richard W. Kaeuper, *University of Rochester;* David Kaiser, *Carnegie-Mellon University;* Jeff Kaufmann, *Muscatine Community College;* Carolyn Kay, *Trent University;* William R. Keylor, *Boston University;* Joseph Kicklighter, *Auburn University;* Charles L. Killinger, III, *Valencia Community College;* Alan M. Kirshner, *Ohlone College;* Charlene Kiser, *Milligan College;* Alexandra Korros, *Xavier University;* Cynthia Kosso, *Northern Arizona University;* Lara Kriegel, *Florida International University;* Lisa M. Lane, *Mira Costa College;* David C. Large, *Montana State University;* Catherine Lawrence, *Messiah College;* Bryan LeBeau, *Creighton University;* Robert B. Luehrs, *Fort Hays State University;* Donna J. Maier, *University of Northern Iowa;* Margaret Malamud, *New Mexico State University;* Roberta T. Manning, *Boston College;* Lyle McAlister, *University of Florida;* Therese M. McBride, *College of the Holy Cross;* David K. McQuilkin, *Bridgewater College;* Victor V. Minasian, *College of Marin;* David B. Mock, *Tallahassee Community College;* Robert Moeller, *University of California, Irvine;* R. Scott Moore, *University of Dayton;* Ann E. Moyer, *University of Pennsylvania;* Pierce C. Mullen, *Montana State University;* John A. Nichols, *Slippery Rock University;* Thomas F. X. Noble, *University of Virginia;* J. Ronald Oakley, *Davidson County Community College;* Bruce K. O'Brien, *Mary Washington College;* Dennis H. O'Brien, *West Virginia University;* Maura O'Connor, *University of Cincinnati;* Richard A. Oehling, *Assumption College;* James H. Overfield, *University of Vermont;* Catherine Patterson, *University of Houston;* Sue Patrick, *University of Wisconsin, Barron County;* Peter C. Piccillo, *Rhode Island College;* Peter O'M. Pierson, *Santa Clara University;* Theophilus Prousis, *University of North Florida;* Marlette Rebhorn, *Austin Community College;* Jack B. Ridley, *University of Missouri, Rolla;* Constance M. Rousseau, *Providence College;* Thomas J. Runyan, *Cleveland State University;* John P. Ryan, *Kansas City Community College;* Geraldine Ryder, *Ocean County College;* Joanne Schneider, *Rhode Island College;* Steven Schroeder, *Indiana University of Pennsylvania;* Steven C. Seyer, *Lehigh County Community*

College; Lixin Shao, *University of Minnesota, Duluth;* George H. Shriver, *Georgia Southern University;* Ellen J. Skinner, *Pace University;* Bonnie Smith, *University of Rochester;* Patrick Smith, *Broward Community College;* James Smither, *Grand Valley State University;* Sherill Spaar, *East Central University;* Charles R. Sullivan, *University of Dallas;* Peter N. Stearns, *Carnegie-Mellon University;* Saulius Suziedelis, *Millersville University;* Darryl B. Sycher, *Columbus State Community College;* Roger Tate, *Somerset Community College;* Janet A. Thompson, *Tallahassee Community College;* Anne-Marie Thornton, *Bilkent University;* Donna L. Van Raaphorst, *Cuyahoga Community College;* James Vanstone, *John Abbot College;* Steven Vincent, *North Carolina State University;* Richard A. Voeltz, *Cameron University;* Faith Wallis, *McGill University;* Sydney Watts, *University of Richmond;* Eric Weissman, *Golden West College;* Christine White, *Pennsylvania State University;* William Harry Zee, *Gloucester County College.*

Each author also received invaluable assistance and encouragement from many colleagues, friends, and family members over the years of research, reflection, writing, and revising that went into the making of this text:

Mark Kishlansky thanks Ann Adams, Robert Bartlett, Ray Birn, David Buisseret, Ted Cook, Frank Conaway, Constantine Fasolt, James Hankins, Katherine Haskins, Richard Hellie, Matthew Kishlansky, Donna Marder, Mary Beth Rose, Victor Stater, Jeanne Thiel, and the staffs of the Joseph Regenstein Library, the Newberry Library, and the Widener and Lamont Libraries at Harvard.

Patrick Geary wishes to thank Mary, Catherine, and Anne Geary for their patience, support, and encouragement; he also thanks Anne Picard, Dale Schofield, Hans Hummer, and Richard Mowrer for their able assistance throughout the project.

Patricia O'Brien thanks Elizabeth Sagias for her encouragement and enthusiasm throughout the project and Robert Moeller for his keen eye for organization and his suggestions for writing a gendered history.

MARK KISHLANSKY
PATRICK GEARY
PATRICIA O'BRIEN

FOR QUALIFIED COLLEGE ADOPTERS

Instructor's Resource Manual

Prepared by David B. Mock of Tallahasee Community College, this thorough Instructor's Manual includes an introductory essay on teaching Western civilization and a bibliographic essay on the use of primary sources for class discussion and analytical thinking. Each chapter contains a chapter summary, key terms, list of important geographic locations, discussion questions, and an annotated list of films (not supplied by Longman) that may be used to enrich the course.

Test Bank

Prepared by Chris Howell of Red Rocks Community College, this supplement contains more than 1,200 multiple-choice, true/false, and essay questions. Multiple-choice and true/false questions are referenced by topic and text page number.

TestGen-EQ Computerized Testing System

This flexible, easy-to-master computerized test bank on a dual-platform CD includes all of the items in the printed test bank and allows instructors to select specific questions, edit existing questions, and add their own items to create exams. Tests can be printed in several different fonts and formats and can include figures, such as graphs and tables.

Companion Website *(www.ablongman.com/kishlansky)*

Instructors can take advantage of the Companion Website that supports this text. The instructor section includes teaching links and downloadable maps, tables, and graphs from the text for use in PowerPoint™.

Supplements Central™ *(http://suppscentral.ablongman.com)*

A helpful website where instructors can download supplements including: Instructor's Manuals, Test Banks, TestGens, Power Point™ presentations, as well as CourseCompass®, WebCT, and BlackBoard materials. Instructors will need to request a password from their sales representative to gain access.

Text-Specific Transparency Set

A set of full-color transparency map acetates drawn from *Civilization in the West,* Fifth Edition.

History Video Program

A list of over 100 videos from which qualified college adopters can choose. Restrictions apply.

History Digital Media Archive CD-ROM

This CD-ROM contains electronic images and interactive and static maps, along with media elements such as video. It is fully customizable and ready for classroom presentation. All images and maps are available in PowerPoint™ as well.

CourseCompass *(http://www.ablongman.com/techsolutions)*

Focus on teaching the course, not the technology! CourseCompass combines the strength of Longman content with state-of-the-art technology that simplifies online course management for you. This easy-to-use and customizable program enables you to tailor the content and functionality to meet your individual needs. You can create an online presence—for ANY course you teach—in under an hour. This course contains several dozen primary sources, Western civilization maps from Longman textbooks, and the map exercises from both *Mapping Western Civilization* and *Western Civilization Map Workbook*, all of which you can customize for your own class and text.

BlackBoard *(http://www.ablongman.com/techsolutions)*

Longman's rich Western civilization content is available in BlackBoard's course management system. The BlackBoard format enables you to quickly and easily customize any course to meet your specific needs. This downloadable course contains several dozen primary sources, Western civilization maps from Longman textbooks, and the map exercises from both *Mapping Western Civilization* and *Western Civilization Map Workbook*, all of which you can customize for your own class and text.

WebCT *(http://www.ablongman.com/techsolutions)*

WebCT offers a host of online course management tools. Longman will provide qualified college adopters with a wealth of material to customize their own WebCT course. Available content includes several dozen primary sources, Western civilization maps from Longman textbooks, and the map exercises from both *Mapping Western Civilization* and *Western Civilization Map Workbook*, all of which you can customize for your own class and text. Contact your sales representative for more information.

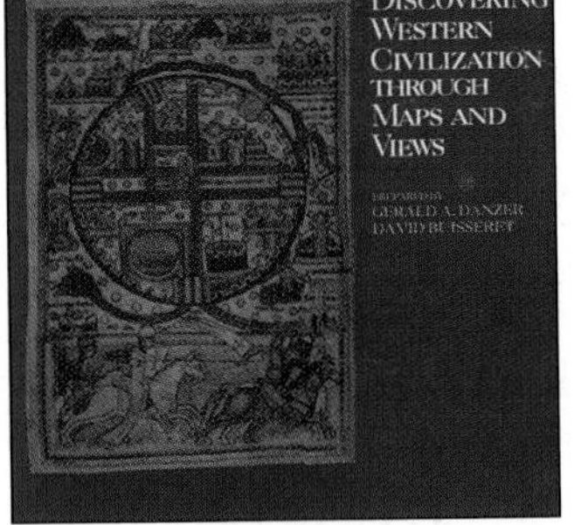

Discovering Western Civilization Through Maps and Views

Created by Gerald Danzer, University of Illinois at Chicago, and David Buisseret, this unique set of 140 full-color acetates contains an introduction to teaching history through maps and a detailed commentary on each transparency. The collection includes cartographic and pictorial maps, views and photos, urban plans, building diagrams, and works of art. Available to qualified college adopters.

FOR STUDENTS

Study Guide

Revised by Paul Brasil of Mountain Community College, this *Study Guide* is available in two volumes. Each chapter includes a summary; a timeline activity; map and geography questions; key terms, people, and events; and identification, multiple-choice, and critical-thinking questions.

Companion Website *(www.ablongman.com/kishlansky)*

Providing a wealth of resources for students using *Civilization in the West*, this Companion Website contains chapter summaries, interactive practice test questions, and web links for every chapter in the text.

Research Navigator and Research Navigator Guide

Research Navigator is a comprehensive website comprising three exclusive databases of credible and reliable source material for research and for student assignments: EBSCO's ContentSelect Academic Journal Database, the New York Times Search by Subject Archive, and "Best of the Web" Link Library. The site also includes an extensive help section. The Research Navigator Guide provides your students with access to the Research Navigator website and includes reference material and hints about conducting online research. **Free to qualified college adopters when packaged with the text.**

Multimedia Edition CD-ROM for *Civilization in the West*

This unique CD-ROM takes students beyond the printed page, offering them a complete multimedia learning experience. It contains the full annotatable textbook on CD-ROM, with contextually placed media—audio, video, interactive maps, photos, and figures—that link students to additional content directly related to key concepts in the text. The CD also contains the *Study Guide*, map workbooks, a primary source reader, and more than a dozen supplementary books, most often assigned in Western civilization courses, including Plato, *The Republic*, and Machiavelli, *The Prince*. **Free to qualified college adopters when packaged with the text.**

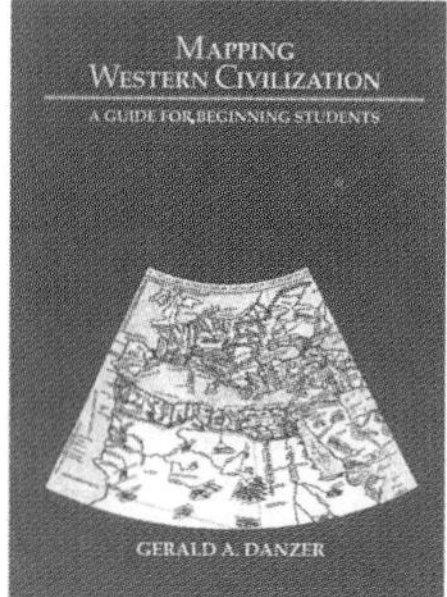

Mapping Western Civilization: Student Activities

Created by Gerald Danzer, University of Illinois at Chicago, this FREE map workbook for students is designed as an accompaniment to *Discovering Western Civilization Through Maps and Views*. It features exercises designed to teach students to interpret and analyze cartographic materials such as historical documents. **Free to qualified college adopters when packaged with the text.**

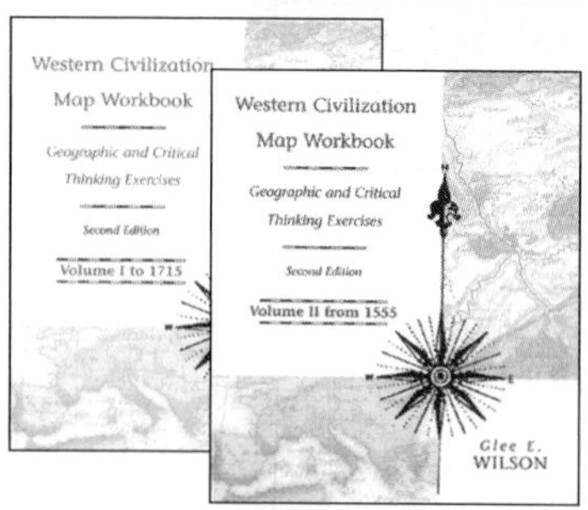

Western Civilization Map Workbook

The map exercises in these two volumes by Glee Wilson test and reinforce basic geography literacy while building critical-thinking skills. **Free to qualified college adopters when packaged with the text.**

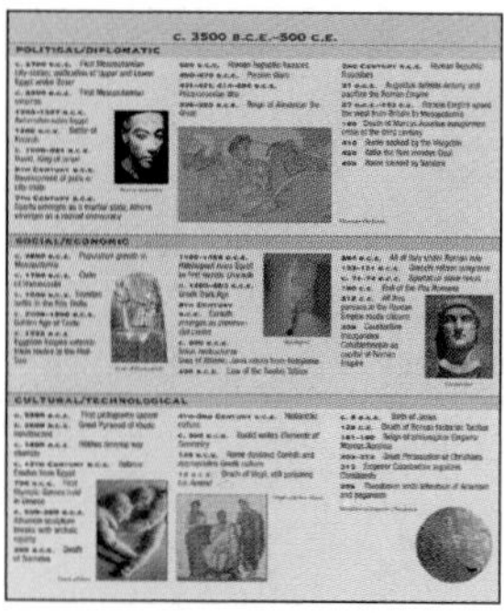

Full-Color Longman Western Civilization Timeline

Noting key events and trends in political and diplomatic, social and economic, and cultural and technological history, this fold-out illustrated timeline provides a thorough and accessible chronological reference guide for Western civilization. **Free to qualified college adopters when packaged with the text.**

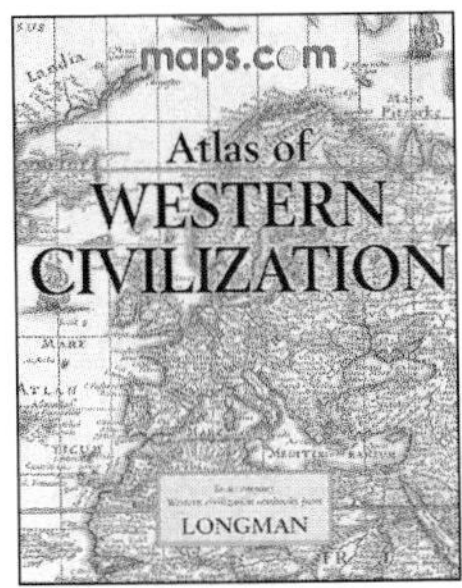

Longman Atlas of Western Civilization

This 52-page atlas features carefully selected historical maps that provide comprehensive coverage for the major historical periods. Each map has been designed to be colorful, easy-to-read, and informative, without sacrificing detailed accuracy. This atlas makes history—and geography—more comprehensible.

A Short Guide to Writing About History, Fourth Edition

Written by Richard Marius, late of Harvard University, and Melvin E. Page, Eastern Tennessee State University, this engaging and practical text helps students get beyond merely compiling dates and facts; it teaches them how to incorporate their own ideas into their papers and to tell a story about history that interests them and their peers. Covering both brief essays and the documented resource paper, the text explores the writing and researching processes, identifies different modes of historical writing, including argument, and concludes with guidelines for improving style.

Longman World History—Primary Sources and Case Studies *(http://longmanworldhistory.com)*

The core of this website is its large database of thought-provoking primary sources, case studies, maps, and images—all carefully chosen and edited by scholars and teachers of world history. The content and organization of the site encourage students to analyze the themes, issues, and complexities of world history in a meaningful, exciting, and informative way. Offered at a significant discount to *A Brief History of Western Civilization: The Unfinished Legacy* users, professors can visit the site for a free three-day trial.

Interpretations of the Western World

General Editor Mark Kishlansky has prepared a customizable database of secondary source readings in Western civilization. Selections are grouped topically so that instructors can assign readings that illustrate different points of view about a given historical debate (e.g., How democratic was Athens? Did the Industrial Revolution improve the standard of living?). Interpretations of the Western World can be packaged at a discount with *A Brief History of Western Civilization: The Unfinished Legacy*, Fourth Edition.

PENGUIN-LONGMAN PARTNERSHIP

The partnership between Penguin Books and Longman Publishers offers your students a discount on the titles below when instructors bundle them with any Longman survey. Visit www.ablongman.com/penguin for more information.

Available Titles

Peter Abelard, *The Letters of Abelard and Heloise*
Dante Alighieri, *Divine Comedy: Inferno*
Dante Alighieri, *The Portable Dante*
Anonymous, *The Song of Roland*
Anonymous, *The Epic of Gilgamesh*
Anonymous, *Vinland Sagas*
Aristophanes, *The Knights, Peace, The Birds, Assemblywomen, Wealth*
Louis Auchincloss, *Woodrow Wilson* (Penguin Lives Series)
Jane Austen, *Emma*

Jane Austen, *Pride and Prejudice*
Jane Austen, *Persuasion*
Jane Austen, *Sense and Sensibility*
Edward Bellamy, *Looking Backward*
Richard Bowring, *Diary of Lady Murasaki*
Charlotte Brontë, *Jane Eyre*
Charlotte Brontë, *Villette*
Emily Brontë, *Wuthering Heights*
Benvenuto Cellini, *The Autobiography of Benvenuto Cellini*
Geoffrey Chaucer, *The Canterbury Tales*
Marcus Tullius Cicero, *Cicero: Selected Political Speeches*
Miguel de Cervantes, *The Adventures of Don Quixote*
Bartolome de las Casas, *A Short Account of the Destruction of the West Indies*
René Descartes, *Discourse on Method and The Meditations*
Charles Dickens, *Hard Times*
Charles Dickens, *Great Expectations*
John Dos Passos, *Three Soldiers*
Einhard, *Two Lives of Charlemagne*
Olaudah Equiano, *The Interesting Narrative and Other Writings*
Jeffrey Gantz (tr.), *Early Irish Myths and Sagas*
Peter Gay, *Mozart* (Penguin Lives Series)
William Golding, *Lord of the Flies*
Kenneth Grahame, *The Wind in the Willows*
Grimm & Grimm, *Grimms' Fairy Tales*
Thomas Hardy, *Jude the Obscure*
Herodotus, *The Histories*
Thomas Hobbes, *Leviathan*
Homer, *The Iliad*
Homer, *Odyssey: Revised Prose Translation*
Homer, *Odyssey Deluxe*
The Koran
Lemisch, *B. Franklin*
Primo Levi, *If Not Now, When?*
Machiavelli, *The Prince*
Karl Marx, *The Communist Manifesto*
John Stuart Mill, *On Liberty*
Jean-Baptiste Molière, *Tartuffe and Other Plays*
Charles-Louis Montesquieu, *Persian Letters*
Sir Thomas More, *Utopia and Other Essential Writings*
Sherwin Nuland, *Leonardo DaVinci*
George Orwell, *1984*
George Orwell, *Animal Farm*
Plato, *Great Dialogues of Plato*
Plato, *The Republic*
Plato, *The Last Days of Socrates*
Marco Polo, *The Travels*
Procopius, *The Secret History*
Jean-Jacques Rousseau, *The Social Contract*
Sallust, *The Jugurthine Wars, The Conspiracy of Cataline*
William Shakespeare, *Hamlet*
William Shakespeare, *Macbeth*
William Shakespeare, *The Merchant of Venice* (Pelican Series)
William Shakespeare, *The Merchant of Venice* (Signet Classics)
William Shakespeare, *Othello*
William Shakespeare, *The Taming of the Shrew*
William Shakespeare, *Twelfth Night*
William Shakespeare, *King Lear*
William Shakespeare, *Four Great Comedies: The Taming of the Shrew, A Midsummer's Night Dream, Twelfth Night, The Tempest*
William Shakespeare, *Four Great Tragedies: Hamlet, Macbeth, King Lear, Othello*
William Shakespeare, *Four Histories: Richard II, Henry IV: Part I, Henry IV: Part II, Henry V*
William Shakespeare, *The Tempest*
Mary Shelley, *Frankenstein*
Aleksandr Solzhenitsyn, *One Day in the Life of Ivan Denisovich*
Sophocles, *The Three Theban Plays*
St. Augustine, *The Confessions of St. Augustine*
Robert Louis Stevenson, *The Strange Case of Dr. Jekyll and Mr. Hyde*
Suetonius, *The Twelve Caesars*
Jonathan Swift, *Gulliver's Travels*
Tacitus, *The Histories*
Voltaire, *Candide, Zadig and Selected Stories*
Goethe, *Faust, Part 1*
Goethe, *Faust, Part 2*
Edith Wharton, *Ethan Frome*
M. Willet, *The Signet World Atlas*
Gary Wills, *Saint Augustine* (Penguin Lives Series)
Virginia Woolf, *Jacob's Room*

ABOUT THE AUTHORS

MARK KISHLANSKY Mark Kishlansky is Frank B. Baird, Jr. Professor of English and European History and has served as the Associate Dean of the Faculty at Harvard University. He was educated at the State University of New York at Stony Brook where he first studied history and at Brown University where he received his Ph.D. in 1977. For 16 years, he taught at the University of Chicago and was a member of the staff that taught Western Civilization. Currently, he lectures on the History of Western Civilization at Harvard. Professor Kishlansky is a specialist on seventeenth-century English political history and has written, among other works, *A Monarchy Transformed, The Rise of the New Model Army* and *Parliamentary Selection: Social and Political Choice in Early Modern England.* From 1984 to 1991 he was editor of the *Journal of British Studies* and is presently the general editor of the *History Compass*, the first on-line history journal. He is also the general editor for Pearson Custom Publishing's source and interpretations databases, which provide custom book supplements for Western Civilization courses.

PATRICK GEARY Holding a Ph.D. in Medieval Studies from Yale University, Patrick Geary has broad experience in interdisciplinary approaches to European history and civilization. He has served as the director of the Medieval Institute at the University of Notre Dame as well as director for the Center for Medieval and Renaissance Studies at UCLA where he is currently Professor of History. He has also held positions at the University of Florida and Princeton University and has taught at the École des Hautes Études en Sciences Sociales in Paris and the University of Vienna. His many publications include *Readings in Medieval History; Before France and Germany: The Creation and Transformation of the Merovingian World; Phantoms of Remembrance: Memory and Oblivion at the End of the First Millennium;* and *The Myth of Nations: The Medieval Origins of Europe.*

PATRICIA O'BRIEN Between 1995 and 1999, Patricia O'Brien worked to foster collaborative interdisciplinary research in the humanities as director of the University of California Humanities Research Institute. Since 1999, she has held the position of Dean of the College of Humanities, Arts, and Social Sciences at the University of California, Riverside. She has held appointments at the University of California, Irvine, Yale University, and at the École des Hautes Études en Sciences Sociales in Paris. Professor O'Brien is a specialist in modern French cultural and social history and has published widely on the history of crime, punishment, cultural theory, urban history, and gender issues. Representative publications include *The Promise of Punishment: Prisons in Nineteenth-Century France;* "The Kleptomania Diagnosis: Bourgeois Women and Theft in Late Nineteenth-Century France" in *Expanding the Past: A Reader in Social History;* and "Michel Foucault's History of Culture" in *The New Cultural History,* edited by Lynn Hunt. Professor O'Brien's commitment to this textbook grew out of her own teaching experiences in large, introductory Western civilization courses. She has benefited from the contributions of her students and fellow instructors in her approach to the study of Western civilization in the modern period.

CHAPTER 14

EUROPE AT WAR, 1555–1648

THE VISUAL RECORD

THE MASSACRE OF THE INNOCENTS

"WAR IS ONE OF THE SCOURGES with which it has pleased God to afflict men," wrote Cardinal Richelieu (1585–1642), the French minister who played no small part in spreading the scourge. War was a constant of European society and penetrated to its very core. It dominated all aspects of life. It enhanced the power of the state, it defined gender roles, it consumed lives and treasure and commodities ravenously. War affected every member of society from combatants to civilians. There were no innocent bystanders. Grain in the fields was destroyed because it was food for soldiers; houses were burned because they provided shelter for soldiers. Civilians were killed for aiding the enemy or holding out against demands for their treasure and supplies. Able-bodied men were taken forcibly to serve as conscripts, leaving women to plant and harvest as best they could.

Neither the ancient temple nor the Roman costume can conceal the immediacy of the picture shown here. It is as painful to look at now as it was when it was created over 350 years ago. Painted by Nicolas Poussin (1594–1665) at the height of the Thirty Years' War, the *Massacre of the Innocents* remains a horrifying composition of power, terror, and despair. The cruel and senseless slaughter of the innocent baby that is about to take place is echoed throughout the canvas. In the background between the executioner's legs can be seen a mother clasping her own child tightly and anticipating the fall of the sword. In the background on the right, another mother turns away from the scene and carries her infant to safety. In the foreground strides a mother holding her dead child. She tears at her hair and cries in anguish. To a culture in which the image of mother and child—of Mary and Jesus—was one of sublime peacefulness and joy, the contrast could hardly have been more shocking.

The picture graphically displays the cruelty of the soldier, the helplessness of the child, and the horror of the mother. By his grip on the mother's hair and his foot on the baby's throat, the warrior shows his brute power. The mother's futile effort to stop the sword illustrates her powerlessness. She scratches uselessly at the soldier's back. Naked, the baby boy raises his hands as if to surrender to the inevitable, as if to reinforce his innocence.

To study Europe at war, we must enter a world of politics and diplomacy, of issues and principles, of judgment and error. There can be no doubt that the future of Europe was decisively shaped by this century of wholesale slaughter, during which dynastic and religious fervor finally ran its course. The survival of Protestantism, the disintegration of the Spanish empire, the rise of Holland and Sweden, the collapse of Poland and Muscovy, the fragmentation of Germany—these were all vital transformations the consequences of which would be felt for centuries. We cannot avoid telling this story, untangling its causes, narrating its course, and revealing its outcome. But neither should we avoid facing its reality. Look again at the painting by Poussin.

LOOKING AHEAD

As we will see in this chapter, warfare in the seventeenth century decisively reshaped power relations of families and states. Protestantism survived after nearly a century of military challenge and the power of the great Habsburg dynasty was finally crushed. In its place rose France, England, and Holland, and a new chapter of European conflict began.

THE CRISES OF THE WESTERN STATES

"Un roi, une foi, une loi"—"One king, one faith, one law." This was a prescription that members of all European states accepted without question in the sixteenth century. Society was an integrated whole, equally dependent on monarchical, ecclesiastical, and civil authority for its effective survival. A European state could no more tolerate the presence of two churches than it could the presence of two kings. But the Reformation had created two churches. The coexistence of Catholics and Protestants in a single realm posed a stark challenge to accepted theory and traditional practice.

The problem proved intractable because it admitted only one solution: total victory. There could be no compromise for several reasons. Religious beliefs were profoundly held. Religious controversy was more than a life-and-death struggle: it was a struggle between everlasting life and eternal damnation. Doomed, too, was the practical solution of toleration. To the modern mind, toleration seems so logical that it is difficult to understand why it took over a century of bloodshed before it came to be grudgingly accepted by the most bitterly divided countries. But toleration was not a practical solution in a society that admitted no principle of organization other than one king, one faith.

▲ Catherine de Médicis (1519–1598), the wife of Henry II of France, was the real power behind the throne during the reigns of her sons Charles IX (1560–1574) and Henry III (1574–1589). Her overriding concern was to ensure her sons' succession and to preserve the power of the monarchy.

The French Wars of Religion

No wars are more terrible than civil wars. The loss of lives and property is staggering, but the loss of communal identity is greater still. Generations pass before societies recover from their civil wars. Such was the case with the French wars of religion.

The Spread of Calvinism and Religious Division. Protestantism came late to France. Not until after Calvin reformed the Church in Geneva and began to export his brand of Protestantism did French society begin to divide along religious lines. By 1560 there were over 2,000 Protestant congregations in France, and their membership totaled nearly 10 percent of the French population. Calvin and his successors achieved their greatest following among the middle ranks of urban society: merchants, traders, and artisans. They also found a receptive audience among aristocratic women, who eventually converted their husbands and children.

However, the wars of religion were brought on by more than the rapid spread of Calvinism. Equally important was the vacuum of power that had been created when Henry II (1547–1559) died in a jousting tournament. Surviving Henry were his extraordinary widow, Catherine de Médicis, three daughters, and four sons, the oldest of whom, Francis II (1559–1560), was only 15 years old. Under the influence of his beautiful young wife, Mary, Queen of Scots, Francis allowed her relatives, the Guise family, to dominate the great offices of state and to exclude their rivals from power. The Guises controlled the two most powerful institutions of the state: the army and the Church.

The Guises were staunchly Catholic, and among their enemies were the Bourbons, princes of the blood with a direct claim to the French throne but also a family with powerful Protestant members. The revelation of a Protestant plot to remove the king from Paris provided the Guises with an opportunity to eliminate their most potent rivals. The Bourbon duc de Condé, the leading Protestant peer of the realm, was sentenced to death. But five days before Condé's execution, Francis II died, and Guise power evaporated. The new king, Charles IX (1560–1574), was only 10 years old and firmly under the grip of his mother, Catherine de Médicis, who now declared herself regent of France.

Civil War. Condé's death sentence convinced him that the Guises would stop at nothing to gain their ambitions. Force would have to be met with force. Protestants and Catholics alike raised armies, and in 1562, civil war ensued. Because of the tangle of motives among the participants, each side in the struggle had different objectives. Catherine wanted peace and was willing to accept almost any strategy for securing it. At first she negotiated with the Bourbons, but she was ultimately forced to accept the fact that the Guises were more powerful. The Guises wanted to suppress Protestantism and eliminate Protestant influence at court. They were willing to undertake the task with or without the king's express support.

Once the wars began, the leading Protestant peers fled the court, but the position of the Guises was not altogether secure. Henry Bourbon, king of Navarre, was the next in line to the throne should Charles IX and his two brothers die without male heirs. Henry had been raised in the Protestant faith by his mother, Jeanne d'Albret, whose own mother, Marguerite of Navarre, was among the earliest protectors of the Huguenots, as the French Calvinists came to be called.

The inconclusive nature of the early battles might have allowed for the pragmatic solution by Catherine de Médicis had it not been for the assassination of the duc de Guise in 1563 by a Protestant fanatic. This act added a personal vendetta to the religious passions of the Catholic leaders. They encouraged the slaughter of Huguenot congregations and openly planned the murder of Huguenot leaders. Protestants gave as good as they got. In open defiance of Valois dynastic interests, the Guises courted support from Spain, while the Huguenots imported Swiss and German mercenaries to fight in France. Noble factions and irreconcilable religious differences were pulling the government apart.

The Saint Bartholomew's Day Massacre. By 1570, Catherine was ready to attempt another reconciliation. She announced her plans for a marriage between her daughter Margaret and Henry of Navarre, a marriage that would symbolize the spirit of conciliation between the crown and the Huguenots. The marriage was to take place in Paris during August 1572. The arrival of Huguenot leaders from all over France to attend the marriage ceremony presented an opportunity of a different kind to the Guises and their supporters. If leading Huguenots could be assassinated in Paris, the Protestant cause might collapse, and the truce that the wedding signified might be turned instead into a Catholic triumph.

Saint Bartholomew was the apostle whom Jesus described as a man without guile. Ironically, it was on his feast day that the Huguenots who had innocently come to celebrate Henry's marriage were led like lambs to the slaughter. On 24 August 1572 the streets of Paris ran red with Huguenot blood. Although frenzied, the slaughter was inefficient. Henry of Navarre and a number of other important Huguenots escaped the carnage and returned to their urban strongholds. In the following weeks the violence spread from Paris to the countryside, and thousands of Protestants paid for their beliefs with their lives.

One King, Two Faiths

The Saint Bartholomew's Day Massacre was a transforming event in many ways. In the first place, it prolonged the wars. A whole new generation of Huguenots now had an attachment to the continuation of warfare: their fathers and brothers had been mercilessly slaughtered. By itself, the event was shocking enough; in the atmosphere of anticipated reconciliation created by the wedding, it screamed out for revenge. And the target for retaliation

Painting of the Saint Bartholomew's Day Massacre. The massacre began in Paris on 24 August 1572, and the violence soon spread throughout France.

was no longer limited to the Guises and their followers. By accepting the results of the massacre, the monarchy sanctioned it and spilled Huguenot blood on itself. For more than a decade, Catherine de Médicis had maintained a distance between the crown and the leaders of the Catholic movement. That distance no longer existed.

The Theory of Resistance. After Saint Bartholomew's Day, Huguenot theorists began to develop the idea that resistance to a monarch whose actions violated divine commandments or civil right was lawful. For the first time, Huguenot writers provided a justification for rebellion. Perhaps most importantly, a genuine revulsion against the massacres swept the nation. A number of Catholic peers now joined with the Huguenots to protest the excesses of the crown and the Guises. These Catholics came to be called the *politiques*, from their desire for a practical settlement of the wars. They were led by the duke of Anjou, who was next in line to the throne when Charles IX died in 1574 and Henry III (1574–1589) became king.

Against them, in Paris and a number of other towns, the Catholic League was formed, a society that pledged its first allegiance to religion. The League took up where the Saint Bartholomew's Day Massacre left off, and the slaughter of ordinary people who professed the wrong religion continued. Matters grew worse in 1584 when the duke of Anjou died. With each passing year it was becoming apparent that Henry III would produce no male heir. After the duke's death, the Huguenot Henry of Navarre was the next in line for the throne. Catholic Leaguers talked openly of altering the royal succession and began to develop theories of lawful resistance to monarchical power. By 1585, when the final civil war began—the war of the three Henrys, named for Henry III, Henry Guise, and Henry of Navarre—the crown was in the weakest possible position. Paris and the Catholic towns were controlled by the League, and the Protestant strongholds were controlled by Henry of Navarre. King Henry III could not abandon his capital or his religion, but neither could he gain control of the Catholic party. The extremism of the Leaguers kept the politiques away from court; and without the politiques there could be no settlement.

In December 1588, Henry III summoned Henry Guise and Guise's brother to a meeting in the royal bedchamber. There, they were murdered by the king's order. The politiques were blamed for the murders—revenge was taken on a number of them—and Henry III was forced to flee his capital. He made a pact with Henry of Navarre, and together royalist and Huguenot forces besieged Paris. All supplies were cut off from the city, and only the arrival of a Spanish army prevented its fall. In 1589, Catherine de Médicis died, her ambition to reestablish the authority of the monarchy in shambles, and in the same year a fanatic priest gained revenge for the murder of the Guises by assassinating Henry III.

Henry IV. Now Henry of Navarre came into his inheritance. But after nearly 30 years of continuous civil war, it was certain that a Huguenot could never rule France. If Henry was to become king of all France, he would have to become a Catholic king. It is not clear when Henry made the decision to accept the Catholic faith—"Paris is worth a Mass," he reportedly declared—but he did not announce his decision at once. Rather, he strengthened his forces, tightened his bonds with the politiques, and urged his countrymen to expel the Spanish invaders. He finally made his conversion public and in 1594 was crowned Henry IV (1589–1610). A war-weary nation was willing to accept him.

In 1598, Henry proclaimed the Edict of Nantes, which granted limited toleration to the Huguenots. It was the culmination of decades of attempts to find a solution to the existence of two religions in one state. It was a compromise that satisfied no one, but it was a compromise that everyone could accept. "One king, two faiths" was as apt a description of Henry IV as it was of the settlement. Yet neither Henry's conversion nor the Edict of Nantes stilled the passions that had spawned and sustained the French wars of religion. Sporadic fighting between Catholics and Huguenots continued, and fanatics on both sides fanned the flames of religious hatred. Henry IV survived 18 attempts on his life before he was finally felled by an assassin's knife in 1610, but by then he had established the monarchy and brought a semblance of peace to France.

CHRONOLOGY

THE FRENCH WARS OF RELIGION

1559	Death of Henry II
1560	Protestant duc de Condé sentenced to death
1562	First battle of wars of religion
1563	Catholic duc de Guise assassinated; Edict of Amboise grants limited Protestant worship
1572	Saint Bartholomew's Day Massacre
1574	Accession of Henry III
1576	Formation of Catholic League
1584	Death of duc d'Anjou makes Henry of Navarre heir to throne
1585	War of the three Henrys
1588	Duc de Guise murdered by order of Henry III
1589	Catherine de Médicis dies; Henry III assassinated
1594	Henry IV crowned
1598	Edict of Nantes

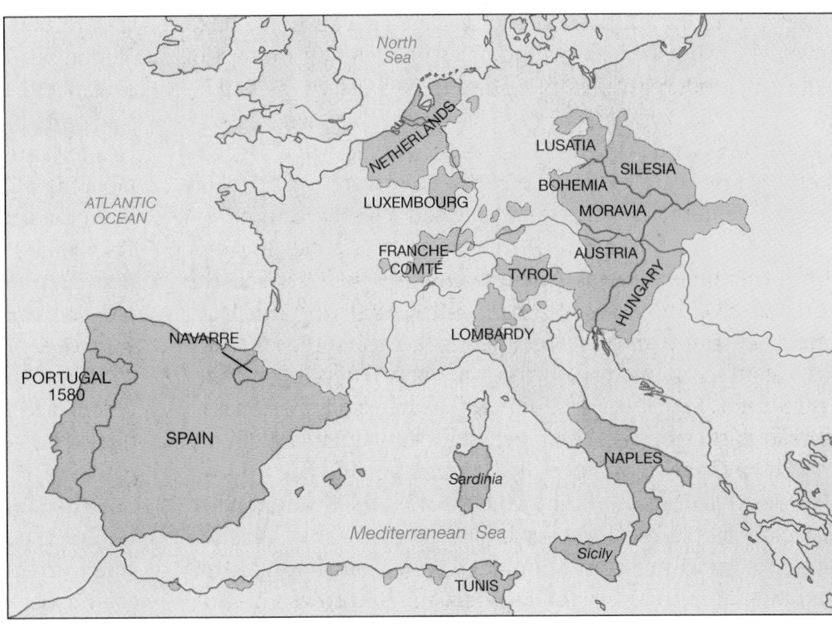

The combined territories of the Spanish and Austrian Habsburgs during the reign of Philip II. Charles V had divided his estates to make it easier for them to be governed.

The World of Philip II

While France was caught up in religious strife, Spain, by the middle of the sixteenth century, had achieved the status of the greatest power in Europe. The dominions of Philip II (1556–1598) of Spain stretched from the Atlantic to the Pacific; his continental territories included the Netherlands in the north and Milan and Naples in Italy. In 1580, Philip became king of Portugal, uniting all the states of the Iberian peninsula. With the addition of Portugal's Atlantic ports and its sizable fleet, Spanish maritime power was now unsurpassed. Philip saw himself as a Catholic monarch fending off the spread of heresy. He came to the throne at just the moment that Calvinism began its rapid growth in northern Europe and provided the impetus for the greatest crisis of his reign: the revolt of the Netherlands.

Though Philip's father, Charles V, amassed a great empire, he had begun only as the Duke of Burgundy. Charles's Burgundian inheritance encompassed a diverse territory in the northwestern corner of Europe. The 17 separate provinces of this territory were called the Netherlands, or the Low Countries, because of the flooding that kept large portions of them under water. The Netherlands, one of the richest and most populous regions of Europe, was an international leader in manufacturing, banking, and commerce. In the southern provinces, French was the background and language of the inhabitants; in the northern ones, Germans had settled, and Dutch was spoken.

The Low Countries had accepted the Peace of Augsburg in a spirit of conciliation in which it was never intended. Here, Catholics, Lutherans, Anabaptists, and Calvinists peaceably coexisted. As in France, this situation changed dramatically with the spread of Calvinism. The heavy concentration of urban populations in the Low Countries provided the natural habitat for Calvinist preachers, who made converts across the entire social spectrum. As Holy Roman Emperor, Charles V may have made his peace with Protestants, but as king of Spain he had not. Charles V had maintained the purity of the Spanish Catholic Church through a careful combination of reform and repression.

Philip II intended to pursue a similar policy in the Low Countries. With papal approval, he initiated a scheme to reform the hierarchy of the Church by expanding the numbers of bishops, and he invited the Jesuits to establish schools for orthodox learning. Simultaneously, he strengthened the power of the Inquisition and ordered the enforcement of the decrees of the Council of Trent. The Protestants sought the protection of their local nobles, who, Catholic or Protestant, had their own reasons for opposing the strict enforcement of heresy laws. Provincial nobles and magistrates resented both the policies that were being pursued and the fact that they disregarded local autonomy. Town governors and noblemen refused to cooperate in implementing the new laws.

The Revolt of the Netherlands

The passive resistance of nobles and magistrates was soon matched by the active resistance of the Calvinists. Unable to enforce Philip's policy, Margaret of Parma, his half-sister, whom Philip had made regent, agreed to a limited toleration. But in the summer of 1566, before this toleration could be put into effect, bands of Calvinists unleashed a storm of iconoclasm in the provinces, breaking stained glass windows and statues of the Virgin and the saints, which they claimed were idolatrous. Helpless in the face of determined Calvinists and apathetic Catholics, local authorities could not protect Church property. Iconoclasm gave way to open revolt. Fearing social rebellion, even the leading Protestant noblemen took part in suppressing these riots.

Rebellion and War. In Spain the events in the Netherlands were treated for what they were: open rebellion. Despite the fact that Margaret had already restored order, Philip II was determined to punish the rebels and enforce the heresy laws. A large military force under the command of the Duke of Alba (1507–1582) was sent from Spain as an army of occupation. Alba lured leading Protestant noblemen to Brussels, where he publicly executed them in 1568. He also established a military court to punish participants in the rebellion, a court that came to be called the Council of Blood. The Council handed down over 9,000 convictions, 1,000 of which carried the death penalty. As many as 60,000 Protestants fled beyond Alba's jurisdiction. Alba next made an example of several small towns that had been implicated in the iconoclasm. He allowed his soldiers to pillage the towns at will before slaughtering their entire populations and razing them to the ground. By the end of 1568, royal policy had gained a sullen acceptance in the Netherlands, but for the next 80 years, with only occasional truces, Spain and the Netherlands were at war.

The Protestants Rebel. Alba's policies had driven Protestants into rebellion, and this forced the Spanish government to maintain its army by raising taxes from the provinces that had remained loyal. Soon the loyal provinces were also in revolt, not over religion but over taxation and local autonomy. Tax resistance and fear of an invasion from France left Alba unprepared for the series of successful assaults Protestants launched in the northern provinces during 1572. The Protestant generals established a permanent base in the northwestern provinces of Holland and Zeeland. By 1575, they had gained a stronghold that they would never relinquish. Prince William of Orange assumed the leadership of the two provinces, which were now united against the tyranny of Philip's rule.

Spanish government was collapsing all over the Netherlands. William ruled in the north, and the States-General, a parliamentary body composed of representatives from the separate provinces, ruled in the south. Margaret of Parma had resigned in disgust at Alba's tactics, and Alba had been relieved of his command when his tactics failed. No one was in control of the Spanish army. The soldiers, who had gone years with only partial pay, now roamed the southern provinces looking for plunder. Brussels and Ghent had both been targets, and in 1576 the worst atrocities of all occurred when mutinous Spanish troops sacked Antwerp. Over 7,000 people were slaughtered, and nearly one-third of the city burned to the ground.

The "Spanish fury" in Antwerp effectively ended Philip's rule over his Burgundian inheritance. The Protestants had established a permanent home in the north. The States-General had established its ability to rule in the south, and Spanish policy had been totally discredited. To achieve a settlement, the Pacification of Ghent of 1576, the Spanish government conceded local autonomy in taxation, the central role of the States-General in legislation, and the immediate withdrawal of all Spanish troops from the Low Countries. This rift among the provinces was soon followed by a permanent split. In 1581, one group of provinces voted to depose Philip II while a second group decided to remain loyal to him. Philip II refused to accept the dismemberment of his inheritance or to recognize the independent Dutch state that now existed in Holland.

Meanwhile, Protestant England under Elizabeth I (1558–1603) had sided with the Dutch Protestants opposing Philip II. During Elizabeth's reign, England and Spain entered a long period of hostility. English pirates raided Spanish treasure ships returning to Europe, and Elizabeth covertly aided both French and Dutch Protestants. Finally, in 1588, Philip decided to invade England. A great fleet set sail from the Portuguese coast to the Netherlands, where a large Spanish army was waiting to be conveyed to England.

The Spanish Armada comprised over 130 ships, many of them the pride of the Spanish and Portuguese navies. They were bigger and stronger than anything possessed by the English, whose forces were largely merchant vessels hastily converted for battle. But the English ships were faster and more easily maneuverable in the unpredictable winds of the English Channel. They also carried guns that could easily be reloaded for multiple firings, whereas the Spanish guns were designed to discharge only one broadside before hand-to-hand combat ensued. With these advantages the English were able to prevent the Armada from reaching port in the Netherlands and to destroy many individual ships as they were blown off course.

Throughout the 1580s and 1590s, Spanish military expeditions attempted to reunite the southern provinces and to

CHRONOLOGY

REVOLT OF THE NETHERLANDS

1559	Margaret of Parma named regent of the Netherlands
1566	Calvinist iconoclasm begins revolt
1567	Duke of Alba arrives in Netherlands and establishes Council of Blood
1568	Protestant Count Egmont executed
1572	Protestants capture Holland and Zeeland
1573	Alba relieved of his command
1576	Sack of Antwerp; pacification of Ghent
1581	Catholic and Protestant provinces split
1585	Spanish forces take Brussels and Antwerp
1609	Twelve Years' Truce

The defeat of the immense armada that Philip II sent to invade England in 1588 dealt a serious blow to Spain's standing in Europe.

conquer the northern ones. But Spanish successes in the south were outweighed by the long-term failure of their objectives in the north. In 1609, Spain and the Netherlands concluded the Twelve Years' Truce, which tacitly recognized the existence of the state of Holland. By the beginning of the seventeenth century, Holland was not only an independent state; it was one of the greatest rivals of Spain and Portugal.

THE STRUGGLES IN EASTERN EUROPE

In eastern Europe, dynastic struggles outweighed the problems created by religious reform. Muscovy remained the bulwark of Eastern Orthodox Christianity, immune from the struggles over the Roman faith. Protestantism did spread into Poland-Lithuania, but its presence was tolerated by the Polish state. The spread of dissent was checked not by repression, but by a vigorous Catholic reformation led by the Jesuits. The domestic crises in the East were crises of state rather than of the church. In Muscovy, the disputed succession that followed the death of Ivan the Terrible plunged the state into anarchy and civil war. Centuries of conflict between Poland-Lithuania and Muscovy came to a head with the Poles' desperate gamble to seize control of their massive eastern neighbor. War between Poland-Lithuania and Muscovy inevitably dominated the politics of the entire region. The Baltic states, most notably Sweden, soon joined the fray.

Kings and Diets in Poland

Until the end of the sixteenth century, Poland-Lithuania was the dominant power in the eastern part of Europe. It was economically healthy and militarily strong. Through its Baltic ports, especially Gdansk, Poland played a central role in international commerce and a dominant role in the northern grain trade. The vast size of the Polish state made defense difficult, and during the course of the sixteenth century it had lost lands to Muscovy in the east and to the Crimean Tartars in the south. But the permanent union with Lithuania in 1569 and the gradual absorption of the Baltic region of Livonia more than compensated for these losses. Matters of war and peace, of taxation, and of reform were placed under the strict supervision of the Polish Diet, a parliamentary body that represented the Polish landed elite. The Diet also carefully controlled religious policy. Roman Catholicism was the principal religion in Poland, but the state tolerated numerous Protestant and Eastern creeds. In the Warsaw Confederation of 1573 the Polish gentry vowed "that we who differ in matters of religion will keep the peace among ourselves."

The biological failure of the Jagiellon monarchy in Poland ended that nation's most successful line of kings. Without a natural heir the Polish nobility and gentry, who officially elected the monarch, had to peddle their throne among the princes of Europe. When Sigismund III (1587–1632) was elected to the Polish throne in 1587, he was also heir to the crown of Sweden. Sigismund accepted the prohibitions against religious repression outlined in the Warsaw Confederation, but he actively encouraged the establishment of Jesuit schools, the expansion of monastic orders, and the strengthening of the Roman Catholic Church.

All of these policies enjoyed the approval of the Polish ruling classes. But the Diet would not support Sigismund's efforts to gain control of the Swedish crown, which he inherited in 1592 but from which he was deposed three years later. If Sigismund triumphed in Sweden, all Poland would get was a part-time monarch. The Polish Diet consistently refused to give the king the funds necessary to invade Sweden successfully. Nevertheless, Sigismund mounted several unsuccessful campaigns against the Swedes that sapped Polish money and manpower.

Muscovy's Time of Troubles

The wars of Ivan the Great and Ivan the Terrible in the fifteenth and sixteenth centuries were waged to secure agricultural territory in the west and a Baltic port in the north. Both objectives came at the expense of Poland-Lithuania. But after the death of Ivan the Terrible in 1584, the Muscovite state began to disintegrate. For years it had been held together only by conquest and fear. Ivan's conflicts with the boyars, the hereditary nobility, created an aristocracy that was unwilling and unable to come to the aid of Ivan's successors. By 1601, the crown was plunged into a crisis of legitimacy known as the Time of Troubles. Ivan had murdered his heir in a fit of anger and left his half-witted son to inherit the throne. This led to a vacuum of power at the center as well as a struggle for the spoils of government. Private armies ruled great swaths of the state, and pretenders to the crown—all claiming to be Dimitri, the lost brother of the last legitimate tsar—appeared everywhere. Ambitious groups of boyars backed their own claimants to the throne. So, too, did ambitious foreigners who eagerly sought to carve up Muscovite possessions.

Muscovy's Time of Troubles was Poland's moment of opportunity. While Muscovy floundered in anarchy and civil war, Poland looked to regain the territory that it had lost to

▼ Eastern Europe (ca. 1550) after the consolidation of Russia and the growth of Poland. The eastern part of Europe was still sparsely populated and economically underdeveloped.

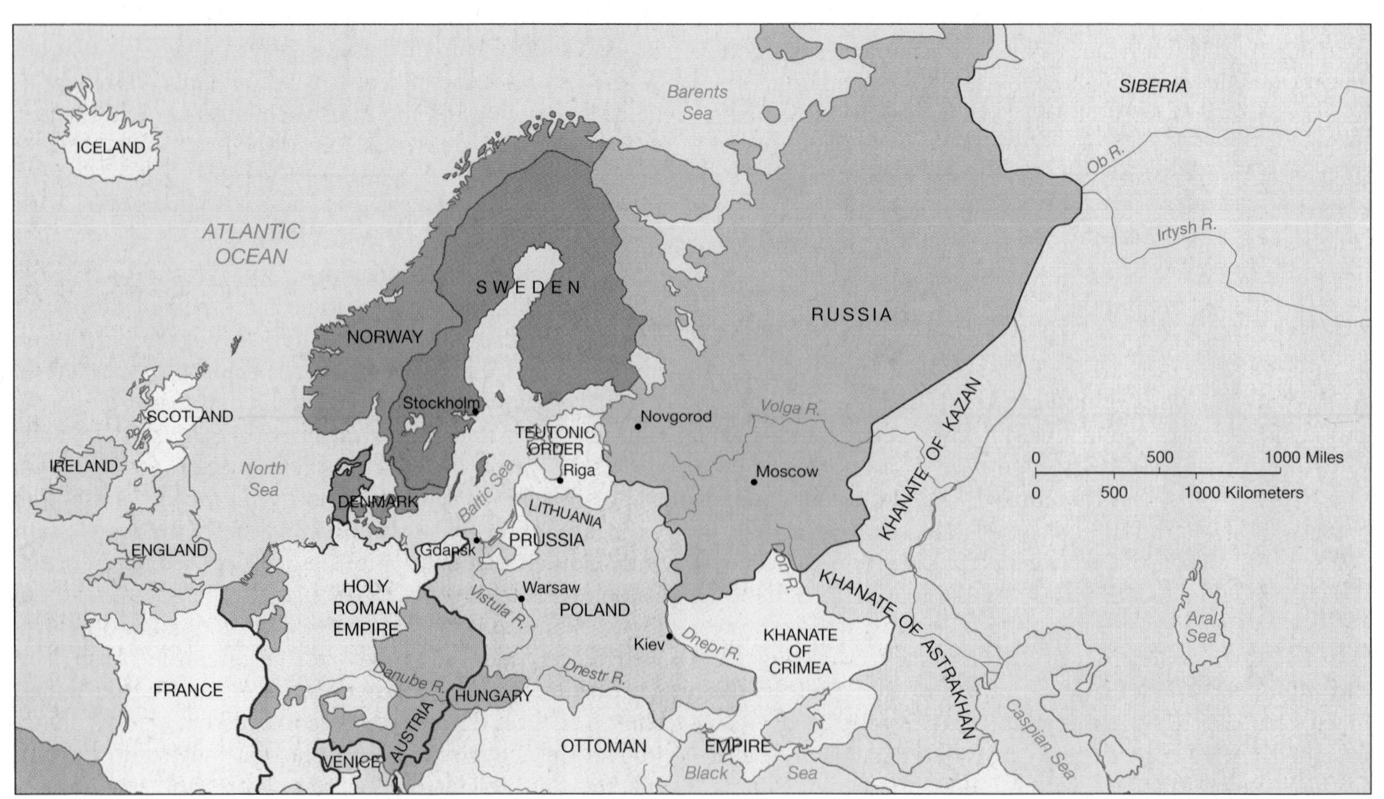

Muscovy over the previous century. Sigismund abandoned war with Sweden to intervene in the struggle for the Russian crown. Polish forces crossed into Muscovy, and Sigismund's generals backed one of the strongest of the false Dimitris, but their plan to put him on the throne failed when he was assassinated. Sigismund used the death of the last false Dimitri as a pretext to assert his own claim to the Muscovite crown. More Polish forces poured across the frontier. In 1610 they took Moscow, and Sigismund proclaimed himself tsar, intending to unite the two massive states.

The Russian boyars, so long divided, now rose against the Polish enemy. The Polish garrison in Moscow was starved into submission, and a native Russian, Michael Romanov (1613–1645), was chosen tsar by an assembly of landholders, the Zemsky Sobor. He made a humiliating peace with the Swedes—who had also taken advantage of the Time of Troubles to invade Muscovy's Baltic provinces—in return for Swedish assistance against the Poles. Intermittent fighting continued for another 20 years. In the end, Poland agreed to peace and a separate Muscovite state but only in exchange for large territorial concessions.

The Rise of Sweden. For the only time in its history, Sweden acquired territories on the European mainland.

The Rise of Sweden

Sweden's rise to power during the seventeenth century was as startling as it was swift. Until the Reformation, Sweden had been part of the Scandinavian confederation ruled by the Danes. Although the Swedes had a measure of autonomy, they were very much a junior partner in Baltic affairs. Denmark controlled the narrow sound that linked the Baltic Sea with the North Sea, and its prosperity derived from the tolls it collected on imports and exports. When, in 1523, Gustav I Vasa led the uprising of the Swedish aristocracy that ended Danish domination, he won the right to rule over a poor, sparsely populated state with few towns or developed seaports. The Vasas ruled Sweden in conjunction with the aristocracy. Although the throne was hereditary, the part played by the nobility in elevating Gustav I Vasa (1523–1560) gave the nobles a powerful voice in Swedish affairs. Through the council of state, known as the Rad, the Swedish nobility exerted a strong check on the monarch.

Sweden's aggressive foreign policy began accidentally. When in the 1550s the Teutonic Knights found themselves no longer capable of ruling in Livonia, the Baltic seaports that had been under their dominion scrambled for new alliances. Muscovy and Poland-Lithuania were the logical choices, but the town of Reval, an important outlet for Russian trade near the mouth of the Gulf of Finland, asked Sweden for protection. After some hesitation, since the occupation of territory on the southern shores of the Baltic would involve great expense, Sweden fortified Reval in 1560. A decade later, Swedish forces captured Narva, farther to the east, and consolidated Sweden's hold on the Livonian coast. By occupying the most important ports on the Gulf of Finland, Sweden could control a sizable portion of the Muscovite trade.

Now only two obstacles prevented the Swedes from dominating trade with Muscovy: Archangel in the north and Riga in the south. In the 1580s, the Muscovites established a port at Archangel on the White Sea. With this new port they opened a trading route to the west around northern Scandinavia. Sweden benefited from the White Sea trade by claiming the northern portions of the Scandinavian peninsula that were needed to make the trade secure. In all of their dealings with Muscovy the Swedes sought further privileges at Archangel while laying plans for its conquest. Riga was a problem of a different sort. As the Swedes secured the northern Livonian ports, more of the Muscovy trade moved to the south and passed through Riga, which would have to be captured or blockaded if the Swedes were to control commerce in the eastern Baltic.

Sigismund's aggressive alliance with the Polish Jesuits had persuaded the Swedish nobility that he would undermine their Lutheran church, and Sigismund was deposed in favor of his uncle Charles IX (1604–1611). War between Sweden and Poland resulted from Sigismund's efforts to regain the Swedish crown, and the Swedes used the opportunity to blockade Riga and to occupy more Livonian territory. The Swedish navy was far superior to any force that the Poles could assemble, but on land, Polish forces were masters. The Swedish invasion force suffered a crushing defeat and had to retreat to its coastal enclaves. The Poles now had an opportunity to retake all of Livonia, but, as always, the Polish Diet was reluctant to finance Sigismund's wars. Furthermore, Sigismund had his eyes on a bigger prize. Rather than follow up its Swedish victory, Poland invaded Muscovy.

Meanwhile, the blockade of Riga and the assembly of a large Swedish fleet in the Baltic threatened Denmark. The Danes continued to claim sovereignty over Sweden and took the opportunity of the Polish-Swedish conflict to reassert it. In 1611, under the energetic leadership of the Danish king Christian IV (1588–1648), Denmark invaded Sweden from both the east and the west. The Danes captured the towns of Kalmar and Alvsborg and threatened to take Stockholm. To end the Danish war, Sweden accepted humiliating terms in 1613, renouncing all claims to the northern coasts and recognizing Danish control of the Arctic trading route.

Paradoxically, these setbacks became the springboard for Swedish success. Fear of the Danes led both the English and the Dutch into alliances with Sweden. These countries all shared Protestant interests, and the English were heavily committed to the Muscovy trade, which was still an important part of Swedish commerce. Fear of the Poles had a similar effect on Muscovy. In 1609 the Swedes agreed to send 5,000 troops to Muscovy to help repel the Polish invasion. In return, Muscovy agreed to cede to Sweden its Baltic possessions. This was accomplished in 1617 and gave Sweden complete control of the Gulf of Finland.

In 1611, during the middle of the Danish war, Charles IX died and was succeeded by his son Gustavus Adolphus (1611–1632), one of the leading Protestant princes of his day. Gustavus's greatest skills were military, and he inherited an ample navy and an effective army. Unlike nearly every other European state, Sweden raised its forces from its own citizens. Gustavus introduced new weapons such as the light mobile gun and reshaped his army into standard-size squadrons and regiments, which were easier to administer and deploy.

The calamitous wars that Gustavus inherited from his father occupied him during the early years of his reign. He was forced to conclude the humiliating peace with the Danes in 1613 and to go to war with the Russians in 1614 to secure the Baltic coastal estates that had been promised in 1609. Gustavus's first military initiative was to resume war with Poland to force Sigismund to renounce his claim to the Swedish throne. In 1621, Gustavus landed in Livonia and in two weeks captured Riga, the capstone of Sweden's Baltic ambitions. Occupation of Riga increased Swedish control of the Muscovy trade and deprived Denmark of a significant portion of its customs duties. Gustavus now claimed Riga as a Swedish port and successfully demanded that ships sailing from there pay tolls to Sweden rather than Denmark. By the mid-seventeenth century, Sweden ranked among the leading Protestant powers.

THE THIRTY YEARS' WAR, 1618–1648

In time, the isolated conflicts that dotted the corners of Europe were joined together. In 1609, Spain and the Dutch Republic had signed a truce that was to last until 1621. In over 40 years of nearly continuous fighting, the Dutch had carved out a state in the northern Netherlands. They used the truce to consolidate their position and increase their prosperity. Spain had reluctantly accepted Dutch independence, but Philip III (1598–1621), like his father before him, never abandoned the objective of recovering his Burgundian inheritance. By the beginning of the seventeenth century, Philip had good reasons for hope. Beginning in the 1580s, Spanish forces had reconquered the southern provinces of the Netherlands. The prosperous towns of Brussels, Antwerp, and Ghent were again under Spanish control, and they provided a springboard for another invasion.

The Twelve Years' Truce gave Spain time to prepare for the final assault. During this time, Philip III attempted to resolve all of Spain's other European conflicts so that he could then give full attention to a resumption of the Dutch war. Circumstance smiled on his efforts. In 1603, the pacific James I (1603–1625) came to the English throne. Secure in his island state, James I desired peace among all Christian princes. He quickly concluded the war with Spain that had begun with the attempted invasion of the Spanish Armada, and he entered into negotiations to marry his heir to a Spanish princess. In 1610, the bellicose Henry IV of France was felled by an assassin's knife. French plans to renew war with Spain were abandoned with the accession of the eight-year-old Louis XIII (1610–1643).

Bohemia Revolts

The Peace of Augsburg had served the German states well. The principle that the religion of the ruler was the religion of the state complicated the political life of the Holy Roman Empire, but it also pacified it. Though rulers had the right to enforce uniformity on their subjects, in practice many of the larger states tolerated more than one religion. By the beginning of the seventeenth century, Catholicism and Protestantism had achieved a rough equality within the German states, symbolized by the fact that of the seven electors who chose the Holy Roman Emperor, three were Catholic, three were Protestant, and the seventh was the emperor himself, acting as king of Bohemia. This situation was not unwelcome to the leaders of the Austrian Habsburg family who succeeded Emperor Charles V. By necessity the eastern Habsburgs were more

WAR IS HELL

No source has better captured the brutality of the Thirty Years' War than the novel Simplicissimus *(1669). In a series of loosely connected episodes, the hero (whose name means "the simplest of the simple") is snatched from his village to serve in marauding armies whose confrontations with local villagers are usually more horrifying than the episode narrated here.*

FOCUS QUESTIONS

How do the peasants respond to the troopers' actions? What does this passage suggest about the breadth of the average villager's experience?

THESE TROOPERS WERE EVEN NOW READY TO MARCH, and had the pastor fastened by a rope to lead him away. Some cried, "Shoot him down, the rogue!" Others would have money from him. But he, lifting up his hands to heaven, begged, for the sake of the Last Judgment, for forbearance and Christian compassion, but in vain; for one of them rode down and dealt him such a blow on the head that he fell flat, and commended his soul to God. Nor did the remainder of the captured peasants fare any better. But even when it seemed these troopers, in their cruel tyranny, had clean lost their wits, came such a swarm of armed peasants out of the wood, that it seemed a wasps'-nest had been stirred. And these began to yell so frightfully and so furiously to attack with sword and musket that all my hair stood on end; and never had I been at such a merrymaking before: for the peasants of the Spessart and the Vogelsberg are as little wont as are the Hessians and men of the Sauerland and the Black Forest to let themselves be crowed over on their own dunghill. So away went the troopers, and not only left behind the cattle they had captured, but threw away bag and baggage also, and so cast all their booty to the winds lest themselves should become booty for the peasants: yet some of them fell into their hands. This sport took from me well-nigh all desire to see the world, for I thought, if 'tis all like this, then is the wilderness far more pleasant.

From Hans Von Grimmelshausen, *The Adventurous Simplicissimus.*

tolerant than their Spanish kinfolk. The head of their house was elected king of Bohemia and king of Hungary, both states with large Protestant populations.

A Fatal Election. In 1617, Mathias, the childless Holy Roman Emperor, began making plans for his cousin, Ferdinand Habsburg, to succeed him. Ferdinand was a very devout and very committed Catholic. To ensure a Catholic majority among the electors, the emperor relinquished his Bohemian title and pressed for Ferdinand's election as the new king of Bohemia. The Protestant nobles of Bohemia forced the new king to accept the strictest limitations on his political and religious powers, but once elected, Ferdinand had not the slightest intention of honoring the provisions that had been thrust on him. His opponents were equally strong willed. When Ferdinand violated Protestant religious liberties, a group of noblemen marched to the royal palace in Prague in May 1618, found two of the king's chief advisers, and hurled them out of an upper-story window.

The Defenestration of Prague, as this incident came to be known, initiated a Protestant counteroffensive throughout the Habsburg lands. Fear of Ferdinand's policies led to Protestant uprisings in Hungary as well as Bohemia. The men who seized control of the government declared Ferdinand deposed and the throne vacant. But they had no candidate to accept their crown. Whatever their religion, princes were always uneasy about the overthrow of a lawful ruler. Whoever came to be called king of Bohemia in place of Ferdinand would have to face the combined might of the Habsburgs. When Emperor Mathias died in 1619, Ferdinand succeeded to the imperial title as Ferdinand II (1619–1637), and Frederick V, one of the Protestant electors, accepted the Bohemian crown.

Frederick V, the "Winter King." Frederick was a sincere but weak Calvinist whose credentials were much stronger than his abilities. His mother was a daughter of Prince William of Orange and his wife, Elizabeth, was a daughter of James I of England. It was widely believed that Elizabeth's resolution that she would "rather eat sauerkraut with a king than roast meat with an elector" decided the issue. No decision could have been more disastrous for the fate of Europe. Frederick ruled a geographically divided German state known as the Palatinate. One hundred miles separated the two segments of his lands, but both were strategically important. The Lower Palatinate bordered on the Catholic Spanish Netherlands and the Upper Palatinate on Catholic Bavaria.

Once Frederick accepted the Bohemian crown, he was faced with a war on three fronts. Ferdinand II had no difficulty enlisting allies to recover the Bohemian crown, since he could pay them with the spoils of Frederick's lands. Spanish troops from the Netherlands occupied the Lower Palatinate, and Bavarian troops occupied the Upper Palatinate. Frederick, by contrast, met rejection wherever he turned. Neither the Dutch nor the English would send more than token aid; both had advised him against breaking the imperial peace. The Lutheran princes of Germany would not enter into a war between Calvinists and Catholics, especially after Ferdinand II promised to protect the Bohemian Lutherans.

At the Battle of the White Mountain in 1620, Ferdinand's Catholic forces annihilated Frederick's army. Frederick and Elizabeth fled to Denmark, and Bohemia was left to face the wrath of Ferdinand, the victorious king and emperor. The retribution was horrible. Mercenaries who had fought for Ferdinand II were allowed to sack Prague for a week. Elective monarchy was abolished, and Bohemia became part of the hereditary Habsburg lands. Free peasants were enserfed and subjected to imperial law. Nobles who had supported Frederick lost their lands and their privileges. Calvinism was repressed and thoroughly rooted out, consolidating forever the Catholic character of Bohemia. Frederick's estates were carved up, and his rights as elector were transferred to the Catholic duke of Bavaria. The Battle of the White Mountain was a turning point in the history of central Europe, for it forced all Protestant nations to arm for war.

CHRONOLOGY	
THE THIRTY YEARS' WAR	
1618	Defenestration of Prague
1619	Ferdinand Habsburg elected Holy Roman Emperor; Frederick of the Palatinate accepts the crown of Bohemia
1620	Catholic victory at battle of the White Mountain
1621	End of Twelve Years' Truce; war between Spain and Netherlands
1626	Danes form Protestant alliance under Christian IV
1627	Spain declares bankruptcy
1630	Gustavus Adolphus leads Swedish forces into Germany
1631	Sack of Magdeburg; Protestant victory at Breitenfeld
1632	Protestant victory at Lützen; death of Gustavus Adolphus
1635	France declares war on Spain
1640	Portugal secedes from Spain
1643	Battle of Rocroi; French forces repel Spaniards
1648	Peace of Westphalia

The War Widens

For the Habsburgs, religious and dynastic interests were inseparable. Ferdinand II and Philip III of Spain fought for their beliefs and for their patrimony. Their victory gave them more than they could have expected. Ferdinand swallowed up Bohemia and strengthened his position in the empire. Philip gained possession of a vital link in his supply route between Italy and the Netherlands. Spanish expansion threatened France. The occupation of the Lower Palatinate placed a ring of Spanish armies around France from the Pyrenees to the Low Countries. The French too searched for allies. But French opinion remained divided over which was the greater evil: Spain or Protestantism.

The Danes Respond. Frederick, now in Holland, refused to accept the judgment of battle. He lobbied for a grand alliance to repel the Spaniards from the Lower Palatinate and to restore the religious balance in the empire. Though his personal cause met with little sympathy, his political logic was impeccable, especially after Spain again declared war on the Dutch. A grand Protestant alliance—secretly supported by the French—brought together England, Holland, a number of German states, and Denmark. It was the Danes who led this potentially powerful coalition. In 1626, a large Danish army under the command of King Christian IV engaged imperial forces on German soil. But Danish forces could not match the superior numbers and the superior leadership of the Catholic mercenary forces under the command of the ruthless and brilliant Count Albrecht von Wallenstein (1583–1634). In 1629, the Danes withdrew from the empire and sued for peace.

If the Catholic victory at the White Mountain in 1620 threatened the well-being of German Protestantism, the Catholic triumph over the Danes threatened its survival. More powerful than ever, Ferdinand II was determined to turn the religious clock back to the state of affairs that had existed when the Peace of Augsburg was concluded in 1555. He demanded that all lands that had then been Catholic but had since become Protestant must now be returned to the Catholic fold. He also proclaimed that because the Peace of Augsburg made no provision for the toleration of Calvinists, they would no longer be tolerated in the empire. These policies together constituted a virtual revolution in the religious affairs of the German states, and they proved impossible to impose. Ferdinand succeeded in only one thing: he united Lutherans and Calvinists against him. Moreover, the costs of the war were heavy even for the victors. Wallenstein, who had over 130,000 men in arms, would no longer take orders from anyone, and Ferdinand II was forced to dismiss him from service.

Protestant Gains. In 1630, King Gustavus Adolphus of Sweden decided to enter the German conflict to protect Swedish interests. While Gustavus Adolphus struggled to construct his alliance, imperial forces continued their triumphant progress. In 1631, they besieged, captured, and put to the torch the town of Magdeburg. Perhaps three-fourths of the 40,000 inhabitants of the town were brutally slaughtered. The sack of Magdeburg marked a turning point in Protestant fortunes. It gave the international Protestant community a unifying symbol that enhanced Gustavus's military efforts. Brandenburg and Saxony joined Gustavus Adolphus, allowing him to open a second front in Bohemia. In the autumn of 1631, this combination overwhelmed the imperial armies. Gustavus won a decisive triumph at Breitenfeld, while the Saxons occupied Prague.

Gustavus Adolphus lost no time in pressing his advantage. While Ferdinand II pleaded with Wallenstein to again lead the imperial forces, the Swedes marched west to the Rhine, easily conquering the richest of the Catholic cities and retaking the Lower Palatinate. In early 1632, Protestant forces plundered Bavaria, but Wallenstein resumed his command and chose to chase the Saxons from Bohemia rather than the Swedes from Bavaria. Not until the winter of 1632 did the armies of Gustavus and Wallenstein finally meet. At the Battle of Lutzen the Swedes won the field but lost their beloved king. Wounded in the leg, the back, and the head, Gustavus Adolphus died. In less than two years he had decisively transformed the course of the war and the course of Europe's future. Protestant forces now occupied most of central and northern Germany.

The Long Quest for Peace

The final stages of the war involved the resumption of the century-old struggle between France and Spain. When the Twelve Years' Truce expired in 1621, Spain again declared war on the Dutch. Dutch naval power was considerable, and the Dutch took the war to the far reaches of the globe, attacking Portuguese settlements in Brazil and in the East and harassing Spanish shipping on the high seas. In 1628, the Dutch captured the entire Spanish treasure fleet as it sailed from the New World. Spain had declared bankruptcy in 1627, and the loss of the whole of the next year's treasure from America exacerbated an already catastrophic situation.

These reversals, combined with the continued successes of Habsburg forces in central Europe, convinced Louis XIII and his chief minister, Cardinal Richelieu, that the time for active involvement in European affairs was now at hand. Throughout the early stages of the war, France had secretly aided anti-Habsburg forces. Gustavus Adolphus's unexpected success dramatically altered French calculations.

Gustavus Adolphus of Sweden, shown at the battle of Breitenfeld in 1631. The battle was the first important Protestant victory of the Thirty Years' War. Gustavus died on the battlefield at Lützen in the following year.

Now it was evident that the Habsburgs could no longer combine their might, and Spanish energies would be drained off in the Netherlands and central Europe. The time had come to take an open stand. In 1635, France declared war on Spain.

France took the offensive first, invading the Spanish Netherlands. In 1636, a Spanish army struck back, pushing to within 25 miles of Paris before it was repelled. Both sides soon began to search for a settlement, but pride prevented them from laying down their arms. Spain toppled first. Its economy in shambles and its citizens in revolt over high prices and higher taxes, it could no longer maintain its many-fronted war. The Swedes again defeated imperial forces in Germany. The Dutch destroyed much of Spain's Atlantic fleet in 1639, and the Portuguese rose up against the union of crowns that had brought them nothing but expense and the loss of crucial portions of their empire. In 1640, the Portuguese regained their independence. In 1643, Spain gambled once more on a knockout blow against the French. But at the Battle of Rocroi, exhausted French troops held out, and the Spanish invasion failed.

By now, the desire for peace was universal. Most of the main combatants had long since perished: Philip III, ever optimistic, in 1621; Frederick V, an exile to the end, in 1632; Gustavus Adolphus, killed at Lutzen in the same year; Wallenstein, murdered by order of Ferdinand II in 1634; Ferdinand himself in 1637; and Louis XIII in 1643, five days before the French triumph at Rocroi. Those who succeeded them did not have the same passions, and after so many decades the longing for peace was the strongest emotion on the Continent.

▼ The Peace of Westphalia, 1648, recognized the new boundaries of European states that included an independent Portugal and United Netherlands. It also recognized the growth of the Ottoman Empire into the Balkans.

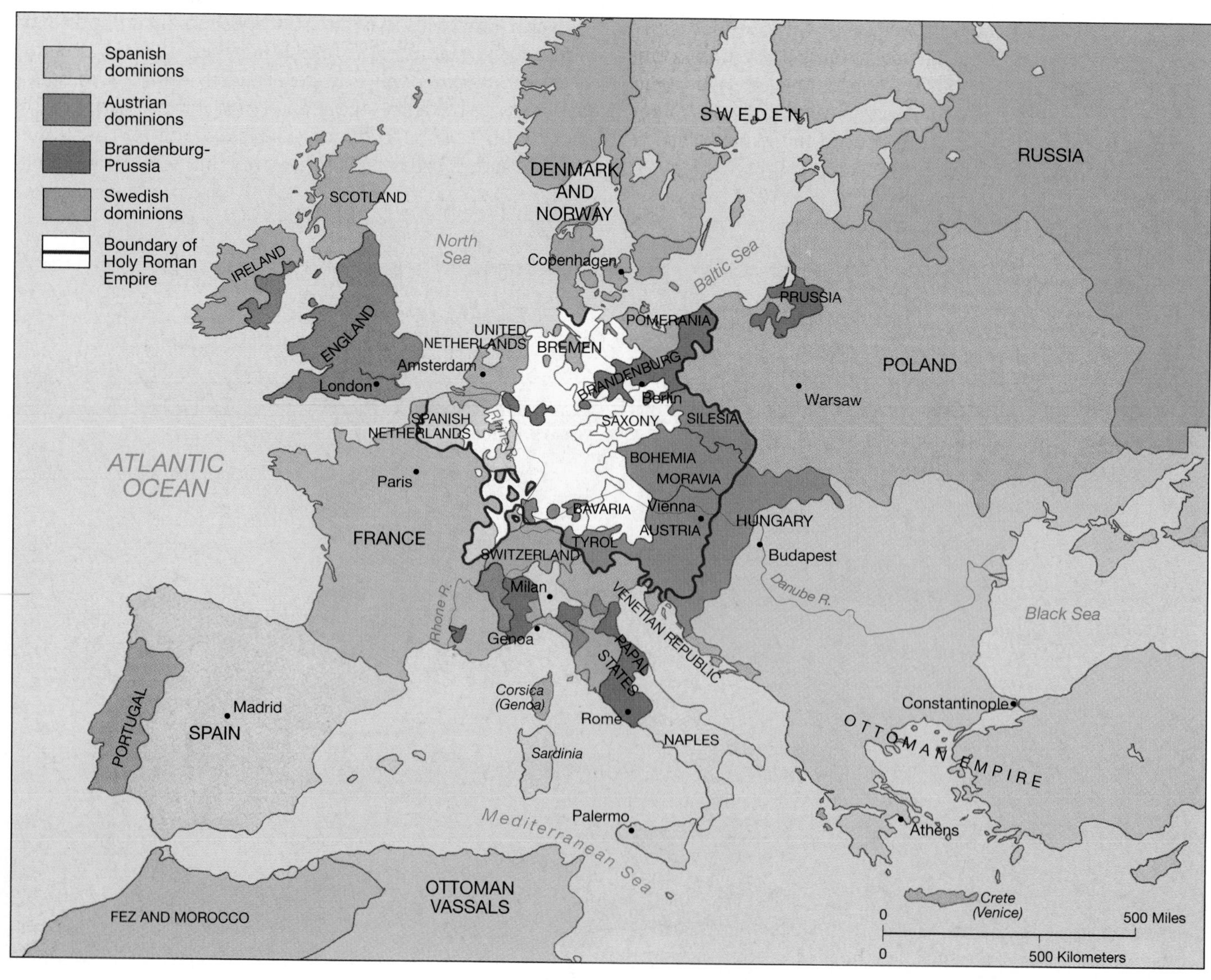

In 1648 a series of agreements, collectively known as the Peace of Westphalia, established the outlines of the political geography of Europe for the next century. Its focus was on the Holy Roman Empire, and it reflected Protestant successes in the final two decades of war. Sweden gained further territories on the Baltic, making it master of the north German ports. France, too, gained in territory and prestige. It kept the vital towns in the Lower Palatinate through which Spanish men and matériel had moved, and though it did not agree to come to terms with Spain immediately, France's fear of encirclement was at an end. The Dutch gained statehood through official recognition by Spain and through the power they had displayed in building and maintaining an overseas empire.

Territorial boundaries were reestablished as they had existed in 1624, giving the Habsburgs control of both Bohemia and Hungary. The independence of the Swiss cantons was now officially recognized as were the rights of Calvinists to the protection of the Peace of Augsburg, which again was to govern the religious affairs of the empire. Two of the larger German states were strengthened as a counterweight to the emperor's power. Bavaria was allowed to retain the Upper Palatinate, and Brandenburg, which ceded some of its coastal territory to Sweden, gained extensive territories in the east. The emperor's political control over the German states was also weakened. German rulers were given independent authority over their states and the imperial diet, rather than the emperor, was empowered to settle disputes. Thus weakened, future emperors ruled in the Habsburg territorial lands with little ability to control, or influence, or even arbitrate German affairs. The judgment that the Holy Roman Empire was neither holy, nor Roman, nor an empire was now irrevocably true.

Conclusion

THE PEACE OF WESTPHALIA put the pieces of the map of European states back together. Protestantism and Catholicism now coexisted, and there was to be little further change in the geography of religion. The northwest of Europe—England, Holland, Scandinavia, and the north German states—was Protestant; the south was Catholic. The empire of the German peoples was now at an end, and the Austro-Hungarian empire was at a beginning. Holland and Sweden had become international powers; Spain and Denmark faded from prominence. Muscovy began a long period of isolation from the West as it attempted to restore a semblance of government to its people.

The costs of the century of nearly continuous warfare were horrific. The population of Germany fell from 15 million in 1600 to 11 million in 1650. The armies brought destruction of all kinds in their wake. Plague again raged in Europe; the town of Augsburg lost 18,000 inhabitants in the early 1630s. Famine, too, returned to a continent that 50 years earlier had been self-sufficient in grain. The war played havoc with all of the economies that it touched. Inflation, devaluation of coinage, and huge public and private debts were all directly attributable to the years of fighting. Furthermore, the toll taken on the spirit of generations that never knew peace is incalculable.

QUESTIONS FOR REVIEW

1. How was Henry IV able to bring peace to France after decades of civil war?
2. What were the political and religious connections between the Armada launched against England by Philip II and the revolt of the Netherlands?
3. How did Sweden rise to become one of Europe's great powers in the first half of the seventeenth century?
4. How did religion help spark and spread the Thirty Years' War?
5. What were the effects of the Peace of Westphalia on political arrangements in the heart of Europe?

DISCOVERING WESTERN CIVILIZATION ONLINE

You can obtain more information about Europe at war at the websites listed below. See also the companion website that accompanies this text: www.ablongman.com/kishlansky, which includes an online study guide and additional resources.

The Crises of the Western States

www.fordham.edu/halsall/mod/modsbook1.html#Conflict
Links to documents on the French wars of religion, the invasion of the Spanish Armada, and the Thirty Years' War.

www.ibiblio.org/wm/paint/tl/north-ren/
Links to pictures and portraits from the late sixteenth and early seventeenth centuries.

www.ibiblio.org/wm/paint/auth/bruegel/death.jpg
A web page depicting Peter Brueghel's *Triumph of Death,* one of the most evocative paintings of the destruction wrought by warfare in early modern Europe.

The Thirty Years' War, 1618–1648

www.yale.edu/lawweb/avalon/westphal.htm
The full text of the Treaty of Westphalia that ended the Thirty Years' War.

SUGGESTIONS FOR FURTHER READING

General Reading

M. S. Anderson, *The Origins of the Modern European State System, 1494–1618* (London: Longman, 1998). A survey of developments stressing war and diplomacy across all of Europe.

Richard Bonney, *The European Dynastic States, 1494–1660* (Oxford: Oxford University Press, 1991). The most up-to-date introduction to the period by a noted historian of France.

Geoffrey Parker, *Europe in Crisis, 1598–1648* (Oxford: Blackwells, 2001). Compelling study of European states in the early seventeenth century.

The Crises of the Western States

Susan Brigden, *New Worlds, Lost Worlds: The Rule of the Tudors, 1485–1603* (New York: Viking, 2001). The latest volume in the new Penguin History of Britain series.

Mack Holt, *The French Wars of Religion, 1562–1629* (Cambridge: Cambridge University Press, 1995). The wars of religion seen in a long perspective.

Jonathan Israel, *The Dutch Republic and the Hispanic World, 1606–1661* (Oxford: Clarendon, 1986). A panoramic survey of the stormy relations between empire and republic.

John Lynch, *Spain, 1516–1598: From Nation State to World Empire* (Cambridge, Mass.: Blackwell, 1994). The most up-to-date survey.

Geoffrey Parker, *Philip II* (Boston: Little, Brown, 1978). The best introduction.

Michael Roberts, *Gustavus Adolphus and the Rise of Sweden* (London: English Universities Press, 1973). A highly readable account of Sweden's rise to power.

Penry Williams, *The Later Tudors* (Oxford: Oxford University Press, 1995). A recent survey in the Oxford history of England.

The Struggles in Eastern Europe

David Kirby, *Northern Europe in the Early Modern Period: The Baltic World, 1492–1772* (London: Longman, 1990). The best single volume on Baltic politics.

Maureen Perrie, *Pretenders and Popular Monarchisms in Early Modern Russia* (Cambridge: Cambridge University Press, 1995). Recent scholarship on the Time of Troubles, focusing on the royal impostors.

Michael Roberts, *The Swedish Imperial Experience* (Cambridge: Cambridge University Press, 1979). Reflections on Swedish history by the preeminent historian of early modern Sweden.

The Thirty Years' War

Ronald G. Asch, *The Thirty Years' War: The Holy Roman Empire and Europe, 1618–1648* (New York: St. Martin's Press, 1997). A narrative survey of this complicated conflict.

J. H. Elliott, *Richelieu and Olivares* (Cambridge: Cambridge University Press, 1984). A comparison of statesmen and statesmanship in the early seventeenth century.

Geoffrey Parker, ed., *The Thirty Years' War*, 2d ed. (London: Routledge, 1997). A revised edition of the standard survey of the conflict.

CHAPTER 15

THE EXPERIENCES OF LIFE IN EARLY MODERN EUROPE, 1500–1650

THE VISUAL RECORD

HAYMAKING

IT IS SUMMER IN THE LOW COUNTRIES. The trees are full, the meadows are green, and bushes hang heavy with fruit. The day has dawned brightly for haymaking. Yesterday, the long meadow was mowed. Today, the hay will be gathered, and the first fruits and vegetables of the season will be harvested. From throughout the village, families come together in labor. Twice each summer, the grass is cut, dried, and stacked. Some of it will be left in the fields for the animals until autumn; some will be carried into large lofts and stored for the winter.

This scene of communal farming was repeated with little variation throughout Europe in the sixteenth century. The village we are viewing is fairly prosperous. We can see at least three horses (still a luxury for farmers) and a large wheeled cart. The houses of the village also suggest comfort. The one at the far right is typical. It contains one floor for living and a loft for storage. The chimney separates a kitchen in the back from the long hall where the family works, sleeps, and entertains itself. The bed—it is not uncommon for there to be only one for the whole family—is probably located near the fireplace. It will be restuffed with straw after the harvest. The spinning wheel probably stands near the single window, which is covered by oiled animal skin, since glass is still much too expensive for use in rural housing. The long end of the hall, farthest from heat and light, will be home to the family's animals once winter sets in. But now, in summer, it is a luxurious space where children can play or parents can claim a little privacy.

The church, easily distinguished by its steeple and arched doorway, is made of brick. The steeple has 16 windows, probably all set with expensive glass and some even with stained glass. The church would have been built over several generations at considerable cost to the villagers. Even the most prosperous houses in the far meadow are all made of timber and thatch, and only the village well, in the middle of the picture, and the chimneys of the houses show any other sign of brick.

In the center of the scene are a large number of laborers. Four men with pitchforks load the cart while two women sweep the hay that falls back into new piles. Throughout the field, men and women, distinguished only by their clothing, rake hay into large stacks for successive loadings of the cart. At least 25 individuals work at these tasks. Men perform the heaviest work of loading the haycart and hammering the scythes; men and women share all the other

work. Although no children appear in the scene, some are undoubtedly at work picking berries and beans.

The scenes of physical labor remind us that the life of ordinary people in the sixteenth century was neither romantic nor despondent, neither quaint nor primitive. It had its own joys and sorrows, its own triumphs and failures. Inevitably, we compare it to our experiences and contrast it to our comforts. By our standards, a sixteenth-century prince endured greater material hardships than a twentieth-century slum resident. There was no running water, no central heating, no lavatories, no electricity. There was no relief for toothache, headache, or numbing pain. Travel was dangerous and exhausting. There was no protection from the open air, and many nights were spent on the bare ground. Waiting for winds to sail was more tedious and uncertain than waiting for planes to fly. Entertainment was sparse and the court jester was no match for stereo and video. But though we cannot help but be struck by these differences, we must not judge life in sixteenth-century Europe by our own standard of living. We must exercise our historical imagination if we are to appreciate the conditions of early modern European society.

LOOKING AHEAD

In this chapter, we will examine the social and economic conditions of early modern European society, dominated as it was by extreme change, and often, hardship. We will see how population growth put pressure on the European economy and how the rich became richer as food prices rose. We will also see how European governments were overwhelmed by changes they could only dimly perceive.

ECONOMIC LIFE

There was no typical sixteenth-century European. Language, custom, geography, and material conditions separated people in one place from those in another. Contrasts between social groups were more striking still. A Muscovite boyar had more in common with an English nobleman than either had with his own country's peasants. A Spanish goldsmith and a German brass maker lived remarkably similar lives when compared to the life of a shepherd anywhere in Europe. No matter how carefully historians attempt to distinguish between country and town life, between social or occupational groups, or between men and women, they are still smoothing out edges that are very rough, turning individuals into aggregates, and sacrificing the particular for the general.

One distinctive sixteenth-century experience that all groups shared, though they could only dimly perceive it, was change. In general, one generation improved on the situation of the last. Agriculture increased; more land was cleared, more crops were grown, and better tools were crafted. On the negative side, irreplaceable resources were lost as more trees were felled, more soil was eroded, and more fresh water was polluted. These changes and dynamic transformations in economic and social conditions affected everyday life in the sixteenth century.

Rural Life

In the sixteenth century, as much as 90 percent of the European population lived on farms or in small towns in which farming was the principal occupation. Villages were small and relatively isolated. They might range in size from a hundred families, as was common in France and Spain, to fewer than 20 families, which was the average size of Hungarian villages. These villages, large or small, prosperous or poor, were the bedrock of the sixteenth-century state. Surplus peasant population fed the towns' insatiable need for laborers and the crowns' for soldiers. The manor, the parish, and the rural administrative district were the institutional infrastructures of Europe. Each organized the peasantry for its own purposes. Manorial rents supported the lifestyle of the nobility; parish tithes supported the works of the Church; and local taxes supported the power of the state. Rents, tithes, and taxes easily absorbed more than half of the wealth produced by the land.

To survive on what remained, the village community had to be self-sufficient. In good times there was enough to eat and some to save for the future. Hard times meant hunger and starvation. One in every three harvests was bad; one in every five was disastrous. Between one-fifth and one-half of the grain harvested had to be saved as seed for the next planting season. When hunger was worst, people faced the agonizing choice of eating or saving their "seed corn."

The Sixteenth-Century Household. Hunger and cold were the constant companions of the average European. In Scandinavia and Muscovy, winter posed as great a threat to survival as starvation did. Everywhere in Europe, homes were inadequate shelter against the cold and damp. Most were built of wood and roofed in thatch. Inside walls were patched with dried mud, and windows were few and narrow. Piled leaves or straw covered the ground and acted as insulation. The typical house was one long room with a stone hearth at the end. The hearth provided both heat and light and belched forth soot and smoke through a brick chimney.

People had relatively few household possessions. The essential piece of furniture was the wooden chest, which was used for storage. A typical family could keep all of its belongings in the chest, which could then be buried or carried away in time of danger. The chest had other uses as well. Its flat top served as a table or bench or a raised surface on which food could be placed. Tables and stools were becoming more common during the sixteenth century, though chairs were still a great luxury. In areas in which spinning, weaving, or other domestic skills were an important part of the family's economy, a long bench was propped against the wall, usually beneath a window. Bedsteads were also becoming more common as the century wore on. They raised the straw mattresses off the ground, keeping them warmer and drier. All other family possessions related to food production. Iron spits and pots, or at least metal rings and clamps for wooden ones, were treasured goods that were passed from generation to generation. Most other implements were wooden. Long-handled spoons, boards known as trenchers used for cutting and eating, and one large cup and bowl were the basic stock of the kitchen. The family ate from the long trencher and passed the bowl and cup. Knives were essential farm tools that doubled for kitchen and mealtime duty, but forks were still a curiosity.

The scale of life was small, and its pace was controlled by nature: up at dawn, asleep at dusk, long working hours in summer, short ones in winter. For most people the world was bounded by the distance that could be traveled on foot. Those who stayed all their lives in their rural villages may never have seen more than a hundred other people at once. Their wisdom, handed down through generations, was of the practical experience that was necessary to survive the struggle with nature.

Reliance on Agriculture. Peasant life centered on agriculture. Technology and technique varied little across the Continent, but there were significant differences depending on climate and soil. Across the great plain, the breadbasket that stretched from the Low Countries to Poland-Lithuania, the most common form of crop growing was still the three-field rotation system. In this method, winter crops such as wheat or rye were planted in one field; spring crops such as barley, peas, or beans were planted in another; and the third field was left fallow. More than 80 percent of what was grown on the farm was consumed on the farm. In most parts of Europe, wheat was a luxury crop, sold at market rather than eaten at home. Wheat bread was prized for its taste, texture, and white color. Rye and barley were the staples for peasants. These grains were cheaper to grow, had higher yields, and could be brewed as well as baked. Most was baked into the coarse black bread that was the mainstay of the peasant diet. Two to three pounds a day for an adult male was an average allotment when grain was readily available. Beer and gruels of grain and skimmed milk or water flavored with fruit juice supplemented peasant fare. In one form or another, grain provided over 75 percent of the calories in a typical diet.

The warm climate and dry weather of Mediterranean Europe favored a two-crop rotation system. With less water and stronger sunlight, half the land had to be left fallow each year to restore its nutrients. Here, fruit, especially grapes and olives, was an essential supplement to diet. With smaller cereal crops, wine replaced beer as a beverage. The fermentation of grapes and grain into wine and beer also provided convenient ways of storing foodstuffs. Wine and olive oil were also luxury products and were most commonly exchanged for meat, which was less plentiful on southern European farms.

Animal husbandry was the main occupation in the third agricultural area of Europe, the mountainous and hilly regions. Sheep, the most common animal, provided the raw material for almost all clothing. Their skins were used for parchment and as window coverings, and they were a ready source of inexpensive meat. In western Europe, their wool was the main export of both England and Spain. Sheep could graze on land that was unsuitable for grain growing, and they could be sheared twice a year to provide a surplus of wool. Pigs were prevalent in woodland settlements. They foraged for food and were kept, like poultry, for slaughter. Oxen were essential as draft animals. In the dairying areas of Europe, cattle produced milk, cheese, and butter; in Hungary and Bohemia, the great breeding center of the Continent, they were raised for export; almost everywhere else, they were used as beasts of burden.

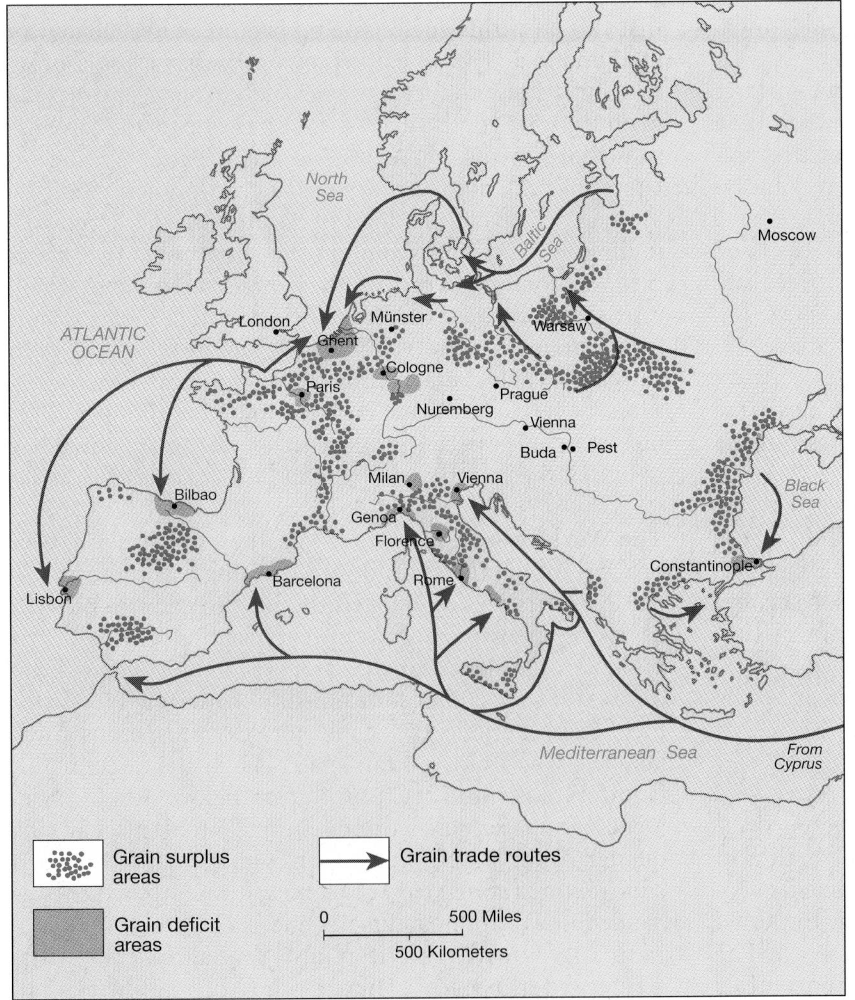

Grain Supply and Trade in Sixteenth-Century Europe. There were two distinct trading routes in northern Europe centering on the Baltic Sea and in southern Europe centering on the Mediterranean Sea.

Most agricultural land was owned not by those who worked it, but by lords who let it out in various ways. The land was still divided into manors, and the manor lord, or *seigneur*, was still responsible for maintaining order, administering justice, and arbitrating disputes. Lords were not necessarily individual members of the nobility; in fact, the lords were more commonly the Church or the state. In western Europe, peasants generally owned between one-third and one-half of the land they worked; eastern European peasants owned little if any land. But by the sixteenth century, almost all peasants enjoyed security of tenure on the land they worked. In return for various forms of rents, they used the land as they saw fit and could hand it down to their children. Rents were only occasionally paid in coin, though money rents became more common as the century progressed. More frequently, the lord received a fixed proportion of the land's yield or received labor from the peasant. Labor service was being replaced by monetary payments in northern and western Europe, but it continued in the east. German and Hungarian peasants normally owed two or three days' labor on the lord's estate each week, while Polish peasants might owe as much as four days. Labor service tied the peasants to the land they worked. Eastern European peasants were less mobile than peasants in the west, and as a result, towns were fewer and smaller in the east.

Though the land in each village was set out in large fields so that crops could be rotated, families owned their own pieces within the field, usually in scattered strips. There were also large common fields used as pasture, as well as common woodlands where animals foraged, fuel was gathered, and game was hunted. Villagers disputed frequently over rights to sticks and branches of trees and over the number of sheep or cows that could be grazed in the meadows, especially when resources were scarce.

Farm work was ceaseless toil. Six or seven times a year, farmers tilled the fields to spread animal manure below the surface of the soil. Although most villages possessed metal plows, the team of draft animals was the single essential component for farming. The births of foals and calves were more celebrated events than the births of children; the death of an ox or a horse was a catastrophe. Calamities lurked everywhere, from rain and drought to locusts and crows. Most farms could support only one family at subsistence level, and excess sons and daughters had to fend for themselves, either through marriage in the village or by migration to a town.

Town Life

In the country, people worked to the natural rhythm of the day and season. In the town, the bell tolled every hour. In the summer, the laborers gathered at the town gates at four in the morning, in the winter at seven. The bell signaled the time for morning and afternoon meals as well as the hour to lay down tools and return home. Wages were paid for hours worked—seven in winter, as many as sixteen in midsummer.

The Heart of Commerce. In all towns, an official guild structure organized and regulated labor. Rules laid down the requirements for training, the standards for quality, and the conditions for exchange. Only those who were officially sanctioned could work in trades, and each trade could perform only specified tasks.

While the life of the peasant community turned on self-sufficiency, that of the town turned on interdependence. The town was one large marketplace in which the circulation of goods dictated the residents' survival. Men and women in towns worked as hard as people on farms, but town dwellers generally received a more varied and more comfortable life in return. This is not to suggest that hunger and hardship were unknown in towns. Urban poverty was endemic and grew worse as the century wore on. In most towns, as much as one quarter of the entire population might be destitute, living on casual day labor, charity, or crime. But the institutional network of support for the poor and homeless was stronger. The urban poor fell victim more often to disease than to starvation.

Towns were distinguished by the variety of occupations that existed within them. The preparation and exchange of food dominated small market towns. Peasants would bring in their finest produce for sale and exchange it for vital manufactured goods such as iron spits or pots for cooking. In smaller towns, there was as much barter as sale; in larger places, money was exchanged for commodities. Women dominated the food trades in most market towns, trading, buying, and selling in the shop fronts that occupied the bottom story of their houses. In these small towns, men divided their time between traditional agricultural pursuits—there were always garden plots and even substantial fields attached to towns—and manufacturing. Almost every town made and distributed to the surrounding area some special product that drew to the town the wealth of the countryside.

The Workforce. In larger towns, the specialization of labor was more intense, and wage earning was more essential. Large traders dominated the major occupations such as baking, brewing, and cloth manufacture, leaving distribution in the hands of the family economy, where there might still be a significant element of bartering. Piecework handicrafts became the staple for less prosperous town families, who prepared raw materials for the large manufacturers or finished products before their sale. Metalworking or glassworking normally took place in one quarter of the town, brewing or baking in another. Each craft required long years of technical training, which was handed down from parents to children.

In large towns there were also specialized trades that women performed. There were 55 midwives in Nuremberg in the middle of the sixteenth century, and a board of women chosen from among the leading families of the town supervised their work. Nursing the sick also seems to have been an exclusively female occupation. So, too, was prostitution, which was officially sanctioned in most large towns in the early sixteenth century. There were official brothels, which were subject to taxation and government control. Public bathhouses served as unofficial brothels for the upper ranks of urban society. They, too, were regulated, especially after the first great epidemic of venereal disease in the early sixteenth century.

Most town dwellers, however, lived by unskilled labor. The most lucrative occupations were strictly controlled, so people who flocked to towns in search of employment usually hired themselves out as day laborers, hauling and lifting goods onto carts or boats or delivering water and food. After the first decades of the century, the supply of laborers exceeded the demand, and town authorities were constantly attempting to expel the throngs of casual workers. The most fortunate of such workers might succeed in becoming servants.

Domestic service was a critical source of household labor. Even families who were on the margins of subsistence employed servants to undertake innumerable household tasks, which allowed parents to pursue their primary occupations. Domestics were not apprentices, though they might aspire to become apprentices to the trade followed in the family with whom they lived. If they had kinship bonds in the town, apprenticeship was a likely outcome. But more commonly, domestics remained household servants, frequently changing employers in hope of more comfortable housing and better food.

Just as towns grew by the influx of surplus rural population, they sustained themselves by the import of surplus agricultural production. Most towns owned vast tracts of land, which they leased to peasants or farmed by hired labor. The town of Nuremberg controlled 25 square miles of forest and farmlands; the region around Toledo was inhabited by thousands of peasants who paid taxes and rents to city landlords. All towns had municipal storehouses of grain to preserve their inhabitants from famine during harvest failures. The diet of even a casual laborer would have been envied by an average peasant. Male grape pickers in Stuttgart received meat, soup, vegetables, wine, and beer; females got soup, vegetables, milk, and bread. In addition they received their wages. It is hardly surprising that towns were enclosed by thick walls and defended by armed guards.

Economic Change

Over the course of the sixteenth century, the European population increased by about one-third, much of the growth taking place in the first 50 years. Rough estimates suggest the rise to have been from about 80 million to 105 million. Patterns of growth varied by region. The population of the eastern part of Europe seems to have increased more steadily across the century, whereas in western Europe there was a population explosion in the early decades. The population of France may have doubled between 1450 and 1550, from 10 million to 20 million, before the wars of religion reversed the trend at the end of the century. The population of England nearly doubled between 1500 and 1600 from more than 2 million to more than 4 million. Europe had finally recovered from the devastation of the Black Death, and by 1600 its population was greater than it had ever been. Demographic growth was even more dramatic in the cities. In 1500, only four cities had populations greater than 100,000; in 1600 there were eight. Fifteen large cities more than doubled their populations. London experienced a phenomenal 400 percent increase.

The rise in population dramatically affected the lives of ordinary Europeans. In the early part of the century, the first phase of growth brought prosperity. Because there was uncultivated land that could be plowed and enough commons and woodlands to be shared, population increase was a welcome development. Even when rural communities began to reach their natural limits, opportunity still existed in the burgeoning towns and cities. At first the cycle was beneficial. Surplus on the farms led to economic growth in the towns. Growth in the towns meant more opportunities for people on the farms.

The first waves of migrants to the towns found opportunity everywhere. Apprenticeships were easy to find, and the shortage of casual labor kept wages at a decent rate. For a short while, rural families could send their younger sons and daughters to the towns and could purchase a few luxury goods for themselves.

This window of opportunity could not remain open forever. With more mouths to feed, more crops had to be planted, and new fields were carved from less fertile areas. In some villages, land was taken from the woodlands or scrublands that were used for animal forage and domestic fuel. In Spain, the land that was reclaimed came at the expense of land used for sheep grazing. This damaged both the domestic and foreign wool trade. It also reduced the amount of fertilizer that was available for enriching the soil. In England and the Low Countries, large drainage projects were undertaken to reclaim land for crops. In the east, so-called forest colonies sprang up, clearing space in the midst of woodlands for new farms.

By midcentury the window of opportunity shut more firmly on people who were attempting to enter the urban economy. Town governments tightened apprenticeship requirements. Guilds raised fees for new entrants and designated only a small number of places where their goods could be purchased. Most apprenticeships were limited to patrimony: one son for each full member. Such restrictions meant that newly arrived immigrants could enter only the less profitable small crafts.

As workers continued to flood into the towns, real wages began to fall, not only among the unskilled but throughout the workforce. A black market in labor developed to take

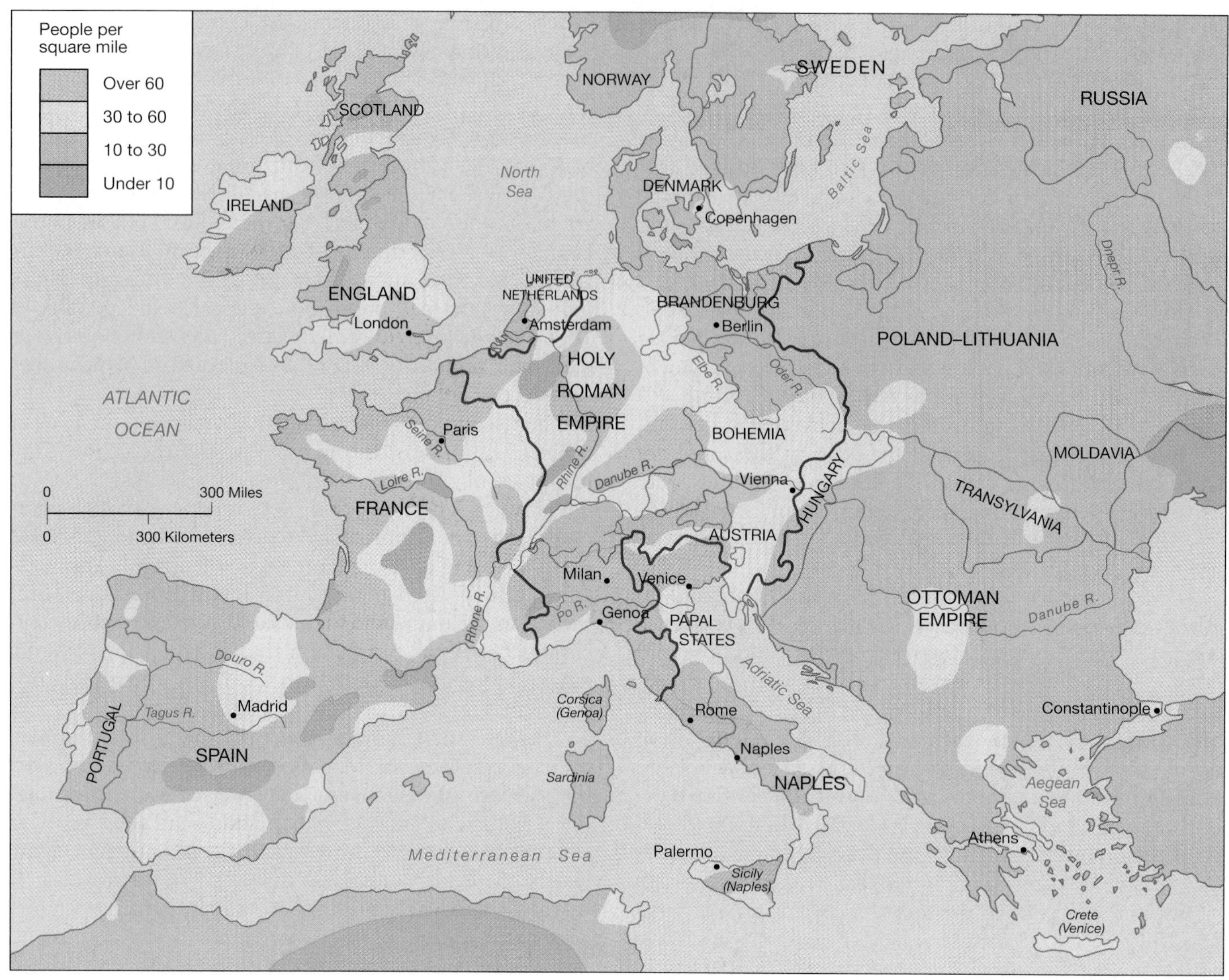

▲ Population Density in Europe, ca. 1600. Most people lived in the western part of the continent on its coastal areas.

advantage of the surplus population. In terms of purchasing power, the wages of a craftsman in the building trade in England fell by half during the sixteenth century. Peasants in the French region of Languedoc who hired out for farm labor lost 56 percent of their purchasing power during the century. Grape pickers, among the least skilled agricultural laborers, endured declines up to 300 to 400 percent.

The fall in real wages took place against a backdrop of inflation that has come to be called the Price Revolution. Over the course of the century, cereal prices increased between fivefold and sixfold, and prices of manufactured goods increased between twofold and threefold. Most of the rapid increase came in the second half of the century, a result of both population growth and the import of precious metals from the New World. Sixteenth century governments understood little about the relationship between money supply and prices. Gold and silver from America flooded the international economy, raising commodity prices. As prices rose, so did the deficits of the state, which was the largest purchaser of both agricultural and manufactured goods. With huge deficits, states began to devalue their coins in the mistaken belief that this would lower their debt. But debased coinage resulted in still higher prices, and higher prices resulted in greater debt. The Price Revolution was felt throughout the Continent and played havoc with government finances, international trade, and the lives of ordinary people.

A 500 percent inflation in agricultural products over a century is not much by modern standards. Compounded, the rate averages less than 2 percent a year. But the Price Revolution did not take place in a modern society or within a modern market economy. In the sixteenth century, this level of rising prices disrupted everything. In the Spanish town of Seville, almost all buildings were rented on 99-year leases to the families who lived and worked in them. This was a fairly common practice throughout Europe. It meant that a landlord who rented a butcher shop and living quarters in 1501 could not raise the rent until 1600! Similarly, lords frequently held the right to purchase agricultural produce at specified prices. That system, similar to today's commodity market, helped both lords and peasants plan ahead, but it assumed steady prices.

Therefore, an enduring increase of prices created profound social dislocation and threw into turmoil all groups and sections of the European economy. Some people became destitute; others became rich beyond their dreams. The towns were particularly hard hit, for they exchanged manufactured goods for food and so suffered when grain prices rose faster than those of other commodities. Landholders who derived their income from rents were squeezed; those who received payment in kind reaped a windfall of more valuable agricultural goods. As long as ordinary peasants consumed what they raised, the nominal value of commodities did not matter. But if some part of their subsistence was obtained by labor, they were in grave peril.

There was now an enormous incentive to produce a surplus for market and to begin to specialize in particular grains that were in high demand. Every small scrap of land that individual peasant families could bring under cultivation would now yield foodstuffs that could be exchanged for manufactured goods that had been unimaginable luxuries a generation earlier. The tendency for all peasants to hold roughly equivalent amounts of land abruptly ceased. The fortunate could now become prosperous by selling their surplus. The unfortunate found ready purchasers for their strips and common rights.

The beneficial cycle now turned vicious. Those who had sold out and left the land looking for prosperity in the towns were forced to return to the land as agrarian laborers. In western Europe, they became the landless poor, seasonal migrants without the safety net of rooted communal life. In eastern Europe, labor service enriched the landed nobility, who were able to sell vast stores of grain in the export market. Poland-Lithuania became a major supplier of cereals to northern Europe. But agricultural surplus from the east could not make up for the great shortfall in the west. By the end of the sixteenth century, the western European states faced a crisis of subsistence.

SOCIAL LIFE

The basic assumption of sixteenth century European society was inequality. The group, rather than the individual, was the predominant unit in society. The first level of the social order was the family and the household, then came the village or town community, and finally the gradations of ranks and orders of society at large. Each group had its own place in the social order, and each performed its own essential function. Society was the sum of its parts.

This traditional social organization was severely tested over the course of the sixteenth century. Economic change reshaped ideas of mobility and drew sharper distinctions between rural and urban life. The growth of towns challenged beliefs about the primacy of agricultural production and the subordinate nature of trade and commerce. The rise to new wealth and prominence of some social groups challenged traditional elites' hold on power and prestige. The transformation of landholding patterns in the villages challenged the stability of rural communities. The rising numbers of poor people challenged the institutions of charitable relief and posed the threat of crime and disorder. Eventually, these developments led to bloody confrontations between social groups.

Social Constructs

Hierarchy was the dominant principle of social organization in the sixteenth century. The hierarchy of masters, journeymen, and apprentices dominated trades; trades themselves existed in a hierarchy. Civic government was a hierarchy of officials led by the elite of councillors and mayors. Among the peasants was the hierarchy of freeholder, laborer, and leaseholder, as well as the more flexible social hierarchy among the ancient and prosperous families and the newer and struggling ones. The family itself was hierarchically organized, with the wife subordinate to her husband, the children to their parents, and the apprentices and servants to their master and mistress. Hierarchy was a principle of orderliness that helped to govern social relations. It is tempting to approach hierarchy through wealth, but the ranks of the nobility cannot be explained by gradations of wealth among nobles, and there were many rich town dwellers who were not members of the governing elite.

Status rather than wealth determined the social hierarchy of the sixteenth century. It conferred privileges and exacted responsibilities according to rank. Status was everywhere apparent. It was confirmed in social conventions such as bowing and hat doffing. In towns and cities, the clothing people were allowed to wear, even the foods they were allowed to eat, reflected status. Status was signified by titles, not just in the ranks of the nobility, but even in ordinary communities of masters and mistresses, goodmen and goodwives, squires and ladies, the English equivalents of a wide variety of European titles. The acceptance of status was an everyday, unreflective act. Inequality was an unquestioned fact of life.

Images that people used to describe both the natural world and their social world reinforced the functional nature of hierarchy. The most elaborate image was that of the Great Chain of Being, a description of the universe in which everything had a place, from God at the top to inanimate objects such as rocks and stones at the bottom. Complex accounts of the Chain listed the nine orders of angels, the multiple ranks of humans, even the degrees of animals and plants, from which lions emerged as kings of the jungle. For ordinary people the Great Chain of Being expressed the belief that all life was interconnected, that every link was a part of a divinely ordered universe and was as necessary as every other.

The second metaphor that was used to describe society stressed this notion of interdependency even more strongly. This was the image of the Body Politic, in which the head ruled, the arms protected, the stomach nourished, and the feet labored. In the state, the king was the head, the church was the soul, the nobles were the arms, the artisans were the hands, and the peasants were the feet. Like the Chain of Being, the Body Politic was a profoundly conservative concept of social organization that precluded the idea of social mobility.

Social Structure

The Great Chain of Being and the Body Politic were static concepts of social organization. But in the sixteenth century, European society was in a state of dynamic change. Fundamentally, all European societies were divided between nobles and commoners, though relationships between the two orders differed from place to place.

The Nobles. Nobility was a legal status that conferred certain privileges on its holders and passed by inheritance from one generation to the next. Each rank had its own privileges, and each was clearly demarcated from the next. The coat of arms was a universally recognized symbol of rank and family connection. Though various systems of title were in use across the Continent, the hierarchy of prince, duke, earl, count, and baron was roughly standard.

Because rulers conferred these titles on individuals, elevating some to higher ranks and others from commoner to noble, the nobility was a political order as well as a social one. Political privileges were among the nobility's most important attributes. In many countries, the highest offices of the state and the military were reserved for members of the nobility. Noblemen were also granted rights of political participation in the deliberative bodies of the state. In England, the peerage was defined as all those who were summoned to the House of Lords. In most parts of central Europe, the nobility alone composed the diets that advised the monarch.

Finally, members of the nobility held economic privileges, a result both of their rank and of their role as lords on the lands they owned. In almost every state, the nobility was exempt from most kinds of taxation. The interests of the nobles conflicted directly with those of the ruler, and the larger the number of tax exemptions for the nobility, the stronger was its power in relation to the monarch. Tax exemptions of the nobility were most extensive in eastern and central Europe. There, the crowns were elective rather than hereditary, allowing the nobles to bargain their support. As Polish agriculture developed into an export industry, exemption from internal tolls and customs gave the nobility a competitive advantage over merchants in the marketing of goods. The nobility in western Europe enjoyed fewer immunities but not necessarily less valuable ones.

Privileges implied obligations. Initially, the nobility was the warrior caste of the state, and its primary obligations were to raise, equip, and lead troops into battle. Much of the great wealth that nobles possessed was at the service of the ruler during times of war, and war was a perpetual activity. By the sixteenth century, the military needs of the state had far surpassed the military power of its nobility. Warfare had become a national enterprise that required central coordination. Nobles became administrators as much as warriors, though it is fair to say that many did both. The French nobility came to be divided into the nobility of the sword and the nobility of the robe—that is, warriors and officeholders.

Nobles also had the obligation of governing at both the national and the local level. At the discretion of the ruler, they could be called to engage in any necessary occupation, no matter how disruptive to their economic or family affairs. They administered their estates and settled the disputes of their tenants. In times of want, they were expected to provide for the needy. The obligation of good lordship was implicitly understood, if not always explicitly carried out, between lord and peasant.

Town Elite and Gentry. The principal distinction in sixteenth-century society was between lord and commoners, but it was not the only one. A new social group was emerging in the towns—a group that had neither the legal nor the social privileges of nobility but performed many of the same functions. The towns remained a separate unit of social organization in most states, enjoying many of the same political and economic privileges as the nobility. Representatives of the towns met with the nobles and the king and were the most important part of the national deliberative assemblies, like the English Parliament or the French estates. Towns were granted legal rights to govern their own citizens, to engage in trade, and to defend themselves by raising and storing arms. Though they paid a large share of most taxes, towns also received large tax concessions.

As individuals, members of the town elite held no special status in society at large. Some were among the richest people in the state, but they had to devise their own systems of honor and prestige. In Venice the *Book of Gold* distinguished the local elite from the ranks of ordinary citizens. In France and Spain, some of the highest officers of leading towns were granted noble status. In England, wealthy guild members could become knights, a rank just below noble status. German burghers, as prosperous townsmen were called, remained caught between noble and common, despised from above because they worked with their hands, envied from below for their wealth and

Georges de La Tour, *The Fortune Teller.* In the painting, which serves as a warning to the naive about the wicked ways of the world, a fashionably dressed young innocent is drawn into the snare of the wily fortune teller.

comfort. In Wurtenberg, the nobility withdrew from the towns and sought the status of free knights.

In rural society the transformation of agricultural holdings in many places also created a group that fit uncomfortably between lords and commoners. The accumulation of larger and larger estates, by purchase from the nobility, the state, or the church, made lords—in the sense of landowners with tenants—of many who were not lords in rank. They received rents and dues from their tenants, administered their estates, and preserved the so-called moral economy that sustained the peasants during hard times. In England, this group came to be known as the gentry, and there were parallel groups in Spain, France, and the Holy Roman Empire. The gentry aspired to the privileges of the nobility. In England, members of the gentry had the right to have a coat of arms and could be knighted. But knighthoods were not hereditary and did not confer membership in the House of Lords. In Spain, the caballeros and hidalgos gained noble privileges but were still of lower status than the grandees.

Social stratification also marked rural communities. In many German villages, a principal distinction was made between those who held land in the ancient part of the settlement—the Esch—and those who held land in those areas into which the village had expanded. The Esch was normally the best land. But interestingly, the holders of the Esch were tied to the lord of the estate, while holders of the less desirable lands were free peasants. Here, freedom to move from place to place was less valued than was the right to live in the heart of the village.

Just the opposite set of values prevailed in English villages, where freeholders were in the most enviable position. They led the movements to break up the common fields for planting and were able to initiate legal actions against their lord. Whenever village land was converted to freehold, unfree tenants would go into debt to buy it. Increasingly, French peasants came to own the land they farmed. They protested against the very title of villein, claiming that its older association with serfdom discouraged others from trading with those so labeled. The distinction between free and unfree went even further in Muscovy, where thousands of starving laborers sold themselves into slavery.

In towns, the order of rank below the elite pertained as much to the kind of work that one performed as it did to the level at which the work was undertaken. The critical division in town life was between those who had the freedom of the city—citizens—and those who did not. Citizenship was restricted to membership in certain occupations and was closely regulated. It could be purchased, but most citizenship was earned by becoming a master in one of the guilds. Only males could be citizens. In Germany, the feminine equivalent for the word that denoted a male citizen meant prostitute! But women who were married to citizens enjoyed their husbands' privileges, and widows of citizens could pass the privileges to their new husbands when they remarried.

Social Change

In the sixteenth century, social commentators believed that change was transforming the world in which they lived. In 1600, a Spanish observer blamed the rise of the rich commoners for the ills of the world. An Englishman commenting on the rise of the gentry could give no better definition of its status than to say that a gentleman was one who lived like a gentleman. In France, the challenge that the new nobility of the robe posed to the old nobility of the sword poisoned relations between these two segments of the ruling elite. The military service class in Muscovy, who were of more use to the Muscovite princes than the traditional landed nobility, posed an even greater threat to the privileges of the boyars.

The New Rich. Pressures on the ruling elites of European society came from above as well as below. The expansion of the state and the power of the prince frequently came as a result of direct conflict with the nobility. Only in east central Europe did the consolidation of the state actually enhance the privileges of the traditional noble orders, and these were areas in which towns were small and urban elites were weak.

Many factors promoted social change during the course of the sixteenth century. First, population increase necessitated an expansion of the ruling orders. With more people to govern, there had to be more governors who could perform the military, political, and social functions of the state. Second, opportunities to accumulate wealth expanded dramatically with the Price Revolution. Traditionally, wealth was calculated in land and tenants rather than in the possession of liquid assets such as gold and silver. But with the increase in commodity prices, surplus producers could rapidly improve their economic position. Moreover, state service became a source of unlimited riches. The profits to be made from tax collecting, officeholding, or the law could easily surpass those to be made from landholding. And the newly rich clamored for privileges.

The New Poor. Social change was equally apparent at the bottom of the social scale, but here it could not be so easily absorbed. The continuous growth of population created a group of landless poor who squatted in villages and clogged the streets of towns and cities. Rough estimates suggest that as many as one-quarter of all Europeans were destitute. This was a staggering figure in great cities, amounting to tens of thousands in London or Paris.

Traditionally, local communities cared for their poor. Widows, orphans, and the handicapped, who would normally constitute over half of the poor in a village or town, were viewed as the "deserving poor," worthy of the care of the community through the Church or private almsgiving. Catholic communities such as Venice created a system of private charity that paralleled the institutions of the Church. Though Protestant communities took charity out of the control of the Church, they were no less concerned about the plight of the deserving poor. In England a special tax, the poor rate, supported the poor. Perhaps the most elaborate system of all existed in the French town of Lyon. There, all the poor were registered and given identity cards. Each Sunday, they would receive a week's worth of food and money. Young girls were provided with dowries, and young boys were taught crafts. But this enlightened system was for the deserving poor only.

Charity was an obligation of the community, but as the sixteenth century wore on, the number of destitute people grew beyond the ability of the local community to care for them. Many of those who now begged for alms fell outside the traditional categories of the deserving poor. They were men and women who were capable of working but incapable of finding more than occasional labor. They left their native communities in search of employment and thus forfeited their claims on local charity. Most wound up in the towns and cities, where as strangers they had no claim on local charity. Poor mothers abandoned their newborn infants on the steps of foundling hospitals or the houses of the rich.

The problem of crime complicated the problems of poverty and vagrancy. Increasing population and increasing wealth equaled increasing crime; the addition of the poor to the equation aggravated the situation. The poor, outsiders to the community without visible means of support, were the easiest targets of official retribution. Throughout the century, numerous European states passed vagrancy laws. In England, the poor were whipped from village to village until they were returned home. Both Venetian and Dutch vagrants were regularly rounded up for galley service. Vagrants in Hungary were sold into slavery. Sexual offenses were criminalized, especially bastardy, since the birth of illegitimate children placed an immediate burden on the community. Prostitutes, who had long been tolerated and regulated in towns, were now persecuted. Rape increased. Capital punishment was reserved for the worst crimes—murder, incest, and grand larceny being most common—but, not surprisingly, executions were carried out mostly on outsiders to the community.

Peasant Revolts

The economic and social changes of the sixteenth century had serious consequences. Most telling was the upswing of violent confrontations between peasants and their lords. Across Europe and with alarming regularity, peasants took up arms to defend themselves from what they saw as violations of traditional rights and obligations. Peasant revolts were not hunger riots. Though they frequently occurred in periods of want, they were not desperate attacks against warehouses or grain silos. Nor

▲ *Feeding the Hungry* by Cornelius Buys, 1504. A maidservant is doling out small loaves to the poor and the lame at the door of a wealthy person's home. The poor who flocked to the towns were often forced to rely on charity to survive.

did those who took part in the revolts form an undisciplined mob. Most revolts chose leaders, drew up petitions of grievances, and organized the rank and file into a semblance of military order. Leaders were literate—drawn more commonly from among the lower clergy or minor gentry than from the peasantry—political demands were moderate, and tactics were sophisticated. But peasant revolts so profoundly threatened the social order that they were met with the severest repression.

Agrarian Changes. It is essential to realize that while peasants revolted against their lords, at bottom their anger and frustration were caused by agrarian changes that could be neither controlled nor understood. As population increased and market production expanded, many of the traditional rights and obligations of lords and peasants became oppressive. One example is that of forest rights. On most estates the forests surrounding a village belonged to the lord. Commonly, the village had its own woodlands in which animals foraged and fuel and building material were available. As population increased, new land was put under the plow, and grain fields pressed up against the forest. There were more animals in the village, and some of them were let loose to consume the young sprouts and saplings. Soon there was not enough food for the wild game that was among the lord's most valuable property. So the game began to feed on the peasants' crops, which were now placed so appetizingly close to the forests. It was a capital crime for a peasant to kill wild game, but neither could the peasants allow the game to consume their crops.

A similar conflict arose over enclosing crop fields. An enclosure was a device—normally a fence or hedge that surrounded an area—to keep a parcel of land separate from the planted strips of land owned by the villagers. It could be used for grazing animals or raising a specialty crop for the market. But an enclosure destroyed the traditional form of village agriculture whereby decisions on which crops to plant were made communally. It became one of the chief grievances of the English peasants. But while enclosures broke up the old field system in many villages, they were a logical response to the transformation of land ownership that had already taken place. As more and more land was accumulated by fewer and fewer families, it made less and less sense for them to work widely scattered strips all over the village. If a family could consolidate its holdings by swaps and sales, it could gain an estate that was large enough to be used for both crops and grazing. An enclosed estate allowed wealthy farmers to grow more luxury crops for market or to raise only sheep on a field that had once been used for grain.

Enclosure was a process that both lord and rich peasant undertook, but it drove the smallholders from the land and was thus a source of bitter resentment for the poorer peasants. It was easy to protest the greed of the lords who, owning the most land, were the most successful enclosers. But enclosures resulted more from the process whereby villages came to be characterized by a very small elite of large landholders and a very large mass of smallholders and landless poor. It was an effect rather than a cause.

From Hungary to England, peasant revolts brought social and economic change into sharp relief. A call for a crusade against Ottoman advances in 1514 provided the opportunity for Hungarian peasants to revolt against their noble landlords. Thousands dropped their plowshares and grasped the sword of a holy war. But, in fact, war against the Ottomans did not materialize. Instead, the mobilized peasants, under the leadership of disaffected army officers and clergymen, issued grievances against the labor service that they owed to their lords as well as numerous violations of customary agricultural practices. Their revolt turned into a civil war and was crushed with great brutality. In eastern England, Ket's Rebellion centered on peasant opposition to enclosure. The rebels occupied Norwich, the second largest city in the realm, but their aspirations were for reform rather than revolution. They, too, were crushed by well-trained forces.

Uprising in Germany. The complexity of these problems is perhaps best revealed in the series of uprisings that are known collectively as the German Peasants' War. It involved tens of thousands of peasants, and it combined a whole series of agrarian grievances with an awareness of the new religious spirit preached by Martin Luther. Luther condemned both lords and peasants—the lords for their rapaciousness, the peasants for their rebelliousness. Though he had a large following among the peasants, his advice that earthly oppressions be passively accepted was not followed. The Peasants' War was directed against secular and ecclesiastical lords, and the rebels attacked both economic and religious abuses. The combination of demands, such as the community's right to select its own minister and the community's right to cut wood freely, attracted a wide following in the villages and small towns of southern and central Germany. The printed demands of the peasantry, the most famous of which was the Twelve Articles of the Peasants of Swabia (1525), helped to spread the movement far beyond its original bounds. The peasants organized themselves into large armies led by experienced soldiers, but ultimately, movements that refused compromise were ruthlessly crushed.

At base, the demands of the peasantry addressed the agrarian changes that were transforming German villages. Population growth was creating more poor villagers who could only hire out as laborers but who demanded a share of common grazing and woodlands. Because the presence of these poor people increased the taxable wealth of the village, they were advantageous to the lord. But the strain they placed on resources was felt by both the subsistence and surplus farmers. Tensions within the village were all the greater in that the landless members were the kin of the landed. If they were to be settled properly on the land, then the lord would have to let the village expand. If they were to be kept on the margins of subsistence, then the more prosperous villagers would have to be able to control their numbers and their conduct. In either case, the peasants needed more direct responsibility for governing the village than existed in their traditional relationship with their lord. Therefore, the peasants of Swabia demanded release of the village peasantry from the status of serfs. They wanted to be allowed to move off the land, to marry out of the village without penalty, and to be free of the death taxes that further impoverished their children. They also wanted stable rents fixed at fair rates, a limit placed on labor service, and a return to the ancient customs that governed relations between lords and peasants. All of these proposals were backed by an appeal to Christian principles of love and charity. They were profoundly conservative.

The demands of the German peasants reflected a traditional order that no longer existed. In many places, the rents and tithes that the peasants wanted to control no longer belonged to the lords of the estates. They had been sold to town corporations or wealthy individuals who purchased them as an investment and expected to realize a fair return. Most tenants did enjoy stable and fixed rents, but only on their traditional lands. As they increased their holdings, perhaps to keep another son in the village or to expand production for the market, they were faced with the fact that rents were higher and land was more expensive than it had been before. Marriage fines, death duties, and labor service were oppressive, but they balanced the fact that traditional rents were very low. In many east German villages, peasants willingly increased their labor service for a reduction in their money rents. It was hardly likely that they could have both. If the peasants were being squeezed, and there can be little doubt that they were, it was not only the lords who were doing the squeezing. The Church took its tenth, the state increased its exactions, and the competition for survival and prosperity among the peasants themselves was ferocious. Peasants were caught between the jaws of an expanding state and a changing economy. When they rebelled, the jaws snapped shut.

PRIVATE AND COMMUNITY LIFE

The great events of the sixteenth century—the discovery of the New World, the consolidation of states, the increasing incidence and ferocity of war, and the reform of religion—all had a profound impact on the lives of ordinary people. However slowly and intermittently these developments penetrated to isolated village communities, they were inextricably bound up with the experiences and world view of all Europeans.

The Family

Sixteenth-century life centered on the family, the primary kinship group. European families were predominantly nuclear, composed of a married couple and their children. In western Europe, a small number of families contained the adult siblings of the family head, uncles and aunts who had not yet established their own families. This pattern was more common in the east, especially in Hungary and Muscovy, where taxation was based on households and thus encouraged extended families. Yet, however families were composed, kinship had a wider orbit than just parents and children. In-laws, step relations, and cousins were considered part of the kin group and could be called on for support in a variety of contexts from charity to employment and business partnerships. In towns, such family connections created large and powerful clans.

In a different sense, family was lineage, the connections between preceding and succeeding generations. This was an important concept among the upper ranks of society, in which ancient lineage, genuine or fabricated, was a valued component of nobility. Even in peasant communities, however, lineage existed in the form of the strips in the field that were passed from generation to generation and named for the family that owned them.

The family was also an economic unit. It was the basic unit for the production, accumulation, and transmission of wealth. Occupation determined the organization of the economic family. Every member of the household had his or her own functions that were essential to the survival of the unit. Tasks were divided by gender and by age, but there was far more intermixture than is traditionally assumed. On farms, women worked at nearly every occupation with the exception of mowing and plowing. In towns, they were vital to the success of shops and trades, though they were denied training in the skilled crafts. As laborers, they worked in the town fields—for little more than half the wages of men performing the same tasks—and in carrying and delivering goods and materials. Children contributed to the economic vitality of the household from an early age.

Finally, the family was the primary unit of social organization. It was in the family that children were educated and the social values of hierarchy and discipline were taught. Authority in the family was strictly organized in a set of three overlapping categories. At the top was the husband, head of the household, who ruled over his wife, children, and servants. All members of the family owed obedience to the head. Children owed obedience to their parents, male or female. Similarly, servants owed obedience to both master and mistress. Male apprentices were under the authority of the wife, mother, and mistress of the household. The importance of the family as a social unit was underscored by the fact that people who were not attached to families attracted suspicion in sixteenth-century society. Single men were often viewed as potential criminals, single women as potential prostitutes.

Though the population of Europe was increasing in the sixteenth century, families were not large. Throughout northern and western Europe, the size of the typical family was two adults and three or four children. Late marriages and breast-feeding helped to control family size. The first restricted the number of childbearing years; the second increased the space between pregnancies. Women married around age 25, men slightly later. Most women could expect about 15 fertile years and seven or eight pregnancies if neither they nor their husband died in the interim. Only three or four children were likely to survive beyond the age of ten. In her fertile years, a woman was constantly occupied with infants. If she used a wet nurse, as many women in the upper ranks of society did, then she was likely to have 10 or 12 pregnancies during her fertile years and correspondingly

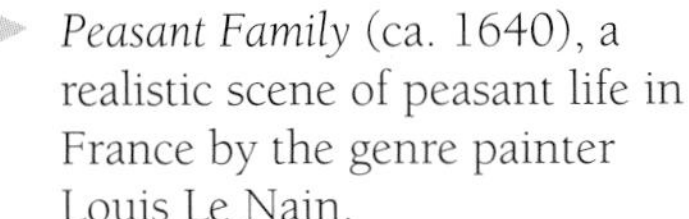

Peasant Family (ca. 1640), a realistic scene of peasant life in France by the genre painter Louis Le Nain.

more surviving children. Constant pregnancy and child care may help explain some of the gender roles that men and women assumed in the sixteenth century. Biblical injunctions and traditional stereotypes help explain others. Whether a woman was pregnant or not, her labor was a vital part of the domestic economy, especially until the first surviving children were strong enough to assume their share. The woman's sphere was the household. On the farm, she was in charge of the preparation of food, the care of domestic animals, the care and education of children, and the manufacture and cleaning of the family's clothing. In towns, women supervised the shop that was part of the household. They sold goods, kept accounts, and directed the work of domestics or apprentices.

The man's sphere was the public one: the fields in rural areas, the streets in towns. Men plowed, planted, and did the heavy reaping work of farming. They made and maintained essential farm equipment and had charge of the large farm animals. They marketed surplus produce and made the few purchases of equipment or luxury goods. Men performed the labor service that was normally due the lord of the estate, attended the local courts in various capacities, and organized the affairs of the village. In towns, men engaged in heavy labor, procured materials for craft work, and marketed their product if it was not sold in the household shop. Only men could be citizens of the towns or full members of most craft guilds, and only men were involved in civic government.

This separation of men and women into the public and the domestic spheres meant that marriage was a blending of complementary skills. Each partner brought to the marriage essential knowledge and abilities that were fundamental to the economic success of the union. Except in the largest towns, nearly everyone was married for at least a part of his or her life. Remarriage was more common for men than for women, however, because a man continued to control the family's property after the death of his wife, whereas a widow might have only a share of it after bequests to children or provisions for apprentices.

While male roles were constant throughout the life cycle, as men trained for and performed the same occupations from childhood to death, female roles varied greatly depending on the situation. While under the care of fathers, masters, or husbands, women worked in the domestic sphere; once widowed, they assumed the public functions of head of household. Many women inherited shops or farmland; most became responsible for the placement and training of their children. But because of the division of labor on which the family depended and because of the inherent social and economic prejudices that segregated public and domestic roles, widows were particularly disadvantaged.

Communities

The family was part of a wider community. On the farm, this community was the rural village; in the town, it was the ward, quarter, or parish in which the family lived. Community life must not be romanticized. Interpersonal violence, lawsuits, and feuds were common in both rural and urban communities. Like every other aspect of society, the community was socially and economically stratified, gender roles were segregated, and resources were inequitably divided. But the community was also the place where people found their social identity. It provided marriage partners for its families, charity for its poor, and a local culture for all of its inhabitants.

Identities and Customs. The two basic forces that tied the rural community together were the lord and the priest. The lord set conditions for work and property ownership that necessitated common decision making on the part of the village farmers. The lord's presence, commonly in the form of an agent, could be both a positive and a negative force for community solidarity. Use of the common lands, the rotation of labor service, and the form in which rents in kind were paid were all decisions that had to be made collectively. Village leadership remained informal, though in some villages, headmen or elders bargained with the lord's agent or resolved petty disputes among the villagers. Communal agreement was also expressed in communal resistance to violations of custom or threats to the moral economy. All these forms of negotiation fused individual families into a community. So, too, in a different way did the presence of the parish priest or minister, who attended all the pivotal events of life—birth, marriage, and death. The church was the only common building of the community; it was the only space that was not owned outright by the lord or an individual family. The scene of village meetings and ceremonies, it was the center of both spiritual and social life. The parish priest served as a conduit for all the news of the community and the focal point for the village's festive life.

Communities were also bound together by their own social customs. In rural parishes, there was the annual perambulation, a walk around the village fields that usually occurred before planting began. It was led by the priest, who blessed the fields as the village farmers followed.

In towns, ceremonial processions were far more elaborate. Processions might take place on saints' days in Catholic communities or on anniversaries of town liberties. The order of the march, the clothing worn by the participants, and the objects displayed reflected the strict hierarchies of the town's local organizations.

Weddings and Festivals. Not all ceremonial occasions were so formal. The most common ceremony was the wedding, a public event that combined a religious rite and a community procession with feasting and festivity. It took different forms in different parts of Europe and in different social groups. Many couples were engaged long before they were married, and in many places it was the engagement that was most important to the individuals and the wedding that was most important to the community. Traditional weddings involved the formal transfer of property, an important event in rural communities where the ownership of strips of land or common rights concerned everyone. The bridal dowry and the groom's inheritance were formally exchanged during the wedding, even if both were small. The public procession, "the marriage in the streets," as it was sometimes called in towns, proclaimed the union throughout the community.

Other ceremonies were equally important in creating a shared sense of identity within the community. In both town and countryside, the year was divided by a number of festivals that defined the rhythm of toil and rest. They coincided with both the seasonal divisions of agricultural life and the central events of the Christian calendar. Christmas and Easter were probably the most widely observed Christian holidays, but Carnival, which preceded Lent, was a frenzied round of feasts and parties that resulted in a disproportionate number of births nine months later. The twelve days of Christmas were only loosely attached to the birth of Jesus and were even abolished by some Protestant churches. The rites of May, which celebrated the rebirth of spring, were filled with sexual play among the young adults of the community. All Hallows' Eve was a celebration for the community's dead. Their spirits wandered the village on that night, visiting kin and neighbors.

In addition to feasting, dancing, and play, festivals often included sports, such as soccer or wrestling, which served to channel aggressions. At such times, village elders would also arbitrate disputes, and marriage alliances or property transactions would be arranged.

Festivals further cemented the political cohesion of the community. Seating arrangements signaled the hierarchy of the community, and public punishment of offenders reinforced deference and social and sexual mores. Youth groups or the village women might band together to shame a promiscuous woman or to place horns on the head of a cuckolded husband. These forms of community ritual worked not only to punish offenders but also to reinforce the social and sexual values of the village as a whole.

Popular Beliefs and the Persecution of Witches

Ceremony and festival are reminders that sixteenth-century Europe was still a preliterate society. Despite the introduction of printing and the millions of books that were produced during the period, the vast majority of Europeans conducted their affairs without the benefit of literacy. Outside a small circle of intellectuals, there was little effective knowledge about either human or celestial bodies. The mysteries of the sun, moon, and stars were as deep as those of health and sickness. But this does not mean that ordinary people lived in a constant state of terror and anxiety. They used the knowledge they did have to form a view of the universe that conformed to their experiences and responded to their hopes.

Magical Practices. These beliefs blended Christian teaching and folk wisdom with a strong strain of magic. Popular belief in magic could be found everywhere in Europe, and it operated in much the same way as science does today. Only skilled practitioners could perform magic. It was a technical subject that combined expertise in the properties of plants and animals with theories about the composition of human and heavenly bodies. It had its own language, a mixture of ancient words and sounds with significant numbers and catch phrases. Magicians specialized. Alchemists worked with rocks and minerals, astrologers with the movement of the stars. Witches were thought to understand the properties of animals especially well.

Magical practices appealed to people at all levels of society. The wealthy favored astrology and paid handsomely to discover which days and months were the most auspicious for marriages and investments. The poorest villagers sought the aid of herbalists to help control the constant aches and pains of daily life. Sorcerers and wizards were called on in more extreme circumstances, such as a threatened harvest or matters of life and death. These magicians competed with the remedies offered by the Church. Special prayers and visits to the shrines of particular saints were believed to have similar curative value. Magical and Christian beliefs were often practiced simultaneously. In some French villages, for example, four-leaf clovers were considered especially powerful if they were found on a particular saint's day. It was not until the end of the century, when Protestant and Catholic leaders condemned magical practices and began a campaign to root them out, that magic and religion came into conflict.

Magical practices served a variety of purposes. Healing was the most common, and many "magical" brews were effective remedies for the minor ailments for which they were prescribed. Most village magicians were women because it was believed that women had unique knowledge and understanding of the body. Magic was also used for predictive purposes. Certain charms and rituals were believed to have the power to affect the weather, the crops, and even human events. As always, affairs of the heart were as important as those of the stomach. Magicians advised the lovesick on potions and spells that would gain them the object of their desires. Finally, it was believed that magic had the power to alter the course of nature and could be used for both good and evil purposes.

The Witchcraft Craze. Magic for evil was black magic, or witchcraft. Witches were believed to possess special powers that put them into contact with the devil and the forces of evil, which they could then use for their own purposes. Belief in the prevalence of good and evil spirits was Christian as well as magical. But the Church had gradually consigned the operation of the devil to the afterlife and removed his direct agency from earthly affairs. Beginning in the late fifteenth century, church authorities began to prosecute large numbers of suspected witches. By the end of the sixteenth century, there was a continent-wide witch craze. Confessions were obtained under torture, as were further accusations.

Witches were usually women, most often unmarried or widowed. In a sample of more than 7,000 cases of witchcraft prosecuted in early modern Europe, over 80 percent of the defendants were women. There is no clear explanation for why women fulfilled this important and powerful role. Belief in women's special powers over the body through their singular ability to give birth is certainly one part of the explanation, for many stories about the origins of witches suggest that they were children fathered by the devil and left to be raised by women. This sexual element of union with the devil and the common belief that older women were sexually aggressive combined to threaten male sexual dominance. Witches were

THE DEVIL'S DUE

Evidence of the supernatural world abounded for the people of premodern Europe. Natural disasters such as plague and human disasters such as war promoted fear of witchcraft. When the world seemed out of balance and the forces of good retreated before the forces of evil, people sought someone to blame for their troubles. Witches were an obvious choice. Accused witches were most commonly women on the margins of society. Once brought before the authorities, many admitted their traffic with Satan, especially under torture. The Witch Hammer *is a set of detailed instructions for the rooting out of witches, including procedures to induce their confessions.*

FOCUS QUESTIONS

What is the point of torture, punishment, or investigation? Is the suspected witch seen as being in control of his or her magic?

THE METHOD OF BEGINNING AN EXAMINATION BY TORTURE IS AS FOLLOWS: First, the jailers prepare the implements of torture, then they strip the prisoner (if it be a woman, she has already been stripped by other women, upright and of good report). This stripping is lest some means of witchcraft may have been sewed into the clothing—such as often, taught by the Devil, they prepare from the bodies of unbaptized infants, [murdered] that they may forfeit salvation. And when the implements of torture have been prepared, the judge, both in person and through other good men zealous in the faith, tries to persuade the prisoner to confess the truth freely; but, if he will not confess, he bids attendants make the prisoner fast to the strappado or some other implement of torture. The attendants obey forthwith, yet with feigned agitation. Then, at the prayer of some of those present, the prisoner is loosed again and is taken aside and once more persuaded to confess, being led to believe that he will in that case not be put to death.

But if, neither by threats nor by promises such as these, the witch cannot be induced to speak the truth, then the jailers must carry out the sentence, and torture the prisoner according to the accepted methods, with more or less of severity as the delinquent's crime may demand. And, while he is being tortured, he must be questioned on the articles of accusation, and this frequently and persistently, beginning with the lighter charges—for he will more readily confess the lighter than the heavier. And, while this is being done, the notary must write down everything in his record of the trial—how the prisoner is tortured, on what points he is questioned, and how he answers.

And note that, if he confesses under the torture, he must afterward be conducted to another place, that he may confirm it and certify that it was not due alone to the force of the torture.

But, if the prisoner will not confess the truth satisfactorily, other sorts of tortures must be placed before him, with the statement that, unless he will confess the truth, he must endure these also. But, if not even thus he can be brought into terror and to the truth, then the next day or the next but one is to be set for a *continuation* of the tortures—not a *repetition*, for they must not be repeated unless new evidence be produced. . . .

And during the interval, before the day assigned, the judge, in person or through approved men, must in the manner above described try to persuade the prisoner to confess, promising her (if there is aught to be gained by this promise) that her life shall be spared.

The judge shall see to it, moreover, that throughout this interval guards are constantly with the prisoner, so that she may not be left alone; because she will be visited by the Devil and tempted into suicide.

From *The Witch Hammer*.

also believed to have peculiar physical characteristics. A group of Italian witches, male and female, were distinguished by having been born with a caul, that is, a membrane around their heads that was removed after birth. Accused witches were strip-searched to find the devil's mark, which might be any bodily blemish. Another strand of explanation lies in the fact that single women existed on the fringes of society, isolated and exploited by the community at large. Their occult abilities thus became a protective mechanism that gave them a function within the community while they remained outside it.

It is difficult to know how important black magical beliefs were in ordinary communities. Most of the daily magic that was practiced was a mixture of charms, potions, and prayers that mingled magical, medical, and Christian beliefs. Misfortunes that befell particular families or social groups were blamed on the activities of witches. The campaign of the established churches to root out magic was directed largely against witches. The churches transposed witches' supposed abilities to communicate with the devil into the charge that they worshiped the devil. Because there was such widespread belief in the presence of diabolical spirits and in the capabilities of witches to control them, Protestant and Catholic church courts could easily find witnesses to testify in support of the charges against individual witches. Over 100,000—perhaps several times that many—condemned witches in Europe were burned, strangled, drowned, or beheaded. Yet wherever sufficient evidence exists to understand the circumstances of witchcraft prosecutions, it is clear that the community itself was under some form of social or economic stress rather than that there was any increase in the presence or use of witches.

Conclusion

POPULATION GROWTH, ECONOMIC DIVERSIFICATION, and social change characterized life in sixteenth-century Europe. It was a century of extremes. The poor were getting poorer, and the rich were getting richer. The early part of the century has been called the golden age of the peasantry; the later part has been called the crisis of subsistence. At all levels of the social scale, the lives of grandparents and grandchildren were dramatically different. For surplus producers, the quality of life improved throughout the century. The market economy expanded. Agricultural surplus was exchanged for more land and a wider variety of consumer goods. Children could be given an education, and domestic and agricultural labor was cheap and plentiful. For subsistence producers, the quality of life eroded. In the first half of the century, their diet contained more meat than it would for the next 300 years. Their children could be absorbed on new farms or sent to towns where there was a shortage of both skilled and unskilled labor. But gradually, the outlook turned bleak. The land could support no more new families, and the towns needed no more labor. As wages fell and prices rose, peasants in western Europe were caught between the crushing burdens of taxation from lord, state, and church and the all-too-frequent catastrophes of poor harvests, epidemic disease, and warfare. In eastern Europe, the peasantry was tied to the land in a new serfdom, which provided minimum subsistence in return for the loss of freedom and opportunity. When peasants anywhere rose up against these conditions, they were cut down and swept away like new-mown hay. The witch-hunts of the sixteenth and early seventeenth centuries reflected troubled times, a pervasive misogyny, and a misguided effort to eliminate the cause of the troubles.

QUESTIONS FOR REVIEW

1. What physical forces and social customs shaped the everyday life of Europe's rural population?
2. What was the nature of demographic change in the sixteenth century, and what was its impact on the European economy?
3. How are the terms "stratification," "hierarchy," and "status" useful for understanding social relations in early modern Europe?
4. How were the different roles of men and women within the family reflected in the different lives of men and women in the wider community?

DISCOVERING WESTERN CIVILIZATION ONLINE

You can obtain more information about life in early modern Europe at the websites listed below. See also the companion website that accompanies this text: www.ablongman.com/kishlansky, which include an online study guide and additional resources.

Social Life

www.fordham.edu/halsall/mod/modsbook04.html
A site with links to sources, pictures, and accounts of everyday life in early modern Europe. A good place to start.

www.fordham.edu/halsall/mod/17france-soc.html
Documents illustrating social conditions in early modern France.

Private Life

Womenshistory.about.com/cs/witches
This site offers historical information about witches and witchcraft in Europe and America and includes links to related sites.

www.englishhistory.net/tudor/life.html
Part of a comprehensive site on Tudor England, this section on life in Tudor England offers information on topics including food and drink, pastimes and entertainment, and mental illness.

SUGGESTIONS FOR FURTHER READING

General Reading

Henry Kamen, *European Society, 1500–1700* (London: Hutchinson, 1984). A general survey of European social history.

Peter Laslett, *The World We Have Lost: Further Explored* (New York: Scribners, 1984). One of the pioneering works on the family and population history of England.

Robert Mandrou, *Introduction to Modern France* (New York: Harper & Row, 1977). Explores a variety of subjects in French social history from the mental to the material world.

Economic Life

Judith Bennett, *Ale, Beer, and Brewsters: Women's Work in a Changing World* (Oxford: Oxford University Press, 1996). An important study of the role of women in one of the most traditional trades.

Fernand Braudel, *Civilization and Capitalism: The Structures of Everyday Life* (New York: Harper & Row, 1981). Part of a larger work filled with fascinating detail about the social behavior of humankind during the early modern period.

Social Life

Peter Blickle, *The Revolution of 1525* (Baltimore, Md.: Johns Hopkins University Press, 1981). A provocative interpretation of the causes and meaning of the German Peasants' War.

Michael Bush, *Noble Privilege* (New York: Holmes & Meier, 1983). An analytic account of the types of privileges enjoyed by the European nobility, based on wide reading.

Edward Muir, *Ritual in Early Modern Europe* (Cambridge: Cambridge University Press, 1997). A fascinating account of the transformations in concepts of time and the body in early modern Europe.

J. L. Price, *Dutch Society, 1588–1713* (New York: Longman, 2001). A general social history of the Dutch "Golden Age."

Barry Reay, *Popular Cultures in England, 1550–1750* (New York: Addison Wesley Longman, 1998). A sound and insightful thematic survey.

Private Life

Peter Burke, *Popular Culture in Early Modern Europe* (New York: Harper & Row, 1978). A lively survey of cultural activities among the European populace.

Roger Chartier, ed., *A History of Private Life, vol. 3, Passions of the Renaissance* (Cambridge, Mass.: Harvard University Press, 1989). A lavishly illustrated study of the habits, mores, and structures of private life from the fifteenth to the eighteenth centuries.

Stuart Clark, *Thinking with Demons: The Idea of Witchcraft in Early Modern Europe* (Oxford: Oxford University Press,

1997). A sensitive reading of the sources for the study of witchcraft.

Beatrice Gottlieb, *The Family in the Western World From the Black Death to the Industrial Age* (Oxford: Oxford University Press, 1994). An outstanding introduction to the transformations in the lives of families.

Ralph Houlbrooke, *The English Family, 1450–1700* (London: Longman, 1984). A thorough survey of family history for the society that has been most carefully studied.

Brian Levack, *The Witch-Hunt in Early Modern Europe* (London: Longman, 1987). A study of the causes and meaning of the persecution of European witches in the sixteenth and seventeenth centuries.

R. Muchembled, *Popular Culture and Elite Culture in France, 1400–1750* (Baton Rouge: Louisiana State University Press, 1985). A detailed treatment of the practices of two conflicting cultures.

Keith Thomas, *Religion and the Decline of Magic* (New York: Scribners, 1971). A gargantuan descriptive and anecdotal account of the forms of religious and magical practice in England.

Merry E. Wiesner, *Women and Gender in Early Modern Europe* (Cambridge: Cambridge University Press, 1993). The best introduction to European women's history.

CHAPTER 16

THE ROYAL STATE IN THE SEVENTEENTH CENTURY

THE VISUAL RECORD

FIT FOR A KING

BEHOLD VERSAILLES, the greatest palace of the greatest king of the greatest state in seventeenth-century Europe. Everything about it was stupendous, a reflection of the grandeur of Louis XIV and of France. Sculptured gardens in dazzling geometric forms stretched for acres, scenting the air with exotic perfumes. Nearly as beautiful as the grounds were the 1,400 fountains, especially the circular basins of Apollo and Latona, the sun god and his mother. The hundreds of water jets that sprayed at Versailles defied nature as well as the senses, for the locale was not well-irrigated and water had to be pumped through elaborate mechanical works all the way from the Seine. Gardens and fountains provided the setting for the enormous palace with its hundreds of rooms for both use and show. Five thousand people, one tenth of whom served the king alone, inhabited the palace. Thousands of others flocked there daily. Most lived in the adjacent town, which had grown from a few hundred people to over 40,000 in a single generation. The royal stables quartered 12,000 horses and hundreds of carriages. The cost of all of this magnificence was equally astounding, estimated to be over 100 million French pounds. Louis XIV ordered the official receipts burned.

Like the marble of the palace, nature itself was chiseled to the requirements of the king. Forests were pared to make leafy avenues or trimmed to conform to the geometric patterns of the gardens. In spring and summer, groves of orange trees grown in tubs were everywhere; in winter and fall they were housed indoors at great expense. Life-size statues and giant carved urns lined the carefully planned walkways that led to breathtaking views or sheltered grottoes. A cross-shaped artificial canal, more than a mile long, dominated the western end of the park.

Despite all the extravagance, the palace was so uncomfortable to live in that Louis had a separate chateau built on the grounds as a quiet retreat. His wife and his mistresses complained constantly of accommodations in which all interior comforts had been subordinated to the external facade of the building. Versailles was a seat of

state as well as the home of the monarch, and it is revealing that the private was sacrificed to the public.

Soldiers, artisans, and the merely curious clogged the three great avenues that led from Paris to the palace. When the king dined in public, hordes of Parisians drove out for the spectacle, filing past the monarch as if he were an exhibit at a museum. The site itself was poorly drained, and the stench of sewage was particularly noxious in the heat and the rain. Even the gardens were too vast to be enjoyed. In the planted areas, the smell of flowers was overpowering while the acres of mown lawn proved unattractive to an aristocracy little given to physical exercise. In these contrasts of failure amid achievement, Versailles stands as an apt symbol of its age: a gaudy mask to hide the wrinkles of the royal state.

Versailles expressed the contradictions of its age. The seventeenth century was an era when the rich got richer and the poor got poorer. It was a time when the monarchical state expanded its power and prestige even as it faced grave challenges to its very existence. It was an epoch of unrelenting war amid a nearly universal desire for lasting peace.

LOOKING AHEAD

The great palaces of European absolute monarchs were designed to intimidate those who visited them. They were the representation of royal power at its apex. As we will learn in this chapter, not since Rome's emperors were at the height of their glory had power been more concentrated in the hands of rulers, and what they had consolidated over centuries they now had to protect against competing dynasties or rebellious subjects.

THE RISE OF THE ROYAL STATE

The wars that dominated the early part of the seventeenth century had a profound impact on the western European states. Not only did they cause terrible suffering and deprivation, but they also demanded efficient and better-centralized states to conduct them. War was both a product of the European state system and a cause of its continued development. As armies grew in size, their material needs grew in volume. As the battlefield spread from state to state, defense became government's most important function. More and more power was absorbed by the monarch and his chief advisers; more and more of the traditional privileges of aristocracy and of towns were eroded. At the center of these rising states, particularly in western Europe, were the king and his court. In the provinces were tax collectors and military recruiters.

Divine Kings

In the early sixteenth century, monarchs treated their states and their subjects as personal property. Correspondingly, rulers were praised in personal terms, for their virtue, their wisdom, or their strength. By the early seventeenth century, the monarchy had been transformed into an office of state. Now rulers embodied their nation, and, no matter what their personal characteristics, they were held in awe because they were monarchs.

Thus, as rulers lost direct personal control over their territory, they gained indirect symbolic control over their nation. This symbolic power was manifested everywhere. By the beginning of the seventeenth century, monarchs had permanent seats of government attended by vast courts of officials, place seekers, and servants. They no longer moved from place to place with their vast entourages. The idea of the capital city emerged, with Madrid, London, and Paris as the models. Here, the grandiose style of the ruler stood proxy for the wealth and glory of the nation. Great display bespoke great pride and strength.

Portraits of rulers conveyed the central message. Elizabeth I was depicted astride a map of England or clutching a rainbow and wearing a gown woven of eyes and ears to signify her power to see and hear her subjects. The Flemish artist Sir Anthony van Dyck (1599–1641) created powerful images of three generations of Stuart kings of England. Diego Velázquez (1599–1660) was court painter to Philip IV of Spain. His series of equestrian portraits of the Habsburgs—kings, queens, princes, and princesses—exude the spirit of the seventeenth-century monarchy, the grandeur and pomp, the power and self-assurance. Peter Paul Rubens (1577–1640) represented 21 separate episodes in the life of Marie de Médicis, queen regent of France.

Monarchy was also glorified in literature. National history, particularly of recent events, enjoyed wide popularity. Its avowed purpose was to draw the connection between the past and the present glories of the state. A popular French history of the period was entitled *On the Excellence of the Kings and the Kingdom of France.* Francis Bacon (1561–1626), who is remembered more as a philosopher and scientist, wrote a laudatory history of England's Henry VII, founder of the Tudor dynasty.

▼ Queen Elizabeth I of England. This portrait was commissioned by Sir Henry Lee to commemorate the queen's visit to his estate at Ditchley. Here the queen is the very image of Gloriana—ageless and indomitable.

In England, the seventeenth century was a period of renaissance. Poets, playwrights, historians, and philosophers gravitated to the English court. Ben Jonson (1572–1637), a commoner whose wit and talent brought him to court, made his mark by writing and staging masques, light entertainment that included music, dance, pantomime, and acting. Jonson's lavish productions, with sets designed by the great architect Inigo Jones (1573–1652), were frequently staged at Christmastime and starred members of the court as players. The masques took for their themes the grandeur of England and its rulers.

Shakespeare and Kingship. Many of the plays of William Shakespeare (1564–1616) also dealt with monarchy. Like Jonson, Shakespeare came from an ordinary family and began his career as an actor and producer of theater. He soon began to write as well as direct his plays, and his company, the King's Players, received royal patronage. He set many of his plays at the courts of princes, and even comedies such as *Measure for Measure* (1604) and *The Tempest* (1611) centered on the power of the ruler to dispense justice and to bring peace to his subjects. Shakespeare's history plays focused entirely on the character of kings. In *Richard II* (1597) and *Henry VI* (three parts, 1591–1594), Shakespeare exposed the harm that weak rulers inflicted on their states, while in *Henry IV* (two parts, 1598–1600) and *Henry V* (1599) he highlighted the benefits to be derived from strong rulers. In Shakespeare's tragedies a flaw in the ruler's personality brought harm to the world around him. In *Macbeth* (1606) this flaw was ambition; in *Hamlet* (1602) it was irresolution. Shakespeare's concentration on the affairs of rulers helped to reinforce their dominating importance in the lives of all of their subjects.

Monarchy and Law. The political theory of the divine right of kings further enhanced the importance of monarchs. This theory held that the institution of monarchy had been created by God and that the monarch functioned as God's representative on earth. One clear statement of divine right theory was actually written by a king, James VI of Scotland, who later became King James I of England (1603–1625). In *The True Law of Free Monarchies* (1598), James reasoned that God had placed kings on earth to rule and had charged them with the obligations "to minister justice; to establish good laws; and to procure peace." God would also judge them in heaven for their transgressions.

The idea of divine origin of monarchy was uncontroversial, and it was espoused not only by kings. The French Estates-General, for example, in 1614 agreed that "the king is sovereign in France and holds his crown from God only." This sentiment echoed the commonplace view of French political theorists. The greatest writer on the subject, Jean Bodin (1530–1596), called the king "God's image on earth." In *The Six Books of the Commonwealth* (1576), Bodin defined the essence of the monarch's power: "The principal mark of sovereign majesty is essentially the right to impose laws on subjects generally without their consent."

Kings were nevertheless bound by the law of nature and the law of nations. They could not deprive their subjects of their lives, their liberties, or their property without due cause established by law. As one French theorist held, "While the kingdom belongs to the king, the king also belongs to the kingdom." Wherever they turned, kings were instructed in the duties of kingship.

The Court and the Courtiers

In reality, the day-to-day affairs of government had grown beyond the capacity of any monarch to handle them. The expansion in the powers of the western states absorbed more officials than ever. At the beginning of the sixteenth century, the French court of Francis I employed 622 officers; at the beginning of the seventeenth century, the court of Henry IV employed over 1,500. Yet the difference was not only in size. Members of the seventeenth-century court were becoming servants of the state as well as of the monarch.

Expanding the court was one of the ways in which monarchs co-opted potential rivals within the aristocracy. In return, those who were favored received royal grants of titles, lands, and income. As the court expanded, so did the political power of courtiers. Royal councils—a small group of leading officeholders who advised the monarch on state business—grew in significance. The council assumed management of the government and soon began to advocate policies for the monarch to adopt.

Yet the court still revolved around the monarch. The monarch appointed, promoted, and dismissed officeholders at will. As befitted this type of personal government, most monarchs chose a single individual to act as a funnel for private and public business. This was the "favorite," whose role combined varying proportions of best friend, right-hand man, and hired gun. Some favorites, like the French Cardinal Richelieu and the Spanish Count-Duke Olivares, were able to transform themselves into chief ministers. Others, like the English Duke of Buckingham, simply remained royal companions. Favorites lasted only as long as they retained their influence with the monarch. Richelieu claimed that it was "more difficult to dominate the four square feet of the king's study than the affairs of Europe." The parallel careers of Richelieu, Olivares, and Buckingham neatly illustrate the dangers and opportunities of the office.

Cardinal Richelieu (1585–1642), a younger son of a minor French noble family, trained for the law and then for a position that his family owned in the Church. He was made a cardinal in 1622. After skillful participation in the meeting of the Estates-General of 1614, Richelieu was

A GLIMPSE OF A KING

Louis de Rouvroy, duc de Saint-Simon, spent much of his career at the court of Louis XIV. His Memoires *provide a fascinating study of life at Versailles, as well as poison pen portraits of the king and his courtiers. Here he describes some habits of the king.*

FOCUS QUESTIONS

How does the king maintain his power over the nobles? Why does so much in this political system depend on personal skills and self-presentation?

HE ALWAYS TOOK GREAT PAINS to find out what was going on in public places, in society, in private houses, even family secrets, and maintained an immense number of spies and tale-bearers. These were of all sorts; some did not know that their reports were carried to him; others did know it; there were others, again, who used to write to him directly, through channels which he prescribed; others who were admitted by the backstairs and saw him in his private room. Many a man in all ranks of life was ruined by these methods, often very unjustly, without ever being able to discover the reason; and when the King had once take a prejudice against a man, he hardly ever got over it. . . .

No one understood better than Louis XIV the art of enhancing the value of a favour by his manner of bestowing it; he knew how to make the most of a word, a smile, even of a glance. If he addressed any one, were it but to ask a trifling question or make some commonplace remark, all eyes were turned on the person so honored; it was a mark of favour which always gave rise to comment. . . .

He loved splendour, magnificence, and profusion in all things, and encouraged similar tastes in his Court; to spend money freely on equipages and buildings, on feasting and at cards, was a sure way to gain his favour, perhaps to obtain the honour of a word from him. Motives of policy and something to do with this; by making expensive habits the fashion, and, for people in a certain position, a necessity, he compelled his courtiers to live beyond their income, and gradually reduced them to depend on his bounty for the means of subsistence.

From duc de Saint-Simon, *Memoires*.

given a court post through the patronage of Queen Marie de Médicis, mother of Louis XIII. The two men made a good match. Louis XIII hated the work of ruling, and Richelieu loved little else.

Though Richelieu received great favor from the king—he became a duke and amassed the largest private fortune in France—his position rested on his managerial abilities. Richelieu never enjoyed a close personal relationship with his monarch, and he never felt that his position was secure. In 1630, Marie de Médicis turned against him, and he was very nearly ousted from office. His last years were filled with suppressing plots to undermine his power or to take his life.

The Count-Duke Olivares (1587–1645) was a younger son of a lesser branch of a great Spanish noble family. By the time he was 20, he had become a courtier with a title, a large fortune, and, most unusually, a university education. Olivares became the favorite of King Philip IV (1621–1665). He was elevated to the highest rank of the nobility and used his closeness to the monarch to gain court appointments for his relatives and political supporters.

But he was more interested in establishing political policy than in building a court faction. His objective was to maintain the greatness of Spain, and he attempted to further the process of centralizing Spanish royal power, which was not very advanced. Olivares's plans for a nationally recruited and financed army ended in disaster. His efforts at tax reform went unrewarded. He advocated the aggressive foreign policy that mired Spain in the Thirty Years' War and the eighty years of war in the Netherlands. As domestic and foreign crises mounted, Philip IV could not resist the pressure to dismiss his chief minister. In 1643, Olivares was removed from office; two years later, physically exhausted and mentally deranged, he died.

The Duke of Buckingham (1592–1628) was also a younger son but was not of the English nobility. He received the aimless education of a country gentleman, spending several years in France learning the graces of fashion and dancing. He was reputedly one of the handsomest men in Europe, and his looks and charm eventually brought him to the attention of Queen Anne, the wife of James I. She recommended Buckingham for a minor office that gave him frequent access to the king, and in less than seven years he rose from commoner to duke, the highest rank of the English nobility.

Along with his titles, Buckingham acquired political power. He assumed a large number of royal offices, among them Admiral of the Navy, and placed his relatives and dependents in many others. Buckingham took his obligations seriously. He began a reform of naval administration, for example, but his rise to power was so sudden that he found enemies at every turn. These increased dramatically when James I died in 1625, but Buckingham still managed to become the favorite and chief minister of the new king, Charles I (1625–1649). With Charles I firmly behind him, his accumulation of power and patronage proceeded unabated, as did the enmity he aroused. In 1628, Buckingham was assassinated by a discontented naval officer. While Charles I wept inconsolably at the news, ordinary Londoners drank to the health of Buckingham's killer.

The Drive to Centralize Government

Richelieu, Olivares, and Buckingham met very different ends, but they shared a common goal: to extend the authority of the monarch over his state and to centralize his control over the machinery of governance. One of the chief means by which kings and councilors attempted to expand the authority of the state was through the legal system.

Administering justice was one of the sacred duties of the monarchy. The complexities of ecclesiastical, civil, and customary law gave trained lawyers an essential role in government. As the need for legal services increased, royal law courts multiplied and expanded. In France, the Parlement of Paris, the main law court of the state, became a powerful institution that contested with courtiers for the right to advise the monarch.

In Spain the *letrados*—university-trained lawyers who were normally members of the nobility—were the backbone of royal government. Formal legal training was a requirement for many of the administrative posts in the state. In Castile, members of all social classes frequently used the royal courts to settle personal disputes. The expansion of a centralized system of justice thus joined the interests of subjects and the monarchy.

In England, central courts situated in the royal palace of Westminster grew, and the lawyers and judges who practiced in them became a powerful profession. They were especially active in the House of Commons of the English Parliament, which, along with the House of Lords, had extensive advisory and legislative powers. More important than the rise of the central courts, however, was the rise of the local ones. The English crown extended royal justice to the counties by granting legal authority to members of the local social elite. These justices of the peace, whose position can be traced to medieval times, became agents of the crown in their own localities. Justices were given power to hear and settle minor cases and to imprison people who had committed serious offenses until the assizes, the semiannual sessions of the county court.

Assizes combined the ceremony of rule with its process. Royal authority was displayed in a great procession to the courthouse that was led by the judge and the county justices, followed by the grand and petty juries of local citizens who would hear the cases and finally by the carts carrying the prisoners to trial. Along with the legal business that was performed, assizes were occasions for edifying sermons, typically on the theme of obedience. Their solemnity, marked by the black robes of the judge, the Latin of the legal proceedings, and the public executions, served to instill a sense of the power of the state in the throngs of ordinary people who witnessed them.

Efforts to integrate center and locality extended to more than the exercise of justice. The monarch also needed officials who could enforce royal policy in localities where the special privileges of groups and individuals remained strong. By the beginning of the seventeenth century, the French monarchy had begun to rely on new central officials known as intendants to perform many of the tasks of the provincial governors. Cardinal Richelieu expanded the use of the intendants, and by the middle of the century they had become a vital part of royal government.

The Lords Lieutenant were a parallel institution created in England. Unlike every other European state, England had no national army. Every English county was required to raise, equip, and train its own militia. Lords Lieutenant were in charge of these trained bands. The lieutenants were chosen from the greatest nobles of the realm, but they delegated their work to members of the local gentry, large landholders who took on their tasks as a matter of prestige rather than profit. Perhaps not surprisingly, the English military was among the weakest in Europe, and nearly all its foreign adventures ended in disaster.

Efforts to centralize the Spanish monarchy could not proceed so easily. The separate regions over which the king ruled maintained their own laws and privileges. Attempts to apply Castilian rules or implant Castilian officials always drew opposition from other regions. In 1625, Olivares proposed a plan to help unify Spain and solve the dual problems of military manpower and military finance. After 1621, Spain was fighting in the Netherlands and Germany. Olivares called for a Union of Arms to which all the separate regions of the empire, including Mexico, Peru, Italy, and the dominions in Iberia, would contribute. Olivares was able to establish at least the principle of unified cooperation, but not all of the Iberian provinces were persuaded to contribute. Catalonia stood on its ancient privileges and refused to grant either troops or funds.

The Taxing Demands of War

More than anything else, the consolidation of the state was propelled by war, which required increased governmental powers of taxation. Perhaps half of all revenue of the western states went to finance war. To maintain its military forces, the state had to squeeze every penny from its subjects. Old taxes had to be collected more efficiently, and new taxes had to be introduced and enforced. Such unprecedented demands for money on the part of the state were always resisted. The privileged challenged the legality of levying taxes; the unprivileged tried to avoid paying them.

The economic hardships caused by the ceaseless military activity touched everyone. Those in the direct path of battle had little left to feed themselves, let alone to provide to the state. The disruption of the delicate cycle of planting and harvesting devastated local communities. Armies plundered ripened grain and trampled seedlings as they moved through fields. The conscription of village men and boys removed vital skills and labor from the community. Peasants were squeezed by the armies for crops, by the lords for rents, and by the state for taxes.

In fact, the inability of the lower orders of European society to finance a century of warfare was clear from the beginning. In Spain and France, much wealth was beyond the reach of traditional royal taxation. The nobility and many of the most important towns had long enjoyed exemption from basic taxes on consumption and wealth. European taxation was regressive, falling most heavily on those who were least able to pay. Rulers and subjects alike recognized the inequities of the system, and regime after regime considered overhauling the national tax system but ultimately settled for new emergency levies. Nevertheless, the fiscal crisis that the European wars provoked did result in an expansion of state taxation.

Military spending also increased in England. War with Ireland in the 1590s and with Spain between 1588 and 1604 depleted the reserves that the crown had obtained when Henry VIII dissolved the monasteries. Disastrous wars against France and Spain in the 1620s provoked fiscal crisis for a monarchy that had few direct sources of revenue. While the great wealth of the kingdom was in land, the chief sources of revenue for the crown were in trade. In the early seventeenth century, customs duties became a lucrative source of income when the judges ruled that the king could determine which commodities could be taxed and at what rate.

Because so much of the crown's revenues derived from commerce and because foreign invasion could come only from the sea, the most pressing military need of the English monarchy was for naval defense. Even during the Armada crisis, the largest part of the English fleet had been made up of private merchant ships pressed into service through the emergency tax of Ship Money. This was a tax on each port town to hire a merchant ship and fit it out for war. In the 1630s, Charles I revived Ship Money and extended it to all English localities.

Still, no matter how much new revenue was provided for war finance, more was needed. New taxes and increased rates of traditional taxation created suffering and a sense of grievance throughout the western European states. Opposition to taxation was not based on greed. The state's right to tax was not yet an established principle. Monarchs received certain forms of revenue in return for grants of immunities and privileges to powerful groups in their state. The state's efforts to go beyond these restricted grants was viewed as theft of private property. In the Ship Money case, challengers argued that the king had no right to such demands except in a case of national emergency. The king argued that such an emergency existed, since pirates were attacking English shipping. But if Charles I did not make a convincing claim for national emergency, the monarchs of France and Spain, the princes of Germany, and the rulers of the states of eastern Europe all did.

Throughout the seventeenth century, monarchy was consolidating its position as a form of government. The king's authority came from God, but his power came from his people. By administering justice, assembling armies, and extracting resources through taxation, the monarch ruled as well as governed. The richer and more powerful the king, the more potent was his state. His subjects began to identify themselves as citizens of a nation and to see themselves in distinction to other nations.

THE CRISES OF THE ROYAL STATE

The expansion of the functions, duties, and powers of the state in the early seventeenth century was not universally welcomed in European societies. The growth of central government came at the expense of local rights and privileges held by organized bodies such as the Church and the towns or by individuals such as provincial officials and aristocrats. The state proved to be a powerful competitor for the meager surplus produced on the land. As rents and prices stabilized in the early seventeenth century, after a long period of inflation, taxation increased, especially with the gathering momentum of the Thirty Years' War. State exactions burdened all segments of society. Peasants lost the small benefit that rising prices had conferred on producers. The surplus that parents had once passed on to children was now taken by the state. Local officials, never altogether popular, came to be seen as parasites and provided easy targets for peasant rebellions. Larger landholders, whose prosperity depended on rents and services from an increasingly impoverished peasantry, suffered along with their tenants. Even the great magnates were appalled by the state's insatiable appetite.

It was not only taxation that aroused opposition. Social and economic regulation meant more laws, more lawyers, and more agents of enforcement. State regulation was disruptive and expensive at a time when the fragile European economy was in decline. The early seventeenth century was a time of hunger in most of western Europe. Subtle changes in climate reduced the length of growing seasons and the size of crops. Bad harvests in the 1620s and 1640s left disease and starvation in their wake. And the wars ground on.

EUROPEAN POPULATION DATA (IN MILLIONS)							
Year	**1550**	**1575**	**1600**	**1625**	**1650**	**1675**	**1700**
England	3.0	—	4.0	4.5	—	5.8	5.8
France	—	20.0	—	—	—	—	19.3
Italy	11.0	13.0	13.0	13.0	12.0	11.5	12.5
Russia	9.0	—	11.0	8.0	9.5	13.0	16.0
Spain	6.3	—	7.6	—	5.2	—	7.0
All Europe	85.0	95.0	100.0	100.0	80.0	90.0	100.0

By the middle of the seventeenth century, a Europe-wide crisis was taking shape. Bread riots and tax revolts had become increasingly common in the early seventeenth century. As the focus of discontent moved from local institutions to the state, the forms of revolt and the participants also changed. Members of the political elite began to formulate their own grievances against the expansion of state power. A theory of resistance, first developed in the French wars of religion, came to be applied to political tyranny and posed a direct challenge to the idea of the divine right of kings. By the 1640s, all of these forces converged, and rebellion exploded across the Continent. In Spain, the ancient kingdoms of Catalonia and Portugal asserted their independence from Castilian rule; in France, members of the aristocracy rose against a child monarch and his regent. In Italy, revolts rocked Naples and Sicily. In England, a constitutional crisis gave way to civil war and then to the first political revolution in European history.

The Need to Resist

Europeans lived more precariously in the seventeenth century than in any period since the Black Death. One benchmark of crisis was population decline. In the Mediterranean, the Spanish population fell from 8.5 million to 7 million, and the Italian population from 13 million to 11 million. The ravages of the Thirty Years' War were most clearly felt in central Europe. Germany lost nearly one-third of its people; Bohemia lost nearly half. England, the Netherlands, and France were hardest hit in the first half of the century and only gradually recovered by 1700. Population decline had many causes, and direct casualties from warfare were only a very small component. The indirect effects of war—the disruption of agriculture and the spread of disease—were far more devastating. Spain alone lost half a million people at the turn of the century and another half million between 1647 and 1652. Severe outbreaks of plague hit England in 1625 and in 1665, and France endured three consecutive years of epidemics from 1629 to 1631.

All sectors of the European economy from agriculture to trade stagnated or declined in the early seventeenth century, but peasants were hardest hit. The surplus from good harvests did not remain in rural communities to act as a buffer for bad ones. Tens of thousands died during the two great subsistence crises in the late 1620s and the late 1640s.

Acute economic crisis led to rural revolt. As the French peasants reeled from visitations of plague, frost, and floods, the French state was raising the taille, the tax on basic commodities that fell most heavily on the lower orders. A series of French rural revolts in the late 1630s protested tax increases. The *Nu-Pieds* ("barefooted") rose against changes in the salt tax; other peasants rose against new levies on wine. These revolts typically began with the murder of a local tax official, the organization of a peasant militia, and the recruitment of local clergy and notables. The rebels forced temporary concessions from local authorities but never achieved lasting reforms. Each revolt ended with the reimposition of order by the state. In England, the largest rural protests, such as the Midland Revolt of 1607, centered on opposition to the enclosure of grain fields and their conversion to pasture.

The most spectacular popular uprisings occurred in Spanish-occupied Italy. In the spring of 1647, in the Sicilian city of Palermo, violence broke out in the wake of a disastrous harvest, rising food prices, and relentless taxation. As grain prices rose, the city government subsidized the price of bread, running up huge debts in the process. When the town governors could no longer afford the subsidies, they decided to reduce the size of the loaf rather than increase its price. The women of the city rioted when the first undersized loaves were placed on sale, and soon the entire city was in revolt. Commoners who were not part of the urban power structure led the revolt, and for a time they achieved the abolition of Spanish taxes on basic foodstuffs. Their success provided the model for a similar uprising in Naples, the largest city in Europe. The revolt began in 1647 after the Spanish placed a tax on fruit. A crowd gathered in protest, burned the customs house, and murdered several local officials. The rebels again achieved the temporary suspension of Spanish taxation. But neither of the Italian urban revolts could attract support from the local governors or the nobility. Both uprisings were eventually crushed.

The Right to Resist

Rural and urban revolts by members of the lower orders of European society were doomed to failure. Not only did the state control vast military resources, but it could count on the loyalty of the governing classes to suppress local disorder. Only when disgruntled local elites joined the angry peasants did the state face a genuine crisis. Traditionally, aristocratic rebellion was sparked by rival claimants to the throne. By the early seventeenth century, however, hereditary monarchy was too firmly entrenched to be threatened by aristocratic rebellions. When Elizabeth I of England died without an heir, the throne passed to her cousin, James I, without even a murmur of discontent. In France the assassination of Henry IV in 1610 left a child on the throne, yet it provoked little more than intrigue over which aristocratic faction would advise him. The principles of hereditary monarchy and the divine right of kings laid an unshakable foundation for royal legitimacy. But if the monarch's right to rule could no longer be challenged, was the method of rule equally unassailable? Were subjects bound to their sovereign in all cases whatsoever?

Resistance Theory. Luther and Calvin had preached a doctrine of passive obedience. Magistrates ruled by divine will and must be obeyed in all things, they argued. Both left a tiny crack in the door of absolute submission, however, by recognizing the right of lesser magistrates to resist their superiors if divine law was violated. During the French civil wars, a broader theory of resistance began to develop. In attempting to defend themselves from accusations that they were rebels, a number of Huguenot writers responded with an argument that accepted the divine right of kings but maintained that kings were placed on earth by God to uphold piety and justice. When they failed to do so, lesser magistrates were obliged to resist them. Because God would not institute tyranny, oppressive monarchs could not be acting by divine right. Therefore, the king who violated divine law could be punished. In the most influential of these writings, *A Defense of Liberty Against Tyrants* (1579), Philippe Duplessis-Mornay (1549–1623) took the critical next step and argued that the king who violated the law of the land could also be resisted.

In the writings of both the French Huguenots and the Dutch Protestants there remained strict limits to this right to resist. These authors accepted divine right theory and restricted resistance to other divinely ordained magistrates.

Logic soon drove the argument further. If it was the duty of lesser magistrates to resist monarchical tyranny, why was it not the duty of all citizens to do so? This question was posed by the Jesuit professor Juan de Mariana (1536–1624) in *The King and the Education of the King* (1598). Since magistrates were first established by the people and then legitimated by God, magistrates were nothing other than the people's representatives. If it was the duty of magistrates to resist the tyranny of monarchs, Mariana reasoned, then it must also be the duty of every individual citizen. "If the sacred fatherland is falling into ruins, he who tries to kill the tyrant will be acting in no ways unjustly."

In his defense of the English Revolution, the great English poet John Milton (1608–1674) built on traditional resistance theory. Kings were instituted by the people to uphold piety and justice. Lesser magistrates had the right to resist monarchs. An unjust king forfeited his divine right and was to be punished like any ordinary citizen. In *The Tenure of Kings and Magistrates* (1649), Milton expanded on the conventional idea that society was formed by a covenant, or contract, between ruler and ruled. The king, in his coronation oath, promised to uphold the laws of the land and to rule for the benefit of his subjects. The subjects promised to obey. Failure to meet obligations—by either side—broke the contract.

Resistance and Rebellion. By the middle of the seventeenth century, resistance theory provided the intellectual justification for a number of attacks on monarchical authority. In 1640, simultaneous rebellions in the ancient kingdoms of Portugal and Catalonia threatened the Spanish monarchy. The Portuguese successfully dissolved the rather artificial bonds that had been created by Philip II and resumed their separate national identity. Catalonia, the easternmost province of Spain, which Ferdinand of Aragon had brought to the union of crowns in the fifteenth century, presented a more serious challenge. Throughout the 1620s, Catalonia, with its rich Mediterranean city of Barcelona, had consistently rebuffed Olivares's attempts to consolidate the Spanish provinces. The Catalan Cortes—the representative institution of the towns—refused to make even small contributions to the Union of Arms or to successive appeals for emergency tax increases. Catalonian leaders feared that these demands were only an entering wedge. They did not want their province to go the way of Castile, where taxation was as much an epidemic as was plague.

Catalonia resisted demands for contributions to the Spanish military effort, but soon the province was embroiled in the French war, and Olivares was forced to bring troops into Catalonia. The presence of the soldiers and their conduct inflamed the local population. In the spring of 1640, an unconnected series of peasant uprisings took place. Soldiers and royal officials were slain, and the Spanish viceroy of the province was murdered. But the violence was not directed only against outsiders. Attacks on wealthy citizens raised the specter of social revolt.

It was at this point that a peasant uprising broadened into a provincial rebellion. The political leaders of Barcelona sanctioned the rebellion and decided to lead it. They declared that Philip IV had violated the fundamental laws of Catalonia and that in consequence their allegiance to the crown of Spain was dissolved. They turned to Louis XIII of France, offering him sovereignty if he would preserve their liberties. In fact, the Catalonians simply exchanged a devil they knew for one they did not. The French happily sent troops into Barcelona to repel a Spanish attempt to crush the rebellion. Now two armies occupied Catalonia. The Catalan rebellion lasted for 12 years. When the Spanish finally took Barcelona in 1652, both rebels and ruler were exhausted from the struggle.

The revolt of the Catalans posed a greater external threat to the Spanish monarchy than it did an internal one. In contrast, the French Fronde, an aristocratic rebellion that began in 1648, was more directly a challenge to the underlying authority of the state. It too began in response to fiscal crises brought on by war. Throughout the 1640s, the French state, tottering on the edge of bankruptcy, had used every means of creative financing that its ministers could devise. Still, it was necessary to raise traditional taxes and to institute new ones. The first tactic revived peasant revolts, especially in the early years of the decade; the second led to the Fronde.

The Fronde was a rebellion against the regency government of Louis XIV (1643–1715), who was only four years old when he inherited the French throne. His mother, Anne of Austria (1601–1666), ruled as regent with the help of her Italian adviser, Cardinal Mazarin (1602–1661). In the circumstances of war, agricultural crisis, and financial stringency, no regency government was going to be popular, but Anne and Mazarin made the worst of a bad situation. They initiated new taxes on officeholders, Parisian landowners, and the nobility. Soon all three groups united against them, led by the Parlement of Paris, the highest court in the land, in which new decrees of taxation had to be registered. When the Parlement refused to register a number of the new taxes proposed by the government and soon insisted on the right to control the crown's financial policy, Anne and Mazarin struck back by having a number of Parlement members arrested. But in 1648, barricades went up in Paris, and the court, along with the nine-year-old king, fled the capital. Quickly, the Fronde—which took its name from the slingshots that children used to hurl stones at carriages—became an aristocratic revolt aimed not at the king but at his advisers. Demands for Mazarin's resignation, the removal of the new taxes, and greater participation in government by nobles and Parlement were coupled with profuse statements of loyalty to the king.

The duc de Condé, leader of the Parisian insurgents, courted Spanish aid against Mazarin's forces, and the cardinal was forced to make concessions to prevent a Spanish invasion of France. The leaders of the Fronde agreed that the crown must overhaul its finances and recognize the rights of the administrative nobility to participate in formulating royal policy. But they had no concrete proposals to accomplish either aim. Nor could they control the deteriorating political situation in Paris and a number of provincial capitals, where urban and rural riots followed the upper-class attack on the state. The catastrophic winter of 1652, with its combination of harvest failure, intense cold, and epidemic disease, brought the crisis to a head. Louis XIV was declared old enough to rule, and his forces recaptured Paris, where he was welcomed as a savior. The Fronde accomplished little other than to demonstrate that the French aristocracy remained an independent force in politics. Like the Catalonian revolt, it revealed the fragility of the absolute state on the one hand, yet its underlying stability on the other.

The English Civil War

The most profound challenge to monarchical authority in the seventeenth century took place in England. In 1603, James I succeeded his cousin Elizabeth I without challenge. He was not a lovable monarch, but he was capable, astute, and generous. His principal difficulties were that he was Scottish and that he succeeded a legend. Elizabeth I had ruled England successfully for over forty years. As the economy soured and the state tilted toward bankruptcy in the 1590s, the queen remained above criticism. She sold off royal lands worth thousands of pounds and ran up huge debts at the turn of the century. Yet the gleaming myth of the glorious virgin queen was not the least bit tarnished, and when she died, the general population wept openly.

At first, James I endeared himself to the English gentry and aristocracy by showering them with the gift of social elevation. On his way to London from Scotland, the first of the Stuart kings knighted thousands of gentlemen. But he showered favor equally on his own countrymen, members of his royal Scottish court who accompanied him to England. A strong strain of ethnic prejudice combined with the disappointed hopes of English courtiers to generate immediate hostility to the new regime. Though he relied on Elizabeth's most trusted ministers to guide state business, James was soon plunged into financial and political difficulties. He never escaped from either.

Charles I. James's financial problems resulted directly from the fact that the tax base of the English monarchy was undervalued. For decades the monarchy had staved off a crisis by selling lands that had been confiscated from the Church in the mid-sixteenth century. But this solution reduced the crown's long-term revenues and made it dependent on extraordinary grants of taxation from Parliament. Royal demands for money were met by parliamentary demands for political reform. The most significant, in 1628, during the reign of Charles I, led to the formulation of the Petition of Right, which restated the traditional English freedoms from arbitrary arrest and imprisonment (habeas corpus), from nonparliamentary taxation, and from the confiscation of property by martial law.

Religious problems mounted on top of economic and political difficulties. Puritans were demanding thoroughgoing church reforms. One of the most contentious issues raised by some Puritans was the survival in the Anglican Church of the Catholic hierarchy of archbishops and bishops. These Puritans demanded the abolition of this episcopal form of government and its replacement with a presbyterial system similar to that in Scotland, in which congregations nominated their own representatives to a national assembly. Neither James I nor his son, Charles I, opposed religious reform, but to achieve their reforms, they strengthened episcopal power. In the 1620s, Archbishop William Laud (1573–1645) rose to power in the English church by espousing a Calvinism so moderate that many denied it was Calvinism at all. Laud preached the beauty of holiness and strove to reintroduce decoration in the church and a formal decorum in the service. One of Laud's first projects after he was appointed archbishop of Canterbury was to establish a consistent divine service in England and Scotland by creating new prayer books.

▼ Charles I by Daniel Myrtens. The antagonism between Charles and Parliament sparked a civil war in England.

It fell to the unfortunate dean of St. Giles Cathedral in Edinburgh to introduce the new Scottish prayer book in 1637. The reaction was immediate: someone threw a stool at his head, and dozens of women screamed that "popery" was being brought to Scotland. Citizens rioted, and the clergy and the nobility resisted the use of the new prayer book. To Charles I the opposition was rebellion, and he began to raise forces to suppress it. But the Scots fought back, and by the end of 1640 an army of Charles's Scottish subjects had successfully invaded England.

Now the fiscal and political problems of the Stuart monarchs came into play. For 11 years, Charles I had managed to live from his own revenues. He had accomplished this by a combination of economy and the revival of ancient feudal rights that struck hard at the governing classes. He levied fines for unheard-of offenses, expanded traditional taxes, and added a brutal efficiency to the collection of revenue. While these expedients sufficed during peacetime, they could not support an army and war. Charles I was again dependent on grants from Parliament, which he reluctantly summoned in 1640.

The Long Parliament. The Long Parliament, which met in November 1640 and sat for thirteen years, saw little urgency in levying taxes to repel the Scots. After all, the Scots were resisting Laud's religious innovations, and many Englishmen agreed that they should be resisted. Parliament proposed a number of constitutional reforms that Charles I reluctantly accepted. The Long Parliament would not be dismissed without its own consent. In the future, Parliaments would be summoned once in every three years. Due process in common law would be observed, and the ancient taxes that the crown had revived would be abolished.

At first, Charles I could do nothing but bide his time and accept these assaults on his power and authority. Once he had crushed the Scots, he would be able to bargain from a position of strength. But as the months passed, it became clear that Parliament had no intention of providing him with money or forces. By the end of 1641, Charles's patience had worn thin. He bungled an attempt to arrest the leaders of the House of Commons, but he successfully spirited his wife and children out of London.

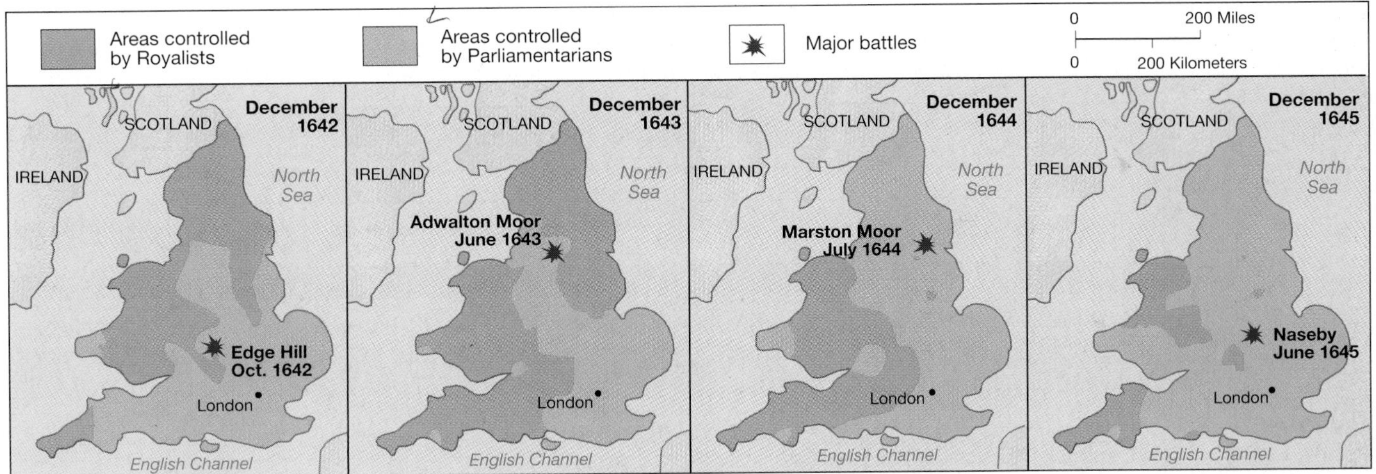

The English Civil War. The maps show the gradual triumph of the parliamentarians whose control of London and the coastal areas gave them a profound logistical advantage during the wars.

Then he too left the capital and headed north, where, in the summer of 1642, he raised the royal standard and declared the leaders of Parliament rebels and traitors. England was plunged into civil war.

There were strong passions on both sides. Parliamentarians believed that they were fighting to defend their religion, their liberties, and the rule of law. Royalists believed that they were fighting to defend their monarch, their church, and social stability. After nearly three years of inconclusive fighting, Parliament won a decisive victory at Naseby in June 1645 and brought the war to an end the following summer. The king was in captivity, bishops had been abolished, a Presbyterian church had been established, and limitations were placed on royal power. All that was necessary to end three years of civil war was the king's agreement to abide by the judgment of battle.

But Charles I had no intention of surrendering either his religion or his authority. Despite the rebels' successes, they could not rule without him, and he would concede nothing as long as opportunities to maneuver remained. In 1647 there were opportunities galore. The war had proved ruinously expensive to Parliament. It owed enormous sums to the Scots, to its own soldiers, and to the governors of London. Each of these elements had its own objectives in a final settlement of the war, and they were not altogether compatible. London feared the parliamentary army, unpaid and camped dangerously close to the capital. The Scots and the English Presbyterians in Parliament feared that the religious settlement that had already been made would be sacrificed by those known as Independents, who desired a more decentralized church. The Independents feared that they would be persecuted just as harshly by the Presbyterians as they had been by the king. In fact, the war had settled nothing.

The English Revolutions

Charles I happily played both ends against the middle until the army decisively ended the game. In June 1647, parliamentary soldiers kidnapped the king and demanded that Parliament pay their arrears, protect them from legal retribution, and recognize their service to the nation. Those in Parliament who opposed the army's intervention were impeached, and when London Presbyterians rose up against the army's show of force, troops moved in to occupy the city. The civil war, which had come so close to resolution in 1647, had now become a military revolution. Religious and political radicals flocked to the army and encouraged the soldiers to support their programs and to resist disbandment. New fighting broke out in 1648, as Charles encouraged his supporters to resume the war. But forces under the command of Sir Thomas Fairfax (1612–1671) and Oliver Cromwell (1599–1658) easily crushed the royalist uprisings in England and Scotland. The army now demanded that Charles I be brought to justice for his treacherous conduct both before and during the war. When the majority in Parliament refused, still hoping to reach an accommodation with the king, the soldiers again acted decisively. In December 1648, army regiments were sent to London to purge the two houses of Parliament of those who opposed the army's demands. The remaining members, contemptuously called the Rump Parliament, voted to bring the king to trial for his crimes against the liberties of his subjects. On 30 January 1649, Charles I was executed, and England was declared to be a commonwealth. The monarchy and the House of Lords were abolished, and the nation was to be governed by what was left of the membership of the House of Commons.

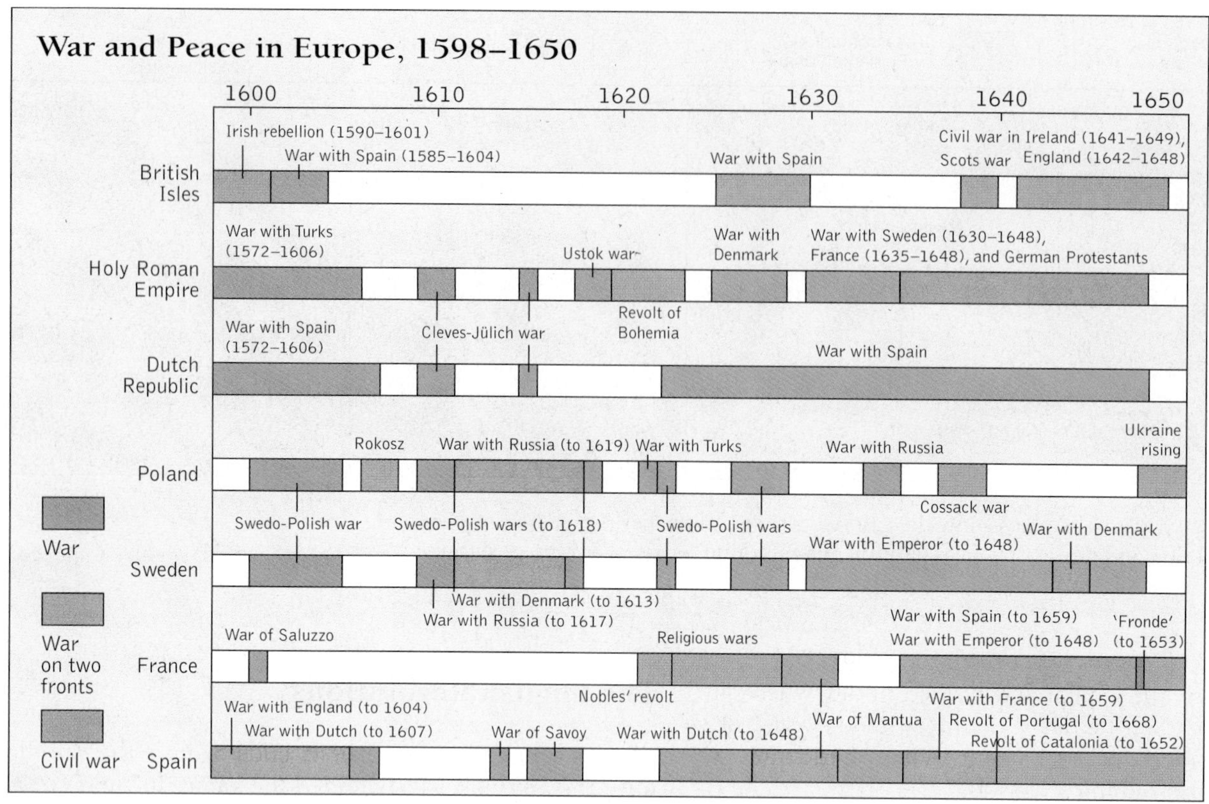

Oliver Cromwell. For four years, the members of the Rump Parliament struggled with proposals for a new constitution, achieving little. In 1653, Oliver Cromwell, with the support of the army's senior officers, forcibly dissolved the Rump and became the leader of the revolutionary government. At first he ruled along with a Parliament that had been handpicked from among the supporters of the commonwealth. When Cromwell's Parliament proved no more capable of governing than had the Rump, a written constitution, The Instrument of Government (1653), established a new polity. Cromwell was given the title Lord Protector, and he was to rule along with a freely elected Parliament and an administrative body known as the council of state.

Cromwell was able to smooth over conflicts and hold the revolutionary cause together through the force of his own personality. He was a devout Puritan who had opposed the arbitrary policies of Charles I and who believed in a large measure of religious toleration for Christians. Though many urged him to accept the crown of England and begin a new monarchy, Cromwell steadfastly held out for a government in which fundamental authority resided in Parliament. Until his death he defended the achievements of the revolution.

But a sense that only a single person could effectively rule a state remained strong. When Cromwell died in 1658, his oldest son Richard was proposed as the new Lord Protector, but Richard had very little experience in either military or civil affairs. Nor did he have the sense of purpose that was his father's greatest source of strength. Without an individual to hold the movement together, the revolution fell apart. In 1659, the army again intervened in civil affairs, dismissing the recently elected Parliament and calling for the restoration of the monarchy. After a period of negotiation in which the king agreed to a general amnesty with only a few exceptions, the Stuarts were restored when Charles II (1649–1685) took the throne in 1660.

Twenty years of civil war and revolution had their effect. Parliament became a permanent part of civil government. Royal power over taxation and religion was curtailed, though in fact Parliament proved more vigorous in suppressing religious dissent than the monarchy ever was. England was to be a reformed Protestant state, though there remained much dispute about what constituted reform. Absolute monarchy had become constitutional monarchy with the threat of revolution behind the power of Parliament and the threat of anarchy behind the power of the Crown.

The "Glorious Revolution." The threats of revolution and of anarchy proved potent in 1685 when James II (1685–1688) came to the throne. A declared Catholic, James attempted to use his power of appointment to foil the constraints that Parliament imposed on him. He elevated Catholics to leading posts in the military and in the central government and began a campaign to pack a new Parliament with his supporters. This proved to be too much for the governing classes, which entered into negotiations with William, Prince of Orange, who was the husband of Mary Stuart, James's eldest daughter. In 1688, William landed in England with a small force. Without support, James II fled to France, the English throne was declared vacant, and William and Mary were proclaimed king and queen of England. There was little bloodshed and little threat of social disorder, and the event soon came to be called the Glorious Revolution. Its achievements were set down in the Declaration of Rights (1689), which was presented to William and Mary before they took the throne. The Declaration reasserted the fundamental principles of constitutional monarchy as they had developed over the previous half-century. Security of property and the regularity of Parliaments were guaranteed. The Toleration Act (1689) granted religious freedom to nearly all groups of Protestants. The liberties of the subject and the rights of the sovereign were to be in balance.

The events of 1688 in England reversed a trend toward increasing power on the part of the Stuarts. This second episode of resistance resulted in the development of a unique form of government, which, a century later, spawned dozens of imitators. John Locke (1632–1704) was the theorist of the Revolution of 1688. He was heir to the century-old debate on resistance, and he carried the doctrine to a new plateau. In *Two Treatises on Government* (1689), Locke developed the contract theory of government. Political society was a compact that individuals entered into freely for their own well-being. It was designed to maintain each person's natural rights: life, liberty, and property. Natural rights were inherent in individuals; they could not be given away. The contract between rulers and subjects was an agreement for the protection of natural rights. When rulers acted arbitrarily, they were to be deposed by their subjects, preferably in the relatively peaceful manner in which James II had been replaced by William III.

The efforts of European monarchies to centralize their power came at the expense of the Church, the aristocracy, and the localities. It was a difficult struggle that took place over decades. In France, the Fronde was an aristocratic backlash; in Spain, the revolt of the Catalans pitted the Castilian crown against a proud ethnic province. In England, the excesses of monarchy were succeeded by the excesses of parliamentary rule. But the lesson that the English ruling elites learned was that for a nation to enjoy the benefits of a powerful central authority, it was necessary to restrain that authority. The Revolution of 1688 helped to create a constitutional balance between ruler and ruled.

THE ZENITH OF THE ROYAL STATE

The midcentury crises tested the mettle of the royal states. Over the long term, the seventeenth-century crises had two different consequences. First, they provided a check to the exercise of royal power. Fear of recurring rebellions had a chilling effect on policy, especially taxation. Reforms of financial administration, long overdue, were one of the themes of the later seventeenth century. Even as royal government strengthened itself, it remained concerned about the impact of its policies. The memory of rebellion also served to control the ambitions of factious noblemen and town oligarchies.

If nothing else, these episodes of opposition to the rising royal states made clear the universal desire for stable government, which was seen as the responsibility of both subjects and rulers. By the second half of the seventeenth century, effective government was the byword of the royal state. The natural advantages of monarchy had to be merged with the interests of the citizens of the state and their desires for wealth, safety, and honor. After so much chaos and instability the monarchy had to be elevated above the fray of day-to-day politics to become a symbol of the nation's power and glory.

In England, Holland, and Sweden a form of constitutional monarchy developed in which rulers shared power, in varying degrees, with other institutions of state. In England it was Parliament, in Holland the town oligarchies, and in Sweden the nobility. But in most other states in Europe there developed a pure form of royal government known as absolutism. Absolute monarchy revived the divine right theories of kingship and added to them a cult of the personality of the ruler. Absolutism was practiced in states as dissimilar as Denmark, Brandenburg-Prussia, and Russia. It reached its zenith in France under Louis XIV, the most powerful of the seventeenth-century monarchs.

The Nature of Absolute Monarchy

Locke's theory of contract provided one solution to the central problem of seventeenth-century government: how to balance the monarch's right to command and the subjects' duty to obey. By establishing a constitutional monarchy, in which power was shared between the ruler and a representative assembly of subjects, England found one path out of this thicket. But it was not a path that many others could follow.

The English solution was most suited to a state that was largely immune from invasion and land war. Constitutional government required a higher level of political participation of citizens than did absolute monarchy. Greater participation meant greater freedom of expression, greater toleration of religious minorities, and greater openness in the institutions of government. All were dangerous. The price that England paid was a half-century of governmental instability.

The alternative to constitutional monarchy was absolute monarchy. It, too, found its leading theorist in England. Thomas Hobbes (1588–1679), in his greatest work, *Leviathan* (1651), argued that before civil society had been formed, humans had lived in a savage state of nature, "in a war of every man against every man." This was a ghastly condition without morality or law. People came together to form a government for the most basic of all purposes: self-preservation. Without government they were condemned to a life that was "solitary, poor, nasty, brutish, and short." To escape the state of nature, individuals pooled their power and granted it to a ruler. The terms of the Hobbesian contract were simple. Rulers agreed to rule; subjects agreed to obey. When the contract was intact, people ceased to live in a state of nature. When it was broken, they returned to it. With revolts, rebellions, and revolutions erupting in all parts of Europe, Hobbes's state of nature never seemed very far away.

For most states of Europe in the later seventeenth century, absolute monarchy became not only a necessity but an ideal. The consolidation of power in the hands of the divinely ordained monarch, who, nevertheless, ruled according to principles of law and justice, was seen as the perfect form of government.

The main features of absolute monarchy were all designed to extend royal control. As in the early seventeenth century, the person of the monarch was revered. Courts grew larger and more lavish in an effort to enhance the glory of the monarchy and thereby of the state. "*L'état, c'est moi*" ("I am the state"), Louis XIV was supposed to have said. As the king grew in stature, his competitors for power all shrank. Large numbers of nobles were herded together at court under the watchful eye of monarchs who now ruled rather than reigned. The king shed the cloak of his favorites and rolled up his own sleeves to manage state affairs. Representative institutions were weakened or cast aside. Monarchs needed standing armies trained in the increasingly sophisticated arts of war, so the military was expanded and made an integral part of the machinery of government. The military profession developed within nations, gradually replacing mercenary adventurers who fought for booty rather than for duty.

Yet the absolute state was never as powerful in practice as it was in theory. Nor did it ever exist in its ideal shape. Absolutism was always in the making, never quite made. Its success depended on a strong monarch who knew his own will and could enforce it. It depended on unity within the state, on the absence or ruthless suppression of religious or political minorities. The absolute ruler needed to control information and ideas to limit criticism of state policy. Ultimately, the absolute state rested on the will of its citizens to support it. The seventeenth-century state remained a loose confederation of regions, many acquired by conquest, whose loyalty was practical rather than instinctive. There was no state police to control behavior or attitudes, no newspapers or mass communication to spread propaganda. Censorship might restrict the flow of forbidden books, but it could do little to dam up the current of ideas.

Absolutism in the East

Frederick William, the Great Elector of Brandenburg-Prussia (1640–1688), made highly effective use of the techniques of absolutism. In 1640, he inherited a scattered and ungovernable collection of territories. The nobility, known as *die Junker*, enjoyed immunity from almost all forms of direct taxation, and the towns had no obligation to furnish either men or supplies for military operations beyond their walls.

When Frederick William attempted to introduce an excise—the commodity tax on consumption that had so successfully financed the Dutch Revolt and the English Revolution—he was initially rebuffed. But military emergency overcame legal precedents. By the 1650s, Frederick William had established the excise in the towns, though not in the countryside.

With the excise as a steady source of revenue, the Great Elector set about forming one of the most capable and best disciplined standing armies of the age. He organized one of the first departments of war to oversee all of the details of the creation of his army, from housing and supplies to the training of young officer candidates. This department was also responsible for the collection of taxes. By integrating military and civilian government, Frederick William established an efficient state bureaucracy that was particularly responsive in times of crisis. The creation of the Prussian army was the force that led to the creation of the Prussian state.

The same materials that forged the Prussian state led to the transformation of Russia. Soon after the young Tsar Peter I, known later as "the Great" (1682–1725), came to the throne, he realized that he could compete with the western states only by learning to play their game.

Like Frederick William, Peter concentrated on military reform. He understood that if Russia was to flourish in a world dominated by war and commerce, it would have to reestablish its hold on the Baltic ports. This meant dislodging the Swedes from the Russian mainland and creating a fleet to protect Russian trade. Neither goal seemed likely. The Swedes were one of the great powers of the age, constant innovators in battlefield tactics and military organization. Peter studied their every campaign. His first wars against the Swedes ended in humiliating defeats, but with each failure came a sharper sense of what was needed to succeed.

First Peter introduced a system of conscription and created a standing army. He unified the military command at the top and stratified it in the field. He established promotion based on merit and established military schools to train cadets for the next generation of officers.

Finally, in 1709, Peter realized his ambitions. At the battle of Poltava the Russian army routed the Swedes, wounding King Charles XII, annihilating his infantry, and capturing dozens of his leading officers. After the battle of

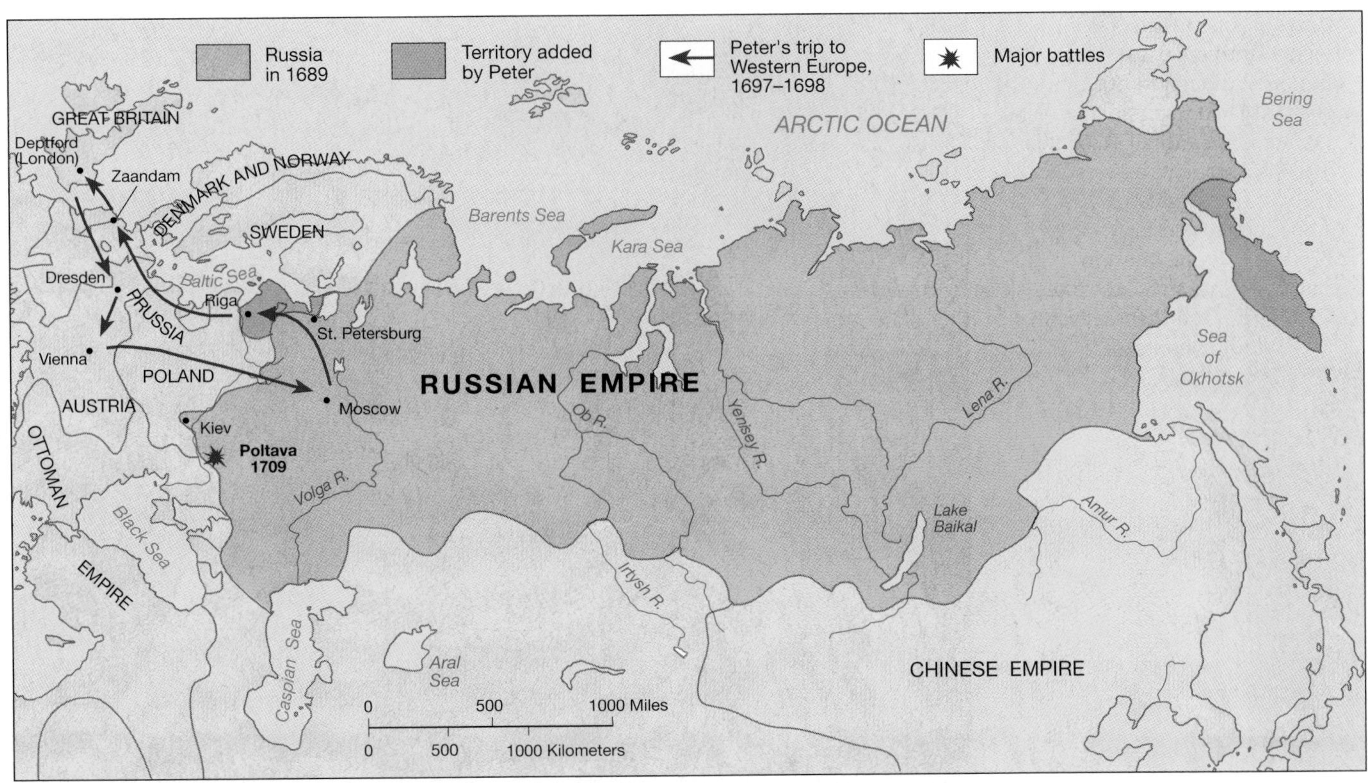

The Expansion of Russia under Peter the Great. Peter added vital territory on the Baltic Sea to the vast Russian empire.

Poltava, Russia gradually replaced Sweden as the dominant power in the Baltic.

As an absolute ruler, Peter the Great's power was unlimited, but it was not uncontested. He secularized the Russian Orthodox church, subjecting it to state control and confiscating much of its wealth. He broke the old military service class, which attempted a coup d'état when he was abroad in the 1690s. By the end of his reign, the Russian monarchy was among the strongest in Europe.

The Origins of French Absolutism

Nowhere was absolutism as successfully implanted as in France. Louis XIII (1610–1643) was only eight years old when he came to the throne, and he grew slowly into his role under the tutelage of Cardinal Richelieu. It was Richelieu's vision that stabilized French government. As chief minister, Richelieu saw clearly that France's survival and prosperity depended on strengthening royal power. He preached a doctrine of *raison d'état* ("reason of state"), in which he placed the needs of the nation above the privileges of its most important groups. Richelieu saw three threats to stable royal government: the Huguenots, the nobles, and the most powerful provincial governors.

Richelieu took measures to control all three. The power of the nobles was the most difficult to attack. The nobles' long tradition of independence from the crown had been enhanced by the wars of religion. The ancient aristocracy, the nobility of the sword, felt themselves to be in a particularly vulnerable position. Their world was changing, and their traditional roles were becoming obsolete. Professional soldiers replaced them at war, professional administrators at government. Mercantile wealth threatened their economic superiority, and the growth of the nobility of the robe—lawyers and state officials—threatened their social standing. They were hardly likely to take orders from a royal minister such as Richelieu.

To limit the power of local officials, Richelieu used intendants to examine their conduct and to reform their administration. He made careful appointments of local governors and brought more regions under direct royal control. Against the Calvinists, who were called Huguenots in France, Richelieu's policy was more subtle. He was less interested in challenging their religion than their autonomy. In 1627, when the English sent a force to aid the Huguenots against the government, Richelieu and Louis XIII abolished the Huguenots' privileges altogether. They were allowed to maintain their religion but not

Anne of Austria acted as a regent during her son's minority, though in practice she delegated most power to her adviser Cardinal Mazarin. This painting emphasizes the piety of the royal family, as Anne, Louis, and his younger brother Philippe kneel in prayer against a backdrop of God, Jesus, and their heavenly and worldly servants.

their special status. Finally, in 1685, Louis XIV revoked the Edict of Nantes, which had guaranteed civil and religious rights to the Huguenots. All forms of Protestant worship were outlawed, and the ministers who were not hunted down and killed were forced into exile. Despite a ban on Protestant emigration, over 200,000 Huguenots fled the country, many of them carrying irreplaceable skills with them to Holland and England in the west and to Brandenburg in the east.

Richelieu's program was a vital prelude to the development of absolute monarchy in France. The cardinal did not act without the full support of Louis XIII, but there can be no doubt that Richelieu was the power behind the throne. Louis XIII hated the business of government and even neglected his principal responsibility of providing the state with an heir. For years, he and his wife slept in separate palaces, and only a freak rainstorm in Paris forced him to spend a night with the queen, Anne of Austria, in 1637. It was the night of the conception of Louis XIV. Louis XIII and Richelieu died within six months of each other in 1642–1643, and the nation again endured the turmoil of a child king.

Louis le Grand

Not quite five years old when he came to the throne, Louis XIV was tutored by Cardinal Jules Mazarin (1602–1661), Richelieu's successor as chief minister. Mazarin was more ruthless and less popular than his predecessor, but like Richelieu, he was an excellent administrator.

The King and His Ministers. In order to pacify the rebellious nobility of the Fronde, who opposed Mazarin's power, Louis XIV was declared to have reached his majority at the age of 13. But it was not until Mazarin died ten years later, in 1661, that the king began to rule.

Louis was blessed with able and energetic ministers. The two central props of his state—money and might—were in the hands of dynamic men, Jean-Baptiste Colbert (1619–1683) and the Marquis de Louvois (1639–1691). Colbert, to whom credit belongs for the building of the French navy, the reform of French legal codes, and the establishment of national academies of culture, was Louis's chief minister for finance. Colbert's fiscal reforms were so successful that in less than six years a debt of 22 million French pounds had become a surplus of 29 million. Colbert achieved this astonishing feat not by raising taxes but by increasing the efficiency of their collection. Until Louis embarked on his wars, the French state was solvent.

To Louvois, Louis's minister of war, fell the task of reforming the French army. During the Fronde, royal troops were barely capable of defeating the makeshift forces of the nobility. By the end of the reign, the army had grown to 400,000, and its organization had been thoroughly reformed.

Louis XIV furthered the practice of relying on professional administrators to supervise the main departments of state and to offer advice on matters of policy. He built on the institution of the intendant that Richelieu had developed with so much success. Intendants were now a permanent part of government, and their duties expanded from their early responsibilities as coordinators and mediators into areas of policing and tax collection. It was through the intendants that the wishes of central government were made known in the provinces.

The Court of Versailles. Though Louis XIV was well served, it was the king himself who set the tone for French absolutism. "If he was not the greatest king he was the best actor of majesty that ever filled the throne," wrote an English observer. The acting of majesty was central to Louis's rule. His residence at Versailles was the most glittering court of Europe. When the court and king moved there permanently in 1682, Versailles became the envy of the Continent. But behind the imposing facade of Versailles stood a well-thought-out plan for domestic and international rule.

Louis XIV attempted to tame the French nobles by requiring their attendance at his court. Louis established a system of court etiquette so complex that constant study was necessary to prevent humiliation. While the nobility studied decorum, they could not plot rebellion. Leading noblemen of France rose at dawn so that they could watch Louis be awakened and hear him speak his first words. Dozens followed him from hall to gallery and from gallery to chamber as he washed, dressed, prayed, and ate. There was no greater concern than the king's health, unless it was the king's mood, which was as changeable as the weather.

During Louis's reign, France replaced Spain as the greatest nation in Europe. Massive royal patronage of art, science, and thought brought French culture to new heights. The French language replaced Latin as the universal European tongue. France was the richest and most populous European state, and Louis's absolute rule finally harnessed these resources to a single purpose. France became a commercial power rivaling the Netherlands, a naval power rivaling England, and a military power without peer. It was not only for effect that Louis took the image of the sun as his own. In court, in the nation, and throughout Europe, everything revolved around him.

Louis XIV made his share of mistakes. His aggressive foreign policy ultimately bankrupted the crown. But without doubt, his greatest error was to persecute the Huguenots. As an absolute ruler, Louis regarded the Huguenots, with their separate communities and distinct forms of worship, as an affront to his authority. Supporters of the monarchy celebrated the revocation of the Edict of Nantes in 1685 as an act of piety. But the persecution of the Huguenots was a social and political disaster for France. The Huguenots who fled to other Protestant states spread stories of atrocities that stiffened European resolve against Louis. Those who remained became an embittered minority who pulled at the fabric of the state at every chance. Nor did the official abolition of Protestantism have much effect on its existence. Against these policies the Huguenots held firmly to their beliefs. There were well over one million French Protestants, undoubtedly the largest religious minority in any state. Huguenots simply went underground, practicing their religion secretly and gradually replacing their numbers. No absolutism, however powerful, could succeed in eradicating religious beliefs.

▼ This Hyacinthe Rigaud portrait of Louis XIV in his coronation robes shows the splendor of *Le Roi Soleil* (the Sun King), who believed himself to be the center of France as the sun is the center of the solar system.

Conclusion

LOUIS XIV GAVE HIS NAME TO THE AGE THAT HE AND HIS NATION DOMINATED, but he was not its only towering figure. The Great Elector, Peter the Great, Louis the Great—so they were judged by posterity—all had forged nations for a new age. Their style of rule showed the royal state at its height, still revolving around the king but more and more dependent on permanent institutions of government that followed their own imperatives. The absolute state harnessed the economic and intellectual resources of the nation to the political will of the monarch, who ruled by incorporating vital elements of the state into the process of government. In England, the importance of the landholding classes was recognized in the constitutional powers of Parliament. The rights of the monarch were balanced against the liberties of the subject. In Prussia, the military power of the Junker was asserted through command in the army, the most important institution of the state. In France, Louis XIV co-opted many nobles at his court, while he made use of a talented pool of lawyers, clergymen, and administrators in his government. A delicate balance existed between the will of the king and the will of the state, a balance that would soon lead these Continental powers into economic competition and military confrontation.

QUESTIONS FOR REVIEW

1. How did war in the seventeenth century contribute to the creation of more powerful monarchical states?
2. What religious and political ideas were developed to justify resistance to monarchical authority?
3. What political and religious problems combined to bring England to civil war, and what results did the conflict produce in English government?
4. How did rulers such as Frederick William of Brandenburg, Peter the Great, or Louis XIV, and theorists such as Hobbes, justify absolute monarchical power?

DISCOVERING WESTERN CIVILIZATION ONLINE

You can obtain more information about the royal state in the seventeenth century at the websites listed below. See also the companion website that accompanies this text: www.ablongman.com/kishlansky, which contains an online study guide and additional resources.

The Crises of the Royal State

www.fordham.edu/halsall/mod/modsbook06.html
Links to sources relating to the reign of Charles I and the revolution against him.

www.baylor.edu/BIC/WCIII/Essays/charles.1.html
Excerpts from primary sources describing the execution of Charles I.

www.thegloriousrevolution.com
A site with links all relating to the Revolution of 1688 in England.

The Zenith of the Royal State

www.kipar.org/
A site on the Golden Age of France in the seventeenth century but with extensive links to English and Dutch materials on a variety of subjects.

www.bc.edu/bc_org/avp/cas/fnart/arch/versailles.html
Views of the gardens and rooms inside the palace with special emphasis on architecture.

www.loc.gov/exhibits/bnf/bnf0005.html
The Library of Congress's exhibition on the Age of Absolutism shows manuscripts, medals, and portraits of leading figures at the French court.

SUGGESTIONS FOR FURTHER READING

General Reading

Euan Cameron, ed., *Early Modern Europe: An Oxford History* (Oxford; New York: Oxford University Press, 1999). Up-to-date essays by leading historians with well-chosen topics and illustrations.

William Doyle, *The Old European Order* (Oxford: Oxford University Press, 1978). An important synthetic essay, bristling with ideas.

Thomas Munck, *Seventeenth Century Europe, 1598–1700* (New York: St. Martin's Press, 1990). The most up-to-date survey.

Quentin Skinner, *The Foundations of Modern Political Thought*, 2 vols. (Cambridge: Cambridge University Press, 1978). A seminal work on the history of ideas from Machiavelli to Calvin.

Lawrence Stone, *The Causes of the English Revolution* (New York: Harper & Row, 1972). A vigorously argued explanation of why England experienced a revolution in the mid-seventeenth century.

The Rise of the Royal State

Yves-Marie Bercé, *The Birth of Absolutism* (London: Macmillan, 1996). A history of France from the reign of Louis XIV to the eve of the Revolution by a leading historian of France.

J. H. Elliott, *Richelieu and Olivares* (Cambridge: Cambridge University Press, 1984). A brilliant dual portrait.

J. H. Elliott and Jonathan Brown, *A Palace for a King* (New Haven, Conn.: Yale University Press, 1980). An outstanding work on the building and decorating of a Spanish palace.

The Crises of the Royal State

Trevor Aston, ed., *Crisis in Europe, 1600–1660* (Garden City, N.Y.: Doubleday, 1967). Essays on the theme of a general crisis in Europe by distinguished historians.

Jonathan Israel, ed., *The Anglo-Dutch Moment* (Cambridge: Cambridge University Press, 1991). Essays by an international team of scholars on the European dimensions of the Revolution of 1688.

M. A. Kishlansky, *A Monarchy Transformed* (London: Penguin Books, 1996). The most recent survey of a remarkable era.

The Zenith of the Royal State

William Beik, *Louis XIV and Absolutism: A Brief Study with Documents* (Boston: Bedford/St. Martin's, 2000). A useful short history and selection of documents by a leading historian of French absolutism.

Joseph Bergin, *The Rise of Richelieu* (New Haven, Conn.: Yale University Press, 1991). A fascinating portrait of a consummate politician.

Claire Constans, *Versailles, Absolutism and Harmony* (New York: Vendome Press, 1998). A richly illustrated architectural history of the center and symbol of French absolutism.

Paul Dukes, *The Making of Russian Absolutism* (London: Longman, 1982). A thorough survey of Russian history in the seventeenth and eighteenth centuries.

H. W. Koch, *A History of Prussia* (London: Longman, 1978). A comprehensive study of Prussian history, with an excellent chapter on the Great Elector.

Geoffrey Parker, *The Military Revolution* (Cambridge: Cambridge University Press, 1988). A lucid discussion of how power was organized and deployed in the early modern state.

David Sturdy, *Louis XIV* (London: Macmillan, 1998). A concise survey of the reign organized topically.

CHAPTER 17

SCIENCE AND COMMERCE IN EARLY MODERN EUROPE

THE VISUAL RECORD

REMBRANDT'S LESSONS

BY THE EARLY SEVENTEENTH CENTURY, interest in scientific investigation had spread out from narrow circles of specialists to embrace educated men and women. One of the more spectacular demonstrations of new knowledge was public dissection, which by law could be performed only on the corpses of criminals. Here the secrets of the human body were revealed both for those who were in training as physicians and for those who had the requisite fee and a strong stomach. Curiosity about the human body was becoming a mark of education. Pictures drawn on the basis of dissections filled the new medical texts like the one on the stand at the feet of the corpse in *The Anatomy Lesson of Dr. Nicolaes Tulp* (1632) by Rembrandt van Rijn (1606–1669).

The painting was commissioned by members of the Amsterdam company of surgeons, the physicians' guild of the early seventeenth century. Rembrandt was to compose the picture so that each of the sitters (whose names are written on the paper one of them holds in his hand), as well as Dr. Tulp, would appear as if he alone were the subject of a portrait. Rembrandt succeeded beyond expectation. Each individual stands out from the group, yet the drama of the scene unifies them. Rembrandt froze the action as Dr. Tulp was demonstrating how the gesture he was making with his left hand looked in the dissected arm of the cadaver.

The Anatomy Lesson established the twenty-five-year-old Rembrandt as one of the most gifted painters in Amsterdam. The group portrait, which Rembrandt brought to new levels of expression, was becoming a favorite genre. It was used to celebrate the leaders of Dutch society, who, unlike the leaders of most other European states, were not princes and aristocrats, but merchants, guild officials, and professionals. Rembrandt captured a spirit of civic pride in his group portraits. Here it was the surgeons' guild; later it would be the leaders of the cloth merchants' guild; another time a militia company.

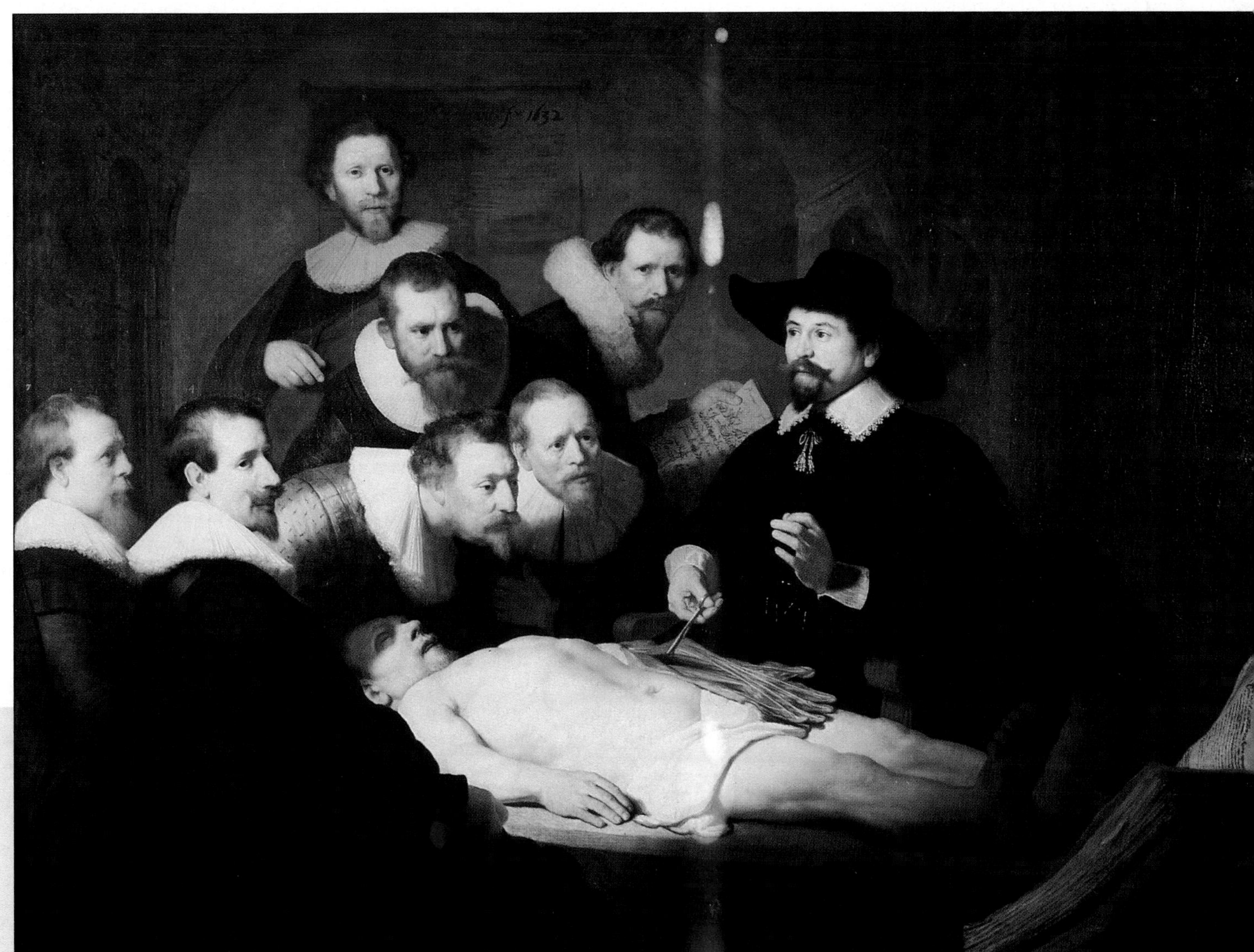

Like the leaders of the surgeons' guild who commissioned their own portrait, the Dutch Republic swelled with pride in the seventeenth century. Its long war with Spain was finally over, and the new state was flourishing. Its ships traveled to all parts of the globe. Bankers and merchants were the backbone of the Dutch Republic. Yet this republic of merchants was also one of the great cultural centers of the Continent. In the burgeoning port of Amsterdam, the fastest-growing city in Europe, artists, philosophers, and mathematicians lived in close proximity. The free exchange of ideas made Amsterdam home to people who had been exiled for their beliefs. The Dutch practiced religious toleration as no one else did. Catholics, Protestants, and Jews all were welcomed and allowed to pursue their own paths without persecution.

LOOKING AHEAD

Freedom of thought and freedom of expression helped develop a new spirit of scientific inquiry, like that portrayed in The Anatomy Lesson of Dr. Nicolaes Tulp. *As this chapter will show, maritime nations such as Holland and England took full advantage of scientific and technological discovery to expand their overseas trade and enrich their citizens. Although much of the new science was seemingly abstract, its practical applications ultimately fueled a new commercial spirit and a new European economy.*

THE NEW SCIENCE

The emergence of the new science challenged the intelligentsia's most basic assumptions and beliefs. Men dropping balls from towers or peering at the skies through a glass claimed that they had disproved thousands of years of certainty about the nature of the universe. New discoveries seemed to loosen the moorings of everything that educated people thought they knew about their world. Although common sense told them that the sun moved from east to west while the earth stood still, the new science insisted that the earth was in constant motion and that it revolved around the sun.

The scientific revolution was the opening of a new era in European history. After two centuries of classical revival, European thinkers had finally come up against the limits of ancient knowledge. Ancient wisdom had served Europeans well, but now the certainties of the past were being called into question. The explanations of the universe and the natural world that had been advanced by Aristotle and codified by his followers no longer seemed adequate. Breaking the hold of Aristotelianism, however, was no easy task. A full century was to pass before even learned people would accept the proofs that the earth revolved around the sun. Even then, the most famous of them—Galileo—had to recant these views or be condemned as a heretic.

The two essential characteristics of the new science were that it was materialistic and mathematical. Its materialism was contained in the realization that the universe was composed of matter in motion. This meant that the stars and planets were made not of some perfect ethereal substance but of the same matter that was found on the earth. They were therefore subject to the same rules of motion as were earthly objects. The mathematics of the new science was contained in the realization that calculation had to replace common sense as the basis for understanding the universe. Mathematics itself was transformed with the invention of logarithms, analytic geometry, and calculus. Scientific experimentation took the form of measuring repeatable phenomena. When Galileo attempted to develop a theory of acceleration, he rolled a brass ball down an inclined plane and recorded the time and distance of its descent one hundred times before he was satisfied with his results.

The new science was a Europe-wide movement. The spirit of scientific inquiry flourished everywhere among the educated. The main contributors to astronomy were a Pole, a Dane, a German, and an Italian. The founder of medical chemistry was Swiss; the best anatomist was Belgian. England contributed most of all—the founders of modern chemistry, biology, and physics. By and large, these scientists operated outside the traditional seats of learning at the universities. Though most were university-trained and not a few taught the traditional Aristotelian subjects, theirs was not an academic movement. Rather, it was a public one that was made possible by the printing press. Once published, findings became building blocks for scientists throughout the Continent and from one generation to the next. Many discoveries were made in the search for practical solutions to ordinary problems, and what was learned fueled advances in technology and the natural sciences. The new science gave seventeenth-century Europeans a sense that they might finally master the forces of nature.

Heavenly Revolutions

Aristotle had presented a view of the physical world that coincided with a view of the spiritual and moral one. The heavens were unchangeable, and therefore they were better than the earth. The sun, moon, and planets were all faultless spheres, unblemished and immune from decay. Their motion was circular because the circle was the perfect form of motion. The earth was at the center of the universe because it was the heaviest planet and because it was at the center of the Great Chain of Being, between the underworld of spirits and the upperworld of gods. The Aristotelian worldview was thus easily incorporated into Christianity. Aristotle's description of the heavens as being composed of a closed system of crystalline rings that held the sun, moon, and planets in their circular orbits around the earth left room for God and the angels to reside just beyond the last ring.

Of course, some problems existed with Aristotle's explanation of the universe as it was preserved in the work of Ptolemy, the greatest of the Greek astronomers. For one thing, if the sun revolved in a perfect circle around the earth, why were the seasons not perfectly equal? If the planets all revolved around the earth in circles, then why did they look nearer or farther, brighter or darker at different times of the year? To solve these problems, a host of ingenious hypotheses were advanced, but all of them eventually withered under the scrutiny of the new science.

In the 1490s, Nicolaus Copernicus (1473–1543) came to the Polish University of Krakow, where the latest astronomical theories were vigorously debated. He became fascinated by astronomy and puzzled by the debate over planetary motion. Copernicus believed, like Aristotle, that the simplest explanations were the best. If the sun was at the center of the universe and the earth was simply another planet in orbit, then many of the most elaborate explanations of planetary motion were unnecessary. "At rest, in the middle of everything is the sun," Copernicus wrote in *On the Revolutions of the Heavenly Spheres* (1543). "For in this most beautiful temple who would place this lamp in another or better position than that from which it can light up the whole thing at the same time?" Because Copernicus accepted most of the rest of the traditional Aristotelian explanation, especially the belief that the planets moved in perfect circles, his sun-centered universe was only slightly better at predicting the position of the planets than the traditional earth-centered one, but Copernicus's idea stimulated other astronomers to make new calculations.

▲ Andreas Cellarius created this artistic depiction of the solar system in the late seventeenth century. The chart portrays the heliocentric universe described by Copernicus and Galileo and the elliptical orbits of the planets posited by Kepler. An outsized earth is shown in four different positions as it orbits the sun.

Brahe and Kepler. Under the patronage of the king of Denmark, Tycho Brahe (1546–1601) built a large observatory to study planetary motion. In 1572, Brahe discovered a nova, a brightly burning star that was previously unknown. This discovery challenged the idea of an immutable universe composed of crystalline rings. In 1577, the appearance of a comet cutting through the supposedly impenetrable rings punched another hole in the old cosmology. Brahe's own views were a hybrid of old and new. He believed that all planets but the earth revolved around the sun and that the sun and the planets revolved around a fixed earth. To demonstrate this theory, Brahe and his students compiled the largest and most accurate mathematical tables of planetary motion yet known. From this research, Brahe's pupil, Johannes Kepler (1571–1630), one of the great mathematicians of the age, formulated laws of planetary motion. Kepler discovered that planets orbited the sun in an elliptical rather than a circular path. This accounted for their movements nearer to and farther from the earth. He further demonstrated that there was a precise mathematical relationship between the speed with which a planet revolved and its distance from the sun. Kepler's findings supported the view that the solar system was heliocentric and that the heavens, like the earth, were made of matter that was subject to physical laws.

Galileo. What Kepler demonstrated mathematically, the Italian astronomer Galileo Galilei (1564–1642) confirmed by observation. With a telescope that he had created by using magnifying lenses and a long tube, Galileo saw parts of the heavens that had never been dreamt of before. In 1610, he discovered four moons of Jupiter, proving conclusively that not all heavenly bodies revolved around the earth. He observed the landscape of the earth's moon and described it as being full of mountains, valleys, and rivers. It was of the same imperfect form as the earth itself. He even found spots on the sun, which suggested that it, too, was composed of ordinary matter. Many of Galileo's scientific discoveries had to do with motion—he was the first to posit a law of inertia—but his greatest contribution to the new science was his popularization of the Copernican theory.

As news of his experiments and discoveries spread, Galileo became famous throughout the Continent, and his support for heliocentrism became a celebrated cause. In 1616, the Roman Catholic Church cautioned him against promoting his views. In 1633, a year after publishing *A Dialogue Between the Two Great Systems of the World*, the Inquisition tried Galileo and forced him to recant the idea that the earth moves. He spent the rest of his life under house arrest. But Galileo insisted that there was nothing in the new science that was anti-Christian. He rejected the view that his discoveries refuted the Bible, arguing that the Bible was often difficult to interpret and that nature was another way in which God revealed himself.

The Natural World

The new science originated from a number of traditions that were anything but scientific. Inquiry into nature and the environment grew out of the discipline of natural philosophy and was nurtured by spiritual and mystical traditions. Much of the most useful medical knowledge had come from the studies of herbalists; the most reliable calculations of planetary motion had come from astrologers. Though the first laboratories and observatories were developed in aid of the new science, practice in them was as much magical as experimental. The modern emphasis on experimentation and empirical observation developed only gradually. What was new about the new science was the determination to develop systems of thought that could help humans to understand and control their environment. There was a greater openness and spirit of cooperation about discoveries than in the past, when experiments were conducted secretly and results were kept hidden away.

Neoplatonism and the New Scientists. Aristotelianism was not the only philosophical system to explain the nature and composition of the universe. During the Renaissance, the writings of Plato attracted a number of Italian humanists, most notably Marsilio Ficino (1433–1499) and Pico della Mirandola (1463–1494). In Florence, they taught Plato's theory that the world was composed of ideas and forms, which were hidden by the physical properties of objects. These Neoplatonic humanists believed that the architect of the universe possessed the spirit of a geometrician and that the perfect disciplines were music and mathematics. These elements of Neoplatonism created an impetus for the mathematically based studies of the new scientists. They were especially important among the astronomers, who used both calculation and geometry in exploring the heavens. But they also served to bolster the sciences of alchemy and astrology. Alchemy was the use of fire in the study of metals, an effort to find the essence of things through their purification. Whereas medieval alchemists mostly attempted to find gold and silver as the essence of lead and iron, the new experimentation focused on the properties of metals in general. Astrology was the study of the influence of the stars on human behavior, calculated by planetary motion and the harmony of the heavenly spheres. Astrologers made careful calculations based on the movement of the planets and were deeply involved in the new astronomy. The Neoplatonic emphasis on mathematics also supported a variety of mystical sciences based on numerology. These were efforts to predict events from the combination of particular numbers.

The most influential of these mystical traditions was that associated with Hermes Trismegistus ("Thrice Greatest"), an Egyptian who was reputed to have lived in the second century C.E. A body of writings that was mistakenly attributed to Hermes was discovered during the Renaissance and formed the basis of a Hermetic tradition. The core of Hermetic thinking was the idea of a universal spirit that was present in all objects and that spontaneously revealed itself. Kepler was one of the many new scientists who were influenced by Hermeticism. His efforts to understand planetary motion derived from his search for a unifying spirit.

Paracelsus. A combination of Neoplatonic and Hermetic traditions was central to the work of the Swiss alchemist Paracelsus (1493–1541), who studied alchemy before becoming a physician. Though he worked as a doctor, his true vocation was alchemy, and he conducted innumerable experiments that were designed to extract the essence of particular metals. Paracelsus taught that all matter was composed of combinations of three principles: salt, sulfur, and mercury. This view replaced the traditional belief in the four elements of earth, water, fire, and air.

The Paracelsian system transformed ideas about chemistry and medicine. Paracelsus rejected the theory that disease was caused by an imbalance in the humors of the body—the standard view of Galen, the great Greek physician of the second century C.E. Instead, Paracelsus argued that each disease had its own cause, which could be diagnosed and remedied. Whereas traditional doctors treated disease by bloodletting or sweating to correct the imbalance of humors, Paracelsus prescribed the ingestion of particular chemicals, especially distilled metals such as mercury, arsenic, and antimony, and he favored administering them at propitious astrological moments.

Boyle and Chemistry. Although established physicians and medical faculties rejected Paracelsian cures and methods, his influence spread among ordinary practitioners. It ultimately had a profound impact on the studies of Robert Boyle (1627–1691), an Englishman who helped to establish the basis of the science of chemistry. Boyle devoted his energies to raising the study of medical chemistry above that of merely providing recipes for the cure of disease. He worked carefully and recorded each step in his experiments. Boyle's first important work, *The Sceptical Chymist*

(1661), attacked both the Aristotelian and Paracelsian views of the basic components of the natural world. Boyle rejected both the four elements and the three principles. Instead, he favored an atomic explanation in which matter "consisted of little particles of all sizes and shapes." Changes in these particles, which would later be identified as the chemical elements, resulted in changes in matter. Boyle's most important experiments were with gases—a word that Paracelsus invented. Boyle formulated the relationship between the volume and pressure of a gas (Boyle's Law), and he invented the air pump.

Medical Science. The new spirit of scientific inquiry also affected medical studies. The study of anatomy through dissection had helped the new scientists to reject many of the descriptive errors in Galen's texts. The Belgian doctor Andreas Vesalius (1514–1564) published the first modern set of anatomical drawings in 1543. But accurate knowledge of the composition of the body did not mean better understanding of its operation. Dead bodies didn't easily yield the secrets of life. Much of what was known about matters as common as reproduction was an inadequate combination of ancient wisdom and the practical experiences of midwives and doctors.

One of the greatest mysteries was how blood moved through the vital organs. William Harvey (1578–1657), an Englishman who had received his medical education in Italy, was interested in the anatomy of the heart. He examined hearts in more than forty species before concluding that the heart worked like a pump and that the valves of the heart chambers allowed the blood to flow in only one direction. He concluded that the blood was pumped by the heart and circulated throughout the entire body.

Sir Isaac Newton. The greatest of all English scientists was the mathematician and physicist Sir Isaac Newton (1642–1727), who brought together the various strands of the new science. He made a great study of Hermetic writings and from them revived the mystical notions of attraction and repulsion. He merged the materialists and Hermeticists, the astronomers and astrologers, the chemists and alchemists. Newton was the first to understand the composition of light, the first to develop a calculus, the first to build a reflecting telescope. He made stunning contributions to the sciences of optics, physics, astronomy, and mathematics. His magnum opus, *Mathematical Principles of Natural Philosophy* (1687), is one of the most important scientific works ever composed. Newton offered a solution to the following problem: If the world was composed of matter in motion, what was motion?

Though Galileo had first developed a theory of inertia—the idea that a body at rest stays at rest—most materialists believed that motion was inherent in objects. In contrast, Newton believed that motion was the result of the interaction of objects and that it could be calculated mathematically. From his experiments he formulated the concept of force and his famous laws of motion: (1) that objects that are at rest or in uniform linear motion remain in such a state unless acted on by an external force; (2) that changes in motion are proportional to force; and (3) that for every action there is an equal and opposite reaction. From these laws of motion, Newton advanced one step further. If the world was no more than matter in motion and if all motion was subject to the same laws, then the movement of the planets could be explained in the same way as the movement of an apple falling from a tree. There was a mathematical relationship between attraction and repulsion—a universal gravitation, as Newton called it—that governed the movement of all objects. Newton's theory of gravity joined Kepler's astronomy and Galileo's physics. The mathematical, materialistic world of the new science was now complete.

Science Enthroned

By the middle of the seventeenth century, the new science was firmly established throughout Europe. Royal and noble patrons supported the enterprise by paying some of the costs of equipment and experimentation. Royal observatories were created for the astronomers, colleges of physicians for the doctors, laboratories for the chemists. Both England and France established royal societies of learned scientists. The French Académie des Sciences (1666) was composed of 20 salaried scientists and an equal number of students, divided among the different branches of scientific learning. The English Royal Society (1662) boasted some of the greatest minds of the age. It was there that Newton first made public his most important discoveries. Scientific bodies were also formed outside the traditional universities. These were the so-called mechanics colleges, such as Gresham College in London, where the practical applications of mathematics and physics were taught.

The establishment of learned scientific societies and practical colleges fulfilled part of the program advocated by Sir Francis Bacon (1561–1626), one of the leading supporters of scientific research in England. In *The Advancement of Learning* (1605), Bacon proposed a scientific method through inductive, empirical experimentation. Bacon believed that experiments should be carefully recorded so that results were both reliable and repeatable, and in his numerous writings he stressed the practical impact of scientific discovery.

Bacon's support for the new science contrasts markedly with the stance taken by the Roman Catholic Church. Embattled by the Reformation and the wars of religion, the Church regarded the new science as another heresy. Not only did it confound ancient wisdom and contradict Church teachings, but it was also a lay movement that was neither directed nor controlled from Rome. Galileo's trial slowed the momentum of scientific investigation in Catholic countries and starkly posed the conflict between authority and knowledge. Nevertheless, the Church's stand was based on more than narrow self-interest. Ever since Copernicus had published his views, a new skepticism had emerged among European intellectuals. Every year new theories competed with old ones, and dozens of contradictory explanations for the most common phenomena were advanced and debated. The skeptics concluded that nothing was known and nothing was knowable. Their position led inevitably to the most shocking of all possible views: atheism.

But the new science was not necessarily an attack on established religion. Few of the leading scientists saw a contradiction between their studies and their faith. Still, by the middle of the century, attacks on the Church were increasing, and some people blamed the new science for them. Therefore, it was altogether fitting that one of the leading mathematicians of the day should provide the method for harmonizing faith and reason.

René Descartes (1596–1650) was trained in one of the best Jesuit schools in France before taking a law degree in 1616. He entered military service in the Dutch Republic and, after the outbreak of the Thirty Years' War, joined the Duke of Bavaria's army. Descartes was keenly interested in mathematics, and during his military travels he met and was tutored by a leading Dutch mathematician. In 1619, he dreamt of discovering the scientific principles of universal knowledge. After this dream, Descartes returned to Holland and began to develop his system. He was on the verge of publishing his views when he learned of Galileo's condemnation. Reading Galileo's *Dialogue Between the Two Great Systems of the World*, Descartes discovered that he himself shared many of Galileo's opinions and had worked out mathematical proofs for them, but he refrained from publishing until 1637, when he brought out the *Discourse on Method*.

In the *Discourse on Method*, Descartes demonstrated how skepticism could be used to produce certainty. He began by declaring that he would reject everything that could not be clearly proven beyond doubt. Thus he rejected the material world, the testimony of his senses, and all known or imagined opinions. He was left only with doubt. But what was doubt if not thought, and what was thought if not the workings of his mind? The only thing of which he could be certain, then, was that he had a mind. Thus his famous formulation: "I think, therefore I am." From this first certainty came another, the knowledge of perfectibility. He knew that he was imperfect and that a perfect being had to have placed that knowledge within him. Therefore a perfect being—God—existed.

Descartes's philosophy, known as Cartesianism, rested on the dual existence of matter and mind. Matter was the material world, which was subject to the incontrovertible laws of mathematics. Mind was the spirit of the creator. Descartes was one of the leading mechanistic philosophers, believing that all objects operated in accord with natural laws. He invented analytic geometry and made important contributions to the sciences of optics and physics on which Newton would later build. But his proof that the new science could be harmonized with the old religion was his greatest contribution.

Astronomy, chemistry, biology, and physics all had their modern origins in the seventeenth century. Because thinking about the natural world was integrated, discoveries in one discipline made possible breakthroughs in another. Though many of the pathbreaking discoveries of the new scientists would not find practical use for centuries, the spirit of discovery had a great impact in an age of commerce and capital. The quest for mathematical certainty and prime movers led directly to improvements in agriculture, mining, navigation, and industrial activity. The new sense of control over the material world provided a new optimism for generations of Europeans and bolstered the desire to expand commerce at home and abroad.

EMPIRES OF GOODS

Under the watchful eye of the European states, a worldwide marketplace for the exchange of commodities had been created. First the Dutch and then the English had established monopoly companies to engage in exotic trades in the East. The Spanish and Portuguese, then the English and French had established colonial dependencies in the Atlantic, which they carefully nurtured in hope of economic gain. Protected trade had flourished beyond the wildest dreams of its promoters. Luxury commodities became staples; new commodities became luxuries. Trade enhanced the material life of all European peoples, though it came at great cost to the Asians, Africans, and Latin Americans whose labor and raw materials were converted into the new crazes of consumption.

Though long-distance trade was never as important to the European economy as was inland and intracontinental trade, its development in the seventeenth and eighteenth centuries had a profound impact on lifestyles, economic policy, and ultimately warfare. The first great commercial power, the Dutch, owed their achievements to innovative techniques, rational management, and a social and cultural environment that supported mercantile activities. Dutch society was freer than any other, open to new capital, new ventures, and new ideas. The Dutch developed the innovative concept of the entrepôt, a place where goods were brought for storage before being exchanged. They pioneered in finance by establishing the Bank of Amsterdam in 1609. They led in shipbuilding by developing as early as 1570 the flyboat, a long flat-hulled vessel that was designed specifically to carry bulky cargoes such as grain. They traded around the globe with the largest mercantile fleet yet known. Because the Dutch dominated the European economy, the French and English began to pass laws to eliminate Dutch competition. The English banned imports that were carried in Dutch ships; the French

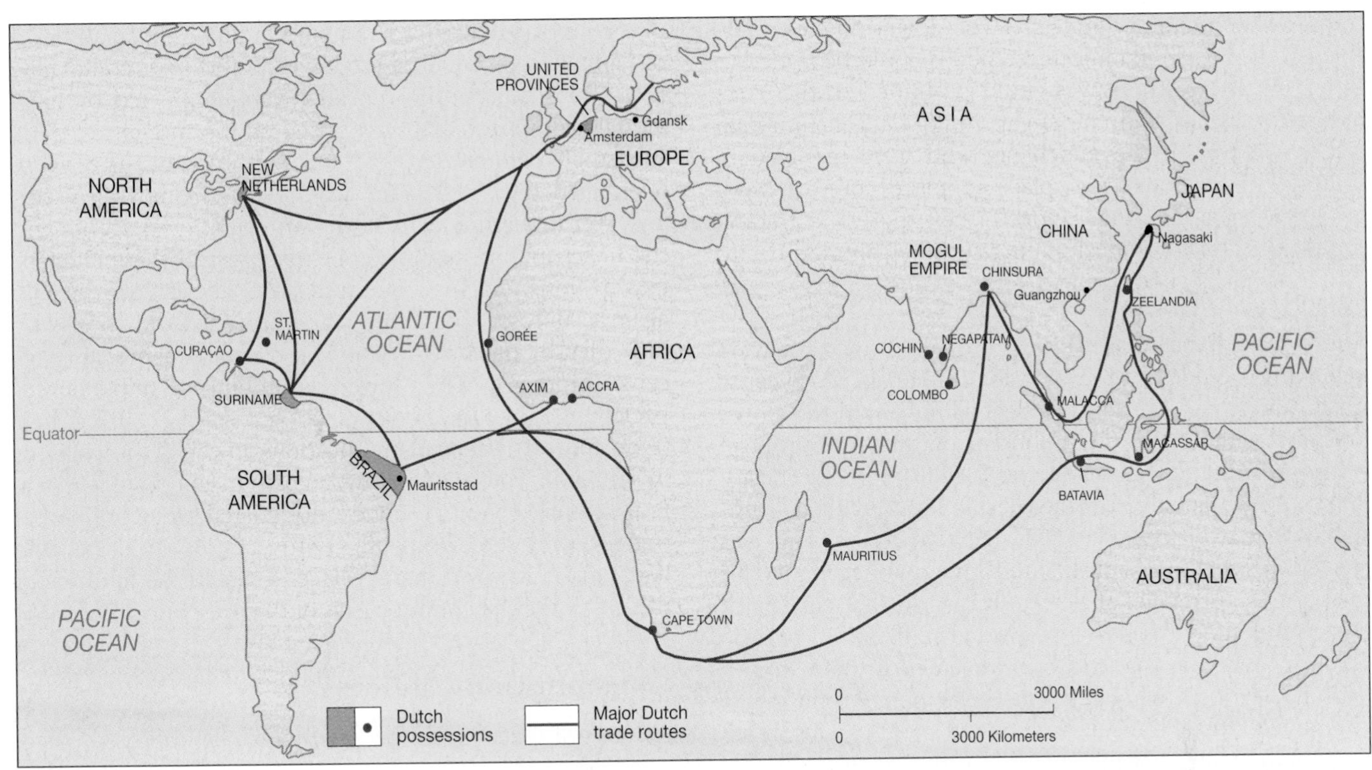

Dutch Trade Routes, ca. 1650. The Dutch were the greatest commercial nation of the seventeenth century.

banned Dutch products. Both policies cut heavily into Dutch superiority, and both ultimately resulted in commercial warfare. By the end of the seventeenth century, England and France surpassed the Dutch.

The Marketplace of the World

By the sixteenth century, all the major trading routes had already been opened. The Spanish moved back and forth across the Atlantic; the Dutch and Portuguese sailed around the tip of Africa to the Indian Ocean. The Baltic trade connected the eastern and western parts of Europe as Danes, Swedes, and Dutch exchanged Polish and Russian raw materials for English and French manufactured goods. The Mediterranean was still a vital artery of intercontinental trade, but its preeminent role was diminishing. In 1600, almost three-quarters of the Asian trade was still land-based, much of it carried through the Middle East to the Mediterranean. A century later, nearly all Asian trade was carried directly to western Europe by Dutch and English vessels. Commercial power was shifting to the northern European states just as dramatically as military and political power.

The Evolution of Long-Distance Travel. The technology that was associated with commerce achieved no major breakthroughs to compare with the great transformations of the fifteenth century, when new techniques of navigation made transatlantic travel possible. There continued to be improvements, however. The new astronomical findings were a direct aid to navigation, as were the recorded experiences of so many practiced sea travelers. The materials that were used to make and maintain ships improved with the importation of pitch and tar from the east and with the greater availability of iron and copper from Scandinavia. The single most important innovation in shipbuilding was the Dutch flyboat, which helped traders gain maximum profit from their journeys to the Baltic. Flyboats sacrificed speed and maneuverability for economy and capacity. They carried no heavy armaments and so were well adapted to the serene Baltic trade.

Innovation, organization, and efficient management were the principal elements of what historians have called the commercial revolution. Concerted efforts to maximize opportunities and advantages accounted for the phenomenal growth in the volume and value of commercial exchange. One of the least spectacular and most effective changes was the replacement of bilateral trade with triangular trade. In bilateral trade, the surplus commodities of one community were exchanged for those of another. For communities with few desirable commodities, bilateral trade meant the exchange of precious metals for goods; and throughout much of the sixteenth and early seventeenth centuries, bullion was by far the most often traded commodity. Triangular trade created a larger pool of desirable goods. British manufactured goods could be traded to Africa for slaves, the slaves could be traded in the West Indies for sugar, and the sugar could be consumed in Britain. Moreover, the merchants who were involved in shifting these goods from place to place could achieve profits on each exchange. Indeed, their motive in trading could now change from dumping surplus commodities to matching supply and demand.

The New Forms of Banking. Equally important were the changes made in the way trade was financed. Because states, cities, and even individuals could stamp their own precious metal, there were hundreds of different European coins with different nominal and metallic values. The influx of American silver further destabilized an already unstable system of exchange. The Bank of Amsterdam was created in 1609 to establish a uniform rate of exchange for the various currencies that were traded in that city. From this useful function developed transfer banking, or giro banking, a system that had been invented in Italy. In giro banking, various merchant firms held money on account and issued bills of transfer from one to another. This transfer system meant that merchants in different cities did not have to transport their precious metals or endure long delays in having their accounts settled.

Giro banking also aided the development of bills of exchange, an early form of checking. Merchants could conclude trades by depositing money in a given bank or merchant house and then having a bill drawn for the sum they owed. Bills of exchange were especially important in international trade, as they made large-scale shipments of precious metals to settle trade deficits unnecessary. By the end of the seventeenth century, bills of exchange had become negotiable; that is, they could pass from one merchant to another without being redeemed. Thus a Dutch merchant could buy French wines in Bordeaux with a bill of exchange drawn on an account in the Bank of Amsterdam. The Bordeaux merchant could then purchase Spanish oranges and use the same bill of exchange as payment. There were two disadvantages to this system: Ultimately, the bill had to return to Amsterdam for redemption, and when it did, the account on which it was drawn might be empty.

The establishment of the Bank of England in 1694 overcame such difficulties. The Bank of England was licensed to issue its own bills of exchange, or bank notes, which were backed by the revenue from specific English taxes. This security of payment was widely sought after, and the Bank of England soon became a clearinghouse for all kinds of bills of exchange. The Bank would buy in bills at a discount, paying less than their face value, and pay out precious metal or their own notes in exchange.

The effects of these and many other small-scale changes in business practice helped to fuel prolonged growth in European commerce. It was the European merchant who made this growth possible, accepting the risks of each individual transaction and building up small pools of capital from which successive transactions could take place. Most mercantile ventures were conducted by individuals or families and were based on the specialized trade of a single commodity. Trade offered high returns because it entailed high risks. The long delays in moving goods and their uncertain arrival, the unreliability of agents and the unscrupulousness of other traders, and the inefficiencies in transport and communication all weighed heavily against success. Merchants who succeeded did so less by luck than by hard work. They used family members to receive shipments. They lowered shipping costs by careful packaging. They lowered protection costs by securing their trade routes. Financial publications lowered the costs of information. Ultimately, lower costs meant lower prices. For centuries, luxury goods dominated intercontinental trade, but by the eighteenth century, European merchants had created a world marketplace in which the luxuries of the past were the common fare of the present.

Consumption Choices

As long-distance trade became more sophisticated, merchants became more sensitive to consumer tastes. Low-volume, high-quality goods such as spices and silks, which were the preserve of the largest trading companies, had reached saturation levels by the early seventeenth century. The price of pepper, the most used of all spices, fell nearly continuously after 1650. Triangular trade allowed merchants to provide a better match of supplies and demands. The result was the rise to prominence of a vast array of new commodities, which not only continued the expansion of trade but also reshaped diet, lifestyles, and patterns of consumption. New products came from both the East and the West. Dutch and English incursions into the Asian trade provoked competition with the Portuguese and enlarged the range of commodities that were shipped back to Europe. An aggressive Asian triangle was created in which European bullion bought Indonesian spices that were exchanged for Persian silk and Chinese and Japanese finished goods. In the Atlantic, the English were quick to develop both home and export markets for a variety of new or newly available products.

The New Commodities. The European trade with Asia had always been designed to satisfy consumer demand rather than to exchange surplus goods. Europeans manufactured little that was desired in Asia, so the chief commodity imported to the East was bullion: tons of South American silver, perhaps one-third of all that was produced. In return came spices, silk, coffee, jewels, jade, porcelain, dyes, and a wide variety of other exotic goods. By the middle of the seventeenth century, the Dutch dominated the spice trade; they obtained a virtual monopoly over cinnamon, cloves, nutmeg, and mace and carried the largest share of pepper. Each year, Europeans consumed perhaps one million pounds of the four great spices and seven million pounds of pepper. Both Dutch and the English competed for preeminence in the silk trade. The Dutch concentrated on Chinese silk, which they used mostly in trade with Japan. The English established an interest in lower-quality Indian silk spun in Bengal.

The most important manufactured articles imported from the East to Europe were the lightweight, brightly colored Indian cottons known as calicoes. Until the middle of the seventeenth century, cotton and cotton blended with silk were used in Europe only for wall hangings and table coverings. The material, which was soft and smooth to the touch, soon replaced linen for use as underwear and close-fitting garments among the well-to-do. The fashion quickly caught on, and the Dutch, who were first to realize the potential of the cotton market, began to export calicoes throughout the Continent. The English and French followed suit, establishing their own trading houses in India and bringing European patterns and designs with them for the Asians to copy.

Along with the new apparel from the East came new beverages. Coffee, which was first used in northern Europe in the early seventeenth century, had become a fashionable drink by the end of the century. Coffee houses sprang up in the major urban areas of northern Europe. As a basic beverage and import commodity, coffee was surpassed in importance only by tea.

Tea and Sugar. While coffee drinking remained the preserve of the wealthy, tea consumption spread throughout European society. It was probably most important in England, where the combination of Chinese tea and West Indian sugar created a phenomenal growth in consumption. In 1706, England imported 100,000 pounds of tea. By the end of the century the number had risen to over 15 million pounds. The English imported most of this tea directly from China, where an open port had been established at Canton. Tea soon became the dominant cargo of the large English merchant ships coming from Asia. Some manufactured goods would be brought to India on the outward voyage, but once the ships had loaded the green and black teas, they sailed directly home. Almost all tea was purchased with bullion, since the Chinese had even less use for European goods than did other Asians. Not until the discovery that the Chinese consumed large quantities of opium, which was grown in India and Southeast Asia, did a triangular trade develop.

The success of tea was linked to the explosive growth in the development of sugar in Europe's Atlantic colonies. The Portuguese found Brazil's hot, humid climate to be well suited for cultivation of the cane plants. The island of Barbados became the first English sugar colony. The planters modeled their development on Brazil, where African slaves were used to plant, tend, and cut the giant canes from which the sugar was extracted. Hot, sweet tea quickly became a popular drink throughout English society. By 1700, the English were sending home over 50 million pounds of sugar besides what they were shipping directly to the North American colonies.

The triangular trade of manufactures—largely reexported calicoes—to Africa for slaves, who were exchanged in the West Indies for sugar, became the dominant form of English overseas trade. Colonial production depended on the enforced labor of hundreds of thousands of Africans. Gold and silver, tobacco, sugar, rice, and indigo were all slave crops. Africans were enslaved by other Africans and then sold to Europeans to be used in the colonies. More than six million black slaves were imported into the Americas during the course of the eighteenth century. Although rum and calicoes were the main commodities exchanged for slaves, the Africans who dominated the slave trade organized a highly competitive market. Every colonial power participated in this lucrative trade. More than three million slaves were imported into the Portuguese colony of Brazil; by the end of the eighteenth century, the sugar island of Saint Domingue held 500,000 slaves and only 35,000 French inhabitants. The English, with their sugar colonies of Barbados and Jamaica and their tobacco colonies of Virginia and Maryland, ultimately came to control the slave trade. The prosperous economies of Newport, Rhode Island, and the English port of Liverpool were built entirely on the slave trade, as were hundreds of plantation fortunes.

Sugar was by far the dominant commodity of the colonial trade, but it was not the only one. Furs and fish had first driven Europeans toward North America, and both remained important commodities. Beaver and rabbit skins were the most common materials for making headgear in an age in which everyone wore a hat. The schools of cod in Canadian waters were among the richest in the world, and the catch was shipped back either salted or dried. The English established an industry on the Newfoundland coast for drying the tons of fish that they caught. In the eighteenth century, rice was grown for export in the southern American colonies, particularly South Carolina. Tobacco was the first new American product to come into widespread use in Europe, and its popularity—despite various official efforts to ban its use as dirty and unhealthy—grew steadily. American tobacco was grown principally in the colonies of Virginia and Maryland and shipped across the ocean, where it was frequently blended with European varieties. Although the English were the principal importers, it was the Dutch who dominated the European tobacco trade, making the most popular blends.

The new commodities flooded into Europe from all parts of the globe. By the middle of the eighteenth century, tea, coffee, cocoa, gin, and rum were among the most popular beverages. These were all products that had been largely unknown a century earlier. Tea and sugar passed from luxury to staple in little more than a generation, and the demand for both products continued to increase. To meet it, the European trading powers needed to create and maintain a powerful and efficient mercantile system.

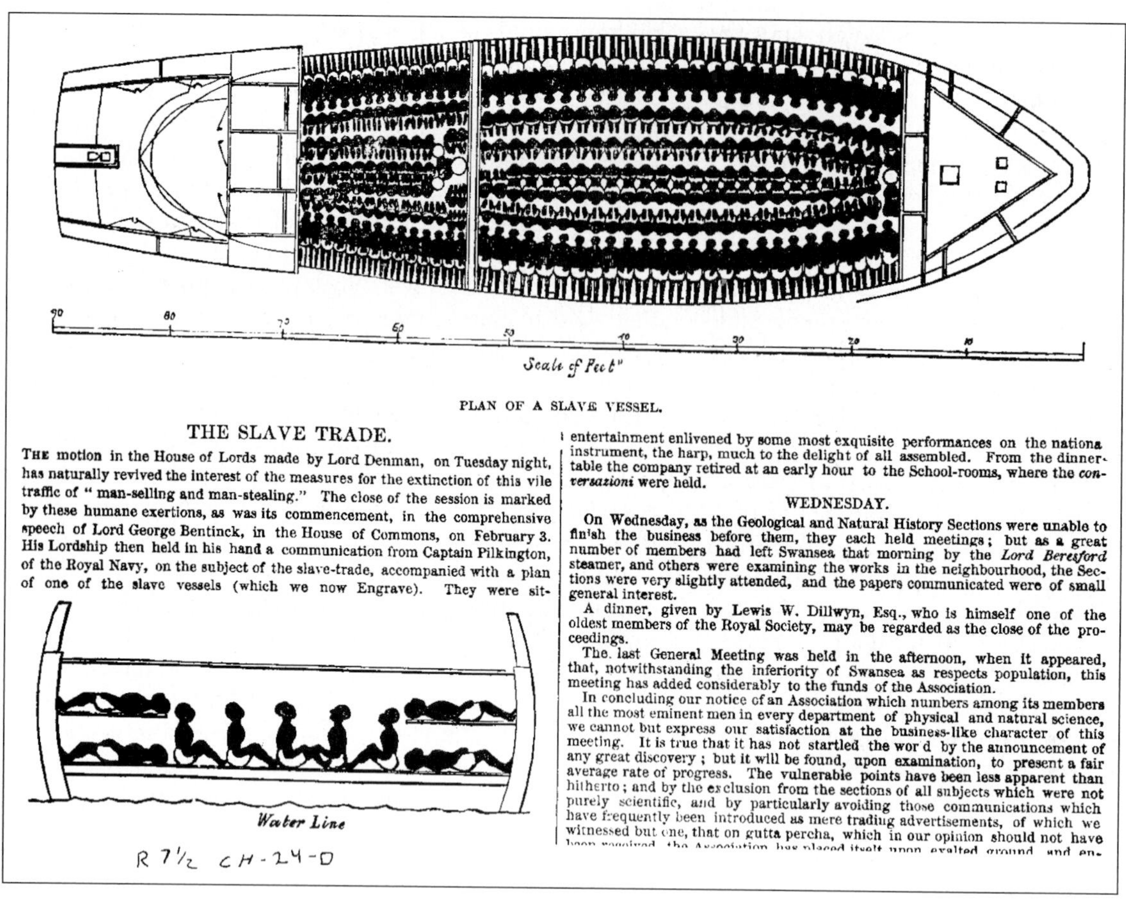

PLAN OF A SLAVE VESSEL.

THE SLAVE TRADE.

THE motion in the House of Lords made by Lord Denman, on Tuesday night, has naturally revived the interest of the measures for the extinction of this vile traffic of "man-selling and man-stealing." The close of the session is marked by these humane exertions, as was its commencement, in the comprehensive speech of Lord George Bentinck, in the House of Commons, on February 3. His Lordship then held in his hand a communication from Captain Pilkington, of the Royal Navy, on the subject of the slave-trade, accompanied with a plan of one of the slave vessels (which we now Engrave). They were sit-

entertainment enlivened by some most exquisite performances on the nationa instrument, the harp, much to the delight of all assembled. From the dinner-table the company retired at an early hour to the School-rooms, where the *conversazioni* were held.

WEDNESDAY.

On Wednesday, as the Geological and Natural History Sections were unable to finish the business before them, they each held meetings; but as a great number of members had left Swansea that morning by the *Lord Beresford* steamer, and others were examining the works in the neighbourhood, the Sections were very slightly attended, and the papers communicated were of small general interest.

A dinner, given by Lewis W. Dillwyn, Esq., who is himself one of the oldest members of the Royal Society, may be regarded as the close of the proceedings.

The last General Meeting was held in the afternoon, when it appeared, that, notwithstanding the inferiority of Swansea as respects population, this meeting has added considerably to the funds of the Association.

In concluding our notice of an Association which numbers among its members all the most eminent men in every department of physical and natural science, we cannot but express our satisfaction at the business-like character of this meeting. It is true that it has not startled the wor d by the announcement of any great discovery; but it will be found, upon examination, to present a fair average rate of progress. The vulnerable points have been less apparent than hitherto; and by the exclusion from the sections of all subjects which were not purely scientific, and by particularly avoiding those communications which have frequently been introduced as mere trading advertisements, of which we witnessed but one, that on gutta percha, which in our opinion should not have

This diagram shows how slaves were packed into cargo holds for the notorious Middle Passage to the Americas. The plan was a model of efficiency, for slave traders sought to maximize profits.

Dutch Masters

For the nearly 80 years between 1565 and 1648 that the Dutch were at war, they grew ever more prosperous. While the economies of most other European nations were sapped by warfare, the Dutch seemed to draw strength from their interminable conflict with the Spanish empire. They did have the advantage of fighting defensively on land and offensively on sea. Land war was terribly costly to the aggressor, which had to raise large armies, transport them to the site of battles or sieges, and feed them while they were there. The defender simply had to fortify strong places, keep its water routes open to secure supplies, and wait for the weather to change. Sea war—or piracy, depending on one's viewpoint—required much smaller outlays for men and matériel and promised the rewards of captured prizes. The Dutch became expert at attacking the Spanish silver fleets, singling out the slower and smaller vessels for capture. The Dutch also benefited from the massive immigration into their provinces of Protestants who had lived and worked in the southern provinces. The immigrants brought vital skills in manufacturing and large reserves of capital for investment in Dutch commerce.

The Dutch grounded their prosperity in commerce. Excellent craftsmen, they took the lead in finishing cloth, refining raw materials, and decorating consumer goods. They were also successful farmers, but their greatest abilities were in trade.

Though the Dutch Republic comprised seven separate political entities, with a total population of about two million, the province of Holland was preeminent among them. Holland contained more than one-quarter of this population, and its trading port of Amsterdam was one of the great cities of Europe. The city had grown from a mid-sized urban community of 65,000 in 1600 to a metropolis of 170,000 50 years later. The port was one of the busiest in the world, for it was built to be an entrepôt. Vast warehouses and docks lined its canals. Visitors were impressed by Amsterdam's bustle, cleanliness, and businesslike appearance. The central buildings were the Bank and the Exchange, testimony to the dominant activities of the residents.

Rembrandt, *The Syndics of the Cloth Guild* (1662). This work was painted for the Drapers' or Cloth Guild and installed at the Guild's headquarters in Amsterdam. The five hatted Syndics look as though they have been caught in a momentary interruption of business. The bareheaded figure in the background is the valet, who unlike the Syndics, was not required to pay for his portrait.

The Dutch dominated all types of European trade. They handled more English coal than England, more French wine than France, more Swedish iron than Sweden. Dutch ships outnumbered all others in every important port of Europe. Goods were brought to Amsterdam to be redistributed throughout the world. Dutch prosperity rested first on the Baltic trade. Even after it ceased to expand in the middle of the seventeenth century, the Baltic trade made up over one-quarter of all of Holland's commercial enterprise. The Dutch also were the leaders in the East Indian trade throughout the seventeenth century. They held a virtual monopoly on the sale of exotic spices and the largest share of the pepper trade. Their imports of cottons and especially of porcelain began new consumer fads that soon resulted in the development of European industries. Dutch potteries began to produce china, as lower-quality ceramic goods came to be known. Dutch trade in the Atlantic was of less importance, but the Dutch did have a colonial presence in the New World, controlling a number of small islands and the rapidly growing mainland settlement of New Netherland. Yet the Dutch still dominated the secondary market in tobacco and sugar, becoming the largest processor and refiner of these important commodities.

In all of these activities the Dutch acted as merchants rather than as consumers. Unlike most other Europeans, they regarded precious metal as a commodity like any other and took no interest in accumulating it for its own sake. This attitude enabled them to pioneer triangular trading and develop the crucial financial institutions that were necessary to expand their overseas commerce. The Dutch were not so much innovators as improvers. They saw the practical value in Italian accounting and banking methods and raised them to new levels of efficiency. They made use of marine insurance to help diminish the risks of mercantile activity. Their legal system favored the creation of small trading companies by protecting individual investments. The European stock and commodity markets were centered in Amsterdam. By the 1670s, over 500 commodities were traded on the Amsterdam exchange, and even a primitive futures market had evolved for those who wanted to speculate.

There were many explanations for the unparalleled growth of this small maritime state into one of the greatest of European trading empires. Geography and climate provided one impetus; the lack of sufficient foodstuffs provided another. Yet there were cultural characteristics as well. One was the openness of Dutch society. Even before the struggle with Spain, the northern provinces had shown a greater inclination toward religious toleration than had most parts of Europe. Amsterdam became a unique center for religious and intellectual exchange. European Jews flocked there, as did Catholic dissidents such as Descartes. They brought with them a wide range of skills and knowledge along with capital that could be invested in trade. There was no real social nobility among the Dutch, and there was certainly no set of values that prized investment in land over investment in trade. The French and Spanish nobility looked with scorn on their mercantile classes and shunned any form of commercial investment. The English, though more open to industry and trade, sank as much of their capital as possible into landed estates and country houses. The Dutch economic elite invested in trade. By the middle of the seventeenth century, the Dutch Republic enjoyed a reputation for cultural creativity that was the envy of the Continent. A truly extraordinary school of Dutch artists led by Rembrandt celebrated this new state born of commerce with vivid portrayals of its people and its prosperity.

Mercantile Organization

Elsewhere in Europe, trade was the king's business. The wealth of the nation was part of the prestige of the monarch, and its rise or fall was part of the crown's power. In all European states except the Dutch Republic, the activities of merchants were scorned by both the landed elite and the salaried bureaucrats. Yet the activities of the mercantile classes took on increasing importance for the state for two reasons. First, imported goods, especially luxuries, were a noncontroversial target for taxation. Customs duties and excise taxes grew all over Europe. Second, the competition for trade was seen as a competition between states rather than between individual merchants. Trading privileges involved special arrangements with foreign powers, arrangements that recognized the sovereign power of European monarchs. In this way, trade could bring glory to the state.

Mercantilism. The competition for power and glory derived from the theory of mercantilism, a set of assumptions about economic activity that were commonly held throughout Europe and that guided the policies of almost every government. Mercantilists believed that the wealth of a nation resided in its stock of precious metal and that economic activity was a zero-sum game. In other words, they believed that there was a fixed amount of money, a fixed amount of commodities, and a fixed amount of consumption. What one country gained, another lost. If England bought wine from France and paid £100,000 in precious metal for it, then England was £100,000 poorer and France was £100,000 richer. If one was to trade profitably, it was absolutely necessary to wind up with a surplus of precious metal. Therefore, it was imperative that governments regulate trade so that the stocks of precious metal were protected from the greed of the merchants. The first and most obvious measure of protection was to prohibit the export of coin except by license, a prohibition that was absolutely unenforceable and was violated more often by government officials than by merchants.

These ideas about economic activity led to a variety of forms of economic regulation. The most common was the monopoly, a grant of special privileges in return for both financial considerations and an agreement to abide by the rules set out by the state. Some monopolies were granted by the crown as a reward for past favors or to purchase future support. Monopolists usually paid considerable fees for their rights, but they could make capital investments with the expectation of long-term gains. This advantage was especially important in attracting investors for risky and expensive ventures such as long-distance trade. Monopolists also benefited the economy as a whole by increasing productive investment at a time when most capital was being used to purchase land, luxury goods, or offices.

The East India Companies. Two monopoly companies, the English and the Dutch East India Companies, dominated the Asian trade. The English East India Company, founded in 1600 with a capital of £30,000, was given the exclusive right to the Asian trade and immediately established itself throughout the Indian Ocean. The Dutch East India Company was formed two years later with ten times the capital of its English counterpart. By the end of the century, the Dutch company employed over 12,000 people. Both companies were joint-stock companies, a new form of business organization. Subscribers owned a percentage of the total value of the company, based on the number of shares they bought, and were entitled to a distribution of profits on the same basis. Initially, the English company determined profits on single voyages and was to distribute all of its assets to its shareholders after a given period. However, changes in legal practice gave the company an identity that was separate from the individuals who held the shares. Now shares could be exchanged without the breakup of the company as a whole. Both Amsterdam and London soon developed stock markets to trade the shares of monopoly companies.

Both East India Companies were remarkably good investments. The Dutch East India Company paid an average dividend of 18 percent for over 200 years. The value of English East India Company shares rose fivefold in the second half of the seventeenth century alone. Few other monopoly companies achieved a record comparable to those of the East India Companies. Companies that failed included the English Royal African Company, founded in 1672 to provide slaves for the Spanish colonies, and the French East Indian and African Companies. The Dutch and English companies were successful because they were able to lower the costs of protecting their ships and cargoes.

Protective Trade Regulations. Monopolies were not the only form of regulation in which seventeenth-century governments engaged. For states with Atlantic colonies, regulation took the form of restricting markets rather than traders. In the 1660s, the English government, alarmed at the growth of Dutch mercantile activity in the New World, passed a series of Navigation Acts designed to protect English shipping. Colonial goods—primarily tobacco and sugar—could be shipped to and from England only in English boats. If the French wanted to purchase West Indian sugar, they could not simply send a ship to the English colony of Barbados loaded with French goods and

ENCOUNTERING PIRATES

The increase in commercial shipping and long-distance trade also meant an increase in assaults at sea. Pirates were a constant threat in the Mediterranean where they were based on the Barbary coast of North Africa and were not unknown as far afield as the English Channel. Pirates had a reputation for ruthlessness and cruelty that far surpassed any of their actual deeds. They were a popular subject for travelers' tales, short fiction, and poetry. Even in the eighteenth century they were associated with buried treasure and deserted islands. This account is from a French sea captain whose ship is accosted on the high seas.

FOCUS QUESTIONS

How did the sailors first defend themselves? What did they fear about the pirates?

MEANWHILE THE SEITIE (a type of boat favored by Mediterranean pirates) had got to within musket-shot of us, and without firing at us she sent over her boat with six men in it dressed like Provencals each with a hat on his head. When they were close enough to be heard they asked us who we were and where we were bound. . . I shouted to them not to come any closer or I would shoot at them, so they returned to their ship where I had observed several Moorish turbans. I told the crew not to fire without my order. And at that moment they all wept and lamented, saying: "Farewell liberty! What will become of our wives and children?" So I said: "We must defend ourselves. Let us commend ourselves to God and the Holy Virgin. If we escape, let us promise to have masses said and to walk barefoot to the first place where we find a church." We sang the *Salve Regina* rather quietly, and I saw that my men were very discouraged, so I stove in the end of a barrel of powder at my cabin doorway, stuck a lighted length of match in the end of my pistol and said in an angry voice: "God Almighty, if anyone fails in his duty, I'll kill him and set the match to this powder. Better to die than end up a slave to these cruel savages."

From Jean Doublet, *Encounter with a Barbary Pirate* (1682).

exchange them for sugar. Rather, they had to make their purchases from an English import-export merchant, and the goods had to be unloaded in an English port before they could be reloaded to be shipped to France. As a result of these protective measures, the English reexport trade skyrocketed. In the year 1700, reexports amounted to nearly 40 percent of all English commerce. With such a dramatic increase in trading, all moved in English ships, shipbuilding boomed, and English ports and coastal towns enjoyed heightened prosperity. For a time, colonial protection proved effective.

The French entered the intercontinental trade later than their North Atlantic rivals, and they were less dependent on trade for their subsistence. French protectionism was as much internal as colonial. Of all the states of Europe, only France could satisfy its needs from its own resources. Achieving such self-sufficiency, however, required coordination and leadership. In the 1670s, Louis XIV's finance minister, Jean-Baptiste Colbert (1619–1683), developed a plan to bolster the French economy by protecting it against European imports. First Colbert followed the English example of restricting the reexport trade by requiring that imports come to France either in French ships or in the ships of the country from which the goods originated. In addition, he used tariffs to make imported goods unattractive in France. He sponsored a drive to increase French manufacturing, especially of textiles, tapestries, linens, glass, and furniture. To protect the investments in French manufacturing, enormous duties were placed on the import of similar goods manufactured elsewhere. The Venetian glass industry, for example, suffered a serious blow from Colbert's tariffs. English woolen manufacturers were also damaged, and the English sought retaliatory measures. At the same time, the English had already begun to imitate this form of protection. In the early eighteenth century, England attempted to limit the importation of cotton goods from India to prevent the collapse of the domestic clothing industry.

The Navigation Acts and Colbert's program of protective tariffs were directed specifically against Dutch reexporters. The Dutch were the acknowledged leaders in all branches of commerce in the seventeenth century. There were many summers when there were more Dutch vessels in London Harbor than there were English ships. In the 1670s, the Dutch merchant fleet was probably larger than the English, French, Spanish, Portuguese, and German fleets combined. Restrictive navigation practices were one way to combat an advantage that the Dutch had built through heavy capital investment and by breaking away from the prevailing theories about the relationship between wealth and precious metals. The English and French Navigation Acts cut heavily into the Dutch trade, and ultimately, both the English and French overtook the Dutch. But protectionism had its price. Just as the dynastic wars were succeeded by the wars of religion, the wars of religion were succeeded by the wars of commerce.

"The discovery of America and that of a passage to the East Indies by the Cape of Good Hope are the two greatest and most important events in the history of mankind." So wrote the great Scottish economist Adam Smith (1723–1790) in *The Wealth of Nations* (1776). For Smith and his generation, the first great age of commerce was coming to an end. The innovations of the Dutch had given way to a settled pattern of international long-distance trade. States now viewed commerce as a part of their national self-interest. They developed overseas empires, which they protected as markets for their goods and sources for their raw materials. The empires were justified by the theory of mercantilism and the demands of a generation of consumers who saw the luxuries of the past as the necessities of the present.

THE WARS OF COMMERCE

The belief that there was a fixed amount of trade in the world was still strong in the late seventeenth century. One country's gains in trade were another's losses. Competition for trade was part of the struggle by which the state grew powerful. It was not inevitable that economic competition would lead to warfare, but restrictive competition was another matter.

Thus the scramble for colonies in the seventeenth century led to commercial warfare in the eighteenth. As the English gradually replaced the Dutch as the leading commercial nation, so the French replaced the English as the leading competitor. Their struggles for the dominance of world markets brought European warfare to every corner of the globe.

The Mercantile Wars

Commercial warfare in Europe began between the English and the Dutch in the middle of the seventeenth century. Both had established aggressive overseas trading companies in the Atlantic and in Asia. In the early seventeenth century, the Dutch were the undisputed leaders. Their carrying capacity and trade monopolies were the greatest in the world. Yet the English were rising quickly. Their Atlantic colonies began to produce valuable new commodities such as tobacco and sugar, and their Asian trade was expanding decade after decade. Conflict was inevitable, and the result was three naval wars fought between 1652 and 1674.

The Dutch had little choice but to strike out against English policy, but they also had little chance of overall success. Their spectacular naval victory in 1667, when the Dutch fleet surprised many English warships at port and burned both ships and docks at Chatham, obscured the fact that Dutch commercial superiority was slipping. In 1664, the English conquered New Netherland on the North American mainland and renamed it New York. With this defeat, the Dutch lost their largest colonial possession. The wars were costly to both states, nearly bankrupting the English crown in 1672. Anglo-Dutch rivalry was finally laid to rest after 1688, when William of Orange, stadtholder of Holland, became William III (1689–1702), king of England.

The Anglo-Dutch commercial wars were just one part of a larger European conflict. Dutch commerce was as threatening to France as it was to England, though in a different way. Under Colbert, France pursued a policy of economic independence. The state supported internal industrial activity through the financing of large workshops and the encouragement of new manufacturing techniques. To protect French products, Colbert levied punitive tariffs on Dutch imports; these tariffs severely depressed both trade and manufacture in Holland. Though the Dutch retaliated with restrictive tariffs of their own—in 1672 they banned the import of all French goods for an entire year—the Dutch economy depended on free trade. The Dutch had much more to lose than did France in a battle of protective tariffs.

The battle that Louis XIV had in mind, though, was more deadly than one of tariffs. Greedily, he eyed the Spanish Netherlands—to which he had a weak claim through his Habsburg wife—and believed that the Dutch stood in the way of his plans. The Dutch had entered into an alliance with the English and Swedes in 1668 to counter French policy, and Louis was determined to crush them in retaliation. He successfully bought off both of Holland's supposed allies, providing cash pensions to the kings of England and Sweden in return for England's active participation and Sweden's passive neutrality in the impending war. In 1672, Louis's army, over 100,000 strong, invaded the Low Countries and swept all before them. Only the opening of the dikes by the Dutch prevented the French from entering the province of Holland itself.

The French invasion coincided with the third Anglo-Dutch war, and the United Provinces found themselves besieged on land and sea. Their international trade was disrupted, their manufacturing industries were in ruins, and their military budget skyrocketed. Only able diplomacy and skillful military leadership prevented their total demise. A separate peace was made with England; and Spain, whose sovereign territory had been invaded, entered the war on the side of the Dutch, as did a number of German states. Louis's hope for a lightning victory faded, and the war settled into a series of interminable sieges and reliefs of fortified towns. The Dutch finally persuaded France to come to terms in the Treaty of Nijmegen (1678–1679). While Louis XIV retained a number of the territories he had taken from Spain, his armies withdrew from the United Provinces, and he agreed to lift most of the commercial sanctions against Dutch goods. The first phase of mercantile warfare was over.

The Wars of Louis XIV

It was Louis XIV's ambition to restore the ancient Burgundian territories to the French crown and to provide secure northern and eastern borders for his state. Pursuit of these aims involved him in conflicts with nearly every other European state. Spain had fought for 80 years to preserve the Burgundian inheritance in the Low Countries. By the Peace of Westphalia (1648), the northern portion of this territory became the United Provinces, while the southern portion remained loyal to the crown and became the Spanish Netherlands. This territory provided a barrier between Holland and France that both states attempted to strengthen by establishing fortresses and bridgeheads at strategic places. In the east, Louis eyed the duchies of Lorraine and Alsace and the large swath of territory farther south known as Franche-Comté. The Peace of Westphalia had granted France control of a number of imperial cities in these duchies, and Louis aimed to link them together. All of these territories were ruled by Habsburgs: Alsace and Lorraine by the Austrian Holy Roman Emperor, Franche-Comté by the Spanish king.

The Balance of Power. In the late seventeenth century, ambassadors and ministers of state began to develop the theory of a balance of power in Europe. This was a belief that no state or combination of states should be allowed to become so powerful that its existence threatened the peace of the others. Behind this purely political idea of the balance of power lay a theory of collective security that knit together the European state system. French expansion in either direction not only threatened the other states that were directly involved but also posed a threat to European security in general.

Louis showed his hand clearly enough in the Franco-Dutch war that had ended in 1679. Though he withdrew his forces from the United Provinces and evacuated most of the territories he had conquered, by the Treaty of Nijmegen France absorbed Franché-Comté as well as portions of the Spanish Netherlands. Louis began plotting his next adventure almost as soon as the treaty was signed. Over the next several years, French troops advanced steadily into Alsace, ultimately forcing the city of Strasbourg, a vital bridgehead on the Rhine, to recognize French sovereignty. Expansion into northern Italy was similarly calculated. Everywhere Louis looked, French engineers rushed to construct fortresses and magazines in preparation for another war.

War finally came in 1688, when French troops poured across the Rhine to seize Cologne. A united German empire led by Leopold I, archduke of Austria, combined with the maritime powers of England and Holland, led by William III, to form the Grand Alliance, the first of the great balance of power coalitions. In fact, the two sides proved to be so evenly matched that the Nine Years' War (1688–1697) settled very little, but it did demonstrate that a successful European coalition could be formed against France. It also signified the permanent shift in alliances that resulted from the Revolution of 1688 in England. Although the English had allied with France against the Dutch in 1672, after William became king he persuaded the English Parliament that the real enemy was France. Louis's greatest objective, to secure the borders of his state, had withstood its greatest test. He might have rested satisfied but for the vagaries of births, marriages, and deaths.

Like his father, Louis XIV had married a daughter of the king of Spain. Philip IV had married his eldest daughter to Louis XIV and a younger one to Leopold I of Austria, who subsequently became the Holy Roman Emperor (1658–1705). Before he died, Philip finally fathered a son, Charles II (1665–1700), who attained the Spanish crown at the age of four but was mentally and physically incapable of ruling his vast empire. For decades it was apparent that there would be no direct Habsburg successor to the Spanish empire. Louis XIV and Leopold I both had legitimate claims to an inheritance that would have irreversibly tipped the European balance of power.

The War of the Spanish Succession. As Charles II grew increasingly feeble, efforts to find a suitable compromise to the problem of the Spanish succession were

▼ War of the Spanish Succession. The great British victories in this war were in the Spanish Netherlands and the Holy Roman Empire. They established Britain as a great power.

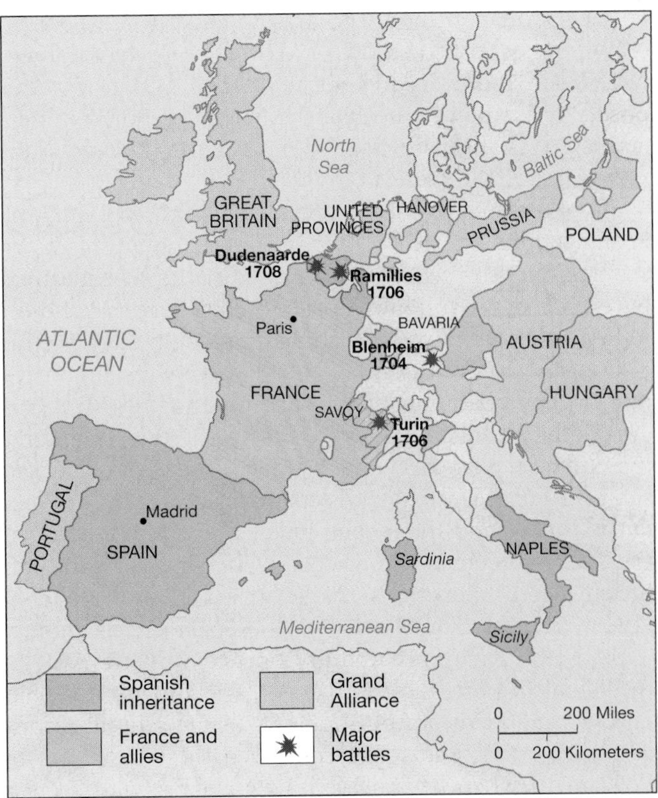

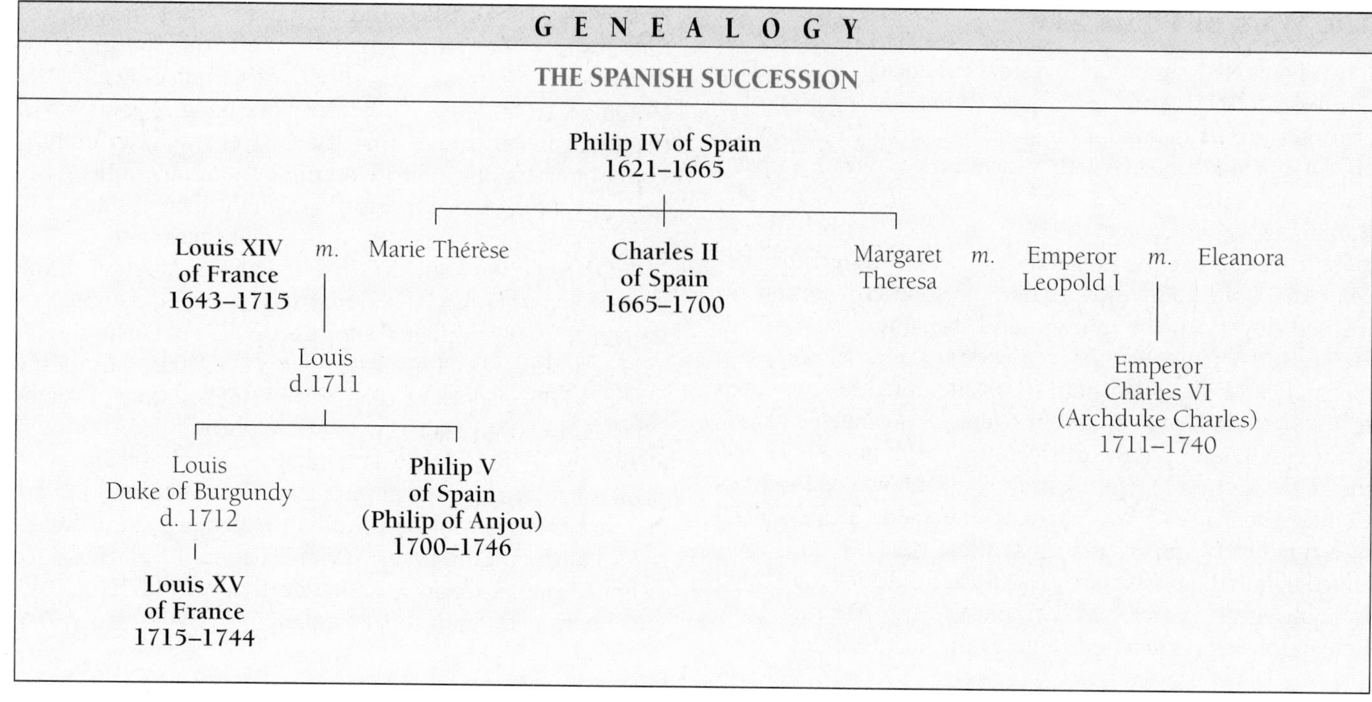

led by William III, who, as stadtholder of Holland, was vitally interested in the fate of the Spanish Netherlands and, as king of England, was equally interested in the fate of the Spanish American colonies. In the 1690s, two treaties of partition were drawn up. The first achieved near universal agreement but was nullified by the death of the German prince who was to inherit the Spanish crown. The second, which would have given Italy to Louis's son and everything else to Leopold's son, was opposed by Leopold, who had neither naval nor commercial interests and who claimed most of the Italian territories as imperial fiefs.

All of these plans had been made without consulting the Spanish, who wanted to maintain their empire intact. To this end, they devised a brilliant plan. Charles II bequeathed his entire empire to Philip of Anjou, the younger grandson of Louis XIV, with two stipulations: that Philip renounce his claim to the French throne and that he accept the empire intact, without partition. If he—or, more to the point, his grandfather, Louis XIV—did not accept these conditions, the empire would pass to Archduke Charles, the younger son of Leopold I. Such provisions virtually ensured war between France and the empire unless compromise between the two powers could be reached. Before terms could even be suggested, however, Charles II died, and Philip V (1700–1746) was proclaimed king of Spain and its empire.

Thus the eighteenth century opened with the War of the Spanish Succession (1702–1714). Emperor Leopold rejected the provisions of Charles's will and sent his troops to occupy Italy. Louis XIV confirmed the worst fears of William III when he provided his grandson with French troops to "defend" the Spanish Netherlands. William III revived the Grand Alliance and initiated a massive land war against the combined might of France and Spain. The allied objectives were twofold: to prevent the unification of the French and Spanish thrones and to partition the Spanish empire so that both Italy and the Netherlands were ceded to Austria. Louis XIV's objective was simply to preserve as much as possible of the Spanish inheritance for the house of Bourbon.

William III died in 1702 and was succeeded by Anne (1702–1714). John Churchill (1650–1722), Duke of Marlborough and commander-in-chief of the army, continued William's policy. England and Holland again provided most of the finance and sea power, but the English also provided a land army that was nearly 70,000 strong. Prussia joined the Grand Alliance, and disciplined Prussian troops helped to offset the addition of the Spanish army to Louis's forces. Churchill defeated French forces in 1704 at Blenheim in Germany and in 1706 at Ramillies in the Spanish Netherlands. France's military ascendancy was over.

Efforts to negotiate a peace settlement took longer than the war itself. The Austrians had taken control of Italy, the English and Dutch had secured the Spanish Netherlands, and the French had been driven back beyond the Rhine. The Allies believed that they could now impose any treaty they pleased on Louis XIV and, along with concessions from France, attempted to oust his grandson, Philip V, from the Spanish throne. This proved impossible to achieve, though it took more than five years to learn the lesson. By then the European situation had taken another strange twist. Both the emperor Leopold and his oldest son had died. Now Leopold's younger son, Archduke Charles, inherited the empire as Charles VI (1711–1740) and raised the prospect of an equally dangerous combined Austrian-Spanish state.

Between 1713 and 1714, a series of treaties at Utrecht settled the War of the Spanish Succession. Spanish possessions in Italy and the Netherlands were ceded to Austria; France abandoned all its territorial gains east of the Rhine and ceded its North American territories of Nova Scotia and Newfoundland to England. England also acquired from Spain Gibraltar, on the southern coast of Spain, and the island of Minorca in the Mediterranean. Both were strategically important to English commercial interests. English intervention in the Nine Years' War and the War of the Spanish Succession did not result in large territorial gains, but it did result in an enormous increase in English power and prestige. Over the next 30 years, England would assert its own imperial claims.

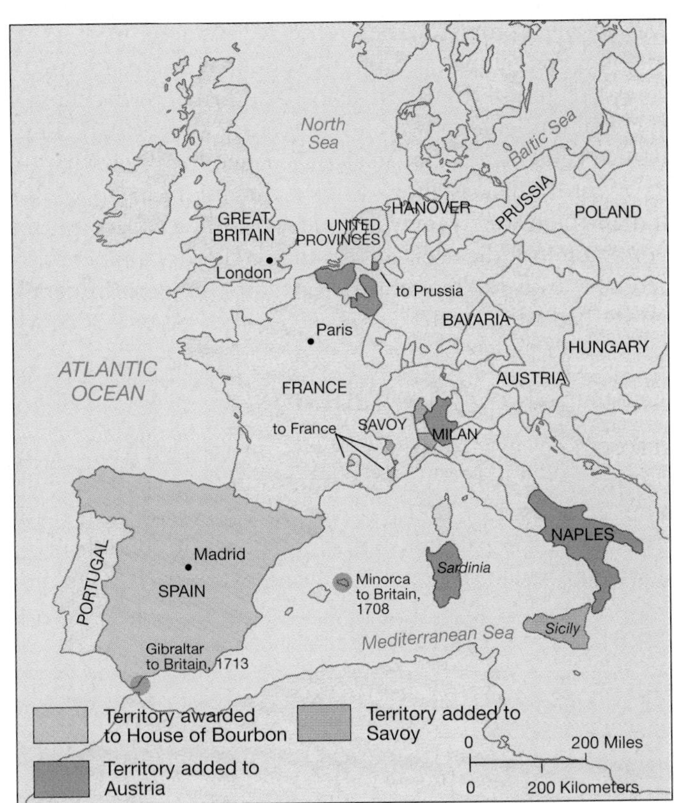

▲ The Treaty of Utrecht, Europe 1714. The treaty redistributed European possessions to create a balance of power.

The Colonial Wars

The Treaty of Utrecht (1713–1714) ushered in almost a quarter century of peace in western Europe. Austrian rule in the Netherlands and Italy remained a major irritant to the Spanish, but Spain was too weak to do more than sulk and snarl. The death of Louis XIV in 1715 quelled French ambitions for a time and even led to an Anglo-French accord, which guaranteed the preservation of the settlement reached at Utrecht. Peace allowed Europe to rebuild its shattered economy and resume the international trade that had been so severely disrupted over the last 40 years. The Treaty of Utrecht had resolved a number of important trading issues, all in favor of Great Britain, as England was known after its union with Scotland in 1707. In addition to receiving Gibraltar and Minorca from Spain, Britain was granted the monopoly to provide slaves to the Spanish American colonies and the right to send one trading ship a year to them. In the East and in the West, Britain was becoming the dominant commercial power in the world.

Part of the reason for Britain's preeminence was the remarkable growth of its Atlantic colonies. Like every other colonial power, the British held a monopoly on their colonial trade. They were far less successful than were the Spanish and French in enforcing the notion that colonies existed only for the benefit of the parent country, but the English Parliament continued to pass legislation aimed at restricting colonial trade with other nations and other nations' colonies. Like most other mercantile restrictions, these efforts were stronger in theory than in practice. Tariffs on imports and customs duties on British goods provided a double incentive for smuggling.

France emerged as Britain's true colonial rival. In the Caribbean, the French had the largest and most profitable of the West Indian sugar islands, Saint Domingue (modern-day Haiti). In North America, France not only held Canada but also laid claim to the entire continent west of the Ohio River. The French did not so much settle their colonial territory as occupy it. They surveyed the land, established trading relations with the Native Americans, and built forts at strategic locations. The English, in contrast, had developed fixed communities, which grew larger and more prosperous by the decade. France decided to defend its colonies by establishing an overseas military presence. Regular French troops were shipped to Canada and installed in Louisbourg, Montreal, and Quebec. The British responded with troops of their own and sent an expeditionary force to clear the French from the Ohio River Valley. This action was the immediate cause of the Seven Years' War (1756–1763).

Although the Seven Years' War had a bitter Continental phase, it was essentially a war for empire between the English and the French. There were three main theaters: the North American mainland, the West Indian sugar plantations, and the eastern coast of India. All over the globe, the British won smashing victories. The British navy blockaded the water route to Canada and ultimately captured Montreal and Quebec. After some initial successes, the French were driven back west across the Mississippi River, and their line of fortresses in the Ohio Valley fell into English hands. The English took all the French sugar islands except Saint Domingue. British success in India was equally complete. The French were chased from their major trading zone, and English dominance was secured.

By the end of the Seven Years' War, Britain had become a global imperial power. In the Peace of Paris (1763), France ceded all of Canada in exchange for the return of its West Indian islands. British dominion in the East Indian trade was recognized and led ultimately to British dominion in India itself. In less than a century, France's ascendancy was broken, and Europe's first modern imperial power had been created.

Conclusion

EUROPEAN COMMERCIAL EXPANSION WAS THE FIRST STEP in a long process that would ultimately transform the material life of all human beings. The quest for new commodities led to the sophistication of transportation, marketing, and distribution—all vital developments for agricultural changes in the future. The ability to move large quantities of goods from place to place and to exchange them between different parts of the globe laid the foundation for organized manufacturing. The practical impact of scientific discovery, as yet only dimly glimpsed, would soon spur the transformation of handicrafts into industries. In the eighteenth century, the material world was still being conquered, and the most unattractive features of this conquest were all too plainly visible. Luxuries for the rich were won by the labors of the poor and the enslaved. (For a discussion of eighteenth-century culture and society, see Chapter 19.) The greed of merchants and the glory of princes made an unholy alliance that resulted in warfare around the globe.

As intercontinental trade made the world grow smaller and increasingly interdependent, the scientific revolution made the universe larger and reduced the earth from its traditional status as the central point of reference to being just one of a family of planets orbiting the sun.

QUESTIONS FOR REVIEW

1. What was new about the methods and ideas of Copernicus, Brahe, Kepler, and Galileo, and why were they threatening to Catholic doctrine?
2. In what ways did the new science build upon traditional ideas associated with alchemy, astrology, and Hermetic thinking? In what ways was it a departure?
3. What new technologies, trading practices, and financial devices assisted the expansion of long-distance trading?
4. Why were the Dutch especially well-suited to participate in the worldwide expansion of European commerce?
5. How did the governments of the various European nations promote their own commercial interests?

DISCOVERING WESTERN CIVILIZATION ONLINE

You can obtain more information about science and commerce in early modern Europe at the websites listed below. See also the companion website that accompanies this text: www.ablongman.com/kishlansky, which contains on online study guide additional resources.

The New Science

www.fordham.edu/halsall/mod/modsbook09.html
Links to sources and other sites dealing with the Scientific Revolution.

www.cuny.edu/multimedia/arsnew/arstoc.html
An interesting site dealing with the relations between Renaissance art and early modern science.

www.lucidcafe.com/library/95dec/newton.html
A miscellany of material on Sir Isaac Newton.

es.rice.edu/ES/humsoc/Galileo/
A site devoted to Galileo that contains pictures of his instruments and guides to his experiments.

Empires of Goods

www.bell.lib.umn.edu/Products/Products.html
A site describing the new products introduced to Europe during the period of global expansion.

www.historyhouse.com/stories/tulip.htm
The story of Tulipmania in seventeenth-century Holland.

SUGGESTIONS FOR FURTHER READING

General Reading

Jan de Vries, *The European Economy in an Age of Crisis* (Cambridge: Cambridge University Press, 1976). A comprehensive study of economic development, including long-distance trade and commercial change.

A. Rupert Hall, *The Revolution in Science, 1500–1750* (London: Longman, 1983). The best introduction to the varieties of scientific thought in the early modern period. Detailed and complex.

Derek McKay and H. M. Scott, *The Rise of the Great Powers, 1648–1815* (London: Longman, 1983). An outstanding survey of diplomacy and warfare.

The New Science

Wilbur Applebaum, ed., *Encyclopedia of the Scientific Revolution: From Copernicus to Newton* (New York: Garland, 2000). A substantial reference resource.

H. F. Cohen, *The Scientific Revolution* (Chicago: University of Chicago Press, 1994). The history of the idea of the scientific revolution and of the events that comprised it.

Stillman Drake, *Galileo* (New York: Hill and Wang, 1980). A short but engaging study of the great Italian scientist.

Lisa Jardine, *Ingenious Pursuits: Building the Scientific Revolution* (New York: Anchor Books, 1999). A new study emphasizing the technical contexts of the scientific revolution and interactions between its major figures.

Steven Shapin, *The Scientific Revolution* (Chicago: University of Chicago Press, 1996). An excellent brief introduction.

Richard Westfall, *The Life of Isaac Newton* (Cambridge: Cambridge University Press, 1993). The best short biography.

Empires of Goods

J. N. Ball, *Merchants and Merchandise: The Expansion of Trade in Europe* (London: Croom Helm, 1977). A good overview of European overseas economies.

John Brewer and Roy Porter, eds., *Consumption and the World of Goods* (New York: Routledge, 1993). An important and wide-ranging collection of studies of the place of consumption in early modern Western history.

K. N. Chaudhuri, *The Trading World of Asia and the English East India Company* (Cambridge: Cambridge University Press, 1978). A brilliant account of the impact of the Indian trade on both Europeans and Asians.

Philip Curtin, *The Atlantic Slave Trade* (Madison: University of Wisconsin Press, 1969). A study of the importation of African slaves into the New World, with the best estimates of the numbers of slaves and their destinations.

Jonathan Israel, *Dutch Primacy in World Trade, 1585–1740* (Oxford: Oxford University Press, 1989). The triumph of Dutch traders and techniques written by the leading authority.

Sidney Mintz, *Sweetness and Power* (New York: Viking Press, 1985). An anthropologist explores the lure of sugar and its impact on Western society.

The Wars of Commerce

Jeremy Black, *A System of Ambition? British Foreign Policy, 1660–1793* (London: Longman, 1991). The best survey of Britain's international relations during the long eighteenth century.

A. C. Carter, *Neutrality or Commitment: The Evolution of Dutch Foreign Policy, 1667–1795* (London: Edward Arnold, 1975). A tightly written study of the objectives and course of Dutch diplomacy.

Paul Langford, *The Eighteenth Century, 1688–1815* (New York: St. Martin's Press, 1976). A reliable guide to the growth of British power.

CHAPTER 18

THE BALANCE OF POWER IN EIGHTEENTH-CENTURY EUROPE

- THE VISUAL RECORD: A Dashing Officer
- GEOGRAPHICAL TOUR: A Grand Tour of Europe in 1714
- THE RISE OF RUSSIA
- THE TWO GERMANIES
- THE GREATNESS OF GREAT BRITAIN

THE VISUAL RECORD

A DASHING OFFICER

FROM THE MIDDLE OF THE SEVENTEENTH CENTURY, Britain was a great sea-faring power. Its navy, built up during the reign of Charles I and the rule of Oliver Cromwell, challenged the Dutch for imperial supremacy in the east and the Spanish for colonial supremacy in the west. Louis XIV actually paid the British government a subsidy to remain neutral in his commercial and territorial wars and even attempted to rent British ships on occasion. The British flag flew on seas worldwide and it would not be long before Britannia ruled the waves. But beginning at the end of the seventeenth century, Great Britain also became a feared landed military power. Under its Dutch king, William III, British armies successfully held the French at bay in the Nine Years' War and inflicted defeat upon them in the brutal War of the Spanish Succession (1702–1714). British generals, such as the Duke of Marlborough, became European-wide celebrities, their feats the subject of story, song, and painting.

Britain's rise to military greatness was as swift as it was unexpected and it lasted for more than one hundred years. The titanic struggle with France dominated the lives of four successive generations and was not finally concluded until the Battle of Waterloo in 1815. Throughout the eighteenth century, the military was present in British society in a way in which it never had been before or would be again. A society that had openly condemned the concept of a standing army now gave way to one in which the presence of uniformed officers was everywhere. Where younger sons had once gone into the church, now they joined the guards. Where the impoverished and luckless had once migrated to London, now they took the King's shilling, as voluntary enlistment was called. The excess agricultural populations of Scotland and Ireland, once doomed to hunger and starvation, now became the raw materials for the greatest fighting men Europe had known.

One indication of the new prominence given soldiers was the painting of their portraits by the most talented artists of the day. This portrait of Captain Robert Orme was painted by Sir Joshua Reynolds, founder and first president of the Royal Academy and one of the greatest portrait artists of the age. Reynolds revived the long tradition of English portrait painting that had reached its height with the Fleming Van Dyck and the Dutch Kneller. But Reynolds was no foreign import. He was born and raised in Devonshire, learned his trade by painting sailors at Plymouth Docks, and even sailed on a naval expedition. Reynolds's military portraits capture that spirit of patriotism, of strength, and of courage that the British expected from their officers. Captain Orme, a member of the prestigious Coldstream Guards, is portrayed in a moment of action, his stead foaming and winded, the message that he carries admitting of no delay. Slaughter rages behind him. In his haste, his hair has come undone and his extended right arm suggests that he is about to mount and gallop away. But in his pause there is a great stillness and confidence. His gaze is suffused with reassurance, the jaw solid, the eyes piercing. This is the image of flesh and blood that carried Britain to its greatness in the wars of the eighteenth century.

LOOKING AHEAD

The balance of power established by the European monarchies in the eighteenth century was achieved on the battlefield. As we shall see in this chapter, in Russia, Prussia, and Austria, noblemen flocked to military service and the military portion of national economies multiplied dramatically. In the east, her neighbors three times carved up Poland. In the west, the continuing struggle between France and Britain resulted in the destabilization of French society that prepared the way for the French Revolution. In the Atlantic, Britain casually lost its North American colonies in a war it fought half-heartedly for a prize it no longer appreciated.

GEOGRAPHICAL TOUR

A Grand Tour of Europe in 1714

In the eighteenth century, young noblemen from every European nation completed their education by taking a grand tour. Usually in company with a tutor, they would visit the palaces, castles, and churches of their neighboring countries, learn a little of the language, and mingle with others of their class who were engaged in a similar experience. Noblemen who took the grand tour in the second decade of the century witnessed the redrawing of Europe's political map as well as a new balance of power among the European states.

The political geography of Europe was reorganized at the beginning of the eighteenth century by two treaties. The Treaty of Utrecht (1713–1714) created a new Europe in the west, and the Treaty of Nystad (1721) did the same in the east. Both agreements reflected the dynamics of change that had taken place over the previous century. The rise of France on the Continent and of Britain's colonial empire around the globe were facts that could no longer be ignored. The decline of Sweden and Poland and the emergence of Russia as a great power were the beginning of a long-term process that would continue to dominate European history.

All of that could be seen on a map of Europe in the early eighteenth century (see **Map A**). France's absorption of Alsace and encroachments into Lorraine would be bones of contention between the French and Germans for two centuries and would ultimately contribute to the outbreak of World Wars I and II. The political footballs of the Spanish Netherlands and Spanish Italy, now temporarily Austrian, continued to be kicked around until the nationalist

▼ **Map A. Europe in 1714.** This map shows Europe as established by the Treaty of Utrecht.

movements of the nineteenth century gave birth to Belgium, Luxembourg, and a united Italy. The emergence of Brandenburg-Prussia on the north German coast and the gradual decline in the power of the Holy Roman Emperor were both vital to the process that created a unified Germany and a separate Austria. In the southeast, the slow but steady reconquest of the Balkans from Ottoman dominion restored the historic southern border of the Continent. The inexorable expansion of Russia was also already apparent.

Expansion of Western Europe

Perhaps the most obvious transformation in the political geography of western Europe was the expansion of European power around the globe.

Colonies in the Americas. In the Atlantic, Spain remained the largest colonial power, controlling all of Mexico and Central America, the largest and most numerous of the Caribbean islands, North America from Colorado to California (as well as Florida), and most of South America (see **Map B**). The other major colonial power in the region was Portugal, which held the richly endowed colony of Brazil.

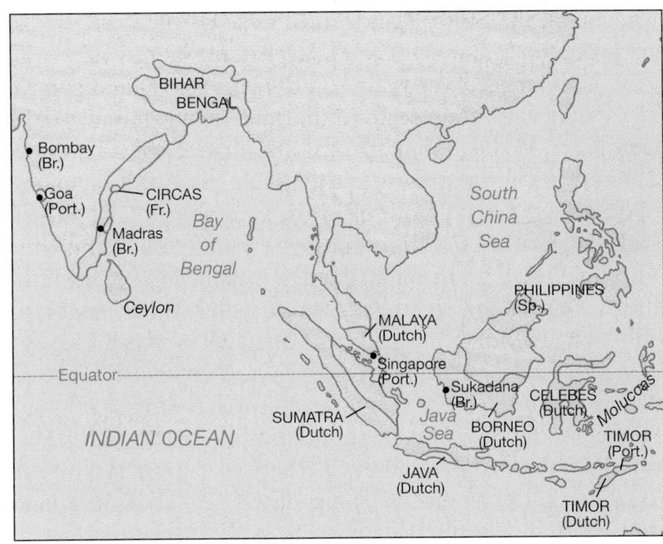

▲ **Map C. India and the East Indies.** The famous spice islands were still controlled by the Dutch while the British gained footholds on both coasts of India.

▼ **Map B. The Americas.** Much of the American continents was still uncharted with most settlements in the coastal areas.

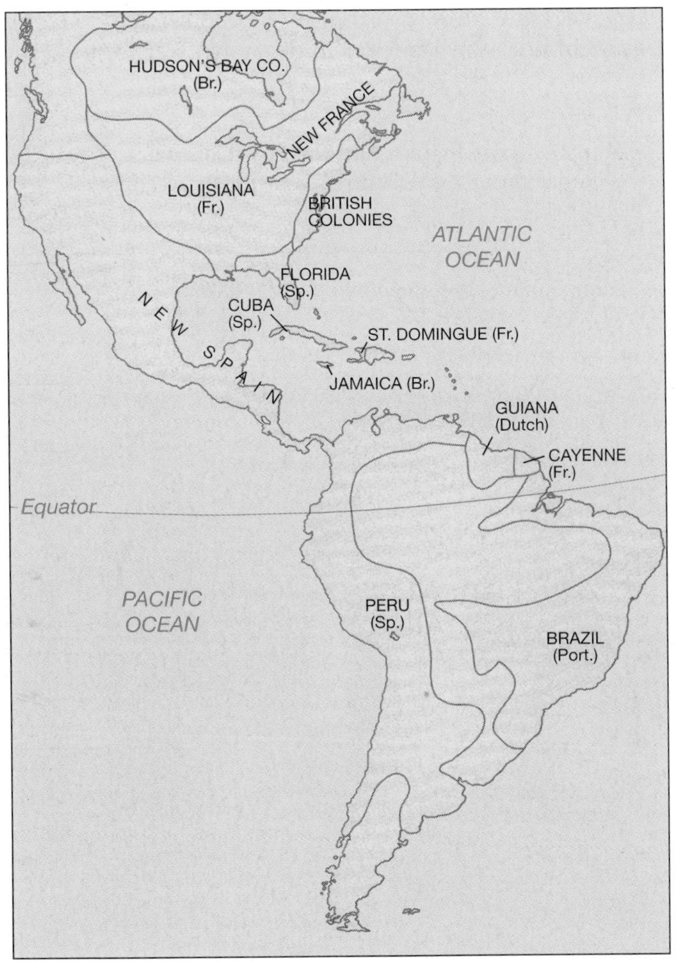

In North America, the French and British shared the eastern half of the continent (see **Map B**). The French controlled most of it. They had landed first in Canada and then slowly made their way down the Saint Lawrence River. New France, as their colonial empire was called, was a trading territory, and it expanded along the Great Lakes and the Ohio, Missouri, and Mississippi Rivers all the way to the Gulf of Mexico. France also claimed the territory of Louisiana, named for Louis XIV, which stretched from New Orleans to Montana. The British settlements ranged along the Atlantic seaboard from Maine to Georgia. Unlike the French, the British settled their territory and were interested in expansion only when their population, which was doubling every 25 years, outgrew its resources. By the early eighteenth century, the ports of Boston, New York, Philadelphia, and Charleston were thriving commercial centers.

Colonies in the Far East. Europeans managed their eastern colonial territories differently than they did those in the Atlantic. Initially, the Portuguese and the Dutch had been satisfied with establishing trading factories—coastal fortresses in Africa and Asia that could be used as warehouses and defended against attack. But in the seventeenth century, the European states began to take control of vital ports and lucrative islands (see **Map C**). Here the Dutch were the acknowledged leaders, replacing the Portuguese, who had begun the process at the end of the sixteenth century. Holland held, by force or in conjunction with local leaders, all the Spice Islands in the Pacific. The Dutch also occupied both sides of the Malay Peninsula and nearly all the coastal areas of the islands in the Java Sea. Dutch control of Ceylon was strategically important for its Indian trade. Compared to the Dutch, all other European states had only a minor territorial presence in the East, with the exception of Spain, which still controlled the Philippines. The British had limited their eastern outposts to trading establishments. Through these they maintained a significant presence in India. During the eighteenth century, the British began to colonize the Indian subcontinent directly (see **Map C**).

Great Britain. Imperial expansion was the most obvious change in the geopolitical boundaries of Europe, but it was not the only one. A brief tour of the western states after the Treaty of Utrecht reveals some others. In 1707, England and Scotland formally joined together to form Great Britain (see **Map D**). In addition to its eastern and western colonies, Britain had also gained control of Gibraltar at the foot of Spain and the island of Minorca in the Mediterranean (see **Map E**). Both territories were strategically important to British commerce.

The Low Countries. Across the English Channel were the Low Countries, now permanently divided between the United Provinces in the north, led by Holland, and the provinces in the south that had remained loyal to the Spanish crown in the sixteenth century (see **Map D**). By 1714, the golden age of the Dutch was over. They lost their predominance in European trade to France and much of their eastern empire to Britain. What the Dutch gained at Utrecht was the right to maintain their forces in the towns along the border between France and the old Spanish Netherlands. The Spanish Netherlands, the original Burgundian inheritance, were now being slowly dismembered. Since the accession of Louis XIV, France had plucked small pieces from the territories that had been contested between France and Spain since the fifteenth century. Between French aggression and the Dutch occupation of such important places as Ghent and Ypres, the ability of the southern provinces to maintain a separate identity suffered a grave blow. The Treaty of Utrecht dealt a still graver blow by assigning sovereignty over this territory to Austria, ostensibly because the emperor was a Habsburg, but really because the balance of power in western Europe demanded it.

France. To the south lay France, still the most powerful nation in Europe despite its losses in the War of the Spanish Succession (see **Map E**). By 1714, Louis XIV had broken forever the danger of Spanish encirclement. Louis had methodically set out to occupy those territories that were strategically necessary to defend his state from invasion. In the northeast, he absorbed the Duchy of Bar. In the north, he absorbed a healthy portion of Flanders. He pushed the eastern boundary of his state to the Rhine by overrunning Alsace and parts of Lorraine (see **Map E**). Strasbourg remained French under the settlement of 1714, testimony to the fact that it was possible to hold France only at the western banks of the Rhine. Finally, farther to the south, Louis had won and held Franche-Comté, once the center of Burgundy. In 1714, France was larger, stronger, and better able to defend its borders than ever before. It was also exhausted.

Spain. As France expanded, Spain contracted. Less than two centuries earlier, a Spanish king had dreamed of being monarch over all of Europe. Now a French Bourbon sat on the great Habsburg throne, and Spain was slowly being sliced to pieces. By 1714, the European territories of the Spanish empire had been reduced to Iberia itself (see **Map E**). However, the loss of its European empire ultimately proved to be a blessing in disguise for Spain, which now entered a new and unexpected phase of growth and influence.

The Empire. The center of Europe remained occupied by the agglomeration of cities, bishoprics, principalities, and small states known collectively as the Holy Roman Empire but now more accurately called the German empire (see Map F). There were still over 300 separate jurisdictions, most of them vulnerable to preying neighbors such as Louis XIV. Bavaria in the south and Saxony, Brandenburg, and Hanover in the north were among the

▼ **Map D. Great Britain and the Low Countries.** Great Britain and the Low Countries were the two leading European commercial nations.

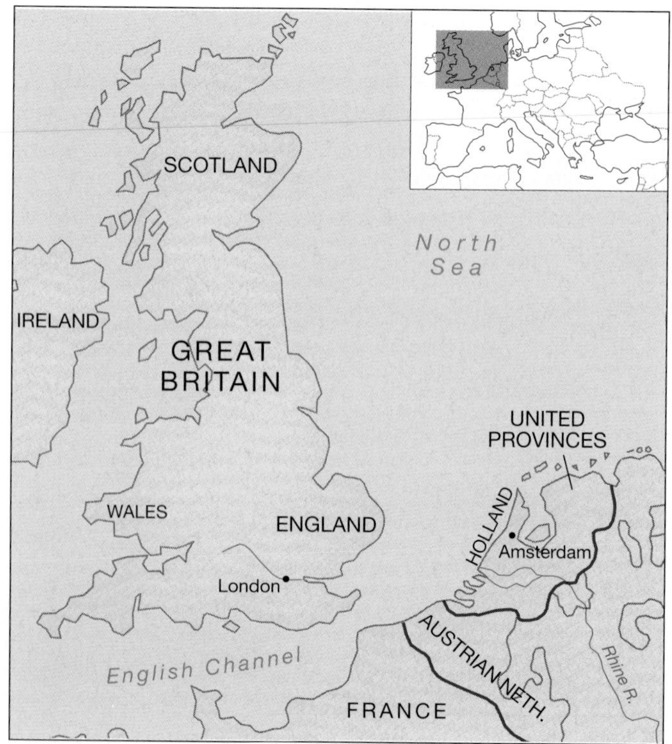

most important of the large states, with the added twist that Hanover was now ruled by the king of Great Britain. The emperor, now officially prohibited from interference in the internal administration of the large states, was less dominant in German affairs than he had been before the Thirty Years' War.

Increasingly, Habsburg power centered on Austria, Bohemia, and Hungary (see **Map F**). This was especially true during the reign of Leopold I (1655–1705). Withstanding threats on all sides, Leopold was able to expand his state to the west and south and bring Austria into the ranks of the great European powers. Such an outcome could hardly have been foreseen in 1683, when the Ottomans besieged Vienna itself and only the arrival of 70,000 Polish-led troops saved the city from falling. From that time forward, Austrian forces scored stunning victories. By 1699, almost all of Hungary had been retaken by Austria; with the Treaty of Passarowitz in 1718, Austria gained the rest of Hungary and Serbia. The Treaty of Utrecht had already granted Austria control of the Netherlands, Lombardy, and Naples, making the Austrian Habsburgs rulers of a European empire (see **Map F**).

Austria's Italian possessions included the vast southern territories of Naples (including Sicily after 1720) and the rich industrial area surrounding Milan in the north. Alongside the Austrian territories a number of independent city-states, including Venice and Genoa, continued to flourish on the Italian peninsula. The Grand Duchy of Tuscany, with its great city of Florence, and the Papal States had expanded over the course of the seventeenth century, absorbing their smaller neighbors until both were large, consolidated territories (see **Map F**). To the west of the Italian states was the Duchy of Savoy (see **Map F**), which grew and prospered. After the War of the Spanish Succession, Savoy was counted among the victors, though it had fought on both sides. Duke Victor Amadeus II became a king when he received the island of Sicily, which he exchanged with Austria for Sardinia in 1720 (see **Map F**).

Thus the Treaty of Utrecht signaled a new configuration of political power. England, France, Prussia, and Austria were the ascending powers; Holland and Spain were the declining ones. Italy and the southern Netherlands were the bones over which the biggest dogs fought. This was western Europe in 1714.

Realignment in Eastern Europe

In eastern Europe it was the Treaty of Nystad (1721), which ended the Great Northern War (1700–1721), that fixed the political geography. Here the emerging powers were Russia and Prussia; those in decline were Sweden and Poland. The critical factor in eastern European politics remained access to the sea. Gaining control of outlets to the Baltic Sea in the north and the Black Sea in the south was the central motivation for the long years of war fought among the eastern states.

▲ **Map E. France and Spain.** The War of the Spanish Succession permanently separated France and Spain.

▲ **Map F. The Holy Roman Empire.** It was still a conglomeration of towns, principalities, and bishoprics, but increasingly the empire was losing political and administrative control over its lands.

Russia. The expansion of Russia is one of the central events in European history, and the early eighteenth century is its pivotal period. During the long years of social and economic recovery after the death of Ivan the Terrible in 1584, Russia had been easy prey for its powerful neighbors Sweden and Poland. Through a series of wars and political pacts, Russia had ceded most of its Baltic territories to Sweden and had relinquished land and population in the west to Poland. Peter the Great (1682–1725) set out to reclaim what had been lost. As a result of the Great Northern War, Russia regained the eastern Baltic coastline from the southeastern end of Finland to Riga in the west (see **Map G**). Russia now controlled all of the vital Baltic ports in the east. Peter built a new capital, Saint Petersburg, on the Gulf of Finland and laid the foundation for the Russian navy.

Sweden. What Russia gained, Sweden lost (see **Map G**). At the height of its power in the middle of the seventeenth century, Sweden had dominated the Baltic. It had occupied all of Finland, controlled the important eastern coast of Norway, and gained a foothold in Germany. Sweden had also captured the southern tip of its own peninsula from the Danes, making the mainland portion of its state whole. But Sweden's century-long rise to power was followed by a rapid period of decline. As a result of the Great Northern War, Sweden lost all of its German territories. Those on the North Sea went to Hanover; those on the Baltic went to Prussia. Livonia, Estonia, and the eastern provinces were returned to Russia, but Sweden was able to hold on to its vital gains from the Danes. Sweden had built its own window to the west at Göteborg on the North Sea, and from there it could carry on direct trade with Britain and the Netherlands.

▼ **Map G. Russia and Sweden.** Sweden's age of territorial expansion was over by the beginning of the eighteenth century.

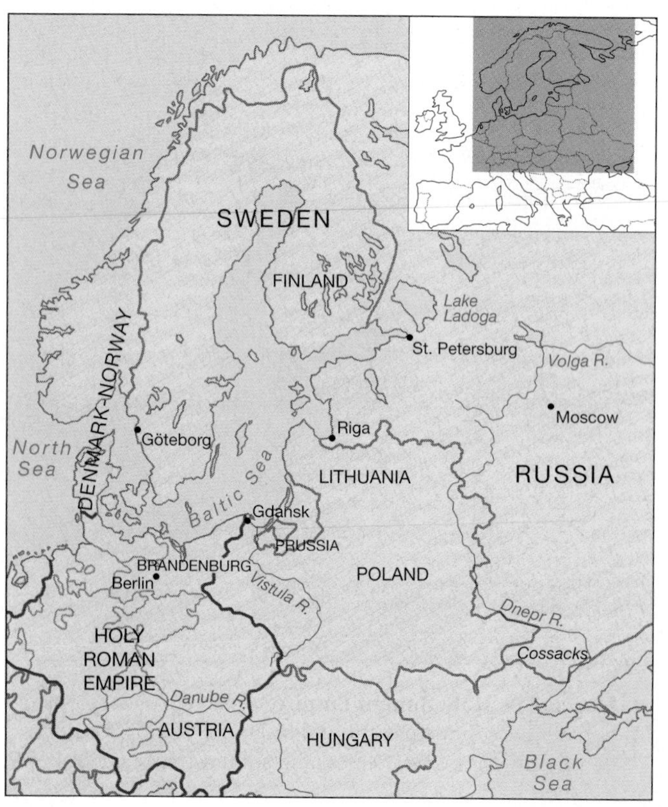

Prussia. Since the end of the Thirty Years' War, Brandenburg-Prussia, a domain of the Holy Roman Empire, had been growing steadily (see **Map G**). From the capital at Berlin the princes of Brandenburg directed the accumulation of small neighboring German lands: Magdeburg and Halle to the southwest, a piece of Pomerania to the northeast. Brandenburg expanded in every direction, but it could do little to join itself to the kingdom of Prussia. A huge swath of Poland separated the two. In the eighteenth century, the determination to expand and close the gap dominated Prussian history.

Poland. This aim meant eventual conflict with Poland, which, despite its political weakness, was one of the largest territories in Europe (see **Map G**). On its southern border it held back Ottoman expansion, while on its eastern border it held back the Russians. Its great port of Gdansk on the Baltic dominated the grain and timber trade with northern Europe as well as local Baltic commerce between Scandinavia and the mainland. Sweden and Russia controlled Poland politically, helping to nominate its elected kings and ensuring that its decentralized form of aristocratic government kept it weak. Except for its Baltic territories, Poland was not yet seen as a great prize to be fought over. By the beginning of the eighteenth century, however, it was a helpless giant ready to be toppled.

Thus a potent Prussia and Russia and a prostrate Poland characterized the realignment of the eastern portion of Europe. At the same time, the separation between east and west was narrowing. Prussia's German orientation and the westernization of Russia led to closer ties with the west.

THE RISE OF RUSSIA

At the beginning of the eighteenth century, Russia was scarcely of concern to the rest of Europe. Peter the Great changed that. The Treaty of Nystad had confirmed the magnitude of his victory over the Swedes in the Great Northern War. The change created consternation in the courts of Europe. Little was known about the Russian ruler or his state. Letters from European merchants stationed in Moscow were the main source of Western knowledge about the vast Muscovite empire. What little mercantile contact there was between Russia and the West was conducted entirely by westerners, who were allowed to live in Moscow in a separate ghetto called "German-town."

Peter the Great sought greater contact with western Europe. Twice he visited Europe to discover the secrets of western prosperity and might. He arranged marriages between the closest heirs to his throne, including his son Alexis, and the sons and daughters of German princes and dukes. By 1721, he had established 21 separate foreign embassies. The sons of the Russian gentry and nobility were sent to the west—sometimes forcibly—to further their education and to learn to adapt to western outlooks. Peter recruited foreign engineers and gunners to serve in his army, foreign architects to build his new capital at Saint Petersburg, foreign scholars to head the new state schools, and foreign administrators to oversee the new departments of state. He borrowed freely from Europe and adapted sensibly. If necessary, he would drag his country kicking and screaming into the modern world.

By 1721, Russia was recognized all over Europe as an emerging power. Its defeat of Sweden had made European monarchs sit up and take notice. Peter's absorption of Sweden's Baltic territories made Russia a power in the north. The Russian navy, built mostly by foreigners, was now capable of protecting Russian interests and defending important ports such as Riga and Saint Petersburg. Even the Dutch, who had long plotted the decline of Swedish might, now became nervous. It was therefore unsettling that the Russian ruler now wished to be recognized as an emperor.

The Reforms of Peter the Great

Peter the Great was not the first Russian tsar to attempt to borrow from the West. The process had been under way for decades. The opening of the northern port of Archangel in 1584 led to direct contact with British and Dutch traders, who brought new ideas and useful products. But Russia was a vast state, and Europe was only one of its neighbors. Russia's religion had come from Byzantium rather than Rome, thus giving Russian Christianity an eastern flavor. Its Asian territories mixed the influence of Mongols and Ottomans; its southern borders met Tartars and Cossacks. While most European states were racially and ethnically homogeneous, Russia was a loose confederation of diverse peoples. Yet the western states posed the greatest threat to Russia in the seventeenth century, and it was to the West that Peter, like his father before him, turned his attention.

Nearly all of Peter's reforms—economic, educational, administrative, social, military—were aimed at enhancing military efficiency rather than civil progress. In his 30 years of active rule, there was only one year—1724—during which he was not at war. Vital reforms such as the poll tax (1724), which changed the basis of taxation from the household to the individual adult male, had enormous social consequences. The new policy of taxing individuals officially erased whole social classes. A strict census, taken (and retaken) to inhibit tax evasion, became the basis for further governmental encroachments on the tsar's subjects. Yet the poll tax was designed not for any of these purposes but to increase tax revenue for war. Similarly, the establishment of compulsory, lifetime military service, which was required of the landowning classes (the nobility and gentry), was undertaken to provide officers and state servants for an expanding military machine.

Although Peter's reforms were developed from little other than military necessity, they constituted a fundamental transformation in the life of all Russian people. The creation of a gigantic standing army and an entirely new navy meant conscription of the Russian peasantry on a grand scale. In a ten-year period of the Great Northern War, the army absorbed 330,000 conscripts, most of whom never returned to their homes. Military service was not confined to the peasantry. Traditionally, the rural gentry raised and equipped the local conscript forces and gave them what training they could. Most of the gentry lived on estates that had been granted to them along with the resident peasants as a reward for their military contributions. Peter the Great intensified the obligations of the gentry. Not only were they to serve the state for life, but they were to accompany their regiments to the field and lead them in battle. When too old for active military service, they were to perform administrative service in the new departments of state.

The expansion of military forces necessitated an expansion of military administration as well. Peter's first innovation was the creation of the Senate, a group of nine senior administrators who were to oversee all aspects of military and civil government. The Senate became a permanent institution of government led by an entirely new official, the Procurator-General, who presided over its sessions and could propose legislation as well as oversee administration. From the Senate emanated 500 officials known as the fiscals, who traveled throughout the state looking for irregularities in tax assessment and collection. They quickly developed into a hated and feared internal police force.

Peter's efforts to reorganize his government went a step further in 1722, when he issued the Table of Ranks. This was an official hierarchy of the state that established the social position or rank of individuals. It was divided into three categories: military service, civil service, and owners of landed estates. Each category contained 14 ranks, and it was decreed that every person who entered the hierarchy did so at the bottom and worked his way up. The creation of the Table of Ranks demonstrated Peter's continued commitment to merit as a criterion for advancement. This standard had been shown in the military, where officers were promoted on the basis of service and experience rather than birth or background. Equally important was Peter's decision to make the military service the highest of the three categories. This reversed the centuries-old positions of the landed aristocracy and the military service class. Though the old nobility also served in the military and continued to dominate state service, the Table of Ranks opened the way for the infusion of new elements into the Russian elite.

Many of the men who were able to advance in the Table of Ranks did so through attendance at the new institutions of higher learning that Peter founded. His initial educational establishments were created to further the military might of the state. The Colleges of Mathematics, Engineering, and Artillery, which became the training grounds for his army officers, were all founded during the Great Northern War. Peter was also interested in liberal education, and he had scores of Western books translated into Russian. He had a press established in Moscow to print original works, including the first Russian newspaper. He decreed that a new, more Westernized alphabet replace the one used by the Russian Orthodox church and that books be written in the vernacular rather than in the formal literary language of religious writers. He also introduced Arabic numerals into official accounting records.

▼ This portrait of Peter the Great by his court painter Louis Caravaque pays homage to Peter's intense interest in naval matters. Ships flying English, Dutch, Danish, and Russian flags prepare for maneuvers under his command.

Peter's reforms of government and society were matched by his efforts to energize the economy. No state in Europe had as many natural resources as did Russia, yet manufacturing barely existed there. Peter took a direct hand in establishing factories for the production of iron, copper, textiles, glass, and leather. The state owned about half of these establishments, most of them on a larger scale than any known in the West. By 1726, more than half of all Russian exports were manufactured goods, and Russia had become the largest producer of iron and copper in the world.

In all of these ways and more, Peter the Great transformed Russia, but the changes did not come without cost. The traditions of centuries were not easily broken. Intrigue against Peter led first to confrontation with the old military elite and later to conflict with his only son, Alexis. It remains unclear whether the plot with which Alexis was connected actually existed or was a figment of Peter's imagination, but it is abundantly clear that Alexis's death in 1718 from torture plunged the state into a succession crisis in 1725. In the end, the great costs of westernization were paid by the masses of people, who benefited little from the changes.

Life in Rural Russia

At the beginning of the eighteenth century, nearly 97 percent of the Russian people lived on the land and practiced agriculture. Their lifestyles and farming methods had changed little for centuries. Most of the country's soil was poor. A harsh climate and low yields characterized Russian agriculture. One-third of the annual harvests during the eighteenth century were poor or disastrous, yet throughout the century, state taxation was making ever larger demands on the peasantry. During Peter's reign alone, direct taxation increased by 500 percent.

The theory of the Russian state was one of service, and the role of Russian peasants was to serve their master. The law code of 1649 formalized a process that had been under way for over a century whereby peasants lost status and became the property of their landlords. During the next century, laws curtailed the ability of peasants to move freely from one place to another, eliminated their right to hold private property, and abolished their freedom to petition the tsar against their masters. At the same time that landlords increased their hold over peasants, the state increased its hold over landlords. They were made responsible for the payment of taxes owed by their peasants and for the military service due from the peasants. By the middle of the eighteenth century, over half of all peasants—6.7 million adult males by 1782—had become serfs, the property of their masters, without any significant rights or legal protection.

Private landlords reckoned their wealth in the number of serfs they owned. Actually, most owned only a small number—fewer than 50—in the middle of the eighteenth century. The small number resulted from the common practice whereby a father's estate was divided among all of his surviving sons. Most members of the gentry were small landholders, constantly in debt and rarely able to meet their financial and service obligations to the state. This life of poverty at the top was, of course, magnified at the bottom. The vast majority of serfs lived in small villages, where they divided up their meager surplus to pay their taxes and drew lots to see who would be sent for military service. When their lords' debts became too heavy, it was the serfs who were foreclosed upon.

If serfs made up the bottom half of the Russian peasantry, there were few advantages to being in the top half among the state peasants. State peasants lived on lands owned by the monarchy itself. Like the serfs, state peasants were subject to the needs of the state for soldiers and workers. Forced labor was used in all of Peter's grandiose projects. Saint Petersburg was built by the backbreaking labor of peasant conscripts. From 1709, when the project began, perhaps as many as 40,000 laborers a year were forced to work on the various sites. The unhealthy conditions of the swampy environment in which the new capital rose claimed the lives of thousands of these workers, as did the appalling conditions of overwork and undernourishment in which they lived.

Many Russian peasants developed a philosophy of submission and a rich folk culture that valued a stubborn determination to endure. For those who would no longer bend to the knout—the heavy leather whip that was the omnipresent enforcer of obedience—only flight or rebellion remained. Hundreds of thousands of serfs fled to state-owned lands in hope of escaping the cruelties of individual landlords. Although severe penalties were imposed for aiding runaway serfs, in fact most state overseers and many private landlords encouraged runaways to settle on their lands. In their social and economic conditions, eighteenth-century Russian peasants were hardly distinguishable from medieval European serfs.

The Enlightened Empress Catherine

Of all the legacies of Peter the Great, perhaps the one of most immediate consequence was that government could go on without him. During the next 37 years, six tsars ruled Russia, "three women, a boy of twelve, an infant, and a mental weakling," as one commentator acidly observed. Although each succession was contested, the government continued to function smoothly, and Peter's territorial conquests were largely maintained. Russia also experienced a remarkable increase in population during this period. Between 1725 and 1762 the population grew from 13 to 19 million, a jump of nearly one-half in a single generation. This explosion of people dramatically increased the wealth of the landholding class, whose members reckoned their status by the number of serfs they owned.

The expansion of the economic resources of the nobility was matched by a rise in their legal status and political power. This period was sarcastically dubbed "the emancipation of the nobility," a phrase that captures not only the irony of the growing gap between rich and poor but also the contrast between the social structures of Russia and those of western Europe. In return for their privileges and status, Peter the Great extended the duties that the landowning classes owed to the state. By granting unique rights, such as the ownership of serfs, to the descendants of the old military service class, Peter had forged a Russian nobility. However, lifetime service was the price of nobility.

To gain and hold the throne, each succeeding tsar had to make concessions to the nobles to win their loyalty. The requirement of service to the state was gradually weakened until finally, in 1762, the obligation was abolished entirely.

Catherine's Accession. The abolition of compulsory service was not the same as the abolition of service itself. In fact, the end of compulsory service enabled Catherine II, the Great (1762–1796), to enact some of the most important reforms of her reign. Her first two acts as empress—having her husband, Peter III, murdered and lowering the salt tax—strengthened her position.

Catherine was a dynamic personality who alternately captivated and terrified those with whom she came into contact. She was influenced on the one hand by the new French ideas of social justice and the nobility of the human race and on the other by the traditional Russian ideas of absolute rule over an enserfed and subhuman population. Catherine handled these contrasting dimensions of her rule masterfully, gaining abroad the reputation as the most enlightened of European monarchs and at home the sincere devotion of her people.

The most important event in the early years of Catherine's reign was the establishment of a legislative commission to review the laws of Russia. Catherine herself wrote the *Instruction* (1767) by which the elected commissioners were to operate. She borrowed her theory of law from the French jurist Baron de Montesquieu (1689–1755) and her theory of punishment from the Italian reformer Cesare Beccaria (1738–1794). Among other things, Catherine advocated the abolition of capital punishment, torture, serf auctions, and the breakup of serf families by sale. Few of these radical reforms were ever put into practice.

In 1775, Catherine restructured local government. Russia was divided into 50 provincial districts, each with a population of between 300,000 and 400,000 inhabitants. Each district was to be governed by both a central official and elected local noblemen. This reform was modeled on the English system of justices of the peace. Previous local reforms had failed because of the absence

CHILDHOOD TRAUMAS

Catherine the Great left a fascinating account of her early years, which is in sharp contrast to her reputation for ruthlessness as a ruler.

FOCUS QUESTIONS

What kinds of attention did Catherine's parents show her? What is the significance of the fact that Catherine tells the story of her coughing attack just after describing her parents' treatment of her?

MY FATHER, WHOM I SAW VERY SELDOM, considered me to be an angel, my mother did not bother much about me. She had had, eighteen months after my birth, a son whom she passionately loved, whereas I was merely tolerated and often repulsed with violence and temper, not always with justice. I was aware of all this, but not always able to understand what I really felt about it.

At the age of seven I was suddenly seized with a violent cough. It was the custom that we should kneel every night and every morning to say our prayers. One night as I knelt and prayed I began to cough so violently that the strain caused me to fall on my left side, and I had such sharp pains in my chest that they almost took my breath away.

Finally, after much suffering, I was well enough to get up and it was discovered, as they started to put on my clothes, that I had in the meantime assumed the shape of the letter Z: my right shoulder was much higher than the left, the backbone running in a zigzag and the left side falling in.

From Catherine the Great, *Memoirs* (1755).

of a resident local nobility. The abolition of compulsory service made possible the establishment of local institutions. In 1785, Catherine issued the Charter of the Nobility, a formal statement of the rights and privileges of the noble class. The Charter incorporated all the gains the nobility had made since the death of Peter the Great, but it also instituted the requirements for local service that had been the basis of Catherine's reforms. District councils with the right to petition the tsar directly became the centerpiece of Russian provincial government.

To train the local nobility for government service, Catherine introduced educational reforms. She broadened the educational system, establishing provincial elementary schools on the Austrian model to train the sons and daughters of the local nobility. To staff these, Catherine created teachers' colleges so that the state would not have to rely on foreign educators. Although the program called for the equal education of women, except in Saint Petersburg and Moscow few women attended either elementary or high schools.

Catherine's reforms did little to enhance the lives of the vast majority of her people. She took no effective action to end serfdom or to soften its rigors. In fact, by grants of state land, Catherine gave away 800,000 state peasants, who became serfs. So, too, did millions of Poles who became her subjects after the partition of Poland in 1793 and 1795.

Pugachev's Revolt. Popular discontent fueled the most significant uprising of the century, Pugachev's Revolt (1773–1775), which took place during Catherine's reign. Emelyan Pugachev (1726–1775) was a Cossack who had been a military adventurer in his youth. Disappointed in his career, he made his way to the Ural Mountains, where he recruited Asian tribesmen and laborers who were forced to work in the mines. By promising freedom and land ownership, he drew peasants to his cause. In 1773, Pugachev declared himself to be Tsar Peter III, the murdered husband of Catherine II. He began with small raiding parties against local landlords and military outposts and soon gained the allegiance of tens of thousands of peasants. In 1774, with an army of nearly 20,000, Pugachev took the city of Kazan and threatened to advance on Moscow. It was another year before state forces could effectively control the rebellion. Finally, Pugachev was betrayed by his own followers and sent to Moscow, where he was executed.

During the reigns of Peter and Catherine the Great, Russia was transformed into an international power. Saint Petersburg, a window to the West, attracted many of Europe's leading luminaries. At court, French was spoken, the latest fashions were worn, and the newest ideas for economic and educational reform were aired. The Russian nobility mingled comfortably with its European counterparts, while the military service class developed into bureaucrats and administrators. Although court society glittered, for millions of peasants the quality of life was no better at the end of the campaign of westernization than it had been at the beginning.

▲ Chained but undaunted, Emelyan Pugachev awaits punishment for leading a peasant rebellion in the southern Urals.

THE TWO GERMANIES

The Thirty Years' War, which ended in 1648, initiated a profound transformation of the Holy Roman Empire. Warfare had devastated imperial territory and left a legacy of political consequences. There were now two empires—a German and an Austrian—though both were ruled by the same person. In the German territories, whether Catholic or Protestant, the Holy Roman Emperor was more a constitutional monarch than the absolute ruler he was in Austria. The larger states such as Saxony, Bavaria, and Hanover made their own political alliances despite the jurisdictional control that the emperor claimed to exercise. Most decisively, so did Brandenburg-Prussia. By the beginning of the eighteenth century, the electors of Brandenburg had become the kings of Prussia, and Prussian military power and efficient administrative structure became the envy of its German neighbors.

The Austrian empire was composed of Austria and Bohemia, the Habsburg hereditary lands, and as much of Hungary as could be controlled. Austria remained the center of the still-flourishing Counter-Reformation and a stronghold of Jesuit influence. The War of the Spanish Succession, which gave the Habsburgs control of the southern Netherlands and parts of Italy, brought Austria an enhanced role in European affairs. Austria remained one of the great powers of Europe and the leading power in the Holy Roman Empire, despite the rise of Prussia. Indeed, from the middle of the eighteenth century the conflict between Prussia and Austria was the defining characteristic of central European politics.

The Rise of Prussia

The transformation of Brandenburg-Prussia from a petty German principality to a great European power was one of the most significant developments of the eighteenth century. Frederick William, the Great Elector (1640–1688), had begun the process of forging Brandenburg-Prussia into a power in its own right by building a large and efficient military machine. At the beginning of the eighteenth century, Prussia was on the winning side in both the War of the Spanish Succession and the Great Northern War. When the battlefield dust had settled, Prussia possessed Pomerania and the Baltic port of Stettin. It was now a recognized power in eastern Europe.

Frederick William I. Frederick William I (1713–1740) and his son Frederick II, the Great (1740–1786), turned this promising beginning into an astounding success. A devout Calvinist, Frederick William I deplored waste and display. The reforms he initiated were intended to subordinate both aristocracy and peasantry to the needs of the state and to subordinate the needs of the state to the demands of the military.

Because of its exposed geographical position, Prussia's major problem was to maintain an efficient and well-trained army during peacetime. Security required a constant state of military preparedness, yet the relaxation of military discipline and the desertion of troops to their homes inevitably followed the cessation of hostilities. Frederick William I solved this problem by integrating the economic and military structures of his state. First he appointed only German officers to command his troops, eliminating mercenaries. Then he placed these noblemen at the head of locally recruited regiments. Each adult male in every district was required to register for military service in the regiment of the local landlord. These reforms dramatically increased the effectiveness of the army by shifting the burden of recruitment and training to the localities.

Yet despite all the attention that Frederick William I lavished on the military—by the end of his reign, nearly 70 percent of state expenditures went to the army—his foreign policy was largely pacific. In fact, his greatest achievements were in civil affairs, reforming the bureaucracy, establishing a sound economy, and raising state revenues. Through generous settlement schemes and by welcoming Protestant and Jewish refugees, Frederick William was able to expand the economic potential of these eastern territories. Frederick William I pursued an aggressive policy of land purchase to expand the royal domain, and the addition of so many new inhabitants in Prussia further increased his wealth. While the major western European powers were discovering deficit financing and the national debt, Prussia was running a surplus.

Frederick the Great. Financial security was vital to Frederick the Great's success. Father and son had quarreled bitterly throughout Frederick's youth, and most observers expected that out of spite, Frederick would tear down all that his father had built up. He and his father were cast in the same mold, however, with the unexpected difference that Frederick was the more ruthless and ambitious. With his throne, Frederick II inherited the fourth largest army in Europe and the richest treasury. He wasted no time in putting both to use. His two objectives were to acquire the Polish corridor of West Prussia that separated his German and Prussian territories and the agriculturally and industrially rich Austrian province of Silesia to the southeast of Berlin. Just months after his coronation, Frederick conquered Silesia, which soon came to dominate the Prussian economy.

It was Frederick's military prowess that earned him the title "the Great." However, his achievements went beyond the military arena. More than his father, Frederick II forged an alliance with the Prussian nobility, integrating the nobles into a unified state. A tightly organized central administration, which depended on the cooperation of the local nobility, directed both military and bureaucratic affairs. At the center, Frederick worked tirelessly to oversee his government. Whereas Louis XIV had proclaimed, "I am the state," Frederick the Great announced, "I am the first servant of the state." He codified the laws of Prussia, abolished torture and capital punishment, and instituted agricultural techniques imported from the states of western Europe. By the end of Frederick's reign, Prussia had become a model for bureaucratic organization, military reform, and enlightened rule.

Austria Survives

Austria was the great territorial victor in the War of the Spanish Succession, acquiring both the Netherlands and parts of Italy. Austrian forces recaptured a large part of Hungary from the Turks, thereby expanding Austria's territory to the south and the east. Charles VI (1711–1740), hereditary ruler of Austria and Bohemia, king of Hungary, and Holy Roman Emperor of the German nation, was recognized as one of Europe's most potent rulers—but appearances were deceptive. The apex of Austrian power and prestige had already passed, and Austria's rivals in eastern Europe, Russia, and Prussia were on the rise.

Decentralized Rule. The difficulties facing Austria ran deep. The Thirty Years' War had made the emperor more an Austrian monarch than an imperial German ruler. On the Austrian hereditary estates, the Catholic Counter-Reformation continued unabated, bringing with it the benefits of Jesuit education, cultural revival, and the religious unity that was necessary to motivate warfare against the Ottomans. But these benefits came at a price. Perhaps as many as 200,000 Protestants fled Austria and Bohemia, taking their skills and capital with them. For centuries the vision of empire had dominated Habsburg rule. This meant that the Austrian monarchy was a multiethnic confederation of relatively autonomous lands loosely tied together by loyalty to a single head. Hungary even elected the Habsburg emperor its king in a separate ceremony. Therefore it was hard for Austria to centralize in the same way as had Prussia.

Austria was predominantly rural and agricultural. Less than 5 percent of the population lived in towns of 10,000 or more; less than 15 percent lived in towns at all. The landed aristocracy exploited serfs to the maximum. Not only were serfs required to give labor service three days a week (and up to six days a week during planting and harvest times), but the nobility maintained a full array of feudal privileges, including the right to mill all grain and brew all beer. When serfs married, when they transferred property, even when they died, they paid taxes to their lord. As a result, they had little left to give the state. In consequence, the Austrian army was among the smallest and poorest of the major powers, despite the fact that it had the most active enemies along its borders.

Lack of finance, lack of human resources, and lack of governmental control were not the only problems facing Charles VI. With no sons to succeed him, Charles feared that his hereditary and elective states would go their separate ways after his death and that the great Habsburg monarchy would end. For 20 years, his abiding ambition was to gain recognition for the principle that his empire would pass intact to his daughter, Maria Theresa. He expressed the principle in a document known as the Pragmatic Sanction, which stated that all Habsburg lands would pass intact to the eldest heir, male or female. Charles VI made concession after concession to gain acceptance of the Pragmatic Sanction. But the leaders of Europe licked their lips at the prospect of a dismembered Austrian empire.

Maria Theresa. In 1740, soon after Maria Theresa (1740–1780) inherited the imperial throne, Frederick of Prussia invaded the rich Austrian province of Silesia and attracted allies for an assault on Vienna. Faced with Bavarian, Saxon, and Prussian armies, Maria Theresa appeared before the Hungarian estates, accepted their crown, and persuaded them to provide her with an army capable of halting the allied advance. Though she was unable to reconquer Silesia, Hungarian aid helped her to hold the line against her enemies.

Maria Theresa and her family. Eleven of Maria Theresa's 16 children are posed with the empress and her husband, Francis of Lorraine. Standing next to his mother is the future emperor Joseph II.

The loss of Silesia, the most prosperous part of the Austrian domains, signaled the need for fundamental reform. The new eighteenth-century idea of building a state replaced the traditional Habsburg concern with maintaining an empire. Maria Theresa and her son Joseph II (1780–1790) began the process of transformation. For Austria, state building meant first the reorganization of the military and civil bureaucracy to clear the way for fiscal reform. As in Prussia, a central directory was created to oversee the collection of taxes and the disbursement of funds. Maria Theresa personally persuaded her provincial estates both to increase taxation and to extend it to the nobles and the clergy. Although her success was limited, she finally established royal control over the raising and collection of taxes.

Maria Theresa also improved the condition of the Austrian peasantry. She established the doctrine that the "peasant must be able to support himself and his family and pay his taxes in time of peace and war." She limited labor service to two days per week and abolished the most burdensome feudal dues. Joseph II ended serfdom altogether. The new Austrian law codes guaranteed peasants' legal rights and established their ability to seek redress through the law. Joseph II hoped to extend reform even further. In the last years of his life, he abolished obligatory labor service and ensured that all peasants kept one-half of their income before paying local and state taxes. Such a radical reform met a storm of opposition and was abandoned at the end of Joseph's reign.

The reorganization of the bureaucracy, the increase in taxation, and the social reforms that created a more productive peasantry revitalized the Austrian state. The efforts of Maria Theresa and Joseph II to overcome provincial autonomy worked better in Austria and Bohemia than in Hungary. The Hungarians declined to contribute at all to state revenues, and Joseph II took the unusual step of refusing to be crowned king of Hungary so that he would not have to make any concessions to Hungarian autonomy. He even imposed a tariff on Hungarian goods sold in Austria. More seriously, parts of the empire had already been lost before the process of reform could begin. Prussia's seizure of Silesia was the hardest blow of all. Yet in 1740, when Frederick the Great and his allies had swept down from the north, few would have predicted that Austria would survive.

The Politics of Power

Frederick the Great's invasion of Silesia in 1740 was callous and cynical. Since the Pragmatic Sanction bound him to recognize Maria Theresa's succession, Frederick calculatingly offered her a defensive alliance in return for which she would simply hand over Silesia. It was an offer she should not have refused. Though Frederick's action initiated the War of the Austrian Succession, he was not alone in his desire to shake loose parts of Austria's territory. Soon nearly the entire Continent became embroiled in the conflict.

The War of the Austrian Succession. The War of the Austrian Succession (1740–1748) resembled a pack of wolves stalking its injured prey. It quickly became a major international conflict involving Prussia, France, and Spain on one side and Austria, Britain, and Holland on the other. Spain joined the fighting to recover its Italian possessions, Saxony claimed Moravia, France entered Bohemia, and the Bavarians moved into Austria from the south. With France and Prussia allied, it was vital that Britain join with Austria to maintain the balance of power. Initially, the British did little more than subsidize Maria Theresa's forces, but once France renewed its efforts to conquer the Netherlands, both Britain and the Dutch Republic joined in the fray.

That the British cared little about the fate of the Habsburg empire was clear from the terms of the treaty that they dictated at Aix-la-Chapelle (Aachen) in 1748. Austria recognized Frederick's conquest of Silesia as well as the loss of parts of its Italian territories to Spain. France, which the British had always regarded as the real enemy, withdrew from the Netherlands in return for the restoration of a number of colonial possessions. The War of the Austrian Succession made Austria and Prussia permanent enemies and gave Maria Theresa a crash course in international diplomacy. She learned firsthand that self-interest rather than loyalty underlay power politics.

The Seven Years' War. This lesson was reinforced in 1756, when Britain and Prussia entered into a military accord at the beginning of the Seven Years' War (1756–1763). Prussian expansion and duplicity had already alarmed both Russia and France, and Frederick II feared that he would be squeezed from both the east and the west. He could hardly expect help from Maria Theresa, so he made overtures to the British, whose interests in protecting Hanover, the hereditary estates of their German-born king, outweighed their prior commitments to Austria. Frederick's actions drove France into the arms of both the Austrians and the Russians, and an alliance that included the German state of Saxony was formed in defense. Thus was initiated a diplomatic revolution in which France and Austria became allies after 300 years as enemies.

Once again, Frederick the Great took the offensive, and once again, he won his risk against the odds. His attack on Saxony and Austria in 1756 brought a vigorous response from the Russians, who interceded on Austria's behalf with a massive army. Three years later, at the battle of Kunersdorf, Frederick suffered the worst military defeat of his career when the Russians shattered his armies. In 1760, his forces were barely one-third of the size of those massed by his opponents, and it was only a matter of time before he was fighting defensively from within Prussia.

In 1762, Russian empress Elizabeth died. She was succeeded by her nephew, the childlike Peter III, a German by birth who worshipped Frederick the Great. When Peter came to the throne, he immediately negotiated peace with Frederick, abandoning not only his allies but also the substantial territorial gains that the Russian forces had made within Prussia. It was small wonder that the Russian military leadership joined in the coup d'état that brought Peter's wife, Catherine, to the throne in 1762. With Russia out of the war, Frederick was able to fend off further Austrian offensives and to emerge with his state, including Silesia, intact.

The Seven Years' War did little to change the boundaries of the German states, but it had two important political results. The first was to establish beyond doubt the status of Prussia as a major power and a counterbalance to Austria in central Europe. The existence of the dual Germanies, one led by Prussia and the other by Austria, was to have serious consequences for German unification in the nineteenth century and the two world wars in the twentieth. The second result of the Seven Years' War was to initiate a long period of peace in eastern Europe. Both Prussia and Austria were financially exhausted from two decades of fighting. Both states needed a breathing spell to initiate administrative and economic improvements, and the period following the Seven Years' War witnessed the sustained programs of internal reforms for which Frederick the Great, Maria Theresa, and Joseph II were famous in the decades following 1763.

The Partitions of Poland. Peace among the eastern European powers did not mean that they abandoned their territorial ambitions. All over Europe, absolute rulers reformed their bureaucracies, streamlined their administrations, increased their sources of revenue, and built enormous standing armies—all over Europe except in Poland, that is. There, the autonomous power of the nobility remained as strong as ever. No monarchical dynasty was ever established, and each elected ruler not only confirmed the privileges of the nobility but usually was forced to extend them. In the Diet, the Polish representative assembly, small special-interest groups could bring legislative business to a halt by exercising their veto power. Given the size of Poland's borders, its army was pathetically inadequate, and

▲ This engraving by Le Mire is called "The Cake of the Kings: First Partition of Poland, 1773." The monarchs of Russia, Austria, and Prussia join in carving up Poland. The Polish king is clutching his tottering crown.

the Polish monarchy was helpless to defend its subjects from the destruction on all sides.

In 1764, Catherine the Great and Frederick the Great combined to place one of Catherine's former lovers on the Polish throne and to turn Poland into a weak dependent. Russia and Prussia had different interests in Poland's fate. For Russia, Poland represented a vast buffer state that kept the German powers at a distance from Russia's borders. It was more in Russia's interest to dominate Polish foreign policy than to conquer its territory. For Prussia, Poland looked like another helpless flower, "to be picked off leaf by leaf," as Frederick observed. Poland seemed especially appealing because Polish territory, including the Baltic port of Gdansk, separated the Prussian and Brandenburg portions of Frederick's state.

By the 1770s, the idea of carving up Poland was being actively discussed in Berlin, Saint Petersburg, and Vienna. In 1772, the three great eastern powers struck a deal. Russia would take a large swath of the grain fields of northeast Poland, which included over one million people; Frederick would unite his lands by seizing West Prussia; and Austria would gain both the largest territories, including Galicia, and the greatest number of people, nearly two million Polish subjects.

In half a century, the balance of power in central Europe had shifted decisively. Prussia's absorption of Silesia and parts of Poland made it a single geographical entity as well as a great economic and military power. Austria fought off an attempt to dismember its empire and went on to participate in the partition of Poland. From one empire there were now two states, and the relationship between Prussia and Austria would dominate central Europe for the next century.

THE GREATNESS OF GREAT BRITAIN

By the middle of the eighteenth century, Great Britain had become the leading power of Europe. It had won its spurs in Continental and colonial wars. Britain was unsurpassed as a naval power, able to protect its far-flung trading empire and to make a show of force in almost any part of the world. Perhaps more impressively, for a nation that did not support a large standing army, British soldiers had won decisive victories in the European land wars. Until the American Revolution, Britain came up a winner in every military venture it undertook. In addition, Britain enjoyed economic preeminence. British colonial possessions in the Atlantic and Indian Oceans poured consumer products into Britain for export to the European marketplaces. Growth in overseas trade was matched by growth in home production. British advances in agricultural technique had transformed Britain from an importer to an exporter of grain. The manufacturing industries that other European states attempted to create with huge government subsidies flourished in Britain through private enterprise.

British military and economic power was supported by a unique system of government. In Britain, the nobility served the state through government. The British constitutional system, devised in the seventeenth century and refined in the eighteenth, shared power between the monarchy and the ruling elite through the institution of Parliament. Central government integrated monarch and ministers with chosen representatives from the localities. Such integration not only provided the crown with the vital information it needed to formulate national policy, but also eased acceptance and enforcement of government decisions. Government was seen as the rule of law, which, however imperfect, was believed to operate for the benefit of all.

The parliamentary system gave Britain some of its particular strengths, but it also had some drawbacks. Politics was a national pastime rather than the business of an elite of administrators and state servants. Decentralization of decision making led to half-measures designed to placate competing interests. Appeals to public opinion, especially by candidates for Parliament, often played on fears and prejudices that divided rather than united the nation. Moreover, the relative openness of the British system hindered diplomatic and colonial affairs, in which secrecy and rapid changes of direction were often the monarch's most potent weapons. These weaknesses came to light most dramatically during the struggle for independence waged by Britain's North American colonists.

The British Constitution

The British Constitution was a patchwork of laws and customs that was gradually sewn together. Many of its greatest innovations came about through circumstance rather than design, and circumstance continued to play an essential role in its development in the eighteenth century. At the apex of the government stood the king, not an absolute monarch like his European counterparts, but not necessarily less powerful for having less arbitrary power. The British people revered monarchy and the monarch. The theory of mixed government depended on the balance of interests represented by the monarchy, the aristocracy in the House of Lords, and the people in the House of Commons. The monarch, as the actual and symbolic leader of the nation and the Supreme Head of the Church of England, was still regarded as divinely ordained and a special gift to the nation. Allegiance to the Anglican Church thus intensified allegiance to the king.

The partnership between the crown and the representative body was best expressed in the idea that the British government was composed of King-in-Parliament. Parliament consisted of three separate organs: monarch, lords, and commons. Though each existed separately as a check on the potential excesses of the others, parliamentary government could operate only when the three functioned together. The king was charged with selecting ministers, initiating policy, and supervising administration. The two houses of Parliament were charged with raising revenue, making laws, and presenting subjects' grievances to the crown.

The House of Commons had 558 members after the union with Scotland in 1707. Most members of the lower house were nominated to their seats. The largest number of seats were located in small towns, where a local oligarchy, or neighboring patron, had a customary right to make nominations that were invariably accepted by the electorate. Even in the largest cities, influential citizens made arrangements for nominating members in order to avoid the cost and confusion of an actual election. Campaigns were ruinously expensive for the candidates—an election in 1754 cost the losing candidates £40,000—and potentially dangerous to the local community, where bitter social and political divisions boiled just below the surface. (For a discussion of European culture and society in the eighteenth century, see Chapter 19.)

The British gentry dominated the Commons, occupying over 80 percent of the seats in any session. Most of these members also served as unpaid local officials in the counties, as justices of the peace, captains of the local militias, or collectors of local taxes. They came to Parliament not only as representatives of the interests of their class, but as experienced local governors who understood the needs of both crown and subject.

Nevertheless, the crown had to develop methods to coordinate the work of the two houses of Parliament and facilitate the passage of governmental programs. The king and his ministers began to use the deep royal pockets of offices and favors to bolster their friends in Parliament. Not only were those employed by the crown encouraged to find a place in the House of Commons, but those who had a place in Parliament were encouraged to take employment from the crown. Despite its potential for abuse, this was a political process that integrated center and locality, and at first it worked rather well. Men with local standing were brought into central offices, where they could influence central policymaking while protecting their local constituents. These officeholders, who came to be called *placemen,* never constituted a majority of the members of Parliament. They formed the core around which eighteenth-century governments operated, but it was a core that needed direction and cohesion. Such leadership and organization were the essential contribution of eighteenth-century politics to the British Constitution.

Parties and Ministers

Although parliamentary management was vital to the crown, it was not the crown that developed the basic tools of management. Rather, these techniques originated within the political community itself, and their usefulness was only slowly grasped by the monarchy. The first and, in the long term, most important tool was the party system. Political parties initially developed in the late seventeenth century around the issue of the Protestant succession. Those who opposed James II because he was a Catholic attempted to exclude him from inheriting the crown. They came to be called by their opponents Whigs, which meant "Scottish horse thieves." Those who supported James's hereditary rights but who also supported the Anglican Church came to be called by their opponents Tories, which meant "Irish cattle rustlers."

The Whigs supported a Protestant monarchy and a broad-based Protestantism. They attracted the allegiance of large numbers of dissenters, heirs to the Puritans of the seventeenth century who practiced forms of Protestantism different from that of the Anglican Church. The struggle between Whigs and Tories was less a struggle for power than one for loyalty to their opposing viewpoints. As the Tories tended to oppose the succession of Prince George of Hanover and the Whigs to support it, it was no mystery which party would find favor with George I (1714–1727). Moreover, as long as there was a pretender to the British throne—another rebellion took place in Scotland in 1745 led by the grandson of James II—the Tories continued to be tarred with the brush of disloyalty.

The division of political sympathies between Whigs and Tories helped to create a set of groupings to which parliamentary leadership could be applied. A national rather than a local or regional outlook could be used to organize support for royal policy as long as royal policy conformed to that national outlook. The ascendancy of the Whigs enabled George I and his son George II (1727–1760) to govern effectively through Parliament, but at the price of dependence on the Whig leaders. Though the monarch had the constitutional freedom to choose his ministers, realistically he could choose only Whigs and practically none but the Whig leaders of the House of Commons. Fortunately for the first two Georges, they found a man who was able to manage Parliament but desired only to serve the crown.

Sir Robert Walpole (1676–1745), who came from a gentry family in Norfolk, was an early supporter of the Hanoverian succession. Once George I was securely on the throne, Walpole became an indispensable leader of the House of Commons. An excellent public speaker, he relished long working days and the details of government, and he understood better than anyone else the intricacies of state finance. Walpole became First Lord of the Treasury, a post that he transformed into first minister of state. From his treasury post, Walpole assiduously built a Whig parliamentary party. He carefully dispensed jobs and offices, using them as bait to lure parliamentary supporters. Walpole's organization paid off both in the passage of legislation desired by the crown and at the polls, where Whigs were returned to Parliament time and again.

From 1721 to 1742, Walpole was the most powerful man in the British government. His long tenure in office was as much a result of his policies as of his methods of governing. He brought a measure of fiscal responsibility to government by establishing a fund to pay off the national debt. In foreign policy, he pursued peace with the same fervor that both his predecessors and his successors pursued war. The long years of peace brought prosperity to both the landed and merchant classes, but they also brought criticism of Walpole's methods. His use of government patronage to

▼ The First British Empire (ca. 1763). The empire was the result of commercial enterprise and Britain's military successes.

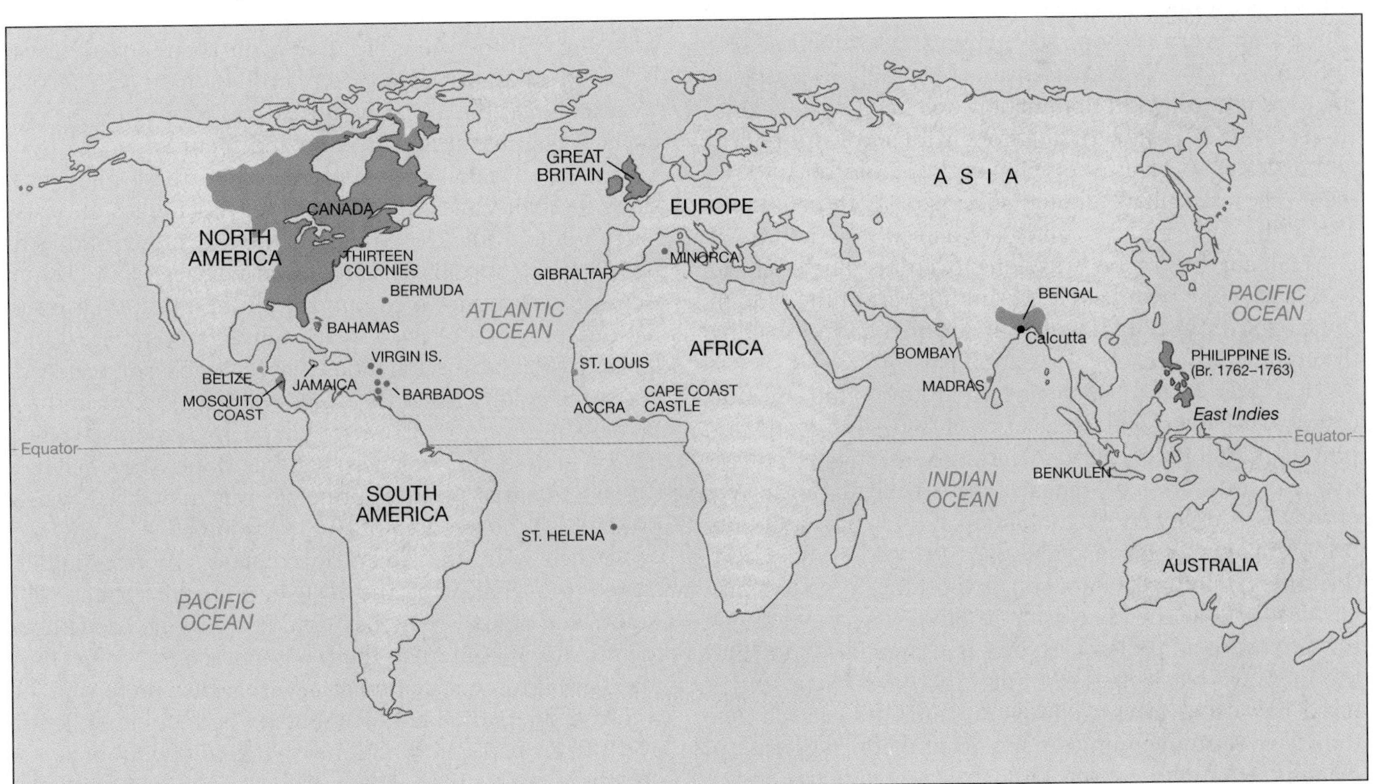

build his parliamentary party was attacked as corruption. So too were the ways in which the pockets of Whig officeholders were lined. During his last decade in office, Walpole struggled to survive. His attempt to extend the excise tax on colonial goods nearly led to his loss of office in 1733. His refusal to respond to the clamor for continued war with Spain in 1741 finally led to his downfall.

Walpole's 20-year rule established the pattern of parliamentary government. The crown needed a "prime" minister who was able to steer legislation through the House of Commons. It also needed a patronage broker who could take control of the treasury and dispense its largess in return for parliamentary backing. Walpole's personality and talents had combined these two roles. Thereafter, they were divided. Those who had grown up under Walpole had learned their lessons well. The Whig monopoly of power continued unchallenged for nearly another 20 years. The patronage network that Walpole had created was vastly extended by his Whig successors. Even minor posts in the customs or the excise offices were exchanged for political favor, and only those approved by the Whig leadership could claim them. The cries of corruption grew louder, and in London a popular radicalism developed in opposition to the Whig oligarchy. The outcry was taken up as well in the North American colonies, where two million British subjects champed at the bit of imperial rule.

CHRONOLOGY

THE NEW EUROPEAN POWERS

1707	England and Scotland unite to form Great Britain
1713–1714	Peace of Utrecht ends War of the Spanish Succession (1702–1714)
1714	British crown passes to House of Hanover
1721	Treaty of Nystad ends Great Northern War (1700–1721)
1721–1742	Sir Robert Walpole leads British House of Commons
1722	Peter the Great of Russia creates Table of Ranks
1740	Frederick the Great of Prussia invades Austrian province of Silesia
1748	Treaty of Aix-la-Chapelle ends War of the Austrian Succession (1740–1748)
1756–1763	Seven Years' War pits Prussia and Britain against Austria, France, and Russia
1773–1775	Pugachev's Revolt in Russia
1774	Boston Tea Party
1775	American Revolution begins
1785	Catherine the Great of Russia issues Charter of the Nobility

America Revolts

Britain's triumph in the Seven Years' War (1756–1763) had come at great financial cost to the nation. At the beginning of the eighteenth century, the national debt stood at £14 million; by 1763 it had risen to £130 million. Then, as now, the cost of world domination was staggering. George III (1760–1820) came to the throne with a taste for reform and a desire to break the Whig stranglehold on government. He was to have limited success on both counts. In 1763, the king and his ministers agreed that reform of colonial administration was long overdue. Such reform would have the twin benefit of shifting part of the burden of taxation from Britain to North America and of making the commercial side of colonization pay.

This was sound thinking all around, and in due course, Parliament passed a series of duties on goods imported into the colonies, including glass, wine, coffee, tea, and most notably sugar. The so-called Sugar Act (1764) was followed by the Stamp Act (1765), a tax on printed papers such as newspapers, deeds, and court documents. Both acts imposed taxes in the colonies similar to those that already existed in Britain. Accompanying the acts were administrative orders designed to cut into the lucrative black market trade. The government instituted new rules for searching ships and transferred authority over smuggling from the local colonial courts to Britain's Admiralty courts. Though British officials could only guess at the value of the new duties imposed, it was believed that with effective enforcement, £150,000 would be raised. All this would go toward paying the vast costs of colonial administration and security.

British officials were perplexed when these mild measures met with a ferocious response. Assemblies of nearly every colony officially protested the Sugar Act and petitioned for its repeal. Riots followed passage of the Stamp Act. Tax collectors were hounded out of office, their resignations precipitated by threats and acts of physical violence. In Massachusetts, mobs that included political leaders in the colony razed the homes of the collector and the lieutenant-governor. However much the colonists might have regretted the violence that was done, they believed that an essential political principle was at stake. It was a principle of the freedom of an Englishman.

At their core, the American colonists' protests underscored the vitality of the British political system. The Americans argued that they could not be taxed without their consent and that their consent could come only through representation in Parliament. Since there were no colonists in Parliament, Parliament had no jurisdiction over the property of the colonists. Taxation without representation was tyranny. There were a number of subtleties to this argument that were quickly lost as political rhetoric and political action heated up. First, the colonists did tax themselves through their own legislatures, and much of that money paid the costs of administration and defense. Second, as a number of pamphleteers pointed out, no one in the colonies had asked the British government to send regiments of the army into North America. The colonists had little reason to put their faith in British protection. Hard-fought colonial victories were tossed away at European negotiating tables, while the British policy of defending Indian rights in the Ohio Valley ran counter to the settlers' interests. When defense was necessary, the colonists had proven themselves both able and cooperative in providing it. A permanent tax meant a permanent army, and a standing army was as loathed in the colonies as it was in Britain.

The passion generated in the colonies over the issue of taxation without parliamentary representation was probably no greater than that generated in Britain. For the British, the principle at issue was parliamentary sovereignty. Once the terms of debate had been so defined, it was difficult for either side to find a middle ground.

Parliamentary moderates managed repeal of the Stamp Act and most of the clauses of the Sugar Act, but they also joined in passing the Declaratory Act (1766), which stated unequivocally that Parliament held sovereign jurisdiction over the colonies "in all cases whatsoever." This claim became more and more difficult to sustain as colonial leaders began to cite the elements of resistance theory that had justified the Revolution of 1688. Then the protest had been against the tyranny of the king; now it was against the tyranny of Parliament. American propagandists claimed that a conspiracy existed to deprive the colonists of their property and rights, to enslave them for the benefit of special interests and corrupt politicians.

The techniques of London radicals who opposed parliamentary policy were adopted by colonists. Newspapers were used to whip up public support; boycotts brought ordinary people into the political arena; public demonstrations such as the Boston Tea Party (1774) were carefully designed to intimidate; and mobs were occasionally given free rein. Though the government had faced down these tactics when they were used in London to support John Wilkes (1725–1797), an ardent critic of royal policy, they were less successful when the crisis lay an ocean away. In 1770, British troops fired on a Boston mob and provided American propagandists with empirical evidence that Britain intended to enslave the colonies. Violence was met by violence, and in 1775, full-scale fighting was under way. Eight years later, Britain withdrew from a war it could not win, and the American colonies were left to govern themselves.

Conclusion

BY THE END OF THE THIRD QUARTER OF THE EIGHTEENTH CENTURY, Europe had a new political configuration. A continent that had once been dominated by a single power—Spain in the sixteenth century and France in the seventeenth—was now dominated by a state system in which alliances among several great powers held the balance. Despite the loss of its American colonies, Great Britain had proved to be the most potent of the states. Its victories over the French in the Seven Years' War and over France and Prussia in the War of the Austrian Succession secured its position. However, this position could be maintained only through alliances with the German states, either Prussia or Austria. The rise of Prussia provided a counterweight to French domination of the Continent. Though these two states became allies in the middle of the century, the ambitions of their rulers made them natural enemies, and it would not be long before French and Prussian armies were again pitted against each other. France, still the wealthiest and most populous of European states, had slumbered through the eighteenth-century reorganization. The legacies of Louis XIV took a long time to reach fruition. He had claimed glory for his state, giving the French people a sense of national identity and national destiny but causing enormous social and economic dislocation. Thus the mid-eighteenth century was to be an age of the greatest literary and philosophical achievement for France, but the late eighteenth century was to witness the greatest social upheaval that Europe had ever known.

QUESTIONS FOR REVIEW

1. What were the great powers of Europe in the eighteenth century and in what ways was there a "balance of power" among them?
2. What did Peter I and Catherine II of Russia accomplish during their reigns that justifies the title "the Great"?
3. How was the tiny state of Brandenburg-Prussia able to make itself into one of Europe's major powers, and what did that mean for the Austrian empire?
4. How did Britain's theory of mixed government and its parliamentary party system assist its rise to become Europe's great imperial power?
5. How and why did the "balance of power" shift during the eighteenth century?

DISCOVERING WESTERN CIVILIZATION ONLINE

You can obtain more information about the balance of power in eighteenth-century Europe at the websites listed below. See also the companion website that accompanies this text: www.ablongman.com/kishlansky, which contains on online study guide and additional resources.

The Rise of Russia

www.english.upenn.edu/~jlynch/FrankenDemo/Places/russia.html

A site detailing the history of Russia from the time of Peter the Great. Includes links to the building of St. Petersburg.

www.fordham.edu/halsall/mod/18catherine.html

A site providing sources from the reign of Catherine the Great.

The Two Germanies

www.hfac.uh.edu/gbrown/philosophers/leibniz/FriedrichGreat/FriedrichGreat.html

A hyper-linked biographical essay on Frederick the Great of Prussia.

The Greatness of Great Britain

www.revolution.h-net.msu.edu/

A site with extensive links to all aspects of the American Revolution.

www.loc.gov/exhibits/declara/declara1.html

An online exhibit at the Library of Congress on the drafting of the Declaration of Independence.

SUGGESTIONS FOR FURTHER READING

General Reading

M. S. Anderson, *War and Society in Europe of the Old Regime, 1618–1789,* 2d ed. (Montreal: McGill-Queen's University Press, 1998). A brief survey of the military history of the period.

Olwen Hufton, *Europe: Privilege and Protest, 1730–1789* (Ithaca, N.Y.: Cornell University Press, 1980). An excellent survey of the political and social history of the mid-eighteenth century.

David Kirby, *Northern Europe in the Early Modern Period* (London: Longman, 1991). Political history from a Baltic perspective, with excellent chapters on Sweden and Russia.

Geographical Tour: Europe in 1714

Derek McKay and H. M. Scott, *The Rise of the Great Powers* (London: Longman, 1983). An outstanding survey of diplomacy and warfare.

The Rise of Russia

M. S. Anderson, *Peter the Great* (London: Thames and Hudson, 1978). A well-constructed, comprehensive biography.

Isabel de Madariaga, *Catherine the Great, a Short History* (New Haven, Conn.: Yale University Press, 1990). The best brief life.

David Longley, *The Longman Companion to Imperial Russia, 1689–1917* (New York: Longman, 2000). A useful reference text with biographical and topical entries.

The Two Germanies

Reed S. Browning, *The War of Austrian Succession* (London: Macmillan, 1995). A comprehensive history of a complicated event.

David Fraser, *Frederick the Great: King of Prussia* (New York: Allen Lane, 2001). The latest biography.

J. Gagliardo, *Germany Under the Old Regime* (London: Longman, 1991). The best single-volume history.

C. A. Macartney, *Maria Theresa and the House of Austria* (Mystic, Conn.: Verry Inc., 1969). Still the best introductory study.

The Greatness of Great Britain

Bernard Bailyn, *The Ideological Origins of the American Revolution* (Cambridge, Mass.: Harvard University Press, 1967). A brilliant interpretation of the underlying causes of the break between Britain and the North American colonies.

John Brewer, *The Sinews of Power: War, Money and the English State, 1688–1783* (Cambridge, Mass.: Harvard University Press, 1990). An influential and clearly written book on the fiscal and military innovations that underwrote English power in the eighteenth century.

J. C. D. Clark, *English Society, 1688–1832* (Cambridge: Cambridge University Press, 1985). A bold reinterpretation of the most important features of English society.

Linda Colley, *Britons* (New Haven, Conn.: Yale University Press, 1992). A lively account of how a nation was forged from Welsh, Scots, and English and how unity and diversity intermixed.

Paul Langford, *A Polite and Commercial People: England 1727–1783* (Oxford: Oxford University Press, 1989). The standard survey in the Oxford history series.

CHAPTER 19

CULTURE AND SOCIETY IN EIGHTEENTH-CENTURY EUROPE

THE VISUAL RECORD

HAPPY FAMILIES

"HAPPY FAMILIES ARE ALL ALIKE," wrote Lev Tolstoy in the nineteenth century, when the idea of a happy family was already a cliché. Such an idea would never have occurred to his eighteenth-century forebears. For them the happy family was doubly new—new in the change in the relationships within the family and new in the stress on happiness itself. Personal happiness was an invention of the Enlightenment, the result of novel attitudes about human aspirations and human capabilities. "Happiness is a new idea in Europe," wrote Louis de Saint-Just (1767–1794). It emerged in response to the belief that what was good brought pleasure and what was evil brought pain. Happiness, both individual and collective, became the yardstick by which life was measured. This meant a reorientation in personal conduct and, most of all, a reorientation of family life. Especially for people with an economic cushion, a pleasurable family life was essential. Husbands and wives were to become companions, filled with romantic love for each other and devoted to domestic bliss. Children were to be doted on, treated not as miniature adults to be lectured and beaten, but as unfilled vessels into which all that was good was to be poured.

Were ever a couple more in love than the husband and wife depicted in *A Visit to the Wet Nurse* by Jean-Honoré Fragonard (1732–1806)? The man clasps his wife's arm to his cheek, she lays her hand on his shoulder. Their sighs are almost audible! Together, they admire the fruit of their love: the baby asleep in the cradle. They have come together to see how the wet nurse is caring for their child. Doubtless it was they who provided the rather opulent bassinet, which contrasts sharply with the other furniture in the room, and the linens and pillows into which the baby has nestled.

At the beginning of the eighteenth century, the use of a wet nurse was still common among the families of the French bourgeoisie, the class to which this couple—judging from their clothes—undoubtedly belongs. As time moved on, however, more and more mothers began to nurse their babies themselves. In part, this change was a response to the higher mortality rate among infants sent out to wet nurses. The unsanitary environment of the towns ran a close race with the neglect that many wet nurses showed their charges. But a wet nurse who could

be supervised, that is, one who lived near enough to be visited but far enough away from the town to enjoy wholesome air, might be the best of both worlds.

But there are two families in this picture, and they are hardly alike. At first glance, the wet nurse looks like an old woman. It is shocking to realize that she cannot be much older than thirty, an age beyond which wealthy families would not hire her for fear either that she would not have much milk or that it would be sour. The two younger children are undoubtedly hers, the youngest probably just weaned so that all of her milk would go to the baby. The wet nurse also spins to earn a little extra.

LOOKING AHEAD

Like much else in the eighteenth century, the world of the family was divided between high and low. As we shall see in this chapter, it was developments in the middle that were most characteristic of eighteenth-century social and cultural developments. The spirit of Enlightenment was spreading from the elites throughout all social ranks, improving education, health, and social welfare. The rapid growth of the bourgeoisie, or the middle class, enhanced the quality of life for tens of thousands and transformed values in the most basic institutions of society.

EIGHTEENTH-CENTURY CULTURE

The eighteenth century spawned a rich and costly culture. Decorative architecture, especially interior design, reflected the increasing sociability of the aristocracy. Entertainment, especially music, became a central part of aristocratic culture. The string quartet made its first appearance in the eighteenth century, and chamber music enjoyed unparalleled popularity.

Musical entertainments in European country houses were matched by the literary and philosophical entertainments of the urban salons. The salons, especially in Paris, blended the aristocracy and bourgeoisie with the leading intellectuals of the age. At formal meetings, papers on scientific or philosophical topics were read and discussed. At informal gatherings, new ideas were examined and exchanged. The most influential thinkers of the day presented the ideas of the Enlightenment, a new European outlook on religion, society, and politics.

The Enlightenment

The Enlightenment was less a set of ideas than it was a set of attitudes. At its core was a critical questioning of traditional institutions, customs, and morals. In 1762, the French philosopher Jean-Jacques Rousseau (1712–1778) published one of the most important works on social theory, *The Social Contract,* which opened with the gripping maxim "Man is born free and everywhere he is in chains." But most of the great thinkers of the Enlightenment were not so much philosophers as savants, knowledgeable popularizers whose skills were in simplifying and publicizing a hodgepodge of new views.

In France, Enlightenment intellectuals were called *philosophes* and claimed all the arts and sciences as their purview. *The Encyclopedia* (35 volumes, 1751–1780), edited by Denis Diderot (1713–1784), was one of the greatest achievements of the age. Entitled the *Systematic Dictionary of the Sciences, Arts, and Crafts,* it attempted to summarize all acquired knowledge and to dispel all imposed superstitions. There was no better definition of a philosophe than that given to them by one of their enemies: "Just what is a philosophe? A kind of monster in society who feels under no obligation towards its manners and morals, its proprieties, its politics, or its religion. One may expect anything from men of their ilk."

The Enlightenment was by no means a strictly French phenomenon. Its greatest figures included the Scottish economist Adam Smith (1723–1790), the Italian legal reformer Cesare Beccaria (1738–1794), and the German philosopher Immanuel Kant (1724–1804). In France it began among antiestablishment critics; in Scotland and the German states it flourished in the universities; and in Prussia, Austria, and Russia it was propagated by the monarchy. The Enlightenment began in the 1730s and was still going strong a half-century later, when its attitudes had been absorbed into the mainstream of European thought.

No brief summary can do justice to the diversity of enlightened thought in eighteenth-century Europe. Because it was an attitude of mind rather than a set of shared beliefs, there are many contradictory strains to follow. In his famous essay *What Is Enlightenment?* (1784), Immanuel Kant described it simply as freedom to use one's own intelligence. "I hear people clamor on all sides: Don't argue! The officer says: Don't argue, drill! The tax collector says: Don't argue, pay. The pastor says: Don't argue, believe." To all of them, Kant replied: "Dare to know! Have the courage to use your own intelligence."

The Spirit of the Enlightenment

In 1734 a small book entitled *Philosophical Letters Concerning the English Nation* appeared in France. Its author, Voltaire (1694–1778), who had spent two years in Britain, demonstrated again and again the superiority of the British. They practiced religious toleration and were not held under the sway of a venal clergy. They valued people for their merits rather than their birth. Their political constitution was a marvel—"The English nation is the only one on earth that has succeeded in controlling the power of kings by resisting them." They made national heroes of their scientists, poets, and philosophers. In all of this, Voltaire contrasted British virtue with French vice. He attacked the French clergy and nobility directly and the French monarchy implicitly. Not only did he praise the genius and accomplishments of Sir Isaac Newton above those of René Descartes, but he also graphically contrasted the Catholic Church's persecution of Descartes with the British state's celebration of Newton.

Voltaire. In France, Voltaire's book *Philosophical Letters* was officially banned and publicly burned, and a warrant was issued for his arrest. The *Philosophical Letters* dropped like a bombshell on the moribund intellectual culture of the Church and the universities and burst open the complacent, self-satisfied Cartesian world view. The book ignited a movement that would soon spread to nearly every corner of Europe.

Born in Paris in 1694 into a bourgeois family with court office, François-Marie Arouet, who later took the pen name Voltaire, was educated by the Jesuits, who encouraged his poetic talents and instilled in him an enduring love of literature. He was a difficult student, especially as he had already rejected the core of the Jesuits' religious doctrine. He was no less difficult as he grew and began a career as a poet and playwright. It was not long before he was imprisoned in the Bastille for penning verses that maligned the honor of the

▲ During the Enlightenment, salons showcased the most influential thinkers of the day. Here, a lecture is being given at the house of Madame Geoffrin.

regent of France. When released from prison, he insulted a nobleman, who retaliated by having his servants publicly beat Voltaire. Voltaire issued a challenge for a duel, a greater insult than the first, given his low birth. He was again sent to the Bastille and was released only on the promise that he would leave the country immediately.

Thus Voltaire found himself in Britain, where he spent two years learning English and writing plays. When he returned to Paris in 1728, it was with the intention of popularizing Britain to Frenchmen. He wrote and produced a number of plays and began writing the *Philosophical Letters,* a work that not only secured his reputation but also forced him into exile at the village of Cirey, where he moved in with the Marquise du Châtelet (1706–1749).

The Marquise du Châtelet, though only 27 at the time of her liaison with Voltaire, was one of the leading advocates of Newtonian science in France. She built a laboratory in her home and introduced Voltaire to experimental science. While she undertook the immense challenge of translating Newton into French, Voltaire worked on innumerable projects: poems, plays, philosophical and antireligious tracts (which she wisely kept him from publishing), and histories. It was one of the most productive periods of his life, and when the Marquise du Châtelet died in 1749, Voltaire was crushed.

Then older than 50, Voltaire began his travels. He was invited to Berlin by Frederick the Great, but the relationship between these two great egotists was predictably stormy and resulted in Voltaire's arrest in Frankfurt. Finally allowed to leave Prussia, Voltaire eventually settled in Geneva, where he quickly became embroiled in local politics and was asked to leave.

Voltaire was tired of wandering and tired of being chased. He was also deeply affected by the tragic earthquake in Lisbon in 1755, when thousands of people attending church services were killed. Optimism in the face of such a senseless tragedy was no longer possible. His black mood was revealed in *Candide* (1759), which was to become his enduring legacy. *Candide* introduced the ivory-tower intellectual Dr. Pangloss, the overly optimistic Candide, and the very practical philosophy "We must cultivate our own garden."

Voltaire's greatest contribution to Enlightenment attitudes was probably his capacity to challenge all authority.

He held nothing sacred. He questioned his own paternity and the morals of his mother; he lived openly with the Marquise du Châtelet and her husband; and he spoke as slightingly of kings and aristocrats as he did of his numerous critics. At the height of the French Revolution, Voltaire's body was removed from its resting place in Champagne and taken with great pomp to Paris and interred in the Pantheon, where the heroes of the nation were put to rest. "Voltaire taught us to be free" was the slogan that the Parisian masses chanted during the funeral procession. It was an ending that was perhaps too solemn and conventional for one as irreverent as Voltaire. When the monarchy was restored after 1815, his bones were unceremoniously dumped in a lime pit.

Hume. Some enlightened thinkers based their critical outlook on skepticism, the belief that nothing could be known for certain. When the Scottish philosopher David Hume (1711–1776) was accused of being an atheist, he countered the charge by saying that he was too skeptical to be certain that God did not exist. Hume's first major philosophical work, *A Treatise of Human Nature* (1739), made absolutely no impression on his contemporaries. Hume worked as a merchant's clerk, a tutor, and finally a private secretary. During these years he continued to write, publishing a series of essays on the subject of morality and rewriting his treatise into *An Enquiry Concerning Human Understanding* (1748), his greatest philosophical work.

Hume made two seminal contributions to Enlightenment thought. He exploded the synthesis of Descartes by arguing that neither matter nor mind could be proved to exist with any certainty. Only perceptions existed, either as impressions of material objects or as ideas. If human understanding was based on sensory perception rather than on reason, then there could be no certainty in the universe. Hume's second point launched a frontal attack on established religion. If there could be no certainty, then the revealed truths of Christian religion could have no basis. In his historical analysis of the origins of religion, Hume argued that "religion grows out of hope or fear." He attacked the core of Christian explanations that were based on either Providence or miracles by arguing that for anyone who understood the basis of human perception, it would take a miracle to believe in miracles.

Montesquieu. In 1749, Hume received in the mail a work from an admiring Frenchman, entitled *The Spirit of the Laws*. The sender was Charles-Louis de Secondat, Baron Montesquieu (1689–1755). Born in Bordeaux, he ultimately inherited both a large landed estate and the office of president of the Parlement of Bordeaux. His novel *Persian Letters* (1721) was a brilliant satire of Parisian morals, French society, and European religion all bound together by the story of a Persian despot who leaves his harem to learn about the ways of the world. The use of the Persian outsider allowed Montesquieu to comment on the absurdity of European customs in general and French practices in particular. The device of the harem allowed him to titillate his audience with exotic sexuality.

After this success, Montesquieu decided to sell his office and make the grand tour. He spent nearly two years in England, for which, like Voltaire, he came to have the greatest admiration. Back in Bordeaux, Montesquieu began to assemble his thoughts for a work of political theory. The two societies that he most admired were those of ancient Rome and present-day Britain, and he studied the forms of their government and the principles that animated them. *The Spirit of the Laws* was published in 1748, and despite its gargantuan size and densely packed examples, it was immediately recognized as a masterpiece. Catherine the Great of Russia kept it at her bedside, and it was the single most influential work for the framers of the United States Constitution.

In both *Persian Letters* and *The Spirit of the Laws*, Montesquieu explored how liberty could be achieved and despotism avoided. He divided all forms of government into republics, monarchies, and despotisms. Each form had its own peculiar spirit: virtue and moderation in republics, honor in monarchies, and fear in despotisms. Like each form, each spirit was prone to abuse and had to be restrained if republics were not to give way to vice and excess, monarchies to corruption, and despotisms to repression. Montesquieu classified regimes as either moderate or immoderate and, through the use of extensive historical examples, attempted to demonstrate how moderation could be maintained through rules and restraints, through the spirit of the law.

For Montesquieu, a successful government was one in which powers were separated and checks and balances existed within the institutions of the state. As befitted a provincial magistrate, he insisted on the absolute separation of the judiciary from all other branches of government. The law needed to be independent, impartial, and just. Montesquieu advocated that law codes be reformed and reduced mainly to regulate crimes against persons and property. Punishment should fit the crime but should be humane. Montesquieu was one of the first to advocate the abolition of torture. Like most Europeans of his age, he saw monarchy as the only realistic form of government, but he argued that for a monarchy to be successful, it needed a strong and independent aristocracy to restrain its tendency toward corruption and despotism. He based his arguments on the example of Britain, which he praised as the only state in Europe in which liberty resided.

Enlightened Education and Social Reform. Enlightened thinkers attacked established institutions, above all the Church. Most were deists who believed in the existence of God on rational grounds only. Following the materialistic ideas of the new science, deists believed that nature conformed to its own material laws and operated without divine intervention. God, in a popular Enlightenment image, was like a clockmaker who constructed the elaborate mechanism, wound it, and gave the pendulum its first swing. After that, the clock worked by itself. Deists were accused of being anti-Christian, and they certainly opposed the ritual forms of both Catholic and Protestant worship as well as the role of the Church in education, for education was the key to an enlightened view of the future.

Jean-Jacques Rousseau attacked the educational system. His tract on education, disguised as the romantic novel *Émile* (1762), argued that children should be taught by appealing to their interests rather than with strict discipline. Education was crucial because the Enlightenment was dominated by the idea of the British philosopher John Locke (1632–1704) that the mind was blank at birth, a *tabula rasa*—"white paper void of all characters"—and that it was filled up by experience. Contrary to the arguments of Descartes, Locke wrote, in *An Essay Concerning Human Understanding* (1690), that there were no innate ideas and no good or evil that was not conditioned by experience. For Locke, as for a host of thinkers after him, good and evil were defined as pleasure and pain. We do good because it is pleasurable, and we avoid evil because it is painful. Morality was a sense experience rather than a theological one. It was also relative rather than absolute. This was an observation that derived from increased interest in non-European cultures. Baron Montesquieu's *Persian Letters* was the most popular novel of a genre that described non-European societies that knew nothing of Christian morality.

By the middle of the eighteenth century, the pleasure/pain principle enunciated by Locke had come to be applied to the foundations of social organization. If personal good was pleasure, then social good was happiness. The object of government, in the words of the Scottish moral philosopher Francis Hutcheson (1694–1746), was "the greatest happiness of the greatest number." This principle was at the core of *Crimes and Punishments* (1764), Cesare Beccaria's pioneering work of legal reform. Laws were instituted to promote happiness within society. They had to be formulated equitably for both criminal and victim. Punishment was to act as a deterrent to crime rather than as retribution. Therefore Beccaria advocated the abolition of torture to gain confessions, the end of capital punishment, and the rehabilitation of criminals through the improvement of penal institutions. By 1776, happiness was established as one of the basic "rights of man," enshrined in the American Declaration of Independence as "life, liberty, and the pursuit of happiness."

It was in refashioning the world through education and social reform that the Enlightenment revealed its orientation toward the future. "Optimism" was a word invented in the eighteenth century to express this feeling of liberation from the weight of centuries of traditions. "This is the best of all possible worlds and all things turn out for the best" was the satirical slogan of Voltaire's Candide. But if Voltaire believed that enlightened thinkers had taken optimism too far, others believed that it had to be taken further still.

Progress, an idea that not all enlightened thinkers shared, was another invention of the age. It was expressed most cogently by the French philosopher the Marquis de Condorcet (1743–1794) in *The Progress of the Human Mind* (1795), in which he developed an almost evolutionary view of human development from a savage state of nature to a future of harmony and international peace.

CHRONOLOGY

MAJOR WORKS OF THE ENLIGHTENMENT

1690	*An Essay Concerning Human Understanding* (Locke)
1721	*Persian Letters* (Baron Montesquieu)
1734	*Philosophical Letters Concerning the English Nation* (Voltaire)
1739	*A Treatise of Human Nature* (Hume)
1740	*Pamela* (Richardson)
1748	*An Enquiry Concerning Human Understanding* (Hume); *The Spirit of the Laws* (Baron Montesquieu)
1751–1780	*Encyclopedia* (Diderot)
1759	*Candide* (Voltaire)
1762	*Émile; The Social Contract* (Rousseau)
1764	*Crimes and Punishments* (Beccaria)
1784	*What Is Enlightenment?* (Kant)
1795	*The Progress of the Human Mind* (Marquis de Condorcet)
1798	*An Essay on the Principles of Population* (Malthus)

The Impact of the Enlightenment

The influence of Enlightenment ideas was felt everywhere, even seeping to the lowest strata of society. Paradoxically, enlightened political reform took firmer root in eastern Europe, where the ideas were imported, than in western Europe, where they originated. It was absolute rulers who were most successful in borrowing Enlightenment reforms.

Enlightened ideas informed the eastern European reform movement that began around mid-century, especially in the areas of law, education, and the extension of religious toleration. Law reforms were influenced by the works of Montesquieu and Beccaria. In Prussia and Russia, the movement to codify and simplify the legal system did not reach fruition in the eighteenth century, but in both places it was well under way. The Prussian jurist Samuel von Cocceji (1679–1755) initiated the reform of Prussian law and legal administration. Cocceji's project was to make the enforcement of law uniform throughout the realm, to prevent judicial corruption, and to produce a single code of Prussian law. The code, finally completed in the 1790s, reflected the principles of criminal justice articulated by Beccaria. In Russia, the Law Commission summoned by Catherine the Great in 1767 never did complete its work. Nevertheless, profoundly influenced by Montesquieu, Catherine attempted to abolish torture and to introduce the Beccarian principle that the accused was innocent until proven guilty. In Austria, Joseph II presided over a wholesale reorganization of the legal system. Courts were centralized, laws were codified, and torture and capital punishment were abolished.

Enlightenment ideas also underlay the efforts to improve education in eastern Europe. The religious orders, especially the Jesuits, were the most influential educators of the age, and the Enlightenment attack on them created a void that had to be filled by the state. Efforts at compulsory education were first undertaken in Russia under Peter the Great, but these were aimed at the compulsory education of the nobility. Catherine extended the effort to the provinces, attempting to educate a generation of Russian teachers. She was especially eager for women to receive primary schooling, although the prejudice against educating women was too strong to overcome. Austrian and Prussian reforms were more successful in extending the reach of primary education, even if its content remained weak.

Religious toleration was the area in which the Enlightenment had its greatest impact in Europe, though again this was most visible in the eastern countries. Freedom of worship for Catholics was barely whispered about in Britain, and neither France nor Spain was moved to tolerate Protestants. Nevertheless, within these parameters there were some important changes in the religious makeup of the western European states. In Britain, Protestant dissenters were no longer persecuted for their beliefs. By the end of the eighteenth century, the number of Protestants outside the Church of England was growing, and by the early nineteenth century, discrimination against such Protestants was all but eliminated. In France and Spain, relations between the national church and the papacy were undergoing a reorientation. Both states were asserting more independence—both theologically and financially—from Rome. The shift was symbolized by disputes over the role of the Jesuits, who were finally expelled from France in 1764 and from Spain in 1767.

In eastern Europe, enlightened ideas about religious toleration did take effect. Catherine the Great abandoned persecution of a Russian Orthodox sect known as the Old Believers. Prussia had always tolerated various Protestant groups, and with the conquest of Silesia it acquired a large Catholic population. Catholics were guaranteed freedom of worship; Frederick the Great even built a Catholic church in Berlin to symbolize this policy. Austria extended enlightened ideas about toleration furthest. Maria Theresa was a devout Catholic and actually increased religious persecution in her realm, but Joseph II rejected his mother's dogmatic position. In 1781, he issued the Patent of Toleration, which granted freedom of worship to Protestants and members of the Eastern Orthodox church. The following year he extended this toleration to Jews. Joseph's attitude toward toleration was as practical as it was enlightened. He believed that the revocation of the Edict of Nantes—which had granted limited toleration to Protestants—at the end of the seventeenth century had been an economic disaster for France, and he encouraged religious toleration as a means to economic progress.

Joseph's belief that religious toleration could promote economic progress was in keeping with the ferment of new ideas on economics in Europe. A science of economics was first articulated during the Enlightenment. A group of French thinkers known as the physiocrats subscribed to the view that land was wealth and thus argued that agricultural activity, especially improved means of farming and livestock breeding, should take first priority in state reforms. Because wealth came from land, taxation should be based only on land ownership, a principle that was coming into increased prominence, despite the opposition of the landowning class. Physiocratic ideas combined a belief in the sanctity of private property with the need for the state to increase agricultural output. Ultimately, the physiocrats, like the great Scottish economic theorist Adam Smith, came to believe that government should cease to interfere with private economic activity. They articulated the doctrine *laissez faire, laissez passer*—"let it be, let it go." The ideas of Adam Smith and the physiocrats ultimately formed the basis for nineteenth-century economic reform.

If the Enlightenment did not initiate a new era, it did offer a new vision, whether in Hume's psychology, Montesquieu's political science, Rousseau's sociology, or Smith's economic theory. All of these subjects, which have had such a powerful impact on contemporary life, had their modern origins in the Enlightenment. As the British poet Alexander Pope (1688–1744) put it, "Know then thyself, presume not God to scan / The proper study of mankind is man." Enlightened thinkers challenged existing ideas and existing institutions. A new emphasis on self and on pleasure led to a new emphasis on happiness. All three fed into the distinctively Enlightenment idea of self-interest. Happiness and self-interest were values that would inevitably corrode the old social order, which was based on principles of self-sacrifice and corporate identity. It was only a matter of time.

EIGHTEENTH-CENTURY SOCIETY

Eighteenth-century society was a hybrid of old and new. It remained highly stratified socially, politically, and economically. Birth and occupation determined wealth, privilege, and quality of life as much as they had in the past. But in the eighteenth century the gulf between top and bottom was being filled by a thriving middle class, a *bourgeoisie*, as they were called in France. There were now more paths toward the middle and upper classes and more wealth to be distributed among people living above the level of subsistence, but at the top of society the nobility remained the privileged order in every European state.

The Nobility

Nobles were defined by their legal rights. They had the right to bear arms, the right to special judicial treatment, and the right to tax exemptions. In Russia, only nobles could own serfs; in Poland, only nobles could hold government office. In France and Britain, the highest court positions were always reserved for noblemen. Nobles dominated the Prussian army. The Spanish nobility, rich or poor, shunned all labor as a right of their heritage. Swedish and Hungarian noblemen had their own legislative chambers, just as the British had the House of Lords.

Though all who enjoyed these special rights were noble, not all nobles were equal. In many states, the noble order was subdivided into easily identifiable groups. The Spanish *grandees,* the upper nobility, were numbered in the thousands; the Spanish *hidalgos,* the lower nobility, were numbered in the hundreds of thousands. In Hungary, out of 400,000 noblemen, only about 15,000 belonged to the landed nobility, who held titles and were exempt from taxes. In England, the elite class was divided between the peers and the gentry. The peers held titles, were members of the House of Lords, and had a limited range of judicial and fiscal privileges. In the mid-eighteenth century there were only 190 British peers. The gentry, which numbered over 20,000, dominated the House of Commons and local legal offices but were not strictly members of the nobility. The French nobility was informally divided into the small group of peers known as the *Grandes*, whose ancient lineage, wealth, and power set them apart from all others; a rather larger service nobility whose privileges derived in one way or another from municipal or judicial service; and what might be called the country nobility, whose small estates and local outlook made their exemption from taxes vital to their survival.

These distinctions among the nobilities of the European states masked a more important one: wealth. As the saying went, "All who were truly noble were not wealthy, but all who were truly wealthy were noble." In the eighteenth century, despite the phenomenal increase in mercantile activity, wealth was still calculated in profits from the ownership of land, and it was the wealthy landed nobility who set the tone of elite life in Europe.

For the wealthy, aristocracy was becoming an international status. The influence of Louis XIV and the court of Versailles lasted for well over a century and spread to town and country life. Most nobles maintained multiple residences. The new style of aristocratic entertainment required more public space on the first floor, while the increasing demand for personal and familial privacy necessitated more space in the upper stories. The result was larger and more opulent homes. Here, the British elite led all others. To the expense of architecture was added the expense of decoration. New materials, such as West Indian mahogany, occasioned new styles, and both drove up costs. The high-quality woodwork and plastering that the English Adam brothers made fashionable was quickly imitated on the Continent. Only the Spanish nobility shunned country estates, preferring to reside permanently in towns.

The building of country houses was only one part of the conspicuous consumption of the privileged orders. Improvements in travel, in both transport and roads, permitted increased contact between members of the national elites. The stagecoach and canals made travel quicker and more enjoyable. The grand tour of historical sites continued to be used as a substitute for formal education. The grand tour was also a means of introducing the European aristocracies to each other. Whether it was a Russian noble in Germany or a Briton in Prussia, all spoke French and shared a common cultural outlook.

Much of that outlook was cultivated in the salons, a social institution begun in the seventeenth century by French women that gradually spread throughout the continent. In the salons, especially those in Paris, the aristocracy and the bourgeoisie mingled with the leading intellectuals of the age, examining and exchanging new ideas. It was in the salons that the impact of the Enlightenment, the great European intellectual movement of the eighteenth century, first made itself felt.

The Bourgeoisie

Bourgeois is a French word, and it carried the same tone of derision in the eighteenth century that it does today. The bourgeois male was a man on the make, scrambling after money or office or title. The bourgeoisie provided the safety valve between the nobility and those who were acquiring wealth and power but who lacked the advantages of birth and position. They served vital functions in all European societies, dominating trade, both nationally and internationally. They made their homes in cities and did much to improve the quality of urban life. They developed their own culture and class identity and permitted successful individuals to enjoy a sense of pride and achievement.

In the eighteenth century, the bourgeoisie was growing in numbers and importance. Some of its members were able to pass into the nobility through the purchase of land or office. But for most, their own social group began to define its own values, which centered on the family and the home. Their homes became a social center for kin and neighbors, and their outlook on family life reflected new personal relationships.

Marriages were made for companionship as much as for economic advantage. Romantic love between husbands and wives was newly valued. So were children, whose futures came to dominate familial concern. Childhood was recognized as a separate stage of life and the education of

The Dutton Family by John Zoffany. This eighteenth-century painting shows the comforts enjoyed by the British upper middle class.

children as one of the most important of parental concerns. The image of the affectionate father replaced that of the hard-bitten businessman; the image of the doting mother replaced that of the domestic drudge.

Urban Elites. In the society of orders, nobility was the acid test. The world was divided into the small number of those who had it and the large number of those who did not. At the apex of the non-noble pyramid was the bourgeoisie, the elites of urban Europe whose place in the society of orders was ambiguous. *Bourgeois*, or *burgher*, simply meant "town dweller," but as a social group it had come to mean "wealthy town dweller." The bourgeoisie was strongest where towns were strongest: in western rather than in eastern Europe and in northern rather than southern Europe with the notable exception of Italy. Holland was the exemplar of a bourgeois republic. More than half of the Dutch population lived in towns, and there was no significant aristocratic class to compete for power. The Regents of Amsterdam were the equivalent of a European court nobility in wealth, power, and prestige, though not in the way in which they had accumulated their fortunes. The size of the bourgeoisie in various European states cannot be absolutely determined. At the end of the eighteenth century, the British middle classes probably constituted around 15 percent of the population, the French bourgeoisie less than 10 percent. By contrast, the Russian and Hungarian urban elites were less than 2 percent of the population of those states.

Like the nobility, the bourgeoisie constituted a diverse group. At the top were great commercial families engaged in the expanding international marketplace and reaping the profits of trade. In wealth and power they were barely distinguishable from the nobility. At the bottom were the so-called petite bourgeoisie: shopkeepers, craftsmen, and industrial employers. The solid core of the bourgeoisie was employed in trade, exchange, and service. Most were engaged in local or national commerce. Trade was the lifeblood of the city, for by itself the city could neither feed nor clothe its inhabitants. Most bourgeois fortunes were first acquired in trade. Finance was the natural outgrowth of commerce, and another segment of the bourgeoisie accumulated or preserved capital through the sophisticated financial instruments of the eighteenth century. While the very wealthy loaned directly to the central government or bought shares in overseas trading companies, most bourgeois participated in government credit markets. They purchased state bonds or lifetime annuities and lived on the interest. The costs of war flooded the urban credit markets with high-yielding and generally stable financial instruments. Finally, the bourgeoisie were members of the burgeoning professions that provided services for the rich. Medicine, law, education, and the bureaucracy were all bourgeois professions, for the cost of acquiring the necessary skills could be borne only by those who were already wealthy.

The bourgeoisie grew as European urbanization continued steadily throughout the eighteenth century. In 1600, only 20 European cities contained as many as 50,000 people; in 1700, that number had risen to 32, and by 1800 it has increased to 48. London, the largest city, had grown to 865,000 people, a remarkable feat considering that in 1665, over one-quarter of the London population died in the Great Plague. In such cities the demand for lawyers, doctors, merchants, and shopkeepers was almost insatiable.

Besides wealth, the urban bourgeoisie shared another characteristic: mobility. The aspiration of the bourgeoisie was to become noble, either through office or by acquiring rural estates. In Britain, a gentleman was still defined by lifestyle: "All are accounted gentlemen in England who maintain themselves without manual labor." Many trading families left their wharves and countinghouses to acquire rural estates and live off rents. In France and Spain, nobility could still be purchased, though the price was constantly going up. For the greater bourgeoisie the transition was easy; for the lesser it was usually just beyond their grasp. The bourgeoisie did not only imagine their discomfort; they were made to feel it at every turn. Despised from above, envied from below, they were the subject of jokes, of theater, and of popular songs. They were the first victims in the shady financial dealings of the crown and court, the first casualties in urban riots. Their one consolation was that as a group they got richer and richer. And as a group they began to develop a distinctive culture that reflected their qualities and aspirations.

Bourgeois Values. Although many members of the bourgeoisie aspired to noble status, others had no desire to wear the silks and furs that were reserved for the nobility or to attend the opening night at the opera decked in jewels and finery. In fact, such ostentation was alien to them. A real tension existed between the values of noble and bourgeois. The ideal noble was idle, wasteful, and ostentatious; the ideal bourgeois was industrious, frugal, and sober. When Louis XVI tried to make household economies in the wake of a financial crisis, critics said that he acted "like a bourgeois."

Even if the bourgeoisie did not constitute a class, they did share certain attitudes that constituted a culture. The wealthy among them participated in the new world of consumption, whether they did so lavishly or frugally. For those who aspired to more than their birth allowed, there was a loosening of the strict codes of dress that reserved certain fabrics, decorative materials, and styles to the nobility. Merchants and bankers could now be seen in colored suits or with pipings made of cloth of gold; their wives could be seen in furs and silks. They might acquire coaches and carriages to take them on the Sunday rides through the town gardens or to their weekend retreats in the suburbs. Parisian merchants, even master craftsmen such as clockmakers, were now acquiring suburban homes although they could not afford to retire to them for the summer months.

Increasingly, the bourgeoisie was also beginning to travel. In Britain, whole towns were established to cater to leisure travelers. The southwestern town of Bath, famous since Roman times for the soothing qualities of its waters, was the most popular of all European resort towns. Brighton, a seaside resort on the south coast, quadrupled in size in the second half of the eighteenth century. Bathing—what we would call swimming—either for health or for recreation, became a middle-class fad, displacing traditional fears of the sea.

Leisure and Entertainment. Leisure activities of the bourgeoisie quickly became commercialized. Theaters and music halls proliferated. Voltaire's plays were performed before packed houses in Paris. In Venice, it was estimated that over 1,200 operas were produced in the eighteenth century. Public concerts were a mark of bourgeois culture, for the court nobility was entertained at the royal palaces or at great country houses.

Theater and concertgoing were part of the new attitude toward socializing that was one of the greatest contributions of the Enlightenment. Enlightened thinkers spread their views in the salons, and the salons soon spawned the academies, local scientific societies that, though led and patronized by provincial nobles, included large numbers of bourgeois members. The academies sponsored essay competitions, built up libraries, and became the local center for intellectual interchange. A less-structured form of sociability took place in the coffeehouses and tearooms that came to be a feature of even small provincial towns. In the early eighteenth century, there were over 2,000 London coffee shops where men—for the coffeehouse was largely a male preserve—could talk about politics, read the latest newspapers and magazines, and indulge their taste for this still-exotic beverage. Parisian clubs, called *societés*, covered a multitude of diverse interests. Literary *societés* were the most popular, maintaining their purpose by forbidding drinking, eating, and gambling on their premises.

Above all, bourgeois culture was literate culture. Wealth and leisure led to mental pursuits—if not always to intellectual ones. The proliferation of relatively cheap printed material had an enormous impact on the lives of those who were able to afford it. Holland and Britain were the most literate European societies and also, because of the absence of censorship, the centers of European printing. This was the first great period of the newspaper and the magazine. The first daily newspaper appeared in London in 1702; 80 years later, 37 provincial towns had their own newspapers, and the London papers were read all over Britain. Then, as now, the newspaper was as much a vehicle for advertisement as for news. News reports tended to be bland, avoiding controversy and concentrating on general national and international events. Advertising, by contrast, tended to be lurid, promising cures for incurable ills and the most exquisite commodities at the most reasonable prices.

For entertainment and serious political commentary the British reading public turned to magazines, of which there were over 150 separate titles by the 1780s. The most famous were *The Spectator*, which ran in the early part of the century and did much to set the tone for a cultured middle-class life, and the *Gentleman's Magazine*, which ran in the mid-century and was said to have had a circulation of nearly 15,000. The longest-lived of all British magazines was *The Ladies' Diary*, which continued in existence from 1704 to 1871 and doled out self-improvement, practical advice, and fictional romances in equal proportion.

The Ladies' Diary was not the only publication aimed at lettered bourgeois women. A growing body of both domestic literature and light entertainment was available to them. This included a vast number of teach-yourself books aimed at instructing women how best to organize domestic life or how to navigate the perils of polite society. Moral instruction, particularly on the themes of obedience and sexual fidelity, was also popular. But the greatest output directed toward women was in the form of fanciful romances, from which a new genre emerged. The novel first appeared in its modern form in the 1740s. Samuel Richardson (1689–1761) wrote *Pamela* (1740), the story of a maidservant who successfully resisted the advances of her master until he finally married her. The story tended to overshadow the overt moral message that was Richardson's original intention.

Family Life. In the eighteenth century, a remarkable transformation in home life was under way, one that the bourgeoisie shared with the nobility: the celebration of domesticity. The image—and sometimes the reality—of the happy home, where love was the bond between husband and wife and between parents and children, came to dominate both the literary and visual arts. Only those who were wealthy enough to afford to dispense with women's work could partake of the new domesticity, and only those who had been touched by Enlightenment ideas could attempt to make the change. But where it occurred, the transformation in the nature of family life was one of the most profound alterations in eighteenth-century culture.

The first step toward the transformation of family relationships was in centering the conjugal family in the home. In the past, the family was a less important structure for most people than the social groups to which they belonged or the neighborhood in which they lived. Marriage was an economic partnership at one end and a means to carry on lineage at the other. Individual fulfillment was not an object of marriage, and this attitude could be seen among the elites in the high level of arranged marriages, the speed with which surviving spouses remarried, and the formal and often brutal personal relationships between husbands and wives.

Patriarchy was the dominant value within the family. Husbands ruled over wives and children, making all of the crucial decisions that affected both the quality of their lives and their futures. As late as the middle of the eighteenth century, a British judge established the "rule of thumb," which asserted that a husband had a legal right to beat his wife with a stick, but the stick should be no thicker than a man's thumb. It was believed that children were stained with the sin of Adam at birth and that only the severest upbringing could clean some of it away. Children were sent out first for wet-nursing, then at around the age of seven for boarding, either at school or in a trade, and finally into their own marriages.

This profile of family life began to change, especially in western Europe, during the second half of the eighteenth century. Though the economic elements of marriage remained strong, romantic and sexual attraction became a factor. Even in earlier centuries, parents did not simply assign a spouse to their children, but by the eighteenth century, adolescents themselves searched for their own marriage partners and exercised a strong negative voice in identifying unsuitable ones.

Companionate Marriage. The quest for compatibility, no less than the quest for romantic love, led to a change in personal relationships between spouses. The extreme formality of the past was gradually breaking down. Husbands and wives began spending more time with each other, developing common interests and pastimes. Their personal life began to change. For the first time, houses were built to afford the couple privacy from their children, their servants, and their guests. Rooms were designed for specific functions and were set off by hallways.

Couples had more time for each other because they were beginning to limit the size of their families. There were a number of reasons for this development, which again pertained only to the upper classes. For one thing, child mortality rates were declining among wealthy social groups. Virulent epidemic diseases like the plague, which knew no class lines, were gradually disappearing, and sanitation was improving. Bearing fewer children had an enormous impact on women's lives, reducing the danger of death and disablement in childbirth and giving women time to pursue domestic tasks. Many couples appear to have made a conscious decision to space births, though success was limited by the fact that the most common technique of birth control was coitus interruptus, or withdrawal.

The transformation in the quality of relationships between spouses was mirrored by an even greater transformation in attitudes toward children. Childhood now took on a new importance for many reasons. With the decline in mortality rates, parents could feel that their emotional investment in their children had a greater chance of fulfillment. Equally important were the new ideas about education, especially Locke's belief that the child enters into the world a blank slate whose personality is created through

LOVE AND MARRIAGE

Frances Brooke (1724–1789) was one of the earliest women novelists in Britain, publishing her first novel, The History of Lady Julia Mandeville, *in 1763. Orphaned at an early age, she settled in London and earned her living as a translator, writer, and editor. Brooke also participated in the thriving magazine culture of mid-eighteenth-century London. In her essay periodical,* The Old Maid, *she addressed domestic and public issues through the voice of a fictional mouthpiece, "Mary Singleton, Spinster." In this excerpt from the first issue of the magazine, the "Old Maid" reflects on her personal history and the circumstances that led to her unmarried state.*

FOCUS QUESTIONS

How does the passage of time affect the Old Maid's recollections about her past? According to this selection, how do parents control the destiny of their children and heirs? What appears to be the role of love in eighteenth-century marriages?

I WAS BORN IN THE NORTH OF ENGLAND, being the eldest daughter of an honest country justice, who having no children but me and a younger sister, proposed leaving his estate, a clear eight hundred a year, betwixt us. My sister married a neighboring gentleman, and I might perhaps have followed her example, having very good offers (upon my word it's true, I have several love letters by me, which I read once a year, on my birthday, by the help of spectacles) but unluckily, at the age of twenty three, I was addressed by a gentleman so very agreeable, and so passionately fond of me, that though he had not a shilling, I unknown to any body, partly from inclination, partly for fear the poor man should hang himself, which he often threatened, engaged myself to him. As it was impossible to get my father's consent, we agreed to wait till his death; and my lover, who was bred to no employment, went in the meantime to reside with an old relation, in a distant country, who had a good estate, and whose son had a friendship for him. After two years of expectation, during which my faithful admirer, who contrived to see me as often as the distance of the place, and his dependent situation would permit, had frequently pressed me to marry him privately, my father died. Though my concern for his death was real, love soon dried up my tears: no one who is not as romantic as I then was can imagine the joy I felt at being able to give my lover such a proof of the disinterestedness of my passion: I sent a servant post with a letter full of fine sentimental rhapsodies which I am now convinced were very foolish, and received the following answer,

> MADAM,
>
> I am sorry for your loss: I have also been so unhappy as to lose my uncle and cousin, who both died of the smallpox within this week: the excess of my grief, and the multiplicity of business I am at present engaged in, by being left heir to my uncle's estate, render it impossible for me to wait upon you. I am much obliged to you for the expressions of regard in your's [sic], and am sorry to tell you, my uncle when dying, insisted on my promise to marry Miss Wealthy, who was intended for my cousin. The will of the dead ought to be sacred therefore it is impossible for me to fulfill the engagement into which we, perhaps imprudently, entered. I expect from your known candor that you will do me the justice to believe no motive but the gratitude and respect I own to the memory of this dear relation, to whose generosity I am so much obliged, could make me give up the hope of being yours. I doubt not your good sense and religion will enable you to bear with becoming fortitude, a shock, which I have need of all the strength of manly reason to support. I sincerely wish you every happiness, and that you may whenever you marry, meet with a man more worthy of you . . .
>
> —J.C.

From *The Old Maid*, Number 1 (November 15, 1755).

early education. This view placed a new responsibility on parents and gave them the concept of childhood as a stage through which individuals passed. This idea could be seen in the commercial sphere as well as in any other. In 1700, there was not a single shop in London that sold children's toys exclusively; by the 1780s, toy shops were everywhere. There were also shops that sold clothes specifically designed for children; children's clothes were no longer simply adult clothes in miniature. Most important of all was the development of materials for the education of children. This took place in two stages. At first, children's books were designed to help adults teach children. Later came books directed at children themselves with large print, entertaining illustrations, and nonsensical characters, usually animals that taught moral lessons.

The commercialization of childhood was, of course, directed at adults. The new books and games for children had to be purchased and used by parents as well. More and more mothers were devoting their time to their children. Among the upper classes, the practice of wet-nursing began to decline. Mothers wanted to nurture their infants both literally by breast-feeding and figuratively by teaching them. Children became companions to be taken on outings to the increasing number of museums or shows of curiosities.

The emergence of the bourgeoisie was one of the central social developments of the eighteenth century. The bourgeois culture, which emphasized a fulfilling home life, leisure pursuits, and literacy, soon came to dominate the values of educated society in general. But the population at large could not share this transformation of family life. Working women could afford neither the cost of instructional materials for their children nor the time to use them. Ironically, working women now began using wet nurses, once the privilege of the wealthy, because increasingly, a working woman's labor was the margin of survival for her family. Working women enjoyed no privacy in the hovels in which they lived with large families in single rooms. Wives and children were still beaten by husbands and fathers. By the end of the eighteenth century, two distinct family cultures coexisted in Europe, one based on companionate marriage and the affective bonds of parents and children and the other based on patriarchal dominance and the family as an economic unit.

The Masses

Although more Europeans were surviving than ever before, with more food, more housing, better sanitation, and even better charities, there was also more misery. Those who would have succumbed to disease or starvation a century before now survived from day to day, beneficiaries—or victims—of increased farm production and improved agricultural marketing. The market economy organized a more effective use of land as large farming enterprises gobbled up smaller units, but it created a widespread social problem. The landless agrarian laborer of the eighteenth century was the counterpart of the sixteenth century wandering beggar. In the cities, the plight of the poor was as desperate as ever. Even the most openhearted charitable institutions were unable to cope with the massive increase in the poor. Thousands of mothers abandoned their children to the foundling hospitals, hoping that they would have a better chance of survival, even though hospital death rates were near 80 percent.

Despite widespread poverty, many members of the lower orders were able to gain some benefit from existing conditions. The richness of popular culture, signified by a spread of literacy into the lower reaches of European society, was one indication of this change. So too were the reforms urged by enlightened thinkers to improve basic education and to improve the quality of life in the cities. For that segment of the lower orders that could keep its head above water, the eighteenth century offered new opportunities and new challenges.

Breaking the Cycle. Of all the legacies of the eighteenth century, none was more fundamental than the

The Snatched Kiss, or *The Stolen Kiss* (1750s), by Jean-Honoré Fragonard, was one of the "series paintings" popular in the late eighteenth century. A later canvas entitled *The Marriage Contract* shows the next step in the lives of the lovers.

steady increase in European population that began around 1740. This was not the first time that Europe had experienced sustained population growth, but it was the first time that such growth was not checked by a demographic crisis. In 1700, the European population is estimated to have been 120 million. By 1800, it had grown 50 percent to over 180 million, with regional variations in the growth rate. While France, Spain, and Italy expanded between 30 and 40 percent, Prussia doubled and Russia and Hungary may have tripled in number. Britain increased by 80 percent from about 5 to 9 million, but the rate of growth was accelerating. In 1695, the English population stood at 5 million. It took 62 years to add the next million and 24 years to add the million after that. In 1781, the population was 7 million, but it took only 13 years to reach 8 million and only 10 more years to reach 9 million. Steady population growth had continued without significant checks for more than half a century.

Ironically, the traditional pattern of European population found its theorist at the very moment that it was about to disappear. In 1798, Thomas Malthus (1766–1834) published *An Essay on the Principles of Population*. Reflecting on the history of European population, Malthus observed the cyclical pattern by which growth over one or two generations was checked by a crisis that significantly reduced population. From these lower levels, new growth began until it was checked and the cycle repeated itself. Because the number of people increased more quickly than did food supplies, the land could sustain only a certain level of population. When that level was near, the population became prone to a demographic check. Malthus divided population checks into two categories: positive and preventive. Positive checks were war, disease, and famine, all of which Malthus believed were natural, though brutal, means of population control. Preventive checks were the means by which societies could limit their growth to avoid the devastating consequences of positive checks. Celibacy, late marriages, and sexual abstinence were among the choices that Malthus approved, though abortion, infanticide, and contraception were also commonly practiced.

Patterns of Population. In the sixteenth and seventeenth centuries, the dominant pattern of the life cycle was high infant and child mortality, late marriages, and early death. All controlled population growth. Infant and child mortality rates were staggering; only half of those born reached the age of 10. Late marriage was the only effective form of birth control, given the strong social taboos against sexual relations outside marriage, for a late marriage reduced a woman's childbearing years. Women in western Europe generally married between the ages of 24 and 26; they normally ceased bearing children around the age of 40. But not all marriages lasted this 14- or 16-year span, since one or the other partner sometimes died. On average, the childbearing period for most women was 10 to 12 years, long enough to endure six pregnancies, which would result in three surviving children.

Three surviving children for every two adults would, of course, have resulted in a 50 percent rise in population in every generation. Celibacy was one limiting factor; urban death rates were another. Perhaps as much as 15 percent of the population in western Europe remained celibate either by entering religious orders that imposed celibacy or by lacking the personal or financial attributes necessary to marry. In the cities, rural migrants accounted for the appallingly high death rates. When we remember that the largest European cities were continuously growing—London from 200,000 in 1600 to 675,000 in 1750, Paris from 220,000 to 576,000, Rome from 105,000 to 156,000, Madrid from 49,000 to 109,000, Vienna from 50,000 to 175,000—then we can appreciate how many countless thousands of immigrants perished from disease, famine, and exposure before they could marry and have children. If urban perils were not enough, there were still the positive checks. Plagues carried away hundreds of thousands of people, wars halved populations of places in their path, and famine overwhelmed the weak and the poor.

The late seventeenth and early eighteenth centuries were a period of population stagnation if not actual decline. Not until the third or fourth decade of the eighteenth century did another growth cycle begin. It rapidly gained momentum throughout the Continent and showed no signs of abating after two full generations. Fertility was increasing as some women were marrying younger, thereby increasing their childbearing years. Illegitimacy rates were also rising.

But increasing fertility was only part of the picture. More significant was decreasing mortality. The positive checks of the past were no longer as potent. European warfare not only diminished in scale after the middle of the eighteenth century, it changed location as well. Rivalry for colonial empires removed the theater of conflict from European communities. So did the increase in naval warfare. As warfare abated, so did epidemic disease. The plague had all but disappeared from western Europe by the middle of the eighteenth century. The widespread practice of quarantine, especially in Hungary, which had been the crucial bridge between eastern and western epidemics, went far to eradicate the scourge of centuries.

Without periodic demographic crises the European population began a gentle but continuous rise. Urban sanitation was becoming more effective. Clean water supplies, organized waste and sewage disposal, and strict quarantines were increasingly part of urban regulations. The use of doctors and trained midwives helped to lower the incidence of stillbirth and decreased the number of women who died in childbirth. Almost everywhere, levels of infant and child mortality were decreasing. More people were being born, and more were surviving to adulthood. The result was renewed population growth. No wonder Malthus was worried.

Agricultural Improvements. In the past, if warfare or epidemic diseases failed to check population growth, famine would have done the job. How the European economy conquered famine in the eighteenth century is a complicated story. There was no single breakthrough that accounts for the ability to feed the tens of millions of additional people who now inhabited the Continent. Holland and Britain used dynamic new agricultural techniques, but most European agriculture was still mired in the time-honored practices that had endured for centuries. Not everyone could be fed or fed adequately. Widespread famine might have disappeared, but slow starvation and chronic undernourishment had not. Hunger was more common at the end of the eighteenth century than at the beginning, and the nutritional content of a typical diet may have reached its lowest point in European history.

Nevertheless, Europe's capacity to sustain rising levels of population can be explained only in terms of agricultural improvement. Quite simply, European farmers were now producing more food and marketing it better. In the most advanced societies, this was a result of conscious efforts to make agriculture more efficient. In traditional open-field agriculture, communities quickly ran up against insurmountable obstacles to growth. The three-field crop rotation system left a significant proportion of land fallow each year, while the concentration on subsistence cereal crops progressively eroded the land that was in production. Common farming was only as strong as the weakest member of the community. There was little incentive for successful individuals to plow profits back into the land, through either the purchase of equipment or the increase of livestock.

Livestock was a crucial variable in agricultural improvement. As long as there was barely enough food for humans to eat, only essential livestock could be kept alive over the winter. Oxen, which were still the ordinary beasts of burden, and pigs and poultry, which required only minimal feed, were the most common. But few animals meant little manure, and without manure the soil could not easily be regenerated.

Around the middle of the seventeenth century, solutions to these problems began to appear. The first change was consolidation of landholdings so that traditional crop rotations could be abandoned. A second innovation was the introduction of fodder crops, some of which—such as clover—added nutrients to the soil, while others—such as turnips—were used to feed livestock. Better grazing and better winter feed increased the size of herds, and new techniques of animal husbandry, particularly crossbreeding, produced hardier strains. It was quite clear that the key to increased production lay in better fertilization, and by the eighteenth century, some European farmers had broken through the "manure barrier." Larger herds, the introduction of clover crops, the use of human waste from towns, and even the first experiments with lime as an artificial fertilizer were all part of the new agricultural methods.

The New Staples. Along with the new crops that helped to nourish both soil and animals came new crops that helped to nourish people. Indian corn, or maize, was a staple crop for Native Americans and gradually came to be grown in most parts of western Europe. Maize not only had higher nutritional value than most other cereals, it also yielded more food per acre than did traditional grains. So, too, did the potato, which also entered the European diet from the New World. The potato grew in poor soil, required less labor, and yielded an abundant and nutritious harvest. It rapidly took hold in Ireland and parts of Prussia, from which it spread into eastern Europe. The potato allowed families to subsist on smaller amounts of land with less capital outlay.

It must be stressed, however, that these new developments involved only a very narrow range of producers. The new techniques were expensive, and knowledge of the new crops spread slowly. Change had to overcome inertia, intransigence, and fear of failure. The most important improvements in agricultural production were more traditional ones. Basically, there was an increase in the amount of land that was used for growing. In Russia, Prussia, and Hungary, hundreds of thousands of new acres came under the plow; in the west, drainage schemes and forest clearance expanded productive capacity.

There was also an upswing in the efficiency with which agricultural products were marketed. From the seventeenth century onward, market agriculture was gradually replacing subsistence agriculture in most parts of Europe. Market agriculture had the advantage of allowing specialization on farms. Single-crop farming enabled farmers to benefit from the peculiarities of their own soil and climate. They could then exchange their surplus for the range of crops they needed to subsist. Market exchange was facilitated by improved transportation and communication and above all by the increase in the population of towns, which provided demand. The new national and international trade in large quantities of grain evened out regional variations in harvests and went a long way toward reducing local grain shortages. The upkeep of roads, the building of canals, and the clearing of waterways created a national lifeline for the movement of grain.

Finally, it is believed that the increase in agricultural productivity owed something to a change in climate that took place in the late eighteenth century. The European climate is thought to have been unusually cold and wet during the seventeenth century, and it seems to have gradually warmed during the eighteenth century.

The Plight of the Poor. Incremental improvements in agriculture, transportation, and climate contributed to the most serious social problem of the eighteenth century: the dramatic population increase of poor people throughout Europe. There was grim irony in the fact that advances in the production and distribution of food and the retreat of war and plague allowed more people to survive from hand to mouth than ever before. Whereas their ancestors had succumbed to quick death from disease or starvation, they eked out a miserable existence of constant hunger and chronic pain with death at the end of a seemingly endless corridor.

It is impossible to gauge the number of European poor or to separate them into categories of greater and greatest misery. The truly indigent—the starving poor—probably made up 10 to 15 percent of most societies, perhaps as many as 20 million people throughout the Continent. They were most prevalent in towns but were an increasing burden on the countryside, where they wandered in search of agricultural employment. The wandering poor had no counterpart in eastern Europe, where serfdom kept everyone tied to the land, but the hungry and unsheltered certainly did. Yet the problem of poverty was not to be seen only among the destitute. In fact, the uniqueness of the poor in the eighteenth century is that they were drawn from social groups that even in the hungry times of the early seventeenth century had been successful subsistence producers.

It was easy to see why poverty was increasing. The relentless advance of population drove up the price of food and drove down the price of wages. In the second half of the eighteenth century, the cost of living in France rose by over 60 percent while wages rose by only 25 percent. In Spain, the cost of living increased by 100 percent while wages rose only 20 percent. Only in Britain did wages nearly keep pace with prices. Rising prices made land more valuable. At the beginning of the eighteenth century, as the first wave of population expansion hit western Europe, smallholdings began to decrease in size. The custom of partible inheritance, by which each son received a

The poverty of eighteenth-century London slums was a favorite subject of the English artist William Hogarth. *Gin Lane* depicts the London poor in alcoholic delirium, their only escape from the misery of their daily lives.

share of land, shrank the average size of a peasant holding below that necessary to sustain an average-size family, let alone a family that was growing larger. In one part of France it was estimated that 30 acres was a survival plot of land in good times. At the end of the seventeenth century, 80 percent of the peasants there owned less than 25 acres.

As holdings contracted, the portion of the family income that was derived from wage labor expanded. In such circumstances, males were more valuable than females, either as farmers or laborers, and there is incontrovertible evidence that European rural communities practiced female infanticide. In the end, however, it became increasingly difficult for the peasant family to remain on the land. Small freeholders were forced to borrow against future crops until a bad harvest led to foreclosure. Many were allowed to lease back their own lands, on short terms and at high rents, but most swelled the ranks of agricultural laborers, migrating during the planting and harvest seasons, suffering cruelly during winter and summer.

Emigration was the first logical consequence of poverty. In places where rural misery was greatest, such as Ireland, whole communities pulled up stakes and moved to America. Frederick the Great attracted hundreds of thousands of emigrants to Prussia by offering them land. But most rural migrants did not move to new rural environments. Rather, they followed the well-trodden paths to the cities. Many traditional domestic crafts were evolving into industrial activities. In the past, peasants supplemented their family income by processing raw materials in the home. Spinning, weaving, and sewing were common cottage industries in which the workers took in the work, supplied their own equipment, and were paid by the piece. Now, especially in the cloth trades, a new form of industrial activity was being organized. Factories, usually located in towns or larger villages, assembled workers together, set them at larger and more efficient machines, and paid them for their time rather than for their output. Families who were unable to support themselves from the land had no choice but to follow the movement of jobs.

Caring for the Poor. Neither state nor private charities could cope with the flood of poor immigrants. Hospitals, workhouses, and, more ominously, prisons were established or expanded to deal with them. Hospitals were residential asylums rather than places for health care. They took in the old, the incapacitated, and, increasingly, the orphaned young. Workhouses existed for those who were capable of work but incapable of finding it. In most places, workhouses, which were supposed to improve the values of the idle poor by keeping them busy, served only to improve the profits of the industrialists, who rented out workhouse inmates at below-market wages. Prisons grew with crime. There were spectacular increases in crimes against property in all eighteenth-century cities, and despite severe penalties that could include hanging for petty theft, more criminals were incarcerated than executed. Enlightened arguments for the reform of prisons and punishment tacitly acknowledged the social basis of most crime. As always, the victims of crime were mostly drawn from the same social backgrounds as the perpetrators. Along with all of their other troubles, it was the poor who were most commonly robbed, beaten, and abused.

Popular Culture. While many people endured unrelieved misery, others lived comfortably by the standards of the age, and almost everyone believed that things were better now than they had ever been before. Popular culture was a rich mixture of family and community activities that provided outlets from the pressures of work and the vagaries of fortune. It was no less sustaining to the population at large than was the purely literate culture of the elite and no less vital as a means of explanation for everyday events than the theories of the philosophers or the programs of the philosophes.

In fact, the line between elite and popular culture in the eighteenth century was a thin one. For one thing, there was still much mixing of social classes in both rural and urban environments. Occasions of display, such as festivals, village fairs, or religious holidays, brought entire communities together and reinforced their collective identities. Moreover, there were many shared elements between the two cultures. All over Europe, literacy was increasing. Nearly half of the inhabitants of France were literate by the end of the eighteenth century, as were perhaps 60 percent of the population in Britain. Men were more likely to have learned to read than women, as were inhabitants of urban areas. More than one-quarter of French women could read, a number that had doubled over the century. As the rates of female literacy rose, so did overall rates, for women took the lead in teaching children.

Popular literacy spawned popular literature in remarkable variety. Religious tracts were found throughout Europe. They contained stories of Catholic saints or Protestant martyrs or proverbs and prayers. Romances, the staple of lending libraries, were usually published and sold in inexpensive installments. The best-selling popular fiction, at least in western Europe, was melodramatic tales of knights and ladies from the age of chivalry.

Popular social activities continued to reflect the violent and even brutal nature of day-to-day existence. Village festivals were still the safety valve of youth gangs who enforced sexual morals by shaming husbands whose wives were unfaithful or women whose reputations were sullied. Many holidays were celebrated by sporting events that pitted inhabitants of one village against those of another. These almost always turned into free-for-alls in which broken bones were common and deaths were not unknown.

Even more popular were the so-called blood sports involving animals. Dogfighting and cockfighting are among those that still survive today. Less attractive to the modern mind were bearbaiting or bull running, in which the object was the slaughter of a large beast over a prolonged period of time. Blood sports were not confined to the masses—fox-hunting and bullfighting were pastimes for the very rich—but they formed a significant part of local social activity.

So too did the tavern or alehouse, which in town or country was the site for local communication and recreation, where staggering amounts of alcohol were consumed. The increased use of spirits—gin, brandy, rum, and vodka—changed the nature of alcohol consumption in Europe. Wine and beer had always been drunk in quantities that we would find astounding, but these beverages were also an important part of people's diet. By contrast, the nutritional content of spirits was negligible. People drank spirits to get drunk, and drunkenness rose to new levels.

Conclusion

EIGHTEENTH-CENTURY EUROPE WAS A SOCIETY OF ORDERS that was gradually transforming itself into a society of classes. In other words, official ranks such as noble and commoner were giving way to a ranking by wealth or poverty. At the top, still vigorous, was the nobility. But the bourgeoisie was growing, and many of its members managed to pass into the nobility through the purchase of land or office. Opulence and poverty increased in step as the fruits of commerce and land enriched the upper orders while rising population impoverished the lower ones. The rise of the new science and of Enlightenment ideas highlighted the contradictions. The attack on traditional authority, especially the Roman Catholic Church, was an attack on a conservative, static world view. Enlightenment thinkers looked to the future, to a new world shaped by reason and knowledge, a world that was ruled benevolently for the benefit of all human beings. Government, society, the individual—all could be improved if only the rubble of the past were cleared away. The Enlightment thinker could hardly have imagined how potent their vision would become.

QUESTIONS FOR REVIEW

1. What were the main elements of Enlightenment thought?
2. What social, moral, and religious traditions were challenged by the ideas of thinkers such as Voltaire, Hume, Montesquieu, and Rousseau?
3. How did the European nobility maintain its social eminence in the face of a new bourgeois culture created by an expanding middle class?
4. Why did Europe's population begin to grow so dramatically in the eighteenth century, and how did society respond to the challenges that it posed?

DISCOVERING WESTERN CIVILIZATION ONLINE

You can obtain more information about culture and society in eighteenth-century Europe at the websites listed below. See also the companion website that accompanies this text: www.ablongman.com/kishlansky, which contains an online study guide and additional resources.

Eighteenth-Century Culture

www.history.evansville.net/enlighte.html
The best starting point for the culture and history of the age of Enlightenment.

andromeda.rutgers.edu/~jlynch/18th/
A gateway to a wealth of sources on many different aspects of eighteenth-century culture.

eserver.org/18th/
A list of links to a wide range of material relating to eighteenth-century literature and culture.

www.fordham.edu/halsall/mod/modsbook10.html
An outstanding collection of texts of Enlightenment writers.

Eighteenth-Century Society

www.bampfa.berkeley.edu/exhibits/newchild/
A site devoted to the nature of childhood in eighteenth-century Britain.

vos.ucsb.edu/browse.asp?id=2738
An inclusive page of links and resources for the study of English literature in the eighteenth century.

SUGGESTIONS FOR FURTHER READING

General Reading

William Doyle, *The Old European Order, 1660–1800*, 2d ed. (Oxford: Oxford University Press, 1992). An important essay on the structure of European societies and the ways in which they held together.

Olwen Hufton, *Europe: Privilege and Protest, 1730–1789* (Ithaca, N.Y.: Cornell University Press, 1980). An excellent survey of the political and social history of the mid-eighteenth century.

Eighteenth-Century Culture

A. J. Ayer, *Voltaire* (New York: Random House, 1986). A brief and vibrant study.

John G. Gagliardo, *Enlightened Despotism* (New York: Thomas Y. Crowell, 1967). A sound exploration of the impact of Enlightenment ideas on the rulers of Europe, with emphasis on the east.

Norman Hampson, *The Enlightenment* (London: Penguin Books, 1982). The best one-volume survey.

Roy Porter, *The Creation of the Modern World: The Untold Story of the British Enlightenment* (New York: Norton, 2000). A substantial but accessible account of the intellectual innovations and cultural contexts of the Enlightenment in Scotland and England.

Daniel Roche, *France in the Enlightenment* (Cambridge, Mass.: Harvard University Press, 1998). A wide-ranging survey of everything from politics to popular culture.

Eighteenth-Century Society: The Nobility

Michael Bush, *Noble Privilege* (New York: Holmes & Meier, 1983). A good analytic survey of the rights of European nobles.

Jonathan Dewald, *The European Nobility, 1400–1800* (Cambridge: Cambridge University Press, 1996). An insightful survey.

Eighteenth-Century Society: The Bourgeoisie

Elinor Barber, *The Bourgeoisie in Eighteenth-Century France* (Princeton, N.J.: Princeton University Press, 1955). Still the best study of the French bourgeoisie.

John Brewer, *The Pleasures of the Imagination: English Culture in the Eighteenth Century* (London: HarperCollins, 1997). A fascinating study of the making of high culture in England.

Jan de Vries, *European Urbanization, 1500–1800* (Cambridge, Mass.: Harvard University Press, 1984). An important, though difficult, study of the transformation of towns into cities, with the most reliable estimates of size and rates of growth.

Olwen Hufton, *The Prospect Before Her: A History of Women in Western Europe* (New York: Alfred Knopf, 1996). A survey of women's history that is particularly strong for the eighteenth century.

Lawrence Stone, *The Family, Sex and Marriage in England, 1500–1800* (New York: Harper & Row, 1979). A controversial but extremely important argument about the changing nature of family life.

Eighteenth-Century Society: The Masses

Peter Burke, *Popular Culture in Early Modern Europe* (New York: Harper & Row, 1978). A wide survey of practices throughout the Continent.

Olwen Hufton, *The Poor in Eighteenth-Century France* (Oxford: Oxford University Press, 1974). A compelling study of the life of the poor.

Robert Muchembled, *Popular Culture and Elite Culture in France, 1400–1750* (Baton Rouge: Louisiana State University Press, 1985). A complex but richly textured argument about the relationship between two cultures.

Roy Porter, *English Society in the Eighteenth Century* (London: Penguin Books, 1982). A breezy, entertaining survey of English social life.

CHAPTER 20

THE FRENCH REVOLUTION AND THE NAPOLEONIC ERA, 1789–1815

THE VISUAL RECORD

EIGHTEENTH-CENTURY REVOLUTION

IN THE SECOND HALF OF THE EIGHTEENTH CENTURY, two separate revolutions toppled regimes on both sides of the Atlantic. In the first of the two great upheavals, the American Revolution, which lasted from 1775 to 1783, the 13 British colonies located along the Atlantic seaboard secured their independence from Great Britain. They formed themselves into the United States, a democratic republic with its own Declaration of Independence and Constitution. While the American Revolution was challenging British rule in the New World, France appeared to be ruled by a stable and powerful monarchy, one so secure in its reign that it was able to lend a helping hand to those colonists opposing England's king George III.

In the image shown here, entitled "Independence of the United States," the unknown artist is glorifying both the king of France, Louis XVI (1774–1791), and the American Revolution. Louis XVI, the king who would be guillotined by radical revolutionaries in 1793, is commemorated in the painting as a great man of revolution, more important by virtue of his position on the monument than even George Washington and Benjamin Franklin. Washington, whose name is misspelled as "Waginston," is not memorialized as father of his country. Instead, the inscription on the pedestal acknowledges Louis as the "Liberator" of America and the seas, an assertion that would have come as a surprise to the colonists struggling to cast off the British yoke. The memorial column itself is topped by images of the French monarchy including a globe with three *fleurs de lys* and the rooster of the French nation.

Next to the monument is the figure of America, symbolized by a half-naked "noble savage" draped in animal skins and feathers holding the scepter of power in his right hand and in his left hand a pole surmounted by a Phrygian cap of ancient Roman origins, which became popular in the

French Revolution as the symbol of liberty. Under his left foot, America is trampling the British lion, next to the broken British trident symbolizing British failure both as a land and sea power.

The landscape is not a New England scene at all, but a tropical scene with palm trees, one of which is wrapped in a banner proclaiming, "In raising myself up, I make myself beautiful." The aura of the New World as an uncharted territory very different from Europe and the French countryside served both to idealize the American continent and to distance its revolution from the political experience of the French. In an exotic terrain, Louis XVI could appear as a "liberator," as unearned as the title might be.

The American Revolution was popular in France and attracted supporters including the French aristocrat and military man, the Marquis de Lafayette, who even went to the New World to fight in the revolutionary army and persuaded the French government to provide financial aid to the American cause.

LOOKING AHEAD

The French Revolution began six years after the American War of Independence ended, and lasted for a decade. The French revolutionaries of 1789 shared many elements in common with their American counterparts, including an awareness of the writings of the same philosophers and intellectuals on both sides of the Atlantic whose works questioned existing institutions and traditions in favor of democracy, liberty, and equality. Yet to understand the Revolution in France, which, like its American predecessor, also embodied new ideas about government and citizenship, one must understand the distinctive nature of French society, economy, and politics in the 50 years or so preceding 1789 and the crisis in the Old Regime. As we shall see in this chapter, the resulting experiments with parliamentary government and representative and participatory democracy were deeply rooted in crises and practices of Old-Regime France. While experimenting with democracy, France contended with internal violence and foreign wars. Until his defeat by the allied European powers, Napoleon was able to consolidate the French state through reform at home and victory abroad, and in so doing was both the heir of the Revolution and its destroyer.

THE CRISIS OF THE OLD REGIME IN FRANCE, 1715–1788

France in the eighteenth century, the age of the Enlightenment, was a state invigorated by new ideas, but it was also dominated by tradition. The traditional institutions of monarchy, Church, and aristocracy defined power and status. Talk of reform, progress, and perfectibility coexisted with the social realities of privileges and obligations determined by birth. The eighteenth century was a time when old ways prevailed even as new political ideas were taking shape.

At the end of the eighteenth century, a number of foreign visitors to France commented on the disparities that characterized French social and political life. One English visitor in particular—Arthur Young (1741–1820), an agronomist writing on his travels in France in the 1780s—observed that although a prosperous land, France was pocked with extreme poverty; that although a land of high culture and great art, it was riddled with ignorance, illiteracy, and superstition; and that although a land with a centralized bureaucracy, it was also saddled with local pettiness and obsolete practices.

The tensions generated by the clash of continuity and change made it an exciting and complex period in France. Reformers talked of progress while peasants still used wooden plows. The *philosophes* glorified reason in a world of violence, superstition, and fear. The great crisis of eighteenth-century France, the French Revolution, destroyed the Old Regime. But the revolution was as much a product of continuities and traditions as it was a product of change and the challenge of new ideas.

The Financial Crisis

By the beginning of the eighteenth century, absolute monarchy in France had extended royal influence into the new areas of policing, administration, lawmaking, and taxation. But none of the changes proved sufficient to meet the growing needs of the French state. Louis XV, like his great-grandfather Louis XIV, laid claim to rule as an absolute monarch. He insisted that "the rights and interests of the nation . . . are of necessity one with my own, and lie in my hands only." Such claims failed to mask the weaknesses of royal rule. Louis XV lacked a sufficiently developed bureaucracy to administer and tax the nation in an evenhanded fashion.

The French monarchy was in a state of perpetual financial crisis across the eighteenth century. The state sought new loans to meet its needs, while already seriously hobbled by the service on existing debts. Borrowing at high rates required the government to pay out huge sums in interest and service fees on the loans that were keeping it afloat. The outlays in turn piled the state's indebtedness ever higher, requiring more loans, and threatening to topple the whole financial structure of the state and the regime itself. The monarchy tried to reduce expenditures, but such attempts were limited by the necessity of maintaining an effective and costly army and navy.

The nadir of Louis XV's reign came in 1763, with the French defeat in the Seven Years' War both on the Continent and in the colonies. In the Treaty of Paris, France ceded territory, including its Canadian holdings, to Great Britain. But France lost more than territories: it lost its footing in the competition with its chief rival, Great Britain, which had been pulling ahead of France in international affairs since the mid-eighteenth century. The war was also a financial debacle, paid for by loans secured against the guarantee of victory. The defeat not only left France barren of funds, it also promoted further expenditures for strengthening the French navy against the superior British fleet. The king saw taxation as the only way out of the financial trap in which he now found himself.

The Political Crisis

The heightened tensions between the monarch and the aristocracy found expression in various institutions, especially the parlements, which were the 13 sovereign courts in the French judicial system, with their seats in Paris and a dozen provincial centers. The magistrates of each parlement were members of the aristocracy, some of them nobles of recent origin and others of long standing, depending on the locale. Following the costly Seven Years' War, the parlements chose to exercise the power of refusal by blocking a proportional tax to be imposed on nobles and commoners alike. The magistrates resisted taxation, arguing that the king was attacking the liberty of his subjects by attempting to tax those who were exempt by virtue of their privileged status.

The king needed the parlements to record royal decrees before they could become law. The recording process conferred real political power on the parlements, which could withhold approval for the king's policies by refusing to register his decrees. When decrees involved taxation, the magistrates often refused to endorse them. By challenging the king, the parlements became a battleground between the elite, who claimed that they represented the nation, and the king, who said the nation was himself.

The king repeatedly attempted to neutralize the power of the parlements by relying instead on his own state bureaucracy. His agents in the provinces, called intendants, were accountable directly to the central government. The intendants, as the king's men, and the magistrates who presided in the parlements represented contradictory claims to power. As the king's needs increased in the second half of the eighteenth century, the situation was becoming intolerable for those exercising power and those aspiring to rule in the name and for the good of the nation. The financial crisis provided the elite of notables, made up of both aristocrats and bourgeois, with the basis for asserting their own ascendancy to political power.

Public opinion emerged as a powerful and critical source for provoking a political crisis in the regime. With the spread of literacy, newspapers, periodicals, and pamphlets addressed a new reading public. Louis XVI and his queen Marie Antoinette were held accountable as tales of their follies spread throughout the land. Public confidence in the monarchy eroded in response to growing accusations of despotism in the press. Public opinion promoted the sense that France formed a single political community, a nation.

The Attempt at Reform

Beginning in the 1770s, the monarchy attempted a succession of reforms in the hope of stabilizing government. The political battles over the reforms provided the aristocracy with the arena to raise larger political issues about the power to govern.

When Louis XV died in 1774, he left to his 20-year-old grandson and heir Louis XVI the legacy of a disastrous deficit. From the beginning of his reign, Louis XVI was caught in the familiar and vicious circle of excessive state spending—above all, military spending—followed by bouts of heavy borrowing.

In inheriting the trouble-ridden fiscal structure, Louis XVI made his own contribution to it. Following in the footsteps of his grandfather, he involved France in a costly war, the War of American Independence (1775–1783), by supporting the 13 colonies in their revolt against Great Britain. The involvement brought the French monarchy to the brink of bankruptcy. Contrary to public opinion, most of the state's expenditures did not go toward lavishing luxuries on the royal court and the royal family at Versailles. They went to pay off loans. More than half of the state budget in the 1780s represented interest on loans taken to pay for foreign military ventures.

Selling Privileges, Raising Taxes. To those who could afford to purchase them, the king continued to sell offices that carried with them titles, revenues, and privileges. He also relied on the sale of annuities that paid high interest rates and that attracted speculators, large and small. The crown had leased out its rights to collect the salt tax in return for large lump-sum advances from the Royal General Farms, a syndicate of about 100 wealthy financier families. The Royal General Farms reaped healthy profits on their annual transactions at the state's expense. The combined revenues collected by the king through the various stratagems were little more than a drop in the vast ocean of debt that threatened to engulf the state.

The existing tax structure proved hopelessly inadequate to meet the state's needs. The *taille*, a direct tax, was levied, either on persons or on land, according to region. Except for those locales where the taille was attached to land, the nobility was always exempt from direct taxation. Members of the bourgeoisie could also avoid the direct tax as citizens of towns enjoying exemption. That meant that the wealthy, those best able to pay, were often exempt. The privileged elite persisted in rejecting the crown's attempts to tax them. Indirect taxes, such as those on salt (the *gabelle*) and on food and drink (the *aide*), and internal and external customs taxes were regressive taxes that weighed heavily on those least able to pay. The peasantry bore the brunt of the nation's tax burden, and Louis XVI knew all too well that he could not squeeze blood from a stone by increasing indirect taxes. A peasantry too weighted down would collapse—or rebel.

Economic Reforms. As one of the first acts of his reign, in 1775 Louis XVI had restored the magistrates to their posts in the parlements, treating their offices as a form of property of which they had been deprived. In his conciliatory act, Louis XVI stressed that the self-interest

▼ This cartoon depicts the plight of the French peasants. An old farmer is bowed down under the weight of the privileged aristocracy and clergy while birds and rabbits, protected by unfair game laws, eat his crops.

of the aristocracy was at odds with the common good of the nation and urged the approval of his programs. Nevertheless, by 1776 the Parlement of Paris was again obstructing royal decrees.

Louis XVI appointed Anne Robert Jacques Turgot (1727–1781) as his first controller-general. Turgot's reformist economic ideas were influenced by Enlightenment philosophes. In order to generate revenues, Turgot reasoned, France needed to prosper economically. The government was in a position to stimulate economic growth by eliminating regulations, economizing at court, and improving the network of roads through a tax on landowners. Each of Turgot's reforms offended established interests, thereby ensuring his early defeat. Emphasis on a laissez-faire economy outraged the guilds; doing away with the forced labor of peasants on the roads (the *corvée*) threatened privileged groups who had never before been taxed.

As he floundered for a solution to his economic difficulties, the king turned to a new adviser, Jacques Necker (1732–1804), a Swiss-born Protestant banker who tried to eliminate costly inefficiencies. He failed too and was forced to resign in 1781.

Calonne's Program. Charles Alexandre de Calonne (1734–1802), appointed controller-general in 1783, had his own ideas of how to bail out the ship of state. He authored a program of reforms that would have shifted the tax burden off those least able to pay and onto those best able to support the state. Specifically, he proposed a tax on land proportional to land values, a measure that would have most seriously affected the land-rich nobility. In addition, taxes that affected the peasantry were to be lightened or eliminated. Finally, Calonne proposed the sale of Church lands for revenues. In an attempt to bypass the recalcitrant parlements, Calonne advised the crown in 1787 to convene an Assembly of Notables made up of 150 individuals from the magistracy, the Church hierarchy, the titled nobility, and municipal bodies for the purpose of enlisting their support for reforms. Louis listened to Calonne, who was denounced by the Assembly of Notables for attacking the rights of the privileged. He too was forced to resign. All of Louis XVI's attempts to persuade the nobility to agree to tax reforms had failed.

Failed Reforms. A new controller-general, Archbishop Loménie de Brienne (1727–1794), recommended emergency loans. The crown once again disbanded the Paris Parlement, which was now threatening to block loans as well as taxes. Aristocratic magistrates insisted on a constitution, in which their own right to govern would be safeguarded and the accountability of the king would be defined. In opposing the royal reforms, nobles spoke of the "rights of man" and used the term *citizen*. They had no sympathy for tax programs that threatened their privileges. By the summer of 1788, Louis XVI had yielded to the condition placed on him by the Paris Parlement: he agreed to convene the Estates-General, a medieval body that had not met since 1614. Necker returned to power to preside over a caretaker government. The monarchy had collapsed and the political system of the Old Regime had come to an end.

THE FIRST STAGE OF THE FRENCH REVOLUTION, 1789–1792

Those who lived through it were sure that there had never been a time like it before. The French Revolution, or the Great Revolution, as it was known to contemporaries, was a time of creation and discovery. The ten years from 1789 to 1799 were punctuated by genuine euphoria and democratic transformations. From the privileged elites who initiated the overthrow of the existing order to the peasants and workers, men and women, who railed against tyranny, the revolution touched every segment of society.

The revolution achieved most in the area of politics. The overthrow of absolutist monarchy brought with it new social theories, new symbols, and new behavior. The excitement of anarchy was matched by the terror of repression. Revolutionary France had to contend with war throughout Europe. The revolution had its dark side of violence and instability: in its wake came internal discord, civil war, and violent repression. In the search for a new order, political forms followed one after the other in rapid succession: constitutional monarchy, republic, oligarchy. The creation of Napoleon's dictatorship at the end of the century signified that the revolution had come to an end.

Revolutionary incidents flared up throughout Europe in the second half of the eighteenth century in the Netherlands, Belgium, and Ireland. Absolute authority was challenged and sometimes modified. Across the Atlantic, American colonists concerned with the principle of self-rule had thrown off the yoke of the British in the War of Independence. But none of the events, including the American Revolution, was so violent in breaking with the old order, so extensive in involving millions of men and women in political action, and so consequential for the political futures of other European states as was the French Revolution. The triumphs and contradictions of the revolutionary experiment in democracy mark the end of the old order and the beginning of modern history. Politics would never be the same again.

Taking Politics to the People

Choosing representatives for the Estates-General in March and April 1789 stirred up hope and excitement in every corner of France. The call for national elections set in motion a politicizing process the king could not control.

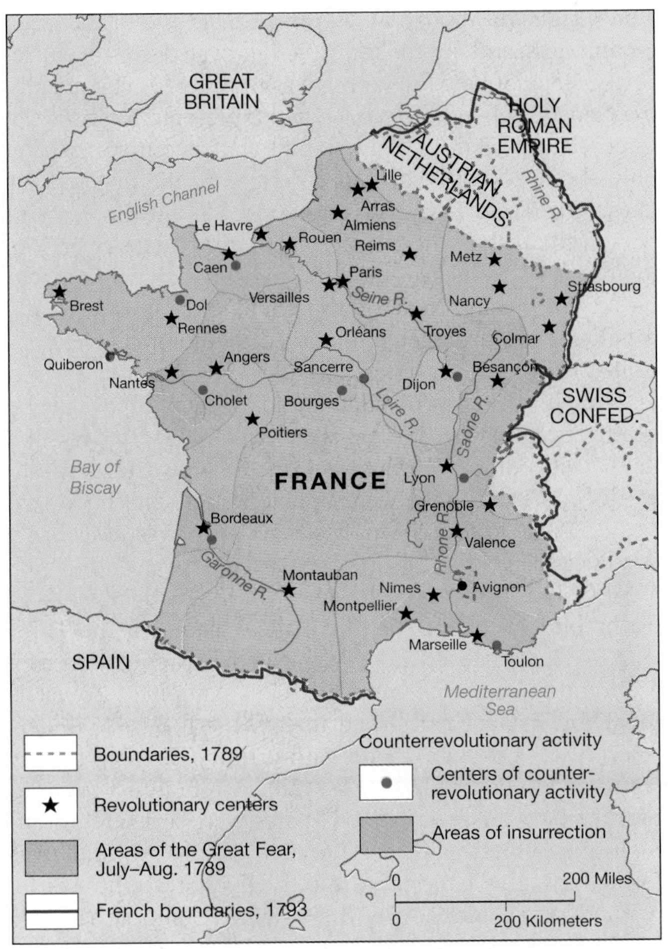

Revolutionary France. The Revolution was not merely a Parisian phenomenon, as this map shows. The forces of the Revolution and the Counterrevolution spread across France. The French borders in 1793 were the result of two years of military expansion in Europe.

Rising Expectations. When Louis XVI announced in August 1788 that the Estates-General would meet at Versailles in May 1789, people from all walks of life hoped for some redress of their miseries. The king hoped that the clergy, nobility, and commoners would somehow solve his fiscal problems. Every social group, from the nobles to the poorest laborers, had its own agenda and its own ideas about justice, social status, and economic well-being.

One in four nobles had moved from the bourgeoisie to the aristocratic ranks in the eighteenth century; two out of every three had been ennobled during the seventeenth or eighteenth centuries. Nobles had succeeded in expanding their economic and social power and they now sought to preserve it. Furthermore, a growing segment of the nobility, influenced by Enlightenment ideas and the example of English institutions, was intent on increasing the political dominance of the aristocracy.

Members of the Third Estate, traditionally excluded from political and social power, were presented with the opportunity of expressing their opinions on the state of government and society. As commoners in the Third Estate, the bourgeoisie embraced within it a variety of professions, from bankers and financiers to businessmen, merchants, entrepreneurs, lawyers, shopkeepers, and artisans. Those who could not read stood in marketplaces and city squares or sat around evening fires and had the political literature read to them. Farmhands and urban laborers realized that they were participating in the same process as their social betters, and they believed they had a right to speak and be heard.

It was a time of great hope, especially for workers and peasants who had been buffeted by the rise in prices, decline in real wages, and the hunger that followed crop failures and poor harvests. There was new promise of a respite and a solution. Taxes could be discussed and changed, the state bureaucracy could be reformed—or better, abolished. Intellectuals discussed political alternatives in the salons of the wealthy. Nobles and bourgeois met in philosophical societies dedicated to enlightened thought. Commoners gathered in cafes to drink and debate. Although the poor often fell outside of the network of communication, they were not immune to the ideas that emerged. In the end, people of all classes had opinions and were more certain than ever of their right to express their ideas. Absolutism was in trouble, though Louis XVI did not know it, as people began to forge a collectively shared idea of politics. People now had a forum—the Estates-General—and a focus—the politics of taxation.

"If Only the King Knew." In conjunction with the political activity and in scheduled meetings, members of all three estates drew up lists of their problems. This process took place in a variety of forums, including guilds and village and town meetings. The people of France drew up grievance lists—known as *cahiers de doléances*—that were then carried to Versailles by the deputies elected to the Estates-General. The grievance lists contained the collective outpouring of problems of each estate and are important for two major reasons. First, they made clear the similarity of grievances shared throughout France. Second, they indicated the extent to which a common political culture, based on a concern with political reform, had permeated different levels of French society. Both the privileged and the nonprivileged identified a common enemy in the system of state bureaucracy to which the monarch was so strongly tied. Although the king was still addressed with respect, new concerns with liberty, equality, property, and the rule of law were voiced.

"If only the king knew!" In that phrase, French men and women had for generations expressed their belief in the inevitability of their fate and the benevolence of their king. They saw the king as a loving and wise father who would not tolerate the injustices visited on his subjects if only he knew what was really happening. In 1789, peasants and workers were questioning why their lives could not be better, but they continued to express their trust in the king. Combined with their old faith was a new hope. The peasants in the little town of Saintes recorded their newly formed expectations:

> Our king, the best of kings and father of a great and wise family, will soon know everything. All vices will be destroyed. All the great virtues of industriousness, honesty, modesty, honor, patriotism, meekness, friendliness, equality, concord, pity, and thrift will prevail and wisdom will rule supreme.

Those who opposed the revolution later alleged that the grievance lists proved the existence of a highly coordinated plot on the part of secret societies out to destroy the regime. They were wrong. Similarities in complaints, demands, and language proved the forging of a new political consciousness, not a conspiracy. Societies and clubs circulated "model" grievance lists among themselves, resulting in the use of similar forms and vocabulary. People were questioning their traditional roles and now had elected deputies who would represent them before the king. In the spring of 1789, a severe economic crisis that heightened political uncertainty swept through France. For a king expected to save the situation, time was running out.

Convening the Estates-General

The elected deputies arrived at Versailles at the beginning of May 1789 carrying in their valises and trunks the grievances of their estates. The opening session of the Estates-General took place in a great hall especially constructed for the event. The 1,248 deputies presented a grand spectacle as they filed to their assigned places to hear speeches by the king and his ministers. Contrasts among the participants were immediately apparent. Seated on a raised throne under a canopy at one end of the hall, Louis XVI was vested in full kingly regalia. On his right sat the archbishops and cardinals of the First Estate, strikingly clad in the pinks and purples of their offices. On his left were the richly and decorously attired nobility. Facing the stage sat the 648 deputies of the Third Estate, dressed in plain black suits, stark against the colorful and costly costumes of the privileged. Members of the Third Estate had announced beforehand that they would not follow the ancient custom for commoners of kneeling at the king's entrance. Fired by the hope of equal treatment and an equal share of power, they had come to Versailles to make a constitution. The opening ceremony degenerated into a moment of confusion over whether members of the Third Estate should be able to wear their hats in the presence of the king. Many saw in the politics of clothing a tense beginning to their task.

The Crisis in Voting by Estate. The tension between commoners and privileged was aggravated by the unresolved issue of how the voting was to proceed. Historically, the Estates-General included equal representation from the three estates of the clergy, nobility, and commoners. Yet only about 200,000 subjects belonged to the first two estates. The Third Estate was composed of all those members of the realm who enjoyed a common identity only in their lack of privilege—more than 28 million French people. Traditionally, each of the three orders was equally weighted. The arrangement favored the nobility, who controlled the first two estates.

The Third Estate was adamant in its demand for vote by head. The privileged orders were equally firm in insisting on vote by order. Paralysis set in, as days dragged into weeks and the Estates were unable to act. The body that was to save France from fiscal collapse was hopelessly deadlocked.

Abbé Emmanuel Joseph Sieyès (1748–1836), a member of the clergy, emerged as the critical leader of the Third Estate. Sieyès had already established his reputation as a firebrand reformer with his eloquent pamphlet, "What Is the Third Estate?" published in January 1789. He understood that although eighteenth-century French society continued to be divided by law and custom into a pyramid of three tiers, these orders or estates were obsolete in representing social realities. The base of the pyramid was formed by the largest of the three estates, those who worked—the bourgeoisie, the peasantry, and urban and rural workers—and produced the nation's wealth. He argued that as long as the First and Second Estates did not share their privileges and rights, they were not a part of the French nation.

Under the influence of Sieyès and the reformist consensus that characterized their ranks, the delegates of the Third Estate decided to proceed with their own meetings. On 17 June 1789, joined by some sympathetic clergy, the Third Estate changed its name to the National Assembly as an assertion of its true representation of the French nation. Three days later, members of the new National Assembly found themselves locked out of their regular meeting room by the king's guard. Outraged by the insult, they moved to a nearby indoor tennis court, where they vowed to stay together for the purpose of writing a constitution. The event, known as the Oath of the Tennis Court, marked the end of the absolutist monarchy and the beginning of a new concept of the state that power resided in the people. The revolution had begun.

The Importance of Public Opinion. The drama of Versailles, a staged play of gestures, manners, oaths, and attire, also marked the beginning of a far-reaching political revolution. Although it was a drama that took place behind closed doors, it was not one unknown to the general public. Throughout May and June 1789, Parisians trekked to Versailles to watch the deliberations and then they brought the news back to the capital. Deputies wrote home to their constituents to keep them abreast of events. Newspapers that reported daily on the wranglings and pamphleteers who analyzed them spread the news throughout the nation. Information, often conflicting, stirred up anxiety; news of conflict encouraged action.

The frustration and stalemate of the Estates-General threatened to put the spark to the kindling of urban unrest. The people of Paris had suffered through a harsh winter and spring under the burdens of high prices (especially of bread), limited supplies, and relentless tax demands. The rioting of the spring had for the moment ceased as people waited for their problems to be solved by the deputies of the Estates-General. The suffering of the urban poor was not new, but their ability to connect economic hardships with the politics at Versailles and to blame the government was. As hopes began to dim with the news of political stalemate, news broke of the creation of the National Assembly. It was greeted with new anticipation.

The Storming of the Bastille

The king, who had temporarily withdrawn from sight following the death of his son at the beginning of June, reemerged to meet with the representatives of each of the three estates and propose reforms, including a constitutional monarchy. But Louis XVI refused to accept the now popularly supported National Assembly as a legitimate body, choosing instead to rely on the three estates for advice. He summoned troops to Versailles and began concentrating soldiers in Paris. Urban dwellers recognized the threat of repression that the troops represented, and crowds decided to meet force with force. To do so, they needed arms, and they knew where to get them.

On 14 July 1789, irate citizens of Paris stormed the Bastille, a royal armory that also served as a prison for a handful of debtors. The storming of the Bastille has become the great symbol of the overthrow of tyranny, but it is significant for another reason. It was an expression of the power of the people to take politics into their own hands. Parisians were following the lead of their deputies in Versailles. They had formed a citizen militia, known as the National Guard, and were prepared to defend their concept of justice and law.

The people who stormed the Bastille were not poor urban rabble, as they were portrayed by their detractors. They were bourgeois and petite bourgeois: shopkeepers, guild members, family men and women, who considered it their right to seize arms to protect their interests. The Marquis de Lafayette (1757–1834), a noble whom the people loved because of his participation in the American Revolution, helped to organize the National Guard. Under his direction the militia adopted the tricolor flag as their standard, replacing the fleur-de-lis of the Bourbons.

The king could no longer dictate the terms of the constitution. By their actions the people in arms had ratified the National Assembly. Louis XVI was forced to yield. Similar uprisings erupted in cities and towns throughout France. National guards in provincial cities modeled themselves after the Parisian militia. Government officials fled their posts, and commoners stood ready to fill the power vacuum that now existed. But the Revolution was not just an urban phenomenon. The peasants had their own grievances and their own way of making a revolution.

The Revolution of the Peasantry

The precariousness of rural life and the increase in population in the countryside contributed to the permanent displacement and destitution of a growing sector of rural society. Without savings and destroyed by poor harvests, impoverished rural inhabitants wandered the countryside looking for odd jobs and eventually begging to survive. All peasants endured common obligations placed on them by the crown and the privileged classes. A bewildering array of taxes afflicted peasants: they owed the tithe to the Church, land taxes to the state, and seigneurial dues and rents to the landlord. In some areas, peasants repaired roads and drew lots for military service. Dues affected almost every aspect of rural life. The labor of women was essential to the survival of the rural family. Peasant women sought employment in towns and cities as seamstresses and servants in order to send money back home to struggling relatives. Children, too, added their earnings to the family pot. In spite of various strategies for survival, the lives of more and more peasant families were disrupted by the end of the eighteenth century, as they were displaced from the land.

In the spring and early summer of 1789, food shortages drove bands of armed peasants to attack manor houses throughout France. In the areas surrounding Paris and Versailles, peasants destroyed game and devastated the forests where the king and his nobles hunted. The peasants suspended their anger as hope grew that the proceedings at Versailles would produce results and relieve their hardship.

The Fear of an Aristocratic Plot. News of the events of Versailles and then of the revolutionary action in Paris did not reassure rural inhabitants. By the end of June, the hope of deliverance from crippling taxes and dues was rapidly fading. The news of the Oath of the Tennis Court and the storming of the Bastille terrified country folk, who saw the actions as evidence of an aristocratic plot that threatened sorely needed reforms. As information moved along postal routes in letters from delegates to their supporters or news was repeated in the Sunday market gatherings, distortions and exaggerations crept in. It seemed to rural inhabitants that their world was falling apart. Some peasants believed that Paris was in the hands of brigands and that the king and the Estates-General were victims of an aristocratic plot.

This state of affairs was aggravated as increasing numbers of peasants, pushed off the land to seek employment as transient farm laborers, were moving from one area to another with the cycles of sowing and harvesting.

The Peasant Revolt. Hope gave way to fear. Beginning on 20 July 1789, peasants in different areas of France reacted with a kind of collective hysteria, spreading false rumors of a great conspiracy. They banded together and marched to the residences of the local nobility, breaking into the chateaus with a single mission in mind: to destroy all legal documents by which nobles claimed payments, dues, and services from local peasants. They drove out the lords and in some cases burned their chateaus, putting an end to the tyranny of the privileged over the countryside.

The members of the National Assembly were aghast at the eruption of rural violence. They knew that to stay in power, they had to maintain peace and protect property. Peasant destruction of seigneurial claims posed a real dilemma for the bourgeois deputies directing the Revolution. If they gave in to peasant demands, they risked losing aristocratic support and undermining their own ability to control events. If they gave in to the aristocracy, they risked a social revolution in the countryside, which they could not police or repress. Liberal members of the aristocracy cooperated with the bourgeois leaders in finding a solution.

In a dramatic meeting that lasted through the night of 4 August 1789, the National Assembly agreed to abolish the principle of privilege. The peasants had won—or thought they had. In the weeks and months ahead, rural people learned that they had lost their own prerogatives—the rights to common grazing and gathering—and were expected to buy their way out of their feudal services.

Women on the March

Women participated with men in both urban and rural revolutionary actions. Acting on their own, women were responsible for the most dramatic event of the early years of the Revolution. On the morning of 5 October 1789, women milling about in the marketplaces of Paris were complaining bitterly about the high cost and shortages of bread. The National Assembly was in session, and the National Guards were patrolling the streets of Paris. But these trappings of political change had no impact on the brutal realities of the marketplace. Women, who were in charge of buying food

A contemporary print of the women of Paris advancing on Versailles. The determined marchers are shown waving pikes and dragging an artillery piece. The women were hailed as heroines of the revolution.

for their families, were most directly in touch with the state of provisioning in the capital. When they were unable to buy bread, their anger exploded. So it was, on the morning of 5 October 1789, that 6,000 Parisian women marched out of the city toward Versailles to bring their protest to the king. Later in the day, Lafayette, sympathetic to the women's cause, led the Parisian National Guard to Versailles to mediate events. The women were armed with pikes and were prepared to use them.

The battle came early the next morning, when the women, tired and cold from waiting all night at the gates of the palace, invaded the royal apartments and chased Marie Antoinette from her bedroom. Several members of the royal guards, hated by the people of Paris for alleged insults against the tricolor cockade, were killed by the irate women, who decapitated them and mounted their heads on pikes. A shocked Louis XVI agreed to return with the crowd to Paris. The crowd cheered the king's decision, which briefly reestablished his personal popularity, though it did not erase his humiliation. Louis XVI was now captive to the Revolution, whose efforts to form a constitutional monarchy he purported to support.

The Trials of Constitutional Monarchy

The disciplined deliberations of committees intent on fashioning a constitutional monarchy replaced the passion and fervor of revolutionary oratory. The National, or Constituent, Assembly divided France into new administrative units—*départements*—for the purpose of establishing better control over municipal governments. Along with new administrative trappings, the government promoted its own rituals. On 14 July 1790, militias from each of the newly created 83 départements of France came together in Paris to celebrate the first anniversary of the storming of the Bastille. A new national holiday was born and, with it, a sense of devotion and patriotism for the new France that had been liberated by the Revolution. In spite of these unifying elements, however, the newly achieved revolutionary consensus showed signs of breaking down.

The Church Stripped of Its Power. On 2 November 1789, Church lands were nationalized. Three months later, legislation dissolved all monasteries and convents, except those that provided aid to the poor or that served as educational institutions. As the French church was stripped of its lands, Pope Pius VI (1775–1799) denounced the principles of the Revolution. In July 1790, the government approved the Civil Constitution of the Clergy; priests now became the equivalent of paid agents of the state. By requiring an oath of loyalty to the state from all practicing priests, the National Assembly created a new arena for dissent: Catholics were forced to choose to embrace or reject the Revolution. Many "nonjuring" priests who refused to take the oath went into hiding.

The wedge driven between the Catholic Church and revolutionary France allowed a mass-based counterrevolution to emerge. Aristocratic émigrés who had fled the country because of their opposition to the Revolution were languishing because of lack of a popular base. From his headquarters in Turin, the king's younger brother, the Comte d'Artois, was attempting to incite a civil war in France. When the revolutionaries decided to attack the Church, not just as a landed and privileged institution but also as a religious one, the counterrevolution expanded rapidly.

Constitutional Monarchy. The Constitution of 1791, completed after more than two years of deliberations, established a constitutional monarchy with a ministerial executive power answerable to a legislative assembly. Louis XVI, formerly the divinely anointed ruler of France, was now "Louis, by the grace of God and the constitutional law of the state, King of the French." In proclaiming his acceptance of the constitution, Louis expressed the sentiments of many when he said, "The end of the revolution is come. It is time that order be reestablished so that the constitution may receive the support now most necessary to it; it is time to settle the opinion of Europe concerning the destiny of France, and to show that French men are worthy of being free."

The Constitution of 1791 marked the triumph of the principles of the Revolution. But before the ink was dry on the final document, the king's actions doomed the new constitution to failure. He pretended to accept the constitutional monarchy, but late one night in June 1791, Louis XVI, Marie Antoinette, and their children disguised themselves as commoners and fled Paris. Louis intended to leave France to join foreign forces opposing the Revolution at Metz. He got as far as Varennes, where he was captured by soldiers of the National Guards and brought back to a shocked Paris. The king had abandoned the Revolution. Although he was not put to death for another year and a half, he was more than ever a prisoner of the Revolution. The monarchy was effectively finished as part of a political solution; with its demise went liberal hopes for a constitutional settlement.

The Revolution's Fiscal Crisis. The revolutionary government faced a fiscal crisis coupled with inflation and foreign war. To establish its seriousness and legitimacy, the National Assembly had been willing in 1789 to absorb the Old Regime's debts. The new government could not sell titles and offices as the king had done, but it did confiscate Church property. In addition, it issued treasury bonds in the form of assignats to raise money. The assignats soon assumed the status of bank-notes, and by spring 1790 they became compulsory legal tender. Initially, they were to be backed by land confiscated from the Church that was now being sold by the state. But the need for money quickly outran the value of the available land. The government continued to print assignats, resulting in the depreciation of French currency in international markets and inflation at home. Assignat-induced inflation produced a sharp decline in the fortunes of bourgeois investors living on fixed incomes. Rising prices meant increased misery for workers and peasants.

New counterrevolutionary groups were becoming frustrated with revolutionary policies. Throughout the winter and spring of 1791–1792, people rioted and demanded that prices be fixed, as the assignat dropped to less than half of its face value. Peasants refused to sell their crops for the worthless paper. Hoarding drove prices up further. Angry crowds turned to pillaging, rioting, and murder.

Foreign war beginning in the fall of 1791 also challenged stability. Some moderate political leaders welcomed war as a blessing in disguise, since it could divert the attention of the masses away from problems at home and could promote loyalty to the Revolution. Others envisioned war as a great crusade to bring revolutionary principles to oppressed peoples throughout Europe. The king and queen, trapped by the Revolution, saw war as their only hope of liberation. Louis XVI could be rightfully restored as the leader of a France defeated by the sovereigns of Europe. Others opposed the war, believing that it would destabilize the Revolution. France must solve its problems at home, they argued, before fighting a foreign enemy. Louis, however, encouraged the ministers and advisers who were eager for battle. In April 1792, France declared war against Austria.

The first stage of the French Revolution ended in the summer of 1792 with the prospect of increased violence both from abroad in international war and at home in mounting civil strife. In its first three years, however, the Revolution had accomplished great things by abolishing aristocratic privilege; by affirming the political principles of liberty, equality, and fraternity; and by asserting constitutional prerogatives of royal accountability. The attempt at constitutional monarchy had failed, but the contours of a new political universe took shape according to bourgeois definitions of political participation, property, and civil liberties. There was little certainty about what political solutions lay ahead, but it was clear that there could be no turning back.

EXPERIMENTING WITH DEMOCRACY: THE REVOLUTION'S SECOND STAGE, 1792–1799

The French Revolution was a school for the French nation. A political universe populated by individual citizens replaced the eighteenth-century world of subjects loyal to their king. A new construction of politics in which all individuals were equal ran counter to prevailing ideas about collective identities defined in guilds and orders. People on all levels of society learned politics by doing it. In the beginning, experience helped. The elites, both noble and bourgeois, had served in government and administration. But the rules of the game under the Old Regime had been very different, with birth determining power.

After 1789, all men were declared free and equal, in opportunity if not in rights. Men of ability and talent, who had served as middlemen for the privileged elite under the Old Regime, now claimed power as their due. Many of them were lawyers, experienced in the problems of exercising power, who had their own ideas about reform. But the school of the Revolution did not remain the domain of a special class. Women demanded their places. Workers seized their rights. And because of the inherent contradictions of representation and participation, experimenting with democracy led to outcomes that did not look very democratic at all.

Declaring Political Rights

The Constitution of 1791 was a statement of faith in a progressive constitutional monarchy. A king accountable to an elected parliamentary body would lead France into a prosperous and just age. The constitution acknowledged the people's sovereignty as the source of political power. It also enshrined the principle of property by making voting rights dependent on property ownership. All men might be equal before the law, but by the Constitution of 1791, only wealthy men had the right to vote for representatives and hold office.

Civil Liberties. All titles of nobility were abolished. In the early period of the Revolution, civil liberties were extended to Protestants and Jews, who had been persecuted under the Old Regime. Previously excluded groups were granted freedom of thought and worship and full civil liberties. Slavery in the colonies was reluctantly outlawed in 1794. Paris revolutionaries had supported the slave rebellion in Saint Domingue (modern-day Haiti) in 1791 even though black independence was at odds with French colonial interests. Led by Toussaint L'Ouverture (1743–1803), black rebels worked to found an independent Haitian state, which was declared in 1804. But the concept of equality with regard to race remained incompletely integrated with revolutionary principles, and Napoleon reestablished slavery in the French colonies in 1802.

Women's Rights. Men were the subject of these newly defined rights. No references to women or their rights appear in the constitutions or the official Declaration of Rights. But women were critical actors in the Revolution from its inception, and their presence shaped and directed the outcome of events, as the women's march to Versailles in 1789 made clear. The Marquis de Condorcet (1743–1794), elected to the Legislative Assembly in 1791, chastised the revolutionaries for overlooking the political rights of women who, he pointedly observed, were half of the human race. He also argued forcefully but unsuccessfully for women's right to be educated. Women remained conspicuously absent from the summit of political power. The Declaration of the Rights of Man and Citizen, adopted by the National Assembly in August 1789, had nothing to say about the rights of women. Olympe de Gouges, a playwright and revolutionary, rewrote the document, entitling her version, which appeared in 1791, Declaration of the Rights of Woman and the Female Citizen. She urged women to demand equal political and legal rights.

The revolutionaries had declared that liberty was a natural and inviolable right, a universal right that was extended to all with the overthrow of a despotic monarch and a privileged elite. The principle triumphed in religious toleration. Yet the revolutionary concept of liberty foundered on the divergent claims of excluded groups of workers, women, and slaves, who demanded full participation in the world of politics. In 1792, revolutionaries confronted the contradictions that were inherent in their political beliefs of liberty and equality, now challenged in the midst of social upheaval and foreign war. In response, the Revolution turned to more radical measures in order to survive.

The Second Revolution: The Revolution of the People

The first revolution of 1789 through the beginning of 1792 was based on liberty—the liberty to compete, to own, and to succeed. The second revolution, which began in 1792, took equality as its rallying cry. This was the revolution of the urban workers, men and women who demanded equality of rights. They were not benefiting from the Revolution, but they had come to believe in their own power as political beings. Organized on the local level into sections, craft workers in cities identified themselves as *sans-culottes*, literally those who did not wear knee breeches, to distinguish themselves from the privileged elite.

On 10 August 1792, the people of Paris invaded the Tuileries Palace, chanting their demands for "Equality!" and "Nation!" Love and respect for the king had vanished. What the people of Paris demanded now was universal manhood suffrage and participation in a popular democracy. Some of the sans-culottes were wealthier than others, some were wage earners, but all shared a common identity as consumers in the marketplace. They wanted government power to be decentralized, with neighborhoods ruling themselves through sectional organizations. When they invaded the Tuileries, the sans-culottes did so in the name of the people. They saw themselves as patriots whose duty it was to brush the monarchy aside. The people were now a force to be reckoned with and feared.

"Terror Is the Order of the Day"

Political factions characterized revolutionary politics from the start. The terms "Left" and "Right," which came to represent opposite ends of the political spectrum, originated in a description of where people sat in the Assembly in relation to the podium. Political designations were refined in successive parliamentary bodies. The Convention was the legislative body elected in September 1792, which succeeded the Legislative Assembly by the latter's own decree and had as its charge determining the best form of government after the collapse of the monarchy. On 21 September 1792, monarchy was abolished in France; the following day the Republic, France's first, came into being. Members of the Convention tried Louis XVI for treason and sentenced him to death by the guillotine in January 1793.

The various political factions of the Convention were described in terms borrowed from geography. The Mountain, sitting in the upper benches on the left, was made up of members of the Jacobin Club (named for its meeting place in an abandoned monastery). The Jacobins were the most radical element, supporting democratic solutions and speaking in favor of the cause of people in the streets.

Jacobin Ascendancy. Both Girondins, the more moderate revolutionary faction, and Jacobins were from the middle ranks of the bourgeoisie, and both groups were dedicated to the principles of the Revolution. At first the two groups were more similar than different. But although the Girondins controlled the ministries, they began to lose their hold on the Revolution and the war. The renewed European war fragmented the democratic movement, and the Girondins were unable to control violence at home. They became prisoners of the Revolution when 80,000 armed Parisians surrounded the National Convention in June 1793.

Girondin power had been eroding in the critical months between August 1792 and June 1793. A new leader was working quietly and effectively behind the scenes to weld a partnership between the popular movement of sans-culottes and the Jacobins. He was Maximilien Robespierre (1758–1794), leader of the Mountain and the Jacobin Club. Robespierre was typical of the new breed of revolutionary politicians. Only 31 years old in 1789, he wrote mediocre poems and attended the local provincial academy to discuss the latest ideas, when he was not practicing law in his hometown of Arras. Elected to the Estates-General, he joined the Jacobin Club and quickly became its leader. He was willing to take controversial stands on issues. Unlike most of his fellow members of the Mountain, including his rival, the popular orator Georges-Jacques Danton (1759–1794), he opposed the war in 1792. Although he was neither an original thinker nor a compelling orator, Robespierre demonstrated that he was a stunning political tactician when he engineered the Jacobin replacement of the Girondins as leaders of the government.

Robespierre and the Reign of Terror. Robespierre's chance for real power came when he assumed leadership of the Committee of Public Safety in July 1793. Facing the threat of internal anarchy and external war, the elected body, the National Convention, yielded political control to the 12-man Committee of Public Safety that ruled dictatorially under Robespierre's direction. The Great Committee, as it was known at the time, orchestrated the Reign of Terror (1793–1794), a period of systematic state repression that meted out justice in the people's name. Summary trials by specially created revolutionary tribunals were followed by the swift execution of the guilty under the blade of the guillotine.

Influenced by *The Social Contract* (1762) and other writings of Jean-Jacques Rousseau, Robespierre believed that sovereignty resided with the people. For him, individual wills and even individual rights did not matter when faced with the will of the nation. As head of the Great Committee, Robespierre oversaw a revolutionary machinery dedicated to economic regulation, massive military mobilization, and a punitive system of revolutionary justice characterized by the slogan "Terror is the order of the day." Militant revolutionary committees and revolutionary tribunals were established in the départements to identify traitors and to mete out harsh justice, especially to members of the bourgeoisie who were perceived as opponents of the government. The civil war, which raged most violently in the Vendée in the west of France, consisted often of primitive massacres that sent probably a quarter of a million people to their deaths. The bureaucratized Reign of Terror was responsible for about 40,000 executions in a nine-month period.

As part of the hated *Ancien Régime*, the Church also came under fire from the revolution. A Cult of the Supreme Being, a civic religion without priests or churches, was established. Its founders were influenced by Rousseau's ideas about nature. The cathedral of Notre Dame de Paris was turned into the Temple of Reason, and the new religion established its own festivals to undermine the persistence of Catholicism.

Women Excluded. By 1793, the Jacobin revolutionaries, who were willing to empower the popular movement of workers, turned against women's participation and denounced it. Olympe de Gouges, a framer of the Declaration of the Rights of Woman and the Female Citizen, was guillotined. Women's associations were outlawed, and the Society of Revolutionary Republican Women was disbanded. Women were declared unfit for political participation because of their biological functions of reproduction and child-rearing. Rousseau's ideas about family policy were probably more influential than his political doctrines. His best-selling books, *La Nouvelle Héloise* (1761) and *Émile* (1762), were moral works that transformed people's ideas about family life. Under his influence, the reading public came to value a separate and private sphere of domestic and conjugal values. Following Rousseau's lead, Robespierre and the Jacobins insisted that women's role as mothers was incompatible with their participation in the political realm.

The Thermidorian Reaction. Robespierre attacked his critics on the Left and on the Right, thereby undermining the support he needed to stay in power. He abandoned the alliance with the popular movement that had been so important in bringing him to power. Using the Terror, Robespierre eliminated his enemies and purged the Jacobins of those who might pose a threat to his control. Charges of conspiracy were leveled against Danton and his followers, who were all guillotined. In the end, Robespierre's enemies—and he had many—were able to turn the tables on him and brand him a traitor. He had saved France from foreign occupation and internal collapse, but he could not save democracy through terror. In the summer of 1794 in the revolutionary month of Thermidor, Robespierre was arrested and guillotined, and the Reign of Terror ceased.

The Revolution did not end with the Thermidorian Reaction, as the fall of Robespierre came to be known, but his execution initiated a new phase. For some, democracy lost its legitimacy. The popular movement was reviled, and "sans-culotte" became a term of derision. Jacobins were forced underground. Price controls were abolished, resulting in extreme hardship for most urban residents. In April 1795, out of desperation, the Jacobins and the sans-culottes renewed their alliance and united to demand "Bread and the Constitution of 1793," but their demands went unheeded, and the popular revolution was suppressed.

The End of the Revolution

In the four years after Robespierre's fall, a new government by committee was established. The Directory, as it was called, offered mediocrity, caution, and opportunism in place of the idealism and action of the early years of the Revolution. There were no heroes or heroines, no great orators. Most people, numbed after years of change, barely noticed that the Revolution was over. Ordinary men in parliamentary institutions effectively did the day-to-day job of running the government. They tried to steer a middle path between royalist resurgence and popular insurrection. This nearly forgotten period in the history of the French Revolution was the fulfillment of the liberal hopes of 1789 for a stable, constitutional rule.

However, the Directory continued to be dogged by European war. A mass army of conscripts and volunteers had successfully extended France's power and frontiers. France expelled foreign invaders and annexed territories, including Belgium, while increasing its control in Holland, Switzerland, and Italy. But the expansion of revolutionary France was expensive and increasingly unpopular. Military defeats and the corruption of the Directory undermined government control. The reinstatement of conscription in 1798 met with widespread resistance. No matter what their political leanings, people were weary. They turned to those who promised stability and peace. Ironically, the savior that France found to answer its needs for peace and a just government was a man of war and a dictator.

CHRONOLOGY

THE FRENCH REVOLUTION

August 1788	Louis XVI announces meeting of Estates-General to be held May 1789
5 May 1789	Estates-General convenes
17 June 1789	Third Estate declares itself the National Assembly
20 June 1789	Oath of the Tennis Court
14 July 1789	Storming of the Bastille
20 July 1789	Revolution of peasantry begins
26 August 1789	Declaration of the Rights of Man and Citizen
5 October 1789	Parisian women march to Versailles; force Louis XVI to return to Paris
February 1790	Monasteries, convents dissolved
July 1790	Civil Constitution of the Clergy
June 1791	Louis XVI and family attempt to flee Paris; are captured and returned
April 1792	France declares war on Austria
10 August 1792	Storming of the Tuileries
22 September 1792	Revolutionary calendar implemented
January 1793	Louis XVI executed
July 1793	Robespierre assumes leadership of Committee of Public Safety
1793–1794	Reign of Terror
1794	Robespierre guillotined
1799	Napoleon overthrows the Directory and seizes power

THE REIGN OF NAPOLEON, 1799–1815

The great debate that rages to this day about Napoleon revolves around the question of whether he fulfilled the aims of the Revolution or perverted them. In his return to a monarchical model, Napoleon resembled the enlightened despots of eighteenth-century Europe. In a modern sense, he was also a dictator, manipulating the French people through a highly centralized administrative apparatus. He locked French society into a program of military expansion that depleted its human and material resources. Yet in spite of destruction and war, he dedicated his reign to building a French state according to the principles of the Revolution.

Bonaparte Seizes Power

In 1795 a young, penniless, and unknown military officer moved among the wealthy and the beautiful of Parisian society and longed for fame. Already nicknamed at school "the Little Corporal" on account of his short stature, he was snubbed because of his background and ridiculed for his foreign accent. Yet within four years this young man had become the ruler of France.

Napoleon's Training and Experience. Napoleon Bonaparte (1769–1821) was a true child of the eighteenth century. He shared the philosophes' belief in a rational and progressive world. Napoleon was born into an Italian noble family in Corsica, which, until a few months before his birth, was part of the Republic of Genoa. He secured a scholarship to the French military school at Brienne, graduating in 1784. He then spent a year at the Military Academy in Paris and received a commission as a second lieutenant of artillery in January 1786.

The Revolution changed everything for Napoleon. It made new posts available as aristocratic generals defected, and it created great opportunities for military men to test their mettle. Foreign war and civil war required military leaders who were devoted to the Revolution. Forced to flee Corsica because he had sided with the Jacobins, Bonaparte crushed Parisian protesters who rioted against the Directory in 1795. The revolutionary wars had begun in 1792 as wars to liberate humanity in the name of liberty, equality, and fraternity. Yet concerns for power, territory, and riches replaced earlier French concerns with defense of the nation and of the Revolution.

This aggrandizement was nowhere more evident than in the Egyptian campaign of 1798, in which Napoleon Bonaparte headed an expedition whose goal was to enrich France by hastening the collapse of the Turkish Empire, crippling British trade routes, and handicapping Russian interests in the region. With Napoleon's highly publicized campaigns in Egypt and Syria, the war left the European theater and moved to the east, leaving behind the original revolutionary ideals.

The Egyptian campaign, which was in reality a disaster, made Napoleon a hero at home. His victories in the Italian campaign in 1796–1797 had launched his political career. As he extended French rule into central Italy, he became the embodiment of revolutionary values and energy.

Napoleon as First Consul. In 1799, Napoleon Bonaparte readily joined a conspiracy that pulled down the Directory, the government he had earlier preserved, and became the First Consul of a triumvirate of consuls.

Napoleon set out to secure his position of power by eliminating his enemies on the Left and weakening those on the Right. He guaranteed the security of property acquired in the Revolution, a move that undercut the royalists, who wanted to return property to its original owners. Through policing forces and special criminal courts, law and order prevailed, and civil war subsided. The First Consul promised a balanced budget and appeared to deliver it. Bonaparte spoke of healing the nation's wounds, especially those opened by religious grievances

Napoleon's Empire. By 1812, Napoleon directly ruled or controlled most of Europe.

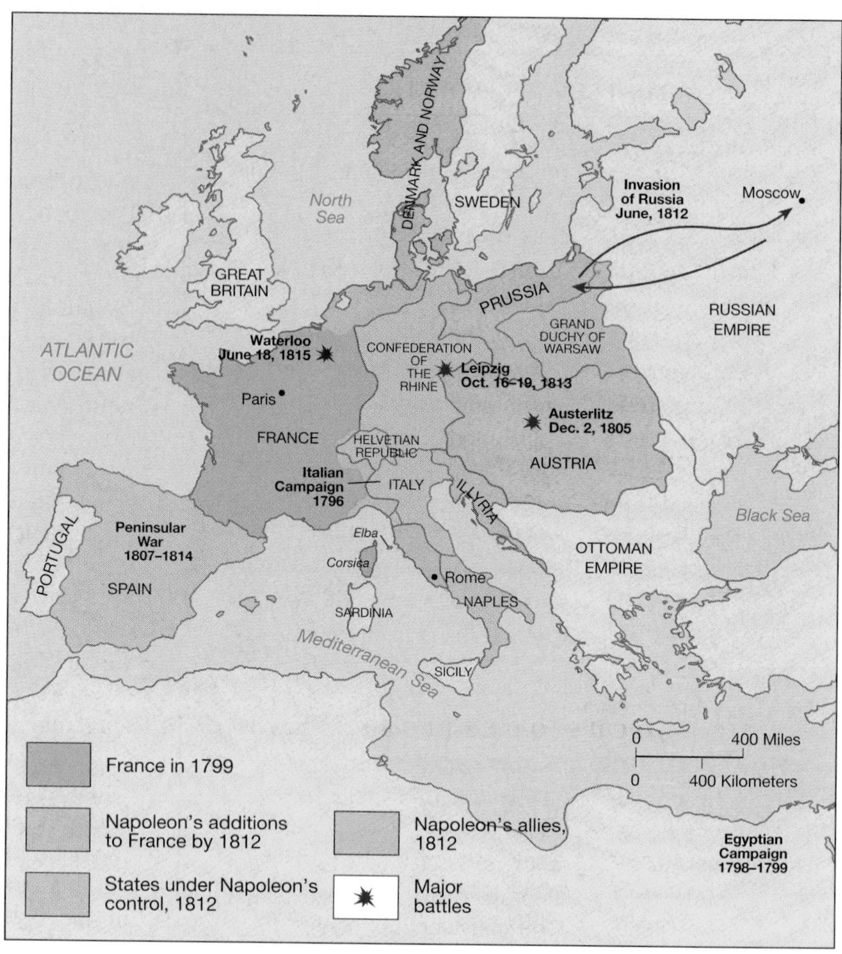

caused by de-Christianization during the Revolution. Realizing the importance of religion in maintaining domestic peace, Napoleon reestablished relations with the pope in 1801 in the Concordat, which recognized Catholicism as the religion of the French and restored the Roman Catholic hierarchy.

Napoleon's popularity as First Consul flowed from his military and political successes and his religious reconciliation. He had come to power in 1799 by appealing for the support of the army. In 1802, Napoleon decided to extend his power by calling for a plebiscite in which he asked the electorate to vote him First Consul for life. Public support was overwhelming. An electoral landslide gave Napoleon greater political power than any of his Bourbon predecessors had known.

Napoleon at War with the European Powers

Napoleon was at war or preparing for war during his entire reign. His military successes, real and apparent, before 1799 had been crucial in his bid for political power. By 1802, he had signed favorable treaties with both Austria and Great Britain. He appeared to deliver a lasting peace and to establish France as the dominant power in Europe. But the peace was short-lived. In 1803, France embarked on an 11-year period of continuous war. Under Napoleon's command, the French army delivered defeat after defeat to the European powers. Austria fell in 1805, Prussia fell in 1806, and the Russian armies of Alexander I were defeated at Friedland in 1807. In 1808, Napoleon invaded Spain to drive out British expeditionary forces intent on invading France. Spain became a satellite kingdom of France, although the conflict continued.

Britain was the one exception to the string of Napoleonic victories. Napoleon initially considered sending a French fleet to invade the island nation. Lacking the strength necessary to achieve this, he turned to economic warfare and blockaded European ports against British trade. Beginning in 1806, the Continental System, as the blockade was known, erected a structure of protection for French manufactures in all continental European markets. The British responded to the tariff walls and boycotts with a naval blockade that cut French commerce off from its Atlantic markets. The Continental System did not break the British economy, however, and the French economy did not flourish when faced with restricted resources and the persistence of a black market in smuggled goods.

Still, by 1810, Napoleon was master of the Continent. French armies had extended revolutionary reforms and legal codes outside France and brought with them civil equality and religious toleration. They had also drained defeated countries of their resources and had inflicted the horrors of war with armies of occupation, forced billeting, and pillage. Napoleon's empire extended across Europe, with only a diminished Austria, Prussia, and Russia remaining independent. He placed his relatives and friends on the thrones of the new satellite kingdoms of Italy, Naples, Westphalia, Holland, and Spain.

THE CIVIL CODE OF THE *CODE NAPOLÉON* (1804)

While still First Consul, Bonaparte assembled a group of the country's leading legal specialists to replace the vast agglomeration of feudal, customary, and canon laws, all with their own courts and procedures, with a unified system based on Roman law. The Civil Code, *along with the* Criminal Code, *made up the* Code Napoléon, *and consisted of 2,281 articles intended to cover all aspects of civil life from birth to death, all civic aspects relating to family and property, contractual responsibilities, and civil liberties. A unified legal system became the basis for economic development and was arguably Napoleon's greatest achievement as ruler of France. The* Civil Code *replaced the Roman Catholic Church as having authority over marriage, and although divorce was permitted in the* Code, *it was outlawed in 1816 and not permitted again until 1884.*

FOCUS QUESTIONS

What rights do men enjoy in this passage that women do not?

What are you able to conclude about the rights of married women who work?

OF THE RESPECTIVE RIGHTS AND DUTIES OF PARENT AND CHILDREN

212. Husband and wife owe each other fidelity, support, and assistance.
213. A husband owes protection to his wife; a wife owes obedience to her husband.
214. A wife is bound to live with her husband and to follow him wherever he deems proper to reside. The husband is bound to receive her, and to supply her with whatever is necessary for the wants of life, according to his means and condition.
215. A wife cannot sue in court without the consent of her husband, even if she is a public tradeswoman or if there is no community or she is separated as to property.
216. The husband's consent is not necessary when the wife is prosecuted criminally or in a police matter.
217. A wife, even when there is no community, or when she is separated as to property, cannot give, convey, mortgage, or acquire property, with or without consideration, without the husband joining in the instrument or giving his written consent.
218. If a husband refuses to allow his wife to sue in court, the Judge may grant the authorization.
219. If a husband refuses to allow his wife to execute and instrument, the wife can cause her husband to be summoned directly before the Tribunal of the First Instance of the common domicile, and such Tribunal shall grant or refuse its consent in the Judges' room after the husband has been heard or has been duly summoned.
220. A wife may, if she is a public tradeswoman, bind herself without the husband's consent with respect to what relates to her trade, and in that case she also binds her husband if there is a community of property between them. She is not considered a public tradeswoman if she merely retails the goods of her husband's business, but only when she has a separate business.
221. When a sentence has been passed upon a husband which carries with it a degrading corporal punishment, even if it has been passed by default, a wife, even of full age, cannot, during the continuance of the punishment, sue in court nor bind herself, unless she has been authorized by the Judge, who may in such cases grant the consent without the husband having been heard or summoned.
222. If a husband has been interdicted or is absent, the Judge may with proper knowledge of the case, authorize the wife to sue in court or to bind herself.
223. Any general authorization, even given by marriage contract, is only valid as to the management of the wife's property.
224. If the husband is a minor, the authorization of the Judge is necessary to the wife, either to sue in court or to bind herself.
225. A nullity based on the want of authorization can only be set up by the wife, the husband, or the heirs.
226. A wife can make a will without her husband's consent.

CHRONOLOGY

THE REIGN OF NAPOLEON

1799	Napoleon establishes consulate, becomes First Consul
1801	Napoleon reestablishes relations with pope, restores Roman Catholic hierarchy
1802	Plebiscite declares Napoleon First Consul for life
1804	Napoleon proclaims himself Emperor of the French
1806	Continental System implemented
1808–1814	France engaged in Peninsular War with Spain
June 1812	Napoleon invades Russia
September 1812	French army reaches Moscow, is trapped by Russian winter
1813	Napoleon defeated at Battle of Nations at Leipzig
March 1814	Napoleon abdicates and goes into exile on island of Elba
March 1815	Napoleon escapes Elba and attempts to reclaim power
15 June 1815	Napoleon is defeated at Waterloo and exiled to island of Saint Helena

The First Empire and Domestic Reforms

Napoleon measured domestic prosperity in terms of the stability of his reign. Through the 1802 plebiscite that voted him First Consul for life, Napoleon maintained the charade of constitutional rule while ruling as virtual dictator. In 1804, he abandoned all pretense and had himself proclaimed emperor of the French. He staged his own coronation and that of his wife Josephine at the cathedral of Notre Dame de Paris.

The Importance of Science and Economic Reforms. Secure in his regime, surrounded by a new nobility that he created on the basis of military achievement and talent, Napoleon set about implementing sweeping reforms in every area of government. He recognized the importance of science for both industry and war. The Revolution had removed an impediment to the development of a national market by creating a uniform system of weights and measures—the metric system, which was established by 1799. Napoleon felt the need to go further. To ensure French predominance in scientific research and application, Napoleon became a patron of science, supporting important work in the areas of physics and chemistry. Building for the future, Napoleon made science a pillar in the new structure of higher education.

The Directory had restored French prosperity through stabilization of the currency, fiscal reform, and support of industry. Napoleon's contribution to the French economy was the much needed reform of the tax system. He authorized the creation of a central banking system. French industries flourished under state protection. The blockade forced the development of new domestic crops such as beet-sugar and indigo, which became substitutes for colonial products. Napoleon extended the infrastructure of roads, so necessary for the expansion of national and European markets.

The New Legal System. Perhaps his greatest achievement was the codification of law, a task begun under the Revolution. Combined with economic reforms, the new Napoleonic Code facilitated trade and the development of commerce by regularizing contractual relations and protecting property rights and equality before the law. The civil laws of the new code carved out a family policy characterized by hierarchy and subordination. Married women were neither independent nor equal to men in ownership of property, custody of children, and access to divorce. Women also lacked political rights. In the Napoleonic Code, women, like children, were subjected to paternal authority. The Napoleonic philosophy of woman's place is well captured in an anecdote told by Madame Germaine de Staël (1766–1817), a leading intellectual of her day. On finding herself seated next to Napoleon at a dinner party, she asked him whom he considered the greatest woman, alive or dead. Napoleon responded, "The one who has had the most children."

Napoleon turned his prodigious energies to every aspect of French life. He encouraged the arts and created a police force. He had monuments built but did not forget about sewers. He organized French administrative life in a fashion that has endured. In place of the popular democratic movement, he offered his own singular authority. In place of elections, clubs, and free associations, he gave France plebiscites and army service. To be sure, Napoleon believed in constitutions, but he thought they should be "short and obscure." For Napoleon, the great problem of democracy was its unpredictability. His regime solved that problem by eliminating choices.

Decline and Fall

Militarily, Napoleon went too far. The first cracks in the French facade began to show in the Peninsular War (1808–1814) with Spain, as Spanish guerrilla tactics proved costly for French troops. But Napoleon's biggest mistake occurred when he decided to invade Russia in June 1812.

The Invasion of Russia and the Battle of Nations. Having decisively defeated Russian forces in 1807, Napoleon entered into a peace treaty with Tsar Alexander I that guaranteed Russian allegiance to French policies. But Alexander repudiated the Continental System in 1810 and appeared to be preparing for his own war against France. Napoleon seized the initiative, sure that he could defeat Russian forces once again. With an army of 500,000 men, Napoleon moved deep into Russia in the summer of 1812. The tsar's troops fell back in retreat, and when Napoleon and his men entered Moscow in September, they found a city in flames. The people of Moscow had destroyed their own city to deprive the French troops of winter quarters. Napoleon's men found themselves facing a severe Russian winter without overcoats, without supplies, and without food. The starving and frostbitten French army was forced into retreat. Fewer than 100,000 men made it back to France.

The empire began to crumble. Britain, unbowed by the Continental System, remained Napoleon's sworn enemy. Prussia joined Great Britain, Sweden, Russia, and Austria in opposing France anew. In the Battle of Nations at Leipzig in October 1813, France was forced to retreat. Napoleon refused a negotiated peace and fought on until the following March, when the victorious allies marched down the streets of Paris and occupied the French capital. Deserted by his allies, Napoleon abdicated in April 1814 in favor of his young son, the titular king of Rome (1811–1832). When the allies refused to accept the young "Napoleon II," the French called on the Bourbon Louis XVIII and crowned him king. Napoleon was then exiled to the Mediterranean island of Elba.

Napoleon's Final Defeat: Waterloo. Still, it was not quite the end for Napoleon. While the European heads of state sat in Vienna trying to determine the future of Europe and France's place in it, Napoleon returned from his exile on Elba. On 15 June 1815, Napoleon once again confronted the European powers in one of the most famous battles in history: Waterloo. With 125,000 loyal French forces, Napoleon seemed within hours of reestablishing the French empire in Europe, but the defeat of his forces was decisive. Napoleon's return proved brief, lasting only 100 days. He was exiled to the island of Saint Helena in the South Atlantic. For the next six years, Napoleon wrote his memoirs under the watchful eyes of his British jailors. He died a painful death on 5 May 1821 from what today is believed to have been cancer.

Conclusion

THE PERIOD OF REVOLUTION AND EMPIRE FROM 1789 TO 1815 radically changed the face of France. A new, more cohesive elite of bourgeois and nobles emerged, sharing power based on wealth and status. Ownership of land remained a defining characteristic of both old and new elites. A new state bureaucracy, built on the foundations of the old, expanded and centralized state power.

The people as sovereign now legitimated political power. Napoleon at his most imperial never doubted that he owed his existence to the people. He channeled democratic forces into enthusiasm for empire. He learned his lessons from the failure of the Bourbon monarchy and the politicians of the Revolution. For 16 years, Napoleon successfully reconciled the Old Regime with the new France. Yet he could not resolve the essential problem of democracy: the relationship between the will of the people and the exercise of political power. The picture in 1815 was not dramatically different from the situation in 1789. The Revolution might be over, but changes fueled by the revolutionary tradition were just beginning. The struggle for a workable democratic culture recurred in France for another century and elsewhere in Europe through the twentieth century.

This 1835 painting by De Boisdenier depicts the suffering of Napoleon's Grand Army on the retreat from Moscow. The Germans were to meet a similar fate more than 100 years later when they invaded Russia without adequate supplies for the harsh winter.

QUESTIONS FOR REVIEW

1. To what extent was the French nobility responsible for the crisis that destroyed the *Ancien Régime?*
2. How did commoners, men and women, transform a crisis of government into a revolution?
3. Why did the leaders of the Revolution resort to a "reign of terror" and what effect did that have on the Revolution?
4. What problems in France and beyond contributed to the rise of Napoleon?
5. What did Napoleon accomplish in France, and what brought about his fall?

DISCOVERING WESTERN CIVILIZATION ONLINE

You can obtain more information about the French Revolution and the Napoleonic Era at the websites listed below. See also the companion website that accompanies this text: www.ablongman.com/kishlansky, which contains an online study guide and additional resources.

The Crisis of the Old Regime in France, 1715–1788

www.fordham.edu/halsall/mod/modsbook05.html
Part of the Modern History Sourcebook sponsored by Fordham University with the goal to direct students to historical documents, this site is devoted to resources discussing absolutism with a subsection on France during the Old Regime.

www.loc.gov/exhibits/bnf/bnf0001.html
Different aspects of French culture as a form of elite power from Charlemagne to Charles de Gaulle are presented by the Library of Congress. Most of the material is from the collections of the Bibliothèque Nationale de France.

www.chateauversailles.fr/en/
Devoted to the history and images of Versailles, this site provides brief essays about the people and events significant to court culture during the seventeenth and eighteenth centuries. It also explores the role of Versailles in French culture after the French Revolution.

The First Stage of the French Revolution, 1789–1792

www.campus.northpark.edu/history/WebChron/WestEurope/AgeRevs.html
A collection of links to chronologies for the "Age of Revolution."

history.hanover.edu/modern/frenchrv.htm
A site devoted to the French Revolution with several links to primary source documents, essays, and bibliographies.

Experimenting with Democracy: The Revolution's Second Stage, 1792–1799

www.fordham.edu/halsall/mod/robespierre-supreme.html
This site contains Robespierre's words on The Cult of the Supreme Being and links to other sites.

The Reign of Napoleon, 1799–1815

www.fordham.edu/halsall/mod/modsbook13.html
This site will direct students to the Modern History Sourcebook section of documents on the French Revolution, Napoleon, and the Napoleonic Wars.

www.napoleon.org/en/home.asp
Sponsored by the Foundation Napoleon for "the furtherance of study and research into the civil and military achievements of the First and Second Empires," this site is aimed at a nonacademic audience, but provides chronologies, essays, images and videos, and links to other sites on Napoleon.

www.womeninworldhistory.com/lesson7.html
This site is part of a teaching unit on Women in World History that provides further pages on all aspects of women's history. It provides testimonies from women working in three different industries: textile workers, miners, and seamstresses.

SUGGESTIONS FOR FURTHER READING

The Crisis of the Old Regime in France, 1715–1788

Keith Michael Baker, *Inventing the French Revolution* (Cambridge: Cambridge University Press, 1992). In a set of essays, Keith Baker views the French Revolution as a basically political event that can only be understood in the context of the changing political culture of the eighteenth century. In examining the political dynamic of the Old Regime, Baker pays special attention to the use of language and the role of public opinion as a political invention.

Roger Chartier, *The Cultural Origins of the French Revolution*, tr. Lydia G. Cochrane (Durham, N.C.: Duke University Press, 1991). Argues for the importance of the rise of critical modes of thinking in the public sphere in the eighteenth century and of long-term de-Christianization in shaping the desire for change in French society and politics.

Daniel Roche, *The People of Paris* (Berkeley: University of California Press, 1987). An essay on popular culture in the eighteenth century in which the author surveys the lives of the Parisian popular classes—servants, laborers, and artisans—and examines their housing, furnishings, dress, and leisure activities.

The First Stage of the French Revolution, 1789–1792

Colin Lucas, ed., *Rewriting the French Revolution* (Oxford: Clarendon Press, 1991). Responding to the historiographic challenge of the bicentenary of the French Revolution, eight scholars present new interpretations in the areas of social development, ideas, politics, and religion.

Timothy Tackett, *Becoming a Revolutionary: The Deputies of the French National Assembly and the Emergence of a Revolutionary Culture* (Princeton: Princeton University Press, 1996). This thoroughly researched collective biography of the cohort of deputies to the National Assembly demonstrates that their practical experience was distinct from that of the nobility. The revolutionary politics of the cohort was forged in their service as deputies in the first year of the Revolution.

Michel Vovelle, *The Fall of the French Monarchy* (Cambridge: Cambridge University Press, 1984). A social history of the origins and early years of the Revolution, beginning with a brief examination of the Old Regime and paying special attention to social and economic changes initiated by the Revolution, the role of the popular classes, and the creation of revolutionary culture.

Experimenting with Democracy: The Revolution's Second Stage, 1792–1799

François Furet, *Interpreting the French Revolution* (Cambridge: Cambridge University Press, 1981). A series of essays challenging many of the assumptions about the causes and outcome of the Revolution and reviewing its historiography. The author argues that political crisis, not class conflict, was the Revolution's primary cause and that revolutionary ideas concerning democracy are central to an understanding of the Reign of Terror.

Dominique Godineau, *The Women of Paris and Their French Revolution* (Berkeley: University of California Press, 1998). A compelling account of the lives of women revolutionaries. Godineau presents women's protests as a mass movement within the Revolution.

Patrice Higonnet, *Goodness Beyond Virtue: Jacobins During the French Revolution* (Cambridge: Harvard University Press, 1998). The author considers the Jacobin politics as a model for modern democrats, not to be reduced to the tragedy of the Terror.

Michael L. Kennedy, *The Jacobin Clubs in the French Revolution, 1793–1795* (New York: Berghahn Books, 2000). The final volume of Kennedy's three-volume history of the Jacobin Club focusing on the period between May 1793 and August 1795.

Sara E. Melzer and Leslie Rabine, eds., *Rebel Daughters: Women and the French Revolution* (New York: Oxford University Press, 1992). Contributors from a variety of disciplines examine the importance of women in the French Revolution, with special attention to the exclusion of women from the new politics.

Dorinda Outram, *The Body of the French Revolution: Sex, Class and Political Culture* (New Haven, Conn.: Yale University Press, 1989). Examines how images of the body in the late eighteenth century differed from class to class and how bourgeois attitudes toward physicality resulted in a gendered political discourse in which the hero replaced the king.

The Reign of Napoleon, 1799–1815

Louis Bergeron, *France Under Napoleon* (Princeton, N.J.: Princeton University Press, 1981). An analysis of the structure of Napoleon's regime, its social bases of support, and its opponents.

Jean Tulard, *Napoleon: The Myth of the Saviour* (London: Weidenfeld and Nicolson, 1984). This biography of Napoleon situates his rise to power within the crisis of legitimacy created by the destruction of the monarchy during the Revolution. The Napoleonic empire is presented as a creation of the bourgeoisie, who desired to end the Revolution and consolidate their gains and control over the lower classes.

Isser Woloch, *Napoleon and His Collaborators: The Making of a Dictatorship* (New York: Norton, 2001). Woloch explains the success of Napoleon's regime in terms of the support of his civilian collaborators.

CHAPTER 21

INDUSTRIAL EUROPE

THE VISUAL RECORD

AN IRON FORGE

THE KEY TO INDUSTRIALIZATION was the replacement of muscle with machine. This demanded ingenuity on the part of inventors, capital on the part of investors, and adaptability on the part of workers. Whether in the cotton mills, where water-powered jennies allowed one worker to spin more than 100had before, or in the pits, where engines allowed water to be drained and miners to dig deeper, machinery changed the nature of production and productivity. Technological innovation transformed the nature of work in Britain.

Although we think of industry in terms of factories, labor forces, and mass output, early industry developed within the context of individual producers. Families worked in cottages to spin and weave, iron was refined and shaped by the village smith. The initial stages of the Industrial Revolution involved changing the ways in which these small producers worked. Joseph Wright's depiction of *An Iron Forge* is a case in point, a family portrait that almost resembles a nativity scene except that the birth being celebrated is the machine forging of iron, the miracle product of the age.

Joseph Wright of Derby was born and bred in the English Midlands where the Industrial Revolution first began. He was fascinated by the scientific developments of his age and specialized in paintings that were technically accurate. *An Iron Forge* was one of a number of industrial scenes that Wright painted in the 1770s when advances in technology were changing the face of rural life. The small shop must have once been that of an ordinary blacksmith, but now it has been transformed into a forge. Outside of the picture a giant water wheel turns a rod that is attached to the drum in the bottom left-hand corner of the painting. The drum turns a shaft which lifts the heavy tilting hammer until it strikes the wooden beam above it. The hammer then falls with the force of its weight to strike the bar of iron that is held in place on the anvil by the iron forger's assistant. No human could swing so heavy a hammer or shape so large a bar of iron so easily. Every detail is precise, in imitation of the mechanical process. For example, the anvil sits in a pan filled with wooden chips which act as a cushion to absorb the shock of the hammer blows. The tiled floor and bricked walls absorb the flying sparks as the red hot metal is molded into bars.

While the machinery is drawn precisely and the technology of the forge is represented accurately, it is the artist's imagination that creates the scene. Though the iron forger who gazes proudly upon his family is portrayed with huge, muscular arms and a powerful torso, he is not engaged in toil. He represents enlightened industry, able to stand above the backbreaking work that had previously been associated with smithing. Indeed, of the three workmen in the picture, only one is actually laboring and he is simply holding the tongs which keeps the iron in place. It is the machine that labors—the drum turning, the cam lifting, the hammer falling—and the people who benefit—proud parents, healthy and happy children. All are the product, the artist seems to be saying, of the new industrialization.

LOOKING AHEAD

As this chapter will discuss, industrialization began in Great Britain around forges like the one portrayed by Joseph Wright. It was the result of changes in agricultural practices that allowed for a larger population to be supported by fewer farmers. It was powered first by coal and its use in the production of iron and then by steam which allowed for powerful engines to mechanize production. The steam engine also allowed for a revolution in transportation with the development of the railroads. Industrialization transformed every aspect of the British economy and soon spread throughout Europe.

THE TRADITIONAL ECONOMY

For generation after generation, age after age, economic life was dominated by toil. Every activity was labor-intensive. Wood was chopped with an axe. Water was drawn from wells or dragged in buckets from the nearest stream. Everything that was consumed was pulled or pushed or lifted, and by the middle of the eighteenth century, nearly eight out of ten Europeans still tilled the soil.

Although the traditional economy was dominated by agriculture, an increasing amount of labor was devoted to manufacture. The development of a secure and expanding overseas trade created a worldwide demand for consumer goods. In the countryside, small domestic textile industries grew up. Families would take in wool for spinning and weaving to supplement their income from agriculture. When times were good, they would expend proportionately less effort in manufacturing; when times were bad, they would expend more. Their tasks were set by an entrepreneur who provided raw materials and paid the workers by the piece. Wages paid to rural workers were lower than those paid to urban laborers because rural workers' wages were not subject to guild restrictions and because they supplemented farm income. Though domestic industry increased the supply of manufactures, it demanded even more labor from an already overworked sector of the traditional economy.

By the eighteenth century, the process that would ultimately transform the traditional economy was already under way. It began with the Agricultural Revolution (discussed below), one of the great turning points in human history. Before it occurred, the life of every community and of every citizen was always a hostage of nature. The struggle to secure an adequate food supply was the dominant fact of life to which nearly all productive labor was dedicated. After the Agricultural Revolution, an inadequate food supply was a political rather than an economic fact of life. Fewer and fewer farmers were required to feed more and more people. In Britain, where nearly 70 percent of the population was engaged in agriculture at the end of the seventeenth century, less than 2 percent worked on farms at the end of the twentieth century. By the middle of the nineteenth century, the most advanced economies were capable of producing vast surpluses of basic commodities. The Agricultural Revolution was not an event, and it did not happen suddenly. It would not deserve the label "revolution" at all were it not for its momentous consequences: Europe's escape from the shackles of the traditional economy.

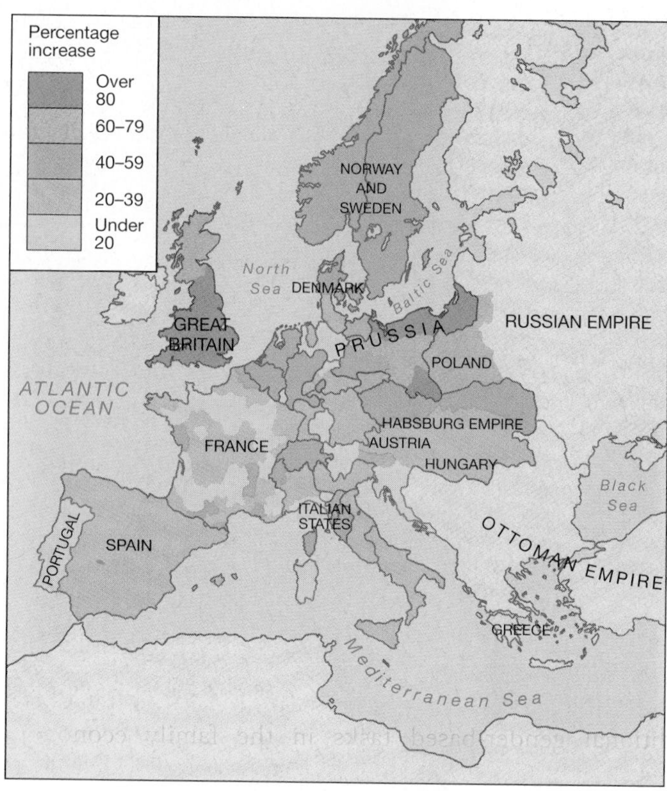

▲ Population Growth in Europe, 1800–1850. While the populations of Britain and Prussia exploded, those of France and Spain grew slowly, leaving them behind as industrialization took shape.

Rural Manufacture

By the end of the eighteenth century, the European population was reaching the point at which another check on its growth might be expected. Between 1700 and 1800, total European population had increased by nearly 50 percent, and the rate of growth was continuing to accelerate. This vast expansion of rural population placed a grave strain on agricultural production. Decade by decade, more families attempted to eke out an existence from the same amount of land. The gains made from intensive cultivation were now lost to overpopulation.

The crisis of overpopulation meant that not only were there more mouths to feed, there were more bodies to clothe. This increased the need for cloth and thus for spinners and weavers. Traditionally, commercial cloth production was the work of urban artisans, but the expansion of the marketplace and the introduction of new fabrics, especially cotton and silk, had eroded the monopoly of most of the clothing guilds. Merchants could sell as much finished product as they could find, and the teeming rural population provided a tempting pool of inexpensive labor for anyone who was willing to risk the capital to purchase raw materials. Initially, farming families took manufacturing work into their homes to supplement their income. Spinning and weaving were the most common occupations, and they were treated as occasional work, reserved for the slow times in the agricultural cycle.

This was known as cottage industry. It was side-employment, less important and less valuable than the vital agricultural labor that all members of the family undertook.

But by the middle of the eighteenth century, cottage industry was developing in a new direction. As landholdings grew smaller, even good harvests did not promise subsistence to many families. This oversupply of labor was soon organized into the putting-out system, which mobilized the resources of the rural labor force for commercial production of large quantities of manufactured goods. The characteristics of the putting-out system were similar throughout Europe. The entrepreneur purchased raw materials, which were "put out" to the homes of workers, where the manufacture took place, most commonly spinning or weaving. The finished goods were returned to the entrepreneur, who sold them at a profit, with which he bought raw materials to begin the process anew.

Putting-out required only a low level of skill and inexpensive common tools. Rural families did their own spinning, and rural villages did their own weaving. Thus putting-out demanded little investment, in either plant, equipment, or education. Nor did it inevitably disrupt traditional gender-based tasks in the family economy. Spinning was women's work, weaving was men's, and children helped at whichever task was under way.

As long as rural manufacture supplemented agricultural income, it was seen as a benefit for everyone involved—the entrepreneur, the individual worker, and the village community. But gradually, the putting-out system came to dominate the lives of many rural families. Spinning and weaving became full-time occupations for families that kept no more than a small garden. But without agricultural earnings, piecework rates became starvation wages, and families who were unable to purchase their subsistence were forced to rely on loans from the entrepreneurs who set them at work. Long hours in dank cottages performing endlessly repetitive tasks became the lot of millions of rural inhabitants. And their numbers increased annually. Whereas the sons of farmers waited to inherit land before they formed their families, the sons of cottage weavers needed only a loom to begin theirs. They could afford to marry younger and to have more children, for children could contribute to manufacturing from an early age. Consequently, the expansion of the putting-out system contributed to overpopulation. The putting-out system was labor-intensive, and as long as there were ready hands to employ, there was little incentive to seek more efficient techniques.

The Agricultural Revolution

The continued growth of Europe's population necessitated an expansion of agricultural output. In most places, this was achieved by intensifying traditional practices, bringing more land into production, and using more labor to work the land. But in the most advanced European economies, first in Holland and then in England, traditional agriculture underwent a long but dynamic transformation, an Agricultural Revolution. It was a revolution of technique rather than technology. Many of the methods that were to increase crop yields had been known for centuries but had never been practiced as systematically as they came to be from the seventeenth century onward and had never been combined with a commercial attitude toward farming. It was the owners' willingness and ability to invest capital in their land that transformed subsistence farming into commercial agriculture.

Enclosures. As long as farming was practiced in open fields, there was little incentive for individual landowners to invest in improvements to their scattered strips. Commercial agriculture was more suited to large estates than small ones and was more successful when the land could be utilized in response to market conditions rather than the necessities of subsistence. The consolidation of estates and the enclosure of fields were thus the initial steps in a long-term process of change.

In England, where enclosure was to become most advanced, it was already under way in the sixteenth century. Prosperous families had long been consolidating their strips in the open fields, and at some point, the lord of the manor and the members of the community agreed to carve up the common fields and make the necessary exchanges to consolidate everyone's lands. Perhaps as much as three-quarters of the arable land in England was enclosed by agreement before 1760. Enclosure by agreement did not mean that the breakup of the open-field community was always a harmonious process. Riots before or after agreed enclosures were not uncommon. Poor farmers who had once enjoyed the right to use certain strips of land for cultivation and pasture often found themselves reduced to working as hired hands for larger landowners.

Opposition to enclosure by agreement led, in the eighteenth century, to enclosure by act of Parliament. Parliamentary enclosure was legislated by government, a government that was composed for the most part of large landowners. A commission would view the community's lands and divide them, usually by a prescribed formula. Between 1760 and 1815, more than 1.5 million acres of farmland were enclosed by act of Parliament. During the late eighteenth century, the Prussian and French governments emulated this practice by ordering large tracts of land enclosed.

The enclosure of millions of acres of land was one of the largest expenses of the new commercial agriculture. As hedging or fencing off the land and plowing up the commons proceeded, more and more agricultural activity become market-oriented. Single crops were sown in large enclosed fields and exchanged at market for the mixture of goods that had previously been grown in the village.

Market production turned farmers' attention from producing a balance of commodities to increasing the yield of a single commodity.

Agricultural Innovations. The first innovation was the widespread cultivation of fodder crops such as clover and turnips. Crops like clover restore nutrients to the soil as they grow, shortening the period in which land has to lie fallow. Moreover, farm animals grazing on clover or feeding on turnips return more manure to the land, further increasing its productivity. Turnip cultivation had begun in Holland and was brought to England in the sixteenth century. But it was not until the late seventeenth century that Viscount Charles "Turnip" Townshend (1675–1738) made turnip cultivation popular. Townshend and other large Norfolk landowners developed a new system of planting known as the four-course rotation, in which wheat, turnips, barley, and clover succeeded one another. This method kept the land in productive use, and both the turnip and clover crops were used to feed larger herds of animals.

The ability of farmers to increase their livestock was as important as their ability to grow more grain. Not only were horses and oxen more productive than humans—a horse could perform seven times the labor of a man while consuming only five times the food—but the animals also refertilized the land as they worked. Light fertilization of a single acre of arable land required an average of 25,000 pounds of manure. But animals competed with humans for food, especially during the winter months, when little grazing was possible. To conserve grain for human consumption, some livestock had to be slaughtered in the autumn. Therefore the development of the technique of meadow floating was a remarkable breakthrough. By flooding low-lying land near streams in the winter, English and Dutch farmers could prevent the ground from freezing during their generally mild winters. When the water was drained, the land beneath it would produce an early grass crop on which the beasts could graze. This meant that more animals could be kept alive during the winter.

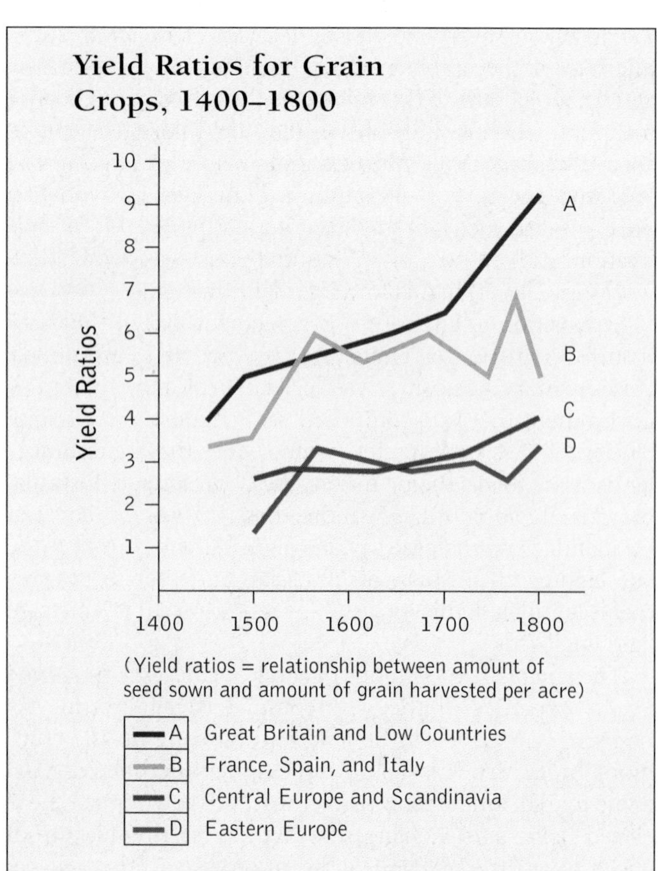

The relationship between animal husbandry and grain growing became another feature of commercial agriculture. In many areas, farmers could choose between growing grain and pasturing animals. When prices for wool or meat were relatively higher than those for grain, fields could be left in grass for grazing. When grain prices rose, the same fields could be plowed. Consolidated enclosed estates made this convertible husbandry possible. The decision to hire field workers or shepherds could be taken only by large agricultural employers.

Convertible husbandry was but the first step in the development of a true system of regional specialization in agriculture. Different soils and climates favored different uses of the land. In southern and eastern England, the soil was thin and easily depleted by grain growing. Traditionally, these light soil areas had been used almost exclusively for sheep rearing. On the other hand, the clay soils of central England, though poorly drained and hard to work, were more suited to growing grain. The new agricultural techniques reversed the pattern. The introduction of fodder crops and increased fertilization rejuvenated thin soils, and southeastern England became the nation's breadbasket. Large enclosed estates provided a surplus of grain throughout the eighteenth century. By the 1760s, England was exporting enough grain to feed over half a million people. Similarly, the midland clays became the location of great sheep runs and cattle herds. Experiments in herd management, crossbreeding, and fattening all resulted in increased production of wool, milk, meat, leather, soap, and tallow for candles.

There can be no doubt about the benefits of the transformation of agricultural practices that began in Holland and England in the seventeenth century and spread slowly to all corners of the Continent over the next 200 years. Millions more mouths were fed at lower cost than ever before. In 1700, each person engaged in farming in England produced enough food for 1.7 people; in 1800, each produced enough for 2.5 people. Cheaper food allowed more discretionary spending, which fueled the demand for consumer goods, which in turn employed more rural manufacturers. But there are no benefits without costs. The transformation of agriculture was also a transformation in a way of life. The open-field village was a community; the enclosed estate was a business. The plight of the rural poor was tragic enough in villages of kin and neighbors, where face-to-face charity might be returned from one generation to the next. As landless laborers, however, the rural poor became fodder for the factories, the "dark satanic mills" that came to disfigure the land. For the destitute, charity was now bestowed on them in anonymous parish workhouses or by the good works of the comfortable middle class. In all of these ways the Agricultural Revolution changed the face of Europe.

THE INDUSTRIAL REVOLUTION IN BRITAIN

Like the changes in agriculture, the changes in manufacturing that began in Britain during the eighteenth century were more revolutionary in consequence than in development. A workforce that was predominantly agricultural in 1750 had become predominantly industrial a century later. A population that for centuries had centered on the south and east was now concentrated in the north and west. Liverpool, Manchester, Glasgow, and Birmingham mushroomed into giant cities. While the population of England grew by 100 percent between 1801 and 1851, from about 8.5 million to over 17 million, the populations of Liverpool and Manchester grew by over 1,000 percent.

It was the replacement of animal muscle by hydraulic and mineral energy that made this continued population growth possible. Water and coal drove machinery that dramatically increased human productivity. In 1812, one woman could spin as much thread as 200 women had in 1770. What was most revolutionary about the Industrial Revolution was the wave after wave of technological innovation and the hundreds of adjustments in technique that applied new ideas in one industry to another, that opened bottlenecks and solved problems.

The Industrial Revolution was a sustained period of economic growth and change brought about by the application of mineral energy and technological innovations to the process of manufacturing. It took place largely during the century between 1750 and 1850, though different industries moved at different paces and sustained economic growth continued in Britain until the First World War. It is difficult to define precisely the timing of the Industrial Revolution because, unlike a political event, an economic transformation does not happen all at once. Nor are new systems and inventions ever really new. Coal miners had been using rails and wheeled carriages to move ore since the seventeenth century; in the sixteenth century, "Jack of Newbury" had housed his cloth workers in a large shed. The one was the precursor of the railroad and the other was the precursor of the factory, but each preceded the Industrial Revolution by more than a century. Before 1750, innovations made their way slowly into general use, and after 1850 the pace of growth slowed appreciably. By then, Britain had a manufacturing economy, less than one-quarter of its labor force engaged in agriculture, and nearly 60 percent was involved in industry, trade, and transport.

Britain First

The Industrial Revolution occurred first in Britain, but even in Britain, industrialization was a regional phenomenon rather than a national one. Many areas of Britain remained untouched by innovations in manufacturing methods and agricultural techniques, though none remained unaffected by the prosperity that industrialization brought. This was the result of both national conditions and historical developments. When industrialization spread to the Continent, it took hold, as it had in Britain, in regions where mineral resources were abundant or where domestic manufacturing was a traditional activity. There was no single model for European industrialization, however often contemporaries looked toward Britain for the key to unlock the power of economic growth.

Water and Coal. Among Britain's blessings, water was foremost. Britain was favored by an internal water system that tied inland communities together. In the eighteenth century, no place in Britain was more than 70 miles from the sea or more than 30 miles from a navigable river. Water transport was far cheaper than hauling goods overland; a packhorse could carry 250 pounds of goods on its back or move 100,000 pounds by walking alongside a river pulling a barge. Small wonder that river transport was one of the principal interests of merchants and traders. Beginning in the 1760s, private concerns began to invest in the construction of canals, first to move coal from inland locations to major arteries and then to connect the great rivers themselves. Over the next 50 years, several hundred miles of canals were built by authority of Navigation Acts, which allowed for the sale of shares to raise capital. In 1760, the Duke of Bridgewater (1736–1803) lived up to his name by completing the first great canal. Among the beneficiaries were the people of Manchester, where the price of coal was halved.

Coal was the second of Britain's natural blessings. Britain's reserves of wood, especially those near centers of population, were nearly depleted by the eighteenth century. Coal had been in use as a fuel for several centuries, it was abundant, and it was easily transported on water. The location of large coalfields along waterways was a vital condition of its early use. As canals and roadways improved, more inland coal was brought into production for domestic use. Yet it was in industry rather than in the home that coal was put to its greatest use. Here again, Britain was favored, for large seams of coal were also located near large seams of iron.

Economic Infrastructure. The factors that contributed to Britain's early industrialization were not only those of natural advantage. Over the course of years, Britain had developed an infrastructure for economic advancement. The transformation of domestic handicrafts to industrial production depended as much on the abilities of merchants as on those of manufacturers. The markets for domestic manufacturing had largely been overseas, where British merchants built up relationships over generations. Export markets were vital to the success of industrialization as production grew dynamically, and most ventures needed a quick turnaround of sales to reinvest their profits in continued growth. Equally important, increased production meant increased demand for raw materials: Swedish bar iron for casting, Egyptian and American cotton for textiles, Oriental silk for luxuries. The expansion of shipping mirrored the expansion of the economy, tripling during the eighteenth century to over one million tons of cargo capacity.

The expansion of shipping, agriculture, and investment in machines, plant, and raw material all required capital. Not only did capital have to exist, but it had to be made productive. Profits in agriculture, especially in the south and east, had somehow to be shifted to investment in industry in the north and west. The wealth of merchants, which flowed into London, had to be redistributed throughout the economy. Short-term investments had to give way to long-term financing. At the end of the seventeenth century, the creation of the Bank of England had begun the process of constructing a reliable banking system. The Bank of England dealt almost entirely with government securities, but it also served as a bill broker. It bought the debts of reputable merchants at a discount in exchange for Bank of England notes. Bank of England notes could then be exchanged between merchants, and this increased the liquidity of the English economy, especially in London. It also became the model for provincial banking by the middle of the eighteenth century. In 1700, there were just 12 provincial banks; by 1790, there were nearly 300.

Though the banking system was vital to large enterprises, in fact the capital for most industry was raised locally, from kin and neighbors, and it grew by plowing profits back into the business. At least at the beginning, manufacturers were willing to take risks and to work for small returns to ensure the survival and growth of their business.

Minerals and Metals

The Industrial Revolution could not have occurred without coal. It was the black gold of the eighteenth century, the fuel that fed the furnaces and turned the engines of industrial expansion. The coal produced by one miner generated as much energy as 20 horses. Coal mining was the first capital-intensive industry in Britain and was already well developed by the seventeenth century. Only the very wealthy could afford to invest in coal mining, and the largest English coalfields were owned by landed families of means who were able to invest agricultural profits in mining.

Early Coal Mining. The technical problems of coal mining grew with demand. As surface seams were exhausted it became necessary to dig deeper shafts, to lower miners farther underground, and to raise the coal greater heights to the surface. Underground mining was extremely dangerous, however, and in addition to frequent cave-ins, miners struggled against inadequate ventilation and light.

But by far the most difficult mining problem was water. As pits were sunk deeper, they reached pools of groundwater, which enlarged as the coal was stripped away from the earth. The pit acted like a riverbed and was quickly filled. Water drainage presented the greatest obstacle to deep-shaft mining. Women and children could carry the water out in large skin-lined baskets, which were attached to a winding wheel and pulled up by horses. Primitive pumps, also horse-powered, had been devised for the same purpose. Neither method was efficient or effective when shafts sank deeper. In 1709, Thomas Newcomen (1663–1729) introduced a steam-driven pump, which enabled water to be sucked through a pipe directly from the pit bottom to the surface. Though the engine was expensive to build and needed tons of coal to create the steam, it could raise the same amount of water in a day as 2,500 humans, and within 20 years of its introduction there were 78 engines draining coal and metal mines in England.

Innovations like Newcomen's engine helped to increase coal output at just the time that it became needed as an industrial fuel. Between 1700 and 1830, coal production increased tenfold, despite the fact that deeper and more difficult seams were being worked. Eventually, the largest demand for coal came from the iron industry. In 1793, just two ironworks consumed as much coal as the entire population of Edinburgh. Like coal mining, iron making was both capital- and labor-intensive, requiring expensive furnaces, water-powered bellows, and mills in which forged iron could be slit into rods or rolled into sheets. Iron making depended on an abundance of wood, for it took the charcoal derived from ten acres of trees to refine one ton of iron ore. Because each process in the making of iron was separate, furnaces, forges, and mills were located near their own supplies of wood. The shipping of the bulky ore, pig iron, and bar iron added substantially to its cost.

The great innovations in the production of iron came with the development of techniques that allowed for the use of coal rather than wood charcoal in smelting and forging. As early as 1709, Abraham Darby (ca. 1678–1717), a Quaker nail maker, experimented with smelting iron ore with coke, coal from which most of the gas has been burned off. Iron coking greatly reduced the cost of fuel in

▲ Women and children often labored in horrible conditions that were cramped, lacked fresh air, and offered little sunlight.

the first stages of production, but because most ironworks were located in woodlands rather than near coal pits, the method was not widely adopted. Moreover, although coke made from coal was cheaper than charcoal made from wood, coke added its own impurities to the iron ore. Nor could it provide the intense heat needed for smelting without a large bellows. The cost of the bellows offset the savings from the coke until James Watt (1736–1819) invented a new form of steam engine in 1775.

The Steam Engine. Like most innovations of the Industrial Revolution, James Watt's steam engine was an adaptation of existing technology. Although Watt is credited with the invention of the condensing steam engine, one of the seminal creations in human history, the success of his work depended on the achievements of numerous other people. An instrument maker in Glasgow, Watt was asked to repair a model of a Newcomen engine and immediately realized that it would work more efficiently if there were a separate chamber for the condensation of the steam. Though his idea was sound, Watt spent years attempting to implement it. He did not succeed until he became partners with the Birmingham iron maker and manufacturer Matthew Boulton (1728–1809). At Boulton's works, Watt found craft workers who could make precision engine valves, and at the foundries of John Wilkinson (1728–1808) he found workers who could bore the cylinders of his engine to exact specifications. Watt later designed the mechanism to convert the traditional up-and-down motion of the pumping engine into rotary motion, which could be used for machines and ultimately for locomotion.

Watt's engine received its first practical application in the iron industry. Wilkinson became one of the largest customers for steam engines, using them for pumping, moving wheels, and ultimately increasing the power of the blast of air in the forge. Increasing the heat provided by coke in the smelting and forging of iron led to the transformation of the industry. In the 1780s, Henry Cort (1740–1800), a naval contractor, experimented with a technique for using coke as fuel in removing the impurities from pig iron. The iron was melted into puddles and stirred with rods. The gaseous carbon that was brought to the surface burned off, leaving a purer and more malleable iron than even charcoal could produce. Because the iron had been purified in a molten state, Cort reasoned, it could be rolled directly into sheets rather than first being made into bars. He erected a rolling mill adjacent to his forge and combined two separate processes into one.

Puddling and rolling had an immediate impact on iron production. Charcoal was no longer needed. From mineral to workable sheets, iron could be made entirely with coke, so ironworks moved to the coalfields. Forges, furnaces, and rolling machines were brought together and powered by steam engines. By 1808, output of pig iron had grown from 68,000 to 250,000 tons and that of bar iron from 32,000 to 100,000 tons.

Cotton Is King

Traditionally, British commerce was dominated by the woolen cloth trade, in which techniques of production had not changed for hundreds of years. During the course of the seventeenth century, new fabrics appeared on the domestic market, particularly linen, silk, and cotton. It was cotton that captured the imagination of the eighteenth-century consumer, especially brightly colored, finely spun Indian cotton.

Domestic Industries. Spinning and weaving were organized as domestic industries. Work was done in the home on small, inexpensive machines to supplement the income from farming. Even the widespread development of full-time domestic manufacturers did not satisfy the increased demand for cloth. Limited output and variable quality characterized British textile production throughout the early part of the eighteenth century. The breakthrough came with technological innovation. Beginning in the mid-eighteenth century, a series of new machines dramatically increased output and, for the first time, allowed English textiles to compete with Indian imports.

The first innovation was the flying shuttle, invented by John Kay (1704–1764) in the 1730s. A series of hammers drove the shuttle, which held the weft, through the stretched warp on the loom. The flying shuttle allowed weavers to work alone rather than in pairs, but it was adopted slowly, for it increased the demand for spun thread, which was already in short supply. The spinning bottleneck was opened by James Hargreaves (d. 1778), who devised a machine known as the jenny. The jenny was a wooden frame containing a number of spindles around which thread was drawn by means of a hand-turned wheel. The first jennies allowed for the spinning of eight threads at once, and improvements brought the number to more than 100. Jennies replaced spinning wheels by the tens of thousands. The jenny was a crucial breakthrough in redressing the balance between spinning and weaving, though it did not solve all problems. Jenny-spun thread was not strong enough to be used as warp, which continued to be wheel spun.

The need to provide stronger warp threads was ultimately solved by the development of the water frame. It was created in 1769 by Richard Arkwright (1732–1792), whose name was also to be associated with the founding of the modern factory system. Arkwright's frame consisted of a series of water-power-driven rollers, which stretched the cotton before spinning. These stronger fibers could be spun into threads that were suitable for warp, and English manufacturers could finally produce an all-cotton fabric. It was not long before another innovator realized that the water frame and the jenny could be combined into a single machine, one that would produce an even finer cotton yarn than that made in India. The mule, so named because it was a cross between a frame and a jenny, was invented by Samuel Crompton (1753–1827). It was the decisive innovation in cotton cloth production. By 1811, ten times as many threads were being spun on mules as on water frames and jennies combined.

The original mules were small machines that could be used for domestic manufactures. But increasingly, the mule followed the water frame into purposely built factories, where it became larger and more expensive. The need for large rooms to house the equipment and the need for a ready source of running water to power it provided an incentive for the creation of factories where

▼ In the eighteenth century, a number of British inventors patented new machines that transformed the British textile industry and marked the beginning of the Industrial Revolution. Among the inventions was the spinning jenny, invented by James Hargreaves in 1764, and named for his daughter. The jenny, which permitted the spinning of a number of threads at the same time, made possible the automatic production of cotton thread.

manufacturers could maintain control over the quality of products through strict supervision of the workforce.

Cotton Factories. Richard Arkwright constructed the first cotton factories in Britain, all of which were designed to house water frames. The organization of the cotton industry into factories was one of the pivotal transformations in economic life. Domestic spinning and weaving took place in agricultural villages; factory production took place in mill towns. The location of the factory determined population movements, and from the first quarter of the eighteenth century onward, a great shift toward the northeast of England took place. Moreover, the character of the work itself changed. The operation of heavy machinery reversed the traditional gender-based tasks. Mule spinning became men's work; hand-loom weaving was taken over by women. The mechanization of weaving took longer than that of spinning because of difficulties in perfecting a power loom and because of opposition to its introduction by workers known as Luddites, who organized machine-breaking riots in the 1810s. The Luddites attempted to maintain the traditional organization of their industry and the independence of their labor. For a time, hand-loom weavers managed to survive by accepting lower and lower piece rates. But their competition was like that of a horse against an automobile. In 1820, there were over 250,000 hand-loom weavers in Britain; by 1850, the number was fewer than 50,000. Weaving as well as spinning became factory work.

The transformation of cotton manufacture had a profound effect on the overall growth of the British economy. It increased shipping because the raw material had to be imported, first from the Mediterranean and then from America. American cotton, especially after 1794, when American inventor Eli Whitney (1765–1825) patented his cotton gin, fed a nearly insatiable demand. In 1750, Britain imported less than five million pounds of raw cotton; a century later the volume had grown to 588 million pounds. And to each pound of raw cotton, British manufacturers added the value of their technology and of their labor. By the mid-nineteenth century, nearly half a million people earned their living from cotton, which alone accounted for over 40 percent of the value of all British exports. Cotton was undeniably the king of manufactured goods.

The Iron Horse

The first stage of the Industrial Revolution in Britain was driven by the production of consumer goods. Pottery, cast-iron tools, clocks, toys, and textiles, especially cottons, were all manufactured in quantities that had been unknown in the early eighteenth century. These products fed a ravenous market at home and abroad. The greatest complaint of industrialists was that they could not get enough raw materials or fuel, nor could they ship their finished products fast enough to keep up with demand. Transportation was becoming a serious stumbling block to continued economic growth. Even with the completion of the canal network that linked the major rivers and improvement in highways and tollways, raw materials and finished goods moved slowly.

It was the need to ship increasing amounts of coal to foundries and factories that provided the spur for the development of railways. Ever since the seventeenth century, coal had been moved from the seam to the pit on rails, constructed first of wood and later of iron. Broad-wheeled carts pulled by horses ultimately ran from the seam to the dock. By 1800, there were perhaps 300 miles of iron rail in British mines. In the same year, Watt's patent on the steam engine expired, and inventors began to apply the engine to a variety of mechanical tasks.

Richard Trevithick (1771–1833) was the first to experiment with a steam-driven carriage. George Stephenson (1781–1848), who is generally recognized as the father of the modern railroad, made a vital improvement in engine power by increasing the steam pressure in the boiler and exhausting the smoke through a chimney. In 1829, he won a £500 prize with his engine "the Rocket," which pulled a load three times its own weight at a speed of 30 miles per hour and could actually outrun a horse.

The First Railways. In 1830, the first modern railway, the Manchester-to-Liverpool line, was opened. Like the Duke of Bridgewater's canal, it was designed to move coal and bulk goods, but surprisingly, its most important function came to be moving people. In its first year the Manchester-Liverpool line carried over 400,000 passengers, who generated double the revenue derived from freight. Investors in the Manchester-Liverpool line, who pocketed a comfortable 9.5 percent when government securities were paying 3.5 percent, learned quickly that links between population centers were as important as those between industrial sites. The London-Birmingham and London-Bristol lines were both designed with passenger traffic in mind. Railway building was one of the great boom activities of British industrialization. By 1835, Parliament had passed 54 separate acts establishing over 750 miles of railways. By 1852, over 7,500 miles of track were in use.

From Goods to Passengers. By the 1850s, coal was the dominant cargo shipped by rail, and the speedy, efficient service continued to drive prices down. The iron and steel industries were modernized on the back of demand for rails, engines, and cast-iron seats and fittings. In peak periods—and railway building was a boom-and-bust affair—as much as one-quarter of the output of the rolling mills went into domestic railroads, and much more went into continental systems. The railways also consumed massive amounts of bricks for beddings, sidings, and especially bridges, tunnels, and stations. Finally, the railways were a

▲ Honoré Daumier (1808–1879), *The Third-Class Carriage*. Daumier captured a human condition peculiar to the modern era: "the lonely crowd."

leading employer of labor, surpassing the textile mills in peak periods.

Most of all, the railroads changed the nature of people's lives. Whole new concepts of time, space, and speed emerged to govern daily activities. The cheap railway excursion was born to provide short holidays or even daily returns. Over six million people visited London by train to view the Crystal Palace exhibition in 1851, a number equivalent to one-third of the population of England and Wales. By speeding all forms of communication, the railways brought people together and helped to develop a sense of national identity.

Entrepreneurs and Managers

The Industrial Revolution in Britain was not simply invented. Too much credit is given to a few breakthroughs, and too little is given to the ways in which they were improved and dispersed. The Industrial Revolution was an age of gadgets when people believed that new was better than old and that there was always room for improvement. "The age is running mad after innovation," the English moralist Dr. Johnson wrote. "All the business of the world is done in a new way; men are hanged in a new way." Societies for the advancement of knowledge sprang up all over Britain. Journals and magazines promoted new ideas and techniques. Competitions were held for the best invention of the year, and prizes were awarded for agricultural achievements. Practical science rather than pure science was the hallmark of industrial development.

Yet technological innovation was not the same as industrialization. A vital change in economic activity took place in the organization of industry. Putters-out, with their circulating capital and hired laborers, could never make the economies necessary to increase output and quality while simultaneously lowering costs. This was the achievement of industrialists, producers who owned workplace, machinery, and raw materials and who invested fixed capital by plowing back their profits. Industrial enterprises came in all sizes and shapes. As late as 1840, fewer than 10 percent of the cotton mills employed more than 500 workers. Most were family concerns with under 100 employees, and many of them failed. There were over 30,000 bankruptcies in the eighteenth century, testimony both to the risks of business and the willingness of entrepreneurs to take them.

To survive against these odds, successful industrialists had to be both entrepreneurs and managers. As entrepreneurs they raised capital, almost always locally from relatives, friends, or members of their church. Quakers were especially active in financing each other's enterprises. The industrial entrepreneur also had to understand the latest methods for building and powering machinery and the most up-to-date techniques for performing the work. One early manufacturer claimed "a practical knowledge of every process from the cotton-bag to the piece of cloth." Finally, entrepreneurs had to know how to market their goods. In these functions, industrial entrepreneurs developed logically from putters-out.

But industrialists also had to be managers. The most difficult task was organization of the workplace. Most gains in productivity were achieved through the specialization of function. The processes of production were divided and subdivided until workers performed a basic task over and over. The education of the workforce was the industrial manager's greatest challenge. Workers had to be taught how to use and maintain their machines and disciplined to apply themselves continuously. At least at the beginning, it was difficult to staff the factories. Many employed children as young as the age of seven from workhouses or orphanages, who, though cheap to pay, were difficult to train and discipline. It was the manager's task to break old habits of intermittent work, indifference to quality, and petty theft of materials. Families were preferred to individuals, for then parents could instruct and supervise their children. There is no reason to believe that industrial managers were more brutal masters than were farmers or that children were treated better in workhouses than in mills. Labor was a business asset, what was sometimes called "living machinery," and its control with carrots and sticks was the industrial manager's chief concern.

Who were the industrialists who transformed the traditional economy? Because British society was relatively open, they came from every conceivable background: dukes and orphans, merchants and salespeople, inventors and improvers. Though some went from rags to riches, like Richard Arkwright, who was the thirteenth child of a poor barber, it was extremely difficult for a laborer to acquire the capital necessary to set up a business. Wealthy landowners were prominent in capital-intensive aspects of industries, for example, owning ironworks and mines but few established factories. Most industrialists came from the middle classes, which comprised only one-third of the British population but provided as many as two-thirds of the first generation of industrialists. These included lawyers, bankers, merchants, and people who were already engaged in manufacturing, as well as tradespeople, shopkeepers, and self-employed craft workers. The career of every industrialist was unique, as a look at two—Josiah Wedgwood and Robert Owen—will show.

Josiah Wedgwood. Josiah Wedgwood (1730–1795) was the thirteenth child of a long-established English potting family. He worked in the potteries from childhood, but a deformed leg made it difficult for him to turn the wheel. Instead, he studied the structure of the business. His head teemed with ideas for improving ceramic manufacturing, but it was not until he was 30 that he could set up on his own and introduce his innovations. These encompassed both technique and organization, the entrepreneurial and managerial sides of his business.

Wedgwood developed new mixtures of clays that took brilliant colors in the kiln and new glazes for both "useful" and "ornamental" ware. He was repelled by the disorder of the traditional pottery, with its waste of materials, uneven quality, and slow output. When he began his first works, he divided the making of pottery into distinct tasks and separated his workers among them. He invested in schools to help train young artists, in canals to transport his products, and in London shops to sell them. Wedgwood was a marketing genius. He named his famed cream-colored pottery Queen's ware and made special coffee and tea services for leading aristocratic families. He would then sell replicas by the thousands. In less than 20 years, Wedgwood pottery was prized all over Europe, and Wedgwood's potting works were the standard of the industry.

Robert Owen. Robert Owen (1771–1858), the son of a small tradesman, was apprenticed to a clothier at the age of 10. As a teenager he worked as a shop assistant in Manchester, where he audaciously applied for a job as manager of a cotton mill. At 19, he was supervising 500 workers and learning the cotton trade. Owen was immediately successful, increasing his workers' output and introducing new materials to the mill. In 1816, he entered a partnership to purchase the New Lanark mill in Scotland. Owen found conditions in Scotland much worse than those in Manchester. Over 500 workhouse children were employed at New Lanark, where drunkenness and theft were endemic. Owen believed that to improve the quality of work, one had to improve the quality of the workplace. He replaced old machinery with new, reduced working hours, and instituted a monitoring system to check theft. To enhance life outside the factory, he established a high-quality company-run store, which plowed its profits into a school for village children.

Owen was struck by the irony that in the mills, machines were better cared for than humans. He thought that with the same attention to detail that had so improved the quality of commodities, he could make even greater improvements in the quality of life. He prohibited children under the age of 10 from mill work and instituted a ten-hour day for child labor. His local school took infants from one year old, freeing women to work and ensuring each child an education. Owen instituted old-age and disability pensions, funded by mandatory contributions from workers' wages. Taverns were closed, and workers were fined for drunkenness and sexual offenses. In the factory and the village, Owen established a principle of communal regulation to improve both the work and the character of his employees. New Lanark became the model of the world of the future, and each year, thousands of people made an industrial pilgrimage to visit it.

The Wages of Progress

Robert Owen ended his life as a social reformer. His efforts to improve the lot of his workers at New Lanark led to experiments to create ideal industrial communities throughout the world. He founded cooperative societies, in which all members shared in the profits of the business, and supported trade unions in which workers could better their lives. His followers planted colonies in which goods were held in common and the fruits of labor belonged to the laborers. Owen's agitation for social reform was part of a movement that produced results of lasting consequence. The Factory Act (1833) prohibited factory work by children under the age of nine, provided two hours of daily education, and effectively created a 12-hour day in the mills until the Ten Hours Act (1847). The Mines Act (1842) prohibited women and children from working underground.

Nor was Owen alone in dedicating time and money to the improvement of workers' lives. The rapid growth of unplanned cities exacerbated the plight of people who were too poor and overworked to help themselves. Conditions of housing and sanitation were appalling even by nineteenth-century standards. *The Report on the Sanitary Condition of the Laboring Population in Britain* (1842), written by Edwin Chadwick (1800–1890), so shocked Parliament and the nation that it helped to shift the burden of social reform to the government. The Public Health Act (1848) established boards of health and the office of medical examiner. The Vaccination Act (1853) and the Contagious Diseases Act (1864) attempted to control epidemics.

The movement for social reform began almost as soon as industrialization. The Industrial Revolution initiated profound changes in the organization of British society. Cities sprang up from grain fields almost overnight. The lure of steady work and high wages prompted an exodus from rural Britain and spurred an unremitting boom in population. In 1750, about 15 percent of the population lived in urban areas; by 1850, about 60 percent did. Industrial workers married younger and produced more children than their agricultural counterparts. For centuries, women had married in their middle twenties, but by 1800, age at first marriage had dropped to 23 for the female population as a whole and to nearly 20 in the industrial areas. This was in part because factory hands did not have to wait until they inherited land or money and in part because they did not have to serve an apprenticeship. Early marriage and large families also signified a belief that things were better now and would be even better soon.

Expansion of Wealth. The Industrial Revolution brought a vast expansion of wealth and a vast expansion of people to share it. Agricultural and industrial change made it possible to support comfortably a population over three times that of the seventeenth century, when it was widely believed that England had reached the limits of expansion. Despite the fact that population doubled between 1801 and 1851, per capita income rose by 75 percent, which means that had the population remained stable, per capita income would have increased by a staggering 350 percent. At the same time, untold millions of pounds had been sunk into canals, roads, railways, factories, mines, and mills.

But the expansion of wealth is not the same as the improvement in the quality of life, for wealth is not equally distributed. An increase in the level of wealth may mean only that the rich are getting richer more quickly than the poor are getting poorer. Similarly, economic growth over a century involved the lives of several generations, which experienced different standards of living. One set of parents may have sacrificed for the future of their children; another may have mortgaged it. Moreover, economic activity is cyclical. Trade depressions, like those induced by the War of 1812 and the American Civil War, which interrupted cotton supplies, could have disastrous short-term effects. The Great Hunger of the 1840s was a time of agrarian crisis and industrial slump. The downturn of 1842 threw 60 percent of the factory workers in the town of Bolton out of work at a time when there was neither unemployment insurance nor a welfare system. Finally, quality of life cannot be measured simply in economic terms. People with more money to spend may still be worse off than their ancestors, who may have preferred leisure to wealth or independence to the discipline of the clock.

There are no easy answers to the quality-of-life question. It seems clear that in the first stages of industrialization, only the wealthy benefited economically, though much of their increased wealth was reinvested in expansion. Under the impact of population growth, the Napoleonic wars, and regional harvest failure, real wages seem to have fallen from the levels reached in the 1730s. Industrial workers were not substantially better off than agricultural laborers when the high cost of food and rent is considered. But beginning around 1820, there is convincing evidence that the real wages of industrial workers were rising, despite the fact that more and more work was semiskilled and unskilled machine-minding and more of it was being done by women, who were generally paid only two-thirds as much as men. Thus, in the second half of the Industrial Revolution, both employers and workers saw a bettering of their economic situation. This was one reason why rural workers flocked to the cities to take the lowest-paid and least desirable jobs in the factories.

EXPLOITING THE YOUNG

The condition of child laborers was a concern of English legislators and social reformers from the beginning of industrialization. Most of the attention was given to factory workers, and most legislation attempted to regulate the age at which children could begin work, the number of hours they could be made to work, and the provision of schooling and religious education during their leisure. It was not until the mid-1840s that a parliamentary commission was formed to investigate the condition of child labor in the mines. In this extract, the testimony of the child is confirmed by the observations of one of the commissioners.

FOCUS QUESTIONS

How does Mr. Franks's account differ from Ellison Jack's own?

Why do you think Ellison offers information about her level of literacy and knowledge of the Bible?

ELLISON JACK, 11-YEARS-OLD GIRL COAL-BEARER at Loanhead colliery, Scotland: I have been working below three years on my father's account; he takes me down at two in the morning, and I come up at one and two next afternoon. I go to bed at six at night to be ready for work next morning: the part of the pit I bear in the seams are much on the edge. I have to bear my burthen up four traps, or ladders, before I get to the main road which leads to the pit bottom. My task is four or five tubs: each tub holds 4G cwt. I fill five tubs in twenty journeys.

I have had the strap when I did not do my bidding. Am very glad when my task is wrought, as it sore fatigues. I can read, and was learning the writing; can do a little; not been at school for two years; go to kirk occasionally, over to Lasswade: don't know much about the Bible, so long since read.

R. H. Franks, Esq., the sub-commissioner: A brief description of this child's place of work will illustrate her evidence. She has first to descend a nine-ladder pit to the first rest, even to which a shaft is sunk, to draw up the baskets or tubs of coals filled by the bearers; she then takes her creel (a basket formed to the back, not unlike a cockle-shell flattened towards the neck, so as to allow lumps of coal to rest on the back of the neck and shoulders), and pursues her journey to the wall-face, or as it is called here, the room of work. She then lays down her basket, into which the coal is rolled, and it is frequently more than one man can do to lift the burden on her back. The tugs or straps are placed over the forehead, and the body bent in a semicircular form, in order to stiffen the arch.

"Child Labor in the Coal Mines," Testimony to the Parliamentary Investigative Committee (1842).

Social Costs. But economic gain had social costs. The first was the decline of the family as a labor unit. In both agricultural and early industrial activity, families labored together. Workers would not move to mill towns without the guarantee of a job for all members of their family, and initially, they could drive a hard bargain. The early factories preferred family labor to workhouse conscripts, and it was traditional for children to work beside their parents, cleaning, fetching, or assisting in minding the machines. Children provided an essential part of family income, and the youngest children were the agency of care for infirm parents. Paradoxically, it was the agitation for improvement in the conditions of child labor that spelled the end of the family work unit. At first, young children were barred from the factories, and older ones were allowed to work only a partial adult shift. Though reformers intended that schooling and leisure be substituted for work, the separation of children from parents in the workplace ultimately made possible the substitution of teenagers for adults, especially as machines replaced skilled human labor. The individual worker now became the unit of labor, and during economic downturns it was adult males with their higher salaries who were laid off first.

The decline of the family as a labor unit was matched by other changes in living conditions when rural dwellers migrated to cities. Many rural habits were unsuited to both factory work and urban living. The tradition of "Saint Monday," for example, was one that was deeply rooted in the pattern of agricultural life. Little effort was expended at the beginning of the work week, and progressively more was expended toward the end. Sunday leisure was followed by Monday recovery, a slow start to renewed labor. The factory demanded constant application, six days a week. Strict rules were enforced to keep workers at their stations and their minds on their jobs. More than efficiency was at stake. Early machines were not only crude, they were dangerous, with no safety features to cover moving parts. Maiming accidents were common in the early factories, the fault of both workers and machines. Similarly, industrial workers entered the world of the cash economy. Most agricultural workers were used to being paid in kind and to barter exchange. Money was an unusual luxury that was associated with binges of food, drink, and frivolities. This made adjustment to the wage packet as difficult as adjustment to the clock. Cash had to be set aside for provisions, rent, and clothing. On the farm, the time of a bountiful harvest was the time to buy durable goods; in the factory, "harvest time" was always the same.

Such adjustments were not easy, and during the course of the nineteenth century a way of life passed from England forever. For some, its departure caused profound sorrow; for others, it was an occasion of good riddance. A vertically integrated society in which lord of the manor, village worthies, independent farmers, workers, and servants lived together interdependently was replaced by a society of segregated social classes. By the middle decades of the nineteenth century, a class of capitalists and a class of workers had begun to form and had begun to clash. The middle classes abandoned the city centers and built exclusive suburban communities in which to raise their children and insulate their families. Conditions in the cities deteriorated under the pressure of overcrowding, lack of sanitation, and the absence of private investment. The loss of interaction between these different segments of society had profound effects on the struggle to improve the quality of life for everyone. Leaders of labor saw themselves as fighting against profits, greed, and apathy; leaders of capital saw themselves as battling drunkenness, sloth, and ignorance. Between these two stereotypes there was little middle ground.

THE INDUSTRIALIZATION OF THE CONTINENT

Though Britain took the first steps along the road to an industrial economy, it was not long before other European nations followed. There was intense interest in "the British miracle," as it was dubbed by contemporaries. European ministers, entrepreneurs, even heads of state visited British factories and mines in the hope of learning the key industrial secrets that would unlock the prosperity of a new age. The Crystal Palace exhibition of manufacturing and industry, held in London in 1851, was the occasion for a Continent-wide celebration of the benefits of technology. By then, many European nations had begun the transformation of their own economies and had entered a period of sustained growth.

There was no single model for the industrialization of the continental states. Contemporaries continually made comparisons with Britain, but in truth the process of British industrialization was not well suited to any part of the Continent but the coal-rich regions in Belgium and the Rhineland. Nevertheless, all of Europe benefited from the British experience. No one else had to invent the jenny, the mule, or the steam engine. Therefore although industrialization began later on the Continent, it could progress more quickly. France and Germany were building a railroad system within years of Britain, despite the fact that they had to import most of the technology, raw materials, and engineers.

Britain shaped European industrialization in another way. Its head start made it very difficult for follower nations to compete against British commodities in the world market. This meant that European industrialization would be directed first and foremost to home markets, where tariffs and import quotas could protect fledgling industries. Though European states were willing to import vital British products, they placed high duties on British-made consumer goods and encouraged higher-cost domestic production. Britain's competitive advantage demanded that European governments become involved in the industrialization of their countries, financing capital-intensive industries, backing the railroads, and favoring the establishment of factories.

European industrialization was therefore not the thunderclap that occurred in Britain. In France, it was a slow, accretive development that took advantage of traditional skills and occupations and gradually modernized the marketplace. In Germany, industrialization had to overcome the political divisions of the empire, the economic isolation of the petty states, and the wide dispersion of vital resources. Regions rather than states industrialized in the early nineteenth century, and parts of Austria, Italy, and Spain imported machinery and techniques and modernized their traditional crafts. But most of these states and most of the eastern part of Europe remained tied to a traditional agrarian-based economy that provided neither labor for industrial production nor purchasing power for industrial goods. These areas quickly became sources for raw materials and primary products for their industrial neighbors.

France: Industrialization Without Revolution

The experience of France in the nineteenth century demonstrates that there was no single path in industrialization. Each state blended its natural resources, historical experiences, and forms of economic organization in unique combinations. While some mixtures resulted in explosive growth, as in Britain, others made for steady development, as in France.

French industrialization was keyed to domestic rather than export markets and to the application of new technology to a vast array of traditional crafts. France possessed a pool of highly skilled and highly productive labor, a manufacturing tradition that was oriented toward the creation of high-quality goods, and consumers who valued taste and fashion over cost and function. While the British dominated the new mass market for inexpensive cottons and cast-iron goods, a market with high sales but low profit margins, the French were producing luxury items whose scarcity kept both prices and profits high.

Two decisive factors determined the nature of French industrialization: population growth and the French Revolution.

Slow Growth. From the early eighteenth to the mid-nineteenth century, France grew slowly. In 1700, the French population stood at just under 20 million; in 1850, it was under 36 million, a growth rate of 80 percent. In contrast,

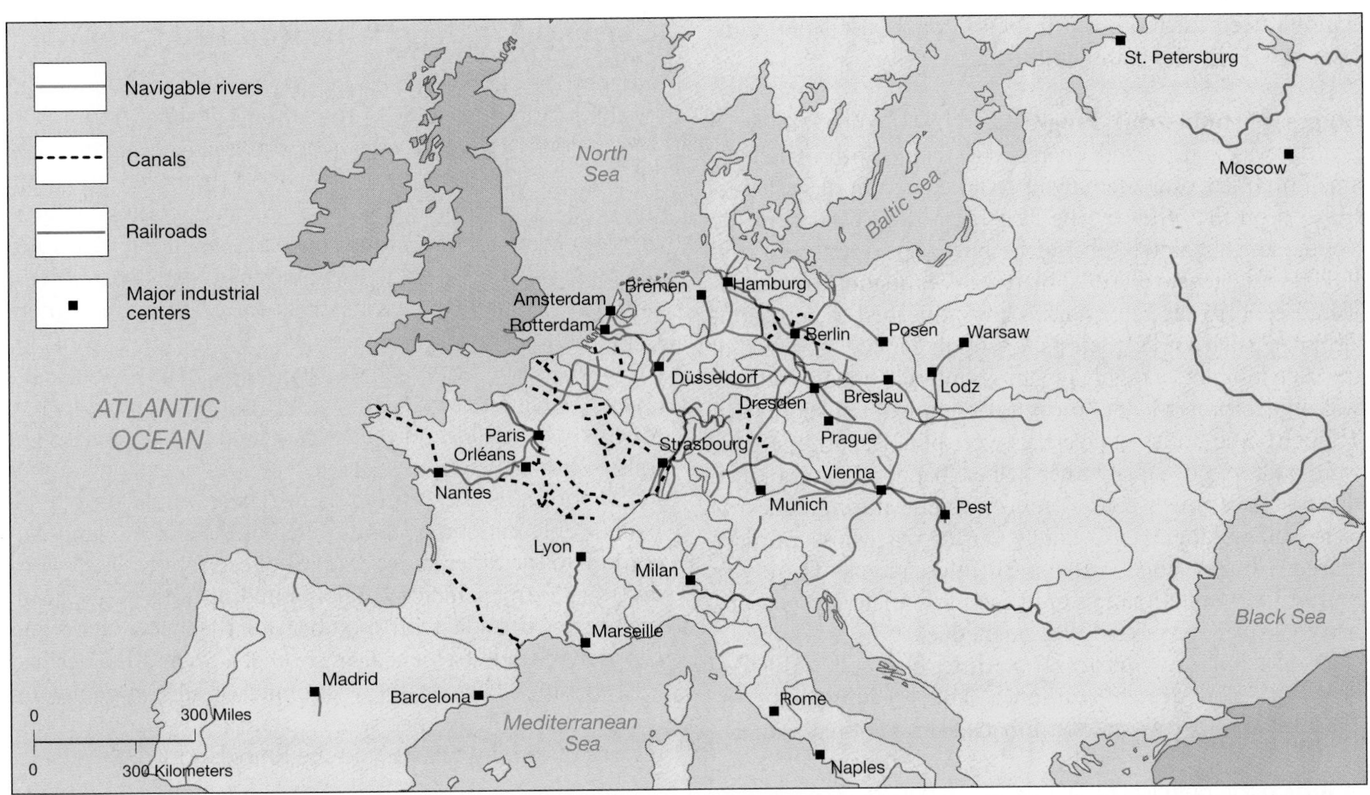

▲ The Industrial Revolution on the Continent. The major developments took place in Germany and in the coastal areas along the English Channel where there were better natural resources or pools of labor.

Germany grew 135 percent, from 15 to 34 million, and England grew 300 percent, from 5 to 20 million, during the same period. Nevertheless, France remained the most populous nation in western Europe, second on the Continent only to Russia. Because of its moderate population growth, France was not pressured by the force of numbers to abandon its traditional agricultural methods, nor did it face a shortage of traditional supplies of energy. Except during crop failures, French agriculture could produce to meet French needs, and more than enough wood remained for domestic and industrial use.

The Impact of the French Revolution. The consequences of the French Revolution are less clear. Throughout the eighteenth century, the French economy performed at least as well as had the British and better in many areas. French overseas trade had grown spectacularly until it was checked by military defeat in the Seven Years' War (1756–1763). French agricultural output increased steadily, while French rural manufactures flourished. A strong guild tradition still dominated urban industries, and although it restricted competition and limited growth, it also helped to maintain standards for the production of high-quality goods that made French commodities so highly prized throughout the world. The Revolution disrupted every aspect of economic life. Some of its outcomes were unforeseen and unwelcome. For example, Napoleon's Continental System, which attempted to close European markets to Britain, resulted in a shipping war, which the British won decisively and which eliminated France as a competitor for overseas trade in the mid-nineteenth century. But other outcomes were the result of direct policies, even if their impact could not have been entirely predicted. Urban guilds and corporations were abolished, opening trades to newcomers but destroying the close-knit groups that trained skilled artisans and introduced innovative products. Similarly, the breakup of both feudal and common lands to satisfy the hunger of the peasantry had the effect of maintaining a large rural population for decades.

Despite the efforts of the central government, there had been little change in the techniques used by French farmers over the course of the eighteenth century. French peasants clung tenaciously to traditional rights that gave even the smallest landholder a vital say in community agriculture. Landlords were predominantly absentees, less interested in the organization of their estates than in the dues and taxes that could be extracted from them. Therefore the policies of successive revolutionary governments strengthened the hold of small peasants on the land. With the abolition of many feudal dues and with careful family planning, smallholders could survive and pass a meager inheritance on to their children. French agriculture was able to supply the nation's need for food, but it could not release large numbers of workers for purely industrial activity.

Stages of Industrial Progress. Thus French industrial growth was constrained on the one hand by the relatively small numbers of workers who could engage in manufacturing and on the other by the fact that a large portion of the population remained subsistence producers, cash-poor and linked only to small rural markets. Throughout the eighteenth century, the French economy continued to be regionally segregated rather than nationally integrated. The size of the state inhibited a highly organized internal trade, and there was little improvement of the infrastructure of transportation. Though some British-style canals were built, canals in Britain were built to move coal rather than staple goods, and France did not have much coal to move. Manufacturing concerns were still predominantly family businesses whose primary markets were regional rather than international. There was no national capital market until the mid-nineteenth century, and there were precious few regional ones.

It was not until midcentury that sustained industrial growth became evident in France. This was largely the result of the construction of railroads on a national plan, financed in large part by the central government. Whereas in Britain the railways took advantage of a national market, in France they created one. They also gave the essential stimulation to the modernization of the iron industry, of machine making, and of the capital markets.

The disadvantages of being on the trailing edge of economic change were mitigated for a time by conventional practices of protectionism. Except in specialty goods, agricultural produce, and luxury products, French manufacturers could not compete with either British or German commodities. Had France maintained its position as a world trader, this comparative disadvantage would have been devastating. But defeat in the wars of commerce had led to a drawing inward of French economic effort. Marseilles and Bordeaux, once bustling centers of European trade, became provincial backwaters in the nineteenth century. But the internal market was still strong enough to support industrial growth, and domestic commodities could be protected by prohibitive tariffs, especially against British textiles, iron, and, ironically, coal.

While France achieved industrialization without an industrial revolution, it also achieved economic growth within the context of its traditional values. Agriculture may not have modernized, but the ancient village communities escaped the devastation that modernization would have brought. The orderly progression of generations of farming families characterized rural France until the shattering experiences of the Franco-Prussian War (1870) and the First World War (1914–1918). Nor did France experience the mushroom growth of new cities, with all of their problems of poverty, squalor, and homelessness. Slow population growth ameliorated the worst of the social diseases of industrialization, while traditional rural manufacturing softened the transformation of a way of life.

Germany: Industrialization and Union

The process of industrialization in Germany was dominated by the historic divisions of the empire of the German peoples. Before 1815 there were over 300 separate jurisdictional units within the empire, and after 1815 there were still more than 30. These included large advanced states such as Prussia, Austria, and Saxony as well as small free cities and the personal enclaves of petty nobles who had guessed right during the Napoleonic wars. Political divisions had more than political impact. Each state clung tenaciously to its local laws and customs, which favored its citizens over outsiders. Merchants who lived near the intersection of separate jurisdictions could find themselves liable for several sets of tolls to move their goods and several sets of customs duties for importing and exporting them. These would have to be paid in different currencies at different rates of exchange according to the different regulations of each state. Small wonder that German merchants exhibited an intense localism, preferring to trade with members of their own state and supporting trade barriers against others. Such obstacles had a depressing effect on the economies of all German states but pushed with greatest weight against the manufacturing regions of Saxony, Silesia, and the Rhineland.

Agriculture. Most of imperial Germany was agricultural land that was suited to a diversity of uses. The mountainous regions of Bavaria and the Austrian alpine communities practiced animal husbandry. There was a grain belt in Prussia, where the soil was poor but the land was plentiful, and one in central Germany in which the soil was fertile and the land was densely occupied. The Rhine Valley was one of the richest in all of Europe and was the center of German wine production. While English farmers were turning farms into commercial estates, German peasants were learning how to make do with less land.

Agricultural estates were organized differently in different parts of Germany. In the east, serfdom still prevailed. Peasants were tied to the land and its lord and were responsible for labor service during much of the week. Methods of cultivation were traditional, and neither peasants nor lords had much incentive to adopt new techniques. In central Germany, the long process of commuting labor service into rents was nearly complete by the end of the eighteenth century. The peasantry was not yet free, as a series of manorial relationships still tied them to the land, but they were no longer mere serfs. Finally, western Germany was dominated by free farmers who either owned or leased their lands and who had a purely economic relationship with their landlords. The restriction of peasant mobility in much of Germany posed difficulties for the creation of an industrial workforce. As late as 1800, over 80 percent of the German population was engaged in agriculture, a proportion that would drop slowly over the next half century.

Though Germany was well endowed with natural resources and skilled labor in a number of trades, it had not taken part in the expansion of world trade during the seventeenth century, and the once bustling Hanseatic ports had been far outdistanced by the rise of the Atlantic economies. The principal exported manufacture was linen, which was expertly spun and woven in Saxony and the Prussian province of Silesia. The linen industry relied on the putting-out system and some factory spinning, especially after the introduction of British mechanical innovations. But even the most advanced factories were still being powered by water, and so they were located in mountainous regions where rapidly running streams could turn the wheels. Neither linens nor traditional German metal crafts could compete on the international markets, but they could find a wider market within Germany if only the problems of political division could be resolved.

The Zollverein. The problems of political division were especially acute for Prussia after the reorganization of European boundaries in 1815. Prussian territory now included the coal- and iron-rich Rhineland provinces, but a number of smaller states separated these areas from Prussia's eastern domain. Each small state exacted its own tolls and customs duties whenever Prussian merchants wanted to move goods from one part of Prussia to the other. Such movement became more common in the nineteenth century as German manufacturing began to grow in step with its rising population. Between 1815 and 1865, the population of Germany grew by 60 percent, to over 36 million. This was an enormous internal market, nearly as large as France, and the Prussians resolved to make it a unified trading zone by creating a series of alliances with smaller states, known as the Zollverein (1834). The Zollverein was not a free-trade zone, like the British Empire, but rather a customs union in which member states adopted the liberal Prussian customs regulations. Every state was paid an annual portion of receipts based on its population, and every state—except Prussia—increased its revenues as a result. Prussia gained the ability to move goods and materials from east to west. It also forced Hanover and Saxony into the Zollverein and kept its powerful rival Austria out. Prussia's economic union soon proved to be the basis for the union of the German states.

The creation of the Zollverein was vital to German industrialization. It permitted the exploitation of natural advantages, such as plentiful supplies of coal and iron, and it provided a basis for the building of railroads. Germany was a follower nation in the process of industrialization. Seeking to learn from England, it brought British equipment and engineers to Germany, and German manufacturers sent their children to England to learn the latest techniques in industrial management. Friedrich Engels (1820–1895) worked in a Manchester cotton factory, where he observed the appalling conditions of the industrial labor force and wrote *The Condition of the Working Class in England* (1845). Steam engines were installed in German coal mines, if not in factories, and the process of puddling revolutionized iron making, though most iron was still smelted with charcoal rather than coke. Coal was plentiful in Prussia, but it was found at the eastern and western extremities of Germany. Therefore the railroads were the key to tapping German industrial potential. Here, they were a cause rather than a result of industrialization. The agreements that were hammered out in the creation of the Zollverein made possible the planning necessary to build single rail lines across the boundaries of numerous states.

Germany imported most of its engines directly from Britain and so adopted the standard British gauge for its system. As early as 1850, there were over 3,500 miles of rail in Germany, with important roads linking the manufacturing districts of Saxony and the coal and iron deposits of the Ruhr. Twenty years later, Germany was second only to Britain in the amount of track that had been laid and opened. By then, Germany was no longer simply a follower. German engineers and machinists, trained in Europe's best schools of technology, were turning out engines and rolling stock second to none. And the railroads transported a host of high-quality manufactures, especially durable metal goods that came to carry the most prestigious trademark of the late nineteenth century: "Made in Germany."

The Lands That Time Forgot

Nothing better demonstrates the point that industrialization was a regional rather than a national process than a survey of the states that did not develop industrial economies by the middle of the nineteenth century. These states ranged from the Netherlands, which was still one of the richest areas in Europe, to Spain and Russia, which were the poorest. Also included were Austria-Hungary, the states of the Italian peninsula, and Poland. In all of these nations there was some industrial progress. The Bohemian lands of Austria contained a highly developed spinning industry; the Spanish province of Catalonia produced more cotton than Belgium; and the Basque region was rich in iron and coal. Northern Italy mechanized its textile production, particularly silk spinning, while in the regions around both Moscow and Saint Petersburg, factories were run on serf labor. Nevertheless, the economies of all these states remained nonindustrial and, except that of the Netherlands, dominated by subsistence agriculture.

There were many reasons why these states were unable to develop their industrial potential. Some, such as Naples and Poland, were simply underendowed with resources; others, such as Austria-Hungary and Spain, faced difficulties of transport and communications that could not easily be overcome. Spain's modest resources were located on its northern and eastern edges, while a vast arid plain dominated the center. To move raw materials and finished products from one end of the country to the other was a daunting task, made more difficult by a lack of waterways and the rudimentary condition of Spanish roads. Two-thirds of Austria-Hungary was either mountains or hills, a geographic feature that presented obstacles that not even the railroads could easily solve. But there was far more than natural disadvantage behind the failure of these parts of Europe to move in step with the industrializing states. Their social structure, agricultural organization, and commercial policies all hindered the adoption of new methods, machines, and modes of production.

The leaders of traditional economies maintained tariff systems that insulated their own producers from competition. But protection was sensible only when it protected rather than isolated. Inefficiently produced goods of inferior quality were the chief results of the protectionist policies of the follower nations. Failure to adopt steam-powered machines made traditionally produced linens and silks so expensive that smuggling occurred on an international scale. Though these goods might find buyers in domestic markets, they could not compete in international trade, and one by one the industries of the follower nations atrophied. The economies that remained traditionally organized came to be exploited for their resources by those that had industrialized. Traditional agriculture could not produce the necessary surplus of either labor or capital to support industry, and industry could not economize sufficiently to make manufactured goods cheap enough for a poor peasantry.

There was more than irony in the fact that one of the first railroads built on the Continent was built in Austria but designed to be powered by horses rather than engines. The first railways in Italy linked royal palaces to capital cities; those in Spain radiated from Madrid and bypassed most centers of natural resources. In these states, the railroads were built to move the military rather than passengers or goods. They were state-financed, were occasionally state-owned, and almost always lost money. They were symbols of the industrial age, but in these states they were symbols without substance.

Conclusion

THE INDUSTRIALIZATION OF EUROPE IN THE EIGHTEENTH CENTURY was an epochal event in human history. The constraints on daily life that nature imposed were loosened for the first time. No longer did population growth in one generation mean famine in the next. No longer was it necessary for the great majority of people to toil in the fields to earn their daily bread. Manufacture replaced agriculture as humanity's primary activity, though the change was longer and slower than the burst of industrialization that took place in the first half of the nineteenth century. For the leaders, Britain especially, industrialization brought international eminence. British achievements were envied, British inventors were celebrated, and Britain's constitutional and social organization was lauded. A comparatively small island nation had become the greatest economic power in Europe. Industrialization had profound consequences for economic life, but its effects ran deeper than that. The search for new markets would result in the conquest of continents; the power of productivity unleashed by coal and iron would result in the first great arms race. Both would reach fruition in World War I, the first industrial war. For better or worse, we still live in the industrial era that began in Britain in the middle of the eighteenth century.

QUESTIONS FOR REVIEW

1. Why did early manufacturing develop in the countryside, and what effect did that have on manufacturing practices and social relations?
2. In what ways were the ideas about organization of manufacturers such as Josiah Wedgwood and Robert Owen as significant as new technology in the development of industry in Britain?
3. How did British society address some of the changes in peoples' lives that were brought about by industrialization?
4. How did industrialization on the Continent differ from industrialization in England?
5. Why did some nations develop little industry at all?

DISCOVERING WESTERN CIVILIZATION ONLINE

You can obtain more information on industrial Europe at the websites listed below. See also the companion website that accompanies this text: www.ablongman.com/kishlansky, which contains an online study guide and additional resources.

The Industrial Revolution in Britain

www.history.rochester.edu/steam/hart/
A nineteenth-century account of the life of James Watt and his role as inventor of the steam engine with links to the history of the steam engine.

www.womeninworldhistory.com/lesson7.html
Sponsored by Women in World History Curriculum, this site details the plight of women's work in industrial England.

www.spartacus.schoolnet.co.uk/IRchild.main.htm
This site chronicles child labor in Britain, including life in the factory and first-hand experiences.

www.fordham.edu/halsall/mod/modsbook14.html
An outstanding collection of documents on the Industrial Age with links.

The Industrialization of the Continent

www.fordham.edu/halsall/mod/indrevtabs1.html
Charts and statistics about industrialization in Europe.

SUGGESTIONS FOR FURTHER READING

General Reading

T. S. Ashton, *The Industrial Revolution* (Oxford: Oxford University Press, 1997). A compelling brief account of the traditional view of industrialization.

Niall Ferguson, *The Cash Nexus: Money and Power in the Modern World, 1700–2000* (New York: Basic Books, 2001). A transnational history of the role of finance in the making of the modern world.

Jordan Goodman and Katrina Honeyman, *Gainful Pursuits: The Making of Industrial Europe, 1600–1914* (London: Edward Arnold, 1988). A brief overview of the entire process of industrialization.

David S. Landes, *The Wealth and Poverty of Nations: Why Some Are So Rich and Some So Poor* (New York: W. W. Norton, 1998). A controversial and sweeping argument about Western economic dominance of the modern world.

The Traditional Economy

Richard Brown, *Society and Economy in Modern Britain, 1700–1850* (London: Routledge, 1991). A comprehensive survey.

E. A. Wrigley, *Continuity, Chance and Change* (Cambridge: Cambridge University Press, 1988). Explores the nature of the traditional economy and the way in which Britain escaped from it.

The Industrial Revolution in Britain

François Crouzet, *The First Industrialists* (Cambridge: Cambridge University Press, 1985). An analysis of the social background of the first generation of British entrepreneurs.

Martin Daunton, *Progress and Poverty: An Economic and Social History of Britain, 1700–1850* (Oxford: Oxford University Press, 1995). The best single-volume survey on the Industrial Revolution and its effects on British society.

Phyllis Deane, *The First Industrial Revolution*, 2d ed. (Cambridge: Cambridge University Press, 1979). The best introduction to the technological changes in Britain.

Peter Mathias, *The First Industrial Nation*, 2d ed. (London: Methuen, 1983). A general survey of British industrialization.

Joel Mokyr, *The Lever of Riches: Technological Creativity and Economic Progress* (New York: Oxford University Press, 1992). A compelling argument concerning the role of technology by a leading econometrician.

Kenneth Morgan, *The Birth of Industrial Britain: Economic Change, 1750–1850* (London; New York: Longman, 1999). A brief synthesis with selections of sources and an up-to-date bibliography.

E. P. Thompson, *The Making of the English Working Class* (New York: Random House, 1966). A brilliant and passionate study of the ways laborers responded to the changes brought about by the industrial economy.

The Industrialization of the Continent

W. O. Henderson, *The Rise of German Industrial Power* (Berkeley: University of California Press, 1975). A chronological study of German industrialization that centers on Prussia.

Tom Kemp, *Industrialization in Nineteenth-Century Europe*, 2d ed. (London: Longman, 1985). Survey of the process of industrialization in the major European states.

Herbert Kisch, *From Domestic Manufacture to Industrial Revolution: The Case of the Rhineland Textile Districts* (New York: Oxford University Press, 1989). A scholarly study of the slow pace of industrialization in Germany.

Roger Price, *The Economic Transformation of France* (London: Croom Helm, 1975). A study of French society before and during the process of industrialization.

Clive Trebilcock, *The Industrialization of the Continental Powers, 1780–1914* (London: Longman, 1981). A complex study of Germany, France, and Russia.

CHAPTER 22

POLITICAL UPHEAVALS AND SOCIAL TRANSFORMATIONS, 1815–1850

- THE VISUAL RECORD: Potato Politics
- GEOGRAPHICAL TOUR: Europe in 1815
- THE NEW IDEOLOGIES
- PROTEST AND REVOLUTION

THE VISUAL RECORD

POTATO POLITICS

VEGETABLES HAVE HISTORIES TOO. But none has a more interesting history in the West than the humble potato. First introduced to northern Europe from the Andean highlands of South America at the end of the sixteenth century, it rapidly became a staple of peasant diets from Ireland to Russia. The potato's vitamins, minerals, and high carbohydrate content provided a rich source of energy to Europe's rural poor. It was simple to plant, it required little or no cultivation, and it did well in damp, cool climates. Best of all, it could be grown successfully on the smallest plots of land. One acre could support a family of four for a year.

In his painting *Planting Potatoes*, the French painter Jean-François Millet (1814–1875) depicts the peasants in a reverent posture, bowing as field laborers might in prayer (as they do in Millet's more sentimental work, *The Angelus*). The couple's baby sleeps swaddled in a basket shaded by the tree. Millet, the son of a wealthy peasant family, understood well the importance of the potato in the peasant family diet.

But the fleshy root not only guaranteed health; it also affected social life. Traditionally, peasants had delayed marrying and starting families because of the unavailability of land. Now the potato allowed peasants who had only a little land to marry and have children earlier. In peasant homes where family members did putting-out work for local entrepreneurs, potato cultivation drew little labor away from the spinning wheel and loom. It permitted prosperous farmers to devote more land to cash crops, since only a small portion was required to feed a family. Most commonly, however, the potato was the single crop grown by most Irish farm workers. As the sole item of diet, it provided life-sustaining nutrients and a significant amount of the protein so necessary for heavy labor. The Irish adult male ate an average of twelve to fourteen pounds of cooked potatoes a day—a figure that may seem preposterous to us today.

Proverbs warned peasants against putting all their eggs in one basket, but no folk wisdom prepared the Irish for the potato disaster that struck them. In 1845, a fungus from America destroyed the new potato crop. Although peasants were certainly accustomed to bad harvests and crop failures, they had no precedent for the years of blight

that followed. From 1846 to 1850, famine and the diseases resulting from it—scurvy, dysentery, cholera, and typhus fever—killed over a million people in what became known as the Great Hunger. Within five years the Irish population was reduced by almost 25 percent.

The Irish potato famine has been called the "last great European natural disaster," but it was as much a social and political disaster as a natural one. The government of the United Kingdom of Great Britain and Ireland seemed powerless to stop the famine. The repeal of protective trade barriers to allow the Irish to buy cheaper grain was of no help to the penniless farmers, and although emergency work relief and soup kitchens were briefly offered, they were withdrawn when a banking crisis hit England. The workhouses created under the Irish Poor Law system were not intended to deal with such disasters. Mass deaths and mass graves were the inevitable result.

LOOKING AHEAD

As the wealth of European societies expanded in the nineteenth century, so did the number of those who lived on the edge, poised between unemployment and starvation. The Irish Great Hunger was the most striking example of the problem that plagued all Western societies in the first half of the nineteenth century: what to do with the poor. In this chapter, we shall see that while the boundaries of European nations were redefined following the Napoleonic Wars in order to create stability, the economic hardships of peasants and workers continued to plague and disrupt European societies internally. The new ideologies of the first half of the nineteenth century grappled with the challenge of reshaping state and society. But social inequities continued to fuel protest and revolution between 1815 and 1850 and pulled down governments across Europe.

GEOGRAPHICAL TOUR

Europe in 1815

Peasants like those depicted by Millet in his painting *Planting Potatoes* (see this chapter's Visual Record) seldom traveled beyond their own villages. Of course, all that changed with Napoleon's quest for empire. Napoleon placed in motion large armies of peasants and workers crisscrossing the continent, and no one state on its own had been able to defeat his conscript armies. In the end, those combined powers who were victorious in defeating Napoleon's empire learned a lesson on the territorial and political interdependence of Europe. They now saw the whole of Europe as one entity and conceived of peace in terms of a general European security.

The primary goal of the leaders of Russia, Austria, Prussia, and France who met in 1815 was to devise the most stable territorial arrangement possible. That goal entailed redrawing the map of Europe (see **Map A**). During the negotiations, traditional claims of the right to rule came head to head with new ideas about stabilization. The equilibrium that was established in 1815 made possible a century-long European peace. Conflicts erupted, to be sure, but they took on the characteristics of the new system that was constructed at Vienna in 1815.

The Congress of Vienna

In 1814, representatives of the victorious Allies agreed to convene in the Austrian capital of Vienna for the purposes

▼ **Map A. Europe, 1815.** In a series of treaties following Napoleon's defeat, the European powers redrew the map of Europe to create the most stable territorial arrangement and ensure European security. At the center of Europe stood the German confederation, outlined here in red.

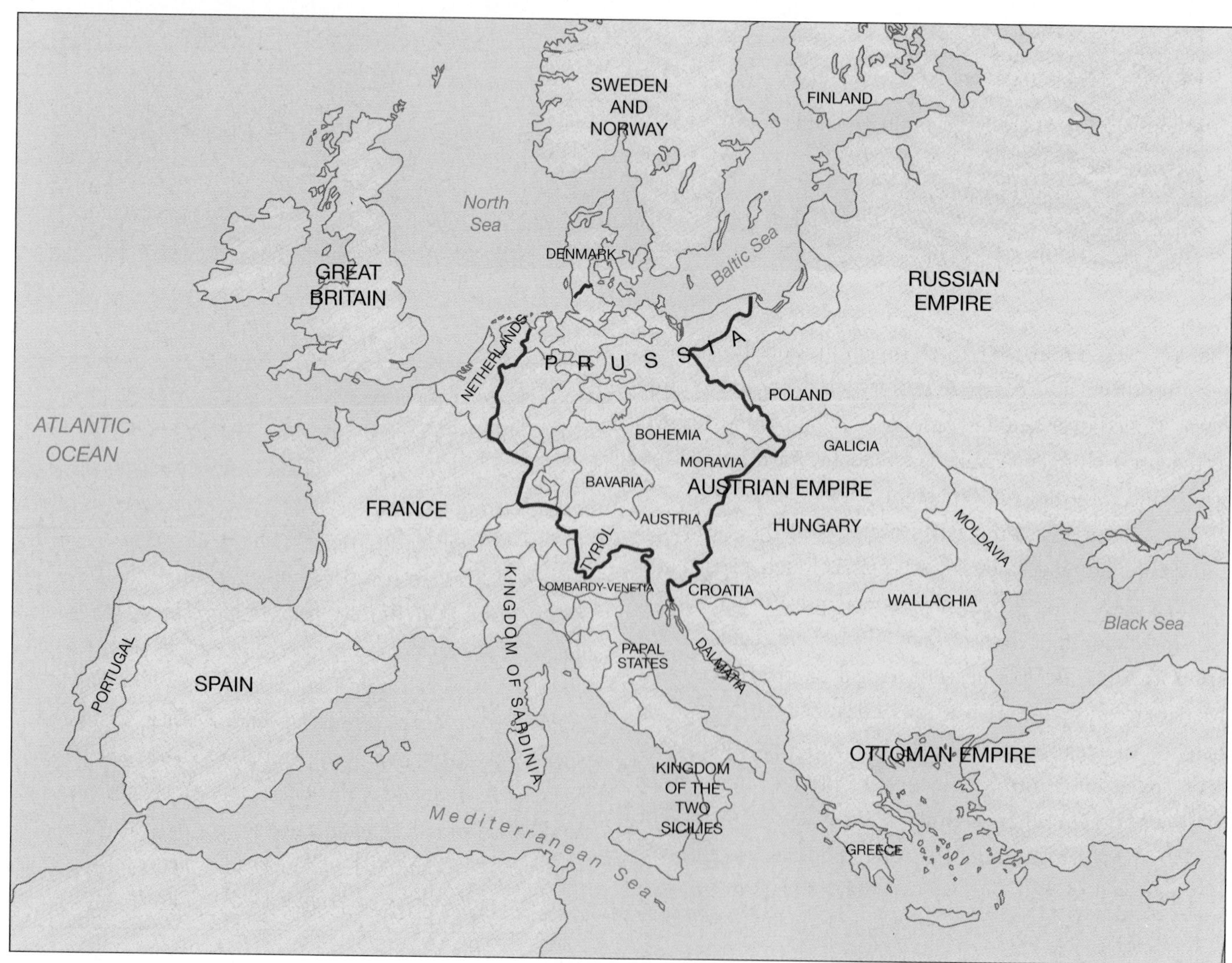

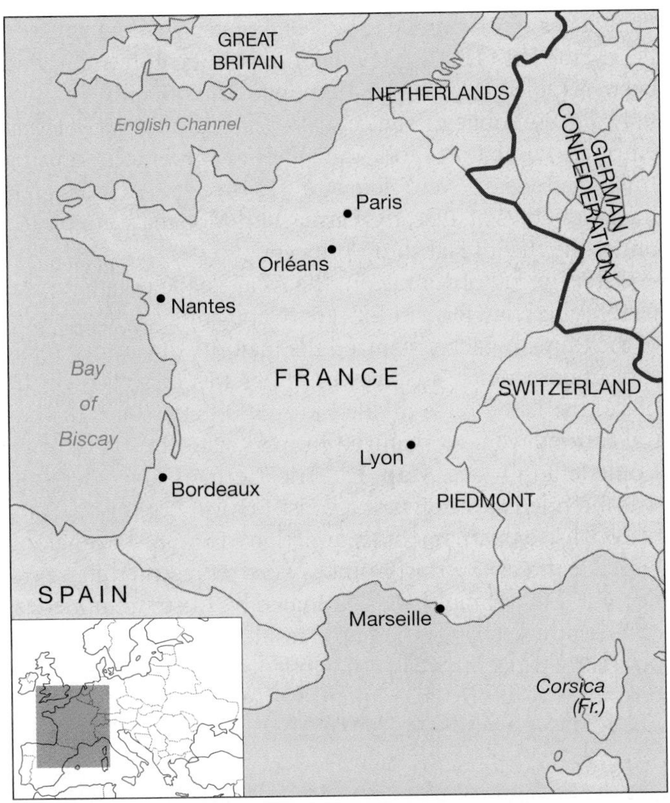

▲ **Map B. France, 1815.** In determining the borders of France, European heads of state were torn between the need to punish and control France and the importance of reconciliation with France for a stable Europe. The Second Peace of Paris of November 1815 permitted France to return to the borders of 1790 and to resume its role as one of the Great Powers.

of mopping up the mess created in Europe by French rule and restoring order to European monarchies.

The central actors whose personalities dominated the Congress of Vienna were the Austrian minister of foreign affairs Prince Klemens von Metternich (1773–1859), the British foreign secretary Viscount Castlereagh (1769–1822), the French minister of foreign affairs Charles Maurice de Talleyrand (1754–1838), the Russian tsar Alexander I (1801–1825), and the Prussian king Frederick William III (1797–1840). In spite of personal eccentricities and occasionally outright hostilities among Europe's leaders, all shared a concern with reestablishing harmony in Europe.

Settling with France. Because of the concern with establishing harmony at the time of Napoleon's defeat, the peace that was enforced against France was not a punitive one. After Napoleon's abdication in 1814, the Four Powers decided that leniency was the best way to support the restored Bourbon monarchy. After 1793, royalist émigrés referred to the young son of the executed Louis XVI as Louis XVII, although the child died in captivity and never reigned. In 1814, the Great Powers designated the elder of the two surviving brothers of Louis XVI as the appropriate candidate for the restored monarchy. Because of the circumstances of his restoration, the new king, Louis XVIII (1814–1815, 1815–1824), bore the ignominious image of returning "in the baggage car of the Allies." Every effort was made not to weigh him down with a harsh settlement. The First Peace of Paris, signed by the Allies with France in May 1814, had established French frontiers at the 1792 boundaries, which included Avignon, Venaissin, parts of Savoy, and German and Flemish territories, none of which had belonged to France in 1789.

Even after the hundred-day return of Napoleon, the "Usurper," the Second Peace of Paris of November 1815 somewhat less generously declared French frontiers to be restricted to the boundaries of 1790 (see **Map B**) and exacted from France an indemnity of 700 million francs. An army of occupation consisting of 150,000 troops was also placed on French soil at French expense but was removed ahead of schedule in 1818.

New Territorial Arrangements. The dominant partnership of Austria and Britain at the Congress of Vienna resulted in treaty arrangements that served to restrain the ambitions of Russia and Prussia. No country was to receive territory without giving up something in return, and no one country was to receive enough territory to make it a

▼ **Map C. Kingdom of the Netherlands.** As a buffer on France's northernmost border, the new Kingdom of the Netherlands was a forced union of two regions with different languages and religions. The union lasted only until 1831 when the southern provinces revolted to form Belgium.

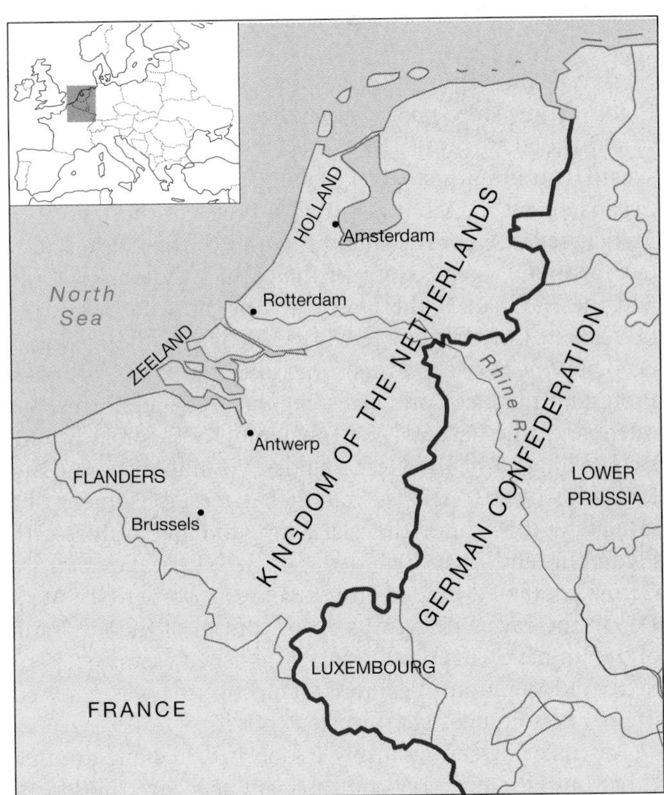

▲ **Map D. Italian Peninsula, 1815.** Austria gained major territorial concessions on the Italian peninsula. The Austrian empire now included Lombardy and Venetia. Austria was also influential throughout the peninsula in the Papal States, the three small duchies (Tuscany, Parma, Modena), and the Kingdom of the Two Sicilies.

present or future threat to the peace of Europe. To contain France, some steps taken before the Congress were ratified or expanded. In June 1814, the Low Countries had been set up as a unitary state as a buffer against future French expansion on the Continent and a block to the revival of French sea power. The new Kingdom of the Netherlands (see **Map C**), created out of the former Dutch Republic and the Austrian Netherlands, was placed under the rule of William I of Orange (1815–1840). The Catholic southern provinces were thus uneasily reunited with the Protestant northern provinces, regions that had been separated since the Peace of Westphalia in 1648. Great Britain gave William I of the Netherlands two million pounds to fortify his frontier against France. The reestablishment of a monarchy that united the island kingdom of Sardinia with Piedmont and that included Savoy, Nice, and part of Genoa contained France on its southeast border (see **Map D**). To the east, Prussia was given control of the left bank of the Rhine. Switzerland was reestablished as an independent confederation of cantons. Bourbon rule was restored in Spain on France's southwestern border.

Austria's power was firmly established in Italy, through either outright territorial control or influence over independent states (see **Map D**). The Papal States were returned to Pope Pius VII (1800–1823), along with territories that had been Napoleon's Cisalpine Republic and the Kingdom of Italy. The Republic of Venice was absorbed into the Austrian empire. Lombardy and the Illyrian provinces on the Dalmatian coast were likewise restored to Austria. The Italian duchies of Tuscany, Parma, and Modena were placed under the rule of Habsburg princes.

After the fall of Napoleon, the Allies made no attempt to restore the Holy Roman Empire. Napoleon's Confederation of the Rhine, which organized the majority of German territory under French auspices in 1806, was dissolved. In its place, the lands once divided into 300 petty states in central Europe were reorganized into 38 states in the German Confederation (see **Map E**). The German Confederation was intended as a bulwark against France, not to serve any nationalist or parliamentary function. The 38 states, along with Austria as the thirty-ninth, were represented in a new Federal Diet at Frankfurt, dominated by Austrian influence.

All of these changes were the result of carefully discussed but fairly uncontroversial negotiations. The question of Poland was more problematic. Successive partitions by

▼ **Map E. German Confederation.** The league of German states created in 1815 replaced the Holy Roman Empire. The 39 states, of which 35 were monarchies and 4 were free cities, existed to ensure the independence of its member states and support in case of external attack. The member states of Austria and Prussia lay partially outside of the Confederation.

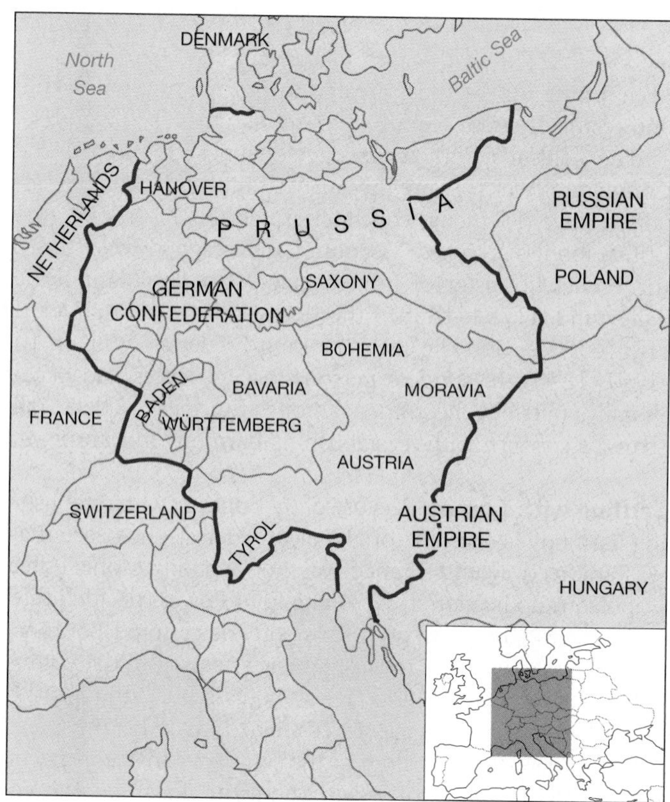

Russia, Austria, and Prussia in 1772, 1793, and 1795 had completely dismembered the land that had been Poland. Napoleon had reconstituted a small portion of Poland as the Grand Duchy of Warsaw. The Congress's dilemma was what to do with this Napoleonic creation and with Polish territory in general. Fierce debate over Poland threatened to shatter congressional harmony (see **Map F**).

Tsar Alexander I of Russia argued for a large Poland that he intended to be fully under his influence. Frederick William III of Prussia contended that if a large Poland were to be created, Prussia would expect compensation by absorbing Saxony (see **Map G**). Both Great Britain and France distrusted Russian and Prussian territorial aims. In the midst of the crisis over Poland, Talleyrand, the wily and brilliant French negotiator, persuaded Britain and Austria to sign a secret treaty with France to preserve an independent Polish territory. He then deliberately leaked news of the secret agreement of these powers to go to war, if necessary, to block Russian and Prussian aims. Alexander I and Frederick William III immediately backed down.

In the final arrangement, Prussia retained the Polish territory of Posen, and Austria kept the Polish province of Galicia (see **Map F**). Krakow, with its population of 95,000, was declared a free city. Finally, a kingdom of Poland, nominally independent but in fact under the tutelage of Russia, emerged from what remained of the Grand Duchy of Warsaw. It was a solution that benefited no one in particular and disregarded Polish wishes.

▲ **Map G. Saxony.** In 1806, Saxony had sided with France against Prussia and remained allies with the French for the remainder of the wars. With Napoleon's defeat in 1815, about 40 percent of Saxony became part of Prussia.

▼ **Map F. Poland, 1815.** An independent kingdom in name only, Poland was under the influence of Russia. Prussia carved off Posen, and Austria maintained control of Galicia. Krakow was defined by treaty as an independent republic.

In addition to receiving Polish territories, Prussia gained two-fifths of the kingdom of Saxony (see **Map G**) as well as territory on the left bank of the Rhine, the Duchy of Westphalia, and Swedish Pomerania. With these acquisitions, Prussia doubled its population to around 11 million people. The Junkers, the landed class of east Prussia, reversed many of the reforms of the Napoleonic period. The new territories that Prussia gained were rich in waterways and resources but geographically fragmented. The dispersal of holdings that was intended to contain Prussian power in central Europe spurred Prussia to find new ways of uniting its markets. In this endeavor, Prussia constituted a future threat to Austrian power over the German Confederation.

In Scandinavia, Russia's conquest of Finland was acknowledged by the members of the Congress. In return, Sweden acquired Norway from Denmark. Unlike Austria, Prussia, and Russia, Great Britain made no claim to territories at the Congress. Having achieved its aim of containing France, its greatest rival for dominance on the seas, Britain returned the French colonies it had seized in war.

For the time being, the redrawing of the territorial map of Europe had achieved its pragmatic aim of guaranteeing the peace. It was now left to a system of alliances to preserve that peace.

The Alliance System

Only by joining forces had the European powers been able to defeat Napoleon, and the necessity of a system of alliances was recognized even after the battles were over. Two alliance pacts dominated the post-Napoleonic era: the renewed Quadruple Alliance and the Holy Alliance.

The Quadruple Alliance (see **Map H**), signed by the victorious powers of Great Britain, Austria, Russia, and Prussia in November 1815, was intended to protect Europe against future French aggression and to preserve the status quo. In 1818, having completed its payment of war indemnities, France joined the pact, which now became the Quintuple Alliance. The five powers promised to meet periodically over the next 200 years to discuss common problems and to ensure the peace.

▼ **Map H. Quadruple Alliance.** This Alliance grew out of the need of the Great Powers to create a stable Europe, and had as its initial impulse the creation of a buffer against a future French threat. Austria, Great Britain, Prussia, and Russia entered into the agreement as the basis for defining the balance of power in Europe.

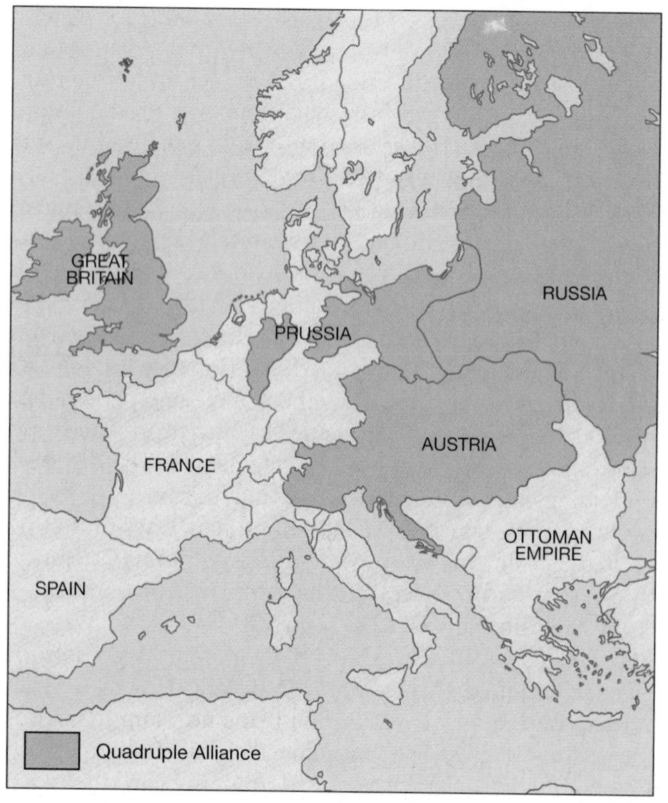

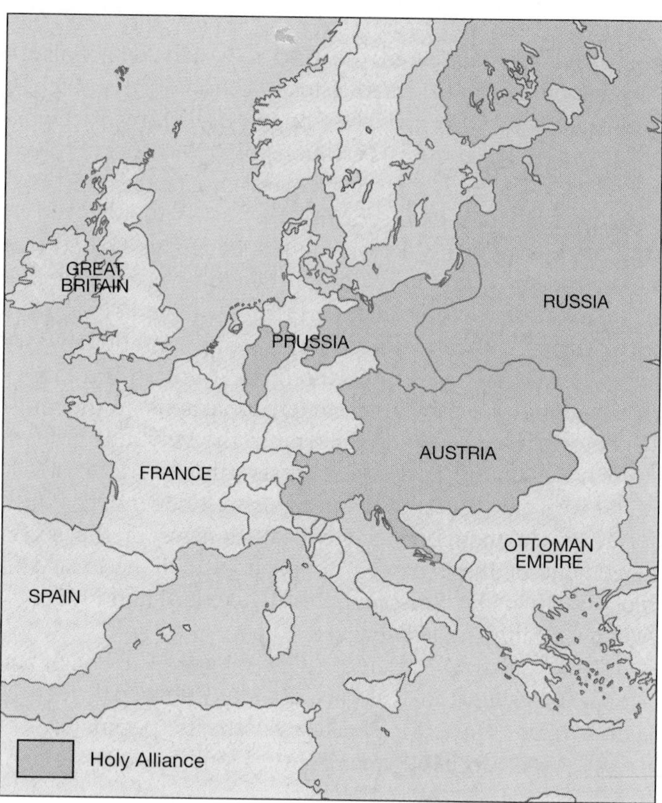

▲ **Map I. Holy Alliance.** Under the influence of the religious mysticism of the Russian Tsar Alexander I, Emperor Francis I of Austria and King Frederick William III of Prussia entered an accord to treat each other according to the precepts of the Christian religion. As a counterweight to the Quadruple Alliance, it served as a justification for repression against dissent.

The Holy Alliance (see **Map I**) was the brainchild of Alexander I and was heavily influenced by his mystical view of international politics. In this pact, the monarchs of Prussia, Austria, and Russia agreed to renounce war and to protect the Christian religion. The Holy Alliance spoke of "the bonds of a true and indissoluble brotherhood . . . to protect religion, peace, and justice." Russia was able to give some credibility to the alliance with the sheer size of its army. Career diplomats were aware of the hollowness of the Holy Alliance as a treaty arrangement, but it did indicate the willingness of Europe's three eastern autocracies to intervene in the affairs of other states.

The concept of Europe acting as a whole, through a system of periodic conferences, marked the emergence of a new diplomatic era. However, conflict was inherent in the commitment of parliamentary governments to open consultation and the need for secrecy in diplomacy. Dynastic regimes sought to intervene in smaller states to buoy up despots. That certainly seemed to be the case in 1822, when the European powers met to consider restoring the

CHRONOLOGY	
THE ALLIANCE SYSTEM	
May 1814	First Peace of Paris
23 September 1814–9 June 1815	Congress of Vienna
26 September 1815	Formation of the Holy Alliance
20 November 1815	Second Peace of Paris; Formation of the Quadruple Alliance
November 1818	Quadruple Alliance expands to include France in Quintuple Alliance
1823	French restoration of Bourbon Monarchy in Spain

Bourbon monarchy in Spain. The British, acting as a counterbalance to revolutionary tendencies, refused to cooperate and blocked united action by the Alliance. France took military action on its own in 1823, restored King Ferdinand VII, and abolished the Spanish constitution.

In both the Congress of Vienna and the system of alliances that succeeded it, European nations aimed to establish a balance of power that recognized legitimate rulers and preserved the peace. The upheaval of the French Revolution and the revolutionary and Napoleonic wars had made clear that the interdependence of nations was a guarantee of survival. Europe's statesmen hoped that by keeping the peace abroad, domestic peace would follow.

THE NEW IDEOLOGIES

After 1815, the world was changing in many ways. As national boundaries were being redefined, the ways in which Europeans regarded their world was also being transformed. Steam-driven mechanical power in production and transportation steadily replaced human and animal power. In deference to what it was replacing, the new mechanical force was measured in units of horsepower. The new technology challenged old values; new definitions of worth emerged from the changing world of work. The fixed, caste-like distinctions of the old aristocratic world were under attack or in disarray. Western intellectuals struggled to make sense of the new age and their place in it.

The political and economic upheavals of the first half of the nineteenth century encouraged a new breed of thinkers to search for ways to explain the transformations of the period. Before midcentury, Europeans witnessed one of the most intellectually fertile periods in the history of the West. This era gave birth to new ideologies—liberalism, nationalism, romanticism, conservatism, and socialism—that came to shape the ideas and institutions of the present day.

The New Politics of Preserving Order

European states had been dealing with war for over two decades. Now they faced the challenge of peace. The revolution and Napoleon had not only meant military engagements; they had also brought the force of revolutionary ideas to the political arena, and these ideas did not retire from the field after Waterloo. Nor did treaties restore an old order, despite their claims. Governments throughout Europe had to find new ways to deal with the tension between state authority and individual liberty. Conservative and liberal thinkers took very different paths in the pursuit of political stability.

Conservatism. Conservatism represented a dynamic adaptation to a social system in transition. In place of individualism, conservatives stressed the established institutions of European society; in place of reason and progress, conservatives advocated gradual, evolutionary growth and social stability. They opposed an abrupt break with tradition. Liberty, argued British statesman Edmund Burke (1729–1797) in *Reflections on the Revolution in France* (1790), must emerge out of the gradual development of the old order, not its destruction. On the Continent, conservatives Louis de Bonald (1754–1840) and Joseph de Maistre (1753–1821) defended the monarchical principle of authority against the onslaught of revolutionary events.

Conservatism took a reactionary turn in the hands of the Austrian statesman Prince Klemens von Metternich. The Carlsbad decrees of 1819 are a good example of the "Metternich system" of espionage, censorship, and university repression in central Europe, which sought to eliminate any constitutional or nationalist sentiments that had arisen during the Napoleonic period. The German Confederation approved the decrees against free speech and civil liberties and set up mechanisms to root out "subversive" university students. Students who had taken up arms in the Wars of Liberation (1813–1815) against France had done so in hopes of instituting liberal and national reforms. Metternich's system aimed at uprooting these goals. Student fraternities were closed, and police became a regular fixture in the university. Political expression was driven underground for at least a decade. Metternich set out to crush liberalism, constitutionalism, and parliamentarianism in central Europe.

Liberalism. The term *liberal* was first used in a narrow, political sense to indicate the Spanish party of reform that supported the constitution modeled on the French document of 1791. But the term assumed much broader connotations in the first half of the nineteenth century as its appeal spread among the European middle classes. Two main tenets of liberalism asserted the freedom of the individual and the corruptibility of authority. As a political doctrine, liberalism built on Enlightenment rationalism and embraced the right to vote, civil liberties, legal equality, constitutional government, parliamentary sovereignty, and a free-market economy. Liberals firmly believed that less government was better government and that noninterference would produce a harmonious and well-ordered world. They also believed that human beings were basically good and reasonable and needed freedom in which to flourish. The sole end of government should be to promote that freedom.

Liberal thinkers grappled with the political conflicts of the revolutionary period and the economic disruptions brought on by industrialization. The Great Revolution at the end of the eighteenth century spawned a vast array of liberal thought in France. Republicans, Bonapartists, and constitutional monarchists cooperated as self-styled "liberals," who shared a desire to preserve the gains of the Revolution while ensuring orderly rule. Liberal ideas also influenced a variety of political movements in the United States, including those demanding the liberation of slaves and the extension of legal and political rights to women.

By the mid-nineteenth century, liberal thinking constituted a dominant strain in British politics. Jeremy Bentham (1748–1832) founded utilitarianism, a fundamentally liberal doctrine that argued for "the greatest happiness of the greatest number" in such works as *Introduction to the Principles of Morals and Legislation*. Bentham believed that government could achieve positive ends through limited and "scientific" intervention. John Stuart Mill (1806–1873) forged his own brand of classical liberalism in his treatise *On Liberty* (1859). Mill went beyond existing political analyses to apply economic doctrines to social conditions in *Principles of Political Economy* (1848). He espoused social reform for the poor and championed the equality of women and the necessity of birth control. David Ricardo (1772–1823), in *Principles of Political Economy and Taxation* (1817), outlined his opposition to government intervention in foreign trade and elaborated

▼ *Liberty Leading the People* (1831) by Eugène Delacroix captures the spirit of the French romantics, who looked upon revolutionary action as a way to achieve union with the spirit of history.

his "iron law of wages," which contended that wages would stabilize at the subsistence level. Increased wages would cause the working classes to increase, and the resulting competition in the labor market would drive wages down to the subsistence level.

Romanticism and Change

Unlike liberalism and conservatism, which were fundamentally political ideologies, romanticism designated a variety of literary and artistic movements throughout Europe that spanned the period from the late eighteenth century to the mid-nineteenth century. One could be a liberal and a romantic just as easily as one could be a conservative and a romantic.

The Romantic World View. Above all, in spite of variations, romantics shared similar beliefs and a common view of the world. Among the first romantics were the English poets William Wordsworth (1770–1850) and Samuel Taylor Coleridge (1772–1834), whose collaborative *Lyrical Ballads* (1798) exemplified the iconoclastic romantic idea that poetry was the result of "the spontaneous overflow of powerful feelings," rather than a formal and highly disciplined intellectual exercise. Romantics in general rebelled against the confinement of classical forms and refused to accept the supremacy of reason over emotions.

Intellectuals, Artists, and Freedom. By rooting artistic vision in spontaneity, romantics endorsed a concept of creativity based on the supremacy of human freedom. The artist was valued in a new way as a genius through whose insight and intuition great art was created. Intuition, as opposed to scientific learning, was endorsed as a valid means of knowing. Building on the work of the eighteenth-century philosopher Immanuel Kant (1724–1804), romanticism embraced subjective knowledge. Inspiration and intuition took the place of reason and science in the romantic pantheon of values.

Germaine de Staël (1766–1817), whose writings influenced French political theory after 1815, is often hailed as the founder of French romanticism. She wrote histories, novels, literary criticism, and political tracts that opposed the tyranny of Napoleonic rule. Like many other romantics, she was greatly influenced by the writings of Jean-Jacques Rousseau, and through him she discovered that "the soul's elevation is born of self-consciousness." The recognition of the subjective meant for De Staël that women's vision was as essential as men's for the flowering of European culture.

The supremacy of emotions over reason found its way into the works of the great romantic composers of the age: Louis Hector Berlioz (1803–1869), the French composer who set Faust's damnation to music; Polish virtuoso Frédéric Chopin (1810–1849); and Hungarian concert pianist Franz Liszt (1811–1886). Artists such as J. M. W. Turner (1775–1851), the English landscape painter, and Eugène Delacroix (1798–1863), the leader of the French romantic school in painting, shared a rebellious experimentation with color and a rejection of classical conventions and forms.

In the postrevolutionary age of the years between 1815 and 1850, romanticism claimed to be no more than an aesthetic stance in art, letters, and music, a posture that had no particular political intent. Yet its validation of the individual as opposed to the caste or the estate was a revolutionary doctrine that helped to define a new political consciousness.

Reshaping State and Society

As another legacy of the French Revolution, the concept of the nation as a source of collective identity and political allegiance became a political force after 1815. Just as nationalism put the needs of the people at the heart of its political doctrine, so did socialism focus on the needs of society and especially of the poor.

Nationalism. In its most basic sense, nationalism before 1850 was the political doctrine that glorified the people united against the absolutism of kings and the tyranny of foreign oppressors. The success of the French Revolution and the spread of Napoleonic reforms boosted nationalist doctrines, which were most fully articulated on the Continent. In Germany, Johann Gottfried von Herder (1744–1803) rooted national identity in German folk culture. *The Fairy Tales* (1812–1814) of the brothers Jacob Ludwig Grimm (1785–1863) and Wilhelm Carl Grimm (1786–1859) had a similar national purpose. The brothers painstakingly captured in print the German oral tradition of peasant folklore. The philosophers Johann Fichte (1762–1814) and Georg Wilhelm Friedrich Hegel (1770–1831) emphasized the importance of the state. There was a new concern with history, as nationalists sought to revive a common cultural past.

In the period between 1830 and 1850, many nationalists were liberals and many liberals were nationalists. The nationalist yearning for liberation meshed with the liberal political program of overthrowing tyrannical rule. Giuseppe Mazzini (1805–1872) represented the new breed of liberal nationalist. A less-than-liberal nationalist was political economist Georg Friedrich List (1789–1846), who formulated a statement of economic nationalism to counter the liberal doctrines of David Ricardo. Arguing that free trade worked only for the wealthy and powerful, List advocated a program of protective tariffs for developing German industries. British free trade, he perceived, was merely economic imperialism in disguise. List was one of the few nationalists who did not wholeheartedly embrace liberal economic doctrines. Beyond ideology and political practices, nationalism began to capture the imagination of groups who resented foreign domination.

Expanding state bureaucracies did little to tame the centrifugal forces of nationalist feeling and probably exacerbated a desire for independence in eastern and central Europe, especially in the Habsburg-ruled lands.

Nationalists valued the authenticity of the vernacular and folklore over the language and customs imposed by a foreign ruler. Herder and the brothers Grimm were German examples of the romantic appreciation of the roots of German culture. While French romantics emphasized the glories of their revolutionary heritage, German romantics stressed the importance of history as the source of one's identity. By searching for the self in a historic past, and especially in the Middle Ages, they glorified their collective cultural identity and national origins.

Socialism. Socialists rejected the world as it was. Socialism, like other ideologies of the first half of the nineteenth century, grew out of the changes in the structure of daily life and the structure of power. There were as many stripes of socialists as there were of liberals, nationalists, and conservatives.

Socialist thinkers in France theorized about alternative societies in which wealth would be more equitably distributed. To Henri de Saint-Simon (1760–1825) the accomplishments and potential of industrial development represented the highest stage in history. In a perfect and just society, productive work would be the basis of all prestige and power. The elite of society would be organized according to the hierarchy of its productive members, with industrial leaders at the top.

Like Saint-Simon, the French social theorist Pierre Joseph Proudhon (1809–1865) recognized the social value of work. But unlike Saint-Simon, Proudhon refused to accept the dominance of industrial society. Proudhon gained national prominence with his ideas about a just society, free credit, and equitable exchange. In his famous pamphlet *What Is Property?* (1840), Proudhon answered, "Property is theft." However, this statement was not an argument for the abolition of private ownership. Proudhon reasoned that industrialization had destroyed workers' rights, which included the right to the profits of their own labor. In attacking "property," in its meaning of profits amassed from the labor of others, Proudhon was arguing for a socialist concept of limited possession—people had the right to own only what they had earned from their own labor—and for a potentially anarchist concept of limited government—people had the right to rule themselves.

At least one socialist believed in luxury. Charles Fourier (1772–1837), an unsuccessful traveling salesman, devoted himself to the study and improvement of society and formulated one of the most trenchant criticisms of industrial capitalism. In numerous writings between 1808 and his death, this eccentric, solitary man put forth his vision of a utopian world organized into units called phalanxes that took into account their members' social, sexual, and economic needs. With a proper mix of duties, everyone in the phalanx would work only a few hours a day. In Fourier's scheme, work was not naturally abhorrent, but care had to be taken to match temperaments with tasks. Women and men fulfilled themselves and found pleasure and gratification through work. People would be paid according to their contributions in work, capital, and talent. In Fourier's phalanxes, every aspect of life would be organized communally, although neither poverty nor property would be eliminated. Education would help to dispel discord, and rich and poor would learn to live together in perfect harmony.

Charles Fourier's work, along with that of Saint-Simon and Proudhon, became part of the tradition of utopian thinking that can be traced back to Thomas More in the sixteenth century. Because he believed in the ability of individuals to shape themselves and their world, Fourier intended his critique of society to be a blueprint for living. Fourier's followers set up communities in his lifetime—40 phalanxes were established in the United States alone—but because of financial frustrations and petty squabbling, all of them failed.

The emancipation of women was an issue acknowledged by socialists as well as liberals. Some social reformers, including Fourier, put the issue of women's freedom at the center of their plans to redesign society. Other social reformers joined with conservative thinkers in arguing that women must be kept in their place, which was in the home.

Socialists, along with other ideologues in the decades before the middle of the nineteenth century, were aware of how rapidly their world was changing. Many believed that a revolution that would eliminate poverty and the sufferings of the working class was at hand. Followers of Saint-Simon, Fourier, and Proudhon all hoped that their proposals and ideas would change the world and prevent violent upheaval. Not all social critics were so sanguine.

In January 1848, two young men, one a philosopher living in exile and the other a businessman working for his father, began a collaboration that would last a lifetime with the publication of a short tract entitled *The Communist Manifesto.* Karl Marx (1818–1883) and Friedrich Engels (1820–1895) described the dire situation of the working classes throughout the 1840s. The growing poverty and alienation of the proletariat, the authors promised, would bring to industrialized Europe a class war against the capitalists. Exploited workers were to prepare themselves for the moment of revolution by joining with each other across national boundaries: "Workers of the world unite. You have nothing to lose but your chains." In light of subsequent events, the *Manifesto* appears to be a work of great predictive value. But neither Marx nor Engels could know that the hour of revolution was at hand.

Intellectuals and reformers hoped with the force of their ideas to reshape the world in which they lived. The technology of industrial production informed people's values and required a new way of looking at the world. Liberals, nationalists, romantics, conservatives, and socialists addressed the challenges of a changing economy in a political universe buffeted by democratic ideas. Rather than providing neat answers, ideologies fueled actions, and often violent protest and revolution erupted in the streets.

PROTEST AND REVOLUTION

For European societies that had remained stable, if not stagnant, for centuries, the changes in the first half of the nineteenth century were undoubtedly startling and disruptive. New factories created the arena for exploitation and misery. More people than ever before lived in cities, and national populations faced the prospect of becoming urban. Urban congestion brought crime and disease; patterns of consumption demonstrated beyond dispute that people were not created equal. A new European society that challenged existing political ideas and demanded new political formulations was in the process of emerging.

Causes of Social Instability

The fabric of stability began unraveling throughout Europe beginning in the 1820s. The forces of order reacted to protest with repression everywhere in Europe. Yet armed force proved inadequate to contain the demands for political participation and the increased political awareness of whole segments of the population. Workers, the middle class, and women's political organizations now demanded, through the vote, the right to govern themselves.

Urban Miseries. In 1800, two of every one hundred Europeans lived in a city. By 1850, the number of urban dwellers per hundred had jumped to five and was rising rapidly. England, where one of every two inhabitants lived in a city, had become an urban society by midcentury. London was the fastest-growing city in Europe.

Massive internal migration caused most urban growth. People from the same rural areas often lived together in the same urban neighborhoods and even in the same boardinghouses. Irish emigrants, for example, crowded together in the "Little Dublin" section of London. Until midcentury, many migrants returned to their rural homes for the winter when work, especially in the building trades, was scarce in the city. Young migrant women who came to the city to work as servants sent money home to support rural relatives or worked to save a nest egg—or dowry—in order to return to the village permanently. Before 1850, 20 percent of the workers in London were domestics, and most of these were women.

Despite the neighborhood support networks that migrants constructed for themselves, the city was not always a hospitable place. Workers were poorly paid, and women workers were more poorly paid than men. When working women were cut free of the support of home and family, uncounted numbers were forced into part-time prostitution to supplement meager incomes. More and more women resorted to prostitution as a means of surviving in times of unemployment. It is conservatively estimated that there were 34,000 prostitutes in Paris in 1850 and 50,000 in London. Increased prostitution created an epidemic of venereal diseases, especially syphilis, for which there was no cure until the twentieth century.

Urban crime also grew astronomically, thefts accounting for the greatest number of crimes. Social reformers identified poverty and urban crowding as causes of the increase in criminal behavior. In 1829, both Paris and London began to create modern urban police forces to deal with the challenges to law and order. Crime assumed the character of disease in the minds of middle-class reformers. Statisticians and social scientists, themselves a new urban phenomenon, produced massive theses on social hygiene, lower-class immorality, and the unworthiness of the poor. The pathology of the city was widely discussed. Always at the center of the issue was the "social question": the growing problem of what to do with the poor.

The "Social Question." State-sponsored work relief expanded after 1830 for the deserving poor: the old, the sick, and children. Able-bodied workers who were idle were regarded as undeserving and dangerous, regardless of the causes of their unemployment. Performance of work became an indicator of moral worth, as urban and rural workers succumbed to downturns in the economic cycle. Those who were unable to work sought relief, as a last resort, from the state. What has been called "a revolution in government" took place in the 1830s and 1840s, as legislative bodies increased regulation of everything from factories and mines to prisons and schools.

Some argued, as in the case of the Irish famine, that the government must do nothing to intervene because the problem would correct itself, as Thomas Malthus had predicted 40 years earlier, through the "natural" means of famine and death that would keep population from outgrowing available resources and food supplies. The Irish population, one of the poorest in Europe, had indeed doubled between 1781 and 1841, and for Malthusians the Irish famine was the fulfillment of their vision that overpopulation would be corrected by war, disease, or famine. Poverty was a social necessity; by interfering with it, this first group insisted, governments could only make matters worse.

Others contended that poverty was society's problem, not a law of nature. Therefore, it was the social responsibility of the state to take care of its members. The question of how to treat poverty, or "the social question" as it came to be known among contemporaries, underlay many of the protests and reforms of the two decades before 1850 and fueled the revolutionary movements of 1848. Parliamentary legislation attempted to improve the situation of the poor and especially the working class in the 1830s and 1840s.

In 1833, British reformers turned their attention to the question of child labor. Parliament passed the Factory Act of 1833, which prohibited the employment of children under nine years of age and restricted the work week of children between the ages of 9 and 13 to 48 hours. No child in this age group could work more than nine hours a day. Teenagers between 13 and 18 years of age could work no more than 69 hours a week. By modern standards these "reformed" workloads present a shocking picture of the heavy reliance on child labor. The British Parliament commissioned investigations, compiled in the "Blue Books," that reported the abusive treatment of men, women, and children in factories. Similar studies existed for French and Belgian industry.

The British legislation marked an initial step in state intervention in the workplace. Additional legislation over the next three decades further restricted children's and women's labor in factories and concerned itself with improvement of conditions in the workplace. At bottom the social question was: What was the state's responsibility in caring for its citizens?

The Revolutions of 1830

Few Europeans who were alive in 1830 remembered the age of revolution from 1789 to 1799. Yet the legends were kept alive from one generation to the next. Secret political organizations perpetuated Jacobin republicanism. Mutual-aid societies and artisan associations preserved the rituals of democratic culture. A revolutionary culture seemed to be budding in the student riots in Germany and in the revolutionary waves that swept across southern and central Europe in the early 1820s. Outside Manchester, England, in August 1819 a crowd of 80,000 people gathered in St. Peter's Field to hear speeches for parliamentary reform and universal male suffrage. The cavalry swept down on them in a bloody slaughter that came to be known as the "Peterloo" massacre, a bitter reference to the Waterloo victory four years before.

Poor harvests in 1829 followed by a harsh winter left people cold, hungry, and bitter. Misery fueled social

▼ This engraving by J. W. Lowry shows child labor in the textile factories. The meager wages of children were often necessary for the survival of their families.

protest, and the convergence of social unrest with long-standing political demands touched off apparently simultaneous revolutions all over Europe. Governmental failures to respond to local grievances sparked the revolutions of 1830. Highly diverse groups of workers, students, lawyers, professionals, and peasants rose up spontaneously to demand a voice in the affairs of government.

The French Revolution of 1830. In France, the late 1820s was a period of increasing political friction. Charles X (1824–1830), the former comte d'Artois, had never resigned himself to the constitutional monarchy accepted by his brother and predecessor, Louis XVIII. When Charles assumed the throne in 1824, he dedicated himself to a true restoration of kingship as it existed before the Revolution. To this end, he realigned the monarchy with the Catholic Church and undertook several unpopular measures, including approval of the death penalty for people who were found guilty of sacrilege. The king's bourgeois critics, heavily influenced by liberal ideas about political economy and constitutional rights, sought increased political power through their activities in secret organizations and in public elections. The king responded to his critics by relying on his ultraroyalist supporters to run the government. In May 1830, the king dissolved the Chamber of Deputies and ordered new elections. The elections returned a liberal majority that was unfavorable to the king. Charles X retaliated with what proved to be his last political act, the Four Ordinances, in which he censored the press, changed the electoral law to favor his own candidates, dissolved the newly elected Chamber, and ordered new elections.

Opposition to Charles X might have remained at the level of political wrangling and journalistic protest had it not been for the problems plaguing the people of Paris. A severe winter in France had driven food prices up by 75 percent. The king underestimated the extent of hardship and the political volatility of the population. Throughout the spring of 1830, prices continued to rise and Charles continued to blunder. In a spontaneous uprising in the last days of July 1830, workers took to the streets of Paris. The revolution that they initiated spread rapidly to towns and the countryside, as people throughout France protested the cost of living, hoarding by grain merchants, tax collection, and wage cuts. In "three glorious days" the restored Bourbon regime was pulled down, and Charles X fled to England.

The people fighting in the streets demanded a republic, but they lacked organization and political experience. Liberal bourgeois politicians quickly filled the power vacuum. They presented Charles's cousin, the duc d'Orléans, as the savior of France and the new constitutional monarch. This July Monarchy, born of a revolution, put an end to the Bourbon Restoration. Louis-Philippe, the former duc d'Orléans, became king of the French. The Charter that he brought with him was, like its predecessor, based on restricted suffrage, with property ownership a requisite for voting.

Unrest in Europe. Popular disturbances did not always result in revolution. In Britain, rural and town riots erupted over grain prices and distribution, but no revolution followed. German workers broke their machines to protest low wages and loss of control of the workplace, but no prince was displaced. In Switzerland, reformers found strength in the French revolutionary example. Ten Swiss cantons granted liberal constitutions and established universal manhood suffrage, freedom of expression, and legal equality.

In southern Europe, Turkish overlords ruled Greece as part of the Ottoman Empire. The longing for independence smoldered in Greece throughout the 1820s as public pressure to support the Greeks mounted in Europe. Greek insurrections were answered by Turkish retaliations throughout the Ottoman Empire. The sultan of Turkey had been able to call on his vassal, the pasha of Egypt, to subdue Greece. In response, Great Britain, France, and Russia signed the Treaty of London in 1827, pledging intervention on behalf of Greece. In a joint effort, the three powers defeated the Egyptian fleet. Russia declared war on Turkey the following year, seeking territorial concessions from the Ottoman Empire. Following the Russian victory, Great Britain and France joined Russia in declaring Greek independence. The concerted action of the three powers in favor of Greek independence was neither an endorsement of liberal ideals nor a support of Greek nationalism. The British, French, and Russians were reasserting their commitment, made at the Congress of Vienna, to territorial stability.

Belgian Independence. The overthrow of the Bourbon monarch in France served as a model for revolution in other parts of Europe. In the midst of the Greek crisis the Belgian provinces revolted against the Netherlands. The Belgians' desire to have their own nation struck at the heart of the Vienna settlement. Provoked by a food crisis similar to that in France, Belgian revolutionaries took to the streets in August 1830. Belgians protested the deterioration of their economic situation and made demands for their own Catholic religion, their own language, and constitutional rights. Bitter fighting on the barricades in Brussels ensued, and the movement for freedom and independence spread to the countryside.

The Great Powers disagreed about what to do. Russia, Austria, and Prussia were all eager to see the revolution crushed. France, having just established the new regime of the July Monarchy, and Great Britain, fearing the involvement of the central and eastern European powers in an area where Britain had traditionally had interests, were reluctant to intervene. A provisional government in Belgium set about the task of writing a constitution. All five great powers recognized Belgian independence, with the proviso that Belgium was to maintain the status of a neutral state.

The Forgotten Revolutions. Russia, Prussia, and Austria were convinced to accept Belgian independence because they were having their own problems in eastern and southern Europe. Revolution erupted in Warsaw when Polish army cadets and university students revolted in November 1830 to demand independence and a constitution. Landed aristocrats and gentry helped to establish a provisional government but soon split over how radical reforms should be. Polish peasants refused to support either landowning group. Within the year, Russia brought in 180,000 troops to crush the revolution and reassert its rule over Poland.

In February 1831, the Italian states of Modena and Parma rose up to throw off Austrian domination of northern Italy. The revolutionaries were ineffective against Austrian troops. Revolution in the Papal States resulted in French occupation that lasted until 1838 without serious reforms. Nationalist and republican yearnings were driven underground, kept alive there in the Young Italy movement under the leadership of Giuseppe Mazzini.

Although the revolutions of 1830 are called "the forgotten revolutions" of the nineteenth century, they are important for several reasons. First, they made clear to European states how closely tied together were their fates. True to the principles of the Vienna settlements of 1815, European leaders preserved the status quo and maintained the balance of power. Revolutions in Poland and Italy were contained by Russia and Austria without interference from the other powers. Where adaptation was necessary, as in Greece and Belgium, the Great Powers were able to compromise on settlements, even though the solutions ran counter to previous policies. Heads of state were willing to use the forces of repression to stamp out protest. The international significance of the revolutions reveals a second important aspect of the events of 1830: the vulnerability of international politics to domestic instability.

Finally, the 1830 revolutions exposed a growing awareness of politics at all levels of European society. If policies in 1830 revealed a shared consciousness of events and shared values among ruling elites, the revolutions disclosed a growing awareness among the lower classes of the importance of politics in their daily lives. In a dangerous combination, workers and the lower classes throughout Europe were politicized, yet they continued to be excluded from political power.

Reform in Great Britain

The right to vote had been an issue of contention in the revolutions of 1830 in western Europe. Only the Swiss cantons enforced the principle of one man, one vote. The July Revolution in France had doubled the electorate, but still only a tiny minority of the population (less than 1 percent) enjoyed the vote. Universal male suffrage had been mandated in 1793 during the Great Revolution but not implemented. Those in power believed that the wealthiest property owners were best qualified to govern, in part because they had the greatest stake in politics and society. One also needed to own property to hold office, since those who served in parliaments received no salary.

The Rule of the Land. Landowners also ruled Britain. Migration to cities had depleted the population of rural areas, but the electoral system did not adjust to these changes. Large towns had no parliamentary representation, while dwindling county electorates maintained their parliamentary strength. Areas that continued to enjoy representation greater than that justified by their population

This English cartoon of 1832 is titled *The Clemency of the Russian Monster.* It shows Nicholas I in the guise of a bear with menacing teeth and claws addressing the Poles after crushing their rebellion against Russian rule.

were dubbed "rotten boroughs" or "pocket boroughs" to indicate a corrupt and antiquated electoral system. In general, urban areas were grossly underrepresented, as the wealthy few controlled county seats. Liberal reformers tried to rectify the electoral inequalities by reassigning parliamentary seats on the basis of density of population.

After much parliamentary wrangling and popular agitation, the Great Reform Bill of 1832 proposed a compromise. Although the vast majority of the population still did not have the vote, the new legislation strengthened the industrial and commercial elite in the towns, enfranchised most of the middle class, opened the way to social reforms, and encouraged the formation of political parties. In the 1830s, new radical reformers, disillusioned with the 1832 Reform Bill because it strengthened the power of a wealthy capitalist class, argued that democracy was the only answer to the problems plaguing British society.

The Chartist Movement. In 1838, a small group of labor leaders, including representatives of the London Working Men's Association, an organization of craft workers, drew up a document known as the People's Charter. The single most important demand of the Charter was that all men must have the vote. In addition, Chartists petitioned for a secret ballot, salaries for parliamentary service, elimination of property qualifications to run for office, equal electoral districts, and annual elections.

Chartism blossomed in working-class towns and appeared to involve all members of the family. Women organized Chartist schools and Sunday schools in radical defiance of local church organizations. Many middle-class observers were sure that the moment for class war and revolutionary upheaval had arrived. The government responded with force to the perceived threat of armed rebellion and imprisoned a number of Chartist leaders. The final moment for Chartism occurred in April 1848, when 25,000 Chartist workers, inspired by revolutionary events on the Continent, assembled in London to march on the House of Commons. They carried a newly signed petition demanding the enactment of the terms of the Charter. In response, the government deputized nearly 200,000 "special" constables in the streets. These deputized private citizens were London property owners and skilled workers who were intent on holding back a revolutionary rabble. Tired, cold, and rain-soaked, the Chartist demonstrators disbanded. No social revolution took place in Great Britain, and the dilemma of democratic representation was deferred.

Workers Unite

The word *proletariat* entered European languages before the mid-nineteenth century to describe those workers afloat in the labor pool who owned nothing, not even the tools of their labor, and who were becoming appendages to the new machines that dominated production.

Luddism. Mechanization deprived skilled craftworkers of control of the workplace. In Great Britain, France, and Germany, groups of textile workers destroyed machines in protest. Machine-breakers tyrannized parts of Great Britain from 1811 to 1816 in an attempt to frighten masters. The movement was known as Luddism after its mythical leader, Ned Ludd. Workers damaged and destroyed property for more control over the work process, but such destruction met with severe repression. From the 1820s to the 1850s, sporadic but intense outbursts of machine-breaking occurred in continental Europe. Skilled workers, fearing that they would be pulled down into the new proletariat because of mechanization and the increased scale of production, organized in new ways after 1830.

Uprisings and strikes in France increased dramatically from 1831 to 1834 and favored the destruction of the monarchy and the creation of a democratic republic. Many French craft workers grew conscious of themselves as a class and embraced a socialism that was heavily influenced by their own traditions and contemporary socialist writings. Republican socialism spread throughout France by means of a network of traveling journeymen and tapped into growing economic hardship and political discontent with the July Monarchy. Government repression drove worker organizations underground in the late 1830s, and secret societies proliferated.

Women in the Workforce. Women were an important part of the workforce in the industrializing societies. Working men were keenly aware of the competition with cheaper female labor in the factories. Women formed a salaried workforce in the home, too. To produce cheaply and in large quantities, some manufacturers turned to subcontractors for the simpler tasks in the work process. These new middlemen contracted out work such as cutting and sewing to needy women, who were often responsible for caring for family members in their homes.

Cheap female labor, paid by the piece, allowed employers to profit by keeping overhead costs low and by driving down the wages of skilled workers. Trade unions opposed women's work both in the home and in the factories. Women's talents, union leaders explained, were more properly devoted to domestic chores. Unions argued that their members should earn a wage "sufficient to support a wife and children." Unions consistently excluded women workers from their ranks.

French labor leader Flora Tristan, speaking not only as a worker but also as a wife and mother, had a very different answer for those who wanted to remove women from the workplace and assign them to their "proper place" in the home. She recognized that working women needed to work in order to support themselves and their families. Tristan told audiences in Europe and Latin America that the emancipation of women from their "slave status"

FLORA TRISTAN AND THE RIGHTS OF WORKING WOMEN

Flora Tristan (1803–1844) was a feminist and socialist who in the 1830s was actively involved in efforts to reintroduce divorce and to abolish the death penalty. She made her greatest political efforts for the creation of an international union of workers. The education of women was, Tristan asserted, essential for the success and prosperity of the working class. She toured slums in England and traveled across France on lecture tours to promote workers' unions and the education of women. The excerpt below is taken from her important book, L'Union Ouvrière, *1843. Tristan's argument for women's education is based not only on the claims of women to basic human rights, but on her assertion that educated women held the key to the betterment of families, the working class, and the whole society.*

FOCUS QUESTIONS

Why is education so important in Tristan's justification of women's rights? Would you describe Tristan as a reformer or a revolutionary?

. . . [I]T IS IMPERATIVE, in order to improve the intellectual, moral, and material condition of the working class, that women of the lower classes be given a rational and solid education, conducive to the development of their good inclinations, so that they may become skillful workers, good mothers, capable of raising and guiding their children, and of tutoring them in their school work, and so that they may act as moralizing agents in the life of the men on whom they exert an influence from the cradle to the grave.

Do you begin to understand, you, men, who cry shame before even looking into the question, why I demand rights for woman? Why I should like her to be placed on a footing of absolute equality with man in society, and that she should be so by virtue of the legal right every human being brings at birth?

I demand rights for women because I am convinced that all the misfortunes in the world result from the neglect and contempt in which woman's natural and inalienable rights have so far been held. I demand rights for woman because it is the only way she will get an education, and because the education of man in general and man of the lower classes in particular depends on the education of woman. I demand rights for woman because it is the only way to obtain her rehabilitation in the Church, the law, and society, and because this preliminary rehabilitation is necessary to achieve the rehabilitation of the workers themselves. All the woes of the working class can be summed up in these two words: poverty and ignorance, ignorance and poverty. Now, I see only one way out of this labyrinth: begin by educating women, because women have the responsibility of educating male and female children. . . .

As soon as the dangerous consequences of the development of the moral and physical faculties of women—dangerous because of women's current slave status—are no longer feared, woman can be taught with great care so as to make the best possible use of her intelligence and work. Then, you, men of the lower classes, will have as mothers skillful workers who earn a decent salary, are educated, well brought up, and quite capable of raising you, of educating you, the workers, as is proper for free men. You will have well brought up and well educated sisters, lovers, wives, friends, with whom daily contacts will be most pleasant for you. Nothing is sweeter or more agreeable to a man's heart than the sensible and gracious conversation of good and well educated women.

was essential if the working class as a whole was to enjoy a better future.

Working women's only hope, according to Tristan, lay in education and unionization. She urged working men and women to join together to lay claim to their natural and inalienable rights. In some cases, working women formed their own organizations, like that of the Parisian seamstresses who joined together to demand improved working conditions. On the whole, however, domestic workers in the home remained isolated from other working women, and many women in factories feared the loss of their jobs if they engaged in political activism. The wages of Europe's working women remained low, often below subsistence level.

Revolutions Across Europe, 1848–1850

Europeans had never experienced a year like 1848. Beginning soon after the ringing in of the New Year, revolutionary fervor swept through nearly every European country. By year's end, regimes had been created and destroyed. France, Italy, the German states, Austria, Hungary, and Bohemia were shaken to their foundations. Switzerland, Denmark, and Romania experienced lesser upheavals. Great

Britain had survived reformist agitation, and famine-crippled Ireland had endured a failed insurrection.

Hindsight reveals warning signs in the two years before the 1848 cataclysm. Beginning in 1846, a severe famine racked Europe. Lack of grain drove up prices. An increasing percentage of disposable income was spent on food for survival. Lack of spending power severely damaged markets and forced thousands of industrial workers out of their jobs. The famine hurt everyone—the poor, workers, employers, and investors—as recession paralyzed the economy.

The food crisis took place in a heavily charged political atmosphere. Throughout Europe during the 1840s, middle and lower classes had intensified their agitation for democracy. Chartists in Great Britain argued for a wider electorate. Bourgeois reformers in France campaigned for universal manhood suffrage. The movement was known as the "banquet" campaign because its leaders attempted to raise money by giving speeches at subscribed dinners. In making demands for political participation, those who were agitating for the vote necessarily criticized those who were in power. Freedom of speech and freedom of assembly were demanded as inalienable rights. The food crisis and political activism were the ingredients of an incendiary situation.

In addition to a burgeoning democratic culture, growing demands for national autonomy based on linguistic and cultural claims spread through central, southern, and eastern Europe. Although the revolts in Poland in 1846 failed, they encouraged similar movements for national liberation among Italians and Germans. Even in the relatively homogeneous nation of France, concerns with national mission and national glory grew among the regime's critics. National unity was primarily a middle-class ideal. Liberal lawyers, teachers, and businessmen from Dublin to Budapest to Prague agitated for separation from foreign rule. Austria, with an empire formed of numerous ethnic minorities, had the most to lose. Since 1815, Metternich had been ruthless in stamping out nationalist dissent. By the 1840s, nationalist claims were assuming a cultural legitimacy that was difficult to dismiss or ignore.

France Leads the Way. The events in France in the cold February of 1848 ignited the conflagration that swept Europe. On 22 February, bourgeois reformers had staged their largest banquet to date in Paris in support of extension of the vote. City officials became nervous at the prospect of thousands of workers assembling for political purposes and canceled the scheduled banquet. This was the spark that touched off the powder keg. In a spontaneous uprising, Parisians demonstrated against the government's repressive measures. Skilled workers took to the streets not only in favor of the banned banquet but also with the hope that the government would recognize the importance of labor to the social order. Shots were fired; a demonstrator was killed. The French Revolution of 1848 had begun.

Events moved quickly. The National Guard, a citizen militia of bourgeois Parisians, defected from Louis-Philippe. Many army troops that were garrisoned in Paris crossed the barricades to join revolutionary workers. The

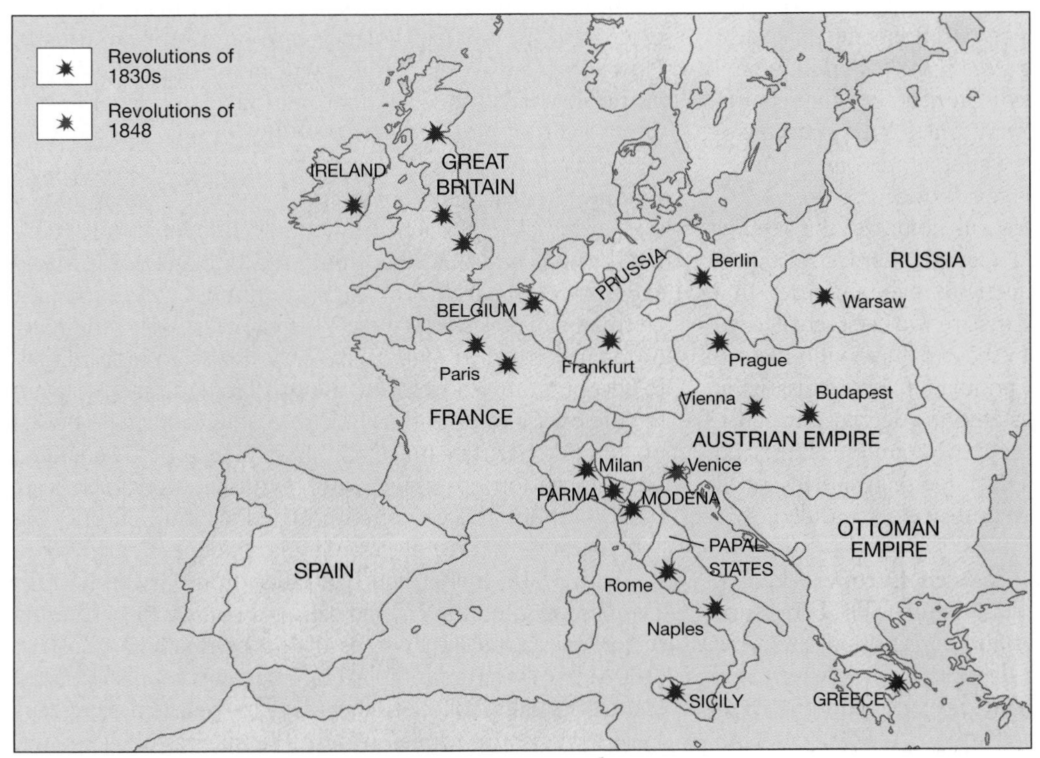

Revolutions of 1830 and 1848. In less than a generation, Europe saw two major revolutions sweep across it from west to east. France experienced the full force of both events, which pulled down successive regimes.

king attempted some reform, but it was too little and too late. Louis-Philippe fled. The Second Republic was proclaimed at the insistence of the revolutionary crowds on the barricades. The Provisional Government, led by the poet Alphonse de Lamartine (1790–1869), included members of both factions of political reformers of the July Monarchy: moderates who sought constitutional reforms and an extension of the suffrage and radicals who favored universal manhood suffrage and social programs to deal with poverty and work. Only the threat of popular violence held this uneasy alliance together.

The people fighting in the streets had little in common with the bourgeois reformers who assumed power on 24 February. Workers made a social revolution out of a commitment to their right to work, which would replace the right to property as the organizing principle of the new society. Only one member of the new Provisional Government was a worker, and he was included as a token symbol of the intentions of the new government. The government acknowledged the demand of the right to work and set up two mechanisms to guarantee workers' relief. First, a commission of workers and employers was created to act as a grievance and bargaining board and to settle questions of common concern in the workplace. Headed by the socialist Louis Blanc (1811–1882) and known as the Luxembourg Commission, the worker-employer parliament was an important innovation but accomplished little other than deflecting workers' attention away from the problems of the Provisional Government. The second measure was the creation of "national workshops" to deal with the problems of unemployment in Paris. Workers from all over France poured into Paris with the hope of finding jobs. However, the workshops had a residency requirement that even Parisians had difficulty meeting. As a result, unemployment skyrocketed. Furthermore, the government was going bankrupt trying to support the program. The need to raise taxes upset peasants in the provinces. National pressure mounted to repudiate the programs of the revolution.

French workers were too weak to dominate the revolution. The government recalled General Louis Cavaignac (1802–1857) from service in Algeria to maintain order. In a wave of armed insurrection, Parisian workers rebelled in June of 1848. Using troops from the provinces who had no identification with the urban population and employing guerrilla techniques he had mastered in Algeria, Cavaignac put down the uprising. The Second Republic was placed under the military dictatorship of Cavaignac until December, when presidential elections were scheduled.

Revolutions in Central and Eastern Europe. France was not alone in undergoing revolution in 1848. Long-suppressed desires for civil liberties and constitutional reforms erupted in widespread popular disturbances in Prussia and the German states. Fearing a war with France and unable to count on Austria or Russia for support, the princes who ruled Baden, Württemberg, Hesse-Darmstadt, Bavaria, Saxony, and Hanover followed the advice of moderate liberals and acceded quickly to revolutionary demands. In Prussia, King Frederick William IV (1840–1861) preferred to use military force to respond to popular demonstrations. Only in mid-March 1848 did the Prussian king yield to the force of the revolutionary crowds building barricades in Berlin by ordering his troops to leave the city and by promising to create a national Prussian assembly. The king was now a prisoner of the revolution.

Meanwhile, the collapse of absolute monarchy in Prussia gave further impetus to a constitutional movement among the liberal leaders of the German states. The governments of all the German states were invited to elect delegates to a national parliament in Frankfurt. The Frankfurt parliament, which was convened in May 1848, had as its dual charge the framing of a constitution and the unification of Germany. It was composed, for the most part, of members of the middle class, with civil servants, lawyers, and intellectuals predominating. In spite of the principle of universal manhood suffrage, there was not a single worker among the 800 men who were elected. To most parliamentarians, who were trained in universities and shared a social and cultural identity, nationalism and constitutionalism were inextricably related.

As straightforward as the desire for a German nation appeared to be, it was complicated by two important facts. First, there were non-German minorities living in German states. What was to be done with the Poles, Czechs, Slovenes, Italians, and Dutch in a newly constituted and autonomous German nation? Second, there were Germans living outside the German states under Habsburg rule in Austria, in Danish Schleswig and Holstein, in Posen (Poznan), in Russian Poland, and in European Russia. How were they to be included within the linguistically and ethnically constituted German nation? After much wrangling over a "small" Germany that excluded Austrian Germans and a "large" Germany that included them, the Frankfurt parliament opted for the small-Germany solution in March 1849. The crown of the new nation was offered to the unpredictable Frederick William IV of Prussia (1840–1861), head of the largest and most powerful of the German states. Unhappy with his capitulation to the revolutionary crowd in March 1848, the Prussian king refused to accept a "crown from the gutter." He had his own plans to rule over a middle-European bloc, but not at the behest of liberal parliamentarians. The attempt to create a German nation crumbled with his unwillingness to lead.

Revolution in Austrian-dominated central Europe was concentrated in three places: Vienna, Budapest, and Prague. By April 1848, Metternich had fallen from power, and the Viennese revolutionaries had set up a constituent assembly. In Budapest, the initial steps of the patriot Lajos Kossuth (1802–1894) toward establishing a separate Hungarian state seemed equally solid, as the Magyars defeated Habsburg troops. Habsburg armies were more successful in Prague, where they crushed the revolution in June 1848.

In December 1848, Emperor Ferdinand I (1835–1848), whose authority had been weakened irreparably by the overthrow of Metternich, abdicated in favor of his 18-year-old nephew, Franz Josef I (1848–1916).

Italian Nationalism. The Habsburg empire was also under siege in Italy, where the Kingdom of the Two Sicilies, Tuscany, and Piedmont declared new constitutions in March 1848. Championed by Charles Albert of Piedmont, Venice and Lombardy rose up against Austria. Nationalist sentiments had percolated underground in the Young Italy movement, founded in 1831 by Giuseppe Mazzini. Mazzini (1805–1872), a tireless and idealistic patriot, favored a democratic revolution. In spite of a reputation for liberal politics, Pope Pius IX (1846–1878) lost control of Rome and was forced to flee the city. Mazzini became head of the Republic of Rome, created in February 1849.

The French government decided to intervene to protect the pope's interests and sent in troops to defeat the republicans. One of Mazzini's disciples, Giuseppe Garibaldi (1807–1882), returned from exile in South America to undertake the defense of Rome. Garibaldi was a capable soldier who had learned the tactics of guerrilla warfare by joining independence struggles in Brazil and Argentina. Although his legion of poorly armed patriots and soldiers of fortune, known from their attire as the Red Shirts, waged a valiant effort to defend the city from April to June 1849, they were no match for the highly trained French army. French troops restored Pius IX as ruler of the Papal States.

Meanwhile, from August 1848 to the following spring, the Habsburg armies fought and finally defeated each of the revolutions throughout the Austrian Empire. Austrian success can be explained in part because the various Italian groups of Piedmontese, Tuscans, Venetians, Romans, and Neapolitans lacked coordination and central organization. Both Mazzini and Pius IX had failed to provide the focal point of leadership necessary for a successful national movement. By the fall of 1849, Austria had solved the problems in its own capital and with Italy and Hungary by military dominance. Austria understood that a Germany united under Frederick William IV of Prussia would undermine Austrian dominance in central Europe.

Europe in 1850. In 1850, Austrians threatened the Prussians with war if they did not give up their plans for a unified Germany. In November of that year, Prussian ministers signed an agreement with their Austrian counterparts in the Moravian city of Olmutz. The convention became known as "the humiliation of Olmutz" because Prussia was forced to accept Austrian dominance or go to war. In every case, military force and diplomatic measures prevailed to defeat the national and liberal movements within the German states and the Austrian Empire.

By 1850, a veneer of calm spread over central Europe. In Prussia the peasantry was emancipated from feudal dues, and a constitution, albeit conservative and based on a three-class system, was established. Yet beneath the surface was the deeper reality of Austrian decline and Prussian challenge. The great Habsburg Empire had needed to call on outside help from Russia to defeat its enemies within. The imperial giant was again on its feet, but for how long? In international relations, Austria's dominance in the German Confederation had diminished, as Prussia assumed greater political and economic power.

The 1848 revolutions spelled the end to the concert of Europe as it had been defined in the peace settlement of 1815. The European powers were incapable of united action to defend established territorial interests.

The revolutions of 1848 failed in part because of the irreconcilable split between moderate liberals and radical

CHRONOLOGY

PROTEST AND REVOLUTION

August 1819	Peterloo Massacre
1824	Charles X assumes French throne
1827	Treaty of London to support liberation of Greece
July 1830	Revolution in Paris; creation of July Monarchy under Louis-Philippe
August 1830	Revolution in Belgium
November 1830	Revolution in Poland
1831–1838	Revolutions in Italian states
1831–1834	Labor protests in France
1832	Britain's Great Reform Bill
1838	Drawing up the first People's Charter in Britain
1846	Beginning of food crisis in Europe; revolts in Poland
1846–1848	Europewide movements for national liberation
February 1848	Revolution in France; overthrow of the July Monarchy; proclamation of the French Second Republic and creation of Provisional Government
March 1848	Uprisings in some German states; granting of a constitution in Prussia
March 1848–June 1849	Revolutions in Italy
April 1848	Revolutions in Vienna, Budapest, Prague
May 1848	Frankfurt Assembly
June 1848	Second revolution in Paris, severely repressed by army troops under General Cavaignac
December 1848	Presidential elections in France; Louis Napoleon wins

democrats. The participation of the masses had frightened members of the middle classes who were committed to moderate reforms that did not threaten property. In France, working-class revolutionaries had attempted to replace property with labor as the standard of status. Property triumphed. In the face of more extreme solutions, members of the middle class were willing to accept the increased authority of existing rule as a bulwark against anarchy. In December 1848, Prince Louis Napoleon, nephew of the former emperor, was elected president of the Second Republic by a wide margin. The first truly modern French politician, Louis Napoleon managed to appeal to everyone—workers, bourgeois, royalists, and peasants—by making promises that were vague or unkeepable. Severe repression forced radical protest into hiding. The new Bonaparte bided his time until the moment in 1851 when he seized absolute power.

Similar patterns emerged elsewhere in Europe. In Germany, the bourgeoisie accepted the dominance of the old feudal aristocracy as a guarantee of law and order. Repressive government, businessmen were sure, would restore a strong economy. The attempts in 1848 to create new nations based on ethnic identities were in shambles by 1850.

Nearly everywhere throughout Europe, constitutions had been systematically withdrawn with the recovery of the forces of reaction. With the French and Swiss exceptions, the bids for the extension of the franchise failed. The propertied classes remained in control of political institutions. Radicals willing to use violence to press electoral reforms were arrested, killed, or exiled. There seemed to be no effective opposition to the rise and consolidation of state power. The 1848 revolutions have been called a turning point at which modern history failed to turn. Contemporaries wondered how so much action could have produced so few lasting results.

Conclusion

THE PERCEPTION THAT NOTHING HAD CHANGED WAS WRONG. The revolutions of 1848 and subsequent events galvanized whole societies to political action. Conservatives and radicals alike turned toward a new realism in politics. Governments could no longer ignore economic upheavals and social dislocations if they wanted to survive. Revolutionaries also learned that the state could wield powerful forces of repression. The state wielded powerful forces of violence against which nationalists, socialists, republicans, and liberals had all been proved helpless. Organizing, campaigning, and lobbying were newly learned political skills, as was outreach across class lines—from bourgeoisie to peasantry—around common political causes. In these ways, 1848 was a turning point in the formation of a modern political culture.

QUESTIONS FOR REVIEW

1. What problems did European peacemakers confront at the Congress of Vienna and how did they attempt to resolve the problems?
2. How did industrialization change European families?
3. In what ways were liberalism and nationalism compatible with each other; how were they in conflict?
4. What are the connections between various ideologies—for instance, liberalism, romanticism, or socialism—and the revolutions of 1830 and 1848?

DISCOVERING WESTERN CIVILIZATION ONLINE

You can obtain more information about political upheavals and social transformations between 1815 and 1850 at the websites listed below. See also the companion website that accompanies this text: www.ablongman.com/kishlansky, which contains an online study guide and additional resources.

Geographical Tour: Europe in 1815

www.fordham.edu/halsall/mod/modsbook16.html
The site provides documents, discussions, and bibliographies on the Congress of Vienna and charts the development of conservative thought.

The New Ideologies

www.fordham.edu/halsall/mod/modsbook18.html
A collection of links to primary documents and bibliographies on liberalism.

www.fordham/edu/halsall/mod/modsbook17.html
www.nationalismproject.org/
These sites provide links to primary documents and bibliographies on nationalism.

www.fordham.edu/halsall/mod/modsbook15.html
This site provides links to primary texts on romantic philosophy and literature.

vos.ucsb.edu/index.asp
This comprehensive database for humanities research provides links to general resources, criticism, and primary texts. Type "Romantics" into the search function for resources on romantic philosophy and literature.

www.Marxists.org/archive/index.htm
The site provides translated texts of Marx and Engels as well as other prominent Social Democrats and Communists.

Protest and Revolution

www.ohiou.edu/~Chastain/index.htm
This site contains the "Encyclopedia of Revolutions of 1848," a large collection of essays by academic and other authors about the revolutions of 1848 in Europe.

www.spartacus.schoolnet.co.uk/IRchild.htm
A collection of biographies of reformers and promoters of child labor, electronic texts of major child labor legislation, and excerpts from primary sources concerning child labor in nineteenth-century Britain.

www.spartacus.schoolnet.co.uk/women.htm
The site contains links to biographies of major figures, essays on the major organizations and societies, and electronic texts of the women's movement in Britain.

www.fordham/edu/halsall/mod/modsbook19.html
The site provides documents, discussions, bibliographies, and other links on the revolutions of 1848.

SUGGESTIONS FOR FURTHER READING

Geographical Tour: Europe in 1815

Tim Chapman, *The Congress of Vienna: Origins, Processes, and Results* (New York: Routledge, 1998). A brief, comprehensive survey of how the European powers victorious against Napoleon redrew Europe's frontiers. It follows the impact of the Settlement to its demise in the twentieth century.

Robert Gildea, *Barricades and Borders, Europe 1800–1914* (Oxford: Oxford University Press, 1996). A synthetic overview of economic, demographic, political, and international trends in European society.

Robin Okey, *The Habsburg Monarchy: From Enlightenment to Eclipse* (New York: St. Martin's Press, 2001). An informative survey of Austrian rule from the mid-eighteenth century to the end of World War I, which contains an annotated bibliography and materials drawn from historiographic material in Magyar, Serbo-Croat, Czech, and other eastern European language sources.

The New Ideologies

Jonathan Beecher, *Charles Fourier: The Visionary and His World* (Berkeley: University of California Press, 1986). An intellectual biography that traces the development of Fourier's theoretical perspective and roots it firmly in the social context of nineteenth-century France.

Craig Calhoun, *The Question of Class Struggle: Social Foundations of Popular Radicalism During the Industrial Revolution* (Chicago: University of Chicago Press, 1982). Presents popular protest of eighteenth- and early nineteenth-century England as the reaction of communities of artisans defending their traditions against encroaching industrialization.

Gareth Stedman Jones, *Languages of Class: Studies in English Working Class History, 1832–1982* (Cambridge: Cambridge University Press, 1983). A series of essays on topics such as working-class culture and Chartism that examine the development of class consciousness.

Denis Mack Smith, *Mazzini* (New Haven, Conn.: Yale University Press, 1994). Mazzini is presented as an important force in legitimizing Italian nationalism by associating it with republicanism and the interests of humanity.

Protest and Revolution

Maurice Agulhon, *The Republican Experiment, 1848–1852* (Cambridge: Cambridge University Press, 1983). Traces the Revolution of 1848 from its roots to its ultimate failure in 1852 through an analysis of the republican ideologies of workers, peasants, and the bourgeoisie.

Clive Church, *Europe in 1830: Revolution and Political Change* (London: Allen & Unwin, 1983). Considers the origins of the 1830 revolutions within a wider European crisis through a comparative analysis of European regions.

R. J. W. Evans and Hartmut Pogge von Strandmann, eds., *The Revolutions in Europe, 1848–1849: From Reform to Reaction* (Oxford: Oxford University Press, 2000). A focused collection of articles on the mid-nineteenth-century collapse of authority across Europe.

Alan J. Kidd, *State, Society, and the Poor in Nineteenth-Century England* (New York: St. Martin's Press, 1999). This volume is part of the *Social History in Perspective* series; it provides an overview of poverty in industrializing England, the role of the poor laws, public welfare, and charitable organizations in the nineteenth century.

Catherine J. Kudlick, *Cholera in Post-Revolutionary Paris: A Cultural History* (Berkeley: University of California Press, 1996). Examines the cultural values of ruling elites and demonstrates the role disease played in shaping political life and class identity in nineteenth-century France.

Patricia O'Brien, *The Promise of Punishment: Prisons in Nineteenth-Century France* (Princeton: Princeton University Press, 1982). An overview of the creation of the penitentiary system in nineteenth-century France and the rise of the new science of punishment, criminology, and the eventual appearance of alternatives to the penitentiary system.

Redcliffe N. Salaman, *The History and Social Influence of the Potato*, revised impression edited by J. G. Hawkes (Cambridge: Cambridge University Press, 1985). The classic study of the potato. A major portion of the work is devoted to the potato famine.

Jonathan Sperber, *Revolutionary Europe, 1780–1850* (New York: Longman, 2000). Considers the revolutions of 1848 within the context of economic and social changes rooted in Old Regime politics and society and from the perspective of the twenty-first century.

CHAPTER 23

STATE BUILDING AND SOCIAL CHANGE IN EUROPE, 1850–1871

- THE VISUAL RECORD: The Birth of the German Empire
- BUILDING NATIONS: THE POLITICS OF UNIFICATION
- REFORMING EUROPEAN SOCIETY
- CHANGING VALUES AND THE FORCE OF NEW IDEAS

THE VISUAL RECORD

THE BIRTH OF THE GERMAN EMPIRE

ALTHOUGH NOT ORDINARILY A FANCIFUL MAN, Otto von Bismarck (1815–1898) wrote to his wife that he imagined himself a midwife assisting at a momentous birth. The birth in his daydream was the proclamation of the German Empire on 21 January 1871. As the Prussian statesman stood in the Versailles Palace outside Paris on that fateful day, surrounded by German aristocrats, he could not forget the years of struggle and planning—the precarious pregnancy, so to speak—that had preceded this joyous event.

The newly established Second Reich, successor to the Holy Roman Empire (962–1806), united the German states into a single nation. The unification had involved years of foreign wars and diplomatic maneuverings. The placid, glossy scene painted by Anton von Werner (1843–1915) hardly suggests Bismarck's strong emotions on this momentous day. The richly marbled and mirrored room, the site of the birth of the German Empire, figures as prominently in the tableau as the uniformed princes and aristocrats, who, with sabers, helmets, and standards raised, cheer the new emperor. The choice of the Hall of Mirrors as the meeting place for the German princes was intended as an assertion of German superiority in Europe. The great hall, after all, had been built by Louis XIV to reflect and glorify the power of absolutist France. Here, the kings of France had presided over lavish ceremonies and opulent receptions. Here, Napoleon I had honored his generals, victorious in conquering central Europe. Here, not long before, Napoleon III had danced on the parqueted floors with Queen Victoria of Britain. And now, here meet the representatives of the German princes who have successfully combined forces to defeat the French Second Empire in only six weeks of war in the fall of 1870, to complete the French humiliation.

The painting shows King William I of Prussia on the dais, flanked by his son Crown Prince Frederick William, and his son-in-law, Friedrich I, the Grand Duke of Baden, whose upraised hand signals the cheer for the new emperor. At the foot of the steps, like a loyal retainer, stands the self-described midwife, Otto von Bismarck, who is singled out in his pure white uniform. Yet there is something amiss. The new German emperor stands to one side of the canvas while Bismarck commands its center. If most eyes

of the cheering princes turn to the emperor, ours are pulled to the chancellor of the new Reich. In both hands Bismarck holds both the document proclaiming the empire and his Prussian military helmet. The artist has shown that it was Bismarck's event, for it was Bismarck who crafted a united Germany.

Bismarck created this new "state of princes," the German Empire, through "iron and blood"—force and military conquest—and not by democratic means. Conservative state building succeeded in unifying Germany where the liberal ideology of representative government had failed.

To Bismarck's left, in profile facing the emperor, stands Count Helmuth von Moltke (1800–1891), head of the Prussian General Staff and the man responsible for reorganizing the Prussian army with Bismarck's support. Medals for bravery and service to his sovereign adorn Moltke's chest. With one foot forward, Moltke is a man of action, almost caught in midstride, a man ready to move into the future.

LOOKING AHEAD

In this chapter, we will examine the period between 1850 and 1871, when unification of territories was an important part of the process of building a nation in both Germany and Italy. Successful statesmen were diplomats who used alliances to further national interests. They were also realists willing to use force to further national interests. The existing nation-states of France, Great Britain, and Russia, with little in common save their commitment to progress, pursued different paths to state reform and consolidation of national power.

The changing values and force of new ideas so evident in the political realm also characterized the changing world of the home and family. Just as realism was a dominant force in politics, realism in arts and sciences became a means of promoting material progress. With the convergence of these changes in a variety of realms, Europeans witnessed the birth of the modern age in the third quarter of the nineteenth century.

BUILDING NATIONS: THE POLITICS OF UNIFICATION

The revolutions of 1848 had occurred in a period of political experimentation. Radicals enlisting popular support had tried and failed to reshape European states for their own nationalist, liberal, and socialist ends. Governments in Paris, Vienna, Berlin, and a number of lesser states had been swept away as revolutions created a power vacuum but no durable solutions. To fill that vacuum, a new breed of politicians emerged in the 1850s and 1860s, men who understood the importance of the centralized nation-state and the need of reforms from above. They shared a new realism about means and ends, and about using foreign policy successes to further domestic programs.

The Crimean War

In 1849 and 1850, Russia had fulfilled its role as policeman of Europe by supporting Austria against Hungary and Prussia. Yet Russia was not merely content to keep the peace; it sought greater power to the south in the Balkans. The narrow straits connecting the Black Sea with the Aegean Sea were controlled by the Ottoman Empire. Russia hoped to benefit from Ottoman weakness caused by internal conflicts and gain control of the straits as an outlet for the Russian fleet to the Mediterranean.

At the center of the hope for Ottoman disintegration lay the "Eastern Question," the term that was used in the nineteenth century to designate the problems surrounding the European territories controlled by the Ottoman Empire. Each of the Great Powers—Russia, Great Britain, Austria, Prussia, and France—hoped to benefit territorially from the collapse of Ottoman control. In 1853, Great Power rivalry over the Eastern Question created an international situation that led to war.

In 1853, the Russian government demanded that the Turkish government recognize Russia's right to protect Greek Orthodox believers in the Ottoman Empire. The Turkish government refused Russian demands, and the Russians ordered troops to enter the Danubian Principalities of Moldavia and Wallachia, which were held by the Turks.

In October 1853, the Turkish government, counting on support from Great Britain and France, declared war on Russia. Russia easily prevailed over its weaker neighbor to the south. In a four-hour battle, a Russian squadron destroyed the Turkish fleet off the coast of Sinope. Tsar Nicholas I (1825–1855) drew up the terms of a settlement with the Ottoman Empire and submitted them to Great Britain and France for review.

The two western European powers, fearing Russian aggrandizement at Turkish expense, responded by declaring war on Russia on 28 March 1854, a date that marked a new phase in the Crimean War. The Italian kingdom of Sardinia also joined the war against Russia in January 1855, hoping to make its name militarily and win recognition for its aim to unite Italy into a single nation. Although Great Britain, France, and the Italian state of Sardinia did not have explicit economic interests, they were motivated by ambition, prestige, and rivalry in the Balkans.

British and French troops landed in the Crimea, the Russian peninsula extending into the Black Sea, in September 1854, with the intention of capturing Sevastopol, Russia's heavily fortified chief naval base on the Black Sea. The allies laid siege to the fortress at Sevastopol, which fell on 11 September 1855 after 322 days of battle. The defeated Russians abandoned Sevastopol, blew up their forts, and sank their own ships. Facing the threat of Austrian entry into the war, Russia agreed to preliminary peace terms.

In the Peace of Paris of 1856, Russia relinquished its claim as protector of Christians in Turkey. The British gained the neutralization of the Black Sea. The mouth of the Danube was returned to Turkish control, and an international commission was created to oversee safe navigation on the Danube. The Danubian Principalities were placed under joint guarantee of the powers, and Russia gave up a small portion of Bessarabia. In 1861, the Principalities were united in the independent nation of Romania.

The Crimean War had dramatic and enduring consequences. Russia ceased to play an active role in European affairs and turned toward expansion in central Asia. Its withdrawal opened up the possibility for a move by Prussia in central Europe.

Unifying Italy

The Kingdom of Sardinia, meanwhile, was leading the drive for Italian reunification. Italy had not been a single political entity since the end of the Roman Empire in the west in the fifth century. The movement to reunite Italy culturally and politically was known as the *Risorgimento* (literally, "resurgence").

Cavour's Political Realism. In 1848, both Giuseppe Mazzini's Young Italy movement and Giuseppe Garibaldi's Red Shirts had sought a united republican Italy achieved through direct popular action, but they had failed. It took a politician of aristocratic birth to recognize that Mazzini's and Garibaldi's model of revolutionary action was doomed against the powerful Austrian military machine. Mazzini was a moralist. Garibaldi was a fighter. But Camillo Benso di Cavour (1810–1861) was an opportunistic politician and a realist.

As premier of Sardinia from 1852 to 1859 and again in 1860–1861, Cavour was well placed to launch his campaign for Italian unity. The Kingdom of Sardinia, whose

▲ The Unification of Italy. By 1860, the majority of the Italian "boot" was under the rule of Piedmont-Sardinia. By 1870, the unification was complete.

principal state was Piedmont, had made itself a focal point for unification efforts. Its king, Carlo-Alberto (1831–1849), had stood alone among Italian rulers in opposing Austrian domination of the Italian peninsula in 1848 and 1849. Severely defeated by the Austrians, he was forced to abdicate. He was succeeded by his son Victor Emmanuel II (1849–1861), who had the good sense to appoint Cavour as his first minister. From the start, Cavour undertook liberal administrative measures that included tax reform, stabilization of the currency, improvement of the railway system, the creation of a transatlantic steamship system, and the support of private enterprise. With these programs, Cavour created for Sardinia the dynamic image of progressive change. He involved Sardinia in the Crimean War, thereby securing its status among the European powers.

Most important, however, was Cavour's alliance with France against Austria in 1858. The alliance was quickly followed by an arranged provocation against the Habsburg monarchy. Austria declared war in 1859 and was easily defeated by French forces in the battles of Magenta and Solferino. The peace settlement joined Lombardy to the Piedmontese state.

Cavour's approach was not without its costs. His partnership with a stronger power meant sometimes following France's lead, and the need to cajole French support meant enriching France with territorial gain in the form of Nice and Savoy. However, Sardinia got more than it gave up. In the summer of 1859, revolutionary assemblies in Tuscany, Modena, Parma, and the Romagna, wanting to eject their Austrian rulers, voted in favor of union with the Piedmontese. By April 1860, these four areas of central Italy were under Victor Emmanuel II's rule. Sardinia had doubled in size to become the dominant power on the Italian peninsula.

Southern Italians took their lead from events in central Italy and, in the spring of 1860, initiated disorders against the rule of King Francis II (1859–1861) of Naples. Uprisings in Sicily inspired Giuseppe Garibaldi to return from his self-imposed exile to organize his own army of Red Shirts, known as the Thousand, who liberated Sicily and then crossed to the Italian mainland to expel Francis II from Naples. Garibaldi next turned his attention to the liberation of the Holy City, where a French garrison protected the pope.

As Garibaldi's popularity as a national hero grew, Cavour became alarmed at the competition in uniting Italy

▼ In this British cartoon of 1860, Garibaldi surrenders his power to Victor Emmanuel II, king of Piedmont-Sardinia (soon to be king of a united Italy). The caption reads "Right Leg in the Boot at Last."

and took secret steps to block the advance of the Red Shirts and their leader. To seize the initiative, Cavour directed the Piedmontese army into the Papal States. After defeating the pope's troops, Cavour's men crossed into the Neapolitan state and scored important victories against forces loyal to the king of Naples. Cavour proceeded to annex southern Italy for Victor Emmanuel II, using plebiscites to seal the procedure.

A King for a United Italy. At this point, in 1860, Garibaldi yielded his own conquered territories to Sardinia, making possible the declaration of a united Italy under Victor Emmanuel II, who reigned as king of Italy from 1861 to 1878.

The new king of Italy was now poised to acquire Venetia, which was under Austrian rule, and Rome, which was ruled by Pope Pius IX, and Victor Emmanuel devoted much of his foreign policy in the 1860s to these ends. In 1866, when Austria lost a war with Prussia, Italy struck a deal with the victor and gained control of Venetia. When Prussia prevailed against France in 1870, Victor Emmanuel took over Rome. The boot of Italy, from top to toe, was now a single nation. The pope remained in the Vatican, opposed to an Italy united under King Victor Emmanuel II.

Unifying Germany

In this age of realistic politicians, Prussian statesman Otto von Bismarck (1815–1898) emerged as the supreme practitioner of *Realpolitik*, the ruthless use of any means, including illegal and violent ones, to advance a country's interests. Bismarck was a Junker, an aristocratic estate-owner from east of the Elbe River, who entered politics in 1847. In the 1850s, he became aware of Prussia's future in the center of Europe; he saw that the old elites must be allied with the national movement to survive.

Prussia's Seven Weeks' War with Austria. In 1850, Prussia had been forced to accept Austrian dominance in central Europe or go to war. Throughout the following decade, however, Prussia systematically undermined Austrian power and excluded Austria from German economic affairs. In 1862, at the moment of a crisis provoked

The Unification of Germany. Under Bismarck's direction, Prussia used military conquest as the means of unifying the 38 disparate states of the German Confederation into the German Empire and gaining territory from Austria and France.

by the king over military reorganization, Bismarck became minister-president of the Prussian cabinet and foreign minister. He overrode the parliamentary body, the Diet, by reorganizing the army without a formally approved budget. In 1864, he constructed an alliance between Austria and Prussia for the purpose of invading Schleswig, a predominantly German-speaking territory controlled by the king of Denmark. Within five days of the invasion, Denmark yielded the duchies of Schleswig and Holstein, now to be ruled jointly by Austria and Prussia.

Counting on the neutrality of France and Great Britain, the support of Sardinia, and good relations with Russia, Bismarck promoted a crisis between Austria and Prussia over management of the formerly Danish territories and led his country into war with Austria in June 1866. In this Seven Weeks' War, Austrian forces proved to be no match for the better-equipped and better-trained Prussian army. Bismarck dictated the terms of the peace, excluding Austria from a united, Prussian-dominated Germany. In 1867, in response to pressures from the subject nationalities, the Habsburg Empire transformed itself into a dual monarchy of two independent and equal states under one ruler, who would be both the emperor of Austria and the king of Hungary. In spite of the reorganization, the problem of nationalities persisted, and ethnic groups began to agitate for total independence from imperial rule.

The Franco-Prussian War. Bismarck's biggest obstacle to German unification was laid to rest with Austria's defeat. The south German states continued to resist the idea of Prussian dominance, but growing numbers of people in Baden, Württemberg, Bavaria, and the southern parts of Hesse-Darmstadt recognized the value of uniting under Prussian leadership.

Many French observers were troubled by the Prussian victory over Austria and were apprehensive about what a united Germany might portend for the future of French dominance in Europe. Napoleon III attempted unsuccessfully to contain Prussian ambitions through diplomatic maneuverings. Instead, France found itself stranded without important European allies. In the spring of 1870, Bismarck seized the initiative and provoked a crisis with France. The issue of succession to the Spanish throne provided the pretext. On 13 July 1870, the Prussian king (later Emperor William I) sent a message to Napoleon III reporting a meeting with the French ambassador. Bismarck skillfully edited this "Ems Dispatch" to suggest that the French ambassador had insulted the Prussian king, then leaked news of the incident to the press in both countries.

As a direct result of this contrived misunderstanding, France declared war on Prussia in July 1870. As Bismarck hoped, the southern German princes immediately sided with the Prussian king. Unlike the Germans, who were well prepared for war, the French had not coordinated deployment with the new technology of the railroad. Although French troops had the latest equipment, they were sent into battle without instructions on how to use it. And they were outnumbered almost two to one. All these factors combined to spell disaster for the French. Within a matter of weeks it was obvious that France had lost the Franco-Prussian War. The path was now clear for the declaration of the German Empire in January 1871.

Prussian Dominance of United Germany. In unifying Germany, Bismarck built on the constitution of the North German Confederation formed in 1867, which guaranteed Prussian dominance. Bismarck used the bureaucracy as a mainstay of the emperor. The new Reichstag—the national legislative assembly—was to be elected by means of universal male suffrage, but it was not sovereign, and the chancellor was accountable only to the emperor.

The United States: Civil War and Reunification

In the 1860s, another crisis in state building was resolved across the Atlantic. The United States cemented political unity through the use of force in its Civil War (1861–1865). The president of the United States, Abraham Lincoln (1809–1865), mobilized the superior resources of the industrial Northern states against the heavily agrarian, slave-owning South. The United States worked to achieve national unity and territorial integrity in another sense through ongoing expansion westward by eliminating and subduing Native American peoples.

With the emancipation of the slaves, republican democracy appeared to triumph in the United States. Newly created European nation-states followed a different path: Plebiscites were manipulated by those in power in Italy, and a neo-absolutism emerged in Germany. Yet the Civil War in the United States and the successful bids for unification in Italy and Germany shared remarkable similarities. In all three countries, wars eventually resulted in a single national market and a single financial system without internal barriers. Unified national economies, particularly in Germany and the United States, paved the way for significant economic growth and the expansion of industrial power.

Nationalism and Force

The personification of nation-states was one of the great achievements of statesmen throughout Europe between 1850 and 1870. The language and symbols they put in place created the nation itself, a new political reality whose forms contained a modern political consciousness. The nation-state became an all-knowing being whose rights had to be protected, whose destiny had to be assured.

The nation was above all a creation that minimized or denied real differences in dialect and language, regional loyalties, local traditions, and village identities. No power was acknowledged to exist above the nation-state, and no power could sanction the nation's actions but itself. Force was an acceptable alternative to diplomacy. Violence and nationalism were inextricably linked in the unification of both Italy and Germany in the third quarter of the nineteenth century.

National unification had escaped the grasp of liberals and radicals between 1848 and 1850 with the failure of revolutionary and reform movements. In the 1850s and 1860s, those who were committed to radical transformations worked from within the existing system. The new realists subordinated liberal nationalism to conservative state-building. Under newly dynamic conservative leadership, military force would validate what intellectuals and idealistic revolutionaries had not been able to legitimate through ideological claims.

REFORMING EUROPEAN SOCIETY

After the revolutions of 1848, government repression silenced radical movements throughout Europe. But repression could not maintain social harmony and promote growth and prosperity. In the third quarter of the nineteenth century, Europe's leaders recognized that reforms were needed to build dynamic and competitive states. Three different models for social and political reform developed in France, Great Britain, and Russia after 1850. All three sets of reforms took place in unified nation-states. The three societies had little in common with each other ideologically, but all reflected a commitment to progress and an awareness of the state's role and responsibility in achieving it.

The Second Empire in France, 1852–1870

One model was that of France, where the French emperor worked through a highly centralized administrative structure and with a valued elite of specialists to achieve social and economic transformation.

Napoleon III. Under Napoleon III's direction the Second Empire achieved economic expansion and industrial development. A new private banking system enabled the pooling of investors' resources to finance industrial expansion. Napoleon III and his advisers believed that prosperity was the answer to all social problems. Between 1852 and 1860, the government supported a massive program of railroad construction. Jobs multiplied, and investment increased. Agriculture expanded as railroad lines opened new markets. The rich got richer, but the extreme poverty of the first half of the nineteenth century was diminishing. Brutal misery in the city and countryside did not disappear, but on the whole, the standard of living increased as wages rose faster than prices.

Rebuilding Paris. The best single example of the energy and commitment of the imperial regime was the rebuilding of the French capital. Before midcentury, Paris was one of the most unsanitary, crime-ridden, and politically volatile capitals in Europe. Within 15 years it had been transformed into a city of lights, wide boulevards and avenues, monumental vistas, parks, and gardens. Poor districts were cleared to make way for the elegant apartment buildings of the Parisian bourgeoisie. As workers from all over France migrated to the capital in search of jobs, the population nearly doubled, increasing by just under one million in the 1850s and 1860s. Wide, straight Parisian avenues served as an international model that was copied in Mexico City, Brussels, Madrid, Rome, Stockholm, and Barcelona between 1870 and 1900.

The new housing that was built within the city was too expensive for the poor, who were pushed out to the suburbs. A volatile population of poor people encircled the city of monuments and museums. Paris as the radical capital of France was being physically dismantled, and a new, more conservative political entity rose in its place as the middle classes took over the heart of the city. This process was very different from the development of other urban areas such as London, where the middle class fled to the suburbs, leaving behind the problems of urban life.

The Foreign Policy of the Second Empire. Just as a new Paris would make France a center of Western culture, Napoleon III intended his blueprint for foreign policy to restore France to its pre-1815 status as the greatest European power. By involving France in both the Crimean War and the war for Italian unification, Napoleon III returned France to adventurous foreign policies, acquired Nice and Savoy from Sardinia, and reversed the settlements of 1815.

French construction of the Suez Canal between the Red Sea and the Mediterranean created tensions with Great Britain, which was protective of its own dominance in the Mediterranean and the Near East. Nevertheless, the free-trade agreement between the British and the French in 1860 was a landmark in overseas policy and a commitment to liberal economic policies.

The Second Empire's involvement in Mexico was a fiasco. The Mexican government had been chronically unable to pay its foreign debts, and France was Mexico's largest creditor. Napoleon III hoped that by intervening in Mexican affairs, he could strengthen ties with Great Britain and Spain, to whom the Mexicans also owed money. With the backing of Mexican conservatives who opposed Mexican president Benito Juárez (1806–1872), Napoleon III supported the Austrian archduke Maximilian (1832–1867) as emperor of Mexico. After he was crowned in 1863, the new Mexican emperor struggled to rule in an enlightened manner, but he was stymied from the beginning by his ineptitude and lack of popular support. Following the recall of the 34,000 French troops that, at considerable expense, were keeping Maximilian's troubled regime in place, Maximilian was captured and executed by a firing squad in the summer of 1867. The Mexican disaster damaged the prestige of Napoleon III's regime in the international arena, and in 1870 the humiliatingly rapid defeat of French imperial forces in the Franco-Prussian War ended the experiment in liberal empire.

The Victorian Compromise

Great Britain provided another model of reform, which was fostered through liberal parliamentary democracy. In government by "amateurs," with local rather than a highly centralized administration, British legislation alternated between a philosophy of freedom and one of protection. But reforms were always hammered out by parliamentary means with the support of a gradually expanding electorate.

Parliamentary Reforms. In contrast to France, Britain enjoyed apparent social harmony without revolution and without civil war. The relative calm of British society in the middle of the nineteenth century owed much to the fact that Great Britain had an enormously productive capitalist economy of sustained growth.

The stability and calm were undoubtedly exaggerated, however, for Great Britain at midcentury had its share of serious social problems. British slums rivaled any in Europe. Poverty, disease, and famine ravaged the kingdom. Social protests of the 1840s raised fears of upheavals similar to those in continental Europe. Yet Great Britain avoided a revolution. One explanation for the relative calm lay in Britain's parliamentary tradition, which emphasized liberty as the birthright of English citizens and was able to adapt to the demands of an industrializing society. Adaptation was slow, but it achieved a compromise among competing social interests. The great compromise of Victorian society was the reconciliation of industrialists' commitment to unimpeded growth with the workers' need for the state's protection.

As part of a pattern of slow democratization, the Reform Bill of 1832 gave increased political power to the industrial and manufacturing bourgeoisie, who joined a landed aristocracy and merchant class. But the property qualification meant that only 20 percent of the population could vote. In 1867, under conservative leadership, a second Reform Bill was introduced. Approval of this bill doubled the electorate, giving the vote to a new urban population of shopkeepers, clerks, and workers. In 1884, farm laborers were enfranchised. Women, however, remained barred from voting until after World War I.

Gladstone and Disraeli. The lives and careers of two men, William Ewart Gladstone (1809–1898) and Benjamin Disraeli (1804–1881), exemplify the particular path the British government followed in maintaining public peace. Rivals and political opponents, both men served as prime ministers and both left their mark on the age.

William Gladstone was a classical liberal who believed in free enterprise and opposed state intervention. Good government, according to Gladstone, should remove obstacles to talent, competition, and individual initiative but should interfere as little as possible in economy and society. Gladstone's first term as prime minister (1868–1874) significantly advanced the British liberal state. Taking advantage of British prosperity, Gladstone abolished tariffs, cut defense expenditures, lowered taxes, and sponsored sound budgets. He furthered the liberal agenda by disestablishing the Anglican Church in Ireland in 1869. The Church had been the source of great resentment to the vast

William Gladstone rides in an omnibus in this painting titled *One of the People* by Alfred Morgan. This mode of transport was thought of as a social leveler because all classes of people could afford the fares.

majority of Irish Catholics, who had been forced to pay taxes to support the Protestant state church.

Gladstone reformed the army and the civil service. His government introduced the secret ballot. Finally, the Liberal Party stressed the importance of education for an informed electorate and passed an Education Act that aimed to make elementary schooling available to everyone. These reforms added up to a Liberal philosophy of government. Liberal government was above all an attack on privilege. It sought to remove restraints on individual freedom and foster opportunity and talent.

During these years, another political philosophy—conservatism—also left its mark on British government. Under the flamboyant leadership of Benjamin Disraeli, the Conservative Party, trusting the state to correct and protect, supported state intervention and regulation on behalf of the poor and disadvantaged. Disraeli sponsored the Factory Act of 1875, which set a maximum of 56 hours on the factory work week. The Public Health Act established a sanitary code. The Artisans Dwelling Act defined minimum housing standards. Probably the most important conservative legislation was the Trade Union Act, which permitted picketing and other peaceful labor tactics.

Disraeli championed protection against free trade. Unlike the Liberals, he insisted on the importance of traditional institutions such as the monarchy, the House of Lords, and the Church of England. His work in organizing a national party machinery facilitated the adaptation of the parliamentary system to mass politics. His methods of campaigning and building a mass base of support were used by successful politicians regardless of political persuasion.

As the intersecting careers of Gladstone and Disraeli demonstrate, the British model combined free enterprise with intervention and regulation. The clear issues and the clear choices of the two great parties—Liberal and Conservative—dominated parliamentary life after midcentury. In polarizing parliamentary politics, they also invigorated it.

The terms "liberal" and "conservative" hold none of the meaning today that they did for men and women in the nineteenth century. Classical liberalism has little in common with its twentieth-century counterpart, which favors an active, interventionist state. Disraeli is a far more likely candidate for the twentieth-century liberal label than is Gladstone, Britain's leading nineteenth-century liberal statesman.

Reforming Russia

Russia offered a third model for reform in the nineteenth century. Like Britain, Russia had avoided revolution at midcentury and hoped to preserve social peace. Yet the Russian model for reform stood in dramatic contrast to Britain's. Russia was an unreformed autocracy in which the tsar held absolute power. Without a parliament, without a constitution, and without civil liberties for his subjects, the Russian ruler governed through a bureaucracy and a police force. Economically, Russia was a semifeudal agrarian state with a class of privileged aristocrats supported by serf labor on their estates.

A Serf-Holding Nation. For decades—since the reign of Alexander I (1801–1825)—the tsars and their advisers realized that they were out of step with developments in western Europe. An awareness was growing that serfdom was uncivilized and morally wrong, as critics compared the Russian practice with the atrocities of American slavery. Among the European powers, only Russia remained a serf-holding nation. Russian serfs were tied to the land and owed dues and labor services in return for the lands they held. Peasant protests mounted, attracting public attention to the plight of the serfs. But in spite of growing moral concern, there were many reasons to resist the abolition of serfdom. How were serf-holders to be compensated for the loss of labor power? What was to be the freed serfs' relationship to the land?

Alexander II and the Emancipation of the Serfs. Hesitation about abolition evaporated with the Russian defeat in the Crimean War. The new tsar, Alexander II (1855–1881), viewed Russia's inability to repel an invasion force on its own soil as proof of its backwardness. Russia had no railroads and was forced to transport military supplies by carts to the Crimea. It took three months to provision troops; the enemy could do so in three weeks. Liberating the serfs would permit a well-trained reserve army to exist without fear of rebellion and would also create a system of free labor, so necessary for industrial development.

In March 1861, the tsar signed the emancipation edict that liberated 52 million serfs. Serfdom was eliminated in Poland three years later. Alexander II, who came to be known as the "Tsar-Liberator," compromised between landlord and serf by allotting land to freed peasants while requiring from the former serfs redemption payments that were spread out over a period of 49 years. To guarantee repayment, the land was granted not directly to individual peasants but to the village commune (*mir*), which was responsible for collecting redemption payments. The peasant paid the state in installments; the state reimbursed the landowner in the form of interest-bearing bonds and redemption certificates. Neither serf nor landholder benefited from these financial arrangements, which kept the former serf under heavy obligations and prevented the landlord from making needed capital improvements. The real winner in the abolition of serfdom was the state, which expanded its bureaucratic hierarchy and financial infrastructure.

The Great Reforms. The tsar introduced a vast array of "Great Reforms"—emancipating the serfs, creating local parliamentary bodies (*zemstvos*), reorganizing the judiciary, modernizing the army—yet Russia was not sufficiently liberalized or democratized to satisfy the critics of autocracy. Between 1860 and 1870, a young generation of intelligentsia, radical intellectuals who were influenced by the rhetoric of revolution in western Europe, protested against the existing order, traveling from village to village to educate the peasants and in some cases to attempt to radicalize them.

The Populist Movement. The radicals paid dearly for their commitment to populism when they were subjected to mass trials and repression in the late 1870s. Some of these critics fled into exile to reemerge as revolutionaries in western Europe, where they continued to oppose the tsarist regime and helped to shape the tradition of revolution and dissent in Western countries. Other educated men and women who remained in Russia chose violence as the only effective weapon against absolute rule. Terrorists who called themselves "Will of the People" decided to assassinate the tsar; in the "emperor hunt" that followed, numerous attempts were made on the tsar's life.

In response to attempts on his life and the assassination of public officials, which were intended to cripple the central regime, Alexander II put the brakes on reform in the second half of his reign. The Great Reforms could not be undone, however, and had set in motion sweeping economic and social changes. The state encouraged capitalist growth and witnessed the rise of a professional middle class and the formation of an embryonic factory proletariat. Yet reforms had increased expectations for an equally dramatic political transformation that failed to materialize. In the end, the Will of the People movement succeeded in its mission. In St. Petersburg in 1881, a terrorist bomb killed Alexander II, the Tsar-Liberator.

The Politics of Leadership

Political modernization was not achieved in Russia; and in western and central Europe, modern politics emerged only after 1850. Until that time, traditional political institutions had prevailed. When faced with revolutionary upheavals, regimes aimed for stability and preservation of their control. Only after 1850 did political leaders emerge who understood the world of politics and directed it to their own ends. Three statesmen typified the new approach to the public world of power: Camillo di Cavour, Otto von Bismarck, and Louis Napoleon.

The Demise of Royal Authority. In old-regime Europe, power flowed downward from the monarch, who was perched atop a hierarchically organized social system that is often depicted as a pyramid. In the first half of the nineteenth century, men and women learned that those in power could be questioned. The good of the people was the primary justification for government. Power now flowed upward from the citizens to their appointed and elected representatives. The new power brokers were those who could control and direct the flow, not merely be carried along or swept away by it. These were realists in the same tradition as Machiavelli and reflected the new political culture of the nineteenth century. They understood the importance of public opinion, which they used as a tool for the shaping of consensus, the molding of support. They also appreciated the power of the press.

The Supremacy of the Nation-State. The new political men also shared, to varying degrees, a disregard for traditional morality in decision making. The nation-state was the supreme justification for all actions. *Realpolitik* meant that statesmen had to think in terms of military capability, technological dominance, and the acceptable use of force. In the gamesmanship of statecraft, they were risk takers.

However, modern European statesmen did not share a common ideological outlook. Cavour leaned toward liberal ideas, while Bismarck was unquestionably conservative, and Louis Napoleon held a blend of liberal and conservative views. Yet these leaders enacted similar policies and sponsored similar legislation to strengthen and promote their states.

CHANGING VALUES AND THE FORCE OF NEW IDEAS

Just as the political world was undergoing transformation, the social, material, and intellectual world was also changing. As feminist thinkers struggled against entrenched prejudice against women, other thinkers brought new insights to the study of human society, some of which worked to impede women's progress toward equality. The third quarter of the nineteenth century opened an era that was especially rich in creativity in the natural and applied sciences.

The Politics of Homemaking

Industrialization had separated the workplace from the home, which was now glorified as a comfortable refuge from the harsh outside world. In 1870, an article in a popular Victorian magazine asserted, "Home is emphatically man's place of rest, where his wife is his friend who knows his mind, where he may be himself without fear of offending, and relax the strain that must be kept out of doors: where he may feel himself safe, understood, and at ease." Managing this domestic haven and her children was the middle-class woman's task, and "home economics" was invented during this period to help her organize her work.

This ideal of domestic order and tranquility was beyond the reach of the vast majority of the population.

Working-class wives and mothers often had to earn wages if their families were to survive. In 1866, women constituted a significant percentage of the French labor force, including 45 percent of all textile workers. At the height of the rhetoric about the virtues of domesticity, as many as 40 percent of married Englishwomen worked in mills in industrial areas such as Lancashire. Others performed piecework in their homes so that they could care for their children.

Many middle-class women protested against the ideology that confined them to the domestic sphere. Earlier in the century, the great novelist Jane Austen had to keep a piece of muslin work on her writing table in the family drawing room to cover her papers lest visitors detect evidence of literary activity. In the next generation, Florence Nightingale refused to accept the embroidery and knitting to which she was assigned at home. She and other women questioned the limited, subordinate role that society offered them. Middle-class women's demands for equal treatment became more persistent after 1870. Patterns of behavior changed within the family, and they were not fixed immutably in social practice. Woman's place and woman's role proved to be much-disputed questions in the new politics of homemaking.

▼ This female aboveground coal-mine worker was photographed in 1864 by Arthur J. Munby. Such women, who sorted the coal, had low status and no prospects.

Realism in the Arts

Realism in the arts and literature was a rejection of romantic idealism and subjectivity. The realist response to the disillusionment with the political failures of the post-1848 era characterized a wide array of artistic and literary endeavors. Realists depicted the challenges of urban and industrial growth by confronting the alienation of modern life.

The Social World of the Artist. The term *realism* was first used to describe the paintings of Gustave Courbet (1819–1877). In *The Artist's Studio* (1855), Courbet portrayed himself surrounded by the intellectuals and political figures of his day. He may have been painting a landscape, but contemporary political life crowded in; a starving Irish peasant and her child crouch beneath the easel. Of his unrelenting canvases, none more fittingly portrays the harsh realism of bourgeois life than the funeral ceremony depicted in *Burial at Ornans* (1849–1850) or better depicts the brutality of workers' lives than *Stone Breakers* (1849).

Other artists shared Courbet's desire to reject the conventions prevailing in the art world in favor of portraying reality in its natural and social dimensions. Jean-Francois Millet's paintings of peasants and workers (see p. 440) sought for a truth deeper than a surface beauty. Images of ordinary people, the working classes, and the poor populated realist art. Realist artists often strove to make a social commentary by capturing scenes from the daily life of the poor that would not have been considered fit subjects for art a generation before.

Realist Novels. After midcentury, idealization in romantic literature yielded to novels depicting the objective and unforgiving social world. Through serialization in journals and newspapers, fiction reached out to mass audiences, who obtained their "facts" about modern life through stories that often cynically portrayed the monotony of daily existence. In *Hard Times* (1854), set in the imaginary city of Coketown, Charles Dickens (1812–1870) created an allegory that exposed the sterility and soullessness of industrial society.

Gustave Flaubert (1821–1880), the great French realist novelist, critiqued the Western intellectual tradition in his unfinished *Dictionary of Accepted Ideas* (1881). His best-known work, *Madame Bovary* (1856), recounts the story of a young country doctor's wife whose desire to escape from

▲ Gustave Courbet (1819–1877), *Burial at Ornans*. This painting portrays the harsh realm of a bourgeois funeral ceremony.

the boredom of her provincial existence leads her into adultery and eventually results in her destruction. Flaubert was put on trial for obscenity and violating public morality with his tale of the unrepentant Emma Bovary. Mary Ann Evans (1819–1890), writing under the pseudonym George Eliot, was also concerned with moral choices and responsibilities in her novels, including *Middlemarch* (1871–1872), a tale of idealism disappointed by the petty realities of provincial English life.

The problem of morality in the realist novel is nowhere more apparent than in the works of the Russian writer, Fyodor Dostoyevsky (1821–1881), whose protagonists wrestle with a universe where God no longer exists and where they must shape their own morality. The impoverished student Raskolnikov in *Crime and Punishment* (1866) justifies his brutal murder of an old woman that occurs in the opening pages of the novel. Realist art and literature addressed an educated elite public but did not flinch before the unrelenting poverty and harshness of contemporary life. The morality of the realist vision lay in depicting the social evils for what they were: failures of a smug and progressive middle class.

Charles Darwin and the New Science

Science had a special appeal for a generation of Europeans disillusioned with the political failures of idealism in the revolutions of 1848. It was not an age of great scientific discovery, but rather one of synthesis of previous findings and their technological applications. Science was, above all, to be useful in promoting material progress.

The preeminent scientist of the age, Charles Darwin (1809–1882), was a great synthesizer. As a young man, he sailed around the world on the *Beagle* (1831–1836) as the ship's naturalist, collecting specimens and fossils. His greatest finds were in South America and especially on the Galapagos Islands. He spent the next 20 years of his life writing about his observations. The result, *On the Origin of Species by Means of Natural Selection* (1859), was a book that changed the world.

Darwin's argument was a simple one: Life forms originate in struggle and perpetuate themselves through struggle. The outcome of this struggle was determined by "natural selection," or what came to be known as "survival of the fittest." Better-adapted individuals survived; others died out. Competition between species and within species produced a dynamic model of organic evolution and progress based on struggle. Darwin did not use the word "evolution" in the original edition, but a positivist belief in an evolutionary process permeated the text. Force explained the past and would guarantee the future, as the fittest survived. The general public found these ideas to be applicable to a whole range of human endeavors and to theories of social organization.

Karl Marx and the Science of Society

Another iconoclastic thinker of this creative period was Karl Marx (1818–1883). "Just as Darwin discovered the law of development of organic nature, Marx discovered the law of development of human history." So spoke Friedrich Engels (1820–1895), longtime friend of and collaborator with Karl Marx, over Marx's grave. The son of a Prussian lawyer, Marx had rejected the study of the law to become a philosopher. As a brilliant young scholar, Marx developed a materially grounded view of society. In 1844, he joined forces with Friedrich Engels, a wealthy German businessman whose father owned factories in Manchester, England. Engels had just written *The Condition of the Working Classes in England in 1844,* an exposé of the social costs of industrialization. Marx and Engels found that they were kindred spirits, both moved by the struggles of the poor and the economic exploitation of workers.

The philosophy of Marx and Engels was built on a materialist view of society in which human beings were defined not by their souls but by their labor. Labor was a struggle to transform nature by producing commodities that are useful for survival. Building on this fundamental concept of labor, Marx and Engels saw society as being divided into two camps: those who own property and those who do not. For Marx, every social system is divided into classes and carries within it the seeds of its own destruction. In a world of commerce and manufacturing, the capitalist bourgeoisie exploit labor for low wages; they are the new aristocracy against whom workers will eventually rebel.

Marx was more than an observer; he was a critic of capitalism who espoused revolutionary change. His labor theory of value was the wedge that he drove into the self-congratulatory rhetoric of the capitalist age. Labor is the source of all value, he argued, yet the bourgeois employers deny workers the profit of their work by refusing to pay them a decent wage. Instead, they pocket the profits. Workers are separated, or alienated, from the product of their labor. But more profoundly, in a capitalist system, all workers are alienated from the creation that makes them human; they are alienated from their labor.

The force of Karl Marx's ideas mobilized thousands of contemporaries who were aware of the injustices of capitalism. Few thinkers have left a more lasting legacy than Karl Marx. His legacy survived distortion, opposition, and criticism from ideologues and scholars. Marx was a synthesizer who combined economics, philosophy, politics, and history in a wide-ranging critique of industrial society.

Marxism spread across Europe as workers responded to its message. Political parties coalesced around Marxist beliefs and programs, and Marxists were beginning to be heard in associations of workers. In London in 1864, they helped to found the International Working Men's Association, an organization of workers dedicated to "the end of all class rule." The promise of a common association of workers transcending national boundaries became a compelling idea to those who envisioned the end of capitalism. In 1871, Marx and his followers turned to Paris for proof that the revolution was at hand.

A New Revolution?

Soundly defeated on 2 September 1870, Napoleon III and his fighting force of 100,000 men became Prussia's prisoners of war. With the emperor's defeat, the Second Empire collapsed. But even with the capture of Napoleon III, the city of Paris refused to capitulate. The dedication of Parisians to the ongoing war with the Prussians was evident from the first. The regime's liberal critics in Paris seized the initiative to proclaim France a republic. If a corrupt and decadent empire could not save the nation, then France's Third Republic could.

The Siege of Paris. In mid-September 1870, two German armies surrounded Paris and began a siege that lasted for over four months. Bismarck's troops were intent on bringing the city to its knees not by fighting but by cutting off its vital supply lines. By November, food and fuel were dwindling, and Parisians were facing starvation. Undaunted, they began to eat dogs, cats, and rats. Soon horses disappeared from the streets, and the zoo was depleted of animals.

CHRONOLOGY

STATE BUILDING AND SOCIAL CHANGE

1853–1856	Crimean War
1859	Austria declares war on Kingdom of Sardinia; France joins forces with Italians
1860	Piedmont-Sardinia annexes duchies in central Italy; France gains Nice and Savoy
3 March 1861	Emancipation of Russian serfs
14 March 1861	Kingdom of Italy proclaimed with Victor Emmanuel II as king
1861–1865	American Civil War
1863	Maximilian crowned emperor of Mexico
1863	Prussians and Austrians at war with Denmark
1866	Seven Weeks' War between Austria and Prussia; Italy acquires Venetia
1867	Emperor Maximilian executed
July 1870	Franco-Prussian War begins
2 September 1870	French Second Empire capitulates with Prussian victory at Sedan
20 September 1870	Italy annexes Rome
18 January 1871	German Empire proclaimed
March–May 1871	Paris Commune

Despite food and fuel shortages, the proud Parisians fought on. The Germans began a steady bombardment of the city beginning in January 1871. Although Parisians continued to resist through three weeks of shelling, the rest of France wanted an end to the war. The Germans agreed to an armistice to allow French national elections. French citizens outside Paris repudiated the war and returned an overwhelmingly conservative majority to seek peace. Thus the siege came to an end, but it left deep wounds that continued to fester.

The Paris Commune. Parisians felt betrayed by the rest of France. Through four months in a besieged city, they had sacrificed, suffered, and died. The war was over, but Paris was not at peace. The new national government, safely installed outside Paris at Versailles, attempted in March 1871 to disarm the Parisian citizenry by using army troops. Parisian men, women, and children poured into the streets to protect their cannons and to defend their right to bear arms. In the fighting that followed, the Versailles troops were driven from the city, and Paris was under siege again.

The spontaneity of the March uprising was soon succeeded by organization. Citizens rallied to the idea of the city's self-government and established the Paris Commune, as other French cities followed the capital's lead. Parisians were still at war, not against a foreign enemy but against the rest of France. The defense of the Commune lasted for 72 days. Armed women formed their own fighting units, the city council regulated labor relations, and neighborhoods ruled themselves. The short-lived Paris Commune ended in May 1871, as government troops reentered the city and brutally crushed it. In one "Bloody Week," 25,000 Parisians were massacred, and 40,000 others were arrested and tried. Such reprisals inflamed radicals and workers all over Europe. The example of the Commune became a rallying cry for revolutionary movements throughout the world and inspired the future leaders of the Russian revolutionary state.

The Commune was important at the time, but not as a revolution. It offered two lessons: First, it demonstrated the power of patriotism. Competing images of the nation were at stake, one Parisian and the other French, but no one could deny the power of national identity to inspire a whole city to suffer and to sacrifice. Second, the Commune made clear the power of the state. No revolutionary movement could succeed without controlling the massive forces of repression that were at the state's command. The Commune had tried to recapture a local, federal view of the world but failed to take sufficient account of the power of the state that it opposed.

RED WOMEN IN PARIS

Louise Michel, a schoolteacher and a member of the Paris Commune, was one of the many women and men who took up arms to defend the Commune against the forces of the government in Versailles. Men's and women's vigilance committees (Michel attended both) met to ensure that the Commune set up by the people would survive. The Communards believed that the Versailles government would limit their hard-won freedoms by creating a new king of France. When the Versailles government attacked Paris, the Communards fought back.

FOCUS QUESTIONS

Why were the cannons so important to these men and women?

Can you guess why the soldiers refused to fire on the crowd?

LEARNING THAT THE VERSAILLES SOLDIERS WERE TRYING to seize the cannon, men and women of Montmartre swarmed up the Butte in a surprise maneuver. Those people who were climbing believed they would die, but they were prepared to pay the price.

The Butte of Montmartre was bathed in the first light of day, through which things were glimpsed as if they were hidden behind a thin veil of water. Gradually the crowd increased. The other districts of Paris, hearing of the events taking place on the Butte of Montmartre, came to our assistance.

The women of Paris covered the cannon with their bodies. When their officers ordered the soldiers to fire, the men refused. The same army that would be used to crush Paris two months later decided now that it did not want to be an accomplice of the reaction. They gave up their attempt to seize the cannon from the National Guard. They understood that the people were defending the Republic by defending the arms that the royalists and imperialists would have turned on Paris in agreement with the Prussians. When we had won our victory, I looked around and noticed my poor mother, who had followed me to the Butte of Montmartre, believing that I was going to die.

On this day, the eighteenth of March, the people wakened. If they had not, it would have been the triumph of some king; instead it was a triumph of the people. The eighteenth of March could have belonged to the allies of kings, or to foreigners, or to the people. It was the people's.

From Louise Michel, *The Red Virgin: Memoirs of Louise Michel* (1981).

Conclusion

WESTERN SOCIETIES HAD CROSSED THE THRESHOLD into the modern age in the third quarter of the nineteenth century. Strong states from Great Britain to Russia were committed to creating and preserving the conditions of industrial expansion. The machine age, railroads, and metallurgy were spreading industrial development much more widely through western and central Europe than had been possible before 1850. Italians and Prussians, in attempting to join the ranks of nation-states, realized that the goal of a strong nation could be achieved only with industrial development and social reforms.

State building in Western societies went hand in hand with growth in the social responsibilities of government. The national powers that would dominate world politics and economy in the twentieth century all underwent modernizing transitions in the 1860s. These included the United States, France, Great Britain, and Germany. The Austrian empire, too, undertook programs to modernize its government and economy, and the Russian empire established social reforms of unparalleled dimensions. New nations came into existence in this period through the limited use of armed force. With the establishment of the German Empire, Otto von Bismarck, the most realistic of politicians, was intent on preserving the peace in Europe by balancing the power of the great European states. Europeans prided themselves on being both modern and realistic in the third quarter of the nineteenth century. Peace was possible if it was armed and vigilant. Reform, not revolution, many were sure, was the key to the future progress of European societies.

QUESTIONS FOR REVIEW

1. How did the process of creating nation-states in Germany and Italy differ?
2. What social and political circumstances explain the different reforms undertaken in France, Britain, and Russia?
3. How did industrialization change women's lives, and how did such changes depend on a woman's social class?
4. What were the connections between Darwin's ideas about nature and Marx's ideas about society?
5. What forces inspired the creation of the Paris Commune, and what did its fate suggest about the possibility of revolution in the late nineteenth century?

DISCOVERING WESTERN CIVILIZATION ONLINE

You can obtain more information about state building and social change in Europe between 1850 and 1871 at the websites listed below. See also the companion website that accompanies this text: www.ablongman.com/kishlansky, which contains an online study guide and additional resources.

Building Nations: The Politics of Unification

www.hillsdale.edu/academics/history/war/index.htm
Electronic texts of officers' and soldiers' accounts of the battles of the Crimean War.

www.fordham.edu/halsall/mod/modsbook23.html
This site focuses on documents relating to the unification of Italy and the Risorgimento.

www.fordham.edu/halsall/mod/germanunification.html
This site provides translations of major primary documents concerning the unification of Germany.

Reforming European Society

www.victorianweb.org
A comprehensive collection of links to Victorian England.

campus.northpark.edu/history/WebChron/WestEurope/LiberalAge.html
A collection of links to chronologies for the "Age of Liberalism," 1848–1914.

www.fordham.edu/halsall/mod/modsbook39.html
This site, a repository for links to the Russian Revolution, provides links to documents on nineteenth-century tsarist Russia.

Changing Values and the Force of New Ideas

www.kings.edu/womens_history/florence.html
Annotated bibliography of literature on Florence Nightingale.

csf.colorado.edu/psn/marx/Archive/1852-18brum/
The electronic text of Karl Marx, *Eighteenth Brumaire of Napoleon*.

www.nal.vam.ac.uk/projects/1851.html
This site draws upon the collection of the National Library of Art in London to chronicle the Great Exhibition of 1851.

web.clas.ufl.edu/users/rhatch/05-DARWIN-PAGE.html
Web page of Professor Robert Hatch of the University of Florida, which provides links to bibliographies, texts, and other resources on Charles Darwin.

dwardmac.pitzer.edu/Anarchist_Archives/pariscommune/Pariscommunearchive.html
A Pitzer College political studies site providing summaries of the major players and events of the Paris Commune as well as an extensive bibliography.

www.fordham.edu/halsall/women/womensbook.html
This section of the Modern History Sourcebook focuses on women's history from antiquity to the present. The sub-chapter on modern European women's history provides links to texts on the structure of working women's lives as well as texts on feminism and the suffrage movement.

SUGGESTIONS FOR FURTHER READING

Building Nations: The Politics of Unification

Derek Beales, *The Risorgimento and the Unification of Italy* (London: Allen & Unwin, 1982). Drawing a distinction between unification and national revival, Beales situates the period of unification within the larger process of cultural and political revival.

David Blackbourn, *The Long Nineteenth Century: A History of Germany, 1780–1918* (New York: Oxford University Press, 1998). This book examines the emergence of Germany from the late eighteenth century through the First World War in terms of politics, economics, and culture.

Denis Mack Smith, *Cavour* (London: Weidenfeld and Nicolson, 1985). Smith contrasts Cavour and his policies with Garibaldi and Mazzini and considers the challenge of regionalism to the unification process.

Reforming European Society

Jane Burbank and David Ransel, eds., *Imperial Russia: New Histories for the Empire* (Bloomington: Indiana University Press, 1998). A collection of essays using new methodologies for understanding Russian history in the eighteenth and nineteenth centuries.

Catherine Hall, Keith McClelland, and Jane Rendall, *Defining the Victorian Nation: Class, Race, Gender and the British Reform Act of 1867* (Cambridge: Cambridge University Press, 2000). This co-authored study presents a cultural, social, and gender history of the extension of the vote in 1867, accompanied by strong bibliographic aids.

Sudhir Hazareesingh, *From Subject to Citizen: The Second Empire and the Emergence of Modern French Democracy* (Princeton: Princeton University Press, 1998). In showing the relationship between the local and the national, the author provides a reevaluation of the emergence of republican citizenship in the Second Empire.

Margaret Homans, *Royal Representations: Queen Victoria and British Culture, 1837–1876* (Chicago: University of Chicago Press, 1998). Victoria is examined as a key to British culture through her roles as monarch, symbol, and wife and mother.

Alain Plessis, *The Rise and Fall of the Second Empire, 1852–1871*, tr. Jonathan Mandelbaum (Cambridge: Cambridge University Press, 1985). Discusses the Second Empire as an important transitional period in French history, when the conflict was between traditional and modern values in political, economic, and social transformations.

Changing Values and the Force of New Ideas

Jenni Calder, *The Victorian Home* (London: B. T. Batsford, 1977). A cultural and social history of Victorian domestic life in which the author describes both bourgeois and working-class domestic environments.

Bonnie G. Smith, *Ladies of the Leisure Class: The Bourgeoises of Northern France in the Nineteenth Century* (Princeton, N.J.: Princeton University Press, 1981). Explores the impact of industrialization on the lives of bourgeois women in northern France and demonstrates how the cult of domesticity emerged in a particular community.

Robert Tombs, *The Paris Commune, 1871* (London: Longman, 1999). A synthetic overview of the events of the Commune and their impact on the course of French and European history.

Martha Vicinus, *Independent Women: Work and Community for Single Women, 1850–1920* (Chicago: University of Chicago Press, 1985). Chronicles the choices that Victorian women made to live outside the norms of marriage and domesticity in various women's communities, including sisterhoods, nursing communities, colleges, boarding schools, and settlement houses.

CHAPTER 24

THE CRISIS OF EUROPEAN CULTURE, 1871–1914

THE VISUAL RECORD

SPEEDING TO THE FUTURE

"WE WANT TO DEMOLISH MUSEUMS and libraries." These are the words not of an anarchist or a terrorist but of a poet. The Italian writer Emilio Marinetti (1876–1944) endeavored, symbolically at least, through the power of his pen, to destroy the citadels of Western culture at the beginning of the twentieth century. Marinetti was not alone in wanting to pull down all that preserved art and learning in the West. Joined by other artists and writers who called themselves futurists, Marinetti represented a desire to break free of the past. By shocking complacent bourgeois society with their art, futurists hoped to fashion a new and dynamic civilization. Although they were a small group with limited influence, their concerns were shared by a growing number of intellectuals who judged European culture to be in the throes of a serious moral and cultural crisis. Futurist ideas also reflected the growing preoccupation with the future common among European men and women who spurned the value of tradition.

The futurist painter Umberto Boccioni (1882–1916) captures an aspect of the dynamic intensity of this changing world in his *Riot in the Galleria* (1910). The painting is set in front of a respectable, Italian coffee shop frequented by well-dressed middle-class men and women. In a flurry of light and shadow, a rush of figures moves toward two women engaged in a brawl at center. That the brawlers are female underscores the irrationality of the incident; yet the brawl itself is not what compels our attention. Rather, it is the movement of the crowd, like moths to a flame, that Boccioni intends us to see. The objects in motion are little more than vibrations in space, faceless and indistinguishable as individuals. The crowd does not walk or run. It appears instead to be in flight. The crowd moves without forethought, attracted by the violence and the possibility of participating in it. Those on the periphery who have not yet joined the frenzy look as though they too will soon be swept into the action.

In the violence of the riot we are shown beauty of movement that surpasses that of an orderly waltz. Boccioni uses the warm glow of the electric lights, symbol of the modern age, to illuminate a "new reality." Golden tones, warm oranges and rosy hues, shadowed in delicate purples, create a mosaic whose beauty in the play of color is strangely at odds with the theme of the two brawling figures who activate the crowd. There is no meaning beyond the movement.

Riot in the Galleria reflects the early twentieth-century preoccupation with change. European society seemed to many contemporaries to be moving into an abyss, a world of tumultuous change but one without values. Technology was transforming Europe with breakneck speed. New forms of communication and transportation—the telephone, the wireless telegraph, the bicycle, the automobile, the airplane—were obliterating traditional understandings of time and space. The cinema and the X-ray altered visual perception and redefined the ways in which people saw the world around them. Science undermined how people thought about themselves by challenging moral and religious values as hollow and meaningless. The natural sciences threw into doubt the existence of a creator.

Like the political revolutionaries of an earlier age, futurist artists issued manifestoes. They sought the liberation of the human spirit from a world that could no longer be understood or controlled. Liberation could be achieved only through immersion in mass society and rapid change. Ironically, Boccioni met his death in 1916 as a soldier in the war that he welcomed as a purifying event.

LOOKING AHEAD

As Europe passed from the nineteenth to the twentieth century, the new, grand scale of industrial production and political life was matched by the emergence of mass society. As this chapter will discuss, the need for regulation and control in mass democracy challenged the liberal, nineteenth-century emphasis on individual rights and parliamentary rule in Great Britain, Germany, France, and Austria. Mass democracy drew new social groups, workers and peasants, into the political arena, but it also continued to exclude others, including women, ethnic minorities, and Jews, whose pursuit of inclusion further challenged parliamentary forms.

The sciences and the new scientific study of society known as the social sciences contributed to attempts to understand how the physical world functioned, its predictability, and its improvement through technological and applied advances in knowledge. A new consciousness shaped ideas about family life, gender roles, and patterns of consumption as Europeans entered the twentieth century.

EUROPEAN ECONOMY AND THE POLITICS OF MASS SOCIETY

Between 1871 and 1914 the scale of European life was radically altered. Industrial society had promoted largeness as the norm, as growing numbers of people worked under the same roof. Large-scale heavy industries fueled by new energy sources dominated the economic landscape. Great Britain, the leader of the first phase of the industrial revolution of the eighteenth century, slipped in prominence as an industrial power at the end of the nineteenth century, as Germany and the United States devised successful competitive strategies of investment, protection, and control.

Regulating Boom and Bust

The organization of factory production throughout Europe and the proximity of productive centers to distribution networks meant ever greater concentration of populations in urban areas. Like factories, cities were getting bigger at a rapid rate and were proliferating in numbers. With every passing year, fewer people remained on the land, and those who stayed were increasingly linked to cities and tied into national cultures by new transportation and communications networks.

The Need for Regulation. Between 1873 and 1895, an epidemic of slumps battered the economics of European nations. These slumps, characterized by falling prices, downturns in productivity, and declining profits, did not strike European nations simultaneously, nor did they affect all countries with the same degree of severity. But the slumps of the late nineteenth century and the boom period of intense economic expansion from 1895 to 1914 did teach industrialists, financiers, and politicians one important lesson: alternating booms and busts in the business cycle were dangerous and had to be regulated. Workers and their families suffered even more as the job market periodically shrank.

Too much of a good thing brought on the steady deflation of the last quarter of the nineteenth century. In the world economy there was an overproduction of agricultural products—a sharp contrast to the famines that had ravaged Europe only 50 years earlier. Overproduction resulted from two new factors in the world economy: technological advances in crop cultivation and the low cost of shipping and transport, which had opened European markets to cheap agricultural goods from the United States, Canada, and Argentina. The drop in food prices affected purchasing power in other sectors and resulted in long-term deflation and unemployment.

Financiers, politicians, and businessmen dedicated themselves to eliminating the boom-and-bust phenomenon, which they considered dangerous. The application of science and technology to industrial production required huge amounts of capital. The two new sources of power after 1880, petroleum and electricity, could be developed only with heavy capital investment. Large mechanized steel plants were too costly for small family firms of the scale that had industrialized textile production so successfully earlier in the century. Heavy machinery, smelting furnaces, buildings, and transport were all beyond the means of the small entrepreneur.

To raise the capital necessary for the new heavy industry at the end of the nineteenth century, firms had to look outside themselves to the stock market, banks, or the state to find adequate capital resources. But investors and especially banks refused to invest without guarantees on their capital. Because investment in heavy industry meant tying up capital for extended periods of time, banks insisted on safeguards against falling prices. The solution that they demanded was the elimination of uncertainty through the regulation of markets.

Cartels. Regulation was achieved through the establishment of cartels, combinations of firms in a given industry united to fix prices and to establish production quotas. Cartels were agreements among big firms intent on controlling markets and guaranteeing profits. Trusts were another form of collaboration that resulted in the elimination of unprofitable businesses. Firms joined together horizontally within the same industry; for example, all steel producers agreed to fix prices and set quotas. Or they combined vertically by controlling all levels of the production process from raw materials to the finished product and all other ancillary products necessary to or resulting from the production process. Firms in Great Britain, falling behind in heavy industry, failed to form cartels and for the most part remained in private hands. But heavy industry in Germany, France, and Austria, to varying degrees, sought regulation of markets and prices through international cartels.

Banks, which had been the initial impetus behind the transformation to a regulated economy, in turn formed consortia to meet the need for greater amounts of capital. A consortium, paralleling a cartel, was a partnership among banks, often international in character, in which interest rates and the movement of capital were regulated by mutual agreement. The state, too, played an important role in directing the economy. In capital-poor Russia, the state used indirect taxes on the peasantry to finance industrialization and railway construction at the end of the nineteenth century. Russia also needed to import capital, primarily from France after 1887.

Throughout Europe, nation-states protected domestic industries by erecting tariff barriers against foreign goods. Only Great Britain among the major powers stood by a policy of free trade. Europe was split into two tiers—the haves and have-nots: those countries with a solid industrial core and those that had remained unindustrialized. This division had a geographic character, the north and west of Europe being heavily developed and capitalized and the southern and eastern parts of Europe remaining heavily agricultural. For both the haves and have-nots, tariff policies were an attractive form of regulation by the state to protect established industries and to nurture industries that were struggling for existence.

Challenging Liberal England

Great Britain experienced the transformation in political organization and social structure before other European nations. But after 1870, changes in politics influenced by the scale of the new industrial society spread to every European country. The policies that the emerging mass society generated were making clearer the contradictions inherent in the ideal of democracy. Mass demands were pushing aside the liberal emphasis on individual rights valued by parliamentary governments everywhere.

Great Britain had avoided revolution and social upheaval in the nineteenth century. Its strong parliamentary tradition was based on a homogeneous ruling elite. Aristocrats, businessmen, and financial leaders shared a common educational background in England's elitist educational system of public schools and the universities of Oxford and Cambridge. Schooling produced a common outlook and common attitudes toward parliamentary rule, whether in the Conservative or the Liberal Party, and guaranteed a certain stability in policies and legislation.

▼ A union leader addresses striking British coal miners in 1912. Labor unions became increasingly militant after the turn of the century as rising unemployment and declining real wages cut into the gains of the working class.

Trade Unions. In the 1880s, issues of unemployment, public health, housing, and education challenged the attitudes of Britain's ruling elite and fostered the advent of independent working-class politics. Between 1867 and 1885, extension of suffrage increased the electorate fourfold. Protected by the markets of its empire, the British economy did not experience the roller-coaster effect of recurrent booms and busts after 1873. But after 1900, wages stagnated as prices continued to rise, and workers responded by supporting militant trade unions.

Trade unions, drawing on a long tradition of working-class associations, were all that stood between workers and the economic dislocation caused by unemployment, sickness, or old age. In addition, new unions of unskilled and semiskilled workers flourished, beginning in the 1880s and 1890s. A Scottish miner, James Keir Hardie (1856–1915), attracted national attention as the spokesman for a new political movement, the Labour Party, whose goal was to represent workers in Parliament. In 1892, Hardie was the first independent working man to sit in the House of Commons. Hardie and his party convinced trade unions that it was in their best interests to support Labour candidates instead of Liberals in parliamentary elections after 1900. By 1906, the new Labour Party had 29 seats in Parliament. Intellectuals now joined with trade unionists in demanding public housing, better public sanitation, municipal reforms, and improved pay and benefits for workers.

Parliamentary Reforms. The existence of the new Labour Party pressured Conservatives and Liberals to develop more enlightened social programs. After 1906, under threat of losing votes to the Labour Party, the Liberal Party heeded the pressures for reform. The "new" Liberals supported legislation to strengthen the right of unions to picket peacefully. Led by David Lloyd George (1863–1945), who was chancellor of the exchequer, Liberals sponsored the National Insurance Act of 1911. The act provided compulsory payments to workers for sickness and unemployment benefits.

In order to gain approval to pay for this new legislation, Lloyd George recognized that Parliament itself had to be renovated. The Parliament Bill of 1911 reduced the House of Lords, dominated by Conservatives resistant to proposed welfare reforms, from its status as equal partner with the House of Commons. Commons could and now did raise taxes without the consent of the House of Lords to pay for new programs that benefited workers and the poor.

Extraparliamentary Protest. Social legislation did not silence unions and worker organizations. Between 1910 and 1914, waves of strikes broke over England. Coal miners, seamen, railroad workers, and dockers protested against stagnant wages and rising prices.

The high incidence of strikes was a consequence of growing distrust of Parliament and of a regulatory state bureaucracy responsible for the social welfare reforms. Labour's voice grew more strident. The Trade Unions Act of 1913 granted unions legal rights to settle their grievances with management directly. Only the outbreak of war in 1914 ended the possibility of a general strike by miners, railwaymen, and transport workers. The question of Irish home rule also plagued Parliament. In Ulster in northern Ireland, army officers of Protestant Irish background threatened to mutiny. In addition, women agitating for the vote shattered parliamentary complacence. The most advanced industrial nation, with its tradition of peaceful parliamentary rule, had entered the age of mass politics.

Political Struggles in Germany

During his reign as chancellor of the German Empire (1871–1890), Otto von Bismarck formed shrewd alliances that hampered the development of parliamentary government. He repeatedly and successfully blocked the emergence of fully democratic participation. In Germany, all males had the right to vote, but the German parliament, the Reichstag, enjoyed only restricted powers in comparison to the British Parliament. Bismarck's objective remained always the successful unification of Germany, and he promoted cooperation with democratic institutions and parties only as long as that goal was enhanced.

Bismarck and the German Parliament. Throughout the 1870s, the German chancellor collaborated with the German liberal parties in constructing the legal codes, the monetary and banking system, the judicial apparatus, and the railroad network that pulled the new Germany together. Bismarck backed German liberals in their antipapal campaign, in which the Catholic Church was depicted as an authority in competition with the German nation-state. The anti-Church campaign, launched in 1872, was dubbed the *Kulturkampf* ("struggle for civilization") because its supporters contended that it was a battle waged in the interests of humanity.

The legislation of the *Kulturkampf* expelled Jesuits from Germany, removed priests from state service, attacked religious education, and instituted civil marriage. Many Germans grew concerned about the social costs of such widespread religious repression, and the Catholic Center Party increased its parliamentary representation by rallying Catholics as a voting bloc in the face of state repression. With the succession of a new pontiff, Leo XIII (1878–1903), Bismarck negotiated a settlement with the Catholic Church, cutting his losses and bringing the *Kulturkampf* to a halt.

The Social Democrat Party. Bismarck's repressive policies also targeted the Social Democratic Party. The Social Democrats were committed to a Marxist critique of capitalism and to international cooperation with other socialist parties. Seeing them as a threat to stability in Germany and in Europe as a whole, Bismarck set out to smash them. In 1878, using the opportunity for repression presented by two attempts on the emperor's life, Bismarck outlawed the fledgling Socialist Party. The Anti-Socialist Law forbade meetings among socialists, fundraising, and distribution of printed matter. Nevertheless, individual Social Democratic candidates stood for election in this period and learned quickly how to work with middle-class parties to achieve electoral successes. By 1890, Social Democrats had captured 20 percent of the electorate and controlled 35 Reichstag seats in spite of Bismarck's anti-Socialist legislation.

Throughout the 1880s, as his ability to manage Reichstag majorities declined and as Socialist strength steadily mounted, Bismarck grew disenchanted with universal manhood suffrage. Beginning in 1888, the chancellor found himself at odds with the new emperor Wilhelm II (1888–1918) over his foreign and domestic policies. The young emperor dismissed Bismarck in March 1890 and abandoned the chancellor's anti-Socialist legislation. The Social Democratic Party became the largest Marxist party in the world and, by 1914, the largest single party in Germany. During the period when the Social Democratic movement was outlawed, Bismarck and Wilhelm II used social welfare legislation to win mass support, including accident insurance, sick benefits, and old age and disability benefits. But such legislation did not undermine the popularity of socialism, nor did it attract workers away from Marxist programs, as the electoral returns demonstrated.

Unable to defeat social democracy by force or by state-sponsored welfare policies, Bismarck's successors set out to organize mass support. Agrarian and industrial interests united strongly behind state policies. An aggressive foreign policy was judged to be the surest way to win over the masses.

In the end, the Reichstag failed to defy the absolute authority of Emperor Wilhelm II, who was served after 1890 by a string of ineffectual chancellors. Despite its constitutional forms, Germany was ruled by a state authoritarianism in which the bureaucracy, the military, and various interest groups exercised influence over the emperor. A high-risk foreign policy that had a mass appeal was one way to circumvent a parliamentary system incapable of decision making. Constitutional solutions had been short-circuited in favor of authoritarian rule.

Political Scandals and Mass Politics in France

The Third Republic in France had an aura of the accidental about its origins and of the precarious about its existence. Yet appearances were misleading. Founded in 1870 with the defeat of Napoleon III's empire by the Germans, the Third Republic claimed legitimacy by placing itself squarely within the revolutionary democratic tradition.

Creating Citizens. The Third Republic successfully worked toward the creation of a national community based on a common identity of citizens. Compulsory schooling, one of the great institutional transformations of French government in 1885, socialized French children in common values, patriotism, and identification with the nation-state. Old ways, local dialects, superstitious practices, and peasant insularity dropped away or were modified under the persistent pressure of a centralized curriculum of reading, writing, arithmetic, and civics. Compulsory service in the army for the generation of young men of draft age served the same end of communicating national values to a predominantly peasant population. Technology also accelerated the process of shaping a national citizenry, as railroad lines tied people together and new and better roads made distances shrink.

A truly national and mass culture emerged in the period between 1880 and 1914. French people were not necessarily more political, but they were political in a new way that enabled them to identify their own local interests with national issues.

The Boulanger Affair. A political crisis, known as the Boulanger Affair, temporarily threatened the stability of the republic and served as a good indication of the extent of the transformation in French political life at the end of the nineteenth century.

As minister of war, General Georges Boulanger (1837–1891) became a hero to French soldiers when he undertook needed reforms of army life. He won over businessmen by leading troops against strikers. Above all, he cultivated the image of a patriot ready to defend France's honor at any cost. But Boulanger was a shallow man who owed his success to a carefully orchestrated publicity campaign that made him the most popular man in France by 1886.

Boulanger's potential in the political arena attracted the attention of right-wing backers, including monarchists who hoped eventually to restore kingship to France. Supported by big-money interests that favored a strengthened executive and a weaker parliamentary system, Boulanger undertook a nationwide political campaign, hoping to appeal to those who were unhappy with the Third Republic and promising vague constitutional reforms. By 1889, Boulanger was able to amass enough national support to frighten the defenders of parliamentary institutions. The charismatic general ultimately failed in his bid for power and fled the country because of allegations of treason. But he left in his wake an embryonic mass movement on the Right that operated outside the channels of parliamentary institutions.

The Dreyfus Affair. A very different kind of crisis began to take shape in 1894 with the controversy surrounding the trial of Captain Alfred Dreyfus (1859–1935) that came to be known simply as "the Affair." Dreyfus was an Alsatian Jewish army officer who was accused of selling military secrets to the Germans. His trial for treason served as a lightning rod for xenophobia—the hatred of foreigners, especially Germans—and anti-Semitism, the hatred of Jews. Dreyfus was stripped of his commission and honors and sentenced to solitary confinement for life on Devil's Island, a convict colony off French Guiana in South America.

Illegal activities and outright falsifications by Dreyfus's superiors to secure a conviction came to light in the mass press and divided the nation. Those who supported Dreyfus's innocence, the pro-Dreyfusards, were for the most part on the left of the political spectrum and spoke of the republic's duty to uphold justice and freedom. The anti-Dreyfusards were associated with the traditional institutions of the Catholic Church and the army and considered themselves to be defending the honor of France.

The Affair represented the ability of an individual to seek redress against injustice. On the national level, the Affair represented an important transformation in the nature of French political life. Existing parliamentary institutions had been found wanting. They were unable to cope with the mass politics stirred up by Dreyfus's conviction. The newspaper press vied with parliament and the courts as a forum for investigation and decision making.

The crises provoked by Boulanger's attempt to gain power and the Dreyfus Affair demonstrated the major role of the press and the importance of public opinion in exerting pressure on the system of government. The press emerged as a myth-maker in shaping and channeling public opinion. Émile Zola (1840–1902), the great French novelist, spearheaded the pro-Dreyfusard movement with his damning article *"J'accuse!"* ("I Accuse!"), in which he pointed to the military and the judiciary as the "spirits of social evil" for persecuting an innocent man. The article appeared in a leading French newspaper and was influential in securing Dreyfus's eventual exoneration and the discovery of the real culprit, one of Dreyfus's colleagues on the General Staff. The Third Republic was never in danger of collapsing, but it was transformed. The locus of power in parliament was challenged by pressure groups outside of it.

Defeating Liberalism in Austria

In the 1870s, the liberal values of the bourgeoisie dominated the Austro-Hungarian Empire. The Habsburg monarchy had adjusted to constitutional government, which was introduced throughout Austria in 1860. Faith in parliamentary government based on a restricted suffrage had established a tenuous foothold. After setbacks of 1848 and the troublesome decade of the 1860s, when Prussia had trounced Austria and Bismarck had routed the hope of an Austrian-dominated German Empire, the Austrian bourgeoisie counted on a peaceful future with a centralized multinational state dedicated to order and progress.

By 1900, however, the urban and capitalist middle class that ruled Austria by virtue of a limited suffrage based on property had lost ground to new groups that were essentially anticapitalist and antiliberal in their outlook. The new groups were peasants, workers, urban artisans and shopkeepers, and the colonized Slavic peoples of the empire. Bourgeois politics and laissez-faire economics had offered little or nothing to these varied groups, who were now claiming the right of participation. Mass parties were formed based on radical pan-Germanic feeling, anticapitalism that appealed to peasants and artisans, hatred of the Jews shared by students and artisans, and nationalist aspirations that attracted the lower middle classes.

The political experiences of Great Britain, Germany, France, and Austria between 1871 and 1914 make clear the common challenges confronting western parliamentary systems in a changing era of democratic politics. In spite of variations, each nation experienced its own challenge to liberal parliamentary institutions, and each shaped its own responses to a new international phenomenon—the rise of the masses as a political force.

OUTSIDERS IN MASS POLITICS

By the end of the nineteenth century, a faceless, nameless electorate had become the basis of new political strategies and a new political rhetoric. A concept of class identification of workers was devalued in favor of interest-group politics in which lobbies formed around single issues to pressure European governments. But the apparently all-inclusive concept of mass society continued to exclude some groups: women, ethnic minorities, and Jews. Women and ethnic minorities learned to incorporate strategies and techniques of politics and organization that permitted them to challenge the existing political system. Others, including anarchists, rejected both the organizational techniques of mass society and the values of the nation-state. Outsiders, then, were both those intent on being integrated into mass politics and those who sought its destruction.

Feminists and Politics

Women's drive for emancipation had been a recurrent motif of European political culture throughout the nineteenth century. In the areas of civil liberties, legal equality with men, and economic autonomy, only the most limited reforms had been enacted. The glorification of domesticity was a kind of recognition of women's unique contribution to society, but it was also a means of keeping women "in their place."

Women's Rights. European women who worked outside of the family were paid one-third to one-half of what men earned for the same work. In Great Britain, women did not enjoy equal divorce rights until the twentieth century. In France, married women had no control over their own incomes; all their earnings were considered their husband's private property. From the Atlantic to the Urals, women were excluded from economic and educational opportunities.

Growing numbers of women, primarily from the middle classes, began calling themselves "feminist," a term that was coined in France in the 1830s. The new feminists throughout western Europe differed from earlier generations in their willingness to organize mass movements and to appropriate the techniques of interest-group politics. The first international congress of women's rights, held in Paris in 1878, initiated an era of international cooperation and exchange among women's organizations. Women's groups now positioned themselves for sustained political action.

On the whole, feminist organizations were divided into two camps. In the first group were those who agitated for the vote; the second included those who thought the vote was beside the point and that the central issues were economic, social, and legal reforms of women's status.

Movements for the Vote. The lessons of the new electoral politics were not lost on feminists seeking women's emancipation through the vote. Leaders like Hubertine Auclert (1848–1914) in France and Emmeline Pankhurst (1858–1928) in Great Britain recognized the need for a mass base of support. If women's organizations were to survive as competing interest groups, they needed to form political alliances, control their own newspapers and magazines, and keep their cause before the public eye.

There was a growing willingness on the part of a variety of women's organizations to use mass demonstrations, rallies, and violent tactics. No movement operated more effectively in this regard than the British suffrage movement. In 1903, a group of eminently respectable middle-class and aristocratic British women formed the Women's Social and Political Union (WSPU). At the center of the movement was Emmeline Pankhurst, a middle-aged woman of frail and attractive appearance who had a will of iron and a gift for oratory. Mrs. Pankhurst and her two daughters, Christabel (1880–1958), a lawyer by training, and Sylvia (1882–1960), an artist, succeeded in keeping women's suffrage before the British public and brought the plight of British women to international attention.

Women's demands for political power were the basis of an unheralded revolution in Western culture. In Great Britain, the decade before the Great War of 1914 was a period of profound political education for women seeking the vote. An unprecedented 250,000 women gathered in Hyde Park in 1908 to hear more about female suffrage. Laughed at by men, ridiculed in the press, and taunted in public demonstrations, women activists refused to be quiet and to know their place.

Mrs. Pankhurst and others advocated violence against personal property to highlight the violence done to women by denying them their rights. Militant women set mailboxes on fire or poured glue and jam over their contents, threw bombs into country houses, and slashed paintings in the National Gallery. These tactics seemed to accomplish little before the war, although they certainly kept the issue of women's suffrage in the public eye until the outbreak of war in 1914.

European women did not gain the right to vote easily. In France and Germany, moderate and left-wing politicians opposed extension of the vote to women because they feared that women would strengthen conservative candidates. Many politicians thought that women were not "ready" for the vote and that they should receive it only as

CONSTANCE LYTTON

Civil disobedience by British women demanding the right to vote often led to their arrest. In protest, incarcerated suffragettes went on hunger strikes to publicize their cause. The British government responded with a brutal policy of force-feeding of prisoners. Constance Lytton, a British aristocrat and suffragette, recounts here the agony of being forcibly fed in prison. Her own health was seriously weakened by the experience.

FOCUS QUESTIONS

How did Constance Lytton express civil disobedience? Why was the government intent on force-feeding women incarcerated in this way, a practice not common with other prisoners?

[THE PRISON'S SENIOR MEDICAL OFFICER] urged me to take food voluntarily. I told him that was absolutely out of the question, that when our legislators ceased to resist enfranchising women then I should cease to resist taking food in prison. . . . I offered no resistance to being placed in position, but lay down voluntarily on the plank bed. Two of the wardresses took hold of my arms, one held my head and one my feet. One wardress helped to pour the food. The doctor leant on my knees as he stooped over my chest to get at my mouth. I shut my mouth and clenched my teeth. . . . The doctor offered me the choice of a wooden or steel gag; he explained elaborately, as he did on most subsequent occasions, that the steel gag would hurt and the wooden one not, and he urged me not to force him to use the steel gag. But I did not speak nor open my mouth, so that after playing about for a moment or two with the wooden one he finally had recourse to the steel. He seemed annoyed at my resistance and he broke into a temper as he plied my teeth with the steel implement. . . . The pain of it was intense and at last I must have given way for he got the gag between my teeth, when he proceeded to turn it much more than necessary until my jaws were fastened wide apart, far more than they could go naturally. Then he put down my throat a tube which seemed to me much too wide and was something like four feet in length. The irritation of the tube was excessive. I choked the moment it touched my throat until it had got down. Then the food was poured in quickly; it made me sick a few seconds after it was down and the action of the sickness made my body and legs double up, but the wardresses instantly pressed back my head and the doctor leant on my knees. The horror of it was more than I can describe. I was sick over the doctor and wardresses, and it seemed a long time before they took the tube out. As the doctor left he gave me a slap on the cheek, not violently, but, as it were, to express his contemptuous disapproval, and he seemed to take for granted that my distress was assumed. . . . I had been sick over my hair, which, though short, hung on either side of my face, all over the wall near my bed, and my clothes seemed saturated with it, but the wardresses told me they could not get me a change that night as it was too late, the office was shut. I lay quite motionless, it seemed paradise to be without the suffocating tube, without the liquid food going in and out of my body and without the gag between my teeth. Before long I heard the sounds of the forced feeding in the next cell to mine. It was almost more than I could bear, it was Elsie Howey, I was sure. When the ghastly process was over and all quiet, I tapped on the wall and called out at the top of my voice, which wasn't much just then, "No surrender," and there came the answer past any doubt in Elsie's voice. "No surrender."

From Constance Lytton, *Prisons and Prisoners* (1914).

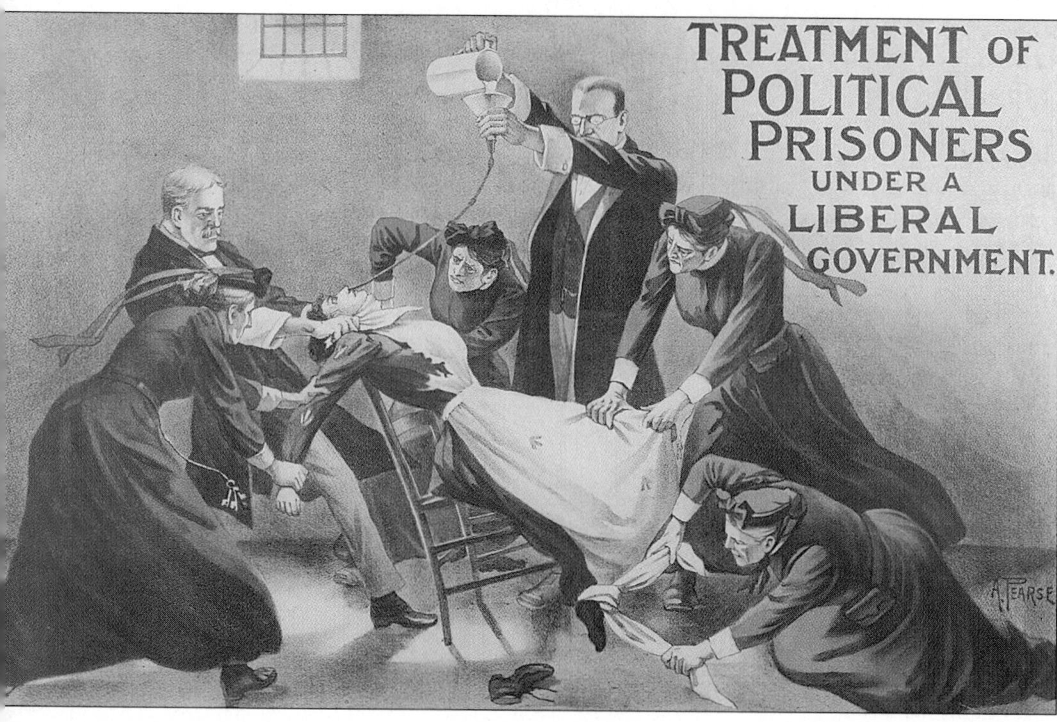

This British suffragette poster, published by the Women's Social and Political Union, graphically depicts the extreme methods used to force-feed women prisoners. A prison guard pulls back the prisoner's head, others hold down her arms and legs, and another ties her foot to the chair. A doctor holds a hose through which he forces gruel into the woman's nose.

a reward—an unusual concept in democratic societies. Not until 1918 were British women granted limited suffrage, and not until 1928 did they gain voting rights that were equal to those of men. Only after war and revolution was the vote extended to other women in the West: Germany in 1918, the United States in 1920, and France at the end of World War II.

Women and Social Reform. Not all activist women saw the right to vote as the solution to women's oppression. Those who agitated for social reforms for poor and working-class women parted ways with the miltant suffragists. Sylvia Pankhurst, for example, left her mother and sister to their political battles to work for social reform in London's poverty-stricken East End. Women socialists were concerned with working-class women's "double oppression" in the home and in the workplace. Working-class women, most notably in Germany, united feminism with socialism in search of a better life.

The women's movements of the period from 1871 to 1914 differed socially and culturally from nation to nation. Yet there is a sense in which the women's movements constituted an international phenomenon. The rise in the level of women's political consciousness occurred in the most advanced Western countries almost simultaneously and had a predominantly middle-class character. In spite of concerted efforts, however, women remained on the outside of societies that excluded them from political participation, access to education, and social and economic equality.

The Jewish Question and Zionism

Two million eastern European Jews migrated westward between 1868 and 1914 in search of peace and refuge. Seventy thousand settled in Germany. Others continued westward, stopping in the United States. Another kind of Jewish migration took place in the nineteenth century: the movement of Jews from rural to urban areas within nations. In eastern Europe, Jewish migrations coincided with downturns in the economic cycle, and Jews became scapegoats for the high rates of unemployment and high prices that seemed to follow in their wake. Most migrants were peddlers, artisans, or small shopkeepers who were seen as threatening to small businesses. Differing in language, culture, and dress, they were viewed as alien in every way.

Anti-Semitism. The term "anti-Semitism," meaning hostility to Jews, was first used in 1879 to give a pseudoscientific legitimacy to bigotry and hatred. Persecution was a harsh reality for Jews in eastern Europe at the end of the nineteenth century. In Russia, Jews could not own property and were restricted to living in certain territories. Organized massacres, or pogroms, in Kiev, Odessa, and Warsaw followed the assassination of Tsar Alexander II in 1881 and occurred again after the failed Russian revolution of 1905. Russian authorities blamed the Jews, who were perennially perceived as outsiders, for the assassination and revolution and the social instability that followed them. Pogroms resulted in the death and displacement of tens of thousands of eastern European Jews.

In western Europe, Jews considered themselves to be assimilated into their national cultures, identifying with their nationality as much as with their religion. Austrian and German Jews were granted full civil rights in 1867 on the principle that citizens of all religions enjoyed full equality. In France, Jews had been legally emancipated since the end of the eighteenth century. But the western and central European politics of the 1890s had a strong dose of anti-Semitism. Demagogues such as Georg von Schönerer (1842–1921) of Austria were capable of whipping up a frenzy of riots and violence against Jews. Western and central European anti-Semitism assumed a new level of virulence at the end of the nineteenth century. Fear of an economic depression united aristocrat and worker in blaming a Jewish conspiracy. German anti-Semitism proliferated in the 1880s. "It is like a horrible epidemic," the scholar Theodor Mommsen (1817–1903) observed.

Fear of the Jews was connected with hatred of capitalism. In France and Germany, Jews controlled powerful banking and commercial firms that became the targets of blame in hard times. Upwardly mobile sons of Jewish immigrants entered the professions of banking, trading, and journalism. They were also growing in numbers as teachers and academics. In the 1880s, more than half of Vienna's physicians (61 percent in 1881) and lawyers (58 percent of barristers in 1888) were Jewish. Their professional success only heightened tensions and condemnations of Jews as an "alien race." Anti-Semitism served as a violent means of mobilizing mass support, especially among the groups that felt threatened by capitalist concentration and large-scale industrialization. For anti-Semitic Europeans, Jews embodied the democratic, liberal, and cosmopolitan tendencies of the new culture that they were consciously rejecting in their new political affiliations.

▼ Jewish Migration. Persecution and expulsions drove two million Jews out of Russia and eastern Europe between 1868 and 1914. Some settled in central Europe; others traveled to Palestine and the Americas.

Zionism. A Jewish leadership emerged in central and western Europe that treated anti-Semitism as a problem that could be solved by political means. For the generation at the end of the nineteenth century, the assimilation of their fathers and mothers was not the answer. Jews needed their own nation, it was argued, since they were a people without a nation. Zionism was the solution to what Jewish intellectuals called "the Jewish problem." Zion, the ancient homeland of biblical times, would provide a national territory, and a choice, to persecuted Jews. Zionism became a Jewish nationalist movement dedicated to the establishment of a Jewish state. Although Zionism did not develop mass support in western Europe among assimilated Jews, its program for national identity and social reforms appealed to a large following of eastern European Jews in Galicia (Poland), Russia, and the eastern lands of the Habsburg Empire—those directly subjected to the extremes of persecution.

Theodor Herzl (1860–1904), an Austrian Jew born in Budapest, was the founder of Zionism in its political form. As a student in Vienna, he encountered discrimination, but his commitment to Zionism developed as a result of his years as a journalist in Paris. Herzl observed the anti-Semitic attacks in republican France that were provoked by the scandals surrounding the misappropriation of funds by prominent French politicians and business leaders during the failed French attempt to build a Panama canal and the divisive conflict over the Dreyfus Affair in the 1890s. He came to appreciate how deeply embedded anti-Semitism was in European society, and he despaired of the ability of corrupt parliamentary governments to uproot it. In *The Jewish State* (1896), Herzl concluded that Jews must have a state of their own. Under his direction, Zionism developed a world organization with the aim of establishing a Jewish homeland in Palestine.

Jews began emigrating to Palestine. With the financial backing of Jewish donors such as the French banker Baron de Rothschild, nearly 90,000 Jews had established settlements there by 1914. Calculated to tap a common Jewish identification with an ancient heritage, the choice of Palestine as a homeland was controversial from the beginning, and the problems arising from the choice have persisted to the present day.

Maurycy Minkowski, *After the Pogrom* (ca. 1910). Minkowski's works depict Jewish life in Poland before the Russian Revolution. In this painting he has expertly captured the weariness, hopelessness, and fear of the refugees who have interrupted their flight to rest. The sense of isolation and dislocation evoked in the painting may derive from the deaf and mute artist's personal perception of profound separation and detachment.

The promised land of the Old Testament, Zion is a holy place in Judaism. The Austrian psychoanalyst Sigmund Freud (1815–1939), who described himself as "a Jew from Moravia," was sympathetic to the Zionist cause but critical of the idea of Palestine as a Jewish state. He considered the idea unworkable and one that was bound to arouse Christian and Islamic opposition. Freud feared that Palestine would arouse the suspicions of the Arab world and challenge "the feelings of the local natives." He would have preferred a "new, historically unencumbered soil."

Some Jewish critics of Zionism thought that a separate Jewish state would prove that Jews were not good citizens of their respective nation-states and would exacerbate hostilities toward Jews as outsiders. Yet Zionism had much in common with the European liberal tradition, because it sought in the creation of a nation-state for Jews the solution to social injustice. Zion, the Jewish nation in the Middle East, was a liberal utopia for the Jewish people. Zionism learned from other mass movements of the period the importance of a broad base of support. By the time of the First Zionist Congress, held in Basel, Switzerland, in 1897, it had become a truly international movement. Zionism did not achieve its goals before World War I, and the Jewish state of Israel was not recognized by the world community until 1948.

Workers and Minorities on the Margins

Changes in the scale of political life paralleled the rise of heavy industry and the increasing urbanization of European populations. New industrial and financial leaders assumed positions among Europe's ruling elite. A new style of politics brought new political actors into the public arena at the beginning of the twentieth century. Extraparliamentary groups grew in influence and power and exerted pressure on the political process. The politics of mass society made clear the contradictions inherent in democracy. Propaganda, the ability to control information, became the avenue to success.

In 1892, the trial in Paris of a bomb-throwing anarchist named Ravachol attracted great public attention. He and other French anarchists had captured the popular imagination with their threats to destroy bourgeois society by bombing private residences, public buildings, and restaurants. Ravachol's terrorist deeds represented the extreme rejection of participation in electoral politics. The public was frightened—but also fascinated. Ravachol opposed the state and the capitalist economy as the dual enemy that could be destroyed only through individual acts of random physical violence. For his crimes he was condemned to death and publicly executed.

The best-known anarchists of the late nineteenth century were those, like Ravachol, who engaged in terrorist assassinations and bombings. Although not all anarchists were terrorists intent on destruction, all shared a desire for a revolutionary restructuring of society. Most anarchists were loners. They dreamed of the collapse of the capitalist system with its exploitation and inequality and of the emergence of a society based on personal freedom, autonomy, and justice. Anarchists spurned the Marxist willingness to organize and participate in parliamentary politics. They disdained the tyranny of new organizations and bureaucracies that worked for gradual reforms at the expense of principles of justice.

There was no single anarchist doctrine, but the varieties of anarchism all shared a hope in a future free from constraints. Mikhail Bakunin (1814–1876), a member of the Russian nobility, absorbed the works and the message of the French social critic Pierre-Joseph Proudhon. Bakunin became Europe's leading anarchist spokesman. Unlike Proudhon, Bakunin was a man of revolutionary action who espoused the use of violence to achieve individual liberation. He believed that all existing institutions must be swept away before ownership of production could be collectivized. Bakunin broke with Marx, whom he considered a "scientific bourgeois socialist," out of touch with the mass of workers.

Bakunin's successor in international anarchist doctrine was also a Russian of aristocratic lineage: Prince Petr Kropotkin (1842–1921). Kropotkin united communism and anarchism, arguing that goods should be communally distributed, "from each according to his ability, to each according to his needs," a principle that Louis Blanc had expressed earlier. On the basis of his own empirical observations, Kropotkin argued that competition and dominance were not laws of nature and instead stressed human interdependence.

It is difficult to measure the extent of Bakunin's or Kropotkin's influence, since whatever followers they might have inspired were not overtly or formally organized. Anarchism's greatest appeal was in the less industrialized parts of southern Europe: Spain, Italy, and southern France. In these countries, grass-roots anarchism germinated in working-class communities. In the second half of the nineteenth century, Russia too had developed a strong populist tradition that was similar to anarchism in its opposition to state tyranny. But anarchism was primarily a western European phenomenon.

Anarchism had special appeal to workers in trades that were staggering under the blows of industrial capitalism. Calling themselves anarcho-syndicalists, artisans—especially in France—were able to combine local trade union organization with anarchist principles. But, unlike union movements in the industrialized countries of Great Britain and Germany, French trade unions remained small, weak, and local. The contrast between the Labour Party in Great Britain and the German Social Democrats on the one hand and the French anarcho-syndicalists on the other highlighted the split between advanced industrial countries and less-developed areas of Europe, where an artisan class was attempting to preserve autonomy and control.

The problems of disaffected groups in general intensified before 1914. Anarchists and anarcho-syndicalist workers deplored the centralization and organization of mass society. Yet anarchism posed no serious threat to social stability because of the effectiveness of policing in most European states. As Friedrich Engels observed at the turn of the century, random violence directed against politics and the economy was no match for the repressive forces at the command of the nation-state. The politics of mass society excluded diverse groups, including women, Jews, and ethnic minorities, from participation. Yet the techniques, values, and organization of the world of politics remained available to all these groups. It was the outbreak of war in 1914 that silenced, temporarily at least, the challenge of these outsiders.

SHAPING THE NEW CONSCIOUSNESS

By the turn of the century, the customs and ideas of the nineteenth century were giving way to a new era. The new world was eliminating the difference between night and day, shrinking distance, and sending images through space. People could see for the first time into solid mass, even into their own bodies. These feats, once the stuff of fable and magic, became reality between 1880 and 1914. The people of the West used science and technology to reshape the world and their understanding of it.

Science changed how people thought and how they lived. It improved the quality of life by defeating diseases, improving nutrition, and lengthening life spans. But scientific knowledge did not come without costs. Scientific discoveries led to new forces of destruction. Scientific ideas challenged moral and religious beliefs. Science was invoked to justify racial and sexual discrimination. Traditional values and religious beliefs also did combat with the new god of science, as philosophers proclaimed that God was dead.

The Authority of Science

New scientific disciplines claimed to study society with methods similar to those applied to the study of bacilli and the atom. A traditional world of order and hierarchy gave way to a new way of perceiving reality. The discoveries of science had ramifications that extended beyond the laboratory, the hospital, and the classroom.

Discoveries in the Physical Sciences. Scientific discoveries in the last quarter of the nineteenth century pushed outward the frontiers of knowledge. In physics, James Clerk Maxwell (1831–1879) discovered the relationship between electricity and magnetism. Maxwell showed mathematically that an oscillating electric charge produces an electromagnetic field and that such a field radiates outward from its source at a constant speed—the speed of light. His theories led to the discovery of the electromagnetic spectrum, comprising radiation of different wavelengths, including X-rays, visible light, and radio waves. This discovery had important practical applications for the development of the electrical industry and led to the invention of radio and television. Within a generation the names of Edison, Westinghouse, Marconi, Siemens, and Bell entered the public realm.

Discoveries in the physical sciences succeeded one another with great rapidity. The periodic table of chemical elements was formulated in 1869. Radioactivity was discovered in 1896. Two years later, Marie Curie (1867–1934) and her husband Pierre (1859–1906) discovered the elements radium and polonium. At the end of the century, Ernest Rutherford (1871–1937) identified alpha and beta rays in radioactive atoms. Building on the new discoveries, Max Planck (1858–1947), Albert Einstein (1879–1955), and Niels Bohr (1885–1962) dismantled the classical physics of absolute and determined principles and left in its place modern physics based on relativity and uncertainty. In 1900, Planck propounded a theory that renounced the emphasis in classical physics on energy as a wave phenomenon in favor of a new "quantum theory" of energy as emitted and absorbed in minute, discrete amounts.

In 1905, Albert Einstein formulated his special theory of relativity, in which he established the relationship of mass and energy in the famous equation $E = mc^2$. In 1916, he published his general theory of relativity, a mathematical formulation that created new concepts of space and time. Einstein disproved the Newtonian view of gravitation as a force and instead saw it as a curved field in the time-space continuum created by the presence of mass. No one at the time foresaw that applying Einstein's theory that a particle of matter could be converted into a great quantity of energy would unleash the most destructive human-made power in history: the atomic and hydrogen bombs, which Einstein, a pacifist, lived to see developed.

Achievements in Biology. Though the discoveries in the physical sciences were the most dramatic, the biological sciences, too, witnessed great breakthroughs. Research biologists dedicated themselves to the study of disease-causing microbes and to the chemical bases of physiology. French chemist Louis Pasteur (1822–1895) studied microorganisms to find methods of preventing the spread of diseases in humans, animals, and plants. He developed methods of inoculation to provide protection against anthrax in sheep, cholera in chickens, and rabies in animals and humans.

The pace of breakthroughs in biological knowledge and medical treatment was staggering. The malaria parasite was isolated in 1880. The control of diseases such as yellow fever contributed to improvement in the quality of life. Knowledge burst the bounds of disciplines, and new fields developed to accommodate new concerns. Research in human genetics, a field that was only starting to be understood, was begun in the first decade of the twentieth century. The studies of Austrian botanist Gregor Mendel (1822–1884) in the crossbreeding of peas in the 1860s led to the Mendelian laws of inheritance.

Applied Knowledge. Biological discoveries resulted in new state policies. Public health benefited from new methods of prevention and detection of diseases caused by germs. A professor at the University of Berlin, Rudolf Virchow (1821–1902), discovered the relationship between microbes, sewage, and disease that led to the development of modern sewer systems and pure water for urban populations. Biochemistry, bacteriology, and physiology promoted a belief in social progress through state programs. After 1900, health programs to educate the general public spread throughout Europe.

Discoveries that changed the face of the twentieth century proliferated in a variety of fields. This was a time of firsts in all directions: airplane flights and deep-sea expeditions, based on technological applications of new discoveries, pushed out boundaries of exploration above the land and below the sea. In 1909, the same year that work began in human genetics, U.S. explorer Robert E. Peary (1856–1920) reached the North Pole. In that year, too, plastic was first manufactured, under the trade name Bakelite. Irish-born British astronomer Agnes Mary Clerke (1842–1907) did pioneering work in the new field of astrophysics. Rutherford proposed a new spatial reality in his theory of the nuclear structure of the atom, which stated that the atom can be divided and consists of a nucleus with electrons revolving around it.

Establishing the Social Sciences

Innovations in the social sciences paralleled the drama of discovery in the biological and physical sciences. The "scientific" study of society purported to apply the methods of observation and experimentation to human interactions. After 1870, sociology, economics, history, psychology, anthropology, and archaeology took shape at the core of new social scientific endeavors. But just as scientific advances could be applied to destructive ends, so, too, did the social sciences promote inequities and prejudices in the Western world.

Archaeology and Economics. Archaeology uncovered lost civilizations. Heinrich Schliemann (1822–1890), who discovered Troy, and Sir Arthur Evans (1851–1941), who began excavations in Crete in 1900, used scientific procedures to reconstruct ancient cultures. Historians, too, applied new techniques to the study of the past. German historian Leopold von Ranke (1795–1886) eschewed a literary form of historical writing that relied on legend and tradition in favor of objective, "scientific" history based on documentation and other forms of material evidence.

The social scientific study of economics came to the aid of businessmen. The neoclassical economic theory of Alfred Marshall (1842–1924) and others recognized the centrality of individual choice in the marketplace while dealing with the problem of how businesses can know they have produced enough to maximize profits. Economists who were concerned with how individuals responded to prices devised a theory of marginal utility, by which producers could calculate costs and project profits on the basis of a pattern of response of consumers to price changes.

Psychology and Human Behavior. "Scientific" psychology developed in a variety of directions. Wilhelm Wundt (1832–1920) established the first laboratory devoted to psychological research in Leipzig in 1879. From his experiments he concluded that thought is grounded in physical reality. The Russian physiologist Ivan Pavlov (1849–1936) won fame with a series of experiments demonstrating the conditioned reflex in dogs. Sigmund Freud (1859–1939) greatly influenced the direction of psychology with his theory of personality development and the creation of psychoanalysis, the science of the unconscious. Freudian probing of the unconscious was a model that was greatly at odds with the behavioral perspective of conditioned responses based on Pavlov's work.

Émile Durkheim (1858–1917), regarded as the founder of modern sociology, studied suicide as a social phenomenon. He pitted sociological theory against psychology and argued that deviance was the result not of psychic disturbances but of environmental factors and hereditary forces.

Heredity became a general explanation for behavior of all sorts. Everything from poverty, drunkenness, and crime to a declining birthrate could be attributed to biologically determined causes. For some theorists, this reasoning teetered on the edge of racism and ideas about "better blood." Intelligence was now measured "scientifically" for the first time with IQ tests developed at the Sorbonne by the psychologist Alfred Binet (1857–1911) in the 1890s. But the tests did not acknowledge the importance of cultural factors in the development of intelligence, and they manipulated science to legitimize a belief in natural elites.

The "New Woman" and the New Consciousness

As women continued to be excluded from national political participation, the right to vote was gradually being extended to all men in western Europe, regardless of property or social rank. New scientific ideas colluded with political prejudices to justify denying women equal rights. The natural sciences had a formative impact on prevailing views of gender relations and female sexuality and were used to prove women's inferiority.

Biology and Woman's Destiny. In *The Descent of Man* (1871), Charles Darwin had concluded that the mental power of men was higher than that of women. French physiologist Paul Broca (1824–1880), a contemporary of Darwin, countered in 1873 that the skull capacity of the two sexes was very similar and that a case for inferiority could not be based on measurement. But Broca was atypical. Most scientific opinion argued in favor of female frailty and inferiority. These "scientific" arguments justified excluding women from educational opportunities and from professions such as medicine and law. There was also a generalized fear in Western societies that women who tried to exceed their "natural" abilities would damage their reproductive functions and neglect their nurturing roles.

The New Woman. In this age of scientific justification of female inferiority, the "new woman" emerged. All over Europe the feminist movement had demanded social, economic, and political progress for women. But the "new woman" phenomenon exceeded the bounds of the feminist movement and can be described as a general cultural phenomenon. The "new woman" was characterized by intelligence, strength, and sexual desire—in every way man's equal. The Norwegian playwright Henrik Ibsen (1828–1906) created a fictional embodiment of the phenomenon in Nora, the hero of *A Doll's House* (1879), who was typical of the restive spirit of independence among wives and mothers who were confined to suffocating households and relegated to the status of children.

The new woman's pursuit of independence included control over her own body. Margaret Sanger (1879–1966), an American, advocated birth control to help women take charge of their reproductive lives. She was arrested several times for her activities but helped to get laws passed that allowed doctors to disseminate information about birth control. Annie Besant (1847–1933) played a similar role in Great Britain. Aletta Jacobs (1849–1929), the first woman to practice medicine in Holland, opened a contraceptive clinic in 1882. Discussions of contraception brought into the public arena the premise that women, like men, were sexual beings. By 1900, sexuality and reproduction were openly connected to discussions of women's rights.

Scientific discoveries had worked to change the world. At the same time, scientific authority was invoked by those intent on preserving traditional values. But as the uncertainty over gender roles at the beginning of the twentieth century makes clear, science was a way of thinking as well as a body of doctrine. Traditional ideas might be scientifically justified, but they would not go unchallenged.

Conclusion

THE PACE OF CHANGE IN SOCIETY AND CULTURE was accelerating in the years leading up to World War I. By 1914, many Europeans felt threatened by all these changes and new ideas. Elitist politicians devised schemes to exploit new opportunities; intellectuals talked of the possibility, even the desirability, of new manipulative dictatorships; and idealist dreams of democracy collided with the realities of mass politics. As the press fanned flames of controversy, social unrest seemed likely. Even the notion of retreat to a tranquil home and hearth was threatened by angry feminist activists. Imperialism also reached its culmination in the years 1870 to 1914 as the more powerful Western countries vied with each other for the possession of colonial territories.

QUESTIONS FOR REVIEW

1. Why did European economies run through cycles of boom and bust in the late nineteenth century, and how did European governments attempt to regulate the economy?
2. What challenges did liberal ideals and institutions confront in England, Germany, France, and Austria?
3. What social forces brought women and others into the new mass politics of the late nineteenth century?
4. What new ideas were being generated in psychology and the social sciences at the turn of the century, and what impact did that have on the way Europeans thought about gender relations?

DISCOVERING WESTERN CIVILIZATION ONLINE

You can obtain more information about the crisis of European culture between 1871 and 1914 at the websites listed below. See also the companion website that accompanies this text: www.ablongman.com/kishlansky, which contains an online study guide and additional resources.

European Economy and the Politics of Mass Society

www.spartacus.schoolnet.co.uk/socialism.htm
This is a fairly comprehensive site on the English labor movement, including texts, biographies of major figures, and other links.

www.erziehung.uni-giessen.de/studis/Robert/inhver_e.html
A brief overview of the development of social welfare legislation in Germany in the latter half of the nineteenth century.

www2.h-net.msu.edu/~habsweb/sourcetexts
Sponsored by the H-Net Discussion list HABSBURG, this site provides electronic texts relating to the creation of the Dual Monarchy.

Outsiders in Mass Politics

www.spartacus.schoolnet.co.uk/women.htm
This site contains links to biographies of major figures, essays on the major organizations and societies, and electronic texts of the women's movement in Britain.

www.genesis.ac.uk
This mapping project on women's history research sources is provided by the Women's Library of London and the Research Support Libraries Programme.

Shaping the New Consciousness

www.loc.gov/exhibits/freud
A Library of Congress virtual exhibit on the life and times of Sigmund Freud.

users.rcn.com/brill/freudarc.html
An exhaustive collection of links to archives, electronic texts, bibliographies, and other resources on Freud and the history of psychoanalysis.

www.fordham.edu/halsall/science/sciencesbook.html
A comprehensive collection of links to primary source materials, websites, and bibliographies on major scientists, discoveries, and theories in the nineteenth century.

SUGGESTIONS FOR FURTHER READING

European Economy and the Politics of Mass Society

Edward Arnold, ed., *The Development of the Radical Right in France: From Boulanger to Le Pen* (New York: St. Martin's Press, 2000). Part I examines Boulangism, Socialism, anti-Semitism, right-wing working-class politics, and the roots of right-wing radicalism.

Sudhir Hazareesingh, *Political Traditions in Modern France* (New York: Oxford University Press, 1994). In examining the particularities of French political life, the author focuses on the relationship between political movements and ideologies since 1789.

Martin P. Johnson, *The Dreyfus Affair* (New York: St. Martin's Press, 1999). A concise and comprehensive overview of the Affair as a defining event in French history.

Kevin Repp, *Reformers, Critics, and the Paths of German Modernity, 1890–1914* (Cambridge, Mass.: Harvard University Press, 2000). The author looks at the reformers, intellectuals, and activists who shaped the modernist movement in Germany.

Carl E. Schorske, *Fin-de-Siècle Vienna: Politics and Culture* (New York: Alfred A. Knopf, 1980). A series of essays describing the break with nineteenth-century liberal culture in one of Europe's great cities as artists, intellectuals, and politicians responded to the disintegration of the Habsburg Empire.

Outsiders in Mass Politics

June Purvis and Sandra Stanley Holton, eds., *Votes for Women* (New York: Routledge, 2000). The editors have brought together a collection of essays that reappraise the history of British suffragism by examining the activities of various women's groups and individuals from the nineteenth century to the interwar period.

Richard Stites, *The Women's Liberation Movement in Russia: Feminism, Nihilism, and Bolshevism, 1860–1930* (Princeton, N.J.: Princeton University Press, 1978). Situates the Russian women's movement within the contexts of both nineteenth-century European feminism and twentieth-century communist ideology and traces its development from the early feminists through the rise of the Bolsheviks to power. Includes a discussion of the Russian Revolution's impact on the status of women.

Sophia A. van Wingerden, *The Women's Suffrage Movement in Britain, 1866–1928* (New York: St. Martin's Press, 1999). A chronological overview of the history of the British suffrage movement.

Shaping the New Consciousness

Geoffrey Crossick and Serge Jaumain, eds., *Cathedrals of Consumption: The European Department Store, 1850–1939* (Aldershot: Ashgate Publishing, 1999). A collection of articles about the creation of department stores in different European countries from the perspectives of culture, consumption, gender, and urban life.

Stephen Kern, *The Culture of Time and Space, 1880–1918* (Cambridge, Mass.: Harvard University Press, 1983). Describes how late nineteenth-century technological advances created new modes of thinking about and experiencing time and space.

Robert A. Nye, *Crime, Madness, and Politics in Modern France: The Medical Concept of National Decline* (Princeton, N.J.: Princeton University Press, 1984). Nye shows how the medical concept of deviance was linked to a general cultural crisis in fin-de-siècle France.

Theodore M. Porter, *The Rise of Statistical Thinking, 1820–1900* (Princeton, N.J.: Princeton University Press, 1986). This work traces the origins of modern statistical innovation of the early 1900s and shows the interdependence of the natural and social sciences.

William M. Reddy, *Money and Liberty in Modern Europe: A Critique of Historical Understanding* (Cambridge: Cambridge University Press, 1987). This essay on the role of money in modern Europe contends that its widespread use in exchange influenced social structure. Arguing that monetary exchange intensified existing social inequities, Reddy examines the expansion of commerce in France, Germany, and England.

Vanessa Schwartz, *Spectacular Realities: Early Mass Culture in Fin-de-Siècle Paris* (Berkeley: University of California Press, 1998). This work examines the formation and emergence of mass urban culture in late nineteenth-century Paris.

John Tosh, *A Man's Place: Masculinity and the Middle-Class Home in Victorian England* (New Haven, Conn.: Yale University Press, 1999). This work examines the private world of the domestic sphere to take account of men and argues that Victorian masculinity was constructed not only in terms of work and male associations but also in terms of the home.

CHAPTER 25

EUROPE AND THE WORLD, 1870–1914

- THE VISUAL RECORD: Politics of Mapmaking
- THE EUROPEAN BALANCE OF POWER, 1870–1914
- THE NEW IMPERIALISM
- THE EUROPEAN SEARCH FOR TERRITORY AND MARKETS
- RESULTS OF A EUROPEAN-DOMINATED WORLD

THE VISUAL RECORD

THE POLITICS OF MAPMAKING

BEFORE PEOPLE KNEW HOW TO WRITE, they drew maps. Yet in 1885, only one-ninth of the land surface of the earth had been surveyed. Within the next decade, however, centuries-old ignorance diminished as cartographers, surveyors, and compilers fanned out around the globe to probe peninsulas and chart continents. By 1900, every continent, including Antarctica, had been explored and its measure taken.

This great leap forward in knowledge did not produce a standardized and uniform map of the world. State officials argued for the primacy of their own national traditions, symbols, colors, and units of measurement, and they blocked attempts at standardization. Mapmakers from Europe and the United States began to gather regularly at international conventions with the goal of devising a uniform map of the world that would satisfy everyone. Their attempts failed repeatedly.

One particular meeting in Paris in 1875 chose the meter as the standard unit of measurement for the world map. Supporters argued that the meter could provide mapmakers with a common language, easily understood and easily divisible. The British countered with yards and miles, unscientifically developed units of measurement to which they had been committed for centuries. Mapmakers who acknowledged the logic of the meter could not agree on which prototype meter should be taken as standard, though most agreed that the meter should be measured in reference to the arc of the meridian.

However, the prime meridian, the place on a map that indicates zero longitude, was itself not a fixed phenomenon. The debate over where the prime meridian should be located is a perfect example of the politics of mapmaking. Unlike the equator, which is midway between the north and south poles, zero longitude can be drawn anywhere. As a result, maps of different national origins located the prime meridian to enhance their own claims to importance. Paris, Philadelphia, and Beijing were just three of the sites for zero longitude on nineteenth-century maps.

Uniformity, the cartographers insisted, would have advantages for everyone. Not least of all, a standardized map would make standardized timekeeping easier.

Standard time could be calculated according to zones of longitude. Germany had five different time zones in 1891. In France, every city had its own time taken from solar readings. The United States had over 200 time zones from one coast to the other. In industrial societies with railroad timetables and legal contracts, time had to be controlled, and it had to be exact. Time had to be standardized. Specialists proposed that the Royal Observatory in Greenwich, England, was the best place to locate the prime meridian in order to calculate a standard time system. The French balked, insisting on Paris as the only candidate for the designation. In the end, there was compromise. The metric system prevailed as the standard for measurement, and the prime meridian passed through the Royal Greenwich Observatory, where standard time was calculated for most of the globe. All of this was possible for the first time only at the end of the nineteenth century, and the key to standardization was determined by geopolitical dominance. Great Britain, the most powerful imperial power, became the starting point for measuring time and space.

The accompanying map provides a dramatic example of the conquest of territories by the British Empire in 1886. The inset map in the upper right shows the extent of British territories a century earlier, and so the map demonstrates the growth of the empire. The figures at the borders of the map include both the colonizers (British prospectors, explorers, military men) and the colonized (native men and women of various conquered territories), all looking toward the figure of Brittania sitting atop the "world."

LOOKING AHEAD

This chapter begins by considering the territorial arrangements and conflicts within Europe between 1870 and 1914 that created a new kind of foreign policy based on mutual interests and national vulnerabilities. The chapter then turns to European rivalries in the global arena and the territorial and market expansion into Africa and Asia that characterized the new imperialism. Finally, the chapter considers how imperial encounters changed both the colonized and the colonizer and produced interdependent markets and a new world economy.

THE EUROPEAN BALANCE OF POWER, 1870–1914

Between 1870 and 1914, European states were locked in a competition within Europe for dominance and control. The politics of geography combined with rising nationalist movements in southern Europe and the Ottoman Empire to create a mood of increasing confrontation among Europe's great powers. The European balance of power that Bismarck had so carefully crafted began to disintegrate with his departure from office in 1890. By 1914, a Europe divided into two camps was no longer the sure guarantee of peace that it had been a generation earlier.

The Geopolitics of Europe

The map of Europe had been redrawn in the two decades after 1850. By 1871, Europe consisted of the Big Five—Britain, France, Germany, Austria-Hungary, and Russia—and a handful of lesser states. The declaration of the German Empire in 1871 and the emergence of Italy with Rome as its capital in 1870 unified numerous disparate states. Although not always corresponding to linguistic and cultural differences among Europe's peoples, national boundaries appeared to be fixed, with no country aspiring to territorial expansion at the expense of its neighbors. But the creation of the two new national units of Germany and Italy had legitimized nationalist aspirations and the militarism necessary to enforce them.

The Three Emperors' League. Under the chancellorship of Otto von Bismarck, Germany led the way in forging a new alliance system based on the realistic assessment of power politics within Europe. In 1873, Bismarck joined together the three most conservative powers of the Big Five—Germany, Austria-Hungary, and Russia—into the Three Emperors' League. Consultation about mutual interests and friendly neutrality were the cornerstones of this alliance. Identifying one's enemies and choosing one's friends in this new configuration of power came in large part to depend on geographic weaknesses. The Three Emperors' League was one example of the geographic imperatives driving diplomacy. Bismarck was determined to banish the specter of a two-front war by isolating France on the Continent.

Each of the Great Powers had a vulnerability, a geographic Achilles' heel. Germany's vulnerability lay in its North Sea ports. German shipping along its only coast could easily be bottlenecked by a powerful naval force. Such an event, the Germans knew, could destroy their rapidly growing international trade. What was worse, powerful land forces could encircle Germany. As Britain's century-old factories slowly became obsolete under peeling coats of paint, Germany enjoyed the advantages of a latecomer to industrialization, forced to start from scratch by investing in the most advanced machinery and technology. The German Reich was willing to support industrial expansion, scientific and technological training, and social programs for its workers. Yet as Germany surged forward to seize its share of world markets, it was acutely aware that it was hemmed in on the Continent. Germany could not extend its frontiers the way Russia had to the east. German gains in the Franco-Prussian war in Alsace and Lorraine could not be repeated without risking greater enmity. German leaders saw the threat of encirclement as a second geographic weakness. Bismarck's awareness of these geographic facts of life prompted his engineering of the Three Emperors' League in 1873, two years after the founding of the German Empire.

Austria-Hungary was Europe's second largest landed nation and the third largest in population. The same factors that had made it a great European power—its size and its diversity—now threatened to destroy it. The ramshackle empire of Europe was weakened by the centrifugal forces of linguistic and cultural diversity, by nationalities clamoring for independence and self-rule, and by an unresponsive political system. Austria-Hungary remained backward agriculturally and unable to respond to the industrial challenge of western Europe. It seemed most likely to collapse from social and political pressures.

Russia's vulnerability was reflected in its preoccupation with maintaining free access to the Mediterranean Sea. Russia, clearly Europe's greatest landed power, was vulnerable because it could be landlocked by frozen or blockaded ports. The ice that crippled its naval and commercial vessels in the Baltic Sea drove Russia east through Asia to secure another ice-blocked port on the Sea of Japan at Vladivostok in 1860 and to seek ice-free Chinese ports. Russia was equally obsessed with protecting its warm-water ports on the Black Sea. Whoever controlled the strait of the Bosporus controlled Russia's grain export trade, on which its economic prosperity depended.

The Ottoman Empire. Another great decaying conglomeration was the Ottoman Empire, bridging Europe and Asia. Politically feeble and on the verge of bankruptcy, the Ottoman Empire with Turkey at its core comprised a vast array of ethnically, linguistically, and culturally diverse peoples. In the hundred years before 1914, increasing social unrest and nationalist bids for independence had plagued the Ottoman Empire. As was the case with the Habsburgs in Austria-Hungary, the Ottomans maintained power with increasing difficulty over these myriad ethnic groups struggling to be free. The Ottoman Empire, called "the sick man of Europe" by contemporaries, found two kinds of relations sitting at its bedside: those who would do anything to ensure its survival, no matter how weak, and those who hoped to hasten its demise. Fortunately for

A Punch cartoon shows European leaders trying to keep the lid on the simmering kettle of Balkan crises.

the Ottoman Empire, rivalry among its enemies helped to preserve it.

The Ottomans had already seen parts of their holdings lopped off in the nineteenth century. Britain had acquired Cyprus, Egypt, Aden, and Sudan from the Ottomans. Germany insinuated itself into Turkish internal affairs and financed the Baghdad Railway in an attempt to link the Mediterranean to the Persian Gulf. Russia acquired territories on the banks of the Caspian Sea and had plans to take Constantinople. But it was the volatile Balkan Peninsula that threatened to upset the European power balance. The Balkans appeared to be ripe for dismemberment. Internally, the Slavs sought independence from their Habsburg and Turkish oppressors. External pressures were equally great, with each of the major powers following its own geopolitical agenda.

The Instability of the Alliance System

The system of alliances formed between and among European states was guided by two realities of geopolitics: the tension between France and Germany and Russia's fear of becoming landlocked.

Franco-German Tensions. A major destabilizing factor in the European balance of power was the tension between France and Germany. France had lost its dominance on the Continent in 1870–1871, when it was easily defeated by Prussia at the head of a nascent German Empire. With its back to the Atlantic, France faced the smaller states of Belgium, Luxembourg, Switzerland, and Italy and the industrially and militarily powerful Germany. France had suffered the humiliation of losing territory to Germany—Alsace and Lorraine in 1871—and was well aware of its continued vulnerability. Geopolitically, France felt trapped and isolated and in need of powerful friends as a counterweight to German power.

Russian Aspirations and the Congress of Berlin. Ostensibly, Russia had the most to gain from the extension of its frontiers and the creation of pro-Russian satellites. It saw that by championing pan-Slavic nationalist groups in southeastern Europe, it could greatly strengthen its own position at the expense of the two great declining empires, Ottoman Turkey and Austria-Hungary. Russia hoped to draw the Slavs into its orbit by fostering the creation of independent states in the Balkans. A Serbian revolt began in two Ottoman provinces, Bosnia and Herzegovina, in 1874. International opinion pressured Turkey to initiate reforms. Serbia declared war on Turkey on 30 June 1876; Montenegro did the same the next day. Britain, supporting the Ottoman Empire because of its trading interests in the Mediterranean, found itself in a delicate position of perhaps condemning an ally when it received news of Turkish atrocities against Christians in Bulgaria. Prime Minister Disraeli insisted that Britain was bound to defend Constantinople because of British interests in the Suez Canal and India. While Britain stood on the sidelines, Russia, with Romania as an ally, declared war against the Ottoman Empire. The war was quickly over; Russia captured all of Armenia and forced the Ottoman sultan, Abdul Hamid II (1842–1918), to sue for peace on 31 January 1878.

Although Great Britain was not largely landlocked as were Germany and Russia, the British had some reason to fear a possible naval blockade. And although the question of Irish home rule was a nationalities problem for Britain, it paled in comparison with Austria-Hungary's internal challenge. As an island kingdom, however, Great Britain relied on imports for its survival. The first of the European nations to become an urban and industrial power, Britain was forced to do so at the expense of its agricultural sector. It could not feed its own people without importing foodstuffs. Britain's geographic vulnerability was its dependence on access to its empire and the maintenance of open sea lanes. Britain saw its greatest menace as coming from the rise of other sea powers—notably Germany.

Bismarck, a seemingly disinterested party acting as an "honest broker," hosted the peace conference that met at Berlin. The British succeeded in blocking Russia's intentions for a Bulgarian satellite and keeping the Russians from taking Constantinople. Russia abandoned its support of Serbian nationalism, and Austria-Hungary occupied Bosnia and Herzegovina. The peace that was concluded at the 1878 Congress of Berlin disregarded Serbian claims, thereby ensuring continuing conflict over the nationalities question.

The Berlin Congress also marked the emergence of a new estrangement among the Great Powers. Russia felt betrayed by Bismarck and abandoned in its alliance with Germany. Bismarck in turn cemented a Dual Alliance between Austria-Hungary and Germany in 1879 that survived until the collapse of the two imperial regimes in 1918. The Three Emperors' League was renewed in 1881, now with stipulations regarding the division of the spoils in case of a war against Turkey.

In 1882, Italy was asked to join the Dual Alliance with Germany and Austria-Hungary, thus converting it into the Triple Alliance, which prevailed until the beginning of World War I in 1914. Germany, under Bismarck's tutelage, signed treaties with Italy, Russia, and Austria-Hungary and established friendly terms with Great Britain. However, a new Balkan crisis in 1885 shattered the illusion of stable relations.

Hostilities erupted between Bulgaria and Serbia. Russia threatened to occupy Bulgaria, but Austria stepped in to prevent Russian domination of the Balkans, thus threatening the alliance of the Three Emperors' League. Russia was further angered by German unwillingness to support its interests against Austrian actions in the Balkans. Germany maintained relations with Russia in a new Reinsurance Treaty drawn up in 1887, which stipulated that each power would maintain neutrality should the other find itself at war. Bismarck now walked a fine line, balancing alliances and selectively disclosing the terms of secret treaties to nonsignatory countries with the goal of preserving the peace. His successor described Bismarck as the only man who could keep five glass balls in the air at the same time.

Bismarck was dismissed from the chancellorship in 1890 by the Kaiser Wilhelm II, a long-time enemy of Bismarck who came to the throne in 1888. Germany now found itself unable to juggle all the glass balls. Under Wilhelm II, Germany allowed the arrangement with Russia to lapse. Russia, in turn, allied itself with France in 1894. Also allied with Great Britain, France had broken out of the isolation that Bismarck had intended for it two decades earlier. The Triple Entente came into existence following the Anglo-Russian understanding of 1907. Now it was the Triple Entente of Great Britain, France, and Russia against the Triple Alliance of Germany, Austria-Hungary, and Italy.

There was still every confidence that these two camps could balance each other and preserve the peace. But from 1908–1909 the unresolved Balkan problem threatened to topple Europe's precarious peace. Against Russia's objections, Austria-Hungary annexed Bosnia and Herzegovina, the provinces it had occupied since 1878. Russia supported Serbia's discontent over Austrian acquisition of these predominantly Slavic territories that Serbia believe should be united with its own lands. Unwilling to risk a European war at this point, Russia was ultimately forced to back down under German pressure. Germany had to contend with its great geopolitical fear: hostile neighbors, France and Russia, on its western and eastern frontiers.

A third Balkan crisis erupted in 1912 when Italy and Turkey fought over the possession of Tripoli in North Africa. The Balkan states took advantage of this opportunity to increase their holdings at Turkey's expense. This action quickly involved Great Power interests once again. A second war broke out in 1913 over Serbian interests in Bulgaria. Russia backed Serbia against Austro-Hungarian support of Bulgaria. The Russians and Austrians prepared for war, while the British and Germans urged peaceful resolution. Although hostilities ceased, Serbian resentment toward Austria-Hungary over its frustrated nationalism was greater

CHRONOLOGY

EUROPEAN CRISES AND THE BALANCE OF POWER

1871	German Empire created
1873	Three Emperors' League: Germany, Austria-Hungary, and Russia
1874	First Balkan crisis: Serbian revolt in Bosnia and Herzegovina
1875	Russo-Turkish War
1876	Serbia declares war on Turkey; Montenegro declares war on Turkey
1878	Congress of Berlin
1879	Dual Alliance: Germany and Austria-Hungary
1881	Three Emperors' League renewed
1882	Triple Alliance: Germany, Austria-Hungary, and Italy
1885	Second Balkan crisis: Bulgaria versus Serbia
1887	Reinsurance Treaty between Germany and Russia
1894	Russia concludes alliance with France
1907	Triple Entente: Great Britain, France, and Russia
1908	Austria-Hungary annexes Bosnia and Herzegovina
1912	Third Balkan crisis: Italy versus Turkey
1913	War erupts between Serbia and Bulgaria

than ever. Britain, in its backing of Russia, and Germany, in its support of Austria-Hungary, were enmeshed in alliances that could involve them in a military confrontation.

THE NEW IMPERIALISM

The concept of empire was certainly not invented by Europeans in the last third of the nineteenth century. Before 1870, European states had controlled empires. The influence of Great Britain stretched beyond the limits of its formal holdings in India and South Africa. Russia held Siberia and central Asia, and France ruled Algeria and Indochina. Older empires, such as Spain, had survived from the sixteenth century, but as hollow shells. What, then, was new about the "new imperialism" practiced by England, France, and Germany after 1870?

In part, the new imperialism was the acquisition of territories on an intense and unprecedented scale. Industrialization created the tools of transportation, communication, and domination that permitted the rapid pace of global empire building. Above all, the new imperialism meant domination by the industrial powers over the nonindustrial world. The United States also participated in the new imperialism, less by territorial acquisition than by developing an "invisible" empire of trade and influence in the Pacific. The forms of imperialism may have varied from nation to nation, but the basically unequal relationship between an industrial power and an undeveloped territory did not.

Only nation-states commanded the technology and resources that were necessary for the new scale of imperialist expansion. Rivalry among a few European nation-states—notably, Great Britain, France, and Germany—was a common denominator that set the standards by which these nations and other European states gained control of the globe by 1900. Why did the Europeans create vast empires? Were empires built for economic gain, military protection, or national glory? Questions about motives may obscure common features of the new imperialism. Industrial powers sought to take over nonindustrial regions, not in isolated areas but all over the globe. In the attempt, they necessarily competed with one another, successfully adapting the resources of industrialism to the needs of conquest.

The Technology of Empire

For Europeans at the end of the nineteenth century, the world had definitely become a smaller place. Technology based on steam, iron, and electricity—the great forces of western industrialization—were responsible for shrinking the globe. Technology not only allowed Europeans to accomplish tasks and to mass-produce goods efficiently, but it also altered the previous conception of time and space.

Steam, which powered factories, proved equally efficient as an energy source in transportation. Great iron steamships fueled by coal replaced the smaller, slower, wind-powered, wooden sailing vessels that had plied the sea for centuries. Steamships could carry large cargoes of people and goods and could meet schedules as precisely as railroads could. Just as the imperial Romans had used their network of roads to link far-flung territories to the capital, Europeans used sea-lanes to join their colonies to the home country.

Until 1850, Europeans ventured no farther on the African continent than its coastal areas. Now the installation of coal-burning boilers on smaller boats permitted navigation of previously uncharted rivers. Steam power made exploration and migration possible and greatly contributed to knowledge of terrain, natural wealth, and resources. Smaller, steam-powered vessels also increased European inland trade with China, Burma, and India.

Engineering Empire. While technology improved European mobility on water, it also literally moved the land. To accommodate the new iron- and then steel-hulled ships, harbors were deepened and canals were constructed. One of the greatest engineering feats of the century was the construction of a hundred-mile-long canal across the Isthmus of Suez in Egypt. Completed in 1869, the Suez Canal joined the Mediterranean and Red Seas and created a new, safer trade route to the East. No longer did trading vessels have to make the long voyage around Africa's Cape of Good Hope. The French built the Suez Canal under the supervision of Ferdinand de Lesseps (1805–1894), a diplomat with no technical or financial background who was able to promote construction because of concessions he received from Said Pasha of Egypt. The canal could accommodate ships of all sizes. Great Britain purchased a controlling interest in the Suez Canal in 1875 to benefit its trade with India.

De Lesseps later presided over the initial construction of the Panama Canal in the Western Hemisphere. The combination of French mismanagement, bankruptcy, and the high incidence of disease among work crews enabled the United States to acquire rights to the Panama project and complete it by 1914. Fifty-one miles long, the Panama Canal connected the Atlantic and Pacific Oceans across the Isthmus of Panama by a waterway containing a series of locks. Now the passage from the Atlantic to the Pacific took less than eight hours—significantly less time than the various overland routes or the voyage around the tip of South America. Both the Suez and Panama Canals saved travel time, which meant higher profits.

Technology also increased the speed of communication. In 1830, it took about two years for a person who sent a letter from Great Britain to India to receive a reply. In 1850, steam-powered mail boats shortened the time required for the same round-trip correspondence to about two or three months. But the real revolution in communication came through electricity. Thousands of miles of copper telegraph wire laced countries together; insulated underwater cables linked continents to each other. By the late nineteenth century, a vast telegraph network connected Europe to every major area of the world. In 1870, a telegram from London to Bombay arrived in a matter of hours, instead of months, and a response could be received back in London on the same day. Faster communications extended power and control throughout empires. Now Europeans could communicate immediately with their distant colonies, dispatching troops, orders, and supplies. This communication network eliminated the problem of overextension that had plagued Roman imperial organization in the third century. For the first time, continents that Europeans had discovered five centuries earlier were brought into daily contact with the West.

Medical Advances. Technological advances in other areas helped to foster European imperialism in the nineteenth century. Advances in medicine allowed European men and women to penetrate disease-laden swamps and jungles. After 1850, European explorers, traders, missionaries, and adventurers carried quinine pills. The bitter-tasting derivative of cinchona-tree bark, quinine was discovered to be an effective treatment for malaria. This treatment got its first important test during the French invasion of Algeria in 1830, and it allowed the French to stay healthy enough to conquer that North African country between 1830 and 1847. David Livingstone (1813–1873) and Henry M. Stanley (1841–1904) were just two of the many explorers who crossed vast terrains and explored the waterways of Africa after malaria, the number one killer of Europeans, had been controlled.

Europeans carried the technologies of destruction as well as survival with them into less-developed areas of the world. New types of firearms that were produced in the second half of the nineteenth century included breech-loading rifles, repeating rifles, and machine guns. The new weapons gave the advantages of both accurate aim and rapid fire. The spears of African warriors and the primitive weaponry of Chinese rebels were no match for sophisticated European arms, which permitted their bearers to lie down while firing and to remain undetected at distances of up to half a mile.

The new technology did not cause the new imperialism. The Western powers used technological advances as a tool for establishing their control of the world. Viewed as a tool, however, the new technology does explain how vast areas of land and millions of people were conquered so rapidly.

Motives for Empire

If technology was not the cause but only a tool, what explains the new imperialism of the late nineteenth century? There are no easy or simple explanations. Individuals made their fortunes overseas, and heavy industries such as the Krupp firm in Germany prospered with the expansion of state-protected colonies. Yet many colonies were economically worthless. Tunisia and Morocco, acquired for their strategic and political importance, constituted an economic loss for the French, who poured more funds into their administration than they were able to extract. Each imperial power held one or more colonies whose costs outweighed the return. Yet this does not mean that some Europeans were simply irrational in their pursuit of empire and glory.

Economics. The test for economic motivation cannot simply be reduced to a balance sheet of debits and credits; in the end, an account of state revenues and state expenditures provides only a static picture of the business of empire. Even losses cannot be counted as proof against the profit motive in expansion. In modern capitalism, profits, especially great profits, are often predicated on risks. Portugal and Italy took great risks and failed as players in the game in which the great industrial powers called the shots. Prestige through the acquisition of empire was one way of keeping alive in the game. Imperialism was influenced by business interests, market considerations, and the pursuit of individual and national fortunes. Not by accident did the great industrial powers control the scramble and dictate the terms of expansion. Nor was it merely fortuitous that Great Britain, the nation that provided the model for European expansion, dedicated itself to the establishment of a profitable worldwide network of trade and investment. Above all, the search for investment opportunities, whether railroads in China or diamond mines in South Africa, lured Europeans into a world system that challenged capitalist ingenuity and imagination. Acquiring territory was only one means of protecting investments. But other benefits were associated with the acquisition of territory that cannot be reduced to economic terms, and those too must be considered.

Geopolitics. Geopolitics, or the politics of geography, is based on the recognition that certain areas of the world are valuable for political reasons. The term, first used at the end of the nineteenth century, described a process that was well under way in international relations. Statesmen influenced by geopolitical concerns recognized the strategic value of certain lands. France, for example, occupied thousands of square miles of the Sahara to protect its interests in Algeria.

Other territory was important because of its proximity to sea routes. Egypt had significance for Great Britain not because of its inherent economic potential but because it allowed the British to protect access to lucrative markets in India through the Suez Canal. Beginning in 1875, the British purchased shares in the canal. By 1879, Egypt was under the informal dual rule of France and Great Britain. The British used the deterioration of internal Egyptian politics to justify their occupation of the country in 1882.

Protected access to India also accounted for Great Britain's maintenance of Mediterranean outposts, its acquisition of territory on the east coast of Africa, and its occupation of territory in southern Asia.

A third geopolitical motive for annexation was the necessity of having fueling bases throughout the world for coal-powered ships. Islands in the South Pacific and the Indian Ocean were acquired primarily to serve as coaling stations for the great steamers carrying manufactured goods to colonial ports and returning with foodstuffs and raw materials. Ports along the southern rim of Asia served the same purpose. The need to protect colonies, fueling ports, and sea lanes led to the creation of naval bases like those on the Red Sea at Djibouti by the French, in southeast Asia at Singapore by the British, and in the Hawaiian Islands at Honolulu by the Americans.

In turn, the acquisition of territories justified the increase in naval budgets and the size of fleets. Britain still had the world's largest navy, but by the beginning of the twentieth century, the United States and Germany had entered the competition for dominance of sea-lanes. Japan expanded its navy as a vehicle for its own claims to empire in the Pacific.

The politics of geography was land- as well as sea-based. As navies grew to protect sea-lanes, armies expanded to police new lands. Between 1890 and 1914, military expenditures of Western governments grew phenomenally; war machines doubled in size. Governments became consumers of heavy industry; their predictable participation in markets for armaments and military supplies helped to control fluctuations in the business cycle and to reduce unemployment at home. A side effect of the growing importance of geopolitics was the increased influence of military and naval leaders in foreign and domestic policy making.

Nationalism. Many European statesmen in the last quarter of the nineteenth century gave stirring speeches about the importance of empire as a means of enhancing national prestige. In his Crystal Palace speech of 1872, Benjamin Disraeli, British prime minister in 1868 and from 1874–1880, put the challenge boldly to the British:

> I appeal to the sublime instinct of an ancient people. . . . The issue is not a mean one. It is whether you will be content to be a comfortable England, modelled and moulded upon Continental principles and meeting in due course an inevitable fate, or whether you will be a great country, an imperial country, a country where your sons, when they rise, rise to paramount positions and obtain not merely the esteem of their countrymen but command the respect of the world.

National prestige was not an absolute value but one that was weighed relatively. Possessing an empire may have

Great Britain originally opposed construction of the Suez Canal but soon recognized its crucial role in the route to India. In this cartoon, *The Lion's Share*, British Prime Minister Disraeli purchases a controlling interest in the Suez Canal Company from the khedive of Egypt. The British lion in the foreground guards the key to India, the symbol of the canal.

meant "keeping up with the Joneses," as it did for smaller countries such as Italy. Imperial status was important to a country like Portugal, which was willing to go bankrupt to maintain its territories. But prestige without economic power was the form of imperialism without its substance. Nation-states could, through the acquisition of overseas territories, gain bargaining chips to be played at the international conference table. In this way, smaller nations hoped to be taken seriously in the system of alliances that preserved the balance of power in Europe.

Western newspapers deliberately fostered the desire for the advancement of national interests. Newspapers competed for readers, and their circulations often depended on the passions they aroused. Filled with tales calculated to titillate and entertain, and with advertisements promising miracle cures, newspapers wrested foreign policy from the realm of the specialist and transformed politics into another form of entertainment. The drama and vocabulary of sporting events, whose mass appeal as a leisure activity also dates from this era, were now applied to imperialist politics. Whether it was a rugby match or a territorial conquest, readers backed the "home" team, disdained the opposition, and competed for the thrill of victory. This marked quite a change for urban dwellers whose grandparents worked the land and did not look beyond the horizon of their home villages. Newspapers forged a national consciousness whereby individuals identified with collective causes that they did not fully comprehend. Some observed what was happening with a critical eye, identifying a deep-seated need in modern men and women for excitement in their lives.

Information conveyed in newspapers shaped opinion, and opinion, in turn, could influence policy. Leaders had

JOSEPH CHAMBERLAIN'S SPEECH TO THE BIRMINGHAM RELIEF ASSOCIATION

Joseph Chamberlain (1836–1914) was an English businessman and statesman and, from 1873 to 1876, the mayor of one of Great Britain's leading industrial cities, Birmingham. He was a national advocate for an expansionist colonial policy as the means of keeping his country strong. On 22 January 1894, with no regard for African people, he spoke before a community group to convince them that British imperialism helped the working class.

FOCUS QUESTIONS

What are the motives evoked by Chamberlain to justify colonial expansion? How does he appeal to the patriotism of the English working classes?

BELIEVE ME, if in any one of the places [in Africa] to which I have referred any change took place which deprived us of that control and influence of which I have been speaking, the first to suffer would be the working-men of this country. Then, indeed, we should see a distress which would not be temporary, but which would be chronic, and we should find that England was entirely unable to support the enormous population which is now maintained by the aid of her foreign trade. If the working-men of this country understand, as I believe they do—I am one of those who have had good reason through my life to rely upon their intelligence and shrewdness—if they understand their own interests, they will never lend any countenance to the doctrines of those politicians who never lose an opportunity of pouring contempt and abuse upon the brave Englishmen, who, even at this moment, in all parts of the world are carving out new dominions for Britain, and are opening up fresh markets for British commerce, and laying out fresh fields for British labour. [Applause.] If the Little Englanders[i] had their way, not only would they refrain from taking the legitimate opportunities which offer for extending the empire and for securing for us new markets, but I doubt whether they would even take the pains which are necessary to preserve the great heritage which has come down to us from our ancestors. [Applause.]

When you are told that the British pioneers of civilisation in Africa are filibusters[ii], and when you are asked to call them back, and to leave this great continent to the barbarism and superstition in which it has been steeped for centuries, or to hand over to foreign countries the duty which you are unwilling to undertake, I ask you to consider what would have happened if 100 or 150 years ago your ancestors had taken similar views of their responsibility? Where would be the empire on which now your livelihood depends? We should have been the United Kingdom of Great Britain and Ireland; but those vast dependencies, those hundreds of millions with whom we keep up a mutually beneficial relationship and commerce would have been the subjects of other nations, who would not have been slow to profit by our neglect of our opportunities and obligations. [Applause.]

From Joseph Chamberlain, M.P., *Foreign and Colonial Speeches* (1897).

[i] Britain's anti-imperialists.

[ii] A person engaged in a private military action against a foreign government.

to reckon with this new creation of "public opinion." In a typical instance, French newspaper editors promoted feverish public outcry for conquest of the Congo by pointing out the need to revenge British advances in Egypt. "Colonial fever" was so high in France in the summer of 1882 that French policy makers were pressured to pursue claims in the Congo basin without adequate assessment or reflection. As a result, the French government evicted Belgians and Portuguese from the northern Congo territory and enforced questionable treaty claims rather than risk public censure for appearing weak and irresolute.

Public opinion was certainly influential, but it could be manipulated. In Germany, the government often promoted colonial hysteria through the press to advance its own political ends. Chancellor Otto von Bismarck used his power over the press to support imperialism and to influence electoral outcomes in 1884. His successors were deft at promoting the "bread and circuses" atmosphere that surrounded colonial expansion to direct attention away from social problems at home and to maintain domestic stability.

The printed word was also manipulated in Britain during the Boer War (1899–1902), critics asserted, by business interests to keep public enthusiasm for the war effort high. J. A. Hobson (1858–1940), himself a journalist and theorist of imperialism, denounced the "abuse of the press" in his hard-hitting *Psychology of Jingoism* (1901), which appeared while the war was still being waged. Hobson recognized "jingoism" as the appropriate term for the "inverted patriotism whereby the love of one's own nation is transformed into hatred of another nation, and [into] the fierce craving to destroy the individual members of that other nation."

Jingoism was not a new phenomenon in 1900, nor was it confined to Britain. Throughout Europe, a mass public appeared increasingly willing to support conflict to defend national honor. Xenophobia, hatred of foreigners, melded with nationalism, both nurtured by the mass press, to put new pressures on the determination of foreign policy. Government elites, who formerly operated behind closed doors far removed from public scrutiny, were now accountable in new ways to faceless masses. Even in autocratic states such as Austria-Hungary, the opinion of the masses was a powerful political force that could destroy individual careers and dissolve governments.

Every nation in Europe had its jingoes, those who were willing to risk war for national glory. Significantly, the term "jingo" was coined in 1878 during a British showdown with the Russians over Turkey. The sentiment was so strong that "the Russians shall not have Constantinople" that the acceptability of war was set to music:

We don't want to fight,
But, by jingo, if we do,
We've got the men,
We've got the ships,
We've got the money too.

This was the most popular music-hall song in Britain that year, and long after the crisis had faded, the tune and its lyrics lingered.

To varying degrees, all of these factors—economics, geopolitics, and nationalism—motivated the actions of the three great imperialist powers—Britain, France, and Germany—and their less-powerful European neighbors. The same reasons account for the global aspirations of non-European nations such as the United States and Japan. None of these powers acted independently; each was aware of what the others were doing and tailored its actions accordingly. Imperialism followed a variety of patterns but always with a built-in component of emulation and acceleration. It was both a cause and a proof of a world system of states in which the actions of one nation affected the others.

The nineteenth-century liberal belief in progress encouraged Europeans to impose their beliefs and institutions on captive millions. After all, industrial society had given Europe the technology, the wealth, and the power to tame nature and dominate the world. Imperialists moralized that they had not only the right but also the duty to develop the nonindustrialized world for their own purposes.

THE EUROPEAN SEARCH FOR TERRITORY AND MARKETS

Most western Europeans who read about the distant regions that their armies and political leaders were bringing under control regarded these new territories as little more than entries on a great tally sheet or as distinctively colored areas on a map. The daily press recorded the numbers of square miles acquired and the names of the peoples in the occupied territories, and that was that. Few Europeans looked on imperialism as a relationship of power between two parties and, like all relationships, one influenced by both partners. Fewer still understood or appreciated the distinctive qualities of the conquered peoples.

The areas that European imperialism affected varied widely in their political organization. Large states existed in some parts of Africa; elsewhere, states were small or even nonexistent. Whatever the situation, however, Europeans, filled with the racist prejudices of the period, considered African governmental institutions too ineffectual to produce the economic change and growth of trade they then wanted. Military takeover and direct rule by European officials seemed the only feasible way to establish empire in Africa and extract the goods and labor these officials sought. In Asia, by contrast, societies such as India and China were territorially large and had efficient institutions of government dominated by established political hierarchies. Although they were more difficult to conquer, their leaders were more likely to cooperate with the imperial powers because their own interests were often similar to those of the Westerners.

For these reasons, European empire builders pursued a variety of models: formal military empires (as in Africa), informal empires (as in China), or formal but indirect rule over hierarchical societies (as in India).

The Scramble for Africa: Diplomacy and Conflict

In the mid-1860s, a committee of the British Parliament recommended that Britain withdraw from the scattering of small colonies it possessed in West Africa, arguing that they were costly anachronisms in an era of free trade. Just 30 years later, in 1898, the president of France, in commenting on French policies of the previous 20 years, remarked that "We have behaved like madmen in Africa, having been led astray by irresponsible people called the 'colonialists.'" The "mad" event that had altered the political landscape of Africa was the so-called "scramble for Africa," a partitioning of Africa that is usually considered as extending from around 1875 to around 1912. By its end, Europeans controlled virtually all Africa.

One cannot detect one single reason for the scramble as it actually took place on the ground. Africa is a large and complex continent, and the reasons for which Europeans pursued specific pieces of African territory were similarly complex. The explanations for the acquisition of a given colony, therefore, depend largely on the historical context of that particular case. In certain areas, such as the West African Sudanic and Sahara desert zones, ambitious French military men sought to advance their careers by carving out grand colonies. The existence of valuable minerals motivated the scramble for the area now called Zimbabwe, the Zambian/Zairian copper belt, and other areas. Along the West African coast, chronic disputes between traders working in an economy soured by a deterioration in the terms of trade seemed to require European annexation. Some colonies, such as present-day Uganda and Malawi, were created to please missionaries already working there. Britain took Egypt, and France occupied Djibouti for strategic reasons. As often as not, as in Mozambique, Tanzania, Namibia, and Botswana, some Europeans seized areas to keep other Europeans from doing the same thing.

Yet there were also basic historical factors that underlay the scramble as a whole. One was the rapid development after 1870 of pseudoscientific racist ideas asserting that Europeans were a superior race and that Africans were inferior. Charles Darwin himself had explicitly suggested the applicability of the concept of evolution to humans. Intellectuals such as Herbert Spencer (1820–1903) quickly took up his suggestion and popularized it as Social Darwinism. According to Social Darwinists, the races of humankind not only occupied distinct positions in a staged sequence of development over time, whites being the most advanced and blacks the least so, but also were engaged in a natural conflict with each other. Social Darwinism's strongest message was that the fittest were destined to prevail, an idea that was especially welcome to the energetic racists of the later nineteenth century because it could be used to justify as "natural" the wars of imperial expansion on which they were then embarking.

The Drive for Markets and Profits. A second underlying factor was the atmosphere created by an economic downturn in Europe that lasted from 1873 until 1896. This downturn, coupled with Germany's fast rise to economic power during the 1870s and 1880s, was deeply unsettling to many Europeans. Protectionist policies springing from new economic anxieties eroded earlier faith in free trade, and many Europeans became keen to acquire African territory just in case it should turn out to be useful in the long run. Even Britain, long the major champion of free trade, became ever more protectionist and imperialistic as the century neared its end.

Historians generally agree that the person who provided the catalyst for the scramble was Leopold II, king of the Belgians (1865–1909). His motive was greed. Early in 1876, Leopold read a report about the Congo River basin that claimed that it was "mostly a magnificent and healthy country of unspeakable richness" that could in "from 30 to 36 months begin to repay any enterprising capitalist." Leopold, an ambitious and frustrated king ruling over a small country, went to work at once to acquire this area, one-third the size of the United States, for himself. Cloaking himself in the mantle of philanthropy and asserting that all he desired was to stamp out the remnants of the East African slave trade, he organized the International African Association in late 1876.

His association soon established stations on the region's rivers and robbed the people of much valuable ivory. Meanwhile, Leopold himself skillfully lobbied for formal recognition of his association's right to rule the Congo basin. France and Portugal, also covetous of the area, objected, and after much diplomatic wrangling, an international conference was finally held in Berlin in late 1884 to decide the question. The Berlin Conference was important not only because it yielded the Congo basin to Leopold as the Congo Free State, but also because it laid down the ground rules for the recognition of other colonial claims in Africa. No longer would merely planting a flag in an area be considered adequate to establish sovereignty; instead, the creation of a real presence calculated to produce "economic development" would be needed. If by panicking the European states, Leopold's actions began the scramble, the Berlin Conference organized and structured it. However, it is clear in retrospect that the scramble would have occurred even without Leopold II's greedy intervention.

European Agreements and African Massacres. In dividing Africa, the European states were remarkably cooperative. Although Britain did threaten Portugal with war in 1890 in a dispute about the area around Lake Malawi, and although it appeared for a while that Britain and France were headed toward armed conflict in 1898 over control of the headwaters of the Nile, peaceful diplomatic settlements were always worked out. Deals that traded one piece of territory for another were common, and peace was maintained. Diplomats did not consider Africa worth a European war.

Yet despite the importance of diplomatic compromise among European states during the scramble, every instance of European expansion in Africa, no matter what its specific motive, was characterized by a readiness to shoot Africans. With Hiram Maxim's invention in 1884 of a machine gun that could fire eleven bullets per second, and with the banning by the Brussels Convention of 1890 of the sale of modern weapons to Africans, the military advantage passed overwhelmingly to the imperialists. As the British poet Hilaire Belloc (1870–1953) tellingly observed,

> *Whatever happens, we have got*
> *The Maxim Gun, and they have not.*

The conquest of "them" became more like hunting than warfare. In 1893, for example, in Zimbabwe, 50 Europeans, using only six machine guns, killed 3,000 Ndebele people in less than two hours. In 1897, in northern Nigeria, a force of 32 Europeans and 500 African mercenaries defeated the 31,000-man army of the emir of Sokoto. Winston Churchill, reporting on the battle of Omdurman in the Sudan in 1898, summed up well the nature of such warfare:

> The [British] infantry fired steadily and stolidly, without hurry or excitement, for the enemy were far away and the officers careful. Besides the soldiers were interested in the work and took great pains. . . . And all the time out on the plain on the other side bullets were shearing through flesh, smashing and splintering bone; blood spouted from terrible wounds; valiant men were struggling on through a hell of whistling metal, exploding shells, and spurting dust—suffering, despairing, dying.

After five hours of fighting, the numbers killed were 20 Britons, 20 Egyptian allies, and over 11,000 Sudanese.

Ethiopia as Exception. One exception to the general rule of easy conquest was Ethiopia. The history of the country illustrates the importance of guns in the dynamics of the scramble. In the middle of the nineteenth century, the emperor of Ethiopia possessed little more than a grand title. Yet while the empire had broken down into its ethnic and regional components, the dream of a united empire was still alive. It was pursued by the emperors of the time, Amharic-speakers with their political base on the fertile plateau that constituted the heartland of the country. In their successful efforts to rebuild the empire, they relied increasingly on modern weapons imported from Europe and stockpiled.

By the early 1870s, however, the emperor realized that his achievements in rebuilding the empire were endangered not merely by the resistance of those whom he was then trying to force into his empire, but, more ominously, by the outside world, especially by Egypt to the north and the Sudan to the west. Furthermore, the opening of the

▲ A contemporary cartoon characterized King Leopold of the Belgians as a monstrous snake crushing the life out of the black population of the Congo Free State. The territory was under the personal rule of the Belgian king from 1885 to 1908.

Suez Canal in 1869 had made the Red Sea and its surrounding areas attractive not only to Egypt but also to European countries eager to protect their trade routes to Asia. By the end of the 1870s, as the scramble for Africa was seriously getting under way, France, Britain, and Italy all became interested in acquiring land in the region. After Britain occupied Egypt in 1882, France took Djibouti (1884) and Italy seized Eritrea (1885), both on the Red Sea.

The emperor, Menelik II (1889–1913), realized that he could exploit rival European interests in the area by playing off one European power against the others to obtain the weapons he needed for expanding his empire's boundaries. He therefore gave certain concessions to France in return for French weapons. Italy, upset at the growing French influence, offered weapons as well, and Menelik accepted them. Russia and Britain joined in. More and more modern weapons flowed into Ethiopia during the 1870s and 1880s and into the early 1890s, and Menelik steadily strengthened his ability both to suppress internal dissent and to block foreign encroachment.

Then, in the early 1890s, Menelik's strategy of balancing one European power against another began to unravel. In 1889, he had signed the Treaty of Wichale with Italy, granting it certain concessions in return for more arms shipments. Italy then claimed that Ethiopia had thus become an Italian protectorate and moved against Menelik when he objected. By 1896, Italy was ready for a major assault on the Ethiopian army, heady with the confident racism of the time that it could defeat the "primitive" Ethiopians with ease. General Oreste Baratieri (1841–1901), the commander of Italy's 18,000-man army in Eritrea, was wisely cautious, however, understanding that modern weapons functioned the same way whether they were fired by Africans or Italians. Knowing that Menelik's army of some 100,000 troops had very long supply lines, Baratieri decided to wait until Menelik could no longer supply his troops with food. Then, he assumed, Menelik's soldiers would simply disappear, and the Italians would walk in. But the prime minister of Italy, Francesco Crispi (1819–1901), wanted a quick, glorious victory to enhance his political reputation and ordered Baratieri to send his army into battle at once. Hopelessly outnumbered, the Italians lost over 8,000 men on 1 March 1896 at the decisive battle of Adowa. With its army destroyed and its artillery lost to the Ethiopians, Italy had no choice but to negotiate a peace.

France and Britain soon ratified Italy's acceptance of Ethiopia as a sovereign state with its greatly expanded imperial boundaries. As a consequence of its victory at Adowa—and attesting to the crucial importance of modern weaponry for survival in late nineteenth-century Africa—Ethiopia was the only African country aside from the U.S. quasi-colony of Liberia that Europeans did not occupy in the scramble for Africa. After 1896, Menelik, with his access to modern weapons assured by his country's international recognition, successfully continued his campaigns to extend his control over the Ethiopian empire's subordinate peoples.

Gold, Empire Building, and the Boer War

Europeans were as willing to shoot white Africans as they were black Africans during the scramble as they seized land and resources. In South Africa, for example, the British engaged in a long war over possession of the world's largest supply of gold with a group of white Africans, the Afrikaners, or Boers, settlers of Dutch and French Huguenot background who had developed their own unique identity during the eighteenth and early nineteenth centuries.

Afrikaner Rule. After the Great Trek (1837–1844), in which a large number of Afrikaners had withdrawn from British control by leaving the Cape Colony, the British had grudgingly recognized the independence of the Orange Free State and the Transvaal, the Afrikaner republics in the interior, in a series of formal agreements. The British complacently believed that the Afrikaners, economically weak and geographically isolated, could never challenge British preeminence in the region. Two events of the mid-1880s shattered their complacence. First, in 1884, Germany, Britain's greatest international competitor, inserted itself into the region by annexing Namibia as part of the scramble. The British, aware that the Germans and the Afrikaners were sympathetic to each other, worried about the German threat to their regional hegemony and economic prospects.

Britain's War in South Africa. British fear of the Germans was redoubled in 1886 when, in the Transvaal Republic, in the Witwatersrand area, the world's largest deposits of gold were discovered. A group of British diamond mine owners who had grown rich exploiting the Kimberley diamond fields after their discovery in 1867 moved in quickly to develop the Witwatersrand's gold, which, because it lay deep in the ground, could be mined only with the investment of large amounts of capital. The best-known of these investors was Cecil Rhodes (1853–1902), a businessman and Cape Colony politician who was intent on expanding his wealth through an extension of British power to the north. Rhodes and his colleagues quickly identified Afrikaner governmental policies on agriculture, tariffs, and labor control as major impediments to profitable gold production. Therefore, in 1895 they organized, with the connivance of members of the British government, an attempt to overthrow the Afrikaner government of the Transvaal. This attempt, led by Dr. L. S. Jameson (1853–1917), Rhodes's lieutenant, involved the invasion of the Transvaal by British South African police and came to be known as the Jameson Raid. It was faultily executed, however, and, to Rhodes's utter humiliation, it failed.

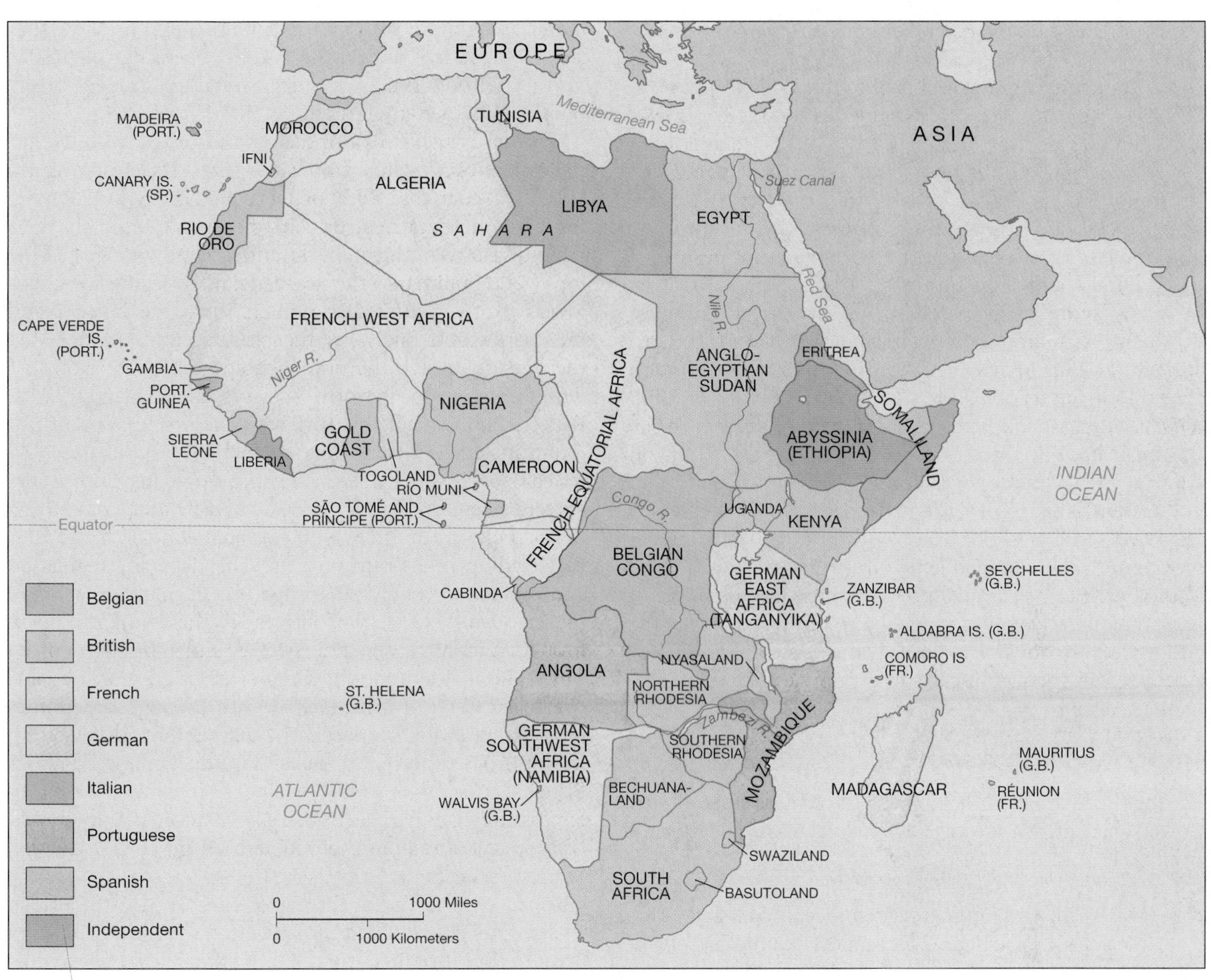

Africa, 1914. Before 1800, Africa was controlled by numerous African states. By 1914, all of Africa, with the exceptions of Ethiopia and Liberia, was under the control or oversight of European powers.

The failure of the Jameson Raid prompted the British government to send a new agent, Alfred Milner (1854–1925), to the area in 1897. An ardent advocate of expanding the British Empire and of keeping German influence in the region to a minimum, and well aware of the importance of gold to Britain's financial position in the world, Milner was determined to push the Afrikaners into uniting with the British in South Africa, through either diplomacy or war. By 1899 it was clear that war was inevitable, and in October, British demands provoked a declaration of war from the Afrikaners. The British confidently expected to have the war over by Christmas, but the Afrikaners carried out a guerrilla war against inept British generals, and the so-called Boer War dragged on and on.

The British eventually sent 350,000 troops to South Africa, but these forces, even when reinforced by thousands of African auxiliaries, could not decisively defeat the 65,000 Afrikaner fighting men. Casualties were high on both sides, not merely from the fighting, but also because typhus epidemics broke out in the concentration camps in which the British interned Afrikaner women and children as they pursued their scorched-earth policies in the countryside. By the war's end, 25,000 Afrikaners, 22,000 British imperial troops, and 12,000 black Africans had died. Britain had also suffered great international criticism for having treated white Afrikaners as if they were black Africans.

In April 1902, the British accepted the conditional surrender of the Afrikaners. The British annexed the Afrikaner republics to the empire and took the opportunity to make the gold industry efficient. But they promised the Afrikaners that no political decisions regarding the majority black African population's political role in a future

South Africa would be taken before returning governmental power to the Afrikaners. This crucial concession ensured that segregation would remain the model for race relations in South Africa throughout the twentieth century.

When World War I broke out in 1914, the scramble for Africa was over, and the map of the continent was colored in imperial inks. France had secured the largest chunk, some four million square miles of mostly tropical forests and deserts. Britain had the second largest empire, richer in minerals and agricultural potential than France's. Germany proudly possessed two West African colonies, Togo and Cameroon, as well as Namibia in southern Africa and Tanganyika in East Africa. Belgium had been forced to assume control over Leopold II's Congo in 1908 after scandals made his continued control unacceptable. Portugal had finally consolidated its feeble hold on Angola, Mozambique, and Portuguese Guinea. Italy had colonies in Libya, Eritrea, and Somalia, while Spain was left with some bits of coast. Only Ethiopia and Liberia were politically independent. Now that they had conquered Africa, the colonial powers had to face the issue of how their new colonies could be made to pay. And the conquered Africans had to face the issue of how they might regain their political and economic independence.

Imperialism in Asia

During the first half of the nineteenth century, strong Asian powers had grown stronger. China increased its control over inner Asian territories; Vietnam and Siam, predecessor to modern Thailand, enhanced their powers in southeast Asia. By the end of the nineteenth century, Asian political dynasties had suffered reversals. China had been permanently weakened in inner Asia; Vietnam had fallen under French colonial rule; Siam had lost half its territories. India had long constituted an important part of the British Empire. By contrast, Japan became an aggressive power, itself an imperial presence.

India. The British Parliament proclaimed that on New Year's Day, 1877, Queen Victoria (1837–1901) would add the title of Empress of India to her many honors. India, the great jewel in the imperial crown, was a land Victoria had never seen. The queen's new title, not universally popular in Britain and unnoticed by most famine-stricken Indian peasants, in fact changed nothing about the way the British ruled India. Yet it was more than merely a symbolic assertion of dominance over a country that had long been controlled by the British.

India was the starting point of all British expansion, and it stood at the center of British foreign policy. To protect its sea routes to India and to secure its Indian markets, Britain acquired territories and carved out concessions all over the world. Devised by Prime Minister Benjamin Disraeli to flatter an aging monarch, the new title of empress was really a calculated warning to Russia, operating on India's northern frontier in Afghanistan, and to France, busily pursuing its own interests in Egypt.

Formal British rule in India began in 1861 with the appointment of a viceroy, who was assisted by legislative and executive councils. Both of these bodies included some Indian representatives. British rule encountered the four main divisions of the highly stratified Hindu society. At the top were Brahmans, the learned and priestly class, followed by the warriors and rulers, then the farmers and merchants, and finally by the peasants and laborers. On the outside existed the untouchables, a fifth division that was intended to perform society's most menial tasks. Rather than disrupt this divisive caste system, the British found it to their advantage to maintain the status quo.

The special imperial relationship originated in the seventeenth century, when the British East India Company, a joint-stock venture free of government control, began limited trading in Indian markets. The need for regulation and protection firmly established British rule by the end of the eighteenth century. Conquest of the Punjab in 1849 brought the last independent areas under British control. Throughout this period, Britain invested considerable overseas capital in India, and in turn India absorbed one-fifth of total British exports. The market for Indian cotton, for centuries exported to Asia and Europe, collapsed under British tariffs, and India became a consumer of cheap Lancashire cotton. The British also exploited India's agriculture, salt, and opium production for profit.

China. At the end of the eighteenth century, the British traded English wool and Indian cotton for Chinese tea and textiles. But Britain's thirst for Chinese tea grew, while Chinese demand for English and Indian textiles slackened. Britain discovered that Indian opium could be used to balance the trade deficit created by tea. British merchants and local Chinese officials, especially in the entry port of Canton, began to expand their profitable involvement in a contraband trade in opium. The British East India Company held a monopoly over opium cultivation in Bengal. Opium exports to China mounted phenomenally—from 200 chests in 1729 to 40,000 chests in 1838. By the 1830s, opium was probably Britain's most important crop in world markets. The British prospered as opium was pumped into China faster than tea was flowing out. Chinese buyers began paying for the drug with silver.

Concerned with the sharp rise in addiction, the accompanying social problems, and the massive outflow of silver, the Chinese government reacted. As Chinese officials saw it, they were exchanging their precious metal for British poison. Addicts were threatened with the death penalty. In 1839, the Chinese government destroyed British opium in the port of Canton, touching off the Opium War (1839–1842).

Between 1842 and 1895, China fought five wars with foreigners and lost all of them. Defeat was expensive, as China had to pay costs to the winners. Before the end of the century, Britain, France, Germany, and Japan had managed to establish major territorial advantages in their spheres of influence, sometimes through negotiation and sometimes through force. By 1912, over 50 major Chinese ports had been handed over to foreign control as "treaty ports." British spheres included Shanghai, the lower Yangzi, and Hong Kong. France maintained special interests in South China. Germany controlled the Shandong peninsula. Japan laid claim to the northeast.

Spheres of influence grew in importance at the beginning of the twentieth century, when foreign investors poured capital into railway lines, which needed treaty protection from competing companies. Railways furthered foreign encroachment and opened up new territories to foreign claims. As one Chinese official explained it, the railroads were like scissors that threatened to cut China into many pieces. Foreigners established no formal empires in China, but the treaty ports certainly signaled both informal rule and indisputable foreign dominance.

Treaty ports were centers of foreign residence and trade, where rules of extraterritoriality applied. This meant that foreigners were exempt from Chinese law enforcement and that, although present on Chinese territory, they could be judged only by officials of their own countries. Extraterritoriality was a privilege not just for diplomats but for every foreign national. It implied both a distrust of Chinese legal procedures and a cultural arrogance about the superiority of Western institutions. It also provoked resentment and growing antiforeign sentiments among the Chinese.

To preserve extraterritoriality and maintain informal empires, the European powers appointed civilian representatives known as consuls. Often merchants themselves—in the beginning unpaid in their posts—and consuls acted as the chieftains of resident merchant communities, judges in all civil and criminal cases, and spokesmen for the commercial interests of the home country. They clearly embodied the commercial intentions of Western governments. Initially, they stood outside the diplomatic corps; later, they were consigned to its lower ranks. Consuls were brokers for commerce and interpreted the international commercial law that was being forged. Consulates spread beyond China as Western nations used consuls to protect their own interests. In Africa, consuls represented the trading concerns of European governments and were instrumental in the transition to formal rule.

Southeast Asia and Japan. European nations pursued imperialist endeavors elsewhere in Asia, acquired territories on China's frontiers, and took over states that had formerly paid tribute to the Chinese Empire. The British acquired Hong Kong (1842), Burma (1886), and Kowloon (1898). The Russians took over the Maritime Provinces in 1858. The French made gains in Indochina (Annam and Tonkin) in 1884 and extended control over Laos in 1893 and Cambodia in 1884. Thailand was the only country in southeast Asia to escape direct control by the Western powers. Yet it was forced to yield territory it once controlled and to accept the treaty port system with its tariffs and extraterritoriality.

The United States took control of the Philippines from the Spanish during the Spanish-American War over Cuba. Facing continued Filipino resistance, the United States opposed Filipino nationalism with a colonial rule that collaborated with a conservative landowning Filipino oligarchy and fostered an acute Philippine economic dependency on the colonial power.

The Sino-Japanese War of 1894–1895 revealed Japan's intentions to compete as an imperialist power in Asia. The modernized and westernized Japanese army easily defeated the ill-equipped and poorly led Chinese forces. As a result, Japan gained the island of Taiwan. Pressing its ambitions on the continent, Japan locked horns with Russia over claims to the Liaodong peninsula, Korea, and south Manchuria. Following its victory in the Russo-Japanese War of 1904–1905, Japan expanded into all of these areas, annexing Korea outright in 1910. The ease with which the small Asian nation had defeated the Russian giant and contributed to the heightening of anti-imperialist sentiments in China sent a strong message to the West.

CHRONOLOGY

THE NEW IMPERIALISM IN AFRICA AND ASIA

1837–1844	Great Trek
1839–1842	Opium War
1869	Suez Canal completed
1884	Berlin Conference held to regulate imperialism in Africa
1886	Gold discovered in the Transvaal Republic
1894–1895	Sino-Japanese War
1896	Battle of Adowa
1899–1902	Boer War
1900	Boxer Rebellion
1904–1905	Russo-Japanese War

RESULTS OF A EUROPEAN-DOMINATED WORLD

Europeans fashioned the world in their own image, but in the process, Western values and Western institutions underwent profound and unintended transformations.

Family values were articulated in an imperialist context, and race emerged as a key factor in culture. The discovery of new lands, new cultures, and new peoples altered the ways in which European women and men regarded themselves and viewed their place in the world. With the rise of new contenders for power—the United States and Japan—and growing criticism about the morality of capitalism, the Western world was not as predictable in 1914 as it had appeared in 1870.

A World Economy

Imperialism produced an interdependent world economic system with Europe at its center. Industrial and commercial capitalism linked the world's continents in a communications and transportation network that would have been unimaginable in earlier ages. As a result, foreign trade increased from 3 percent of world output in 1800 to 33 percent by 1913. The greatest growth in trade occurred in the period from 1870 to 1914, as raw materials, manufactured products, capital, and men and women were transported across seas and continents by those seeking profits.

Meeting Western Needs. Most trading in the age of imperialism still took place among European nations and North America. But entrepreneurs in search of new markets and new resources saw in Africa and Asia opportunities for protected exploitation. New markets were created in nonindustrialized areas of the world to meet the needs of Western producers and consumers. European landlords and managers trained Kenyan farmers to put aside their traditional agricultural methods and to grow more "useful" crops such as coffee, tea, and sugar. The availability of cheaper British textiles of inferior quality drove Indian weavers away from their handlooms. Chinese silk producers changed centuries-old techniques to produce silk thread and cloth that was suited to the machinery and mass-production requirements of the French. Trade permitted specialization but at the choice of the colonizer, not the colonized. World production and consumption were being shaped to suit the needs of the West.

Investment Abroad. Capital in search of profits flowed out of the wealthier areas of Europe into the nonindustrialized regions of Russia, the Balkans, and the Ottoman Empire, where capital-intensive expenditures (on railways, for instance) promised high returns. Capital investment in overseas territories also increased phenomenally as railroads were built to gain access to primary products. Great Britain led in overseas investment with loans abroad greater than those of its five major competitors—France, Germany, Holland, the United States, and Belgium—combined.

The City of London had become the world's banker, and the adoption of gold as the standard for exchange for most European currencies by 1874 further facilitated the operation of a single, interdependent trading and investment system. Britain remained the world's biggest trading nation, with half of its exports going to Asia, Africa, and South America and the other half to Europe and the United States. But Germany was Britain's fastest-growing competitor, with twice as many exports to Europe and expanding overseas trade by 1914. The United States had recently joined the league of the world's great trading nations and was running a strong third in shares of total trade.

Foreign investments often took the form of loans to governments or to enterprises that were guaranteed by governments. Investors might be willing to take risks, but they also expected protection, as did merchants and industrialists trading in overseas territories. Together, trade and investment interests exerted considerable pressure on European states for control through acquisition and concessions. The vast amounts of money involved help to explain the expectations of state involvement and the reasons why international competition, rivalry, and instability threatened to lead to conflict and to war.

Race and Culture

The West's ability to kill and conquer as well as to cure was, as one Victorian social observer argued, proof of its cultural superiority. Every colonizing nation had its spokesmen for the "civilizing mission" to educate and to convert African and Asian "heathens." Cultural superiority was only a short step from arguments for racial superiority. Prompted by the U.S. involvement in the Philippines, the British poet Rudyard Kipling (1865–1936) characterized the responsibilities of the advanced West as "the White Man's burden." The smug and arrogant attitude of his poem about the white man's mission revealed a deep-seated and unacknowledged racism toward peoples considered "half-devil and half-child."

As was discussed earlier in this chapter, views of cultural superiority received support from the scientific work of Herbert Spencer and Charles Darwin. In the 1880s, popularizers applied evolutionary ideas about animal and plant life to the development of human society. Just as animals could be hierarchically organized according to observable differences, so too, it was argued, could the different races of human beings. Race and culture were collapsed into each other. If Westerners were culturally superior, as they claimed, they must be racially superior as well.

Women and Imperialism

Ideas about racial and cultural superiority were not confined to books by pseudoscientists and to discussions

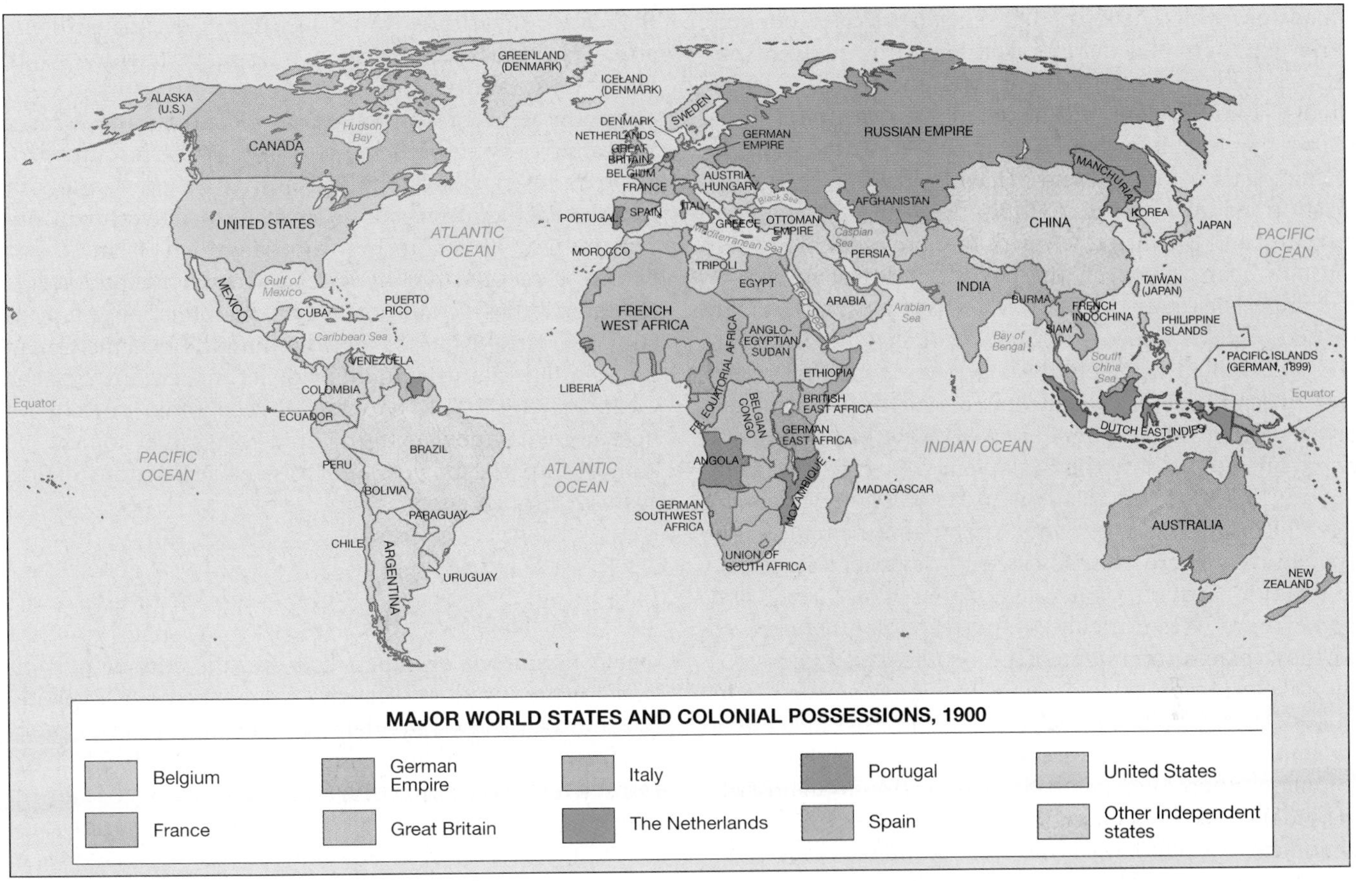

▲ World Colonial Holdings. The European powers, great and small, competed with each other for world empires and world influence between 1870 and 1914.

among policy makers. Public discussions about marriage, reproduction, motherhood, and child-rearing reflected new concerns about furthering "the imperial race"—that is, white Westerners. Women throughout Western societies were advised by reformers, politicians, and doctors to have more children and instructed to take better care of them. "Children [are] the most valuable of imperial assets," one British doctor lectured his readers. Healthy young men were needed in the colonies, they were told, to defend Western values. State officials paid greater attention to infant mortality at the end of the nineteenth century, set up health programs for children, and provided young women with training in home management, nutrition, and child care.

In the poem "The White Man's Burden," Kipling advised, "Send forth the best ye breed." All over Europe, newly formed associations and clubs stressed the need for careful mate selection. In Britain, Francis Galton (1822–1911) founded eugenics, the study of genetics for the purpose of improving inherited characteristics of the race. Imperialism, the propagandists proclaimed, depended on mothers, women who would nurture healthy workers, strong soldiers and sailors, and intelligent and capable leaders. High infant mortality rates and poor health of children were attributed directly to maternal failings, not to environmental factors or poverty. Kaiser Wilhelm II stressed that German women's attention to the "three Ks"—*Kinder, Küche, Kirche* ("children, kitchen, church")—would guarantee a race of Germans who would rule the world. British generals and French statesmen publicly expressed similar sentiments.

Some European women participated directly in the colonizing experience. As missionaries and nurses, they supported the civilizing mission. As wives of officials and managers, they were expected to embody the gentility and values of Western culture. Most men who traded and served overseas did so unaccompanied by women. But when women were present in any numbers, as they were in India before 1914, they were expected to preserve the exclusivity of Western communities.

Ecology and Imperialism

Ecology—the relationship and adjustment of human groups to their environment—was affected by imperial expansion, which dislocated the societies that it touched. Early explorers had disrupted little as they arrived, observed, and then moved on. The missionaries, merchants, soldiers, and businessmen who came later required the inhabitants with whom they came into contact to change their thought and behavior. In some cases, dislocation resulted in material improvements, better medical care, and the introduction of modern technology. For the most part, however, the initial ecological impact of the imperialist was negative. Western men and women carried diseases to people who did not share their immunity. Traditional village life was destroyed in rural India, and African societies disintegrated under the European onslaught. Resistance existed everywhere, but in Africa, as we have seen, only the Ethiopians succeeded in keeping out foreigners. In East Asia, parts of China were subject to foreign influence, while Japan, after being forcibly opened to Western commerce, soon developed imperialist ambitions of its own. Missionaries, merchants, and purveyors of Western culture and technology flocked to all these places to enlighten the natives—and occasionally to learn from them.

Education of native populations had as its primary goal the improvement of administration and productivity in the colonies. When foreigners ruled indirectly through existing indigenous hierarchies, they often created corrupt and tyrannical bureaucracies that exploited natives. The indirect rule of the British in India was based on a pragmatic desire to keep British costs low.

When Asian and African laborers started producing for the Western market, they became dependent on its fluctuations. Victimized for centuries by the vagaries of weather, they now had to contend with the instability and cutthroat competition of cash crops in world markets. Men and women migrated from place to place in the countryside and from the countryside to newly formed cities. Such migrations necessarily affected family life, as individuals married later because they lacked the resources to set up households. Many women, cut free of their tribes (as was the case in Nairobi), turned to prostitution—literally for pennies—as a means of survival.

Some European countries used their overseas territories as dumping grounds for criminals. Imitating the earlier example of the British in Australia, the French developed Guiana and New Caledonia as prison colonies in the hope of solving their social problems at home by exporting undesirables.

The United States provided another variation on imperial expansion. Its westward drive across the North American continent, beginning at the end of the eighteenth century, established the United States as an imperial power in the Western Hemisphere. By 1848, the relatively young nation stretched over 3,000 miles from one ocean to the other. It had met the opposition and resistance of the Native Americans with armed force, decimated them, and concentrated the survivors in assigned territories and, later, on reservations.

At the end of the nineteenth century, the United States, possessing both the people and the resources for rapid industrial development, turned to the Caribbean and the Pacific in pursuit of markets and investment opportunities. By acquiring the Hawaiian Islands and Samoa, it secured fueling bases in the Pacific and access to lucrative East Asian ports. And, by intervening repeatedly in Central America and building the Panama Canal, the United States established its hegemony in the Caribbean by 1914. Growing in economic power and hegemonic influence, the United States had joined the club of imperial powers and was making serious claims against European expansion.

Critiquing Capitalism

One consequence of imperialism was the critique of capitalism it produced. Critics who condemned it as exploitative and racist saw imperialism as an expression of problems that were inherent in capitalism. In 1902, J. A. Hobson (1858–1940) published *Imperialism, A Study,* in which he argued that underconsumption and surplus capital at home drove Western industrial countries overseas in search of a cure for these economic ills. Rather than solving the problems by raising workers' wages and thereby increasing their consumption power and creating new opportunities for investment in home markets, manufacturers, entrepreneurs, and industrialists sought higher profits abroad. Hobson considered these business interests "economic parasites," making large fortunes at the expense of national interests.

In the midst of world war, the future leader of the Russian revolution, Vladimir Ilyich Ulyanov (1870–1924)—or, to use his revolutionary name, Lenin—added his own critique of capitalism. He did not share Hobson's belief that capitalism was merely malfunctioning in its imperialist endeavors. Instead, Lenin argued in *Imperialism, the Highest Stage of Capitalism* (1916) that capitalism is inherently and inevitably imperialistic. Because he was sure that Western capitalism was in the process of effecting its own destruction, Lenin called World War I the final "imperialist war."

Critics, historians, and economists have since pointed out that both works are marred by errors and omissions. Yet they stand at the beginning of almost a century of debate over the morality and economic feasibility of imperialism. Hobson as a liberal and Lenin as a Marxist highlighted the connections between social problems at home—whether in late Victorian England or in prerevolutionary Russia—and economic exploitation abroad. Yet if electoral results and the popular press are any indication, Europeans not only accepted but warmly embraced the responsibilities of empire.

Conclusion

FROM THE VERY BEGINNING OF THE COMPETITION for territories and concessions, no European state could act in Africa or Asia without affecting the interests and actions of its rivals at home. The African scramble made clear how interlocking the system of European states was after 1870. The development of spheres of influence in China underlined the value of world markets and international trade for the survival and expansion of Western nations.

A "balance of power" among states guaranteed national security and independence until the end of the nineteenth century. But between 1870 and 1914, industrialization, technology, and accompanying capital formation created vast economic disparities. Conflict and disequilibrium challenged European stability and balance. Ultimately, it was the politics of geography on the European continent, not confrontations in distant colonies, that polarized the European states into two camps. Despite the unresolved conflicts pervading all of these crises, European statesmen prided themselves on their ability to settle disputes through reason and negotiation. Yet it was the problems at home in Europe and not abroad in the colonies that were to exacerbate geopolitical vulnerabilities and detonate a conflict far worse than the world had ever seen.

QUESTIONS FOR REVIEW

1. What geopolitical factors made the European balance of power so unstable around the turn of the century?
2. What social, political, and economic forces encouraged the nations of Europe to create overseas empires in the late nineteenth century?
3. How and why did European imperialism differ in Africa and Asia?
4. How did imperial expansion around the globe transform the lives of Europeans at home?

DISCOVERING WESTERN CIVILIZATION ONLINE

You can obtain more information about Europe and the world between 1870 and 1914 at the websites listed below. See also the companion website that accompanies this text: www.ablongman.com/kishlansky, which contains an online study guide and additional resources.

The European Balance of Power, 1870–1914

www.fordham.edu/halsall/mod/modsbook38.html

This site is part of a larger site on World War I primary and secondary sources, but it contains a section on the developments among the great powers from the 1870s to 1914.

The New Imperialism

www.fordham.edu/halsall/mod/modsbook34.html

A comprehensive site of links arranged by continent to primary source materials and bibliographies on imperialism.

The European Search for Territory and Markets

www.hum.port.ac.uk/slas/francophone/bibliographies.htm

A collection of bibliographies on the partition of Africa and the impact of colonization in Africa.

www.geocities.com/Vienna/5048/TREATY01.html

This site is devoted to the treaties that gave foreign governments access to political and commercial power in China.

www.chinaexhibit.org

A virtual museum exhibit of photographs taken in 1903 of the Chinese countryside after the Boxer Rebellion.

SUGGESTIONS FOR FURTHER READING

The European Balance of Power, 1870–1914

Norman Rich, *Great Power Diplomacy, 1814–1914* (New York: McGraw-Hill Higher Education, 1992). This work surveys diplomatic activities from the end of the Napoleonic Wars to the eve of World War I.

Alan Sked, *The Decline and Fall of the Habsburg Empire, 1815–1918* (London: Longman, 1989). An overview of the Habsburg Empire's history from Metternich to World War I. The author interprets the various historiographical debates over the collapse of Habsburg rule. Rather than treating the late empire as a case of inevitable decline, the book examines the monarchy as a viable institution within a multinational state.

The New Imperialism

David Cannadine, *Ornamentalism: How the British Saw Their Empire* (New York: Oxford University Press, 2001). The author approaches the history of the British Empire as interconnected with the history of the British nation and considers this "entire interactive system" in terms of a social construction and social perceptions.

Richard Drayton, *Nature's Government: Science, Imperial Britain, and the 'Improvement' of the World* (New Haven, Conn.: Yale University Press, 2000). A fascinating examination of the role scientists, and especially botanists, played as partners with bureaucratic government in British imperial expansion.

Daniel R. Headrick, *The Tentacles of Progress: Technology Transfer in the Age of Imperialism, 1850–1940* (New York: Oxford University Press, 1988). Argues that the transfer of technology to Africa and Asia by the Western imperial powers produced colonial underdevelopment.

Robert H. MacDonald, *The Language of Empire: Myths and Metaphors of Popular Imperialism, 1880–1918* (Manchester: Manchester University Press, 1994). In studying the new metaphors of imperialism, the author examines the role of mythmakers, such as Rudyard Kipling, and popular fiction in shaping imperial perceptions and experiences. The author argues that the very shaping of language about non-European lands and peoples helped determine the form empire took in Great Britain.

The European Search for Territory and Markets

Winfried Baumgart, *Imperialism: The Idea and Reality of British and French Colonial Expansion, 1880–1914* (New York: Oxford University Press, 1982). Principally concerned with the motives that led to imperial expansion, the author argues that motives were many and that each action must be studied in its specific social, political, and economic context.

Raymond F. Betts, *The False Dawn: European Imperialism in the Nineteenth Century* (Oxford: Oxford University Press, 1976). Explores the ideology of empire and the process of cultural transmission through colonial institutions.

Eric Hobsbawm, *The Age of Empire, 1875–1914* (New York: Pantheon, 1987). A wide-ranging interpretive history of the late nineteenth century that spans economic, social, political, and cultural developments.

Thomas Pakenham, *The Scramble for Africa* (New York: Random House, 1991). A narrative history of how Europeans subdivided Africa among themselves.

Results of a European-Dominated World

Barbara Bush, *Imperialism, Race and Resistance: Africa and Britain, 1919–1945* (New York: Routledge, 1999). The study begins with an examination of the impact of the First World War on west and south African race, culture, repression, and resistance through World War II.

Anna Davin, "Imperialism and Motherhood," *History Workshop*, no. 5 (Spring 1978): 9–65. Davin's article links imperialism and economic expansion with the increasing intervention of the state in family life. The author offers an analysis of an ideology that focused on the need to increase population in support of imperial aims and that led to the social construction of motherhood, domesticity, and individualism.

Johannes Fabian, *Language and Colonial Power: The Appropriation of Swahili in the Former Belgian Congo* (Cambridge: Cambridge University Press, 1986). Demonstrates how colonial power was exercised in the Belgian Congo through the study of the growth of Swahili as a lingua franca. The author pays particular attention to the uses of Swahili in industrial and other work situations.

Anne McClintock, *Imperial Leather: Race, Gender, and Sexuality in the Colonial Contest* (New York: Routledge, 1995). By using novels, diaries, advertisements, and other sources, the author demonstrates the relationship between images of domestic life and an ideology of imperial domination and focuses on the role of women in the colonial experience.

Paul B. Rich, *Race and Empire in British Politics* (Cambridge: Cambridge University Press, 1986). An intellectual history of ideas about race in the imperial tradition. Focusing on the years between 1890 and 1970, the author examines the political dimensions of race and race ideology in British society.

CHAPTER 26

WAR AND REVOLUTION, 1914–1920

THE VISUAL RECORD

SELLING THE GREAT WAR

ADVERTISING IS A POWERFUL INFLUENCE IN MODERN LIFE. The leaders of European nations discovered its power in the years of world war from 1914 to 1918. When death counts mounted, prices skyrocketed, and food supplies dwindled, the frenzy and fervor for the war flagged. Then governments came to rely more heavily on the art of persuasion. For the first time in history, war had to advertise.

Political leaders came to realize that the advertising techniques developed by business leaders in the early years of the twentieth century could be useful. Governments took up the "science" of selling—not products but the idea of war. Citizens had to be persuaded to join, to fight, to work, to save, and to believe in the national war effort. Warring nations learned how to organize enthusiasm and how to mobilize the masses in support of what proved to be a long and bloody conflict.

The German poster shows a dramatic appeal to women to support war work. A stern soldier whose visage and bearing communicate strength and singleness of purpose is backed up by an equally determined young woman. She is in the act of handing him a grenade as she stands with him, facing the unseen enemy. The poster reminds us of the centrality of women's work to the waging of a new kind of war in the twentieth century. The battlefront had to be backed up by a "home front"—a term that was used for the first time in the Great War—of working men, women, and even children.

Early war posters stressed justice and national glory. Later, as weariness with the war spread, the need for personal sacrifice became the dominant theme. Look at the sad female figure rising from a sea of suffering and death in the second poster. The woman, both goddesslike and vulnerable, symbolizes Great Britain. She is making a plea for action, seeking soldiers for her cause. This appeal for volunteers for the armed forces was unique to Great Britain, where conscription was not established until 1916. The dark suffering and death in the water, lapping at her robes, are reflected in her eyes. She evinces a fierce determination as she exhorts, "Take up the sword

of justice." In February 1915, Germany declared the waters around the British Isles to be a war zone. All British shipping was subject to attack as well as neutral merchant vessels, which were attacked without warning. In May 1915, the *Lusitania* was sunk, taking with it over 1,000 lives, including 128 Americans. The poster frames an illuminated horizon where a ship that is probably the *Lusitania* goes down. We need not read a word to understand the call to arms against the perfidy of an enemy who has killed innocent civilians. The female figure's determined jaw, clenched fist, and outstretched arms communicate the nobility of the cause and the certainty of success.

Civilians had to be mobilized for two reasons. First, soldiers at the front had to be constantly replenished from civilian reserves. Second, the costs of the war in food, equipment, and productive materials were so high that civilian populations had to be willing to endure great hardships to produce supplies for soldiers at the front. Nations at war used advertising to coordinate civilian and military contributions to a common cause.

LOOKING AHEAD

The European governments proudly "selling" war to their citizens in 1914 expected quick victories. Instead, they experienced a prolonged global war, costly in human life and material destruction, stretching out over four devastating years. Military technology and timetables called the tune in a defensive war fought from the trenches with sophisticated weapons capable of maiming and killing in new ways. The intervention of the United States and German defeat preceded a peace that reshaped Europe as a whole in fundamental ways. In the case of Russia, the war signaled political and social collapse and a revolution of unprecedented scale.

THE WAR EUROPE EXPECTED

In 1914, Europe stood confidently at the center of the world. Covering only seven percent of the earth's surface, Europe dominated the world's trade and was actively exporting both its goods and its culture all over the globe. The values of nineteenth-century liberalism permeated the self-confident world view of European men and women in 1914. They assumed that they could discover the rules that governed the world and use them to fashion a better civilization.

Many Europeans took stability and harmony for granted as preconditions for progress; yet they also recognized the usefulness of war. No one expected or wanted a general war, but liberal values served the goals of limited war, just as they had justified imperial conquest. Statesmen decided that there were rules to the game of war that could be employed in the interests of statecraft. Science and technology also served the interests of war. Statesmen and generals were sure that modern weapons would prevent a long war. Superiority in armed force became a priority for European states seeking to protect the peace.

The beginning of the modern arms race resulted in "armed peace" as a defense against war. Leaders nevertheless expected and planned for a short and limited war. Previous confrontations among European states had been limited in duration and destruction, as in the case of Prussia and France in 1870, or confined to peripheries, as squabbles among the Great Powers in Africa indicated. The alliance system was expected to defend the peace by defining the conditions of war.

As international tensions mounted, the hot summer days of 1914 were a time of hope and glory. The hope was that war, when it came, would be "over by Christmas." The glory was the promise of ultimate victory in the "crusade for civilization" that each nation's leaders held out to their people. When war did come in 1914, it was a choice, not an accident. Yet it was a choice that Europeans did not understand, one whose limits they could not control. Their unquestioned pride in reason and progress that ironically had led them to this war did not survive the four years of barbaric slaughter that followed.

Separating Friends from Foes

At the end of the nineteenth century, the world appeared to be coming together in a vast international network linked by commerce and finance. A system of alliances based on shared interests also connected states to one

European Alliances on the Eve of World War I. Alliance systems divided Europe into two great blocs with few countries remaining neutral.

another. After 1905, the intricate defensive alliances between and among the European states maintained the balance of power between two blocs of nations and helped to prevent one bloc from dominating the other. Yet by creating blocs, alliances identified foes as well as friends. On the eve of the war, France, Great Britain, and Russia stood together in the Triple Entente. Since 1882, Germany, Austria-Hungary, and Italy had joined forces in the Triple Alliance. Other states allied with one or the other of these blocs in pacts of mutual interest and protection. Throughout the world, whether in North Africa, the Balkans, or Asia, the power of some states was intended to balance the power of others. Yet the balance of power did not exist simply to preserve the peace. It existed to preserve a system of independent national societies—nation-states—in a precarious equilibrium. Gains in one area by one bloc had to be offset by compromises in another area to maintain the balance. Nations recognized limited conflict as a legitimate means of preserving equilibrium.

The alliance system of blocs reflected the growing impact of public opinion on international relations. Statesmen had the ability to manipulate the newspaper images of allies as good and rivals as evil. But controlling public opinion served to lock policy makers into permanent partnerships and "blank checks" of support for their allies. Western leaders understood that swings in public opinion in periods of crisis could hobble their efforts to act in the nation's best interest. Permanent military alliances with clearly identified "friends" therefore took the place of more fluid arrangements.

Because of treaty commitments, no country expected to face war alone. Alliances that guaranteed military support permitted weak nations to act irresponsibly, with the certainty that they would be defended by their more powerful partners. France and Germany were publicly committed to their weaker allies, Russia and Austria-Hungary, respectively, in supporting imperialist ambitions in the Balkans from which they themselves derived little direct benefit. The interlocking system of defensive alliances was structured to match strength against strength—France against Germany, for example—thereby making a prolonged war more likely than would be the case if a weak nation confronted a strong enemy. At base, the alliance system stood as both a defense against war and an invitation to it.

Military Timetables

As Europe soon discovered, military timetables restricted a country's options at times of conflict. The crisis of the summer of 1914 revealed the extent to which politicians and statesmen had come to rely on military expertise and strategic considerations for decisions. Military general staffs assumed increasing importance in state policy making. War planners became powerful as war was accepted as an alternative to negotiation. Germany's military preparations are a good example of how war strategy exacerbated crises and prevented peaceful solutions.

The Schlieffen Plan. Alfred von Schlieffen (1833–1913), the Prussian general and chief of the German General Staff from 1891 to 1905 who developed the war plan, understood little about politics but spent his life studying the strategic challenges of warfare. His war plan was designed to make Germany the greatest power on the Continent. The Schlieffen Plan, which he set before his fellow officers in 1905, was bold and daring: in the likely event of war with Russia, Germany would launch a devastating offensive against France. Schlieffen reasoned that France, with its strong military forces, would come to the aid of its ally, Russia. Russia, lacking a modern transportation system, could not mobilize as rapidly as France.

Russia also had the inestimable advantage of the ability to retreat into its vast interior. If Germany were pulled into a war with Russia, its western frontier would be vulnerable to France, Russia's powerful ally. The Schlieffen Plan recognized that France would have to be defeated before Germany could turn its forces eastward against Russia. The Schlieffen Plan thus committed Germany to a war with France, regardless of particular circumstances. Furthermore, with its strategy of invading the neutral countries of Belgium, Holland, and Luxembourg in order to defeat France in six weeks, the plan would have ignored the rights of the neutral countries.

Russia's Mobilization Plan and the French Plan XVII. Germany was not alone in being driven by military considerations. Russian military strategists planned full mobilization if war broke out with Austria-Hungary, which was menacing the interests of Russia's ally Serbia. Russia foresaw the likelihood that Germany would come to the aid of Austria-Hungary. Russia knew, too, that because of its primitive railway network, it would be unable to mobilize troops rapidly. To compensate for this weakness, Russian leaders planned to mobilize *before* war was declared. German military leaders had no choice in the event of full Russian mobilization but to mobilize their own troops immediately and to urge the declaration of war. Once a general mobilization was under way on both sides, conflict could hardly be avoided. Mobilization would mean war.

Like the Schlieffen Plan, the French Plan XVII called for the concentration of troops in a single area with the intention of decisively defeating the enemy. The French command, not well informed about German strengths and strategies, designated Alsace and Lorraine for the immediate offensive against Germany in the event of war. Plan XVII left Paris exposed to the German drive through Belgium that the Schlieffen Plan proposed.

Military leaders throughout Europe argued that if their plans were to succeed, speed was essential. Delays to consider peaceful solutions would cripple military responses. Diplomacy bowed to military strategy. When orders to mobilize went out, armies would be set on the march. Like a row of dominoes falling with the initial push, the two alliance systems would be at war.

Assassination at Sarajevo

A teenager with a handgun started the First World War. On 28 June 1914, in Sarajevo, the sleepy capital of the Austro-Hungarian province of Bosnia, Gavrilo Princip (1895–1918), a 19-year-old Bosnian Serb, repeatedly pulled the trigger of his Browning revolver, killing the designated heir of the Habsburg throne, Archduke Franz Ferdinand, and his wife, Sophie. Princip belonged to the Young Bosnian Society, a group of students, workers, a few peasants, Croats, Muslims, and intellectuals who wanted to free Slavic populations from Habsburg control. Princip was part of a growing movement of South Slavs struggling for national liberation from Austria-Hungary.

Struggle over control of the Balkans had been a long-standing issue that had involved all the major European powers for decades. As Austria-Hungary's ally since 1879, Germany was willing to support Vienna's showdown in the Balkans as a way of stopping Russian advances in the area. The alliance with Germany gave Austria-Hungary a sense of security and confidence to pursue its Balkan aims. Germany had its own plans for domination of the Continent and feared that a weakened Austria-Hungary would undermine its own position in central Europe. Independent Balkan states to the south and east were also a threat to Germany's plans. German leaders hoped that an Austro-Serbian war would remain localized and would strengthen their ally, Austria-Hungary. While Austria-Hungary had Germany's support, Serbia was backed by a sympathetic Russia favoring nationalist movements in the Balkans. Russia had, in turn, been encouraged by France, its ally by military pact since 1894, to take a firm stand in its struggle with Austria-Hungary for dominance among Balkan nationalities.

The interim of five weeks between the assassination of the Archduke Ferdinand and the outbreak of the war was a period of intense diplomatic activity. The assassination gave Austria-Hungary the excuse it needed to bring a troublesome Serbia into line. On 23 July 1914, Austria-Hungary issued an ultimatum to Serbia and secretly decided to declare war regardless of the Serbs' response. The demands were so severe that, if met, they would have stripped Serbia of its independence. Austria's aim was to destroy Serbia. In spite of a conciliatory, although not capitulatory, reply from Serbia to its ultimatum, Austria-Hungary declared war on the Balkan nation on 28 July 1914. Russia mobilized two days later. Germany mobilized in response to the Russian action and declared war on Russia on 1 August and on France on 3 August. France had begun mobilizing on 30 July, when its ally, Russia, entered the war.

Great Britain briefly attempted to mediate a settlement in the Austro-Serbian conflict, but once France declared war, the domino effect of the alliance system was triggered. On 4 August, after Germany had violated Belgian neutrality in its march to France, Great Britain honored its treaty obligations and declared war on Germany. Great Britain entered the war because it judged that a powerful Germany could use ports on the English Channel to invade the British Isles. Italy alone of the major powers remained for the moment outside the conflict. Although Italy was allied with Germany and Austria-Hungary, its own aspirations in the Balkans kept it from fighting for the Austrian cause in 1914.

Self-interest, fear, and ambition motivated the Great Powers in different ways in the pursuit of war. The international diplomatic system that had worked so well to prevent war in the preceding decades now enmeshed European states in interlocking alliances and created a chain reaction. The Austro-Serbian war of July 1914 became a Europe-wide war within a month.

A NEW KIND OF WARFARE

The expectation of a speedy war of decisive victories and domestic glory drove European leaders and their populations to embrace armed conflict as an acceptable means of mediating grievances in 1914. The peace that had been preserved from the end of the nineteenth century to 1914 was a precarious one indeed, predicated as it was on military timetables that planned for war and alliance systems that guaranteed that local disagreements would become international conflicts. The international mechanisms for keeping the peace led directly to war and guaranteed that once war broke out, it would not remain limited and local.

Early in the war, the best-laid plans of political and military leaders collapsed. First, Europe got a war that was not limited but spread quickly throughout Europe and became global. Switzerland, Spain, the Netherlands, and all of Scandinavia remained neutral, but every other European nation was pulled into the war. In August 1914, Japan cast its lot with the Allies, as the Entente came to be known, and in November the Ottoman Empire joined the Central Powers of Germany and Austria-Hungary. In the following year, Italy joined the war, not on the side of its long-term treaty partners, Germany and Austria-Hungary, but on the side of the Allies, with the expectation of benefiting in the Balkans from Austrian defeat. Bulgaria joined Germany and Austria-Hungary in 1915, seeking territory at Serbia's expense. By the time the United States joined the fray in 1917, the war had become a world war.

The second surprise for the European powers was that they did not get a preventive war of movement or one of short duration. Within weeks that pattern had given way to what promised to be a long and costly war of attrition. The war started as German strategists had planned, with

ALL QUIET ON THE WESTERN FRONT

Eyewitness accounts described the horrors of the new trench warfare. But no one captured the war better than the German novelist Erich Maria Remarque (1898–1970), who drew on his own wartime experiences in All Quiet on the Western Front. *Published in 1928 and subsequently translated into 25 languages, this powerful portrayal of the transformation of a school boy into a soldier indicts the inhumanity of war and pleads for peace. Stressing the camaraderie of fighting men and sympathy for the plight of the enemy soldier, Remarque also underscored the alienation of a whole generation—the lost generation of young men who could not go home again after the war.*

FOCUS QUESTIONS

In the final paragraph, the narrator tells us his age. Would you have guessed his age from the opening three paragraphs? How does the narrator's description of his generation transcend enemy lines?

ATTACK, COUNTER-ATTACK, CHARGE, REPULSE—these are words, but what things they signify! We have lost a good many men, mostly recruits. Reinforcements have again been sent up to our sector. They are one of the new regiments, composed almost entirely of young fellows just called up. They have had hardly any training, and are sent into the field with only a theoretical knowledge. They do know what a hand-grenade is, it is true, but they have very little idea of cover, and what is most important of all, have no eye for it. A fold in the ground has to be quite eighteen inches high before they can see it.

Although we need reinforcement, the recruits give us almost more trouble than they are worth. They are helpless in this grim fighting area, they fall like flies. Modern trench-warfare demands knowledge and experience; a man must have a feeling for the contours of the ground, an ear for the sound and character of the shells, must be able to decide beforehand where they will drop, how they will burst, and how to shelter from them.

The young recruits of course know none of these things. They get killed simply because they hardly can tell shrapnel from high-explosive, they are mown down because they are listening anxiously to the roar of the big coal-boxes falling in the rear, and miss the light, piping whistle of the low spreading daisy-cutters. They flock together like sheep instead of scattering, and even the wounded are shot down like hares by the airmen.

Their pale turnip faces, their pitiful clenched hands, the fine courage of these poor devils, the desperate charges and attacks made by the poor brave wretches, who are so terrified that they dare not cry out loudly, but with battered chests, with torn bellies, arms and legs only whimper softly for their mothers and cease as soon as one looks at them.

Their sharp, downy, dead faces have the awful expressionlessness of dead children. . . .

I am young, I am twenty years old; yet I know nothing of life but despair, death, fear, and fatuous superficiality cast over an abyss of sorrow. I see how peoples are set against one another, and in silence, unknowingly, foolishly, obediently, innocently slay one another. I see that the keenest brains of the world invent weapons and words to make it yet more refined and enduring. And all men of my age, here and over there, throughout the whole world see these things; all my generation is experiencing these things with me. What would our fathers do if we suddenly stood up and came before them and proffered our account? What do they expect of us if a time ever comes when the war is over? Through the years our business has been killing;—it was our first calling in life. Our knowledge of life is limited to death. What will happen afterwards? And what shall come out of us?

From Erich Maria Remarque, *All Quiet on the Western Front.*

German victory in battle after battle. The end seemed near. But in less than a month, the war changed in ways that no one had predicted. Technology was the key to understanding the change and to explaining the surprises.

Technology and the Trenches

In nineteenth-century European warfare, armies had relied on mobile cavalry and infantry units whose greatest asset was speed. Rapid advance had been decisive in the Prussian victory over the French in 1870, which had resulted in the formation of the German Empire.

Digging In. Soldiers of the twentieth century were also trained for a moving war, high maneuverability, and maximum territorial conquest. Yet after the first six weeks of battle, soldiers found themselves having to dig ditches and fight from fixed positions. Soldiers on both sides shoveled out trenches four feet deep, piled up sandbags, mounted their machine guns, and began to fight an unplanned, defensive war.

The front lines of Europe's armies in the west wallowed in the trenches that ran from the English Channel to the Swiss frontier. The British and French on one side and the Germans on the other fought each other with machine guns and mortars, backed up by heavy artillery to the rear. Strategists on both sides believed that they could break through enemy lines. As a result, the gruesome monotony of trench warfare was punctuated periodically by infantry offensives in which large concentrations of artillery caused immense bloodshed. Ten million men were killed in this bizarre and deadly combination of old and new warfare. The glamour of battle that attracted many young men disappeared quickly in the daily reality of living in mud with rats and constantly facing death. The British poet Wilfred Owen (1893–1918) wrote shortly before his own death in battle about how the soldier next to him had been shot in the head, soaking Owen in blood: "I shall feel again as soon as I dare, but now I must not."

New Weapons. The invention of new weaponry and heavy equipment had transformed war, but some old ways persisted. In their bright blue coats and red trousers, French and Belgian infantrymen made easy targets. Cavalry units, though largely outmoded, survived even as the railroad made the mobilization, organization, and deployment of mass armies possible. Specialists were needed to control the new war machines that heavy industry had created.

The shovel and the machine gun transformed war. The machine gun was not new in 1914, but its strategic value was not fully appreciated before then. The British had used the Maxim machine gun in Africa, but strategists failed to ask how such a destructive weapon would work against an enemy that was equally armed with machine guns instead of spears. Military strategists continued to plan an offensive strategy when the weaponry developed for massive destruction had pushed them into fighting a defensive war from the trenches. Both sides resorted to concentration of artillery, increased use of poison gas, and unrestricted submarine warfare in desperate attempts to break the deadlock caused by meeting armed force with force.

The new emphasis on total victory drove the Central Powers and the Allies to grisly new inventions. Late in the war, the need to break the deadlock of trench warfare ushered in the airplane and the tank. Neither was decisive in altering the course of the war, although the airplane was useful for reconnaissance and for limited bombing and the tank promised the means of breaking through defensive lines. Chlorine gas was first used in warfare by the Germans in 1915. "Mustard" gas, which was named for its distinctive smell and which caused severe blistering, was introduced two years later. The Germans were the first to use flamethrowers, which were especially effective against mechanized vehicles with vulnerable fuel tanks. Barbed wire, invented in the American Midwest to contain farm animals, became an essential aspect of trench warfare as it marked off the no-man's-land between combatants and prevented surprise attacks.

A typical World War I trench. Millions of soldiers lived amid mud, disease, and vermin, awaiting death from enemy shells. After the French army mutiny in 1916, the troops wrung the concession from their commanders: that they would not have to charge German machine guns while armed only with rifles.

The technology that had been viewed as a proof of progress was now channeled toward engineering new instruments of death. Some new weapons gave rise to their antidotes; for example, the invention of deadly gas was followed soon after by the invention of gas masks. Each side was capable of matching the other's ability to devise new armaments. Deadlocks caused by technological parity forced both sides to resort to desperate concentrations of men and weaponry that resulted not in decisive battles but in ever-escalating casualty rates. As they improved their efficiency at killing, the European powers were not finding a way to end the war.

The German Offensive

German forces seized the offensive in the west and invaded neutral Belgium at the beginning of August 1914. The Belgians resisted stubbornly but unsuccessfully. Belgian forts were systematically captured, and Brussels, the capital, fell under the German advance on 20 August. After the fall of Belgium, German military might swept into northern France with the intention of defeating the French in six weeks.

Germany on Two Fronts. In the years preceding the war, the German General Staff, unwilling to concentrate all of their troops in the west, had modified the Schlieffen Plan by committing divisions to Germany's eastern frontier. The absence of the full German fighting force in the west did not appreciably slow the German advance through Belgium. Yet the Germans had underestimated both the cost of holding back the French in Alsace-Lorraine and the difficulty of maneuvering German forces and transporting supplies in an offensive war. Eventually, unexpected Russian advances in the east also siphoned off troops from the west. German forces in the west were so weakened by their offensive that they were unable to swing west of Paris, as planned, and instead chose to enter the French capital from the northeast by crossing the Marne River. This shift exposed the German First Army on its western flank and opened up a gap on its eastern flank.

The First Battle of the Marne. Despite an initial pattern of retreat and a lack of coordination of forces, Allied French and British troops were ready to take advantage of the vulnerabilities in the German advance. In a series of battles between 6 and 10 September 1914 that came to be known as the First Battle of the Marne, the Allies counterattacked and advanced into the gap. The German army was forced to drop back. In the following months, each army tried to outflank the other in what has been called "the race to the sea." By late fall it was clear that the battles from the Marne north to the border town of Ypres in northwest Belgium near the English Channel had ended an open war of movement on the western front. Soldiers now dug in along a line of battle that changed little in the long three and a half years until March 1918.

The Allies gained a strategic victory in the First Battle of the Marne by resisting the German advance in the fighting that quickly became known as the "miracle" of the Marne. The legend was further enhanced by true stories of French troops being rushed from Paris to the front in taxicabs. Yet the real significance of the Marne lay in the severe miscalculations of military leaders and statesmen on both sides, who had expected a different kind of war. They did not understand that the new technology made a short war unlikely. Nor did they understand the demands that this new kind of warfare would make on civilian populations. Those Parisian taxi drivers foreshadowed how other European civilians would be called on again and again to support the war in the next four years.

"I don't know what is to be done—this isn't war." So spoke Lord Horatio Kitchener (1850–1916), one of the most decorated British generals of his time. He was not alone in his bafflement over the stalemate of trench warfare at the end of 1914. By that time, Germany's greatest fear, a simultaneous war on two fronts, had become a grim reality. The Central Powers were under siege, cut off from the world by the great battlefront in the west and by the Allied blockade at sea. The rules of the game had changed, and the European powers settled in for a long war.

War on the Eastern Front

War on Germany's eastern front was a mobile war, unlike its western counterpart, because there were fewer men and guns in relation to the vast distances.

Russian Tribulations. The Russian army was the largest in the world. Yet it was crippled from the outbreak of the war by inadequate supplies and poor leadership. At the end of August 1914, the smaller German army, supported by divisions drawn from the west, delivered a devastating defeat to the Russians in the one great battle on the eastern front. At Tannenberg the entire Russian Second Army was destroyed, and about 100,000 Russian soldiers were taken prisoner. Faced with this humiliation, General Aleksandr Vasilievich Samsonov (1859–1914), head of the Russian forces, committed suicide on the field of battle.

The German general Paul von Hindenburg (1847–1934), a veteran of the Franco-Prussian war of 1870, had been recalled from retirement to direct the campaign against the Russians because of his intimate knowledge of the area. Assisted by Quartermaster General Erich Ludendorff (1865–1937), Hindenburg followed the stunning victory of Tannenberg two weeks later with another devastating blow to Russian forces at the Masurian Lakes.

The Russians were holding up their end of the bargain in the Allied war effort, but at great cost. They kept the Germans busy and forced them to divert troops to the eastern front, weakening the German effort to knock France out of the war. In the south the tsar's troops defeated the Austro-Hungarian army at Lemberg in Galicia in September. This Russian victory gave Serbia a temporary reprieve. But by mid-1915, Germany had thrown the Russians back and was keeping Austria-Hungary propped up in the war. By fall, Russia had lost most of Galicia, the Polish lands of the Russian Empire, Lithuania, and parts of Latvia and Belorussia to the advancing enemy. These losses amounted to 15 percent of Russia's territory and 20 percent of its population. The Russian army staggered, with over one million soldiers taken as prisoners of war and at least as many killed and wounded.

The Russian army, as one of its own officers described it, was being bled to death. Russian soldiers were poorly led into battle or not led at all because of the shortage of officers. Munitions shortages meant that soldiers often went into battle without rifles, armed only with the hope of scavenging arms from their fallen comrades. Despite these difficulties, the Russians, under the direction of General Aleksei Brusilov (1853–1926), commander of the Russian armies in the southern part of the eastern front, remarkably managed to throw back the Austro-Hungarian forces in 1916 and almost eliminated Austria as a military power. But this was the last great campaign on the eastern front and Russia's last show of strength in the Great War.

Russia Leaves the War. Russia's near destruction of the Austrian army benefited Russia's allies tremendously. To protect its partner, Germany was forced to withdraw eight divisions from Italy, alleviating the Allied situation in the Tyrol, and twelve divisions from the western front, provid-

World War I. The Central Powers were in the unenviable position of fighting wars on two major fronts. The inset shows the stabilized Western Front of trench warfare in northern France and Belgium.

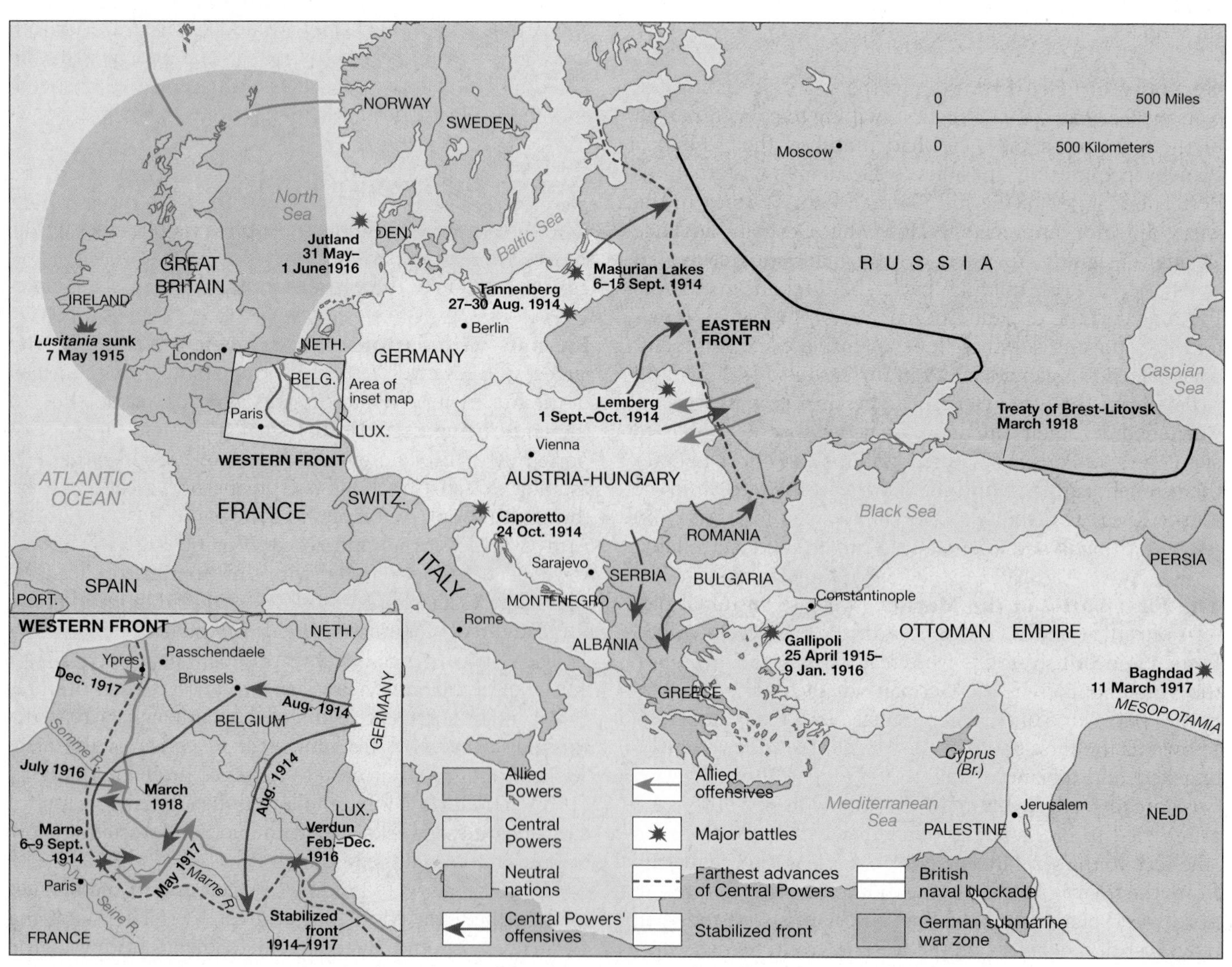

ing relief for the French at Verdun and the British at the Somme. In addition, Russia sent troops to the aid of a new member of the Allied camp, Romania, an act that probably further weakened Brusilov's efforts. In response to Brusilov's challenge, the Germans established control over the Austrian army, assigning military command of the coalition to General Ludendorff.

By the summer of 1917 the tsardom had been overthrown, and a provisional government ruled Russia. Tens of thousands of Russian soldiers were walking away from the war. Russia withdrew from the war and in March 1918 signed a separate peace by which Germany gained extensive territorial advantages and important supply bases for carrying on the war in the west. To protect these territories and their resources, the Germans had to maintain an army on this front. No longer fighting in the east, however, Germany could release the bulk of its forces to fight in the west.

War on the Western Front

Along hundreds of miles of trenches, the French and British tried repeatedly to expel the Germans from northern France and Belgium. Long periods of inactivity were punctuated by orgies of heavy bloodletting. The German phrase "All quiet on the western front" was used in military communiques to describe those periods of uneasy calm before the next violent storm.

Verdun. Military leaders on both sides hoped for a decisive breakthrough that would win the war. In 1916, the Allies planned a joint strike at the Somme, a river in northern France that flowed west into the English Channel, but the Germans struck first at Verdun, a small fortress city in northeast France. By concentrating great numbers of troops, the Germans outnumbered the French five to two. As General Erich von Falkenhayn (1861–1922), chief of the General Staff of the German army from 1914 to 1916, explained it, the German purpose in attacking Verdun was "to bleed the French white by virtue of our superiority in guns."

On the first day of the battle, one million shells were fired. The battlefield was a living hell as soldiers stumbled across corpse after corpse. Against the German onslaught, French troops were instructed to hold out, though they lacked adequate artillery and reinforcements. General Joseph Joffre (1852–1931), commander-in-chief of the French army, was unwilling to divert reinforcements to Verdun.

The German troops advanced easily through the first lines of defense. But the French held their position for ten long, horrifying months of continuous mass slaughter from February to December 1916. General Henri Philippe Pétain (1856–1951) bolstered morale by constantly rotating his troops such that most of the French army—259 of 330 infantry battalions—saw action at Verdun. Nearly starving and poorly armed, the French stood alone in the bloodiest offensive of the war. Attack strategy backfired on the Germans as their own death tolls mounted.

Pétain and his flamboyant general Robert Georges Nivelle (1856–1924) were both hailed as heroes for fulfilling the instruction to their troops: "They shall not pass." Falkenhayn fared less well and was dismissed from his post. Yet no real winners emerged from the scorched earth of Verdun, where observers could see the nearest thing to desert created in Europe. Verdun was a disaster. The French suffered over half a million total casualties. German casualties were almost as high. A few square miles of territory had changed hands back and forth. In the end, no military advantage was gained, though almost 700,000 lives had been lost. Verdun demonstrated that an offensive war under these conditions was impossible.

The Somme. Still, new offensives were devised. The British went ahead with their planned offensive on the Somme in July 1916. For an advance of seven miles, 400,000 British and 200,000 French soldiers were killed or wounded. German losses brought the total casualties of this offensive to one million men. Despite his experience at Verdun, French general Robert Nivelle planned his own offensive in the Champagne region in spring 1917. Nivelle's offensive resulted in 40,000 deaths, and he was dismissed. The French army was falling apart; mutiny and insubordination were everywhere.

The British believed that they could succeed where the French had failed. Under General Douglas Haig (1861–1928), the commander-in-chief of British expeditionary forces on the Continent, the British launched an attack in Flanders through the summer and fall of 1917. Known as the Passchendaele offensive, named for the village and ridge in whose "porridge of mud" much of the fighting took place, this campaign resulted in almost 400,000 British soldiers slaughtered for insignificant territorial gain. The Allies and the Germans finally recognized that "going over the top" in offensives was not working and could not work. The war must be won by other means.

War on the Periphery

Recognizing the stalemate in the west, the Allies attempted to open up other fronts where the Central Powers might be vulnerable. In the spring of 1915, the Allies were successful in convincing Italy to enter the war on their side by promising that it would receive, at the time of the peace, the South Tyrol and the southern part of Dalmatia and key Dalmatian islands, which would assure Italy's dominance over the Adriatic Sea. By thus capitalizing on Italian antagonism toward Austria-Hungary over control of this territory, the Allies gained 875,000 Italian soldiers for their cause. Although these Italian troops were in no way decisive in the fighting that followed, Great Britain, France, and Russia saw the need to build up Allied support in southern Europe to reinforce Serbian attempts to keep Austrian troops beyond its borders. The Allies also hoped that by pulling Germans into this southern front, some relief might be provided for British and French soldiers on the western front.

Germany, in turn, was well aware of the need to expand its alliances beyond Austria-Hungary if it was to compete successfully against superior Allied forces. Trapped as they were to the east and west, the Central Powers established control over a broad corridor stretching from the North Sea through central Europe and down through the Ottoman Empire to the Suez Canal, which was so vital to British interests. In the Balkans, where the war had begun, the Serbs were consistently bested by the Austrians. By late 1915, the Serbs were knocked out of the war, having lost one-sixth of their population through war, famine, and disease. The promise of booty persuaded Bulgaria to join Germany and Austria-Hungary. Over the next year and a half, the Allies responded by convincing Romania and then Greece to join them.

War in the Ottoman Empire. The theater of war continued to expand. Although the Ottoman Empire had joined the war in late 1914 on the side of the Central Powers, its own internal difficulties attenuated its fighting ability. As a multinational empire consisting of Turks, Arabs, Armenians, Greeks, Kurds, and other ethnic minorities, it was plagued by Turkish misrule and Arab nationalism. Hence the Ottoman Empire was the weakest link in the chain of German alliances. Yet it held a crucial position. The Turks could block shipping of vital supplies to Russia through the Mediterranean and Black Seas. Coming to the aid of their Russian ally, a combined British and French fleet attacked Turkish forces at the strait of the Dardanelles in April 1915. In the face of political and military opposition, First Lord of the Admiralty Winston Churchill (1874–1965) supported the idea of opening a new front by sea. Poorly planned and mismanaged, the expedition was a disaster. When the naval effort in the German-mined strait failed, the British foolishly decided to land troops on the Gallipoli peninsula, which extends from the southern coast of European Turkey. There British soldiers were trapped on the rocky terrain, unable to advance against the Turks, unable to fall back. Gallipoli was the first large-scale attempt at amphibious warfare. The Australian and New Zealand forces (ANZACs) showed great bravery in some of the most brutal fighting of the war. Critics in Britain argued that the only success of the nine-month campaign was its evacuation.

Britain sought to protect its interests in the Suez Canal. Turkish troops menaced the canal effectively enough to terrify the British into maintaining an elaborate system of defense in the area and concentrating large troop reinforcements in Egypt. War with the Ottoman Empire also extended battle into the oil fields of Mesopotamia and Persia. This attempt at a new front was initially a fiasco for the British and Russian forces that threatened Baghdad. The Allies proceeded not only without plans but also without maps. They literally did not know where they were going. Eventually, British forces recovered and took Baghdad in 1917, while Australian and New Zealand troops captured Jerusalem. The tentacles of war spread out, following the path of Western economic and imperial interests throughout the world.

War at Sea. Most surprising of all was the indecisive nature of the war at sea. The great battleships of the British and German navies avoided confrontation on the high seas. The only major naval battle of the Great War, the Battle of Jutland in the North Sea, took place in early 1916. Each side inflicted damage on the other but, through careful maneuvering, avoided a decisive outcome

Crew on the deck of a German World War I submarine at sea.

to the battle. Probably the enormous cost of replacing battleships deterred both the British and the Germans from risking their fleets in engagements on the high seas. With the demands for munitions and equipment on the two great land fronts of the war, neither side could afford to lose a traditional war at sea. Instead, the British used their seapower as a policing force to blockade German trade and strangle the German economy.

The German navy, much weaker than the British, relied on a new weapon, the submarine, which threatened to become decisive in the war at sea. During the first months of the war, submarines were used for reconnaissance, but their battle potential became apparent in 1915. Undergoing technological improvements throughout the war, *Unterseebooten*, or U-boats, as German submarines were called, torpedoed six million tons of Allied shipping in 1917. With cruising ranges as high as 3,600 miles, German submarines attacked Allied and neutral shipping as far away as off the shore of the United States and the Arctic supply line to Russia. Outraged neutral powers considered the Germans to be in violation of international law. The Germans also rejected the requirements of warning an enemy ship and boarding it for investigation as too dangerous for submarines, which were no match for battleships above water. The Allies invented depth charges and mines that were capable of blowing German submarines out of the water. These weapons, combined with the use of the convoy system in the Atlantic and the Mediterranean, produced a successful blockade and antisubmarine campaign that put an end to the German advantage.

ADJUSTING TO THE UNEXPECTED: TOTAL WAR

The Great War differed from all previous European experiences and expectations of armed conflict. Technological advances, equally matched on both sides, introduced a war of attrition, defensive and prolonged. Nineteenth-century wars generally lasted six to eight weeks, were confined to one locale, and were determined by a handful of battles marked by low casualties. Such wars had nothing in common with the long, dirty, lice-infested reality of trench warfare with no end in sight to the slaughter.

The period from 1914 to 1918 marked the first time in history that the productive activities of entire populations were directed toward a single goal: military victory. The Great War became a war of peoples, not just of armies. This unexpected war of attrition required civilian populations to adjust to a situation in which what went on at the battlefront transformed life on the home front. For this reason the Great War became known as history's first *total* war.

Adjusting to the revolutionary concept of total war, governments intervened to centralize and control every aspect of economic life. The scale of production and distribution of war-related materials that victory required was unprecedented. To persuade civilians to suffer at home for the sake of the war, leaders pictured the enemy as an evil villain who must be defeated at any cost. The sacrifice required for a total war made total victory necessary. And total victory required an economy that was totally geared to fighting the war.

Mobilizing the Home Front

While soldiers were fighting on the eastern and western fronts, businessmen and politicians at home were creating bureaucratic administrations to control wages and prices, distribute supplies, establish production quotas, and, in general, mobilize human and material resources. The Allies and Central Powers organized civilians of all ages and both sexes to work for the war.

Women's Roles. Women played an essential role on the home front. They had never been isolated from the experiences and hardships of war, but they now found new ways to support the war effort. In cities, women went to work in munitions factories and war-related industries that had previously employed only men. Women filled service jobs, from firefighters to trolley-car conductors, jobs that were essential to the smooth running of industrial society and that men had left vacant. On farms, women literally took up the plow, as both men and horses were requisitioned for the war effort.

By 1918, 650,000 French women were working in war-related industries and in clerical positions in the army, and they had counterparts all over Europe. In Germany, two out of every five munitions workers were women. In Great Britain, the number of women workers jumped from 250,000 at the beginning of the war to five million by the war's end. Women also served in the auxiliary units of the armed services in the clerical and medical corps. In eastern European nations, women entered combat as soldiers. Although most women were displaced from their wartime jobs with the return of men after the armistice, they were as important to the war effort as were the men fighting at the front.

Government Controls. In the first months of the war, the private sector had been left to its own devices, with nearly disastrous results. Shortages, especially of shells, and bottlenecks in production threatened military efforts. Governments were forced to establish controls and to set up state monopolies to guarantee the supplies necessary to wage war. In Germany, industrialists Walter Rathenau (1867–1922) and Alfred Hugenberg (1865–1951) worked with the government. By the spring of 1915, they had eliminated the German problem of munitions scarcity. France was in trouble six weeks after the outbreak of the war: it had used up half of its accumulated munitions supplies in the First Battle of the Marne. German occupation of France's northern industrial basin further crippled munitions production. Through government intervention, France improvised and relocated its war industries. The British government became involved in production, too, by establishing in 1915 the first Ministry of Munitions under the direction of David Lloyd George (1863–1945). Distinct from the Ministry of War, the Ministry of Munitions was to coordinate military needs with the armaments industry.

In a war that leaders soon realized would be a long one, food supplies assumed paramount importance. As the war pulled men off the farms, production declined. Germany, dependent on food imports and isolated from the world market by the Allied blockade, introduced rationing five months after the outbreak of the war. Other Continental nations followed suit. Government agents set quotas for agricultural producers. Armies were fed and supplied at the expense of domestic populations. Great Britain, which enjoyed a more reliable food supply by virtue of its sea power, did not impose food rationing until 1917.

Silencing Dissent

The strains of total war were becoming apparent. Two years of sacrificing and, in some areas, starving began to take their toll among soldiers and civilians on both sides. With the lack of decisive victories, war weariness was spreading. Work stoppages and strikes, which had virtually ceased with the outbreak of war in 1914, began to increase rapidly in 1916. Between 1915 and 1916 in France, the number of strikes by dissatisfied workers increased by 400 percent. Underpaid and tired workers went on strike, staged demonstrations, and protested exploitation. Labor militancy also intensified in the British Isles and Germany. Women were often in the forefront of these protests throughout Europe. Social peace between unions and governments was no longer held together by patriotic enthusiasm for war.

Politicians, too, began to rethink their suspension of opposition to government policies as the war dragged on. Dissidents among European socialist parties regained their prewar commitment to peace. Most Socialists had enthusiastically supported the declarations of war in 1914. By 1916, the united front that political opponents had presented against the enemy was crumbling under growing demands for peace.

In a total war, unrest at home guaranteed defeat. Governments knew that all opposition to war policies had to be eliminated. In a dramatic extension of the police powers of the state, among both the Allies and the Central Powers, criticism of the government became treason. Censorship was enforced. Propaganda became more virulent. Anyone who spoke for peace was no better than the enemy. The governments of every warring nation resorted to harsh measures. Parliamentary bodies were stripped of power, civil liberties were suspended, and democratic procedures were ignored. The civilian governments of Premier Georges Clemenceau (1841–1929) in France and Prime Minister Lloyd George in Great Britain resorted to rule by emergency police power to repress criticism. Under Generals von Hindenburg and Ludendorff in Germany, military rule became the order of the day. Nowhere was government as usual possible in total war.

Every warring nation also sought to promote dissension among the populations of its enemies. Germany aided the Easter Rebellion in Ireland in 1916 in the hope that the Irish demand for independence would damage British fighting strength and morale. Germany also supported separatist movements among minority nationalities in the Russian Empire and was responsible for returning the avowed revolutionary V. I. Lenin under escort to Russia in April 1917. The British engaged in similar tactics. The British foreign secretary Arthur Balfour (1848–1930) worked with Zionist leaders in 1917 in drawing up the Balfour Declaration, which promised to "look with favor" on the creation of a Jewish homeland in Palestine. The British thereby encouraged Zionist hopes among central European Jews, with the intent of creating difficulties for German and Austrian rulers. Similarly, the British encouraged Arabs to rebel against Turks with the same promise of Palestine.

Turning Point and Victory, 1917–1918

For the Allies, 1917 began with a series of crises. Under the hammering of one costly offensive after another, French morale had collapsed, and military discipline was deteriorating. A combined German-Austrian force had eliminated the Allied states of Serbia and Romania. The Italians experienced a military debacle at Caporetto and were effectively out of the war.

"The Blackest Year of the War." The year 1917 was "the blackest year of the war" for the Allies. At the beginning of the year the peril on the sea had increased with the opening of unrestricted U-boat warfare against Allied and neutral shipping. The greatest blow came when Russia, now in the throes of domestic revolution, withdrew. Germany was able to concentrate more of its resources in the west and fight a one-front war. It was also able to use the foodstuffs and raw materials of its newly acquired Russian territories to buoy its home front.

Yet in spite of Allied reversals, the war was not turning in favor of the Central Powers. Both Austria-Hungary and the Ottoman Empire teetered on the verge of collapse, with internal difficulties increasing as the war dragged on. Germany suffered from labor and supply shortages and economic hardship, resulting from the blockade and an economy totally dedicated to waging war.

The war had gone from a stalemate to a state of crisis for both sides. Every belligerent state was experiencing war weariness, and pressures to end the war increased everywhere. Attrition was not working. Attacks were not working. Every country suffered from strikes, food riots, military desertions, and mutinies. Defeatism was everywhere on the rise.

The United States Enters the War. The Allies longed for the entry of the United States into the war. Although the United States was a neutral country, it had become an important supplier to the Allies from early in the war. American trade with the Allies had jumped from $825 million in 1914 to $3.2 billion in 1916. American bankers also made loans and extended credit to the Allies to the amount of $2.2 billion. The United States had made a sizable investment in the Allied war effort, and its economy was prospering.

Beginning with the sinking of the *Lusitania* in 1915, German policy on the high seas had incensed the American public. Increased U-boat activity in 1916 led President Woodrow Wilson (1856–1924) to issue a severe warning to the Germans to cease submarine warfare. However, the Germans were desperate, and the great advantage of submarines was in sneak attacks, a procedure that was against the international rules that required a warning. Germany initiated a new phase of unrestricted submarine warfare on 1 February 1917, when the German ambassador informed the U.S. government that U-boats would sink on sight all ships, including passenger ships, even those that were neutral and unarmed.

German machinations in Mexico were also revealed on 25 February 1917, with the interception of a telegram from Arthur Zimmermann (1864–1940), the German foreign minister. The telegram communicated Germany's willingness to support Mexico's recovery of "lost territory" in New Mexico, Arizona, and Texas in return for Mexican support of Germany in the event of U.S. entry into the war. American citizens were outraged. On 2 April 1917, Wilson, who had won the presidential election of 1916 on the promise of peace, asked the U.S. Congress for a declaration of war against Germany.

The entry of the United States was the turning point in the war, tipping the scales dramatically in favor of the Allies. The United States contributed its naval power to the large Allied convoys that formed to protect shipping against German attacks. In a total war, control and shipment of resources had become crucial issues, and it was in these areas that the U.S. entry gave the Allies indisputable superiority. The United States also sent "over there" tens of thousands of conscripts fighting with the American Expeditionary Forces under the leadership of General John "Black Jack" Pershing (1860–1948). They reinforced British and French troops and gave a vital boost to morale.

The U.S. government was new to the business of coordinating a war effort, but it displayed great ingenuity in creating a wartime bureaucracy that increased a small military establishment of 210,000 soldiers to 9.5 million young men registered before the beginning of summer 1917. By July 1918, the Americans were sending a phenomenal 300,000 soldiers a month to Europe. By the end of the war, two million Americans had traveled to Europe to fight in the war.

The U.S. entry is significant not just because it provided reinforcements, fresh troops, and fresh supplies to the beleaguered Allies. From a broader perspective, it marked a shift in the nature of international politics: Europe could no longer handle its own affairs and settle its own differences without outside help.

U.S. troops, although numerous, were not well trained, and they relied on France and Great Britain for their arms and equipment. But the Germans were aware that they could not hold out indefinitely against this superior Allied force. Austria-Hungary was effectively out of the war. Germany had no replacements for its fallen soldiers, but it was able to transfer troops from Russia, Romania, and Macedonia to the west. Realizing that its only chance of victory lay in swift action, the German high command decided on a bold measure: one great, final offensive that would knock the combined forces of Great Britain, France, and the United States out of the war once and for all by striking at a weak point and smashing through enemy lines. It almost worked.

German Defeat. Known as the Ludendorff offensive, after the general who devised it, the final German push began in March 1918. Secretly amassing tired troops from the eastern front who had been pulled back after the Russian withdrawal, the Germans counted on the element

CHRONOLOGY

FIGHTING THE GREAT WAR

1905	Development of the Schlieffen Plan
28 June 1914	Assassination of Archduke Franz Ferdinand and his wife, Sophie
28 July 1914	Austria-Hungary declares war on Serbia
30 July–4 August 1914	Russia, France, Britain, and Germany declare war in accordance with system of alliances
August 1914	Germany invades Belgium
6–10 September 1914	First Battle of the Marne
1915	Germany introduces chlorine gas
April 1915–January 1916	Gallipoli Campaign
May 1915	Sinking of the *Lusitania*
February–December 1916	Battle at Verdun
1917	First use of mustard gas
2 April 1917	United States enters war
March 1918	Russia withdraws
11 November 1918	Armistice

of surprise to enable them to break through a weak sector in the west. On the first day of spring, Ludendorff struck. The larger German force gained initial success against weakened British and French forces. Yet in spite of breaches in defense, the Allied line held. The Allied Supreme Commander, General Ferdinand Foch (1851–1929), coordinated the war effort that withstood German offensives throughout the spring and early summer of 1918.

The final drive came in mid-July. More than one million German soldiers had already been killed, wounded, or captured in the months between March and July. German prisoners of war gave the French details of Ludendorff's plan. The Germans, now exposed and vulnerable, were placed on the defensive. The German army was rapidly disintegrating. On the other side, tanks, plentiful munitions, and U.S. reinforcements fueled an Allied offensive that began in late September. The German army retreated, destroying property and equipment as it went. With weak political leadership and indecision in Berlin, the Germans held on until early November. The end finally came after four years of war. On 11 November 1918, an armistice signed by representatives of the German and Allied forces took effect.

The war had dragged on for slightly more than four years with great destruction and loss of life on both sides. Of the 70 million who were mobilized, about one in eight were killed. Battlefields of scorched earth and mud-filled ditches, silent at last, scarred once-fertile countrysides as grim memorials to history's first total war. In the end, only the entry of the United States into the war on the side of the Allies brought an end to the misery and bloodletting. The task of settling the peace now loomed.

RESHAPING EUROPE: AFTER WAR AND REVOLUTION

In the aftermath of war, the task of the victors was to devise a settlement that would guarantee peace and stabilize Europe. Russia was excluded from the negotiations because of its withdrawal from the Allied camp in 1917, but much of what happened in the peace settlements reflected concern with the challenge of revolution that the new Soviet Russia represented. A variety of goals marked the peace talks: the idealistic desire to create a better world, the patriotic pursuit of self-defense, the commitment to self-determination of nations (the right of a people to determine their own form of government), and the fixing of blame for the outbreak of the war. In the end, the peace treaties satisfied none of these goals. Meanwhile, Russia's new leaders carefully watched events in the West, looking for opportunities that might permit them to extend their revolution to central Europe.

Settling the Peace

From January to June 1919, an assembly of nations convened in Paris to draw up the new European peace. Although the primary task of settling the peace fell to the

The representatives of the victorious Allies at Versailles: (left to right) David Lloyd George of Great Britain, Vittorio Orlando of Italy, Georges Clemenceau of France, and Woodrow Wilson of the United States.

Council of Four—Premier Georges Clemenceau of France, Prime Minister David Lloyd George of Great Britain, Prime Minister Vittorio Emanuele Orlando of Italy, and President Woodrow Wilson of the United States—small states, newly formed states, and non-European states, Japan in particular, joined in the task of forging the peace. The states of Germany, Austria-Hungary, and Soviet Russia were excluded from the negotiating tables where the future of Europe was to be determined.

Wilson's Fourteen Points. President Wilson, who captured international attention with his liberal views on the peace, was the central figure of the conference. He was firmly committed to the task of shaping a better world. Before the end of the war, he had proclaimed the "Fourteen Points" as a guideline to the future peace and as an appeal to the people of Europe to support his policies. Believing that secret diplomacy and the alliance system were responsible for the events leading up to the declaration of war in 1914, he put forward as a basic principle "open covenants of peace, openly arrived at." Other points included the reduction of armaments, freedom of commerce and trade, self-determination of peoples, and a general association of nations to guarantee the peace. The Fourteen Points were, above all, an idealistic statement of the principles for a good and lasting peace. Point 14, which stipulated "mutual guarantees of independence and territorial integrity" through the establishment of the League of Nations, was endorsed by the peace conference. The League, which the United States refused to join in spite of Wilson's advocacy, was intended to arbitrate all future disputes among states and to keep the peace.

Georges Clemenceau of France was motivated primarily by a concern for his nation's security. France had suffered the greatest losses of the war in both human lives and property destroyed. To prevent a resurgent Germany, Clemenceau supported a variety of measures to cripple Germany as a military force on the Continent. Germany was disarmed. The territory west of the Rhine River was demilitarized, with occupation by Allied troops to last for a period of 15 years. With Russia unavailable as a partner to contain Germany, France supported the creation of a series of states in eastern Europe carved out of former Russian, Austrian, and German territory. Wilson supported these new states out of a concern for self-determination of peoples. Clemenceau supported them for reasons of French security.

Much time and energy were devoted to redrawing the map of Europe. New states were created out of the lands of three failed empires. On the basis of self-determination, Finland, Latvia, Estonia, Lithuania, Poland, Czechoslovakia, Austria, Hungary, and Yugoslavia were all granted nation-state status. However, the rights of ethnic and cultural minorities were violated in some cases because of the impossibility of redrawing the map of Europe strictly according to the principle of self-determination. In spite of good intentions, every new nation had its own national minority, a situation that held the promise of future troubles.

Europe After World War I. The need for security on the Continent led France to support a buffer zone of new nations between Russia and Germany, carved out of the former Austrian Empire. German territory along the French border was demilitarized out of the same concern for protection.

The Treaty of Versailles. The peace conference produced five separate treaties, one with each of the defeated nations: Austria, Hungary, Turkey, Bulgaria, and Germany. The treaty signed with Germany on 28 June 1919, known as the Treaty of Versailles because it was signed in the great Bourbon palace, preceded the others in timing and importance. In that treaty, the Allies imposed blame for the war on Germany and its expansionist aims in the famous War Guilt Clause. If the war was Germany's fault, then Germany must be made to pay punitive reparations.

By 1920, the German people knew that Germany had to make a down payment of $5 billion against a future bill; had to hand over a significant portion of merchant ships, including all vessels of more than 1,600 tons; had to lose all German colonies; and had to deliver coal to neighboring countries. These harsh clauses, more than any other aspect of the peace settlement, came to haunt the Allies in the succeeding decades.

In the end, no nation got what it wanted from the peace settlement. The defeated nations felt that they had been badly abused. The victorious nations were aware of the compromises they had reluctantly accepted. Cooperation among nations was essential if the treaty was to work successfully. It had taken the combined resources of not only France and the British Empire but also Russia with its vast population and the United States with its great industrial and financial might to defeat the power of Germany and the militarily ineffective Austro-Hungarian Empire. A new and stable balance of power depended on the participation of Russia, the United States, and the British Empire. But Russia was excluded from and hostile to the peace settlement, the United States was uncommitted to it, and the British Empire declined to guarantee it. All three Great Powers backed off their European responsibilities at the end of the war. By 1920, all aspects of the treaty, especially the reparations clause, had been questioned and criticized by the very governments that had written them and accepted them. The search for a lasting peace had just begun.

Revolution in Russia, 1917–1920

Russia had gone to war because some of the advisers of Tsar Nicholas II (1894–1917) had persuaded him that the empire was a Great Power with interests beyond its borders. A short, successful war, they said, would strengthen his monarchy against the domestic forces of change. But within the empire the process of modernization was widening social divisions. Little did Nicholas know, when he committed Russia to the path of war instead of revolution, that he guaranteed a future of war *and* revolution or that his own days were numbered.

The Last Tsar. The Romanov dynasty surely needed strengthening. In 1914, Russia was considered backward by the standards of Western industrial society. Russia still recalled a recent feudal past. The serfs had been freed in the 1860s, but the nature of the emancipation exacerbated tensions in the countryside and peasant hunger for land. Russia's limited, rapid industrialization in the 1880s and 1890s was an attempt to catch up with Great Britain, France, and Germany as a world industrial power. But the speed of such change brought with it severe dislocations, especially in the industrial city of Moscow and the capital, St. Petersburg.

In 1905, the workers of St. Petersburg protested hardships due to cyclical downturns in the economy. On a Sunday in January 1905, the tsar's troops fired on a peaceful mass demonstration in front of the Winter Palace, killing and wounding scores of workers, women, and children who were appealing to the tsar for relief. The event, which came to be known as Bloody Sunday, set off a revolution that spread to Moscow and the countryside. In October 1905, the regime responded to the disruptions with a series of reforms that legalized political parties and established the Duma, or national parliament. Peasants, oppressed by their own burdens of taxation and endemic poverty, launched mass attacks on big landowners throughout 1905 and 1906. The government met workers and peasants' demands with a return to repression in 1907. In the half-decade before the Great War, the Russian state stood as an autocracy of parliamentary concessions blended with severe police controls.

What workers had learned in 1905 was the power and the means of independent organization. Factory committees, trade unions, and *soviets*, or elected workers' councils, proliferated. Despite winning a grant of legal status after 1906, unions gained little in terms of ability to act on behalf of their members. Unrest among factory workers revived on the eve of the Great War, a period of rapid economic growth and renewed trade-union activity. Between January and July 1914, Russia experienced 3500 strikes. Although economic strikes were considered legal, strikes that were deemed political were not. With the outbreak of war, all collective action was banned as politically dangerous. Protest stopped, but only momentarily. The tsar certainly weighed the workers' actions in his decision to view war as a possible diversion from domestic problems.

Russia, which had lost a war with Japan in 1904–1905, was still less prepared for war than any of the other belligerents. Undoubtedly, it had more soldiers than other countries, but it lacked arms and equipment. Problems of provisioning such a huge fighting force placed great strains on the domestic economy and on the workforce. Under government coercion to meet the needs of war, industrial output doubled between 1914 and 1917, while agricultural production plummeted. The tsar, who unwisely insisted on commanding his own troops, left the government in the hands of his wife, the Tsarina Alexandra, a German princess by birth, and her eccentric peasant-priest adviser, Rasputin. Scandal, sexual innuendo, and charges of treason surrounded the royal court. The incompetence of a series of unpopular ministers further eroded confidence in the regime.

In the end, the war sharpened long-standing divisions within Russian society. Led by exhausted and starving working women, poorly paid and underfed workers toppled the regime in the bitter winter of March 1917. This event was the beginning of a violent process of revolution and civil war. The tsar abdicated, and all public symbols of the tsardom were destroyed. The banner bearing the Romanov two-headed eagle was torn down; in its place, the Red Flag, the international symbol of revolution, flew over the Winter Palace.

Dual Power. With the tsar's abdication, two centers of authority replaced autocracy. One was the Provisional Government, appointed by the Duma and made up of progressive liberals led by Prince Georgi Lvov (1861–1925), prime minister of the new government, who also served as minister of the interior. Aleksandr Kerenski (1881–1970), the only Socialist in the Provisional Government, served as minister of justice. The members of the new government hoped to establish constitutional and democratic rule.

The other center of authority was the soviets—committees or councils elected by workers and soldiers and supported by radical lawyers, journalists, and intellectuals in favor of socialist self-rule. Party organization and ideological consensus were generally lacking among the soviets, which were quite heterogeneous. The Petrograd Soviet was the most prominent among the councils. (In 1914, the name of St. Petersburg had been changed to the Russian "Petrograd.") This duality of power was matched by duality in policies and objectives and guaranteed a short-lived and unstable regime.

The problems facing the new regime soon became apparent as revolution spread to the provinces and to the battlefront. Peasants, who made up 80 percent of the Russian population, accepted the revolution and demanded land and peace. Without waiting for government directives, peasants began seizing the land. Peasants tried to alleviate some of their suffering by hoarding what little they had. The food crisis of winter persisted throughout the spring and summer, as bread lines lengthened and prices rose. Workers in cities gained better working conditions and higher wages. But wage increases were invariably followed by higher prices that robbed workers of their gains. Real wages declined.

In addition to the problems of land and bread, the war itself presented the new government with other insurmountable difficulties. Hundreds of thousands of Russian soldiers at the front deserted the war, having heard news from home of peasant land grabs and rumors of a new offensive planned for July. The Provisional Government, concerned with Russia's territorial integrity and its position in the international system, continued to honor the tsar's commitments to the Allies by participating in the war. By spring 1917, six to eight million Russian soldiers had been killed, wounded, or captured. The Russian army was incapable of fighting.

The Provisional Government tried everything to convince its people to carry on with the war. In the summer of 1917, the Women's Battalion of Death, composed exclusively of female recruits, was enlisted into the army. Its real purpose, officials admitted, was to "shame the men" into fighting. The all-female unit, like its male counterparts, experienced high losses; 80 percent of the force suffered casualties. The Provisional Government was caught in an impossible situation: it could not withdraw from the war, but neither could it fight. Continued involvement in the lost cause of the war blocked any consideration of social reforms.

Revolution and Civil War in Russia, 1914–1920. Revolutionary and civil unrest was greatest in those areas of Russia with the greatest concentrations of peasants. Kulaks, the more prosperous peasants, were severely repressed for resisting the requisitioning of food after 1918.

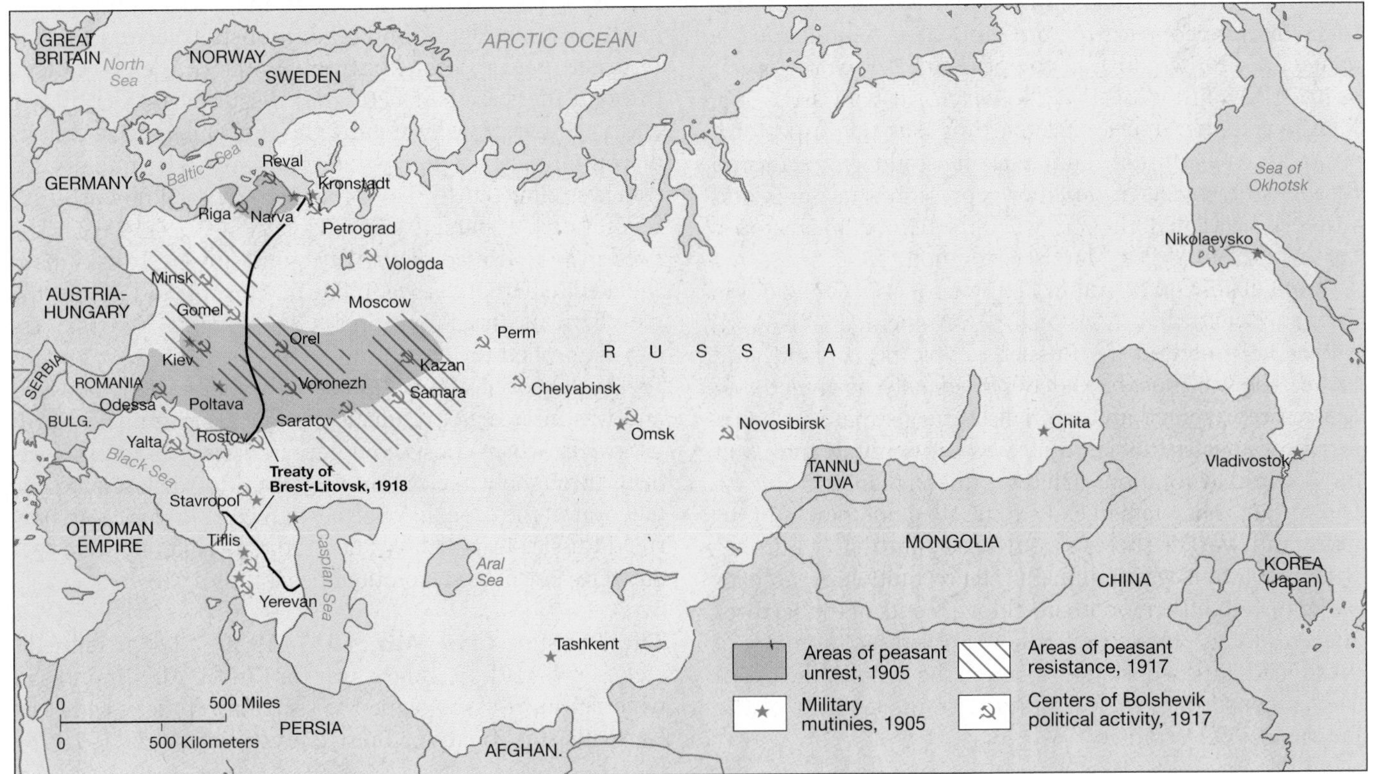

While the Provisional Government was trying to deal with the calamities, many members of the intelligentsia, Russia's educated class, whom the tsar had exiled for their political beliefs, now rushed back from western Europe to take part in the great revolutionary experiment. During the months between February and July 1917, theorists of all stripes put their cases before the people, but it was the Marxists, or Social Democrats, who had the greatest impact on the direction of the revolution.

The Social Democrats believed that there were objective laws of historical development that could be discovered. Russia's future could be understood only in terms of the present situation in western Europe. Like Marxists in the West, the Russian Social Democrats split over how best to achieve a socialist state. The more moderate majority, the Mensheviks (meaning "minority"), wanted to work through parliamentary institutions and were willing to cooperate with the Provisional Government. A smaller faction—despite its name—calling themselves Bolsheviks (meaning "majority") dedicated themselves to preparation for a revolutionary upheaval. After April 1917, the Bolsheviks refused to work with the Provisional Government and organized themselves to take control of the Petrograd Soviet. It had already become an informal national assembly of soviets from all over Russia, and the Bolsheviks argued that it should become the national government.

The leader of the Bolsheviks was Vladimir Ilyich Ulyanov (1870–1924). Best known by his revolutionary name, Lenin, he had just returned from Switzerland to reassume leadership. Forty-seven years old at the time of the revolution, Lenin had spent most of his life in exile or in prison. More a pragmatist than a theoretician, he argued for a disciplined party of professional revolutionaries, a vanguard who would lead the peasants and workers in a socialist revolution against capitalism. In contrast to the Mensheviks, he argued that the time was now ripe for a successful revolution and that it could be achieved through the soviets. Since they represented peasants and workers, he argued, they provided the democratic majority base needed for a true Marxist revolution.

Immediately on arrival in Petrograd, Lenin threw down the gauntlet to the Provisional Government. In his April Theses he promised the Russian people peace, land, and bread. The war must be ended immediately, he argued, because it represented an imperialist struggle that was benefiting capitalists. Russia's duty was to withdraw and wait for a world revolution. This was more than rhetoric on Lenin's part. His years in exile in the West and news of mutinies and worker protests convinced him that a Europe-wide revolution was imminent. His revolutionary policies on land were little more than endorsements of the seizures already taking place all over Russia. Even his promises of bread had little substance. But on the whole, the April Theses constituted a clear critique of the policies of the Provisional Government.

Dissatisfaction with the Provisional Government increased as the war dragged hopelessly on and bread lines lengthened. In the midst of these calamities a massive popular demonstration erupted in July 1917 against the Provisional Government and in favor of the soviets, which excluded the upper classes from voting. The Provisional Government responded with repressive force reminiscent of the tsardom. The July Days were proof of the growing influence of the Bolsheviks among the Russian people. Although the Bolshevik leadership had withdrawn support for the demonstrations at the last moment, Bolshevik rank-and-file party members strongly endorsed the protest. Indisputably, Bolshevik influence was growing in the soviets despite repression and persecution of its leaders. Lenin was forced to flee to Finland.

As a result of the July Days, Kerenski, who had been heading the Ministry of Justice, was named prime minister and continued the Provisional Government's moderate policies. To protect the government from a coup on the right, Kerenski permitted the arming of the Red Guards, the workers' militia units of the Petrograd Soviet. The traditional chasm between the upper and lower classes was widening as the policies of the Provisional Government conflicted with the demands of the soviets.

Lenin and the Bolsheviks Seize Power. The second revolution came in November (October in the Russian calendar). This time it was not a spontaneous street demonstration but the seizure of the Russian capital by the Red Guards of the Petrograd Soviet. The revolution was carefully planned and orchestrated by Lenin and his vanguard of Bolsheviks, who now possessed majorities in the soviets in Moscow, Petrograd, and other industrial centers. Having returned surreptitiously from Finland, Lenin moved through the streets of Petrograd disguised in a curly wig and head bandages, watching the Red Guard seize centers of communication and public buildings. The military action was directed by Lev Bronstein, better known by his revolutionary name, Leon Trotsky (1879–1940). The Bolshevik chairman of the Petrograd Soviet, Trotsky used the Red Guard to seize political control and arrest the members of the Provisional Government. Kerenski escaped and fled the city.

The takeover was achieved with almost no bloodshed and was immediately endorsed by an All-Russian Congress of Soviets, which consisted of representatives of local soviets from throughout the nation who were in session amid the takeover of the capital. A Bolshevik regime under Lenin now ruled Russia. Tsar Nicholas II and the royal family were executed by Bolshevik revolutionaries in July 1918.

The Russian Civil War, 1917–1920. Lenin immediately set to work to end the war for Russia. After months of negotiation, Russia signed a separate peace with the Germans, the Treaty of Brest-Litovsk, in March 1918. By

CHRONOLOGY

THE RUSSIAN REVOLUTION

January–July 1914	Protests and strikes
30 July 1914	Russia enters World War I
March 1917	First Russian Revolution: Abdication of Tsar Nicholas II
March 1917	Creation of Provisional Government
April 1917	Bolsheviks take control of Petrograd
July 1917	Massive demonstration against Provisional Government; Lenin is forced to flee Russia
November 1917	Bolsheviks and Red Guards seize political control in what comes to be known as the October Revolution
March 1918	Russia withdraws from World War I and signs Treaty of Brest-Litovsk
July 1918	Tsar Nicholas II and family are executed

every measure, the treaty was a bitter humiliation for the new Soviet regime. The territorial losses were phenomenal, reducing Russia to the size of its Muscovite period. Russia recognized the independence of Ukraine, Georgia, and Finland; it relinquished its Polish territories, the Baltic states, and part of Belorussia to Germany and Austria-Hungary; and it handed over other territories on the Black Sea to Turkey. Lenin believed that he had no choice; he needed to buy time to consolidate the revolution at home, and he hoped for a socialist revolution in Germany that would soften the enforcement of the terms of the treaty.

The Treaty of Brest-Litovsk was judged a betrayal not only among the Allied powers but also among some Russian army officers who had sacrificed much for the tsar's war. To these military men the Bolsheviks were no more than German agents who held the country in their sway. Lacking sufficient organization, unable to coordinate their movements because the Bolsheviks dominated the country's center, and torn apart by different political goals, the White armies, which were anti-Bolshevik but not all pro-tsarist, ultimately failed to break the Bolshevik hold on the reins of state. But in the three years of civil war between Whites and Reds, the Whites posed a serious threat to Bolshevik policies.

Anti-Bolshevik forces were assisted with materials by the Allies, who intended to keep the eastern front viable. The Allies sent over 100,000 troops and supplies for the purpose of overthrowing the Bolshevik regime by supporting its enemies. Allied support for the White armies came primarily from the United States, Great Britain, France, and Japan and continued beyond the armistice that ended the Great War in 1918. Although Allied intervention did not defeat the Bolsheviks, it played a significant role in shaping Soviet perceptions of the outside world. For generations of Soviet citizens, anti-Bolshevik assistance was seen as the indication of a hostile and predatory capitalist world that was intent on destroying the fledgling Soviet state.

The civil war had another legacy for the future of the Soviet state. To deal with the anarchy caused by the fratricidal struggle, Lenin had to strengthen the government's dictatorial elements at the expense of its democratic ones. The new Soviet state used state police to suppress all opposition. The Marxist goal of dictatorship of the proletariat yielded to the dictatorship of the repressive forces.

In the course of the civil war, Lenin was no more successful than Kerenski and the Provisional Government in solving the problems of food supplies. Human costs of the civil war were high, with over 800,000 soldiers dead on both sides and two million civilian deaths from dysentery and diseases caused by poor nutrition. Industrial production ceased, and people fled the towns to return to the countryside. In 1920, it seemed that Russia could drop no lower. Millions had been killed in war or died from famine. Stripped of territories and sapped of its industrial strength, Russia was a defeated nation. Yet Bolshevik idealism about the success of the proletarian revolution prevailed. By 1920, the major battles of the civil war had been won, although sporadic clashes dragged on into the following year as the Soviet regime extended its control across Siberia, the Ukraine, and the Caucasus. In 1920, Poland, taking advantage of the turmoil in Russia, invaded Russia with French support and succeeded in enlarging Polish boundaries to approximately those after the partition of 1793. (See Chapters 18 and 27.) The Bolshevik leaders, now no longer sure that a world socialist revolution would come to their aid, set out to build their own future.

The Weimar Republic

In September 1918, the leaders of the German High Command, Erich Ludendorff and Paul von Hindenburg, knowing that the German war effort was a lost cause, decided that a constitutional monarchy must be introduced in Germany. Their intention was to save the throne of Emperor William II and to save themselves by handing the responsibility for the government over to the socialist and liberal politicians who were dedicated to ending the war, getting German soldiers home, and demobilizing the army. Popular uprisings in the navy and in urban areas followed, forcing the emperor to abdicate. In spring 1919, a national assembly meeting in the city of Weimar produced Germany's first democratic constitution. The Weimar Republic was born.

The Weimar Republic was in trouble from the start. Germany's first democracy came into existence saddled with a harsh peace. Many Germans identified the new government with defeat and humiliation. The Weimar Republic faced the challenges of establishing its legitimacy and maintaining social peace. Yet it lacked a democratic tradition on which to draw. Traditional ruling groups—the Prussian military and agrarian and bureaucratic elites—preserved their power and privileges even as democratic institutions struggled for existence. Political as well as economic power continued to be concentrated in the hands of the privileged elite that had ruled the Second Reich.

Conclusion

BY EVERY MEASURE, the Great War was disastrously expensive. Some European nations suffered more than others, but all endured significant losses of life, property, and productive capacity. The cost in human lives was enormous. In western Europe, 8.5 million were dead; total casualties amounted to 37.5 million. France lost 20 percent of its men between the ages of 20 and 44, Germany lost 15 percent, and Great Britain lost 10 percent. The war also resulted in huge losses in productive capacity. National economies buckled under the weight of foreign debts and resorted to a variety of methods to bail themselves out, including taxes, loans, and currency inflation. The people of Europe continued to pay for the war long after the fighting had ended.

The big winner in the war was the United States, which was now a creditor nation holding billions of dollars of loans to the Allies and operating in new markets established during the war. The shift was not a temporary move but a structural change. The United States now took its place as a Great Power in the international system. The world of 1914 was gone. What was to replace it was still very much in flux. To the east, Russia was engaged in a vast experiment of building a new society. In the west, the absence of war was not peace.

QUESTIONS FOR REVIEW

1. Why did so many in Europe look forward to war by the summer of 1914, and what had they done to bring it about?
2. How and why did the Great War differ so much from the expectations of both the generals and the majority of Europeans?
3. What is total war, and what made World War I the first such war in history?
4. How was peace at last achieved, and what were the terms of that peace?
5. In what ways did the Great War contribute to revolution in Russia?

DISCOVERING WESTERN CIVILIZATION ONLINE

You can obtain more information about war and revolution between 1914 and 1920 at the websites listed below. See also the companion website that accompanies this text: www.ablongman.com/kishlansky, which contains an online study guide and additional resources.

The War Europe Expected

www.gulib.lausun.georgetown.edu/dept/speccoll/britpost/britpost.htm

www.geocities.com/SoHo/Gallery/8054

These are sites of posters, photos, and art of World War I.

A New Kind of Warfare

www.cc.ukans.edu/~kansite/ww_one/wwi.htm

Site of documents relating to World War I.

www.cc.ukans.edu/~kansite/ww_one/photos/greatwar.htm

A great collection of photos documenting World War I.

Adjusting to the Unexpected: Total War

www.worldwar1.com/

This site on World War I is sponsored by the History Channel.

www.pitt.edu/~pugachev/greatwar/ww1.html

Another comprehensive site containing primary text, summaries, and photos of the major events in World War I.

Reshaping Europe: After War and Revolution

history.acusd.edu/gen/text/versaillestreaty/vercontents.html

This site is devoted to the Versailles Treaty, including the text of all articles of the treaty, suggested readings, maps, photographs, and further links.

www.historyguide.org/europe/rusrev_links.html

This site provides electronic texts in English of Lenin and Trotsky and several other links to sites on the Russian Revolution.

SUGGESTIONS FOR FURTHER READING

The War Europe Expected

Keith Robbins, *The First World War* (Oxford: Oxford University Press, 1984). This study traces the major cultural, political, military, and social developments between 1914 and 1918. Includes a discussion of the course of the land war and modes of warfare.

Jeffrey Verhey, *The Spirit of 1914: Militarism, Myth, and Mobilization in Germany* (Cambridge: Cambridge University Press, 2000). The author captures the fervor and patriotism that surrounded the August experiences and the declaration of war and chronicles the survival of the memory of the "spirit of 1914" in the postwar period.

A New Kind of Warfare

Stéphane Audoin-Rouzeau, *Men at War, National Sentiment and Trench Journalism in France During the First World War* (Providence, R. I.: Berg Publishers, 1992). Using trench newspaper reports, the author is able to capture the daily life of soldiers in the horrors of the bloodiest war in history.

Roger Chickering, *Imperial Germany and the Great War, 1914–1918* (Cambridge: Cambridge University Press, 1998). The author offers a synthetic treatment of the history of the war and its impact on German society.

Frans Coetzee and Marilyn Shevin-Coetzee, eds., *Authority, Identity and the Social History of the Great War* (Providence, R. I.: Berghahn Books, 1995). Recognizing that 1914 marks the beginning of the twentieth century, contributors examine the variety of national responses involved in waging total war and stress the interrelatedness of the home fronts and the battlefronts in affecting individual lives and identities.

Mark Cornwall, *The Undermining of Austria-Hungary: The Battle for Hearts and Minds* (New York: St. Martin's Press, 2000). This study presents extensive research on how propaganda was used by and against Austria-Hungary as a weapon of war.

Paul Fussell, *The Great War and Modern Memory* (New York: Oxford University Press: 2000). This twenty-fifth anniversary edition is a cultural history of World War I, treating the patterns and tendencies in war literature within the framework of a literary tradition. The author argues that the irony that dominates modern consciousness originated in the perception of the war by contemporary artists.

Hew Strachan, ed., *The Oxford Illustrated History of the First World War* (Oxford: Oxford University Press, 1998). This extensively illustrated volume contains 23 chapters on key themes in the history of the Great War covering military issues, the home front, and the role of propaganda.

Adjusting to the Unexpected: Total War

Roger Chickering and Stig Förster, eds., *Great War, Total War: Combat and Mobilization on the Western Front, 1914–1918* (Cambridge: Cambridge University Press, 2000). In a collection of specialist essays, the authors consider the nineteenth-century origins of total industrialized warfare in search of a consensus on what constitutes total war.

Belinda J. Davis, *Home Fires Burning: Food, Politics, and Everyday Life in World War I Berlin* (Chapel Hill: University of North Carolina Press, 2000). This thorough study examines the actions of women, especially poorer women in Berlin during the war and the impact they had on politics and policy.

Susan R. Grayzel, *Women's Identities at War: Gender, Motherhood, and Politics in Britain and France During the First World War* (Chapel Hill: University of North Carolina Press, 1999). A carefully documented cultural history of women's roles in World War I on the French and British home fronts.

Aviel Roshwald and Richard Stites, eds., *European Culture in the Great War: The Arts, Entertainment, and Propaganda, 1914–1918* (Cambridge: Cambridge University Press, 1999). This volume encompasses Europe to include western and eastern Europe and the South Slavic lands and examines the relationship between culture and politics during the war.

Jay Winter, Geoffrey Parker, and Mary Habeck, eds., *The Great War and the Twentieth Century* (New Haven: Yale University Press, 2000). This volume of essays by leading scholars contributes to a comparative history of total war in the twentieth century.

Reshaping Europe: After War and Revolution

Manfred E. Boemeke, Gerald D. Feldman, Elisabeth Glaser, eds., *The Treaty of Versailles: A Reassessment After 75 Years* (Cambridge: Cambridge University Press, 1998). The volume is a synthetic reappraisal of the peace treaty, divergent peace aims, and the postwar context in which it was developed.

Jane McDermid and Anna Hillyar, *Midwives of the Revolution: Female Bolsheviks and Women Workers in 1917* (Athens: Ohio University Press, 1999). This work provides a good overview of the importance of women's actions in the Russian Revolution.

CHAPTER 27

THE EUROPEAN SEARCH FOR STABILITY, 1920–1939

THE VISUAL RECORD

THE HARSH LESSONS OF HYPERINFLATION

FOR MANY WHO SURVIVED THE HORRORS of the Great War, worse disruptions were in store. Inflation, like combat, wreaked havoc with people's lives. During the war, prices had doubled in Great Britain, the United States, Germany, Canada, and Japan. Prices had tripled in France and Sweden; in Italy, they had quadrupled. But all of that was nothing compared to what happened after the war in Germany, Austria, Hungary, Poland, and Russia. Inflation was so great, with prices increasing astronomically—by tens of thousands of times as much—that a new term had to be created for the runaway inflation: hyperinflation. As prices reached staggering heights, currencies collapsed. In Germany in 1918, one prewar gold mark was worth two paper marks; by 1923, it took one billion paper marks to match a single gold mark in value. The currency was worthless.

In war it is important to identify the enemy. So too with hyperinflation did people seek out the adversary. The German expressionist artist George Grosz (1893–1959) was renowned for portraying the decadence and corruption of bourgeois society in the 1920s. In the painting shown here entitled *The Pillars of Society,* Grosz caricatured postwar Germany as composed of corrupt judges, greedy businessmen, mercenary militarists, and hypocritical pacifists.

Many believed that the postwar republican government of Germany was to blame because it had accepted a harsh peace treaty and made reparations payments. Socialists and Communists were singled out for special disdain. Jewish politicians, bankers, and financiers became scapegoats for Germany's economic problems. Confidence in the state evaporated. Inflation began in Germany during the war as the government printed money rather than levying taxes to pay off war debts. After the war, inflation continued because big business, in need of new capital, and organized labor, in search of jobs, benefited from it. The inflation was further aggravated by depreciation of the currencies in central and eastern European countries. The Allied demands for reparations payments further undermined confidence in

the mark. The result was that double-digit inflation turned into hyperinflation in the spring of 1922. When the French army occupied the Ruhr and the German government printed money to subsidize the miners and trainmen who were conducting passive resistance, inflation became astronomical.

More and more paper money came into circulation without any corresponding increase in the amount of goods and services. As the value of money plummeted, prices soared. A handful of apples cost cartloads of paper currency—hundreds of billions of marks—at the height of the inflation in the summer of 1923. People were paid twice a day so that they could rush to stores during their breaks and spend their earnings before their money became worth even less. Working people were malnourished; the unemployed starved. Only one in three German workers was fully employed by the end of 1923. With soaring prices, people lost security and stability just as surely as if they had been in a military upheaval.

LOOKING AHEAD

In this chapter, we shall begin with a geographical tour of Europe that allows us to consider how economic and security issues fueled national and territorial tensions. The Germans blamed the French for their reparations demands and their invading troops for the plight of Germany. Hyperinflation had extremely negative repercussions for democracy, as extremists on both the left and right blamed their liberal political leaders. When the Great Depression that began in 1929 hit European economies, the fear of new inflation prevented governments from using deficit spending to bring back prosperity. In Italy and Germany, fascist dictatorships promised solutions to all economic problems. People, having grown cynical and defiant through suffering, sought security in extraordinary and extrademocratic solutions.

GEOGRAPHICAL TOUR

Europe After 1918

The armistice that ended World War I in 1918 did not stop the process of social upheaval and transformations challenging attempts to restore order throughout Europe (see **Map A**). In 1918, parts of war-torn Europe faced the possibility of revolution. Russia, where revolution had destroyed tsardom, expectantly watched revolutionary developments in countries from the British Isles to eastern Europe. The Bolshevik leaders of Russia's revolution counted on the capitalist system to destroy itself. But that did not happen. By 1921, revolutions had been brutally crushed in Berlin, Munich, and Budapest. The Soviets, meanwhile, had won the civil war against the Whites and survived the intervention of the British, French, Japanese, and Americans. But the new Russian regime was diplomatically isolated and in a state of almost total economic collapse.

In 1917–1918, the United States had played a significant and central role in the waging of war and in the pursuit of peace. Under President Woodrow Wilson, who urged his country to guarantee European security and guide Europe's future, the American nation seemed promising as an active and positive force in international politics. By 1921, however, the United States had retreated to a position not of isolation, but of selective involvement. With one giant, Russia, devastated and isolated, and the other, the United States, reluctant, Europeans faced an uncertain future.

▼ **Map A. Europe After World War I.** The peace settlement dismantled the four great empires in Europe—the Ottoman, Habsburg, Russian, and German—and created new sovereign states.

New Nation-States, New Problems

Before World War I, east-central Europe was a region divided among four great empires: the Ottoman, the Habsburg, the Russian, and the German. Under the pressure of defeat, those empires collapsed into their component national parts, and when the dust of the peace treaties had settled, the region had been molded into a dozen sovereign states (see **Map B**). The victorious Allies hoped that independent states newly created from fragments of empire would buffer Europe from the spread of communism westward and the expansion of German power eastward.

A swath of new independent states cut through the center of Europe. Finland had acquired its independence from Russia in 1917. Estonia, Latvia, and Lithuania, also formerly under Russian rule, comprised the now independent Baltic states (see **Map B**). After more than a century of dismemberment among three empires, Poland became a single nation again. Czechoslovakia was carved out of former Habsburg lands. Austria and Hungary shriveled to small independent states. Yugoslavia was pieced together from a patchwork of territories. Romania swelled, fed on a diet of settlement concessions.

▲ **Map B. East-Central Europe.** A dozen sovereign states were created in East-Central Europe in the hope that they would serve as an independent buffer between Russia and Germany and guarantee peace.

The Instability of Self-Determination. World War I victor nations hoped that the new political geography of Europe would stabilize European affairs; they could not have been more wrong. They erred in three important ways in their calculations. First, many of the new states were internally unstable precisely because of the principle of national self-determination, the idea that nationalities had the right to rule themselves. Honoring the rights of nationalities was simple in the abstract, but application of the principle proved complicated and at times impossible. Religious, linguistic, and ethnic diversity abounded, and recognizing one nationality often meant ignoring the rights of other ethnic groups. In Czechoslovakia, for example, the Czechs dominated the Slovaks and the Germans, even though the Czechs were fewer in number. Ethnic unrest plagued all of eastern Europe. Minority tensions weakened and destabilized the fragile governments.

The struggle for economic prosperity further destabilized the new governments. East-central Europe was primarily agricultural, and the existence of the great empires had created guaranteed markets. The war disrupted the economy and generated social unrest. The peace settlements only compounded the economic problems of the region. When the Habsburg Empire disintegrated, the Danube River basin ceased to be a cohesive economic unit. New governments were saddled with borders that made little economic sense.

Creating cohesive national economic units proved to be an insurmountable task for newly formed governments and administrations that lacked both resources and experience. Low productivity, unemployment, and overpopulation characterized most of east-central Europe. Attempts to industrialize and to develop new markets confronted many obstacles. Much of the land was farmed on a subsistence basis. What agricultural surplus was created was difficult to sell abroad. East-central Europeans, including Poles, Czechs, Yugoslavs, and Romanians, all tied to France through military and political commitments, were excluded from western European markets and were isolated economically from their treaty allies. Economic ties with Germany endured in ways that perpetuated economic dependence and threatened future survival.

Border Disputes. Common borders produced tensions over territories. The peace settlements made no one happy. Poland quarreled with Lithuania, and Czechoslovakia vied with Poland over territorial claims. Poland, as was noted in Chapter 26, actually went to war with Russia for six months in 1920 in an effort to reclaim the Ukraine and expand its borders to what they had been more than a century earlier. The Bolsheviks counterattacked and tried to turn the conflict into a revolutionary war to spread communism to central Europe. The Poles turned the Russians back, and the Treaty of Riga, signed in March 1921, gave Poland much, but not all, of the territory it claimed. The treaty also left the Soviets with yet one more grievance against western capitalists in general and Poland in particular.

Hungary, having lost the most territory in World War I, held the distinction of having the greatest number of territorial grievances against its neighbors—Czechoslovakia, Romania, and Yugoslavia. Yugoslavia made claims against Austria. Bulgaria sought territories controlled by Greece and Romania. Ethnicity, strategic considerations, and economic needs motivated claims for territory. Disputes festered, fed by the intense nationalism that prevented the cooperation necessary for survival.

Germany, the Soviet Union, and Italy further complicated the situation with their own territorial claims against their east-central European neighbors. The new German government refused to accept the loss to Poland of Upper Silesia (see **Map C**) and the "Polish Corridor" that severed East Prussia from the rest of Germany. Russia refused to forget its losses to Romania, Poland, Finland, and the Baltic states. Italy, too weak to act on its own, nevertheless dreamed of expansion into Yugoslavia, Austria, and Albania. The redefined borders of eastern and central Europe produced animosity and the seeds of ongoing conflict. The new states of eastern Europe stood as a picket fence between Germany and Russia, a fence that held little promise of guaranteeing the peace or of making good neighbors.

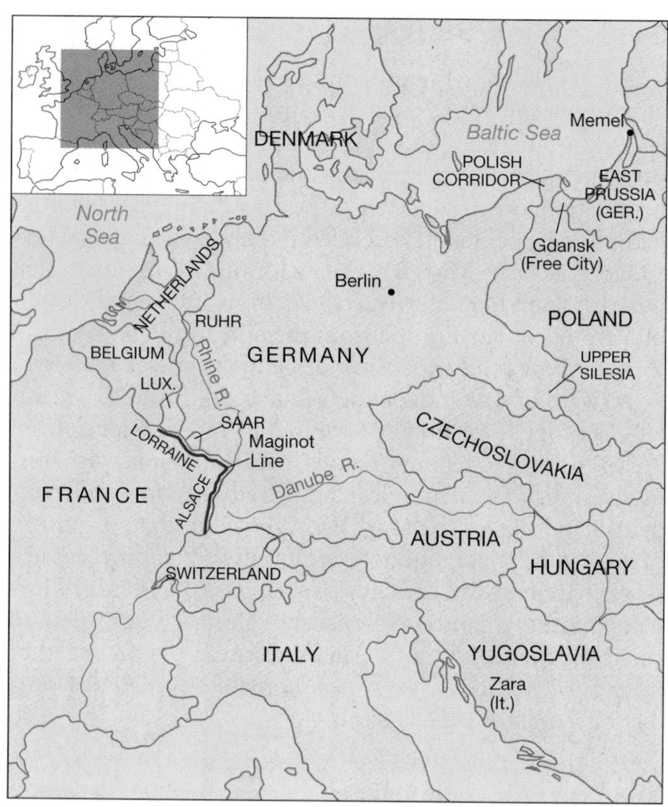

▲ **Map C. Germany.** France hoped to hem Germany in, according to the terms of the peace settlement. France regained from Germany the territories of Alsace and Lorraine that France had lost in the Franco-Prussian War in 1870. In the 1920s, the French began building massive fortifications, known as the Maginot Line, along its frontier with Germany.

German Recovery

From defeat, Germany, the most populous nation in western Europe, with 60 million people, emerged strong. In 1919, the German people endorsed a new liberal and democratic government, the Weimar Republic, so named for the city in which its constitution had been written. The new constitution was unusually progressive, with voting rights for women and extensive civil liberties for German citizens. Because World War I had not been fought in Germany, German transportation networks and industrial plants had escaped serious damage. Its industry was fed by raw materials and energy resources unsurpassed anywhere in Europe outside Russia.

Territorial Advantages and Goals. In east-central Europe, Germany had actually benefited from the dismantling of the Habsburg Empire and the removal of Poland and the Baltic states from Russian control. Replacing its formerly large neighbor to the east were weak states that were potentially susceptible to Germany's influence. Because the governments of east-central Europe feared communism, they were not likely to ally with the Soviet state. The existence of the small buffer states left open the possibility of German collaboration with Russia, since the two large nations might be able to negotiate their interests in the area.

On its western frontier, Germany's prospects were not so bright. Alsace and Lorraine had been returned to France (see **Map C**). From German territory a demilitarized zone had been created in the Rhineland. The Saar district was under the protection of League of Nations commissioners, and the Saar coal mines were transferred to French ownership until 1935, when a plebiscite returned the region to Germany.

Germany's primary foreign policy goal was revision of the treaty settlements of World War I. German statesmen sought liberation of the Rhineland from foreign military occupation, return of the Saar basin, and recovery of the Corridor and Upper Silesia from Poland.

German leaders set economic recovery as the basis of their new foreign policy. In 1922, Germany signed the Treaty of Rapallo with Russia, a peacetime partnership that shocked the western powers. Economics motivated the new Russo-German alliance; German industry needed markets, and the Russians needed loans to reconstruct their economy. Both states wanted to break out of the isolation imposed on them by the victors of World War I. However, Germany quickly learned that markets in Russia were limited and that hopes for recovery depended on financial cooperation with western Europe and the United States. At the end of 1923, Gustav Stresemann (1878–1929) assumed direction of the German Foreign Ministry and began to implement a conciliatory policy toward France and Britain. By displaying peaceful intentions, he hoped to secure U.S. capital for German industry and win the support of the West for the revision of the peace settlement.

The Locarno Treaties. Stresemann joined his French and British counterparts, Aristide Briand (1862–1932) and Austen Chamberlain (1863–1937), in fashioning a series of treaties at Locarno, Switzerland, in 1925. In a spirit of cooperation, Germany, France, and Belgium promised never again to go to war against each other and to respect the demilitarized zone that separated them. Britain and Italy "guaranteed" the borders of all three countries and assured the integrity of the demilitarized zone. The treaties initiated an atmosphere of good will, a "spirit of Locarno," that heralded a new age of security and nonaggression.

However, Germany did not renounce its ambitions in eastern Europe. Stresemann expected Germany to recover the territory that had been lost to Poland. He also knew that Germany must rearm and expand to the east. From the early 1920s until 1933, Germany secretly rearmed in violation of the Treaty of Versailles treaty agreements. Under cover, it rebuilt its army and trained its soldiers and airmen on Russian territory. In violation of the Treaty of Versailles, Germany planned to be once again a great power with the same rights as other European countries.

France's Search for Security

Having learned the harsh lessons of 1870–1871 and 1914–1918, France understood well the threat posed by a united, industrialized, and well-armed Germany. During the years immediately after World War I, France deeply distrusted Germany. France had a smaller population at 40 million people and lower industrial production than Germany. France was devastated by the war, and Germany was not. Even though France had the best-equipped army in the world in 1921, French leaders knew that without the support of Great Britain and the United States, France could not enforce the Treaty of Versailles and keep Germany militarily weak.

The Americans and the British refused to conclude a long-term peacetime alliance with the French. In search of allies on the Continent, therefore, France committed itself to an alliance in the east with Poland and the Little Entente nations of Czechoslovakia, Romania, and Yugoslavia. Treaties with these four states gave France some security in the event of an attack, but the treaties were also liabilities because France would have to fight to defend east-central Europe.

To keep Germany militarily and economically weak, the French attempted to enforce the Treaty of Versailles fully and completely in 1921–1923. They were willing to do so alone if necessary. In 1923, the French army invaded the Ruhr district of Germany and occupied it with the intention of collecting reparations payments. But the Ruhr invasion served only to isolate France further from its wartime allies. In 1924–1925, France decided to cooperate with the United States and Great Britain rather than continue a policy of enforcing the treaty alone and attempting to keep Germany weak. France withdrew its army from the Ruhr and some troops from the Rhineland. It agreed to lower German reparations payments. In addition, by signing the Locarno treaties, France cooperated with the Anglo-American policy that rejected the use of military force against Germany and promoted German economic recovery.

French anxiety about security continued. Nothing indicated the nature of this anxiety more clearly than the construction, beginning in the late 1920s, of the Maginot Line, a system of defensive fortifications between Germany and France (see **Map C**).

Throughout the 1920s, French political leaders tried to engage Great Britain in guaranteeing the security of France and Europe. The British agreed to defend France and Belgium against possible German aggression. However, they stopped short of promising to defend Poland and Czechoslovakia. After settling this matter at Locarno, Britain largely reverted to its prewar pattern of withdrawing from continental Europe and concentrating its attention on the demands of its global empire.

The United States in Europe

The Treaty of Versailles marked the demise of European autonomy. American intervention had boosted French and British morale during the crucial months of 1917. In providing financial help, ships, troops, and supplies, the United States had rescued the Allied powers. After the war, a balance of power in Europe could not be maintained without outside help. Germany had been defeated, but if it recovered, France and Britain alone would probably not be able to contain it. Security and peace now depended on the presence of the United States to guarantee a stable balance of power in Europe and to defend Western hegemony in the world.

However, the United States was unwilling to assume a new role as political leader of Europe and mediator of European conflict. It refused to sign a joint peace, arranging instead a separate peace with Germany. It also refused to join the League of Nations. Following the war, the League had been devised as an international body of nations committed, according to Article 10 of its Covenant, to "respect and preserve as against external aggression the territorial integrity and existing political independence" of others. Germany was excluded from membership until 1926; and the Union of Soviet Socialist Republics (USSR) was denied entry until 1934. Otherwise, the League of Nations claimed a global membership. But the absence of U.S. support and the lack of any machinery to enforce its decisions undermined the possibility of the League's long-term effectiveness. Hopes that the international body could serve as a peacekeeper collapsed in 1931 with the League's failure to deal with the crisis of Japanese aggression against Manchuria.

While the United States persisted in avoiding political and military obligations in Europe, many feared that territorial settlements of the peace held the promise of another war. Even efforts at comprehensive international cooperation like the League of Nations did not overcome the problem of competitive nations, nor did the Kellogg-Briand Pact, which was signed by 23 nations in 1928. Named for U.S. Secretary of State Frank B. Kellogg (1856–1937) and French foreign minister Aristide Briand, who devised the plan, the pact renounced war. In the atmosphere of the 1920s, a time of hope and caution, the agreement carried all the weight of an empty gesture.

CRISIS AND COLLAPSE IN A WORLD ECONOMY

In 1918 the belligerent nations—winners and losers alike—had big bills on their hands. Although nations at war had borrowed abroad and from their own populations through the sale of war bonds, private citizens could not provide all the money needed to finance four years of war.

International Loans and Trade Barriers

France borrowed from Great Britain. Both Great Britain and France took loans from the United States. When these sources proved insufficient, they printed more money. Because more money had claims on the same amount of national wealth, the money in circulation was worth less. When the people who had purchased war bonds were then paid off with depreciated currency, they lost real wealth. Inflation had the same effect as taxation. The people had less wealth, and the government had less debt.

The United States, for the first time in history the leading creditor nation in the world, had no intention of wiping the slate clean by forgiving war debts. Nor did it intend to accept repayment in less-valuable postwar currencies; loans were tied to gold. Britain, France, and Belgium counted on reparations from Germany to pay their war debts and to rebuild their economies. Reparations were calculated on the basis of the damages Germany had inflicted on the Allies. The postwar Reparations Commission determined that Germany owed the victors 132 billion gold marks ($33 billion) to be paid in annual installments of 2 billion gold marks ($500 million) plus 26 percent of the value of German exports.

For the German people and for German leaders, reparations were an unacceptable, punitive levy that mortgaged the prosperity of future generations. Germany, too, wanted to recover from the years of privation of the war. Substantial reparations payments would have transferred real wealth from Germany to the Allies. Transferring wealth would have cut into any increase in the German standard of living in the 1920s, and it would have diminished the investment needed to make the German economy grow. Instead, the German government printed huge amounts of currency. The mark collapsed and world currencies were endangered.

With financial disaster looming, the British and Americans decided to intervene. A plan had to be devised that would permit Germany to prosper while funneling payments to France, which depended on reparations for its own recovery and for its war debt payments to the United States. In 1924, the U.S. banker Charles G. Dawes (1865–1951), along with a group of international financial experts appointed by the Allied governments, devised a solution to the reparations problem. The Dawes Plan aimed to end inflation and restore economic prosperity in Germany by giving Germany a more modest and realistic schedule of payments and by extending a loan from U.S. banks to get payments started.

As important as reparations and war debts are in any understanding of the Western world in the 1920s, they cannot be considered in isolation. Debtor nations, whether Allies paying back loans to the United States or defeated nations paying reparations to the victors, needed to be able to sell their goods in world markets. They saw trade as the principal way to accumulate enough national income to pay back what they owed and to prosper domestically without burying their citizens under a mountain of new taxes.

If trade was to be the stepladder out of the financial hole of indebtedness, open markets and stable currencies were its rungs. Yet the Republican political leaders in the United States insisted on high tariffs to protect domestic goods against imports, and high tariffs prevented Europeans from selling in the United States and earning the dollars they needed to repay war debts.

While blocking imports, the United States planned to expand its own exports to world markets, especially to Europe. The problem for U.S. exporters, however, was the instability of European currencies in the first half of the 1920s. All over Europe, governments allowed inflation to rise with the expectation that depreciating currencies would make their goods cheaper in world markets and hence more salable.

Depreciating European currencies on the one hand meant an appreciating dollar on the other. For the "grand design" of U.S. trade expansion, a strong dollar was no virtue. More and more German marks, British pounds, and French francs had to be spent to purchase U.S. goods. The result was that fewer U.S. exports were sold in European markets. Because two-thirds of Germany's long-term credits came from the United States, Germany's fate was directly linked to the fortunes of U.S. financial centers. Conversely, the soundness of U.S. banks depended on a solvent Germany, which now absorbed 18 percent of U.S. capital exports.

Despite the scaled-down schedule of the Dawes Plan, reparations remained a bitter pill for German leaders and the German public to swallow. In 1929, U.S. bankers devised another plan under the leadership of businessman Owen D. Young (1874–1962), chairman of the board of General Electric. Although the Young Plan initially transferred $100 million to Germany, Germans saw the twentieth century stretching before them as year after year of nothing but humiliating reparations payments. To make matters worse, after 1928, U.S. private loans shriveled in Germany as U.S. investors sought the higher yields of a booming stock market at home.

Europe as a whole made rapid progress in manufacturing production during the second half of the decade and by 1929 had surpassed its prewar (1913) per capita income. Yet structural weaknesses were present. The false security of a new gold standard masked the instability and interdependence of currencies. Low prices prevailed in the agricultural sector, keeping the incomes of a significant segment of the population depressed. But the low rate of long-term capital investment was obscured in the flurry of short-term loans, whose disappearance in 1928 spelled the beginning of the end for European recovery. The protectionist trade policy of the United States conflicted with its insistence on repayment of war debts. Germany's resentment over reparations was in no way alleviated by the Dawes and Young repayment plans. The irresponsibility of U.S. speculation in the stock market pricked the bubble of prosperity. None of these factors operated in isolation to cause the collapse that began in 1929. Taken together, however, they caused a depression of previously unimagined severity in the international economic system.

▲ This poster for the October 1931 British General Election reflects the National Government's concern over mass unemployment and industrial stagnation. The coalition National Government swamped the opposition Labour Party, taking 556 Parliament seats to Labour's 51.

The Great Depression

In the history of the Western world the year 1929 has assumed mythic proportions. During one week in October of that year, the stock market in the United States collapsed. This crash set off the Great Depression in an international economic system that was already plagued with structural problems. It also marked the beginning of a long period of worldwide economic stagnation and depression.

Dependence on the American Economy. A confluence of factors made Europe and the rest of the world vulnerable to reversals in the U.S. economy. Heavy borrowing and reliance on U.S. investment throughout the 1920s contributed to the inherent instability of European economies. Even Great Britain, itself a creditor, relied on short-term loans, but "borrowing short and lending long" proved to be disastrous when loans were recalled. Excessive lending and leniency were fatal mistakes of creditor nations, especially the United States. When, in the summer of 1929, U.S. investors turned off the tap of the flow of capital to search for higher profits at home, a precarious situation began to get worse.

A depression is a severe downturn marked by sharp declines in income and production, as buying and selling slow to a crawl. Depressions were not new in the business cycles of modern economies, but the Great Depression was more serious in extent and duration than any depression before or since. The bottom was not reached until three years after it began. In 1932, one in four American workers was without a job. One in three banks had closed its doors. People lost their homes, unable to pay their mortgages; farmers lost their land, unable to earn enough to survive. The great prosperity of the 1920s had vanished overnight.

The plight of the United States rippled through world markets. Americans stopped buying foreign goods. The Smoot-Hawley Tariff Act, passed by the U.S. Congress in 1930, created an impenetrable tariff fortress against agricultural and manufactured imports. The major trading nations of the world, including Great Britain, enacted similar protectionist measures. U.S. investment abroad dried up.

European nations tried to stanch the outward flow of capital and gold by restricting the transfer of capital abroad. Nevertheless, large amounts of foreign-owned gold ($6.6 billion from 1931 to 1938) were deposited in U.S. banks. In 1931, President Herbert Hoover supported a moratorium on the payment of reparations and war debts. The moratorium, combined with the pooling of gold in the United States, led to a run on the British pound sterling in 1931 and the collapse of Great Britain as one of the world's great financial centers.

Political Repercussions. The gold standard disappeared from the international economy, never to return. So did reparations payments and war debts when the major nations of Europe met without the United States at a special conference held in Lausanne, Switzerland, in 1932. Something else died at the end of the 1920s: confidence in a self-adjusting economy, an "invisible hand" by which the business cycle would be righted. In 1932–1933 the Depression reached its nadir and became a global phenomenon.

Economic hardship transformed political realities. The Labour cabinet in Great Britain was forced to resign, and a new national government composed of Conservative, Liberal, and Labour leaders was formed to deal with the world economic emergency. Republican government was torn by bitter divisions in France. In the United States the Republican Party, which had been in power since 1920, was defeated in 1932. Franklin D. Roosevelt, a Democrat, was elected president in a landslide victory with a mandate to transform the U.S. economy. German democratic institutions were pulled down in favor of fascist dictatorship.

In the decade after the Great War, peace settlements did not promote a stable, international community. Instead, self-determination of peoples created new grounds for national rivalries in eastern Europe, and prewar animosities persisted. The economic interdependence of nation-states through an international system of reparations payments and loans increased the vulnerability of governments to external pressures. With the collapse of world markets and the international finance system in 1929, political stability and international cooperation seemed more elusive than ever.

CHRONOLOGY

INTERNATIONAL POLITICS

1919	Creation of the League of Nations
1920	War between Poland and Russia
1921	Treaty of Riga
1922	Germany and Russia sign Treaty of Rapallo
1923	French and Belgian troops invade the Ruhr district
1924	Dawes Plan
1925	Locarno Treaties
1928	Kellogg-Briand Pact
1929	Young Plan
October 1929	Collapse of the U.S. stock market; beginning of the Great Depression
1935	Saar region returned to German control
1936	Germany stations troops in the Rhineland in violation of the Versailles Treaty

THE SOVIET UNION'S SEPARATE PATH

In the 1920s, the Soviet state was also faced with solving its economic problems. Lenin's successor, Joseph Stalin (1879–1953), obliged the Soviet people to achieve in a single generation what it had taken western Europe a century and a half to accomplish.

The Soviet Regime at the End of the Civil War

Echoing Karl Marx, the Bolshevik leader Lenin declared that the revolution and the civil war had been won in the name of "the dictatorship of the proletariat." The hammer and sickle on the Soviet flag represented the united rule of workers and peasants. But at the end of the civil war in 1921, the Bolsheviks, not the people, were in charge.

The small industrial sector was in total disarray by 1921. Famine and epidemics in 1921–1922 killed and weakened more people than the Great War and the civil war combined. The countryside had been plundered to feed the Red and White armies. The combination of empty promises and a declining standard of living left workers and peasants frustrated and discontented. Urban strikes and rural uprisings defied short-term solutions. The proletarian revolutionary heroes of 1917 were rejecting the new Soviet regime. The Bolshevik Party now faced the task of restoring a country exhausted by war and revolution.

At the head of the Soviet state was Lenin, the first among equals in the seven-man Politburo. The Central Committee of the Communist Party decided "fundamental questions of policy, international and domestic," but in reality the Politburo, the inner committee of the Central Committee, held the reins of power. The broad-based revolutionary coalition had, by the end of World War I, given way to one-party rule.

Among the Politburo seven, three men in particular attempted to leave their mark on the direction of Soviet policy: Leon Trotsky (1879–1940), Nikolai Bukharin (1888–1938), and Joseph Stalin (1879–1953). The great drama of Soviet leadership in the 1920s revolved around how the most brilliant (Trotsky) and the most popular (Bukharin) failed at the hands of the most shrewdly political (Stalin).

In the debate over the direction economic development should take, proposals ranged from a planned economy totally directed from above to an economy controlled from below. In 1920–1921, Leon Trotsky, at that time people's commissar of war, favored a planned economy based on the militarization of labor. Trade unions opposed such a proposal and argued for a share of control over production. Lenin, however, favored a proletarian democracy and supported unions that were organized independently of state control.

The controversy was resolved in the short run at the Tenth Party Congress in 1921, when Lenin chose to steer a middle course between trade union autonomy and militarization by preserving the unions and at the same time insisting on the state's responsibility for economic development. His primary goal was to stabilize Bolshevik rule in its progress toward socialism. He recognized that nothing could be achieved without the peasants. As a result, Lenin found himself embracing a new economic policy that he termed a "temporary retreat" from Communist goals.

The New Economic Policy, 1921–1928

In 1921, Lenin ended the forced requisitioning of peasant produce, which had been in effect during the civil war. In its place, peasants were to pay a tax in kind, that is, a fixed portion of their yield, to the state. Peasants in turn were permitted to reinstate private trade on their own terms. Party leaders accepted this shift in policy because it held the promise of prosperity, so necessary for political stability. Lenin's actions to return the benefits of productivity to the economy, combined with those of the peasants to reestablish markets, created the New Economic Policy (NEP) that emerged in the spring and summer of 1921.

Bukharin's Role. It remained for Nikolai Bukharin, the youngest of the top Bolshevik leaders, to give shape and substance to the economic policy that allowed Russian producers to engage in some capitalist practices. Bukharin tackled Russia's single greatest problem: how could Russia, crippled by poverty, find enough capital to industrialize? Insisting on the need for long-term economic planning, Bukharin counted on a prosperous and contented peasantry as the mainstay of his policy. He also hoped to attract foreign investment in Soviet endeavors as a way of ensuring future productivity.

Bukharin appreciated the importance of landholding to Russian peasants and defended a system of individual farms and private accumulation. Agriculture would operate through a market system, and the peasants would have the right to control their own surpluses. Rural prosperity would generate profits that could be used for gradual industrial development. Bukharin's policy stood in stark contrast to Stalin's later plan to feed industry by starving the agricultural sector.

Collective and large-scale farming had to be deferred indefinitely to reconcile the peasantry to the state—a policy profoundly at odds with the programs of the Communist state to pull down the capitalist system and establish socialism. In 1924, the tax in kind was replaced with a tax in cash. With this shift, the state procured grain through commercial agencies and cooperative organizations instead of directly from the peasants. The move toward Western capitalist models seemed more pronounced than ever to critics of the NEP.

Beginning in 1922, Lenin suffered a series of strokes, which virtually removed him from power by March 1923. When he died on 21 January 1924, the Communist leadership split over the ambiguities of the NEP. The backward nature of agriculture did not permit the kind of productivity that the NEP policy makers anticipated. Cities demanded more food as their populations swelled with the influx of unskilled workers from rural areas. In 1927, peasants held back their grain. The Soviet Union was then experiencing a series of foreign policy setbacks in the West and in China, and Bolshevik leaders spoke of an active anti-Soviet conspiracy by the capitalist powers, led by Great Britain. The Soviet state lowered the price of grain, thereby squeezing the peasantry. The war scare, combined with the drop in food prices, soon led to an economic crisis.

Stalin Takes Charge. By 1928, the NEP was in trouble. Stalin, general secretary of the Communist Party of the Soviet Union, saw his chance. Under his supervision, the state intervened to prevent peasants from disposing of their own grain surpluses. The peasants responded to requisitioning by hoarding their produce and violent rioting. Bukharin and the NEP were in danger. Stalin exploited the internal crisis and external dangers to eliminate his political rivals. Stalin's rival Trotsky had been expelled from the Communist Party in November 1927 on charges that he had engaged in antiparty activities. Banished from Russia in 1929, Trotsky eventually found refuge in Mexico, where he was assassinated in 1940 at Stalin's command.

Bukharin's popularity in the party also threatened Stalin's aspirations. Bukharin was dropped from the Politburo in 1929. He was arrested in 1937 and was tried and executed for alleged treasonous activities the following year. The fate that befell Trotsky and Bukharin was typical of that which afflicted anyone who stood in the way of Stalin's pursuit of dictatorial control. Beneath his apparently colorless personality, Stalin was a dangerous man of great political acumen, a ruthless, behind-the-scenes politician who controlled the machinery of the party to his own ends and was not averse to using violence to achieve them.

Stalin's Rise to Power

Joseph Stalin was born Iosif Vissarionovich Dzhugashvili in 1879. His self-chosen revolutionary name, Stalin, means "steel" in Russian and is as good an indication as any of his opinion of his own personality and will. Stalin, the man who ruled the Soviet Union as a dictator from 1928 until his death in 1953, was not a Russian. He was from Georgia, and he spoke Russian with an accent. Georgia, an area between the Black and Caspian seas, had been annexed by the expanding Russian empire in 1801.

As the only surviving child of his parents, Stalin endured a childhood of brutal poverty. With his mother's support, he nevertheless received an education and entered a seminary. His schooling gave him the opportunity to learn about revolutionary socialist politics. At the turn of the century, Georgia had a strong Marxist revolutionary movement that opposed Russian exploitation. Iosif dropped out of the seminary in 1899 to engage in underground Marxist activities, and he soon became a follower of Lenin.

Stalin's association with Lenin kept him close to the center of power after the October Revolution of 1917. First as people's commissar for nationalities (1920–1923) and then as general secretary of the Central Committee of the Communist Party (1922–1953), Stalin showed natural talent as a political strategist. His familiarity with non-Russian nationalities was a great asset in his dealings with the ethnic diversity and unrest in the vast Soviet state. Unlike other party leaders, who had lived in exile in western Europe before the revolution, Stalin had little knowledge of the West.

After Lenin's death in 1924, Stalin shrewdly bolstered his own reputation by orchestrating a cult of worship for Lenin. In 1929, Stalin used the occasion of his fiftieth birthday to fashion for himself a reputation as the living hero of the Soviet state. Icons, statues, busts, and images of all sorts of both Lenin and Stalin appeared everywhere in public buildings, schoolrooms, and homes. Stalin systematically began eliminating his rivals so that he alone stood unchallenged as Lenin's true successor.

▲ Joseph Stalin.

The First Five-Year Plan

The cult of Stalin coincided with the First Five-Year Plan (1929–1932), which launched Stalin's program of rapid industrialization. Between 1929 and 1937, the period covered by the first two five-year plans (truncated because of their proclaimed success), Stalin laid the foundation for an urban industrial society in the Soviet Union. By brutally squeezing profits out of the agricultural sector, Stalin managed to increase heavy industrial production between 300 and 600 percent.

Stalin committed the Soviet Union to rapid industrialization as the only way to preserve socialism. The failure of revolutionary movements in western Europe meant that the Soviet Union must preserve "socialism in one country," the slogan of the political philosophy that justified Stalin's economic plans. Stalin made steel the idol of the new age. The Soviet state needed heavy machinery to build the future. An industrial labor force was created virtually overnight as peasant men and women were placed at workbenches and before the vast furnaces of modern metallurgical plants. The number of women in the industrial workforce tripled in the decade after 1929. Heavy industrial production soared between 1929 and 1932.

When he first began to deal with the grain crisis of 1928, Stalin did not intend collective agriculture as a solution. But by the end of 1929, the increasingly repressive measures instituted by the state against the peasants had led both to collectivization and to the deportation of *kulaks*, the derisive term for wealthy peasants that literally means "tight-fisted ones." Stalin achieved forced collectivization by confiscating land and establishing collective farms run by the state. Within a few months, half of all peasant farms were collectivized. By 1938, private land was virtually eliminated. The state set prices, controlled distribution, and selected crops with the intention of ensuring a steady food supply and freeing a rural labor force for heavy industry. More as a publicity ploy than as a statement of fact, the First Five-Year Plan was declared a success after only three years. It was a success in one important sense: it did lay the foundations of the Soviet planned economy, in which the state bureaucracy made all decisions about production, distribution, and prices.

Collectivization meant misery for the 25 million peasant families who suffered under it. At least five million peasants died between 1929 and 1932. Collectivization ripped apart the fabric of village life, destroyed families, and sent homeless peasants into exile. Some peasants retaliated by destroying their own crops and livestock. Ultimately, the peasants were to bear the chief burdens of industrialization.

The Comintern, Economic Development, and the Purges

In addition to promoting its internal economic development, the Soviet Union had to worry about survival in a world of capitalist countries.

After the Bolshevik revolution in 1917, Lenin had fully expected that other socialist revolutions would follow throughout the world. But as the prospects for world proletarian revolution evaporated, Soviet leaders sought to protect their revolutionary country from the hostile capitalist world through diplomacy. The end of the Allied intervention in Russia allowed the Bolshevik state to initiate diplomatic relations with the West, beginning with the Treaty of Rapallo signed with Germany in 1921. By 1924, all the major countries of the world—except the United States—had established diplomatic relations with the Soviet Union. In 1928, the Soviet Union cooperated in the preparation of a world disarmament conference to be held in Geneva and joined western European powers in a commitment to peace. The United States and the Soviet Union exchanged ambassadors for the first time in 1933.

The Comintern. In addition to diplomatic relations, the Soviet state in 1919 encouraged various national Communist parties to form an association for the purpose of promoting and coordinating the coming world revolution. This Communist International, or Comintern, was based in Moscow and included representatives from 37 countries by 1920. As it became clear that a world revolution was not imminent, the Comintern concerned itself with the ideological purity of its member parties. Under Lenin's direction the Soviet Communist Party determined policy for all the member parties.

From 1924 to 1929, Bukharin and Stalin shared the view that the Comintern should promote the unity of working classes everywhere and should cooperate with existing worker organizations. In 1929, however, Stalin argued that advanced capitalist societies were teetering on the brink of new wars and revolutions. As a result, the Comintern must seek to sever the ties between Communist parties and social democratic parties in other countries to prepare for the revolutionary struggle. Stalin purged the Comintern of dissenters, and he decreed a policy of noncooperation in Europe from 1929 to 1933. As a result, socialism in Europe was badly split between Communists and democratic socialists, greatly facilitating the triumph of fascist movements, especially Nazism in Germany.

The Second Five-Year Plan, announced in 1933, succeeded in reducing the Soviet Union's dependence on foreign imports, especially in the areas of heavy industry, machinery, and metal works. The basic physical plant for armaments production was in place by 1937, and resources continued to be shifted away from consumer goods to heavy industrial development. This industrial development and the collectivization of agriculture brought growing urbanization. By 1939, one in three Soviet people were living in cities, compared to one in six in 1926. In his commitment to increased production, Stalin introduced into the workplace incentives and differential wage scales that were at odds with the principles and programs of the original Bolshevik revolution. Stricter discipline was enforced; absenteeism was punished with severe fines or loss of employment. Workers who exceeded their quotas were rewarded and honored.

The Great Purge. Amid this rapid industrialization, Stalin inaugurated the Great Purge, actually a series of purges lasting from 1934 through 1938. People whom Stalin believed to be his opponents—real and imagined, past, present, and future—were labeled "class enemies." The most prominent of them were given "show trials." They were intimidated and tortured into false confessions of crimes against the regime and condemned to death or imprisonment. Stalin wiped out the Bolshevik old guard and all potential opposition within the Communist Party to his personal rule. Probably 300,000 people were put to death, among whom were engineers, managers, technologists, and officers of the army and navy. In addition, seven million people were placed in labor camps. The purges dealt a severe blow to the command of the army and resulted in a shortage of qualified industrial personnel,

CHRONOLOGY

THE SOVIET UNION'S SEPARATE PATH

November 1917	Bolsheviks and Red Guard seize power
1919	Creation of the Communist International (Comintern)
1920	Legalization of abortion and divorce
1921	End of the civil war
1921	Introduction of the New Economic Policy
3 April 1922	Stalin becomes secretary general of the Communist party
21 January 1924	Lenin dies
1924–1929	Comintern policy of "Unity of the Working Classes"
1927	Dissatisfied peasants hoard grain
November 1927	Trotsky expelled from Communist party
1928	Stalin introduces grain requisitioning
November 1929	Bukharin expelled from Politburo
1929	Introduction of First Five-Year Plan and the collectivization of agriculture
1929–1933	Comintern policy of noncooperation with Social Democratic parties
1933–1937	Second Five-Year Plan
1934–1938	Great Purge
1936	Abortion declared illegal
1938	Third Five-Year Plan

slowing industrial growth. But Stalin now had unquestioned control of the Party and the country.

Coerced and planned industrial growth brought with it a top-heavy and often inefficient bureaucracy, and that bureaucracy ensured that the Soviet Union was the most highly centralized of the European states. The growing threat of war posed by Nazi Germany meant an even greater diversion of resources from consumer goods to war industries, beginning with the Third Five-Year Plan in 1938.

Women and the Family in the New Soviet State

The building of the new Soviet state exacted particularly high costs from women. Soviet women had been active in the revolution from the beginning. Lenin and the Bolshevik leaders were committed to the liberation of women, who, like workers, were considered to be oppressed under capitalism. Lenin denounced housework as "barbarously unproductive, petty, nerve-wracking, stultifying, and crushing drudgery." In its early days, the Soviet state pledged to protect the rights of mothers without narrowing women's opportunities or restricting women's role to the family.

After the October Revolution of 1917, the Bolsheviks passed a new law establishing equality for women within marriage. In 1920, abortion was legalized. New legislation established the right to divorce and removed the stigma from illegitimacy. Communes, calling themselves "laboratories of revolution," experimented with sexual equality. Russian women were enfranchised in 1917, the first women in a major country to win this right in national elections. The Russian Revolution went further than any revolution in history toward the legal liberation of women within such a short span of time.

These advances, as utopian as they appeared to admirers in western European countries, did not deal with the problems that the majority of Russian women faced. Bolshevik legislation did little to address the economic hardships of peasant and factory women. Although paid maternity leaves and nursing breaks were required by law, these guarantees became a source of discrimination against women workers, who were the last hired and first fired by employers trying to limit expenses. Divorce legislation was hardly a blessing for women with children, since men incurred no financial responsibility toward their offspring in terminating a marriage. Even as legislation was being passed in the early days of the new Soviet state, women were losing ground in the struggle for equal rights and independent economic survival.

By the early 1930s, reforms affecting women were in trouble, largely because of a plummeting birthrate, which alarmed Soviet planners. In 1936, women's right to choose to end a first pregnancy was revoked. In the following decade, all abortions were made illegal. Homosexuality was declared a criminal offense. The family was glorified as the mainstay of the socialist order, and the independence of women was challenged as a threat to Soviet productivity. While motherhood was idealized, the Stalinist drive to industrialize could not dispense with full-time women workers.

Women's double burden in the home and workplace became heavier during Stalin's reign. Most Russian women held full-time jobs in the factories or on the farms. They also worked what they called a "second shift" in running a household and taking care of children. In the industrialized nations of western Europe, the growth of a consumer economy lightened women's labor in the home to some extent. In the Soviet Union, procuring the simplest necessities was women's work that required waiting in long lines for hours. Lack of indoor plumbing meant that women spent hours hauling water for their families at the end of a working day. In such ways, rapid industrialization exacted its special price from Soviet women.

In the 1920s and 1930s, the search for stability and prosperity took the Soviet Union down a very different path from that of the states of western Europe. Rejecting an accommodation with a market economy, Stalin committed the Soviet people to planned rapid industrialization that was accomplished through mass repression and great human suffering and relied on a massive state bureaucratic system.

THE RISE OF FASCIST DICTATORSHIP IN ITALY

Throughout western Europe, parliamentary institutions, representative government, and electoral politics offered no ready solutions to the problems of economic collapse and the political upheaval on the left and the right. Fascism promised what liberal democratic societies failed to deliver: a way out of the economic and political morass. Ruling by means of dictatorship by a charismatic leader, fascism promised an escape from parliamentary chaos, party wranglings, and the threat of communism. It also promised order and security.

Fascism sounded very like socialism. In the Soviet Union, Bolshevik leaders reassured their people that socialism was the only way of dealing with the weaknesses and inequities of the world capitalist system that had been laid bare in the world war. Fascists employed similar language in their initial condemnations of the capitalist economy and liberal political institutions and values.

The word *fascism* is derived from the Latin *fasces*, the name for the bundle of rods with an ax head carried by the magistrates of the Roman Empire. Fascism was rooted in the mass political movements of the late nineteenth century, which emphasized nationalism, antiliberal values, and a politics of the irrational. The electoral successes of the German variant—National Socialism or Nazism—were just beginning in the late 1920s. In the same period, fascist movements appeared in England, Hungary, Spain, and France. But none was more successful than the fascist experiment in Italy.

Mussolini's Italy

Italy was a poor nation. Although Italy was one of the victorious Allies in World War I, Italians felt that their country had been betrayed by the peace settlement of 1919 by being denied the territory and status it deserved. A recently created electoral system based on universal manhood suffrage had produced parliamentary chaos and ministerial instability. People were beginning to doubt the parliamentary regime's hold on the future. It was under these circumstances that the Fascist Party, led by Benito Mussolini (1883–1945), entered politics in 1920 by attacking the large Socialist and Popular (Catholic) parties.

The Rise of Mussolini. Mussolini had begun his political career as a Socialist. He had been arrested numerous times for Socialist political activities and placed under state surveillance. An ardent nationalist, he volunteered for combat in World War I and was promoted to the rank of corporal. Injured in early 1917 by an exploding shell detonated during firing practice, he returned to Milan to continue his work as editor of *Il Populo d'Italia* ("The People of Italy"), the newspaper he founded in 1914 to promote Italian participation in the war.

Mussolini yearned to be the leader of a revolution in Italy, and he recognized the persuasive power of the printed word. Emphasizing nationalist goals and vague measures of socioeconomic transformation, Mussolini identified a new enemy for Italy: Bolshevism. He organized his followers into a highly disciplined Fascist Party, which quickly developed its own national network.

Many Fascists were former socialists and war veterans like Mussolini who were disillusioned with postwar government. They dreamed of Italy as a great world power, as it had been in the days of ancient Rome. Their enemies were not only the Communists with their international outlook but also the big businesses and unions. Panicky members of the lower middle classes sought security against the economic uncertainties of inflation and were willing to endorse violence to achieve it. Near civil war erupted as Italian Communists and Fascists clashed violently in street battles in the early 1920s. The Fascists entered the national political arena and succeeded on the local level in overthrowing city governments.

The March on Rome. On 28 October 1922, the Fascists, still a minority party, undertook their famous March on Rome, which followed similar Fascist takeovers in Milan and Bologna. Mussolini's followers occupied the capital. King Victor Emmanuel III invited Mussolini to form a government. Nationalist conservatives fully expected to be able to use the fascists for their own ends. The accession of the new premier, however, marked the beginning of the end of parliamentary government and the emergence of Fascist dictatorship and institutionalized violence. Rising unemployment and severe inflation contributed to the politically deteriorating situation that helped to bring Mussolini to power.

Destruction and violence became fascism's most successful tools for securing political power. *Squadristi*, armed bands of Fascist thugs, attacked their political enemies, both Catholic and Socialist, destroyed private property, dismantled the printing presses of adversary groups, and generally terrorized both rural and urban populations. By the end of 1922, Fascists could claim a following of 300,000 members, who endorsed the new politics of intimidation.

The Fascists also used intimidation to secure votes. One outspoken Socialist critic of Fascist violence, Giacomo Matteotti, was murdered by Mussolini's subordinates in

1924. The deed threatened the survival of Mussolini's government as 150 Socialist, Liberal, and Popular party deputies resigned in protest. Mussolini chose this moment to consolidate his position by arresting and silencing his enemies. Within two years, Fascists were firmly in control, monopolizing politics, suppressing a free press, creating a secret police force, and transforming social and economic policies. Mussolini made Italy into a one-party dictatorship.

Dealing with Big Business and the Church. In 1925, the Fascist Party entered into an agreement with Italian industrialists that gave industry a position of privilege protected by the state in return for its support. Mussolini presented this partnership as the end to class conflict, but in fact it ensured the dominance of capital and the control of labor and professional groups.

A corrupt bureaucracy run on bribes orchestrated the new relationship between big business and the state. In spite of official claims, Fascist Italy was hurt by the Depression. A large rural sector masked the problems of high unemployment by absorbing an urban workforce that was without jobs. Corporatism, a system of economic self-rule by interest groups, was a sham promoted on paper by Benito Mussolini that had little to do with the dominance of the Italian economy by big business. By lending money to Italian businesses that were on the verge of bankruptcy, the government acquired a controlling interest in key industries, including steel, shipping, heavy machinery, and electricity.

Mussolini, himself an atheist, recognized the importance of the Catholic Church in securing his regime. In 1870, when Italy was unified, the pope was deprived of his territories in Rome. This event, which became known as the "Roman Question," proved to be the source of ongoing problems for Italian governments. In February 1929, in the Lateran Treaty and the accompanying Concordat, Mussolini granted the pope sovereignty over the territory around St. Peter's Basilica and the Vatican. The treaty also protected the role of the Catholic Church in education and guaranteed that Italian marriage laws would conform to Catholic dogma.

By 1929, as the Great Depression loomed, *Il Duce* ("the leader"), as Mussolini preferred to be called, was at the height of his popularity and power. Apparent political harmony had been achieved by ruthlessly crushing fascism's opponents. The agreement with the pope, which restored harmony with the Church, was matched by a new sense of order and accomplishment in Italian society and the economy.

Mussolini's Plans for Empire

As fascism failed to initiate effective social programs, Mussolini's popularity plummeted. In the hope of boosting his sagging image, *Il Duce* committed Italy to a foreign policy of imperial conquest.

Italy had conquered Ottoman-controlled Libya in North Africa in 1911. Now, in October 1935, Mussolini's troops invaded Ethiopia. Using poison gas and aerial bombing, the Italian army defeated the forces of Ethiopian emperor Haile Selassie (1930–1974). European democracies cried out against the wanton attack, but Mussolini proclaimed Ethiopia an Italian territory.

The invasion of Ethiopia exposed the inability of the League of Nations to stop such flagrant violations. Great Britain and France protested Italy's conquest, and a rift opened up between these two western European nations and Italy. Mussolini had distanced himself from Nazi Germany, and he was critical of Hitler's plans for rearmament. Now, however, in light of the disapproval of Britain and France, Mussolini turned to Germany for support. In October 1936, Italy and Germany concluded a friendship alliance. In May 1939, in an agreement known as the Pact of Steel, Germany and Italy drew closer, each agreeing to offer support to the other in any offensive or defensive war.

Mussolini pursued other imperialist goals within Europe. The small Balkan nation of Albania entered into a series of agreements with Mussolini beginning in the mid-1920s that made it dependent financially and militarily on Italian aid. By 1933, Albanian independence had been thoroughly undermined. In order not to be outdone by Hitler, who was at the time dismantling Czechoslovakia, Mussolini invaded and annexed Albania in April 1939.

HITLER AND THE THIRD REICH

Repeated economic, political, and diplomatic crises of the 1920s buffeted Germany's internal stability. Most Germans considered reparations to be an unfair burden that should be resisted in every way possible. The German government did not actually promote inflation to avoid paying reparations, but it did do so to avoid a postwar recession, revive industrial production, and maintain high employment. But in 1923, the moderate inflation that stimulated the economy spun out of control into destructive hyperinflation.

The fiscal problems of the Weimar Republic obscure the fact that in the postwar period, Germany experienced real economic growth. German industry advanced, productivity was high, and German workers flexed their union muscles to secure better wages. Weimar committed itself to large expenditures for social welfare programs, including unemployment insurance. By 1930, social welfare was responsible for 40 percent of all public expenditures, compared to 19 percent before the war. All these changes, apparently fostering the well-being of the German people, aggravated the fears of German big businessmen, who resented the trade unions and the perceived trend toward socialism. The lower middle classes also felt cheated and economically threatened by inflation.

Adolf Hitler salutes a huge crowd of Hitler Youth at a rally. The mass meetings were used by the Nazi mythmakers to enhance Hitler's image as the savior of Germany.

Growing numbers of Germans expressed disgust with parliamentary democracy. The Depression dealt a staggering blow to the Weimar Republic in 1929 as U.S. loans were withdrawn and German unemployment skyrocketed. By 1930, the antagonisms among the parties were so great that the parliament was no longer effective in ruling Germany. As chancellor from 1930 to 1932, Centrist leader Heinrich Brüning (1885–1970) tried to break this impasse by overriding the Weimar constitution. This move opened the door to enemies of the republic, and Brüning was forced to resign.

Hitler's Rise to Power

Adolf Hitler knew how to exploit the Weimar Republic's weaknesses for his own political ends. He denounced the reparations. He made a special appeal to Germans who saw their savings disappearing, first in inflation and then in the Depression. He promised a way out of economic hardship and the reassertion of Germany's claim to status as a world power.

Just as Stalin was born a Georgian and not an ethnic Russian, Adolf Hitler (1889–1945) was born an Austrian outside the German fatherland he came to rule. Hitler came from a middle-class family with social pretensions. Aimlessness and failure marked Hitler's early life. Denied admission to architecture school, he took odd jobs to survive. When war broke out in 1914, he volunteered immediately for service in the German army. Wounded and gassed at the front, he was twice awarded the Iron Cross for bravery in action.

The army provided Hitler with a sense of security and direction. The peace that followed determined his commitment to a career in politics. Hitler profoundly believed in the stab-in-the-back legend: Germany had not lost the war; it had been defeated from within, stabbed in the back by communists, socialists, liberals, and Jews. The Weimar Republic signed the humiliating Treaty of Versailles and continued to betray the German people by taxing wages to pay reparations. His highly distorted and false view of the origins of the Republic and its policies was the basis for his demand that the "Weimar System" be abolished and replaced by a Nazi regime.

The Beer Hall Putsch of 1923. In 1923, Hitler, now leading a small National Socialist German Workers party, the Nazis, attempted to seize control of the Munich municipal government. This effort, known as the Beer Hall Putsch, failed, and Hitler served nine months of a five-year sentence in prison. There he began writing the first volume of his autobiography, *Mein Kampf* ("My Struggle"). In this turgid work, he condemned the decadence of Western society and singled out for special contempt Jews, Bolsheviks, and middle-class liberals. From the Munich episode, Hitler learned that he could succeed against the German republic only from within, by coming to power legally. By 1928, he had a small party of about 100,000 Nazis. Modifying his anticapitalist message, Hitler appealed to the discontented small farmers and tailored his nationalist sentiments to a frightened middle class.

Hitler as Chancellor. Adolf Hitler became chancellor of Germany in January 1933 by legal, constitutional, and democratic means. The Nazi party received its heaviest support from farmers, small businessmen, civil servants, and young people. In the elections of 1930 and 1932 the voters made the Nazi party the largest party in the country—although not the majority one. President Paul von Hindenburg invited Hitler to form a government. Hitler claimed that Germany was on the verge of a Communist revolution, and he persuaded Hindenburg and the Reichstag to consent to a series of emergency laws, which the Nazis used to establish themselves firmly in power. Legislation outlawed freedom of the press and public meetings and approved the use of violence against Hitler's political enemies, particularly the Socialists and the Communists. Within two months after Hitler came to office, Germany was a police state, and Hitler was a "legal" dictator who could issue his own laws without having to gain the consent of either the Reichstag or the president. After carrying out this "legal revolution," the Nazis abolished all other political parties, established single-party rule, dissolved trade unions, and put their own people into state governments and the bureaucracy.

Many observers at the time considered the new Nazi state to be a monolithic structure, ruled and coordinated from the center. However, this was not an accurate observation. Hitler actually issued few directives. Policy was set by an often chaotic jockeying for power among rival Nazi factions. Hitler's political alliance with traditional conservative and nationalist politicians, industrialists, and military men helped to give the state created by Adolf Hitler, which he called the Third Reich, a claim to legitimacy based on continuity with the past. (The First Reich was the medieval German Empire; the Second Reich was the German Empire created by Bismarck in 1871.)

The first of the paramilitary groups that were so important in orchestrating violence to eliminate Hitler's enemies was the Sturmabteilung (SA), or the storm troopers, under Ernst Röhm (1877–1934). Röhm helped Hitler achieve electoral victories by beating up political opponents on the streets and using other thuglike tactics. The SA, also known as Brown Shirts, adopted a military appearance for their terrorist operations. By the beginning of 1934, the SA had 2.5 million members, vastly outnumbering the regular army of 100,000 soldiers.

Heinrich Himmler (1900–1945) headed an elite force within the SA called the Schutzstaffel (SS), or protection squad. SS members wore black uniforms and menacing skull-and-crossbones insignia on their caps. Himmler seized control of political policing and emerged as Röhm's chief rival. In 1934 with the assistance of the army, Hitler and the SS purged the SA and executed Röhm, thereby making the SS Hitler's exclusive elite corps, entrusted with carrying out his extreme programs and responsible later for the greatest atrocities of the Second World War.

Nazi Goals

Hitler identified three organizing goals for the Nazi state: *Lebensraum* ("living space"), rearmament, and economic recovery. The goals were the basis of the new foreign policy Hitler forged for Germany, and they served to fuse that foreign policy with the domestic politics of the Third Reich.

Living Space. Key to Hitler's world view was the concept of *Lebensraum*, living space, by which he considered it the right and the duty of the German master race to be the world's greatest empire, one that would endure for a thousand years. Hitler first stated his ideals about living space in *Mein Kampf*, in which he argued that superior nations had the right to expand into the territories of inferior states. Living space meant for him German domination of central and eastern Europe at the expense of Slavic peoples. Germany had to annex territories, and Hitler's primary target was what he called "Russia and her vassal border states."

Rearmament. Hitler greatly escalated the secret rearmament of Germany begun by his Weimar predecessors

NATIONAL INCOME OF THE POWERS IN 1937 AND PERCENTAGE SPENT ON DEFENSE

	National Income (billions of dollars)	Percentage Spent on Defense
United States	68	1.5
British Empire	22	5.7
France	10	9.1
Germany	17	23.5
Italy	6	14.5
USSR	19	26.4
Japan	4	28.2

in violation of the Treaty of Versailles. He withdrew Germany from the League of Nations and from the World Disarmament Conference, signaling a new direction for German foreign policy. In 1935, he publicly renounced the Treaty of Versailles and declared that Germany was rearming. The following year, he openly defied the French and moved German troops into the demilitarized Rhineland. In 1933, the German state was illicitly spending one billion Reichsmarks on arms, a figure that climbed to 30 billion by 1939.

Hitler knew that preparation for war would require full economic recovery. One of Germany's great weaknesses in World War I had been its dependence on imports of raw materials and foodstuffs. To avoid a repetition of this problem, Hitler instituted a program of autarky, or economic self-sufficiency, by which Germany aimed to produce everything that it consumed. He encouraged the efforts of German industry to develop synthetics for petroleum, rubber, metals, and fats.

Economic Recovery. The state pumped money into the private economy, creating new jobs and achieving full employment after 1936, an accomplishment that was unmatched by any other European nation. Recovery was built on armaments as well as consumer products. The Nazi state's concentration of economic power in the hands of a few strengthened big businesses. The victims of corporate consolidation were the small firms that could no longer compete with government-sponsored corporations such as the chemical giant I.G. Farben.

In 1936, Hitler introduced his Four-Year Plan, which was dedicated to the goals of full-scale rearmament and economic self-sufficiency. Before the third year of the Four-Year Plan, however, Hitler was aware of the failure to develop sufficient synthetic products to meet Germany's needs. But if Germany could not create substitutes, it could take over territories that provided the products Germany lacked. Hitler was committed to territorial expansion from the time he came to power. He rearmed Germany for that purpose. When economists and generals cautioned him, he refused to listen. Instead, he removed his critics from their positions of power and replaced them with Nazis who were loyal to him.

Propaganda, Racism, and Culture

To reinforce his personal power and to sell his program for the total state, Hitler created a Ministry of Propaganda under Joseph Goebbels (1897–1945), a former journalist and Nazi Party district leader in Berlin. Goebbels was a master of manipulating emotions in mass demonstrations. Flying the flag and wearing the swastika signified identification with the Nazi state. With his magnetic appeal, Hitler inspired and manipulated the devotion of hundreds of thousands of those who heard him speak. Leni Riefenstahl, a young filmmaker working for Hitler, made a documentary of a National Socialist Party rally at Nuremberg. In scenes of swooning women and cheering men, her film, called *Triumph of the Will*, recorded the dramatic force of Hitler's rhetoric and his ability to move the German people. Hitler's public charisma masked a profoundly troubled and warped individual. Yet millions, including admirers in western Europe and the United States, succumbed to his appeal.

Targeting the Young and Women. The Nazi total state also sought to regulate family life. Special youth organizations were created for boys and girls between the ages of 10 and 18. After passage of the Hitler Youth Law in 1936, boys were required to join the Hitler Youth, which indoctrinated them with nationalistic and military values. Girls had to join the League of German Girls, which was intended to mold them into worthy wives and mothers. Unmarried girls between the ages of 17 and 21 were eligible to join Faith and Beauty, a voluntary organization that taught mainly middle-class girls etiquette, dancing, fashion consciousness, and beauty care. Woman's natural function, Hitler argued, was to serve in the home. Education for women beyond the care of home and family was a waste. The German Women's Bureau under Gertrud Scholtz-Klink instructed adult women in their "proper" female duties. In an effort to promote large families, the state paid allowances to couples for getting married, subsidized families according to their size, and gave tax breaks to large families. Abortion and birth control were outlawed.

By 1937, the need for women workers conflicted with the goals of Nazi propaganda. With the outbreak of war in 1939, women were urged to work, especially in jobs such as munitions manufacture, formerly held by men. For working women with families, the double burden was a heavy one, as women were required to work long shifts—60-hour work weeks were not unusual—for low wages. Many women resisted entering the workforce if they had other income. At the beginning of 1943, as World War II was raging, female labor became compulsory.

Enemies of the State. Nazi propaganda condemned everything foreign, including Mickey Mouse, who was declared an enemy of the state in the 1930s. Purging foreign influences meant purging political opponents, especially members of the Communist Party, who were rounded up and sent to concentration camps in Germany. Communism was identified as an international Jewish conspiracy to destroy the German *Volk* (people of Aryan descent). Nazi literature also identified "asocials," those who were considered deviant in any way, including homosexuals, who were likewise to be expelled. Euthanasia was used on the mentally ill and the developmentally disabled in the 1930s. Concentration camps were expanded to contain enemies of the state. Later, when concentration camps became sites of extermination and forced labor, gypsies, homosexuals, criminals, and religious offenders had to wear insignia of different colors to indicate their basis for

ADOLF HITLER ON "RACIAL PURITY"

The purity of German blood was a recurrent theme in Hitler's speeches and writings from the beginning of his political career. In attacking both liberalism and socialism, Hitler offered racial superiority as the essence of the National Socialist "revolution." This speech, delivered in Berlin on 30 January 1937, lays out his attack on the concept of individual rights and humanity in favor of the folk community.

FOCUS QUESTIONS

In this diatribe, how does race function to promote the "folk" and to undermine the individual's rights? Is Hitler's goal here to create "a better understanding" among nations?

THE MOST IMPORTANT PLANK in the National Socialist program is to abolish the liberal idea of the individual and the Marxist idea of humanity and to substitute for them the folk community rooted in the soil and held together by the bond of common blood. This sounds simple, but it involves a principle which has great consequences.

For the first time and in the first country our people are being taught to understand that, of all the tasks we have to face, the most noble and the most sacred for all mankind is the concept that each racial species must preserve the purity of blood which God has given to it.

The greatest revolution won by National Socialism is that it has pierced the veil which hid from us the knowledge that all human errors may be attributed to the conditions of the time and hence can be remedied, but there is one error that cannot be set right once it has been made by men—that is, the failure to understand the importance of keeping the blood and the race free from intermingling, and in this way to alter God's gift. It is not for human beings to discuss why Providence created different races. Rather it is important to understand the fact that it will punish those who pay no attention to its work of creation. . . .

I hereby prophesy that, just as knowledge that the earth moves around the sun led to a revolutionary change in the world picture, so will the blood-and-race doctrine of the National Socialist movement bring about a revolutionary change in our knowledge. . . . It will also change the course of history in the future.

This will not lead to difficulties between nations. On the contrary, it will lead to a better understanding between them. But at the same time it will prevent the Jews, under the mask of world citizenship, from thrusting themselves among all nations as an element of domestic chaos. . . .

The National Socialist movement limits its domestic activities to those individuals who belong to one people. It refuses to permit those of a foreign race to have any influence whatever on our political, intellectual, or cultural life. We refuse to give any members of a foreign race a dominant position in our national economic system.

In our folk community, which is based on ties of blood, in the results which National Socialism has obtained by training the public in the idea of this folk-community, lies the deepest reason for the great success of our Revolution.

persecution. The people who received the greatest attention for elimination from Nazi Germany, and then from Europe, were Jews.

Scapegoating Jews. The first measures against the German Jews—their exclusion from public employment and higher education—began in 1933. In 1935, the Nuremberg Laws were enacted to identify Jews, to deprive them of their citizenship, and to forbid marriage and extramarital sexual relations between Jews and non-Jews. On the night of 9 November 1938, synagogues were set afire, and books and valuables owned by Jews were confiscated throughout Germany. Jews were beaten, about 91 were killed, and 20,000 to 30,000 were imprisoned in concentration camps. The night came to be called *Kristallnacht* ("night of broken glass"), which referred to the Jewish shop windows smashed by the Brown Shirts under orders from Goebbels. The government claimed that *Kristallnacht* was an outpouring of the German people's will. An atmosphere of state-sanctioned hatred prevailed.

In addition to anti-Semitism, Hitler also placed other racist theories at the core of his fascist ideology. "Experts" decided that sterilization was the surest way to protect "German blood." In 1933, one of the early laws of Hitler's new Reich decreed compulsory sterilization of "undesirables" to "eliminate inferior genes." The Nazi state decided who these "undesirables" were and forced the sterilization of 400,000 men and women.

The Third Reich delivered on its promises to end unemployment, to improve productivity, to break through the logjam of parliamentary obstacles, and to return Germany to the international arena as a contender for power. Yet Hitler's Nazi government ruled by violence, coercion, and intimidation. With a propaganda machine that glorified the leader and vilified groups singled out as scapegoats for Germany's problems, Hitler destroyed democratic institutions and civil liberties in his pursuit of German power.

DEMOCRACIES IN CRISIS

In contrast to the fascist mobilization of society and the Soviet restructuring of the economy, European democracies responded to the challenges of the Great Depression with small, tentative steps. France and Great Britain were less successful than Nazi Germany in meeting the problems of the Depression. France paid a high price for parliamentary stalemate and was still severely depressed on the eve of war in 1938–1939. Great Britain maintained a stagnant economy and stable politics under Conservative leadership. Internal dissension ripped Spain apart. Its civil war assumed broader dimensions as the Soviet Union, Italy, and Germany struggled over Spain's future while Europe's democratic nations stood by and accepted defeat.

The Failure of the Left in France

France's Third Republic, like most European parliamentary democracies in the 1930s, was characterized by a multiparty system. Genuine political differences often separated one party from another. The tendency to parliamentary stalemate was aggravated by the Depression and by the increasingly extremist politics on both the Left and the Right in response to developments in the Soviet Union and Germany.

The belief of the French people in a private enterprise economy was shaken by the Great Depression, but no new unifying belief replaced it. Distrusting both the New Deal model of the United States and the Nazi response to Depression politics, the Third Republic followed a haphazard, wait-and-see policy of insulating the economy, discouraging competition, and protecting favored interests in both industry and agriculture. France clung to the liberal belief in the self-adjusting mechanism of the market—and suffered greatly for it.

In 1936, an electoral mandate for change swept the Left into power. The new premier, Léon Blum (1872–1950), was a Socialist. Lacking the votes to rule with an exclusively Socialist government, Blum formed a coalition of Left and Center parties that were intent on economic reforms, known as the Popular Front. Before Blum's government could take power, a wave of strikes swept France, and the Popular Front was pushed to intervene. It promised wage increases, paid vacations, and collective bargaining to French workers. The reduced work week of 40 hours caused a drop in productivity, as did the short-lived one-month vacation policy. The government did nothing to prevent the outflow of investment capital from France. Higher wages failed to generate increased consumer demand because employers raised prices to cover their higher operating costs.

German rearmament, now publicly known, forced France into rearmament, which France could ill afford. Blum's government failed in 1937, with France still bogged down in a sluggish and depressed economy. The last peacetime government of the 1930s represented a conservative swing back to laissez-faire policies that put the needs of business above those of workers and brought a measure of revival to the French economy.

The radical Right drew strength from the Left's failures. Right-wing leagues and organizations multiplied, appealing to a frightened middle class. The failure of the Socialists, in turn, drove many sympathizers further to the Left to join the Communist Party. A divided France could not stand up to the foreign policy challenges of the 1930s posed by Hitler's provocations.

Muddling Through in Great Britain

Great Britain was hard hit by the Great Depression in the 1930s; only Germany and the United States experienced comparable economic devastation. The socialist Labour government of the years 1929 to 1931 under Prime Minister Ramsay MacDonald (1866–1937) was unprepared to deal with the 1929 collapse. It took a coalition of moderate groups from the three parties—Liberal, Conservative, and Labour—to address the issues of high unemployment, a growing government deficit, a banking crisis, and the flight of capital. The National Government (1931–1935) was a nonparty, centrist coalition whose members included Ramsay MacDonald, retained as prime minister, and Stanley Baldwin (1867–1947), a Conservative with a background in iron and steel manufacturing.

Slow Recovery. In response to the endemic crisis, the National Government took Britain off the international gold standard and devalued the pound. To protect domestic production, tariffs were established. The British economy showed signs of slow recovery, and the government survived the crisis. Moderates and classical liberals in Great Britain persisted in defending the nonintervention of the government in the economy, despite new economic theories, such as that of John Maynard Keynes (1883–1946), who urged government spending to stimulate consumer demand as the best way to shorten the duration of the Depression.

The British Union of Fascists. Sir Oswald Mosley (1896–1980) promoted a fascist response to Britain's problems. In 1932, he founded the British Union of Fascists (BUF), consisting of goon squads and bodyguards. The BUF was opposed to free-trade liberalism and communism alike. Like other European fascist organizations, BUF squads beat up their political opponents and began attacking Jews, especially eastern European émigrés living in London. Public alarm over increasingly inflammatory and anti-Semitic BUF rhetoric converged with parliamentary denunciation. Popular support for the group was already beginning to erode when the BUF was outlawed in 1936. By this time, anti-Hitler feeling was spreading in Great Britain. In Great Britain, the traditional party system prevailed not because of its brilliant solutions to difficult economic problems but because of the willingness of moderate parliamentarians to cooperate and to adapt, however slowly, to the new need for economic transformation.

The Spanish Republic as Battleground

In 1931, Spain became a democratic republic after centuries of Bourbon monarchy and almost a decade of military dictatorship. In 1936, the voters of Spain elected a Popular Front government. The Popular Front in Spain was more radical than its French counterpart. The property of aristocratic landlords was seized; revolutionary workers went on strike; the Catholic Church and its clergy were attacked. This social revolution initiated three years of civil war. On one side were the Republicans, the Popular Front defenders of the Spanish Republic and of social revolution in Spain. On the other side were the Nationalists, those who sought to overthrow the Republic: aristocratic landowners, supporters of the monarchy and the Catholic Church, and much of the Spanish army.

The Spanish Civil War began in July 1936 with a revolt against the Republic from within the Spanish army. It was led by General Francisco Franco (1892–1975), a tough, shrewd, and stubborn conservative nationalist allied with the Falange, the fascist party in Spain. The conflict soon became a bloody military stalemate, with the Nationalists led by Franco controlling the more rural and conservative south and west of Spain and the Republicans holding out in the cities of the north and east—Madrid, Valencia, and Barcelona.

Almost from the beginning, the Spanish Civil War was an international event. Mussolini sent "volunteer" ground troops to fight alongside Franco's forces. Hitler dispatched technical specialists, tanks, and the Condor Legion, an aviation unit, to support the Nationalists. The Germans regarded Spain as a testing ground for new equipment and new methods of warfare, including aerial bombardment. The Soviet Union intervened on the side of the Republic, sending armaments, supplies, and technical and political advisers. Because the people of Britain and France were deeply divided in their attitudes toward the war in Spain, the British government stayed neutral, and the government of France was unable to aid its fellow Popular Front government in Spain. Although individual Americans volunteered to fight with the Republicans, the U.S. government did not prevent the Texas Oil Company from selling oil to Franco's insurgents, nor did it block the Ford Motor Company, General Motors, and Studebaker from supplying them with trucks.

In response to the Spanish government's pleas for help, 2,800 American volunteers, among them college students, professors, intellectuals, and trade unionists, joined the loyalist army and European volunteers in defense of the Spanish Republic. Britons and antifascist émigrés from Italy and Germany also joined international brigades, which were vital in helping the city of Madrid hold out against the Nationalist generals. The Russians withdrew from the war in 1938, disillusioned by the failure of the French, British, and Americans to come to the aid of the Republicans. Madrid fell to the Nationalists in March 1939. The government that Franco established sent one million of its enemies to prison or concentration camps.

CHRONOLOGY

THE RISE OF FASCISM AND DEMOCRACY IN CRISIS

28 October 1922	Italian Fascists march on Rome
November 1923	Beer Hall Putsch in Munich
1924	Fascists achieve parliamentary majority in Italy
1929	Lateran Treaty between Mussolini and Pope Pius XI
1932	Nazi party is single largest party in German parliament
January 1933	Hitler becomes Chancellor of Germany
30 June 1934	Purge of the SA leaves Hitler and the SS in unassailable position
March 1935	Hitler publicly rejects Treaty of Versailles and announces German rearmament
15 September 1935	Enactment of Nuremberg Laws against Jews and other minorities
3 October 1935	Italy invades Ethiopia
1936	Popular Front government elected in Spain
July 1936	Beginning of Spanish Civil War
October 1936	Rome-Berlin Axis Pact, an Italo-German accord
1936–1937	Popular Front government in France
27 April 1937	Bombing of the Spanish town of Guernica
9 November 1938	*Kristallnacht* initiates massive violence against Jews
March 1939	Fascists defeat the Spanish Republic
April 1939	Italy annexes Albania
May 1939	Pact of Steel between Germany and Italy

Conclusion

THE FRAGILE POSTWAR STABILITY OF THE 1920S crumbled under the pressures of economic depression, ongoing national antagonisms, and insecurity in the international arena. Europe after 1932 was plagued by the consequences of economic collapse, fascist success, and the growing threat of armed conflict. Parliamentary institutions were fighting and losing a tug-of-war with authoritarian movements. A fascist regime was in place in Italy. Dictatorships triumphed in Germany, Spain, and much of eastern and central Europe. Liberal parliamentary governments were threatened by the economic and social challenges of the postwar years.

The exclusion of the Soviet Union from Western internationalism exacerbated the crisis. The Bolshevik revolution had served as a political catalyst among workers in the West, attracting them to the possibility of radical solutions. That potential radicalization aggravated class antagonisms where mass politics prevailed and drove some political leaders to seek antidemocratic solutions in response to social unrest.

QUESTIONS FOR REVIEW

1. What problems for European stability were created or left unresolved by the armistice ending World War I?
2. What did Stalin's victory over Trotsky mean for economic development in the Soviet Union?
3. What is fascism, and why was it so alluring to Italians, Germans, and other Europeans?
4. How were rearmament, anti-Semitism, and economic self-sufficiency all part of Hitler's vision of *Lebensraum?*
5. Why did Europe's remaining democracies prove to be so frail during the 1930s?

DISCOVERING WESTERN CIVILIZATION ONLINE

You can obtain more information about the European search for stability between 1920 and 1939 at the websites listed below. See also the companion website that accompanies this text: www.ablongman.com/kishlansky, which contains an online study guide and additional resources.

Geographical Tour: Europe After 1918

www.library.nwu.edu/govpub/collections/league/index.html
This is the home page of a project to digitize documents published by the League of Nations.

www.fordham.edu/halsall/mod/modsbook40.html
A collection of links to electronic texts and materials on the interwar period, focusing on the cultural crisis in European and American societies as a result of World War I.

craton.geol.brockU.ca/guest/jurgen/bauhaus.htm
A brief history, images, and links to other resources on the famous German school of design, the Bauhaus, and its members.

www.fordham.edu/halsall/mod/modsbook41.html
Comprehensive collection of primary sources and links to materials on the Great Depression in Europe and the United States.

The Soviet Union's Separate Path

www.lib.duke.edu/ias/slavic/nep.htm
This site contains an exhaustive bibliography on Soviet history during the period of the New Economic Policy.

www.loc.gov/exhibits/archives
A virtual exhibit by the Library of Congress on material from the secret archives of the Central Committee of the Communist Party of the USSR.

The Rise of Fascist Dictatorship in Italy

www.fordham.edu/halsall/mod/modsbook42.html
This site refers to fascism in general, but it focuses on a speech of Mussolini and Spanish Civil War materials.

Hitler and the Third Reich

www2.h-net.msu.edu/~german/gtext/nazi/index.html
Sponsored by the H-German list, this is a small collection of electronic texts relating to the rise of the Nazis, the creation of the Third Reich, and World War II.

www.fordham.edu/halsall/mod/modsbook43.html
A collection of primary documents and links on the Weimar Republic and the rise of Nazism.

www.geocities.com/WallStreet/Exchange/5456/third.html
A website of stamps issued during the Third Reich with brief descriptions depicting the cultural values propagated by the Nazis.

Democracies in Crisis

dwardmac.pitzer.edu/anarchist_archives/spancivwar/Spanishcivilwar.html
This site was created by a political studies professor at Pitzer College (see link for Paris Commune in Chapter 23) and contains essays, bibliography, and photographs.

SUGGESTIONS FOR FURTHER READING

Geographical Tour: Europe After 1918

Joseph Rothschild, *East Central Europe Between the Two World Wars* (Seattle: University of Washington Press, 1983). A balanced survey of interwar developments in Poland, Czechoslovakia, Hungary, Yugoslavia, Romania, Bulgaria, Albania, and the Baltic states highlighting internal weaknesses and external vulnerabilities. A concluding chapter covers cultural contributions.

Crisis and Collapse in a World Economy

Gerald Feldman, *The Great Disorder: Politics, Economy and Society in the German Inflation, 1914–1924* (New York: Oxford University Press, 1993). Feldman's monumental study on the German inflation provides a detailed historical account of the economic conditions and monetary policy in Germany during and after the war.

The Soviet Union's Separate Path

Sheila Fitzpatrick, *Everyday Stalinism—Ordinary Life in Extraordinary Times: Soviet Russia in the 1930s* (New York: Oxford University Press, 1999). The author explores the rituals, family life, and institutions of the Stalinist era, what the author calls the "distinctive Stalinist habitat" of Russian urban life in the 1930s.

Chris Ward, ed., *The Stalinist Dictatorship* (New York: Oxford University Press, 1998). A collection of leading Soviet scholars examine Stalin's character, his role within the Soviet Union, and how Stalinism was a lived experience.

The Rise of Fascist Dictatorship in Italy

MacGregor Knox, *Dictatorship, Foreign Policy, and War in Fascist Italy and Nazi Germany* (London: Cambridge University Press, 2000). Expanding on his earlier work on Mussolini's foreign policy, the author offers a comparative perspective of Italy's and Germany's moves from unification to militant dictatorships, the similar forces that shaped their creation, and the differences in expansionist zeal, military traditions, and fighting power.

Zeev Sternhell with Mario Sznajder and Maia Asheri, *The Birth of Fascist Ideology: From Cultural Rebellion to Political Revolution* (Princeton N.J.: Princeton University Press, 1994). Approaches fascism as an ideology rather than a social movement and argues that it was already fully formed before World War I.

Hitler and the Third Reich

Ian Kershaw, *Hitler, 1889–1936: Hubris* (New York: W.W. Norton & Company, 1998); and *Hitler, 1936–1945: Nemesis* (New York: W.W. Norton & Company, 2000). The definitive two-volume biography provides a history of Germany society through Hitler's extraordinary political domination.

Bernd Widdig, *Culture and Inflation in Weimar Germany* (Berkeley: University of California Press, 2001). Through literary and filmic sources, the author provides a cultural analysis of a defining economic event in Germany history.

Democracies in Crisis

Ivan T. Berend, *Decades of Crisis: Central and Eastern Europe Before World War II* (Berkeley: University of California Press, 1998). The author offers a comprehensive overview of central and eastern Europe in the first half of the twentieth century and argues that the region "embarked on a historical 'detour'" in rejecting the parliamentary system and turning to nationalist authoritarian regimes.

Julian Jackson, *The Popular Front in France: Defending Democracy, 1934–1938* (Cambridge: Cambridge University Press, 1988). An in-depth study of Leon Blum's government, with a special emphasis on cultural transformation and the legacy of the Popular Front.

Michael Jackson, *Fallen Sparrows: The International Brigades in the Spanish Civil War* (Philadelphia: American Philosophical Society, 1994). A careful description of the members and activities of the International Brigades, which were organized under the direction of the Comintern to save the Spanish Republic.

Stanley G. Payne, *Fascism in Spain, 1923–1977* (Madison: The University of Wisconsin Press, 1999). The author presents a comprehensive history of Spanish fascism from its origins to the death of Franco.

Michael Richards, *A Time of Silence: Civil War and the Culture of Repression in Franco's Spain, 1936–1945* (Cambridge: Cambridge University Press, 1998). This work examines Spanish society during and after the Spanish Civil War in relation to Franco's policy of "moral and economic reconstruction" based on self-sufficiency.

CHAPTER 28

GLOBAL CONFLAGRATION: HOT WAR AND COLD WAR

THE VISUAL RECORD

PRECURSOR OF WAR

ADOLF HITLER'S ENTRY INTO VIENNA, capital city of his native country of Austria, was planned as a media event. The accompanying photograph displays a triumphant Hitler leading what appears to be a parade on 14 March 1938. Standing in his open Mercedes in order to be visible to thousands of cheering Austrians and protected by thirteen police cars, Hitler was no less the conqueror. The motorcade of limousines moved slowly along the Ringstrasse, Vienna's most important street of monumental public buildings, greeted by wildly cheering crowds. The Nazi swastika fluttered on flagpoles and draped facades. The viewer is left to wonder how the flags and banners could have been manufactured and positioned over the course of a weekend to greet the Fuhrer's unannounced and "friendly visit." The independent nation of Austria had, overnight and with virtually no bloodshed, become part of the German Reich.

On the first page of *Mein Kampf,* Hitler had promised, "Germany-Austria must return to the great German mother-country, and not because of any economic considerations. . . . One blood demands one Reich." By 1938, Hitler had consolidated power at home by removing the non-Nazi conservatives from positions of power in Germany. Now he alone determined foreign policy. As a cornerstone of that policy, Hitler aimed to unite all German people in one nation by extending German control over territories including those not ethnically German, but which could provide "living space" and economic self-sufficiency for the German race. (See "Nazi Goals" in Chapter 27.) Becoming increasingly impatient, Hitler feared that Germany could fail to achieve its destiny as a world power by waiting too long to act. He became more aggressive and willing to use military force as he set out to remove, one by one, the obstacles to German domination of central Europe—Austria, Czechoslovakia, and Poland.

The annexation of Austria was the first step in Hitler's plans for conquest. Using the threat of invasion, Hitler intimidated the Austrian government into legalizing the Nazi party, which thereby brought pro-Nazis into the

Austrian cabinet and German troops into the country. Many Austrians wanted to be joined to Germany; others had no desire to be led by Nazis. A rigged plebiscite in April 1938, organized by Goebbels's Propaganda Ministry, delivered a 99.75 percent vote of approval in Austria for annexation by Germany. With the union of Austria and Germany, the Third Reich claimed a population of 80 million people as it prepared itself for a war to the east. What appeared to be a parade of pomp and circumstance in March 1938 was really the precursor of a terrible conflagration that would last for six years and claim 50 million lives around the globe.

LOOKING AHEAD

This chapter considers the events leading to the outbreak of the war in 1939 and how collaboration and resistance developed across Europe as the German army advanced. Virulent racism played a central role in directing the war against Jews, Slavs, and others identified as inferior by Nazi racial policies. The power of Soviet patriotism and bravery and the entry of the United States into the war ensured Allied victory. Allied cooperation gave way, however, even as the peace was being forged under the direction of the two superpowers. The United States and the Soviet Union faced each other in a war no longer hot, but a Cold War that separated the world into two blocs.

AGGRESSION AND CONQUEST

The years between 1933 and 1939 marked a bleak period in international affairs when the British, the French, and the Americans were unwilling or unable to recognize the dire threat to world peace of Hitler and his Nazi state. The leaders of these countries did not comprehend Hitler's single-minded goal to extend German living space eastward as far as western Russia. They failed to understand the seriousness of the Nazi process of consolidation at home. Their preoccupation with the threat of communism also blinded them to the deadly reality of Hitler's threat, so they took no action against Hitler's initial acts of aggression. The war that began in Europe in 1939 eventually became a great global conflict that pitted Germany, Italy, and Japan—the Axis Powers—against the British Empire, the Soviet Union, and the United States—the Grand Alliance.

Even before war broke out in Europe, there was armed conflict in Asia. The rapidly expanding Japanese economy depended on Manchuria for raw materials and on China for markets. Chinese boycotts against Japanese goods and threats to Japanese economic interests in Manchuria led to a Japanese military occupation of Manchuria and the establishment of the Japanese puppet state of Manchukuo there in 1931–1932. When the powers of the League of Nations, led by Great Britain, refused to recognize this state, Japan withdrew from the League. Fearing that the Chinese government was becoming strong enough to exclude Japanese trade from China, Japanese troops and naval units began an undeclared war in China in 1937. Many important Chinese cities—Peking, Shanghai, Nanking, Canton, and Hankow—fell to Japanese forces. Relentless aerial bombardment of Chinese cities and atrocities committed by Japanese troops against Chinese civilians outraged Europeans and Americans. The governments of the Soviet Union, Great Britain, and the United States gave economic, diplomatic, and moral support to the Chinese government of Chiang Kai-shek. Thus the stage was set for a major military conflict in Asia and in Europe.

Hitler's Foreign Policy and Appeasement

For Hitler, a war against the Soviet Union for living space was inevitable. It would come, he told some of his close associates, in the years 1943–1945. However, he wanted to avoid fighting anew the war that had led to Germany's defeat in 1914–1918. In World War I, Germany fought on two fronts, and German soldiers, civilians, and resources were exhausted. In the next war, Hitler wanted to avoid fighting Great Britain while battling Russia. He convinced himself that the British would remain neutral if Germany agreed not to attack the British Empire. Would they not appreciate his willingness to abolish forever the menace of communism? Were they not Aryans also?

The Campaign Against Czechoslovakia. Encouraged by his success in annexing Austria in 1938, Hitler provoked a crisis in Czechoslovakia in the summer of the same year. He demanded "freedom" for the German-speaking people of the Sudetenland area of Czechoslovakia. His main objective, however, was to smash the Czech state, the major obstacle in central Europe to the launching of an attack on living space farther east.

Western statesmen did not understand Hitler's commitment to destroying Czechoslovakia or his willingness to fight a limited war against the Czechs to do so. Britain, seeking to avoid war, sent Prime Minister Neville Chamberlain (1869–1940) to reason with Hitler. Believing that transferring the Sudetenland, the German-speaking area of Czechoslovakia, to Germany was the only solution—and one that would redress some of the wrongs done to Germany after World War I—Chamberlain convinced France and Czechoslovakia to yield to Hitler's demands.

Appeasement at Munich. Chamberlain's actions were the result of British self-interest. British leaders agreed that their country could not afford another war like the Great War of 1914–1918. Defense expenditures had been dramatically reduced to devote national resources to improving domestic social services, protecting world trade, and fortifying Britain's global interests. Britain understood well its weakened position in its dominions. In the British hierarchy of priorities, defense of the British Empire ranked first, above defense of Europe, and Britain's commitment to western Europe ranked above the defense of eastern and central Europe.

Hitler's response to being granted everything he requested was to renege and issue new demands. His desire for war could not have been more transparent, nor could his unwillingness to play by the rules of diplomacy have been clearer. One final meeting was held at Munich to avert war. On 29 September 1938, one day before German troops were scheduled to invade Czechoslovakia, Mussolini and the French prime minister, Edouard Daladier (1884–1970), joined Hitler and Chamberlain at Munich to discuss a peaceful resolution to the crisis.

At Munich, Chamberlain and Daladier again yielded to Hitler's demands. The Sudetenland was ceded to Germany, and German troops quickly moved to occupy the area. The policy of the British and French was dubbed "appeasement" to indicate the willingness to concede to demands to preserve peace. Appeasement became a dirty word in twentieth-century European history, taken to mean weakness and cowardice. Yet Chamberlain was neither weak nor cowardly. His great mistake in negotiating with Hitler was assuming that Hitler was a reasonable man who, like all reasonable people, wanted to avoid another war.

Chamberlain thought that his mediation at Munich had won for Europe a lasting peace—"peace for our time," he reported. The people of Europe received Chamberlain's assessment with a sense of relief and shame—relief over what had been avoided, shame at having deserted Czechoslovakia. In fact, the policy of appeasement further destabilized Europe and accelerated Hitler's plans for European domination. Within months, Hitler cast aside the Munich agreement by annihilating Czechoslovakia. German troops occupied the western, Czech part of the state, including the capital of Prague. The Slovak eastern part became a German satellite. At the same time, Lithuania was pressured into surrendering Memel to Germany, and Hitler demanded control of Gdansk and the Polish Corridor. No longer could Hitler's goals be misunderstood.

Hitler's War, 1939–1941

In the tense months that followed the Munich meeting and the occupation of Prague, Hitler readied himself for war in western Europe. In May 1939, he formed a military alliance, the Pact of Steel, with Mussolini's Italy. Then Hitler and Stalin, previously self-declared enemies, shocked the West by joining their two nations in a pact of mutual neutrality, the Non-Aggression Pact of 1939. Opportunism lay behind Hitler's willingness to ally with the Communist state that he had denounced throughout the 1930s. A German alliance with the Soviet Union would, Hitler believed, force the British and the French to back down and to remain neutral while Germany conquered Poland—the last obstacle to a drive for expansion eastward—in a short, limited war. Stalin recognized the failure of the western European powers to stand up to Hitler. There was little possibility, he thought, of an alliance against Germany with the virulently anti-Communist Neville Chamberlain. The best Stalin could hope for was that the Germans and the Western powers would fight it out while the Soviet Union waited to enter the war at the most opportune moment. As an added bonus, Germany promised not to interfere if the Soviet Union annexed eastern Poland, Bessarabia, and the Baltic republics of Latvia and Estonia.

Finally recognizing Hitler's intent, the British and the French also signed a pact in the spring of 1939, promising assistance to Poland in the event of aggression. Tensions mounted throughout the summer as Europeans awaited the inevitable German aggression. On 1 September 1939, Germany attacked Poland, and by the end of the month the vastly outnumbered Poles surrendered. Although the German army needed no assistance, the Soviet Union invaded Poland ten days before its collapse, and Germany and the Soviet Union divided the spoils. Not trusting his alliance with Hitler, Stalin took measures to defend the Soviet Union against a possible German attack. The Soviet Union assumed military control in the Baltic states and demanded of Finland territory and military bases from which the city of Leningrad (formerly Petrograd) could be defended. When Finland refused, the Soviets invaded. In the snows of the "Winter War" of 1939–1940, the Finns initially fought the Soviet army to a standstill, much to the encouragement of the democratic West. However, the Finns were eventually defeated in March 1940.

▲ A German motorized detachment rides through a bomb-shattered town during the Nazi invasion of Poland in 1939. The invasion saw the first use of the *blitzkrieg*—lightning war—in which air power and rapid tank movement combined for swift victory.

War in Europe. Hitler's war, the war for German domination of Europe, had begun. But it had not begun the way he intended. Great Britain and France, true to their alliance with Poland and contrary to Hitler's expectations, declared war on Germany on 3 September 1939, even though they were unable to give any help to Poland. In the six months after the fall of Poland, no military action took

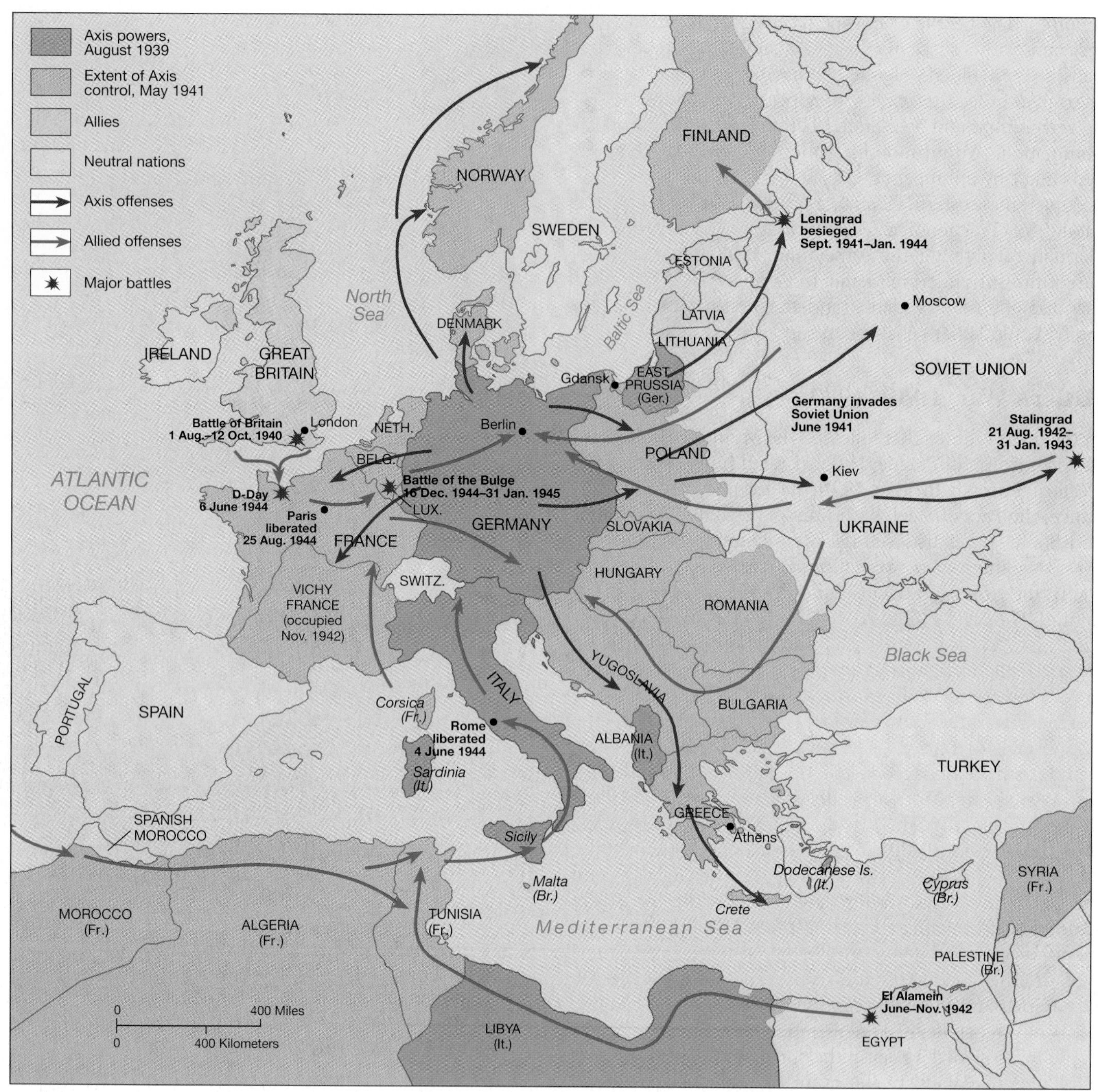

▲ World War II in Europe. Germany was eventually defeated by successful Allied campaigns in north Africa, Italy, eastern Europe, on Germany's two fronts, and by the D-Day landing in northern France in June 1944.

place between Germany and the Allies, because Hitler postponed offensives in northern and western Europe due to poor weather conditions. This strange interlude, which became known as "the phony war," was a period of suspended reality in which France and Great Britain waited for Hitler to make his next move. Civilian morale in France deteriorated among a population that still remembered the death and destruction that France had endured in the Great War. An attitude of defeatism germinated and grew before the first French soldier fell in battle.

With the arrival of spring, Germany attacked Denmark and Norway in April 1940. Then on 10 May 1940, Hitler's armies invaded the Netherlands, Belgium, and Luxembourg. By the third week of May, German mechanized forces were racing through northern France toward the English Channel, cutting off the British and

Belgian troops and 120,000 French forces from the rest of the French army. With the rapid defeat of Belgium, these forces were crowded against the Channel and had to be withdrawn from the beaches of Dunkirk. France, with a large and well-equipped army, nevertheless relied on Allied support and was in a desperate situation without it.

In France, the German army fought a new kind of war called *blitzkrieg* ("lightning war"), so named because of its speed. The British and the French had expected the German army to behave much as it had in World War I, concentrating its striking forces in a swing through coastal Belgium and Holland to capture Paris. French strategists believed that France was safe because of the hilly and forested terrain that they thought was impassable. They also counted on the protection of the fortress wall known as the Maginot Line that France had built in the interwar period. The Maginot Line stretched for hundreds of miles but was useless against mobile tank divisions that outflanked it. With stunning speed, Germany drove its tanks—panzers—through the French defenses at Sedan in eastern France.

The Fall of France. The French could have pinched off the advance of the overextended panzers, but the French army, suffering from severe morale problems, collapsed and was in retreat. On 17 June 1940, only weeks after German soldiers had stepped on French soil, Marshal Henri-Philippe Pétain, the great hero of the battle of Verdun in World War I, petitioned the Germans for an armistice. Three-fifths of France, including the entire Atlantic seaboard, was occupied by the German army and placed under direct German rule. In the territory that remained unoccupied, Pétain created a collaborationist government that resided at Vichy, a spa city in central France, and worked in partnership with the Germans for the rest of the war. Charles de Gaulle (1890–1970), a brigadier general who was opposed to the armistice, fled to London, where he set up a Free French government in exile.

The Battle of Britain. French capitulation in June 1940 followed Italian entry into the war on the side of Germany in the same month. The British were now alone in a war against the two Axis powers as Germany made plans for an invasion of the British Isles from across the English Channel. To prepare the way, the German air force under Reichsmarshal Hermann Göring (1893–1946) launched a series of air attacks against England, which became known as the Battle of Britain. The German air force first attacked British aircraft, airfields, and munitions centers and then shifted targets to major population centers such as London and industrial cities such as Coventry. Between 7 September and 2 November 1940, the city of London was bombed every night. Serious damage was inflicted on the city, and 15,000 people were killed.

Under the leadership of Winston Churchill the British resisted these attacks. Churchill had succeeded Chamberlain as prime minister in 1940. He was a master public speaker who, in a series of radio broadcasts, inspired the people of Britain with the historic greatness of the task confronting them: holding out against Nazism until the forces of the overseas British Empire and the United States could be marshaled to liberate Europe. The British Royal Air Force inflicted serious losses on German aircraft, while British industry was able to maintain steady production of planes, bombs, and armaments. Civilians endured the nightly destruction and air raids in what Churchill termed Britain's "finest hour." Recognizing his lack of success in establishing air superiority over the Channel or in breaking the will of the British people, Hitler abandoned the Battle of Britain and canceled the invasion.

The London Underground was pressed into service as a bomb shelter during the Battle of Britain.

It was not in Great Britain but in the Balkans that Hitler was able to engage the British enemy and inflict serious losses. The British had a presence in the Greek peninsula, where their air units were deployed to support the valiant resistance of the Greeks against Italian aggression. In his original plans for a limited war, Hitler hoped to establish control over the Balkans by peaceful, diplomatic means. But Mussolini's disastrous attempt to achieve military glory by conquering Greece impelled Hitler to make his own plans to attack Greece. Using Bulgaria as the base of operations, Germany invaded Yugoslavia, whose government had been weakened by a recent military coup. The capital of Belgrade fell in April 1941. Internal ethnic enmity between the Croats and the Serbs led to the mutiny of Croatian soldiers and the formation of an autonomous Croatian government in Zagreb that was favorably disposed to the Germans.

German troops then crossed the Yugoslav border into Greece, capturing the capital of Athens on 27 April 1941. German forces then turned their attention to the Greek island of Crete, where fleeing British soldiers sought refuge. In the first mass paratroop attack in history, the Germans rapidly subdued Crete, forcing the British to evacuate to Egypt. The British were routed and experienced humiliating defeat by the German blitzkrieg.

The Balkans were important to Hitler for a number of reasons. Half of Germany's wheat and livestock came from the countries of southeastern Europe. Romanian and Hungarian oil fields supplied Germany's only non-Russian oil. Greece and Yugoslavia were important suppliers of metal ores—including aluminum, tin, lead, and copper—so necessary for industry and the war effort.

The necessity of protecting resources, especially the Romanian oil fields, also gave the area geopolitical importance for Germany. Hitler was well aware of the strategic significance of controlling the Dardanelles in launching an attack against the Soviet Union. Potentially, the British lifeline to its empire could also be cut by control of the eastern Mediterranean.

Collaboration and Resistance

No one nation has ever controlled the Balkans, and Hitler understood that he must rule not by occupation but by collaboration. Collaboration made fewer demands on Germany's troops and resources, as Vichy collaboration in France made clear.

Some Balkan collaborators joined puppet governments out of an ideological commitment to fascism. They were hostile to communism and believed that Hitler's Nazism was far preferable to Stalin's communism. They saw in the German victory the chance to put their beliefs into practice. Some governments collaborated with the Germans out of national self-interest. The government of Hungary allied with Germany in the hope of winning back territory lost at the end of World War I, while Romania allied with the Soviet Union. The government of Slovakia was loyal to the Third Reich because Hitler had given it independence from the Czechs. A German puppet state was set up in the Yugoslav province of Croatia. Other collaborators were pragmatists who believed that by taking political office, they could negotiate with the German conquerors and soften the effects of the Nazi conquest on their people. Hitler had little affection for local ideological fascists and sometimes smashed their movements. He preferred to work with local generals and administrators.

Resistance against German occupation and collaborationist regimes took many forms. Resisters wrote subversive tracts, distributed them, gathered intelligence information for the Allies, sheltered Jews or other enemies of the Nazis, committed acts of sabotage, assassination or other violent acts, and carried on guerrilla warfare against the German army. Resisters ran the risk of endangering themselves and their families, who, if discovered, would be tortured and killed. Resistance movements developed most strongly after the German attack on the Soviet Union in 1941, when the Communist parties of occupied Europe formed the core of the violent resistance against the Nazi regime. Resistance grew stronger when the Germans began to draft young European men for work on German farms and in German factories. Many preferred to go underground rather than to Germany.

One of the great resistance fighters of the Second World War was Josip Broz (1892–1980), alias Tito. He was a Croatian communist and a Yugoslav nationalist. His partisans fought against Italian and German troops and kept ten or more German divisions tied up in Yugoslavia. Tito gained the admiration and the support of Churchill, Roosevelt, and Stalin. After liberation, Tito's organization won 90 percent of the vote in the Yugoslav elections, and he became the leader of the country in the postwar era. Resistance entailed enormous risks and required secrecy, moral courage, and great bravery. On the whole, however, the actions of resistance fighters seldom affected military timetables and did little to change the course of the war and Hitler's domination of Europe.

By the middle of 1941, Hitler controlled a vast continental empire that stretched from the Baltic Sea to the Black Sea and from the Atlantic Ocean to the Russian border. The German army occupied territories and controlled satellites, or Hitler relied on collaborationist governments for support. Having destroyed the democracies of western Europe, with the exception of Great Britain, Hitler's armies absorbed territory and marched across nations at rapid speed with technical and strategic superiority. But military conquest was not the only horror that the seemingly invincible Hitler inflicted on European peoples.

RACISM AND DESTRUCTION

War is hell, as the saying goes. But the horrors perpetrated in World War II exceeded anything ever experienced in Western civilization. In both the European and Asian theaters of battle, claims of racial superiority were invoked to justify inhuman atrocities. The Germans and Japanese used spurious arguments of racial superiority to fuel their war efforts. In Asia, the subjugation of inferior peoples became a rallying cry for conquest. But the Germans and the Japanese were not alone in using racist propaganda. The United States employed racial stereotypes to depict the inferiority of the enemy. They seized the property of Japanese-Americans living on the West Coast and interned them in "relocation" camps.

Nowhere, however, was the use of racism by the state more virulent than in Germany. Nazis used the phrase "the master race" to identify the human beings they considered worthy of living; those not worthy were designated "subhuman." Hatred of certain groups fueled both politics and war. Hitler promised the German people a purified Reich of Aryans "free of the Jews" and the racially and mentally inferior. Slavic peoples—Poles and Russians—he designated as subhumans who could be displaced in the search for Lebensraum and German destiny. With the war in eastern Europe, anti-Semitism changed from a policy of persecution and expropriation in the 1930s into a program of systematic extermination beginning in 1941.

Enforcing Nazi Racial Policies

Social policies that were erected on horrifying biomedical theories discriminated against a variety of social groups in the Third Reich. Beginning in 1933, police harassment of those identified as gypsies began in earnest. In 1936, the Nazi bureaucracy expanded to include the Reich Central Office against the Gypsy Nuisance, which assiduously maintained files on gypsies. Gypsies were subject to all racialist legislation and could be sterilized for their "inferiority" without any formal hearing process. In September 1939, even as the war was beginning, high-ranking Nazis planned the removal of 30,000 gypsies to Poland. Over 200,000 German, Russian, Polish, and Balkan gypsies were killed in the course of the war by internment in camps and by systematic extermination.

Nazi racial policies also singled out mixed-race children for special disgrace. Children born of white German mothers and black fathers were a consequence of the presence of French colonial troops from Senegal, Morocco, and Malaga, who were among the occupation forces in the Rhineland in the 1920s and 1930s. During both the Weimar Republic and the Nazi regime the press attacked these children, who probably numbered no more than 500 to 800 individuals, as "Rhineland bastards." In 1937, without any legal proceedings, the Nazis sterilized them.

People who suffered from hereditary illnesses were also labeled a biological threat to the racial purity of the German people. State doctors devised illegitimate medical tests to establish who was feeble-minded and genetically defective. By treating the society of the Third Reich as one huge laboratory for the production of the racially fit and the "destruction of worthless life," categories were constructed according to subjective criteria that claimed scientific validation. Medical officials examined children, and those who were judged to be deformed were separated from their families and transferred to special pediatric clinics, where they were either starved to death or injected with lethal drugs. In the summer of 1939, the government organized euthanasia programs for adults and identified 65,000 to 70,000 Germans for death. The government required asylums to rank patients according to their race, state of health, and ability to work. These rankings were used to determine candidates for death. In Poland, mental patients were simply shot; in other places they were starved to death. The uncooperative, the sick, and the disabled were purged as racially undesirable.

The category covering the "asocial" was even broader than that covering hereditary illness. Under this designation, criminals, beggars, vagrants, and the homeless could be compulsorily sterilized. Alcoholics, prostitutes, and people with sexually transmitted diseases could be labeled asocial and treated accordingly. These forms of behavior were considered to be hereditary and determined by blood.

Nazi social policies likewise treated homosexuals as "community aliens." The persecution of homosexual men intensified after 1934, when any form of "same-sex immorality" became subject to legal prosecution. "Gazing and lustful intention" were left to the definition of the police and the courts. Criminal sentences could involve a term in a concentration camp. But because homosexuality was judged to be a sickness rather than an immutable biological trait, gays did not become the primary object of Nazi extermination policies that began to be enforced against the "biologically inferior." Treatment of homosexuality might involve psychoanalysis, castration, or indefinite incarceration in a concentration camp.

The badge of homosexual men in Nazi concentration camps during the war was a pink triangle. Although it is not clear how many homosexual men were actually killed by the Nazis, estimates run as high as 200,000. Officials of the Third Reich singled out homosexual men rather than lesbian women because the men's behavior was considered a greater threat to the perpetuation of the German race.

The Destruction of Europe's Jews

In 1933, when Hitler and the Nazis came to power, they did not have a blueprint for the destruction of Europe's

Seizing Jews in Warsaw. Nazi soldiers rounded up men, women, and children for "resettlement" in the east.

Jews. The anti-Semitic policies of the Third Reich evolved incrementally in the 1930s and 1940s. After 1938, German civil servants expropriated Jewish property as rightfully belonging to the state. When the war began, Jews were rounded up and herded into urban ghettos in Germany and in the large cities of Poland. For a time, the German foreign ministry considered the possibility of deporting the more than three million Jews under German control to Madagascar, an island off the southeast coast of Africa. Until 1941, Nazi policies against the Jews were often uncoordinated and unfocused.

The "Final Solution." Confinement in urban ghettos was the beginning of a policy of concentration that ended in annihilation. After identifying Jews, seizing their property, and confining them to ghettos, German authorities began to implement a step-by-step plan for extermination. There appears to have been no single order from Hitler that decreed what became known to German officials as the "Final Solution"—the total extermination of European Jews. But Hitler's recorded remarks make it clear that he knew and approved of what was being done to the Jews. A spirit of shared purpose permeated the entire administrative system from the civil service through the judiciary.

Administrative agencies competed to interpret Hitler's will. SS guards in the camps and police in the streets embraced Hitler's "mission" of destruction. To ensure that the whole process operated smoothly, a planning conference for the Final Solution was held for the benefit of state and party officials at Wannsee, a Berlin suburb, in January 1942. Reinhard Heydrich (1904–1942), head of the Sicherheitsdienst (SD), or Security Service of the SS, led the conference.

Mass racial extermination began with the German conquest of Poland, where both Jews and non-Jews were systematically killed. It continued when Hitler's army invaded the Soviet Union in 1941. This campaign, known as Operation Barbarossa, set off the mass execution of eastern Europeans who were declared to be enemies of the Reich. The tactics of the campaign pointed the way to the Final Solution. To the Nazi leadership, Slavs were subhuman, and by extension, Russian Jews were the lowest of the low, even more despised than German Jews. Nazi propaganda had equated Jews with Communists, and Hitler had used the single word *Judeocommunist* to describe what he considered to be the most dangerous criminal and enemy of the Third Reich, the enemy who must be annihilated at any cost.

The executions were the work of the SS, the elite military arm of the Nazi Party. Special mobile murder squads of the SD under Heydrich were organized behind the German lines in Poland and Russia. Members of the army were aware of what the SS squads were doing and participated in some of the extermination measures. In the spring of 1941, Hitler ordered a massive propaganda campaign to be conducted among the armed forces. This campaign indoctrinated the army to believe that the invasion of the Soviet Union was more than a military campaign; it was a "holy war," a crusade that Germany was waging for civilization. SS chief Heinrich Himmler, probably responding to oral orders from Hitler, set about enforcing Hitler's threats with concrete extermination policies. Fearful that the SS would be outstripped by the regular army in Hitler's favor, Himmler exhorted his men to commit the worst atrocities.

Firing squads shot Russian victims en masse, then piled their bodies on top of one another in open graves. Reviewing these procedures for mass killings, Himmler—ever competitive with other Nazi agencies—suggested a more efficient means of extermination that would require less labor power and would enhance the prestige of the SS. As a result, extermination by gas was introduced; the exhaust fumes of vans were piped into the enclosed cargo areas that served as portable gas chambers. In Poland, Himmler replaced the vans with permanent buildings housing gas chambers, which used Zyklon B, a gas developed for the purpose by the chemical firm I.G. Farben. The chambers could annihilate thousands of people at a time.

The Third Reich began erecting its vast network of death in 1941. The first extermination camp was created in Chelmno, Poland, where 150,000 people were killed between 1941 and 1944. The camps practiced systematic extermination of the groups that were deemed racially inferior, sexually deviant, and politically dangerous. The terms *genocide, judeocide*, and *Holocaust* have been used to describe the mass slaughter of the Jewish people, most of which took place in five major killing centers in what is now Polish territory: Chelmno, Belzec, Sobibor, Treblinka, and Auschwitz.

Many victims, transported for days in sealed railroad cars without food, water, or sanitation facilities, died before ever reaching the camps. Others died within months as forced laborers for the Reich. People of all ages were starved, beaten, and systematically humiliated. Guards taunted their victims verbally, degraded them physically, and tortured them with false hope. Having been promised clean clothes and nourishment, camp internees were herded into "showers" that dispensed gas rather than water. Descriptions of life in the camps reveal a systematized brutality and inhumanity on the part of the German, Ukrainian, and Polish guards toward their victims. In all, 11 million people died by the extermination process—6 million Jews and almost as many non-Jews, including children, the aged, homosexuals, Slavic slave laborers, Soviet prisoners of war, Communists, members of the Polish and Soviet leadership, various resisters, gypsies, and Jehovah's Witnesses.

The words ARBEIT MACHT FREI ("Work Makes You Free") were emblazoned over the main gate at Auschwitz, the largest of the concentration camps. It was at Auschwitz that the greatest number of people died in a single place, including more than one million Jews. The healthy and the young were kept barely alive to work. Hard labor, starvation, and disease—especially typhus, tuberculosis, and other diseases that spread rapidly because of the lack of sanitation—claimed many victims.

On entering the camps, the sick and the aged were automatically designated for extermination because of their uselessness as a labor force. Many children were put to work, but some were designated for extermination. Many mothers chose to accompany their children to their deaths to comfort them in their final moments. Pregnant women too were considered useless in the forced labor camps and were sent immediately to the "showers." The number of German Jewish women who died in the camps was 50 percent higher than the number of German Jewish men. Starvation diets meant that women stopped menstruating. Because the Nazis worried that women of childbearing age would continue to reproduce, women who showed signs of menstruation were killed immediately. Women who were discovered to have given birth in the camp were killed, as were their infants. Family relations were completely destroyed, as inmates were segregated by sex. It soon became clear that even those who were allowed to live were intended only to serve the Nazis' short-term needs.

Resisting Destruction. The impossibility of any effective resistance was based on two essential characteristics of the process of extermination. First, the entire German state and its bureaucratic apparatus were involved in the policies, laws, and decrees of the 1930s that singled out victims while most other Germans stood silently by. There was no possibility of appeal and no place to hide. Those who understood early what was happening and who had enough money to buy their way out emigrated to safer places, including Palestine and the United States. But most countries used immigration quotas to block the entry of German and eastern European refugees. Neither Britain nor the United States was willing to deal with a mass influx of European Jews. Jews in the occupied countries and the Axis nations had virtually no chance to escape. They were trapped in a society where all forces of law and administration worked against them.

A second reason for the impossibility of effective resistance was the step-by-step nature of the process of extermination, which meant that few understood the final outcome until it was too late. Initially, in the 1930s, many German Jews believed that things could get no worse and obeyed the German state as good citizens. Even the policy of removing groups from the ghetto militated against resistance because the hope was that sending 1,000 Jews to "resettlement" would allow the 10,000 Jews who remained behind to be saved. The German authorities deliberately cultivated misunderstanding of what was happening.

Isolated instances of resistance in the camps—rioting at Treblinka, for example—only highlight how impossible rebellion was for physically debilitated people in these heavily guarded centers. In April 1943, in the Warsaw ghetto, Jews organized a resistance movement with a few firearms and some grenades and homemade Molotov cocktails. Starvation, overcrowding, and epidemics made Warsaw, the largest of the ghettos, into an extermination

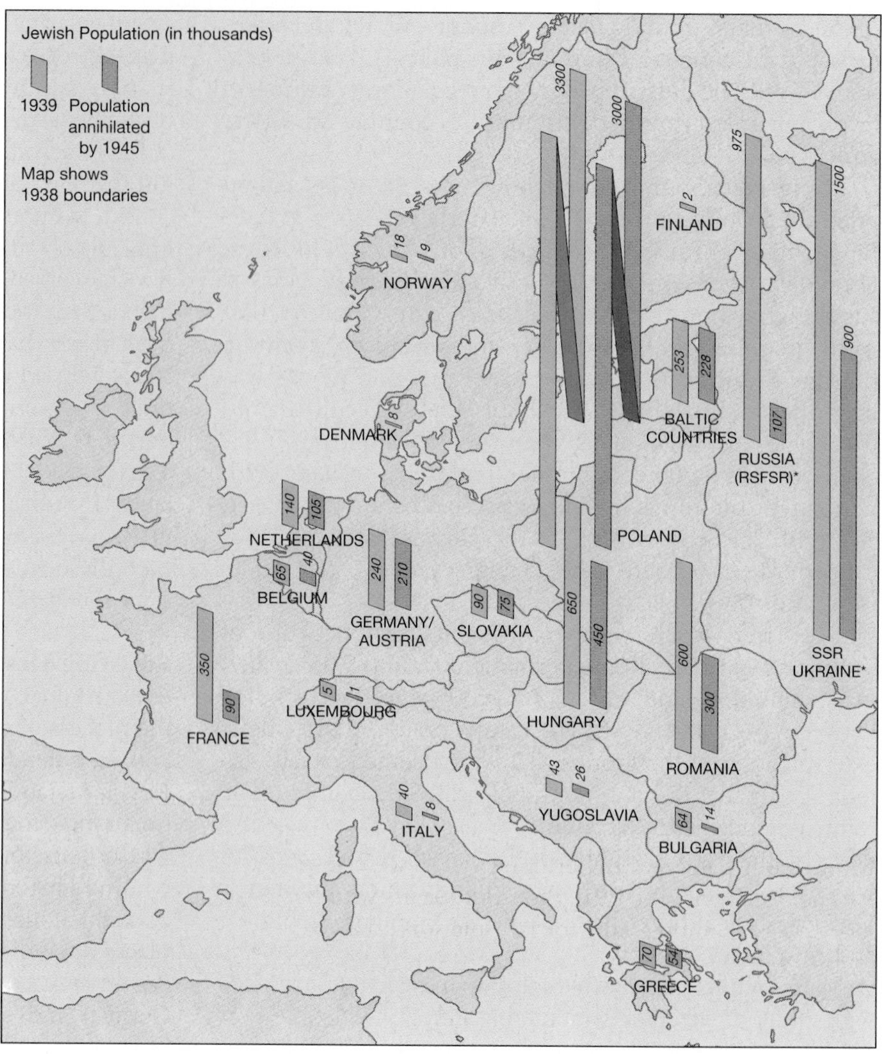

The Holocaust. The greatest loss of Jewish life in the Holocaust took place in Poland and the Soviet Union.

camp. As news reached the ghetto that "resettlement" was the death warrant for tens of thousands of Polish Jews, armed rebellion erupted. It did not succeed in blocking the completion of the Final Solution against the Warsaw ghetto the following year, when the SS commandant proclaimed, "The Jewish Quarter of Warsaw is no more!" Polish and Russian Jews accounted for 70 percent of total Jewish deaths.

Who Knew? It is impossible that killing on such a scale could have been kept secret. Along with those who ordered extermination operations, the guards and camp personnel who were involved in carrying out the directives were aware of what was happening. Those who brought internees to the camps, returning always with empty railroad cars, knew it too. People who saw their neighbors disappearing believed for a time that they were being resettled in the east. But as news filtered back to central and western Europe, it was more difficult to sustain belief in this ruse. People who lived near the camps could not ignore the screams and the fumes of gas and burning bodies that permeated the environs of the camps.

Although it never publicly announced its extermination program, the German government convinced its citizens that the policies of the Nazi state could not be judged by ordinary moral standards. Official propaganda convinced millions that the Reich was the supreme good. Admitting the existence of the extermination program carried with it a responsibility on which few acted, perhaps out of fear of reprisals. There were some heroes, such as Raoul Wallenberg of Sweden, who interceded for Hungarian Jews and provided food and protection for Jews in the Budapest ghetto. The king of Denmark, when informed that the Nazis had ordered Danish Jews to wear the yellow star, stated that he and his family would also wear the yellow star as a "badge of honor." However, heroic acts were isolated and rare.

Collaborationist governments and occupied nations often cooperated with Nazi extermination policies. The French government at Vichy introduced and implemented a variety of anti-Jewish measures. All of this was done without German orders and without German pressure. By voluntarily identifying and deporting Jews, the Vichy government sent 75,000 men, women, and children to their deaths.

As the war dragged on for years, internees of the camps hoped and prayed for rescue by the Allies. But such help did not come. The U.S. State Department and the British Foreign Office had early and reliable information about the nature and extent of the atrocities. But they did not act.

The handful of survivors found by Allied soldiers who entered the camps after Germany's defeat presented a haunting picture of humanity. A British colonel who entered the camp at Bergen-Belsen in April 1945 gave a restrained account of what he found:

> As we walked down the main road of the camp, we were cheered by the internees, and for the first time we saw their condition. A great number were little more than living skeletons. There were men and women lying in heaps on both sides of the track. Others were walking slowly and aimlessly about, vacant expressions on their starved faces.

The sight of corpses piled on top of one another lining the roads, the piles of shoes, clothing, underwear, and gold teeth extracted from the dead shocked those who came to liberate the camps. One of the two survivors of Chelmno summed it up: "No one can understand what happened here."

The Final Solution was a perversion of every value of civilization. The international tribunal for war crimes that met in 1945 in the German city of Nuremberg attempted to mete out justice to the criminals who were responsible for the destruction of 11 million Europeans who had been labeled as demons and racial inferiors. History must record, even if it cannot explain, such inhumanity.

ALLIED VICTORY

At the end of 1941, the situation appeared grim for the British and their dominions and the Americans who were assisting them with munitions, money, and food. Hitler had achieved control of a vast land empire covering nearly all of continental Europe in the west, north, south, and center, as well as much of North Africa. This empire, which Hitler called his "New Order," included territories that were occupied and directly administered by the German army, satellites, and collaborationist regimes. It was fortified by alliances with Italy, the Soviet Union, and Japan. Hitler commanded the greatest fighting force in the world, one that had knocked France out of the war in a matter of weeks, brought destruction to British cities, and conquered Yugoslavia in 12 days. Much of the world was coming to fear German invincibility.

Then, in June 1941, Hitler's troops invaded the Soviet Union, providing the British with an ally. In December, the naval and air forces of Japan attacked U.S. bases in the Pacific, providing the British and the Russians with still another ally. What began as a European war became a world war. This was the war that Hitler did not want and that Germany could not win—a long, total war to the finish against three powers with inexhaustible resources: the British Empire, the Soviet Union, and the United States.

The Soviet Union's Great Patriotic War

Hitler had always considered the Soviet Union Germany's primary enemy. The 1939 Non-Aggression Pact with Stalin was no more than an expedient for Hitler. He rebuked a Swiss diplomat in 1939 for failing to grasp the central fact of his foreign policy:

> Everything I undertake is directed against Russia. If those in the West are too stupid and too blind to understand this, then I should be forced to come to an understanding with the Russians to beat the West, and then, after its defeat, turn with all my concentrated force against the Soviet Union.

Soviet Unpreparedness. On 22 June 1941, when German armies marched into Russia, they found the large Soviet army totally unprepared for war. Stalin's purges in the late 1930s removed 35,000 officers from their posts by dismissal, imprisonment, or execution. Many of the men who replaced them were unseasoned in the responsibilities of leadership. The Russians had not expected the German attack to come so soon, and when the Germans did invade Russian territory, Stalin was so overwhelmed that he fell into a depression and was unable to act for days.

On 3 July 1941, in his first radio address after the attack, Stalin identified his nation with the Allied cause: "Our struggle for the freedom of our country will merge with the struggle of the peoples of Europe and America for their independence, for democratic liberties." He accepted offers of support from the United States and Great Britain. With France defeated and Great Britain crippled, the future of the war depended on Soviet fighting power and U.S. supplies.

German Offensive and Reversals. Hitler's invasion of Russia involved three million soldiers from Germany and Germany's satellites, the largest invasion force in history. It stretched along an immense battlefront from the Baltic Sea to the Black Sea. Instead of exclusively targeting Moscow, the capital, the German army concentrated first on destroying Soviet armed forces and capturing Leningrad in the north and the oil-rich Caucasus in the south. In the beginning, the German forces advanced rapidly in a blitzkrieg across western Russia, where they were greeted as liberators in Ukraine. The Germans took 290,000 prisoners of war and massacred tens of thousands of others in their path through the Jewish settlements of western Russia.

Within four months, the German army had advanced to the gates of Moscow, but they concentrated their forces too late. The Red Army rallied to defend Moscow, as thousands of civilian women set to work digging trenches and antitank ditches around the city. The Soviet people answered Stalin's call for a scorched-earth policy by burning everything that might be useful to the advancing German troops. German troops had also burned much in their path, depriving themselves of essential supplies for the winter months ahead. The German advance was stopped, as the best ally of the Red Army—the Russian winter—settled in. The first snow fell at the beginning of October. By early November, German troops were beginning to suffer the harsh effects of an early and exceptionally bitter Russian winter.

Hitler promised the German people that "final victory" was at hand. So confident was Hitler of a speedy and decisive victory that he sent his soldiers into Russia wearing only light summer uniforms. Hitler's generals knew better and tried repeatedly to explain military realities to him. General Heinz Guderian (1888–1954), commander of the tank units, reported that his men were suffering frostbite, tanks could not be started, and automatic weapons were jamming in the sub-zero temperatures. Back in Germany, the civilian population received little accurate news of the campaign. They began to suspect the worst when the government sent out a plea for woolen blankets and clothing for the troops.

By early December, the German military situation was desperate. The Soviets, benefiting from intelligence information about German plans and an awareness that Japan was about to declare war on the United States, recalled fresh troops from the Siberian frontier and the border with China and Manchuria and launched a powerful counterattack against the poorly outfitted German army outside Moscow. Under the command of General Gyorgi Zhukov (1896–1974), Russian troops, dressed and trained for winter warfare, pushed the Germans back in retreat across the snow-covered expanses. By February, 200,000 German troops had been killed, 46,000 were missing in action, and 835,000 were casualties of battle and the weather. Thus the campaign cost the German army over one million casualties. It probably cost the Soviets twice that number of wounded, missing, captured, and dead soldiers. At the end of the Soviet counterattack in March, the German army and its satellite forces were in a shambles reminiscent of Napoleon's troops, who had been decimated 130 years earlier in the campaign to capture Moscow. An enraged Hitler dismissed his generals for retreating without his permission, and he himself assumed the position of commander-in-chief of the armed forces.

Hitler was not daunted by the devastating costs of his invasion of Russia. In the summer of 1942, he initiated a second major offensive, this time to take the city of Stalingrad. Constant bombardment gutted the city, and the Soviet army was forced into hand-to-hand combat with the German soldiers. But the German troops, once again inadequately supplied and unprepared for the Russian winter, failed to capture the city. The Battle of Stalingrad was over in the first days of February 1943. Of the original 300,000 members of the German Sixth Army, fewer than 100,000 survived to be taken prisoner by the Soviets. Of those, only 5,000 returned to Germany in 1955, when German prisoners of war were repatriated.

Soviet Patriotism. The Soviets succeeded by exploiting two great advantages in their war against Germany: the large Soviet population and their knowledge of Russian weather and terrain. There was a third advantage that Hitler ignored: the Soviet people's determination to sacrifice everything for the war effort. In his successive Five-Year Plans, Stalin had mobilized Soviet society with an appeal to fulfill and surpass production quotas. In the summer of 1941, as Hitler's troops threatened Moscow, Stalin used the same rhetoric to appeal to his Soviet "brothers and sisters" to join him in waging "the Great Patriotic War." The Russian people shared a sense of common purpose, sacrifice, and moral commitment in their loyalty to the nation.

The advancing Germans themselves intensified Soviet patriotism by torturing and killing tens of thousands of peasants who might have willingly cooperated against the Stalinist regime. Millions of Soviet peasants joined the Red Army. Young men of high school age were drafted into the armed forces. Three million women became wage earners for the first time as they replaced men in war industries. Women who remained on the land worked to feed the townspeople and the soldiers. Because the Red Army had requisitioned horses and tractors for combat, grain had to be sown and harvested by hand—and this often meant women's hands. Tens of thousands of Russians left their homes in western Russia to work for relocated Soviet industries in the Urals, the Volga region, Siberia, and Central Asia.

More than 20 million Soviet people—soldiers and civilians, men, women, and children—died in the course of World War II. In addition to those who were killed in battle, millions starved as a direct result of the hardships of war. In 1943, food was so scarce that seed for the next year's crops was eaten. One in every three men born in 1906 died in the war. But Soviet resistance did not flag.

The Great Patriotic War had a profound impact on Soviet views of the world and the Soviet Union's place in it. The Soviet Union sacrificed 10 percent of its population to the war effort and incurred well over 50 percent of all the deaths and casualties of the war. Few families escaped the death of members in the defense of the nation. Soviet citizens correctly considered that they had given more than any other country to defeat Hitler. For the Soviet people their suffering in battle made World War II the Soviet Union's war, and their sacrifice made possible the Allied victory.

The United States Enters the War

Victory still eluded the Allies in western Europe, where another nation, the United States, had now entered the fray. Although a neutral power, the United States began extending aid to the Allies after the fall of France in 1940. Since neither Britain nor the Soviet Union could afford to pay the entire cost of defending Europe against Hitler, the U.S. Congress passed the Lend-Lease Act in 1941. This act authorized President Roosevelt to provide armaments to Great Britain and the Soviet Union without payment.

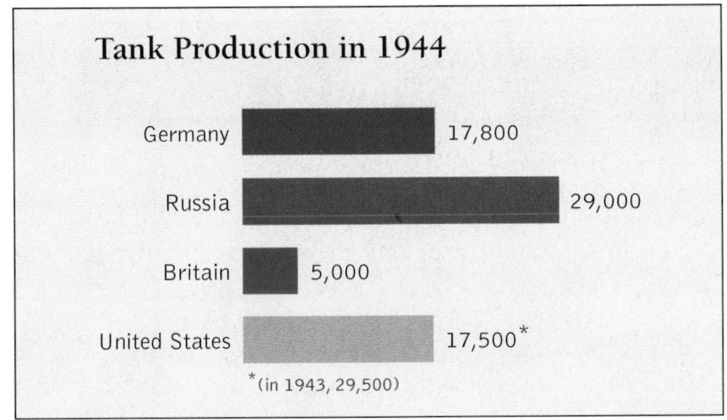

America became "the arsenal of democracy." The United States and Britain sent 4,100 airplanes and 138,000 motor vehicles, as well as steel and machinery, to the Soviet Union for the campaign of 1943. In all, the United States pumped $11 billion worth of equipment into the Soviet war effort between 1941 and 1945. Stalin later told Roosevelt that the Soviet Union would have lost the war with Germany without the help of the Americans and the British.

Japan Attacks. Before the United States entered the war, President Roosevelt and his advisers considered Germany, not Japan, to be America's primary target for a future war. The United States, aware that Japan wanted to expand its control over China and Southeast Asia, initially opposed this expansion through economic embargoes. The presence of the Soviet Union pressing eastward across Asia, coupled with the colonial presences in Asia of Great Britain, France, and the United States, severely constrained Japan's capacity to expand its frontiers and ensure its security. The war in western Europe and the German invasion of the Soviet Union in June 1941 meant that the Japanese could concentrate their attention farther south in China, Indochina, and Thailand. Japan's limited reserves of foreign currency and raw materials drew its attention to the oil and raw materials in Southeast Asia.

In September 1940, Japan joined forces with the Axis Powers of Germany and Italy in the Tripartite Pact, in which the signatories, promising mutual support against aggression, acknowledged the legitimacy of each other's expansionist efforts in Europe and Asia. Japanese-American relations deteriorated after the Japanese invasion of southern Indochina in July 1941. The United States insisted that Japan vacate China and Indochina and reestablish the open door for trade in Asia. However, the United States knew that it was only a matter of time until Japan attacked U.S. interests but was uncertain about where that attack would take place.

On Sunday morning, 7 December 1941, Japan struck at the heart of the U.S. Pacific Fleet, which was stationed at Pearl Harbor, Hawaii. The fleet was literally caught asleep at the switch: 2,300 people were killed, and eight battleships and numerous cruisers and destroyers were sunk or severely damaged. The attack crippled U.S. naval power in the Pacific as the U.S. Navy suffered its worst loss in history in a single engagement. The attack on Pearl Harbor led the United States immediately to declare war on Japan. In President Roosevelt's words, 7 December 1941 was "a date which will live in infamy."

In the next three months, Japan captured Hong Kong, Malaya, and the important naval base at Singapore from the British, taking 60,000 prisoners. In December 1941, the Japanese landed in Thailand and secured immediate agreement for Japanese occupation of strategic spots in the country. They then turned to the Malay peninsula, decisively defeating the British fleet off Malaya and pushing on the ground toward Singapore, which they conquered in February 1942. They conquered British Borneo in January, drove the Dutch from all of Indonesia but New Guinea, pushed U.S. forces in the Philippines into the Bataan peninsula, occupied Burma, and inflicted severe defeats on British, Dutch, and U.S. naval power in East Asia. U.S. General Douglas MacArthur (1880–1964) surrendered the Philippines to the Japanese on 2 January 1942 with the promise to return. With the armies of Germany deep in Russian territory, Australia faced the threat of a Japanese invasion.

Germany Declares War on the United States. Hitler praised the Japanese government for its action against the British Empire and against the United States and its "millionaire and Jewish backers." Germany, with its armies retreating from Moscow, nevertheless declared war on the United States on 11 December 1941. Hitler, in fact, considered that the United States was already at war with Germany because of its policy of supplying the Allies. Within days the United States, a nation with an army smaller than Belgium's, had gone from neutrality to a war in two theaters. Although militarily weak, the United States was an economic giant, commanding a vast industrial capacity and access to resources. The United States grew even stronger under the stimulus of war, increasing its production by 400 percent in two years. It now devoted itself to the demands of a total war and the unconditional surrender of Germany and then Japan.

Winning the War in Europe

The Allies did not always have the same strategies or concerns. President Roosevelt and Prime Minister Churchill had already discussed common goals in the summer of 1941 before U.S. entry into the war. The United States embraced the priority of the European war and the postponement of war in the Pacific. Stalin pleaded for the British and the Americans to open up a second front against Germany in western Europe to give his troops some relief and save Soviet lives. Anglo-American resources were committed to the Pacific to stop the Japanese advance, and the Americans and the British disagreed as to where a second front in Europe might be opened.

PRESIDENT FRANKLIN ROOSEVELT'S REQUEST FOR A DECLARATION OF WAR ON JAPAN, 8 DECEMBER 1941

On 7 December 1941, the Japanese naval and air forces attacked the American naval base at Pearl Harbor in Hawaii, killing and wounding 3,457 military personnel and civilians. Most of the U.S. Pacific fleet was moored in Pearl Harbor, and it sustained severe damage to its naval vessels, battleships, and aircraft. U.S. military and political leaders were taken completely by surprise by the Japanese attack.

FOCUS QUESTIONS

Why is December 7, 1941, called a "day which will live in infamy"? How does Roosevelt's declaration of war reflect outrage over the "infamy"?

TO THE CONGRESS OF THE UNITED STATES: Yesterday, December 7, 1941—a date which will live in infamy—the United States of America was suddenly and deliberately attacked by naval and air forces of the Empire of Japan.

The United States was at peace with that Nation and, at the solicitation of Japan, was still in conversation with its Government and its Emperor looking toward the maintenance of peace in the Pacific. Indeed, one hour after Japanese air squadrons had commenced bombing in Oahu, the Japanese Ambassador to the United States and his colleague delivered to the Secretary of State a formal reply to a recent American message. While this reply stated that it seemed useless to continue the existing diplomatic negotiations, it contained no threat or hint of war or armed attack.

It will be recorded that the distance of Hawaii from Japan makes it obvious that the attack was deliberately planned many days or even weeks ago. During the intervening time the Japanese Government has deliberately sought to deceive the United States by false statements and expressions of hope for continued peace.

The attack yesterday on the Hawaiian Islands has caused severe damage to American naval and military forces. Very many American lives have been lost. In addition, American ships have been reported torpedoed on the high seas between San Francisco and Honolulu.

Yesterday the Japanese Government also launched an attack against Malaya.

Last night Japanese forces attacked Hong Kong.

Last night Japanese forces attacked Guam.

Last night Japanese forces attacked the Philippine Islands.

Last night the Japanese attacked Wake Island.

This morning the Japanese attacked Midway Island.

Japan has, therefore, undertaken a surprise offensive extending throughout the Pacific area. The facts of yesterday speak for themselves. The people of the United States have already formed their opinions and well understand the implications to the very life and safety of our Nation.

As Commander-in-Chief of the Army and Navy I have directed that all measures be taken for our defense.

Always will we remember the character of the onslaught against us.

No matter how long it may take us to overcome this premeditated invasion, the American people in their righteous might will win through to absolute victory. . . .

With confidence in our armed forces—with the unbounded determination of our people—we will gain the inevitable triumph—so help us God.

I ask that the Congress declare that since the unprovoked and dastardly attack by Japan on Sunday, December seventh, a state of war has existed between the United States and the Japanese Empire.

Franklin D. Roosevelt.

The second front came not in western Europe but in the Mediterranean. After the defeat of France in 1940 and the neutralization of the French navy in the Mediterranean, Italy saw a chance to extend its empire in North Africa. With a large army stationed in Libya, Ethiopia, Eritrea, and Italian Somaliland, Mussolini ordered a series of offensives against the Sudan, Kenya, British Somaliland, and Egypt. Most of the Italian advances had been reversed by the British, and 420,000 Italian troops, including African soldiers, were listed as casualties, compared to 3,100 British troops. Germany, however, having succeeded in invading Greece and Yugoslavia, turned its attention to aiding its Axis partner in trouble. In February 1941, Hitler sent General Erwin Rommel (1891–1944), a master strategist of tank warfare, to help the Italians take control of the Suez Canal by launching a counteroffensive in the North African war. Rommel's Axis troops succeeded in entering Egypt and driving the British east of the Egyptian border, thereby dealing the British a serious setback.

The British were simultaneously securing territories in Syria, Palestine, and Iraq to guarantee the oil pipelines of the Persian Gulf for the Allies. Between November 1941 and July 1942 the pendulum swung back and forth between Allied and Axis forces in the Desert War, as the North African campaign came to be known. In August 1942 the Allied forces, now under the command of Bernard Montgomery (1887–1976), launched a carefully planned offensive at El Alamein, and Rommel was forced to retreat to Tunisia.

Now a joint U.S.-British initiative, the first of the war, landed troops in French Morocco and Algeria and advanced into Tunisia, attacking Rommel's Afrika Korps from behind. About 250,000 German and Italian soldiers were taken prisoner, as the Axis powers were decisively defeated in May 1943. Although not a central theater of the war, North Africa provided British forces with important victories and served as a testing ground for the cooperation of Allied forces.

Because of British interests in the Mediterranean, Churchill insisted on a move from North Africa into Sicily and Italy. This strategy was put into effect in 1942. The Italian government withdrew from the war in September, but German troops carried on the fight in Italy. The Anglo-American invasion of Italy did little to alleviate Russian losses, and the Soviet Union absorbed almost the entire force of German military power until 1944. Stalin's distrust of his allies increased. Churchill, Roosevelt, and Stalin met for the first time in late November 1943 in Teheran, Iran. Roosevelt and Churchill made a commitment to Stalin to open a second front in France within six months. Stalin, in turn, promised to attack Japan to aid the United States in the Pacific. The great showdown of the global war was at hand.

On 6 June 1944, Allied troops under the command of the U.S. General Dwight D. Eisenhower (1890–1969) came ashore on the beaches of Normandy in the largest amphibious landing in history. In a daring operation identified by the code name Operation Overlord, 2.2 million U.S., British, and Free French forces, 450,000 vehicles, and 4 million tons of supplies poured into northern France. Allied forces broke through German lines to liberate Paris in late August. The Germans launched a last-ditch counterattack in late December 1944 in Luxembourg and Belgium. This Battle of the Bulge only slowed the Allied advance; in March 1945, U.S. forces crossed the Rhine into Germany. Hitler, meanwhile, refused to surrender and insisted on a fight to the death of the last German soldier. Members of Hitler's own High Command had tried unsuccessfully to assassinate him in July 1944. The final German defeat came in April 1945, when the Russians stormed the German capital of Berlin. Hitler, living in an underground bunker near the Chancellery building, committed suicide on 30 April 1945.

▼ Supplies for the Allied forces pour ashore at the beachheads of Normandy during Operation Overlord in 1944. The invasion began the opening of the second front that Stalin had been urging on the Allies since the German armies thrust into Russia in 1941.

Japanese War Aims and Assumptions

Japan and the United States entered the Pacific war with very different understandings of what was at stake. Initially, the Japanese appealed to Southeast Asian leaders as the liberators of Asian peoples from Western colonialism and imperialism.

Japanese Hegemony in Asia. The approach struck a responsive chord as the Japanese established what they called the Greater East Asia Co-Prosperity Sphere. In November 1943, Burma's leader, Ba Maw, spoke warmly of Japan, but his welcome of the Japanese liberators did not last long. As he bluntly explained in his memoirs, "The brutality, arrogance, and racial pretensions of the Japanese militarists in Burma remain among the deepest Burmese memories of the war years; for a great many people in Southeast Asia these are all they remember of the war."

The Greater East Asia Co-Prosperity Sphere began in 1940 and lasted until the summer of 1945. This reorganization of east and southeast Asia under Japanese hegemony constituted a redefinition of world geography with Japan at the center. The Japanese fashioned a romanticized vision of the family living in harmony, all members knowing their places and enjoying the complementary division of responsibilities and reciprocities that made family life work smoothly. Behind this pleasant image lurked the reality of a brutal power structure forcing subject peoples to accept massively inferior positions in a world fashioned exclusively to satisfy Japanese desires and needs. The Japanese viewed southeast Asia principally as a market for Japanese manufactured goods, a source of raw materials, and a source of profits for Japanese capital invested in mining, rubber, and raw cotton. Plans were made for hydroelectric power and aluminum-refining facilities.

Wartime Japanese nakedly displayed their disdain for the people they conquered in southeast Asia. All subject peoples were to bow on meeting a Japanese, while at public assemblies a ritual bow in the direction of the Japanese emperor was required. This practice dismayed southeast Asians such as Indies Muslims or Philippine Catholics, who regarded Japanese emperor worship as pagan and presumptuous. Japanese holidays, such as the emperor's birthday, were enforced as Co-Prosperity Sphere holidays, and the calendar was reset to the mythical founding of the Japanese state in 660 B.C.E.

The Japanese were less brazen toward the Chinese in their rhetoric, in part because so much of Japanese, and indeed East Asian, civilization had its roots in China. However, Japanese aggression against the Chinese included one of the worst periods of destruction in modern warfare. When the Japanese took over the Nationalist capital of Nanjing in December 1937, 20,000 women were raped, 30,000 soldiers were killed, and another 12,000 civilians died in the more than six weeks of wanton terror inflicted by Japanese soldiers.

Japan's View of the West. With regard to Westerners, Japanese propaganda avoided labeling them as inferior. In part, this reflected Japan's economic and political emulation of the West since the late nineteenth century. Rather than denigrating Western people, the Japanese chose to elevate themselves as a people descended from divine origins. Stressing their unique mythical history gave the Japanese a strong sense of moral superiority, which perhaps led them to misread Westerners. For example, some Japanese mistakenly assumed that individual selfishness and egoism would make Americans and Europeans incapable of mobilizing for a long fight.

Winning the War in the Pacific

The tide in the Pacific war began to turn when the planned Japanese invasion of Australia was thwarted. Fighting in the jungles of New Guinea, Australian and U.S. troops under the command of General Douglas MacArthur turned back the Japanese army. U.S. Marines did likewise with a bold landing at Guadalcanal and months of bloody fighting in the Solomon Islands. In June 1942, within six months of the attack on Pearl Harbor, U.S. naval forces commanded by Admiral Chester Nimitz (1885–1966) inflicted a defeat on the Japanese navy from which it could not recover. In the Battle of Midway, Japan lost four aircraft carriers, a heavy cruiser, over 300 airplanes, and 5,000 men. Midway was the Pacific equivalent of the Battle of Stalingrad.

In the summer of 1943, as the Soviet Union launched the offensive that was to defeat Germany, the United States began to move across the Pacific toward Japan. Nimitz and MacArthur conceived a brilliant plan in which U.S. land, sea, and air forces fought in a coordinated effort. With a series of amphibious landings, they hopped from island to island. Some Japanese island fortresses such as Tarawa were taken; others such as Truk were bypassed and cut off from Japanese home bases. With the conquest of Saipan in November 1944 and Iwo Jima in March 1945, the U.S. forces acquired bases from which B-29 bombers could strike at the Japanese home islands. In the summer of 1945, in the greatest air offensive in history, U.S. planes destroyed what remained of the Japanese navy, crippled Japanese industry, and mercilessly firebombed major population centers. The attack ended with the dropping of atomic bombs on the cities of Hiroshima and Nagasaki. The Japanese government accepted U.S. terms for peace and surrendered unconditionally on 2 September 1945 on the battleship *Missouri* in Tokyo Bay. Four months after the defeat of Germany, the war in Asia was over.

The Fate of Allied Cooperation: 1945

The costs of World War II in terms of death and destruction were the highest in history. An estimated 50 million lives had been lost, including those of 6 million Jews. Most

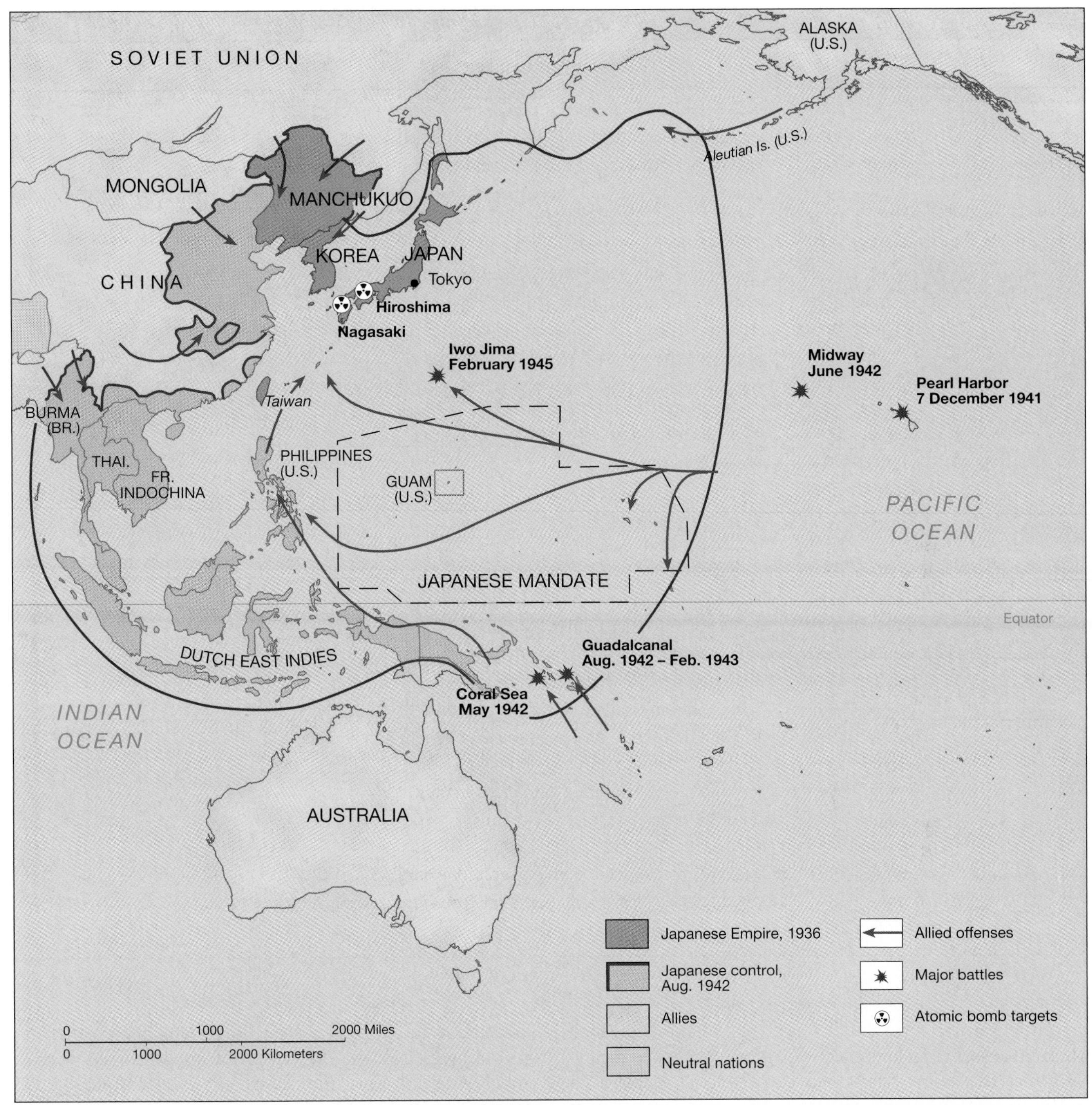

▲ World War II in the Pacific, 1941–1945. Japanese hegemony in Asia was reversed beginning in 1943 by means of coordinated land, sea, and air offensives.

of the dead were Europeans, and most of them were Russians and Poles. An unusually high incidence of civilian deaths distinguished the Second World War from previous wars: well over 50 percent of the dead were noncombatants. Deliberate military targeting of cities explains this phenomenon only in part. The majority of civilian deaths were the result of starvation, enslavement, massacre, and deliberate extermination.

Civilian Populations. The psychological devastation of continual violence, deprivation, injury, and rape of survivors cannot be measured. Terrorizing citizens became an established means of warfare in the modern age. Another phenomenon not matched in the First World War emerged in 1945: mass rape. The Soviet officer corps encouraged the advancing Russian army to use sexual violence against German women and girls. The Russians, treated brutally

CHRONOLOGY

WORLD WAR II

1937	Japan begins undeclared war on China
March 1938	Germany annexes Austria to the German Reich
29 September 1938	Chamberlain, Daladier, Mussolini, and Hitler meet at Munich conference
May 1939	Pact of Steel: military alliance between Italy and Germany
1939	Non-Aggression Pact between Germany and the Soviet Union
1 September 1939	Germany attacks Poland
3 September 1939	Great Britain and France declare war on Germany
April 1940	Germany attacks Denmark and Norway
May 1940	Germany invades the Netherlands, Belgium, Luxembourg, and then France
June 1940	Italy enters the war on the side of Germany
17 June 1940	French Marshal Pétain petitions Germany for an armistice and creates a collaborationist government at Vichy
September 1940	Japan, Germany, and Italy sign Tripartite Pact
September–November 1940	The Battle of Britain
22 June 1941	Germany invades the Soviet Union
1941	First extermination camp created in Chelmno, Poland
7 December 1941	Japan attacks Pearl Harbor; the following day, the United States declares war on Japan
11 December 1941	Germany declares war on the United States
January 1942	Wannsee Conference, where the Final Solution is planned
June 1942	Battle of Midway
September 1942	Italian government withdraws from the war
April 1943	Unsuccessful uprising in the Warsaw ghetto
November 1943	Churchill, Roosevelt, and Stalin meet at Teheran conference
6 June 1944	Allied forces land in northern France—D-Day
February 1945	Churchill, Roosevelt, and Stalin meet at Yalta
March 1945	American forces march into Germany
30 April 1945	Hitler commits suicide
July and August 1945	Churchill, Truman, and Stalin meet at Potsdam
6 August 1945	United States drops atomic bomb on Hiroshima
2 September 1945	Japan surrenders

by Hitler's army, returned the savagery in their advance through eastern and central Europe. Rape became a means of direct retaliation. The Great Patriotic War reached its nadir in central Europe with collective rape as a form of war against civilians. In East Asia, victorious Japanese soldiers raped Chinese women as part of the spoils of war. Japanese military commanders also organized camps of "comfort women," unwilling young women who had been abducted from Korea, the Philippines, and other occupied areas to service the sexual "needs" of Japanese soldiers. Regardless of the country that was involved, victorious armies practiced rape against civilian populations as one of the unspoken aspects of conquest.

Material destruction was also great. Axis and Allied cities, centers of civilization and culture, were turned into wastelands by aerial bombing. The Germans bombed Rotterdam and Coventry. The British engineered the fire-bombing of Dresden. The German army destroyed Warsaw and Stalingrad. The United States leveled Hiroshima and Nagasaki. The nations of Europe were weakened after World War I; after World War II, they were crippled. Europe was completely displaced from the position of world dominance it had held for centuries. The United States alone was undamaged and stronger after the war than before, its industrial capacity and production greatly improved by the war.

The Big Three. What would be the future of Europe? The leaders of the United States, Great Britain, and the Soviet Union—the Big Three, as they were called—met three times between 1943 and 1945: first at Teheran; then in February 1945 at Yalta, a Russian Black Sea resort; and finally in July and August 1945 at Potsdam, a suburb of Berlin. They coordinated their attack on Germany and Japan and discussed their plans for postwar Europe. After Allied victory, the governments of both Germany and Japan would be totally abolished and completely reconstructed. No deals would be made with Hitler or his successors; no peace would be negotiated with the enemy; surrender would be unconditional. Germany would be disarmed and de-Nazified, and its leaders would be tried as war criminals. The armies of the Big Three would occupy Germany, each with a separate zone, but the country would be governed as a single economic unit. The Soviet Union, it was agreed, could collect reparations from Germany. With Germany and Japan defeated, a United Nations organization would provide the structure for a lasting peace in the world.

Stalin expected that the Soviet Union would decide the future of the territories of eastern Europe that the Soviet army had liberated from Germany. This area was vital to the security of the war-devastated Soviet Union; Stalin saw it as a protective barrier against another attack from the west. The Big Three agreed that Romania, Bulgaria, Hungary, Czechoslovakia, and Poland would have pro-Soviet governments. Since Soviet troops occupied these countries in 1945, there was little that the British and the Americans could do to prevent Russian control unless they wanted to go to war against the Soviet Union. Churchill realistically accepted this situation. But for Americans who took seriously the proclamations of President Roosevelt that their country had fought to restore freedom and self-determination to peoples oppressed by tyranny, Soviet power in eastern Europe was a bitter disappointment.

REGULATING THE COLD WAR

With the cessation of the "hot" war that had ripped Europe apart from 1939 to 1945, the armies of the United States and the Soviet Union met on the banks of the Elbe River in 1945. Greeting each other as victors and allies, the occupying armies waited for direction on how to conduct the peace. Europe and Japan were destroyed, leaving the United States and the Soviet Union as indisputably the two richest and strongest nations in the world.

The Two Superpowers

The Soviets understood that they ran a sorry second to the United States in military superiority—the United States was alone in possessing the atomic bomb—and wealth, in which, measured in GNP, the United States was 400 percent richer than the Soviet Union. War had made these two superpowers allies; now the peace promised to make them once again into wary foes. In the three years that followed the war, a new kind of conflict emerged between the two superpower victors, a war that was deemed "cold" because of its lack of military violence but a bitter war nonetheless.

The Cold War emerged as an ideological opposition between communism and capitalist democracies, dominated by the two superpowers—the Soviet Union and the United States—and affecting the entire globe. Drawing on three decades of distrust between the East and the West, the Cold War was related to the economic and foreign policy goals of both superpowers.

Churchill, Roosevelt, and Stalin—the Big Three—at the Yalta Conference. Stalin invoked the Yalta agreements to justify the Soviet Union's control over eastern Europe after the war.

Territorial Gains of the USSR. With the goal of creating a buffer zone of protection, the Soviet Union gained control of territory in eastern Europe. The "Iron Curtain" refers to the post–World War II boundaries that separated capitalist from communist states.

Winston Churchill captured the drama of the new international order in a speech he delivered in Missouri in 1946: "From Stettin in the Baltic to Trieste in the Adriatic an iron curtain has descended across the Continent." The term "iron curtain" described graphically the new fate of Europe, rigidly divided between East and West, a pawn in the struggle of the superpowers.

European Recovery. Cold War conflict initially developed because of differing Russian and American notions about the economic reconstruction of Europe. The Soviet Union realized that U.S. aid to Europe was not a primarily humanitarian program. It was part of an economic offensive in Europe that would contribute to the dominance of U.S. capital in world markets. The United States recognized that the Soviet Union hoped to achieve its own recovery through outright control of eastern Europe. Needing the stability of peace, the Soviets saw in eastern Europe, hostile as the area may have been to forced integration, a necessary buffer against Western competition. The Soviet Union feared U.S. intentions to establish liberal governments and capitalist markets in these states bordering its own frontiers and viewed such attempts as inimical to Soviet interests. For these reasons, Stalin refused to allow free elections in Poland and, by force of occupying armies, annexed neighboring territories that included eastern Finland, the Baltic states, East Prussia, eastern Poland, Subcarpathian Ukraine (Ruthenia), and Bessarabia. Except in the case of East Prussia, these annexations were limited to territories that had once been part of tsarist Russia.

NATO and Other Treaty Alliances. With the aim of containing the Soviet Union, the United States entered into a series of military alliances around the world. To provide mutual assistance should any member be attacked, the United States joined with Belgium, Britain, Canada, Denmark, France, Iceland, Italy, the Netherlands, Norway, and Portugal in 1949 to form the North Atlantic Treaty

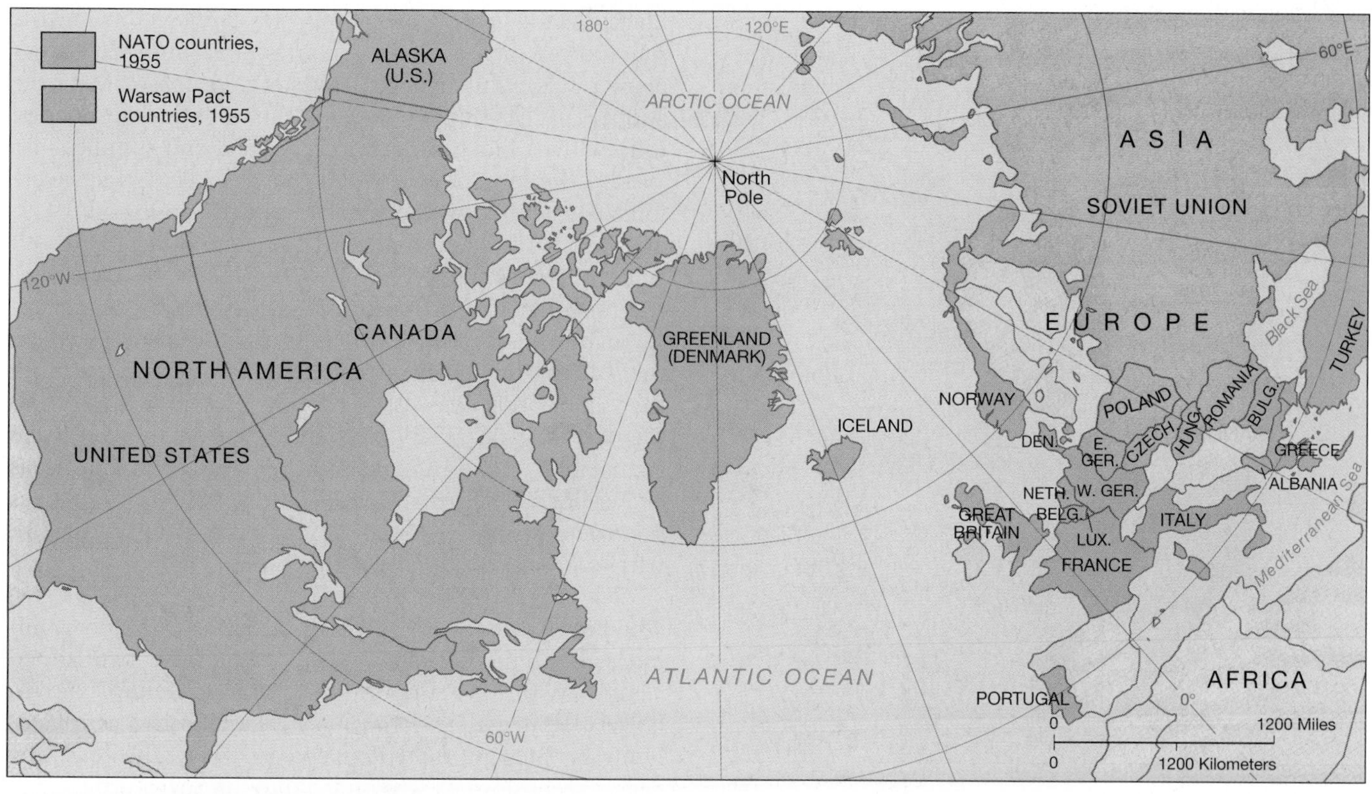

The Cold War: U.S. and Soviet Alliances. The U.S. and Soviet blocs (NATO countries and Warsaw Pact countries, respectively) constituted a balance of power in global politics.

Organization (NATO). Greece and Turkey became members in 1952, West Germany in 1955, and Spain in 1982. The potential military threat of the Soviet Union in western Europe prompted this peacetime military alliance.

A challenge to Cold War power politics came from within the NATO alliance. General Charles de Gaulle, as president of the French Fifth Republic, rejected the straitjacket of U.S. dominance in western Europe and asserted his country's independent status by exploding the first French atomic bomb in 1960. Refusing to place the French military under a U.S. general who served as supreme Allied Commander for NATO, de Gaulle completely withdrew France from participation in NATO by 1966. He forged an independent French foreign policy, taking advantage of the loosening of bloc politics around the mid-1960s.

The Southeast Asia Treaty Organization (SEATO) in 1954 and the Baghdad Pact of 1955 (known as CENTO in 1959) followed. The United States strengthened its military presence throughout the period by acquiring 1,400 military bases in foreign countries for its own forces. The Soviet Union countered developments in the West with its own alliances and organizations. In 1949, the Soviet Union established the Council for Mutual Economic Assistance (Comecon) with bilateral agreements between the Soviet Union and eastern European states. Comecon was Stalin's response to the U.S. Marshall Plan in western Europe. Rather than providing aid, however, Comecon benefited the Soviet Union at the expense of its partners and sought to integrate and control the economies of eastern Europe for Soviet gain. In 1955, Albania, Bulgaria, Romania, Czechoslovakia, Hungary, Poland, and East Germany—all Comecon members—joined with the Soviet Union to form a defensive alliance organization known as the Warsaw Pact. The Soviet Union intended its eastern European allies to serve as a strategic buffer zone against the NATO forces.

The Two Germanys and the World in Two Blocs

In central Europe, Cold War tensions first surfaced over the question of how to treat Germany. The United States and the Soviet Union had very different ideas about the future of their former enemy. In fostering economic reconstruction in Europe, the United States counted on a German economy transfused with U.S. funds that would be self-supporting and stable. The Soviet Union, however, blamed Germany for its extreme destruction and demanded that German resources be siphoned off for Soviet

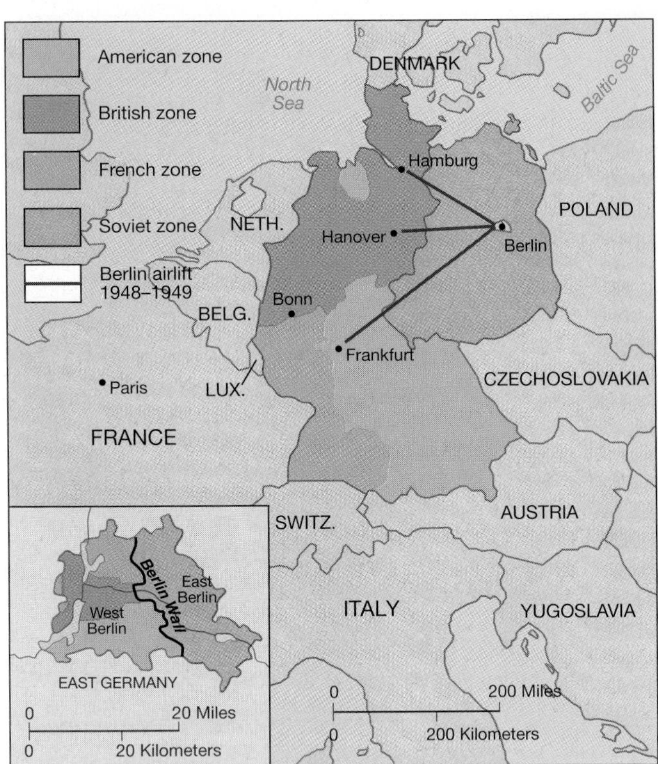

The Division of Germany. Germany was divided into four zones by the victors at the end of World War II. Berlin was in the heart of the Soviet zone, East Germany, and the city itself was divided between East and West sectors.

reconstruction. Stricken as the Soviets were with 20 million dead, millions of homeless refugees surviving in dire poverty, and many cities in ruins, commandeering German labor and stripping Germany of its industrial plant seemed to them only fair.

East and West Germany. With Germany's defeat, its territory had been divided into four zones, occupied by U.S., Soviet, British, and French troops. An Allied Control Commission consisting of representatives of the four powers was to govern Germany as a whole, in keeping with the decisions made at Yalta before the end of the war. As Soviet and U.S. antagonisms over Germany's future deepened, however, Allied rule polarized between East and West. The internal politics of each area were determined by the ideological conflicts between communism and capitalist free enterprise.

Allied attempts to administer Germany as a whole faltered and failed in 1948 over a question of economic policy. The zones of the Western occupying forces (the United States, Great Britain, and France), now administered as a single unit, issued a uniform and stable currency that the Soviets accurately saw as a threat to their own economic policies in Germany. The Soviets blockaded the city of Berlin, which, although it was behind the frontier of the Soviet sector, was being administered in sectors by the four powers and whose western sector promised to become a successful enclave of Western capitalism. With the support of the people of West Berlin, the Allies responded to the Soviet blockade by airlifting food and supplies into West Berlin for a period of almost a year. The Soviets were forced to withdraw the blockade in the spring of 1949. The Berlin blockade hardened the commitment on both sides to two Germanys.

From divided and occupied Germany, two new states came into existence in 1949, their origins separated by less than a month. The Federal Republic of Germany, within the Allied orbit, was established as a democratic, parliamentary regime. Free elections brought the Christian Democrat Konrad Adenauer (1876–1967) to power as chancellor. The German Democratic Republic was ruled as a single-party state under Walter Ulbricht (1893–1973), who took his direction from the Soviet Union.

The Soviet Bloc. The division of Germany became a microcosm of the division of the world into two armed camps. With the support of local Communist parties, Soviet-dominated governments were established in Poland, Hungary, Bulgaria, and Romania in 1947. The following year, Czechoslovakia was pulled into the Soviet orbit.

In 1953, the man who had ruled the Soviet Union for almost three decades died. The death of Joseph Stalin unleashed a struggle for power within the Communist party leadership. It also initiated almost immediately a process of de-Stalinization and the beginnings of a thaw in censorship and repression. After five years of jockeying for power among Stalin's former lieutenants, Nikita Khrushchev emerged victorious and assumed the office of premier in 1958.

De-Stalinization also blossomed in eastern Europe. Discontent over collectivization, low wages, and the lack of consumer goods fueled a latent nationalism among eastern European populations that were resentful of Soviet control and influence. Violence erupted in 1953 in East Berlin as workers revolted over conditions in the workplace, but it was quickly and effectively suppressed. Demands for reforms and liberalization in Poland also produced riots and changes in Communist party leadership. Wladislaw Gomulka (1905–1982), a communist with a nationalist point of view who had survived Stalin's purges, aimed to take advantage of the power vacuum created by the departure of Stalinist leaders. Gomulka refused to back down in the face of severe Soviet pressure and the threat of a Soviet invasion to keep him from power. Elected as the first secretary of the Communist Party in Poland, Gomulka sought to steer his nation on a more liberal course.

Hungarians followed suit with their demands for diversity and for the withdrawal of Hungary from the Warsaw Pact. On 23 October 1956, inspired by the events in Poland, Hungarians rose up in anger against their old-guard Stalinist rulers. Imre Nagy (1896–1958), a liberal

Communist, took control of the government, attempted to introduce democratic reforms, and relaxed economic controls. Moscow responded to liberal experimentation in Hungary by sending tanks and troops into Budapest. Brutal repression and purges followed. The Hungarian experience in 1956 made clear that too much change too quickly would not be tolerated by the Soviet rulers or by hard-line communist leaders in the Eastern Bloc countries. The violent crushing of the Hungarian revolution reminded everyone of the realities of Soviet control and the Soviet Union's defense priorities in Eastern Europe.

The Berlin Wall and Eastern Europe. East Berlin in the late 1950s and early 1960s posed a particular problem for communist rule. Unable to compete successfully in wages and standard of living with the western, capitalist sector of the city, East Berlin saw increasing numbers of its population, especially the educated and professional classes, crossing the line to a more prosperous life. In 1961, the Soviet Union responded to this problem by building a wall that cordoned off the part of the city it controlled. The Berlin Wall eventually stretched for 103 miles, with heavily policed crossing points, turrets, and troops and tanks facing each other across the divide that came to symbolize the Cold War.

In 1968, the policy of de-Stalinization reached a critical juncture in Czechoslovakia. Early in 1968, Alexander Dubcek, Czech party secretary and a member of the younger, educated generation of technocrats, supported liberal reforms in Czechoslovakia. He acted on popular desires for nationalism, the end of censorship, and better working conditions. Above all, he led the way to democratic reforms in the political process that would restore rule to the people. Dubcek spoke of "socialism with a human face," although, unlike the Hungarians in 1956, he made no move to withdraw his country from the Warsaw Pact or to defy Soviet leadership. Moscow nevertheless feared the erosion of obedience within the Eastern bloc and the collapse of one-party rule in the Czech state and sent thousands of tanks and hundreds of thousands of Warsaw Pact troops to Prague and other Czech cities to reestablish control. The Czechs responded with passive resistance. The Soviet invasion made clear that popular nationalism was intolerable in an Eastern Bloc nation.

Alone among eastern European leaders, Marshal Tito of Yugoslavia resisted Soviet encroachment. As a partisan leader of communist resistance during World War II, Tito had heroically battled the Germans. Ruling Yugoslavia as a dictator after 1945, he refused to accede to Soviet directives to collectivize agriculture and to participate in joint economic ventures. Instead of taking sides in the Cold War, he maintained an independent position of neutrality between the East and the West.

Asia. Asia was the next arena for the development of Cold War antagonisms. In 1950, the United States and the United Nations intervened when North Korea attacked South Korea. Korea, formerly controlled by Japan, had been divided after the war as a result of the presence of Russian and U.S. troops. Communist-dominated North Korea refused to accept the artificial boundary between it and Western-dominated South Korea. China, a Communist state after the victory of Mao Zedong (1893–1976) in 1949, intervened in the Korean conflict when U.S. troops advanced on Chinese frontiers in October 1950. After three years of military stalemate, Korea was partitioned at the 38th parallel in 1953. The Soviet Union was not party to the conflict in Korea, but the United States considered China to be in the Soviet camp rather than an independent contender for power.

The United States was heavily committed as a military presence in Southeast Asia after the French withdrawal from Indochina caused by its defeat at Dien Bien Phu in 1954. Arguing the domino theory—that one Southeast Asian country after another would fall like a row of dominoes to communist takeover—the United States also intervened in Laos and Cambodia. Between 1961 and 1973 the United States committed U.S. troops to a full-scale war—though it was officially termed only a "military action"—against communist guerrilla forces throughout the region.

The Middle East. The Middle East was another theater of confrontation between the superpowers. The United States and the Soviet Union used aid to win support of "client" states. The withdrawal, sometimes under duress, of British and French rule in the Middle East and north Africa and the creation of the new state of Israel in 1948 destabilized the area. Egypt and Syria sought Soviet support against the new Israeli state, which was formed out of the part of Palestine that had been under British mandate since 1920 and was dependent on U.S. aid.

Oil, an essential resource for rapid industrialization, was the object of Soviet politicking in Iran after the war. Western oil companies, long active in the area, had won oil concessions in Iran in 1946, but such rights eluded the Soviets. In 1951, a nationalist Iranian government sought to evict Westerners by nationalizing the oil fields. The British blockaded Iranian trade in the Persian Gulf, and the newly formed U.S. espionage organization, the Central Intelligence Agency (CIA), subverted the nationalist government and placed in power the shah of Iran, a leader who was favorable to U.S. interests.

A crisis came in 1956 in Egypt. Egyptian president Gamal Abdel Nasser (1918–1970), a nationalist who came to power through a military coup d'état in 1952, oversaw the nationalization of the Suez Canal. British and French military forces attacked and were forced to withdraw by pressure from both the Soviet Union and the United States, which cooperated in seeking to avert a disaster. However, the Middle East remained a Cold War powder keg, with Israeli and Arab nationalist interests and Soviet and U.S. aid running on a collision course. The expansion of the Israeli state at the expense of its Arab neighbors further exacerbated tensions.

Latin America. The United States was also experiencing Cold War problems closer to home. In 1954, the CIA plotted the overthrow of Guatemala's leftist regime to keep Soviet influence out of the western hemisphere. In 1959, a revolution in Cuba, an island nation only 90 miles off the U.S. coast, resulted in the ejection of U.S. interests and the establishment of a communist regime under the leadership of a young middle-class lawyer, Fidel Castro. In 1962, a direct and frightening confrontation between the United States and the Soviet Union occurred over Soviet missile installations in Cuba. After the Soviet withdrawal from the island, both U.S. President John F. Kennedy and Soviet leader Nikita Khrushchev, intent on averting further nuclear confrontation, pursued policies of "peaceful coexistence." Both sides recognized how close they had come to mutual annihilation in the showdown over Cuba.

Conclusion

THE PRESENCE OF SOVIET ARMIES IN EASTERN EUROPE guaranteed that communism would prevail there after 1945. In western Europe, the U.S. and British presence fostered the existence of parliamentary democracies. Germany was divided. A similar pattern emerged in Asia. The U.S. forces of occupation in Japan oversaw the introduction of democratic institutions. The Soviet Union controlled Manchuria. Korea was divided. The celebration of victory after a war in which 50 million people died did not last long. Nor did the Anglo-American cooperation with the Soviet Union endure. With the defeat of Germany and Japan, the United States and the Soviet Union were the undisputed giants in world politics. Two ideological systems stood facing each other suspiciously across a divided Europe and a divided Asia.

QUESTIONS FOR REVIEW

1. What factors made possible Hitler's diplomatic and military successes between 1933 and 1941?
2. Why did the Nazi regime believe that it needed to destroy the Jews, Gypsies, and other outsiders, and how did it attempt to justify that policy?
3. How did Hitler's invasion of the Soviet Union and the entry of the United States into the war transform the military situation?
4. How did the Allies coordinate their efforts, and what factors strained relations between them?
5. What did it mean for postwar European politics that the Continent was divided by an "iron curtain"?

DISCOVERING WESTERN CIVILIZATION ONLINE

You can obtain more information about World War II and the Cold War at the websites listed below. See also the companion website that accompanies this text: www.ablongman.com/kishlansky, which contains an online study guide and additional resources.

The Coming of World War II

www.yale.edu/lawweb/avalon/imt/munich1.htm
Electronic text of the Munich Pact and ancillary agreements.

www.yale.edu/lawweb/avalon/wwii/yellow/ylbkmenu.htm
Documents on French diplomacy in the 1930s.

www.yale.edu/lawweb/avalon/wwii/bluebook/blbkmenu.htm
Documents on British diplomacy in the 1930s.

Racism and Destruction

www.remember.org/index.html
Cybrary of the Holocaust is an Internet repository for material on the Holocaust. This comprehensive site contains documents and testimonies of camp survivors and liberators, images of the camps, and extensive links to Holocaust-related sites.

www.ushmm.org
Home page of the United States Holocaust Memorial Museum. The site contains a searchable online catalog of both documentary and photographic sources.

www.wiesenthal.com
Home page of the Simon Wiesenthal Center and the Museum of Tolerance. It has an extensive collection of materials related to the Holocaust and anti-Semitism.

www.jewishgen.org/ForgottenCamps/
A virtual museum on the Holocaust with text and images.

sicsa.huji.ac.il/
The site of the Vidal Sassoon International Center for Anti-Semitism that contains an extensive bibliography on the Holocaust.

Allied Victory

www.geocities.com/Athens/Oracle/2691/welcome.htm
This page provides links to a wide variety of sites relating to World War II broken down into topical areas.

www.fordham.edu/halsall/mod/modsbook45.html
A collection of primary source documents and links to materials on World War II.

baby.indstate.edu/gga/gga_cart/gecar127.htm
A collection of maps relating to World War II.

www.uboat.net
The site for information on submarine warfare during World War II.

www.schicklerart.com/auto_exh/RPCWar
Images of World War II from the Soviet perspective.

www.loc.gov/exhibits/wcf/wcf0001.html
A virtual exhibit by the Library of Congress on women journalists, photographers, and broadcasters during World War II.

www.dannen.com/decision
This site contains primary documents relating to the decision to use the atomic bomb.

www.anesi.com/ussbs01.htm
Electronic text of the U.S. Strategic Bombing Survey summary report on operations in the Pacific theater of war.

www.csi.ad.jp/ABOMB
A virtual museum on the development and use of atomic weapons.

www.calvin.edu/academic/cas/gpa
An interesting collection of multimedia documents translated into English on German propaganda during the Nazi period. It also includes Marxist propaganda material from the German Democratic Republic (1949–1989) sponsored by Calvin College.

Regulating the Cold War

www.trumanlibrary.org/whistlestop/study_collections/berlin_airlift/large/berlin_airlift.htm
A virtual exhibit with electronic texts on the Berlin Airlift as presented by the Harry S Truman Library and Museum.

www.fordham.edu/halsall/mod/modsbook46.html
A collection of primary source documents and links to the creation of the United Nations and the outbreak of the Cold War.

cwihp.si.edu/default.htm
This site, sponsored by the Woodrow Wilson International Center for Scholars, provides a comprehensive list of primary documents and images, secondary sources, bibliographies, and working paper series on all aspects of the Cold War.

www.ibiblio.org/expo/soviet.exhibit/entrance.html
A small virtual exhibit on the Cold War with images and electronic texts.

tis.eh.doe.gov/ohre/
A website of documents on radiation experiments using human subjects during the Cold War.

SUGGESTIONS FOR FURTHER READING

The Coming of World War II

Ian Kershaw, *The Nazi Dictatorship* (London: Edward Arnold, 1985). A fine synthesis of key problems of interpretation regarding the Third Reich. Special attention is paid to the interdependence of domestic and foreign policy and the inevitability of war in Hitler's ideology.

Donald Cameron Watt, *How War Came: The Immediate Origins of the Second World War* (London: Heinemann, 1989). An international historian chronicles the events leading to the outbreak of the war.

Racism and Destruction

Renate Bridenthal, Atina Grossmann, and Marion Kaplan, eds., *When Biology Became Destiny: Women in Weimar and Nazi Germany* (New York: Monthly Review Press, 1984). A volume of essays pursuing common themes on the relation between sexism and racism in interwar and wartime Germany.

Raul Hilberg, *The Destruction of the European Jews*, 3 vols. (New York: Holmes and Meier, 1985). An exhaustive study of the annihilation of European Jews beginning with cultural precedents and antecedents. Examines step-by-step developments that led to extermination policies and contains valuable appendixes on statistics and a discussion of sources.

Charles S. Maier, *The Unmasterable Past: History, Holocaust, and German National Identity* (Cambridge, MA: Harvard University Press, 1988). A thoughtful discussion of the historical debate over the Holocaust and the comparative dimensions of the event. Especially valuable in placing the Holocaust within German history.

Michael R. Marrus, *The Holocaust in History* (New York: New American Library, 1987). A comprehensive survey of all aspects of the Holocaust, including the policies of the Third Reich, the living conditions in the camps, and the prospects for resistance and opposition.

Allied Victory

John Campbell, ed., *The Experience of World War II* (New York: Oxford University Press, 1989). This richly illustrated work provides an overview of the Second World War in both the Asian and European theaters in terms of origins, events, and consequences.

Akira Iriye, *The Origins of the Second World War in Asia and the Pacific* (London: Longman, 1987). Examines the events of the 1930s leading up to hostilities in the Pacific theaters, with a special focus on Japanese isolation and aggression.

John Keegan, *The Second World War* (New York: Viking, 1990). Provides a panoramic sweep of "the largest single event in human history," with special attention to warfare in all its forms and the importance of leadership.

Gerhard L. Weinberg, *A World at Arms: A Global History of World War II* (New York: Cambridge University Press, 1994). An overview of the interactions among Germany, the Soviet Union, and Japan, which provides an integrated history of World War II with a helpful bibliographic essay.

Regulating the Cold War

Franz Ansprenger, *The Dissolution of the Colonial Empires* (London: Routledge, 1989). An analysis of Europe's withdrawal from Asia and Africa following the Second World War, beginning with an examination of post–World War I imperialism.

William Roger Louis and Roger Owen, eds., *Suez 1956: The Crisis and Its Consequences* (New York: Oxford University Press, 1989). A series of essays resulting from new research into the origins and consequences of the Suez crisis.

Charles S. Maier, *In Search of Stability: Explorations in Historical Political Economy* (Cambridge: Cambridge University Press, 1987). Covers a wide variety of issues affecting twentieth-century Europe, including the foundation of American international economic policy after World War II and the conditions for stability in western Europe after 1945.

Bruce D. Porter, *The USSR in Third World Conflicts: Soviet Arms and Diplomacy in Local Wars, 1945–1980* (Cambridge: Cambridge University Press, 1984). A case study approach to the Soviet Union's changing postwar policies toward the third world that centers on local wars in Africa and the Middle East.

CHAPTER 29

POSTWAR RECOVERY AND THE NEW EUROPE TO 1989

- THE VISUAL RECORD: Europe in Ruins
- RECONSTRUCTING EUROPE
- CREATING THE WELFARE STATE
- YOUTH CULTURE AND THE "GENERATION GAP"
- TOPPLING COMMUNISM IN THE SOVIET UNION

THE VISUAL RECORD

EUROPE IN RUINS

WHEN THE DUST FROM THE LAST BOMBS SETTLED over Europe's cities, the balance sheets of destruction were tallied. Great cities including London, Cologne, Berlin, Stalingrad, and Warsaw incurred serious damage and human loss. Millions of refugees on the continent found themselves homeless, having lost their loved ones, often all of their personal belongings, and the roofs over their heads. Millions more returned home from battlefronts and concentration camps to rubble, with wounds beyond healing. There were no jobs; there was nothing to eat. Peacetime rationing dipped below wartime levels. For many, the war was far gentler than the peace.

Warsaw in 1946 stands as a stark example of extreme destruction and of startling renewal. At the close of the war, Warsaw was an almost completely destroyed city, consisting of little more than dust, ashes, and the charred hulks of destroyed buildings, with no inhabitants, water, electricity, or sanitation. The scene here, captured by a photographer in early 1946, is not an isolated perspective but rather a landscape typical of Poland's capital after the war. By contrast with this image, Warsaw was recognized in the interwar period of the 1920s and 1930s as a metropolitan center of charm and culture, known for its artists and intellectuals and vibrant urban life.

Warsaw was annihilated not by an atomic bomb, but in stages over a five-year period by flamethrowers, tanks, and dynamite. Unrelenting aerial attacks by German planes against the city and its population systematically destroyed people and buildings in order to bring the civilian population to its knees. The Jewish ghetto was completely eliminated in 1943. The destruction, building by building, was premeditated and methodical. By the end of 1944, Warsaw was no more than a heap of rubble with almost 90 percent of its buildings destroyed. A large portion of its population was wiped out, and those who survived were in detention camps or in flight. Warsaw became known as "the vanished city."

But that is where the postwar story of recovery begins. With the liberation by the Red Army of what was left of the city, the Polish people almost immediately planned for the rebuilding of their capital, helped raise the necessary funds, and volunteered their labor to the great task. Women and children joined the men in clearing the rubble. Aid in the form of food, clothing, and shelter from organizations such as the United Nations Relief and Rehabilitation Administration supported the healing and rebuilding of Warsaw. Civilians returned to the city. By

1951, the population reached 815,000, although still below its 1.3 million inhabitants in 1939.

In rebuilding Warsaw, the Polish people did not ignore the city's historic past by building a modern, postwar metropolis, as did the people of Frankfurt. Instead, they sought to reconstruct Warsaw as it had been in 1939 by recreating monuments and historic buildings in their original form. Often that required architects to consult unconventional sources, including paintings and postcards, in the absence of blueprints and plans. Palaces and castles were reborn, baroque buildings rose up, ornamental gardens were replanted, and ancient vistas and panoramas were brought back to life. The achievement of historical preservation was astounding. By 1951, a large part of the city had been rebuilt, perhaps one of the best examples of how Europeans met the postwar challenge of urban reconstruction and economic revival.

LOOKING AHEAD

Under the tutelage of the two superpowers, the United States and the Soviet Union, Europe diverged on two separate paths of reconstruction and economic integration after 1945. In the West and in the Eastern Bloc, welfare state models emerged for the regulation and social distribution of economic expansion. Slowed prosperity in the late 1960s, combined with the growth of an independent youth culture, helped fuel protests in the East and the West. Dissent and increased détente, prosperity, and rising and unmet consumer expectations throughout the 1980s contributed to the collapse of the Soviet Union. The toppling of communism in the Soviet Union put an end to the Cold War, which had prevailed as a system of stabilization and peace since 1945.

RECONSTRUCTING EUROPE

For victors and vanquished alike, the situation in Europe at the end of the Second World War was dire. Economies geared totally toward war efforts were incapable of the kind of reorientation needed to reconstruct markets and eliminate economic distress. Governments faced political crises as they attempted to restore or establish democratic principles. Moreover, Europe did not have the capital necessary to begin the process of rebuilding. Political disorganization reigned in Berlin, which was divided into sectors, in Germany, which was divided into zones, and in the former European empires, which were in the process of being dismantled. Even the winners were losers as survivors faced a level of human and material destruction unknown in the history of warfare. As one American military observer reported to his superiors in 1947, "Millions of people in the cities are slowly starving." Could Europe rise from these ashes and, if so, in what form?

▼ A brother and sister on the way home from school walk down a deserted street in a bombed-out section of Berlin. They carry tin cans for the hot meals they receive in school.

The Economic Challenge

Economists judged that Europe would need at least 25 years to regain its prewar economic capacity. The worst was also feared: that Europe would never recover as a world economic power. Large-scale population movements made matters worse. Displaced persons by the millions moved across Europe. The release of prisoners of war and slave workers imprisoned during the Third Reich strained already weak economies. Germans were expelled from territories that Germany had controlled before the war. Soviet expansionist policies forced others to flee Estonia, Latvia, and Lithuania. Jews who survived the concentration camps resettled outside Europe, primarily in Palestine and the United States.

European industrial production in 1945 was at one-third of its 1938 level. Housing shortages existed everywhere. France had lost one-fifth of its housing during the war; Germany's 50 largest cities had seen two-fifths of their buildings reduced to rubble. Frankfurt, Düsseldorf, Dresden, Warsaw, and Berlin were virtually destroyed. The transportation infrastructure was severely damaged: railways, roads, and bridges were in shambles all over Europe. Communications networks were in disarray. Industrial machinery that had not been blown up had been worn out in wartime production, and replacement parts were nonexistent. German equipment was dismantled and seized by Soviet soldiers to be used in Russia in place of what the Germans had destroyed.

Agriculture, too, suffered severe reversals. In general, postwar European agriculture was producing at 50 percent of its prewar capacity. Italy suffered greatly, with one-third of its overall assets destroyed. The scarcity of goods converged with ballooning inflation. Black markets with astronomical prices for necessities flourished, as currency rates plummeted. Everywhere, the outlook was bleak. Yet in less than a decade, the situation had been reversed. The solution came from outside Europe.

The Solutions of the Soviet Union and the United States

The two superpowers approached the challenges of economic recovery in Europe from different perspectives. And within Europe itself, nations sought paths to economic prosperity that reflected their histories and social values.

The Soviet Union's Plan for Recovery. The Soviet Union implemented an expansion of its territorial boundaries as a way of reversing some of its drastic losses in the war. Above all, it wanted a protective ring of satellite states as security from attack from the West. Picking up territory from Finland and Poland and parts of East Prussia and eastern Czechoslovakia; forcibly reincorporating the Baltic states of Estonia, Latvia, and Lithuania; and recovering Bessarabia, the Soviet Union succeeded in acquiring sizable territories. In addition, the Soviet state dedicated itself to economic reconstruction behind a protective buffer of satellite states—Poland, East Germany, Czechoslovakia, Hungary, Romania, and Bulgaria—over which Soviet leaders exercised strong control. Yugoslavia and Albania chose to follow a more independent communist path. Lacking the capital necessary to finance recovery, the Soviets sought compensation from eastern and central European territories.

The Soviet Union had its own economic imperatives. Under Stalin's direction the Soviet Union concentrated all its efforts on reconstructing its devastated economy and, to this end, sought integration with eastern European states, whose technology and resources were needed for the rebuilding of the Soviet state. U.S. dominance threatened the vital connection with eastern Europe that the Soviet Union was determinedly solidifying in the postwar years.

The United States' Plan for Recovery. In contrast to the Soviet Union, the United States had incurred relatively light casualties in World War II. Because the fighting had not taken place on the North American continent, U.S. cities, farmlands, and factories were intact. The United States had benefited economically from the conflict in Europe and actually expanded its productivity during the war. In 1945 the United States, which held two-thirds of the world's gold, was producing a full 50 percent of the world's gross national product. A United States bursting with energy and prosperity seemed a real threat to the devastated Soviet Union.

The United States knew that it lacked one important guarantee to secure its growth and its future prosperity: adequate international markets for its goods. In the decade following the Great Depression of 1929, the United States sought to expand its markets. Both Europe and Japan were recognized as potential buyers for U.S. goods, but both areas parried with protectionism to foster their own postdepression recovery. After World War II, the United States intervened in both Europe and Japan to aid reconstruction and recovery. These economies, hungry for capital, no longer opposed U.S. intervention or erected trade barriers against U.S. goods.

By the spring of 1947 it was clear to U.S. policy makers that initial postwar attempts to stabilize European economies and promote world recovery were simply not working. The United States had, earlier in the same year, engineered emergency aid to Turkey and Greece, both objects of Soviet aspirations for control. The aid emerged in an atmosphere of opposition between the United States and the Soviet Union over issues of territorial control in eastern and southern Europe. The Cold War coincided with and reinforced the U.S. need to reconstruct western Europe.

On 5 June 1947, Secretary of State George C. Marshall (1880–1959) delivered the commencement address at Harvard University. In his speech, Marshall introduced the European Recovery Act, popularly known as the Marshall Plan, through which billions of dollars in aid would be made available to European states, both in the east and in the west, provided that two conditions were met: (1) The recipient states had to cooperate with one another in aligning national economic policies and improving the international monetary system, and (2) they had to work toward breaking down trade barriers.

Participating countries included Austria, Belgium, Denmark, France, West Germany, Great Britain, Greece, Iceland, Italy, Luxembourg, the Netherlands, Norway, Sweden, Switzerland, and Turkey. The Soviet Union and eastern European countries were also eligible for aid under the original formulation. But the Soviet Union opposed the plan from the first, wary of U.S. intentions to extend the influence of Western capitalism. Soviet opposition encouraged members of the U.S. Congress, afraid of a communist takeover in Europe, to support the plan.

The amount of U.S. aid to Europe was massive. Over $23 billion was pumped into western Europe between 1947 and 1952. U.S. foreign aid restored western European trade and production while controlling inflation. Dean Acheson (1893–1971), Marshall's successor as secretary of state, described the plan in terms of "our duty as human beings" but nevertheless considered it "chiefly as a matter of national self-interest."

Administering the Marshall Plan

As significant as the gift of funds to European states undoubtedly was, no less important was the whole administrative apparatus that U.S. money brought in its wake. To expend available monies most effectively and to comply with stipulations for cooperation and regulation, the states of western Europe resorted to intensified planning and limited nationalization.

Planning for Recovery. Regulation and state intervention dominated the formulation of economic policy. Special attention was given to workers' welfare through unemployment insurance, retirement benefits, public health, and housing policies. European states recognized the need to provide a safety net for their citizens to avoid the disastrous depression and stagnation of the 1930s, while attempting to rebuild their shattered economies.

The economic theory of John Maynard Keynes, which had been applied successfully by neutral Sweden to its economic policies during the war, came into vogue throughout Europe in 1945, and the postwar era saw the triumph of Keynesian economics. Keynes favored macroeconomic policies to increase productivity and argued for an active role for government in "priming the pump" of economic growth. The government should be responsible, according to Keynes, for the control and regulation of the

THE MARSHALL PLAN

In the rituals that are part of graduation ceremonies, guest speakers often address the challenges of the future awaiting graduates. Not many commencement addresses change the world. The speech given by U.S. Secretary of State George C. Marshall at Harvard University in June 1947 was different. By pledging gifts in aid, the United States helped rebuild war-torn Europe and transform the world's economy.

FOCUS QUESTIONS

What does Marshall mean when he states that this policy is "directed not against any country or doctrine"? How does Marshall explain that the plan for economic recovery is not intended as charity?

THE TRUTH OF THE MATTER is that Europe's requirements for the next three or four years of foreign food and other essential products—principally from America—are so much greater than her present ability to pay that she must have substantial additional help or face economic, social, and political deterioration of a very grave character.

The remedy lies in breaking the vicious circle and restoring the confidence of the European people in the economic future of their own countries and of Europe as a whole. The manufacturer and the farmer throughout wide areas must be able and willing to exchange their products for currencies the continuing value of which is not open to question.

Aside from the demoralizing effect on the world at large and the possibilities of disturbances arising as a result of the desperation of the people concerned, the consequences to the economy of the United States should be apparent to all. It is logical that the United States should do whatever it is able to do to assist in the return of normal economic health in the world, without which there can be no political stability and no assured peace. Our policy is directed not against any country or doctrine but against hunger, poverty, desperation, and chaos. Its purpose should be the revival of a working economy in the world so as to permit the emergence of political and social conditions in which free institutions can exist. Such assistance, I am convinced, must not be on a piecemeal basis as various crises develop. Any assistance that this Government may render in the future should provide a cure rather than a mere palliative. Any government that is willing to assist in the task of recovery will find full cooperation, I am sure, on the part of the United States Government. Any government which maneuvers to block the recovery of other countries cannot expect help from us. Furthermore, governments, political parties, or groups which seek to perpetuate human misery in order to profit therefrom politically or otherwise will encounter the opposition of the United States.

From Department of State Bulletin, 15 June 1947.

economy with the goal of ensuring full employment for its people. Governments could and should check inflation and eliminate boom-and-bust cycles, incurring deficits by spending beyond revenues if necessary.

European Economic Cooperation. U.S. foreign aid contributed mightily to the extension of central planning and the growth of the welfare state throughout western Europe. But money alone could not have accomplished the recovery that took place. The chief mechanism for administering Marshall Plan aid was the Office of European Economic Cooperation (OEEC). This master coordinating agency made the requirements for recovery clear. European states had to stabilize their own economies. Cooperation between the public and private sectors was intended to free market forces, modernize production, and raise productivity. Planning mechanisms, including transnational organizations and networks, resulted in the modernization of production and the assimilation of new techniques, new styles of management, and innovative business practices from the United States.

The major exception to the establishment of central planning agencies and the nationalization of key industries was West Germany. Deciding against the British and French models of planned growth, the West Germans endorsed a free-market policy that encouraged private enterprise while providing state insurance for all workers. What has been described as "a free enterprise economy with a social conscience" produced the richest economy in western Europe by the mid-1950s. Some West German industries had been dismantled, but much of West Germany's productive capacity remained intact in the late 1940s. The wealth of great industrialists such as Krupp, who were serving prison sentences as war criminals, was not expropriated, and their commercial empires stood ready to direct the economic revival. The Krupp and I. G. Farben empires were successfully broken up into smaller units. Industries that were forced to start afresh benefited from the latest technology.

Japan's Recovery. Japanese economic challenges in the postwar era were similar to those of western Europe. As a defeated and occupied nation in 1945, Japan faced a grim future. U.S. aims for Asia were similar to those for Europe: U.S. policy makers sought to create a multilateral system of world trade and preserve the U.S. sphere of influence against communist encroachment. The American general Douglas MacArthur was appointed the Supreme Commander for the Allied Powers and the head of occupation forces in Japan. His mission in Japan was to impose rapid economic change from above. The occupation government set out to erect institutions to promote political democratization and to eliminate militaristic institutions, official patronage, and censorship. Planning, both formal and informal, reshaped the economy as U.S. aid flowed into Japan during the late 1940s and early 1950s. These changes in Japan, as in western Europe, took place alongside growing U.S. fears of communism in the region.

Japan turned its wartime devastation into an advantage by replacing destroyed obsolete factories with the latest technology, obtained by license from foreign firms. Through a combination of bureaucracy and patronage devoted to planned growth, Japan's GNP reached prewar levels by 1956. By 1968, Japan had turned defeat into triumph and stood as the third largest industrial nation in the world.

The abolition of the army and navy was a boon for the Japanese economy, since 28.2 percent of prewar national income had been devoted to support of the military. Postwar demilitarization freed Japan from the financial exigencies of the arms race. Funds that had been used for arms now flowed into investment and new technology. Slowed population growth after 1948 and increased volume in foreign trade contributed to Japanese prosperity.

The United States had succeeded in exporting aspects of its own economy abroad. Through management and planning, recipients of U.S. aid surpassed U.S. goals. A multilateral system of world trade emerged out of the ashes of war.

Western European Economic Integration

European integration, discussed before and during the war, received added impetus in the postwar period. The Marshall Plan reconciled western Europe with West Germany through economic cooperation, although that was by no means its original purpose. Realizing that Europe as a region needed the cooperation of its member states if it was to contend in world markets, associations dedicated to integration began to emerge alongside economic planning mechanisms. The Council of Europe dealt with the "discussion of questions of common concern and by agreements and common action in economic, social, cultural, scientific, legal, and administrative matters and in the maintenance and further realization of human rights and fundamental freedoms." Although not itself a supranational institution with its own authority, the Council of Europe urged a federation among European states. Britain alone rejected all attempts to develop structures of loose intergovernmental cooperation.

Belgium, the Netherlands, and Luxembourg were the first European states to establish themselves as an economic unit—Benelux. Internal customs duties were removed among the three states, and a common external tariff barrier was erected. The Schuman Plan joined France and West Germany in economic cooperation by pooling all coal and steel resources beginning in 1950. The creators of the plan, Jean Monnet (1888–1979) and Robert Schuman (1886–1963) of France, saw it as the first step toward the removal of all economic barriers among European states and as a move toward eventual political integration. In 1951, the Netherlands, Belgium, Luxembourg, France, Italy, and West Germany formed the European Coal and Steel Community (ECSC). While constantly confronting domestic opposition on nationalist grounds, the ECSC succeeded in establishing a "common market" in coal and steel among its member states. In 1957, the same six members created the European Economic Community (EEC) and committed themselves to broadening the integration of markets. This was the beginning of what became known as the Common Market.

The Common Market aimed to establish among its member states a free movement of labor and capital, the elimination of restrictions on trade, common investment practices, and coordinated social welfare programs. National agricultural interests were to be protected. Great Britain was initially a vocal opponent of the Common Market and continued to defend its own trading relationship with its Commonwealth countries. In 1973, Great Britain became a member of the Common Market and joined other European nations in defining common economic policies. The EEC meanwhile achieved the support of the United States in its transitional period, in which it had 15 years to accomplish its aims.

European union was a phenomenon of exclusion as much as inclusion. By its very success, it sharpened antagonisms between the West and the East. While promoting prosperity, European economic unification favored concentration and the emergence of large corporations. Vast individual fortunes flourished under state sponsorship and the rule of the experts. National parliaments were sometimes eclipsed by superfluous new economic decision-making organizations that aimed to make western Europe into a single free-trade area. The Soviet Union, too, relied on state planning to foster rapid economic growth, but it was central planning emanating from Moscow, based on different assumptions and directed toward different ends.

CREATING THE WELFARE STATE

The welfare state, a creation of the post–World War II era throughout Europe, grew out of the social welfare policies of the interwar period and out of the war itself. Welfare programs aimed to protect citizens through the establishment of a decent standard of living available to everyone. The experiences of the Great Depression had done much to foster concern for economic security. In France, the primary concern of the welfare state was the protection of children and the issue of family allowances. In Great Britain, as in Germany, emphasis was placed on unemployment insurance and health-care benefits. Everywhere, however, the welfare state developed a related set of social programs and policies whereby the state intervened in the cycles of individual lives to provide economic support for the challenges of birth, sickness, old age, and unemployment.

Protection of citizenry took varied forms according to Cold War politics. In the Warsaw Pact countries, the need to industrialize rapidly and to dedicate productive wealth to armament and military protection resulted in a nonexistent consumer economy in which the issues of quality of life and protection took a very different direction. Based on a concept of equal access to a minimum standard of living, welfare states did not treat all its members equally. Women were often disadvantaged in social welfare programs, as family needs, men's rights, and the protection of children led to different national configurations.

Prosperity and Consumption in the West

Despite the different paths toward reconstruction after World War II, every western European nation experienced dramatic increases in total wealth. Per capita income was clearly on the rise through the mid-1960s, and there was more disposable wealth than ever before. Prosperity encouraged new patterns of spending based on confidence in the economy. This new consumerism, in turn, was essential to economic growth and future productivity.

The New Consumption. The social programs of the welfare state played an important role in promoting postwar consumption. People began to relax about their economic futures, feeling more secure because of the provisions of unemployment insurance, old-age pensions, and health and accident insurance. In the mid-1950s, all over western Europe, people began to spend their earnings, knowing that accidents, disasters, and sicknesses would be taken care of by the state. Western Europeans even began to buy on credit, spending money they had not yet earned. This, too, was an innovation in postwar markets.

Welfare programs could be sustained only in an era of prosperity and economic growth, since they depended on taxation of income for their funds. However, such taxation did not result in a redistribution of wealth. Wealth remained in the hands of a few and became even more concentrated as a result of phenomenal postwar economic growth. In West Germany, for example, 1.7 percent of the population owned 35 percent of the society's total wealth.

Women's Wages. Just as the welfare state did not redistribute wealth, it did not provide equal pay for equal work. In France, women who performed the same jobs as men in typesetting, for example, and who on average set 15,000 keystrokes per hour at the keyboards compared to 10,000 by men, earned 50 percent of men's salaries and had different job titles. Separate wage scales for women that had been drawn up during the Nazi period remained in effect in West Germany until 1956. The skills associated with occupations performed by women were downgraded, as were their salaries. Women earned two-thirds or less of what men earned throughout western Europe. Welfare state revenues were a direct result of pay-scale inequalities. Lower salaries for women meant higher profits and helped to make economic recovery possible.

The Eastern Bloc and Recovery

In the years before his death in 1953, Joseph Stalin succeeded in making the Soviet Union a vital industrial giant second only to the United States. The Soviet economy experienced dramatic recovery after 1945, in spite of the severe damage inflicted on it during the war. The production of steel, coal, and crude oil skyrocketed under state planning. Heavy industry was the top priority of Soviet recovery, in keeping with prewar commitments to rapid modernization. In addition, the postwar Soviet economy assumed the new burdens of the development of a nuclear arsenal and an expensive program for the exploration of space. Stalin maintained the Soviet Union on the footing of a war economy, restricted occupational mobility, and continued to rely on forced-labor camps.

The Soviet Standard of Living. The Soviet Union's standard of living remained relatively low in these years when western Europe was undergoing a consumer revolution. In the Soviet Union and throughout the Eastern Bloc countries, women's full participation in the labor force was essential for recovery. In spite of their presence in large numbers in highly skilled sectors such as medicine, Soviet and Eastern Bloc women remained poorly paid, as did women in the West. Soviet men received higher salaries for the same work on the grounds that they had to support families.

With Stalin's death, new leaders recognized the need for change, especially with regard to the neglected sectors of agricultural production and consumer products. The Soviet population was growing rapidly, from 170 million in 1939 to 234 million in 1967. Nikita Khrushchev

(1894–1971) promised the Russian people lower prices and a shorter work week, but in 1964, when he fell from power, Russians were paying higher prices for their food than before. With a declining rate of development, the Soviet economy lacked the necessary capital to advance the plans for growth in all sectors. Meanwhile, defense spending nearly doubled in the short period between 1960 and 1968.

Eastern Bloc Economies. The nature of planned Soviet growth exacted heavy costs in the Eastern Bloc countries. Adhering to the Soviet pattern of heavy industrial expansion at the expense of agriculture and consumer goods, East Germany nearly doubled its industrial output by 1955, despite having been stripped of its industrial plants by the Soviet Union before 1948. Czechoslovakia, Bulgaria, Romania, and Yugoslavia all reported significant industrial growth in this period. Yet dislocations caused by collectivization and heavy defense expenditures stirred up social unrest in East Germany, Czechoslovakia, Poland, and Hungary. The Soviet Union responded with some economic concessions but on the whole stressed common industrial and defense pursuits, employing ideological persuasion and military pressure to keep its reluctant partners in line. The slowed growth of the 1960s, the delay in development of consumer durables, and the inadequacy of basic foodstuffs, housing, and clothing were the costs that Eastern Bloc citizens paid for their inefficient and rigid planned economies dedicated to the development of heavy industry. In eastern Europe and the Soviet Union, poverty was virtually eliminated, however, as the state subsidized housing, health care, and higher education, which were available to all.

▲ Many basic needs are provided for under Britain's cradle-to-grave social welfare system. Here mothers and children line up to receive orange juice. Vitamins and milk are also provided for growing children.

Family Strategies

The pressures on European women and their families in 1945 were often greater than in wartime. Severe scarcity of food, clothes, and housing required careful management. After the war, women who had held jobs in the industry and munitions plants were moved out of the workforce to make room for returning men. Changing social policies affected women's lives in the home and in the workplace and contributed to the politicization of women within the context of the welfare state.

Demography and Birth Control. In the aftermath of World War II, prewar concerns with a declining birthrate intensified. In some European countries the birthrate climbed in the years immediately after the war, an encouraging sign to observers who saw in this trend an optimistic conviction that there would be a better future. The situation was more complicated in France and the United States, where the birthrates began to climb even before the war was over. Nearly everywhere throughout Europe, however, the rise in the birthrate was momentary; the United States stood alone in experiencing a genuine and sustained "baby boom" that lasted until about 1960. In Germany and eastern Europe (Poland and Yugoslavia, for example) the costs of the war exacted heavy tolls on families long after the hostilities ended. On average, women everywhere were having fewer children by choice.

Technology had expanded the range of choices in family planning. In the early 1960s, the birth control pill became available on the European and American markets, primarily to middle-class women. Europeans were choosing to have smaller families. The drop in the birthrate had clearly preceded the new technological interventions, which included intrauterine devices (IUDs), improved diaphragms, sponges, and more effective spermicidal creams and jellies. The condom, invented two centuries earlier, was now sold to a mass market. Controversies surrounded the unhealthy side effects of the pill and the dangerous Dalkon shield, an IUD that had not been adequately tested before marketing and resulted in the death or sterilization of thousands of women. Religious leaders spoke out on the moral issues surrounding sexuality without reproduction. Information about their reproductive lives became more accessible to young women. Illegal abortions continued to be an alternative for women. In France and Italy, birth control information was often withheld from the public. Abortion was probably the primary form of birth control in the Soviet Union in the years following the war.

The Family and Welfare. Concurrent with a low birthrate was a return to family life and family values in the years after the war. Those who had lived through the previous 20 years were haunted by the memories of the Great Depression, severe economic hardships, destructive war, and the loss of loved ones. Women and men throughout western Europe and the United States embraced domesticity and a return to normal life, even if they did not opt for large families. Expectations for improved family life placed new demands on welfare state programs. They also placed increased demands on mothers, whose presence in the home was now seen as all-important for the proper development of the child.

European states implemented official programs to encourage women to have more children and to be better mothers. *Pronatalism,* as this policy was known, resulted from an official concern over low birthrates and a decline in family size. Considerations about racial dominance and woman's proper role seem to have affected the development of these policies. In 1945, Lord Beveridge (1879–1960), the architect of the British welfare state, emphasized the importance of women's role "in ensuring the adequate continuance of the British race" and argued that women's place was in the home.

Welfare state programs differed from country to country as the result of a series of different expectations of women as workers and women as mothers. Konrad Adenauer, chancellor of West Germany, spoke of "a will to children" as essential for his country's continued economic growth and prosperity. In Great Britain, the welfare system was built on the ideal of the mother at home with her children. With the emphasis on the need for larger families—four children were considered "desirable" in England—English society focused on the importance of the role of the mother. Family allowances determined by the number of children were tied to men's participation in the workforce; women were defined according to their husband's status. The state welfare system strengthened the financial dependence of English wives on their husbands.

In Great Britain, anxiety about the low birthrate was also tied to the debate over equal pay for women. Opponents of the measure argued that equal pay would cause women to forgo marriage and motherhood and should therefore be avoided. There was a consensus about keeping women out of the workforce and paying them less to achieve that end.

The French system of *sécurité sociale* defined all women, whether married or single, as equal to men. In contrast to the British system, all French women had the same rights of access to welfare programs as men. This may well have reflected the different work history of women in France and the recognition of the importance of women's labor for reconstruction of the economy. As a result, family allowances, pre- and postnatal care, maternity benefits, and child care were provided on the assumption that working mothers were a fact of life. French payments were intended to encourage large families and focused primarily on the needs of children. More and more women entered the paid labor force after 1945, and they were less financially dependent on their husbands than their British counterparts were.

Both forms of welfare state—the British that emphasized women's role as mothers and the French that accepted women's role as workers—were based on different attitudes about gender difference and equality. Women's political consciousness developed in both societies. The women's liberation movements of the late 1960s and early 1970s found their roots in the contradictions of differing welfare policies.

The Beginnings of Women's Protest. The 1960s were a period of protest in Western countries as people demonstrated for civil rights and free expression. The movement against U.S. involvement in Vietnam was fueled by the activism of the black civil rights movement. Pacifist and antinuclear groups united to "ban the bomb." Women participated in all of these movements and, by the end of the 1960s, had begun to question their own place in organizations that did not acknowledge their claims to equal rights, equal pay, and liberation from the oppression of institutions created and run largely by men. A new critique began to form within the welfare state that indicated that there were cracks in the facade.

Feminist criticism of society was not new. A number of Enlightenment authors, both male and female, had pleaded the cause of women's rights. Throughout the nineteenth century, feminism had tended to burst forth during periods of liberalism or revolutionary activism and to remain relatively quiescent during periods of repression. Feminism and liberalism both challenged authority and oppression, and many feminists began their activist careers in liberal causes.

During World War II, feminist issues had been set aside in the national struggles for survival, but not long after the war, one book in particular captured the imagination of many women. *The Second Sex* (1949), by Simone de Beauvoir (1908–1986), a leading French intellectual, analyzed women in the context of Western culture. By examining the assumptions of political theories, including Marxism, in the light of philosophy, biology, history, and psychoanalysis, de Beauvoir uncovered the myths governing the creation of the female self. Showing how the male is the center of Western culture and the female is "other," de Beauvoir urged women to be independent and to resist male definitions. *The Second Sex* became the handbook of the women's movement in the 1960s.

A very different work, *The Feminine Mystique,* appeared in 1963. In this work, American author Betty Friedan voiced the grievances of a previously politically quiescent group of women. Friedan was a suburban homemaker and the mother of three children when she wrote about what she saw as the gap in her own middle-class world between the reality of women's lives and the idealized image of the perfect homemaker. After World War II, women were expected to find personal fulfillment in the domestic sphere. Instead, Friedan found women suffering from "the sickness with no name" and "the nameless desperation" of a profound crisis in identity.

A new politics that centered on women's needs and women's rights slowly took root. The feminist critique did not emerge as a mass movement until the 1970s, by which time the small trickle of feminist writing in the 1960s was becoming a torrent. Youth culture and dissent among the young further informed growing feminist discontent. But the agenda of protest in the 1960s accepted gender differences that social policies reinforced as normal and natural.

YOUTH CULTURE AND THE "GENERATION GAP"

Young people, socialized together in an expanding educational system from primary school through high school, came to see themselves as a distinct social force. They were also socialized by marketing efforts that appealed to their particular needs as a group.

The prosperity that characterized the period from the mid-1950s to the mid-1960s throughout the West provided a secure base from which radical dissenters could launch their protests. The young people of the 1960s were the first generation to come of age after World War II. Although they had no memory of the destruction of that war, they were reminded daily of the imminence of nuclear destruction in their own lives. The combination of the security of affluence and the insecurity of Cold War politics created a widening gap between the world of decision-making adults and the idealistic universe of the young. To the criticisms of parents, politicians, and teachers, the new generation responded that no one over the age of 30 could be trusted.

New styles of dress and grooming signified a rejection of middle-class culture in Europe and the United States. Anthropologists and sociologists in the 1960s began to study youth as if they were a foreign tribe. The "generation gap" appeared as the subject of hundreds of specialized studies. Adolescent behavior was examined across cultures. Sexual freedom and the use of drugs were subjected to special scrutiny. But it was, above all, the politics of the young that baffled and enraged many older observers. When the stable base of economic prosperity began to erode as a result of slowed growth and inflation in the second half of the 1960s, first in western Europe and then in the United States, shrinking opportunities for the young served as a further impetus for political action.

Prosperity and Protest

Increased emphasis on fulfillment through sexual pleasure was one consequence of the technological revolution in birth control devices, and it led to what has been called a revolution in sexual values in Western societies in the 1960s. The sexual revolution drew attention to sexual fulfillment as an end in itself. Women's bodies were displayed more explicitly than ever before in mass advertising to sell products from automobiles to soap. Sex magazines, sex shops, and movies were part of an explosion in the marketing of male sexual fantasies in the 1960s.

Technology allowed women and men to separate pleasure from reproduction but did nothing to alter men's and women's domestic roles. Pleasure was also separated from familial responsibilities, yet the domestic ideal of the woman in the home remained. Some women were beginning to question their exploitation in the sexual revolution. In the early 1970s, this issue became the basis of mass feminist protest.

Just as sexuality was invested with new meaning within the context of protest, so was the use of drugs. Drugs began to pervade Western cultures in apparently harmless ways. At the end of the nineteenth century in the United States, the newly created Coca-Cola actually contained cocaine, a drug derived from the coca shrub. Another ingredient in the soft drink formula was the kola nut, which contains the stimulant caffeine. In the 1950s and 1960s, chemical technology made possible the manufacture of synthetic drugs. Pharmaceutical industries in Europe and the United States expanded by leaps and bounds with the mass marketing of amphetamines, barbiturates, and tranquilizers. Doctors prescribed these new drugs for a variety of problems from obesity to depression to sleeplessness. People discovered that these drugs had additional mood-altering effects.

Marijuana grew in popularity as a safe "recreational" drug, especially among college and university students in the 1960s. In fact, young people were the primary users of drugs of all sorts, including synthetic drugs such as the hallucinogen LSD (lysergic acid diethylamide). Hallucinogens were considered by their proponents to be mind-expanding drugs that enabled the achievement of new levels of consciousness. Such drugs, used by young

▲ The Beatles were the icons of the sixties—an era of pacifism, when young people experimented with sexual liberation, the drug culture, and Eastern mysticism.

people who were affluent enough to afford them, served to widen the gap between the generations still further.

The Protests of 1968

Student protest, which began at the University of California at Berkeley in 1964 as the Free Speech movement, by the spring of 1968 had become an international phenomenon that had spread to other U.S. campuses and throughout Europe and Japan.

The Anti-War Movement and Social Protest. A common denominator of protest, whether in New York, London, or Tokyo, was opposition to the war in Vietnam. Growing numbers of intellectuals and students throughout the world condemned the U.S. presence in Vietnam as an immoral violation of the rights of the Vietnamese people and a violent proof of U.S. imperialism.

Student protesters shared other concerns in addition to opposition to the war in southeast Asia. The growing activism on U.S. campuses was aimed at social reform, student self-governance, and the responsibilities of the university in the wider community. In West Germany, highly politicized radical activists, a conspicuous minority among the students at the Free University of Berlin, directed protest out into the wider society. Student demonstrations met with brutal police repression and violence, and rioting was common.

European students, more than their American counterparts, were also experiencing frustration in the classroom. European universities were unprepared to absorb the huge influx of students in the 1960s. The student-teacher ratio at the University of Rome, for example, was 200 to 1. In Italian universities in general, the majority of over half a million students had no contact with their professors. The University of Paris was similarly overcrowded.

For the most part, student protest was a middle-class phenomenon. In France, for example, only 4 percent of university students came from below the middle class. Higher education had been developed after World War II to serve the increased needs of a technocratic society. Instead of altering the social structure, as politically committed student protesters had hoped, mass education served as a certifying mechanism for bureaucratic and technical institutions. Many of the occupations that students could look forward to were dead-end service jobs or bureaucratic posts.

Protest and the Economy. Student dissent reflected the changing economy of the late 1960s. Inflation was spiraling out of control, economic growth was slowing down, and jobs were being eliminated. One survey estimated that only one in three Italian university graduates in 1967 was able to find a job. The dawning awareness of shrinking career opportunities further aggravated student frustration and dissent.

By the late 1960s, universities and colleges gave students a forum for expressing their discontent in advanced industrial societies. In their protests, student activists rejected the values of consumer society. The programs and politics of the student protesters aimed to transform the world in which they lived. Student protesters in France chanted, "*Métro, Boulot, Dodo,*" a slang condemnation of the treadmill-like existence of those who spent their lives in a repetitive cycle of subway riding (Métro), mindless work (Boulot), and sleep (Dodo).

In May 1968 in France, protest spread beyond the university when workers and managers joined students in paralyzing the French economy and threatening to topple the Fifth Republic. Between 7 and 10 million people went on strike in support of worker and student demands. White-collar employees and technicians joined blue-collar factory workers in the strike. Student demands, based on a thoroughgoing critique of the whole society, proved to be incompatible with the wage and consumption issues of workers. But the unusual if short-lived alliance of students and workers shocked the men who were in power and induced reforms.

TOPPLING COMMUNISM IN THE SOVIET UNION

The Cold War, while it lasted from the post-1945 period to the late 1980s, had provided a way of ordering the world. It served to divide friend from foe, to create spheres of economic interest, and to promote market relations among blocs of nations. Also, in a seemingly contradictory sense, it was a conflict that promoted stability and peace, no matter how uneasy. Even the Soviet action against Czechoslovakia and other expressions of dissent in eastern Europe in 1968 reminded the world of the power of Communist unity in the Eastern Bloc.

Yet the chinks in the façade of unity were already present by the mid-1960s. The use of military intervention to resolve the Czech crisis opened an era governed by what came to be known as the Brezhnev Doctrine. Leonid Brezhnev (1906–1982), general secretary of the Communist Party and head of the Soviet Union from 1966 to 1982, established a policy whereby the Soviet Union claimed the right to interfere in the internal affairs of its allies to prevent counterrevolution. Brezhnev was responsible for the decision to enter Czechoslovakia, arguing that a socialist state was obliged to take action in another socialist state if the survival of socialism was at stake. The Brezhnev Doctrine, the threat of Soviet intervention, influenced domestic politics in eastern Europe through the next decade. After 1968, rigidity and stagnation characterized the actions of the Soviet, East German, and Czechoslovak governments, as well as those of other Eastern Bloc nations.

With repression came protest. At first weak but growing in volume, dissent from within communist countries commanded international attention in the mid-1970s. Criticism of the Soviet Union had been strongly repressed in Eastern Bloc nations. In 1985, the accession to power of Mikhail Gorbachev as general secretary ushered in a new age of openness. A strong critique of domestic and foreign policy aims infused movements for reform throughout the Eastern Bloc, thereby undermining communism and Cold War politics.

Soviet Dissent

In response to state repression during the Brezhnev years, dissidence took on a variety of forms. Some dissenters sought an international forum for their cause.

Jewish Dissenters. Growing numbers of Soviet Jews, for example, petitioned to emigrate to Israel to escape anti-Semitism within the Soviet Union and to embrace their own cultural heritage. Some of the 178,000 who were allowed to emigrate found their way to western Europe and the United States, and stories of persecution were published in the world press. In May 1976, a number of Soviet dissidents, including Jewish protesters, openly declared themselves united for the purpose of securing human rights in the Soviet Union. The state retaliated by charging organizers with anti-Soviet propaganda and handing out harsh prison sentences, which attracted international criticism.

Protest from Intellectuals and Professionals. A vehicle of protest was the self-published, privately circulated manuscripts known as *samizdat*, which became the chief vehicle of dissident communication. For the most part, dissidents were members of a university-trained professional elite. The leading Soviet dissident of the period was Andrei Sakharov (1921–1989), internationally renowned as the father of the Soviet hydrogen bomb and a scientist of great eminence. In 1968, he wrote *Thoughts on Progress, Peaceful Coexistence, and Intellectual Freedom*, a work that opposed Communist party rule in favor of a liberal democratic system. For his dissident activities, Sakharov was sentenced to a life in exile in Gorky in 1980.

Sakharov was not the only figure of stature to engage in protest. The novelist Alexander Solzhenitsyn denounced the abuses of Soviet bureaucracy in his works *One Day in the Life of Ivan Denisovich* and *The Gulag Archipelago*. The historian Roy Medvedev criticized Stalinism and continued to speak out in favor of peace and democratic principles in the Gorbachev years.

For almost three decades, dissidents waged a lonely battle within the Soviet Union for civil liberties, democratic rights, and the end of the nuclear arms race. In the 1980s, it became clear to Soviet watchers in the West that demands for recognition of nationalities were an important part of the dissident movement in the Soviet Union that echoed similar demands throughout eastern Europe. Cultural, religious, ethnic, and ecological concerns and demands for national autonomy joined forces with protests for civil liberties and economic freedom. The reinstatement of Sakharov, one of the Soviet Union's most visible dissidents, as a national hero just before his death and after years of persecution was one of the best barometers of the social revolution that was transforming Soviet politics in the 1980s. The Soviet Union could no longer afford to silence its citizens.

Détente: The Soviets and the West

The nuclear arms race began in earnest during World War II, well before the first atomic bomb was dropped in August 1945. The Germans, the Russians, and the British all had teams exploring the destructive possibilities of nuclear fission during the war. But the Americans had the edge in the development of the bomb. Stalin understood the political significance of the weapon and committed the

Soviet Union to a breakneck program of development following the war.

The Nuclear Club. The result was that the Soviet Union ended the U.S. monopoly and tested its first atomic bomb in 1949. The two countries developed the hydrogen bomb almost simultaneously in 1953. Space exploration by satellite was also considered important in terms of detection and deployment of bombs, and the Soviets pulled ahead in this area with the launching of the first satellite, *Sputnik I,* in 1957. Intercontinental ballistic missiles (ICBMs) followed, further accelerating the pace of nuclear armament.

The atomic bomb and thermonuclear weapons contributed greatly to the shape of Cold War politics. The incineration of Hiroshima and Nagasaki sent a clear message to the world about the power of total annihilation that was available to whoever controlled the bombs. The threat of such total destruction made full and direct confrontation with an equally armed enemy impossible. Both the United States and the Soviet Union, the first two members of the "nuclear club," knew that they had the capability of obliterating their enemy but not before the enemy could respond in retaliation. They also knew that the technology necessary for nuclear arms was available to any industrial power. By 1974, the nuclear club included Great Britain, France, the People's Republic of China, and India. These countries joined the United States and the Soviet Union in spending billions of dollars every year to expand nuclear arsenals and to develop more sophisticated weaponry and delivery systems.

A new vocabulary transformed popular attitudes and values. *Missile gaps, deterrence, first strike, second strike, radioactive fallout,* and *containment* were all terms that colored popular fears. Citizens in the Soviet Union learned of U.S. weapons stockpiling and U.S. deployment of military forces throughout the world. Americans learned that the Soviets had the ability to deliver bombs that could wipe out major U.S. cities. Paranoia on both sides was encouraged by heads of state in their public addresses throughout the 1950s. Traitors were publicly tried, while espionage was sponsored by the state.

The first nuclear test-ban treaty, signed in 1963, prohibited tests in the atmosphere. Arms limitation and nonproliferation were the subjects of a series of conferences between the United States and the Soviet Union in the late 1960s and pointed the way to limitations that were eventually agreed on in the next decade. The United Nations, created by the Allies immediately after World War II to take the place of the defunct League of Nations, established

The first hydrogen bomb test, on 1 November 1952, destroyed an entire island in the Pacific.

CHRONOLOGY

ECONOMIC RECOVERY AND DÉTENTE

1947	Marshall Plan starts U.S. aid to European countries
1949	Soviet Union creates Council for Mutual Economic Assistance (Comecon)
1949	Soviet Union tests its first atomic bomb
1953	United States and Soviet Union develop hydrogen bombs
1957	The Netherlands, Belgium, Luxembourg, France, Italy, and West Germany form the European Economic Community (EEC), also called the Common Market
1963	Soviet Union and United States sign Nuclear Test Ban Treaty
1968	Prague Spring uprising in Czechoslovakia, quelled by Soviet Union

international agencies for the purpose of harnessing nuclear power for peaceful uses. On the whole, however, the arms race persisted, consuming huge amounts of national resources. Conventional forces, too, were expanded to protect Eastern and Western Bloc interests.

The Nuclear Test Ban Treaty of 1963 inaugurated a period of lessening tension between the Eastern and Western Blocs. By the early 1970s, both the United States and the Soviet Union recognized the importance of closer relations between the superpowers. The two nations had achieved nuclear parity. Now, from positions of equality, both sides expressed a willingness to negotiate. The 1970s became the decade of détente, a period of cooperation between the two superpowers. The Strategic Arms Limitation Treaty, known as SALT I, which was signed in Moscow in 1972, limited defensive antiballistic missile systems.

Détente Challenged. The refusal of the United States in 1979 to sign SALT II to limit strategic nuclear weapons ushered in "the dangerous decade" of the 1980s, when the possibility of peaceful coexistence seemed crushed. U.S. President Ronald Reagan, during his first term in office, revived traditional Cold War rhetoric and posturing. Nuclear strategists on both sides were once again talking about nuclear war as possible and winnable. Popular concern over the nuclear arms race intensified in the United States, the Soviet Union, and throughout Europe as the United States pursued the Strategic Defense Initiative (SDI), popularly called "Stars Wars" because of its futuristic science-fiction quality of promised superiority through technology. At the least, the new system threatened an escalation in nuclear defense spending on both sides in its attempt to end the stabilizing parity between the United States and the Soviet Union.

In spite of grandstanding gestures such as the Star Wars initiative, East-West relations after 1983 were characterized, on balance, by less confrontation and more attempts at cooperation between the Soviet Union and the United States. The world political system itself appeared to have stabilized, with a diminution of conflict in the three main arenas of superpower competition: the third world, China, and western Europe. By the end of 1989, leaders in the East and the West declared that the ideological differences that separated them were more apparent than real. They declared an end to the Cold War and sought a new and permanent détente.

The End of the Soviet Union

By the mid-1980s, Soviet leaders were weighing the costs of increasing internal dissent and the promise of benefits from improved relations with the West. During the 40 years that followed World War II, a different kind of leader was being forged in the ranks of the Communist Party among a generation that favored more open political values and dynamic economic growth.

Typical of this new generation of political leaders was Mikhail Gorbachev, who was, above all, a technocrat, someone who could apply specialized technical knowledge to the problems of a stagnant Soviet economy. As the youngest Soviet leader since Stalin, Gorbachev set in motion in 1985 bold plans for increased openness, which he called *glasnost*, and a program of political and economic restructuring, which he dubbed *perestroika*. Appointing men who shared his vision to key posts, especially in the foreign ministry, Gorbachev extended the olive branch of peace to the West and met with President Ronald Reagan in a superpower summit in Geneva. By 1989, many observers inside and outside the Soviet Union felt that a new age was at hand, as the Soviet leader loosened censorship, denounced Stalin, and held the first free elections in the Soviet Union since 1917.

Increased Prosperity. The Soviet Union had undergone dramatic changes after Stalin's death in 1953, and many Stalinist policies were repudiated. The 1960s witnessed increased prosperity, as the population became more urban (180 million people lived in cities by mid-1970) and more literate (the majority of the population remained in school until age 17).

Soviet citizens of the 1960s and 1970s were better fed, better educated, and in better health than their parents and grandparents had been. When people grumbled over food shortages and long lines, the Soviet state reminded them of how far they had come. Yet while economic growth continued throughout the postwar years, the rate of growth was slowing down in the 1970s. Some planners feared that the Soviet Union would never catch up to the United States, Japan, and West Germany. Soviet citizens were increasingly aware of the sacrifices and suffering that economic development had cost them in the twentieth century and of the disparities in the standards of living between the capitalist and communist worlds. Because of outmoded technology, declining older industries, pollution, labor imbalances, critical shortages of foodstuffs and certain raw materials, and a significant amount of hidden unemployment in unproductive industries, discontent spread widely.

Consumer products were either of poor quality or unavailable. Because of limited provisions, people queued an average of two hours every day to purchase food and basic supplies. Housing, when it was available, was inadequate, and there were long waiting lists for vacancies. The black market flourished, with high prices on everything from Western blue jeans to Soviet automobiles. People saw corruption in their ruling elite, whose members wore Western clothes, had access to material goods that were not available to the general population, and lived in luxury.

Production Versus Expectations. The problem was not salaries. Workers were well paid, having more disposable income than ever before; but purchasing power far outstripped supplies. The state system of production, which emphasized quantity over quality, resulted in overproduction of some goods and underproduction of others. The state kept prices low to control the cost of living, but low prices were a problem because they did not provide sufficient incentive for the production of better-quality goods.

Programs between 1985 and 1988 promised more than they delivered. Modest increases in output were achieved, but people's expectations about food and consumer goods were rising faster than they could be met. The Soviet Union did not increase imports of consumer durables or food to meet the demand, nor did quality improve appreciably. Rising wages only gave workers more money that they could not or would not spend on Soviet products. The black market was a symbol both of the state's economic failures and of the growing consumerism of Soviet citizens. Rather than purchase poor-quality goods, Soviets chose to purchase foreign products at vastly inflated prices.

Although his economic reforms broke sharply with the centralized economy established by Stalin in the 1930s, Gorbachev candidly warned that he would not implement a consumption revolution in the near future. Many critics, including Boris Yeltsin, believed that Gorbachev did not go far or fast enough. In place of a controlled economy, Gorbachev offered a limited open market that was free of state controls for manufacturing enterprises organized on a cooperative basis and for light industry. He loosened restrictions on foreign trade, encouraged the development of the private sector, and decentralized economic decision making for agriculture and the service sector.

Reforming the Soviet State. Price increases and the importation of foreign goods, the two measures that were essential for progress in the Soviet consumer economy, had been resisted by Gorbachev's predecessors as politically explosive. The state kept prices down to maintain the low cost of living. In contrast to the ingrained conservatism of his predecessors, Gorbachev represented experimentation, innovation, vitality, and a willingness to question old ways. For him, economic and political reforms had to be accomplished in concert; in other words, the economy could be restructured only by "a democratization of our society at all levels."

Gorbachev's foreign policy also served his economic goals. Military participation in decision making declined as state expenditures on defense were cut. The Soviet Union had always borne larger military costs than had the United States. Gorbachev recognized that Cold War defense spending must decline if the Soviet Union was to prosper. Consumer durables had to take the place of weapons on the production lines. But there the transformation was bound to be slow. Gorbachev met with U.S. President Ronald Reagan and agreed to systematic arms reduction and greater cooperation. In 1989, in a stunning reversal of the Brezhnev doctrine, the Soviet state refused to intervene in the upheavals that were sweeping eastern Europe.

Tensions became most apparent over how Communist Party rule, which operated on the principles of centralization and power flowing from the top, could be coordinated with the demands for freedom and autonomy that Gorbachev's own reforms fostered. To gain credibility and backing, Gorbachev supported the formation of new parliamentary bodies, including a 2,250-member Congress of People's Deputies in 1988. The new Congress soon became the forum for attacks on the Communist Party and the KGB. In the first free elections held in the Soviet Union since 1917, Communist Party officials suffered further reversals in March 1989. Early in 1990, Gorbachev ended the party's constitutional monopoly of power; the party's control of Soviet political life was finished. New parties proliferated, some defending the old order but many demanding a total break with the past and with communist ideology and programs.

Harshly criticized by Boris Yeltsin, who was elected president of the Russian republic in 1990 and was calling for true democracy and decisive economic action, Gorbachev attempted to retrench by increasing control over the media and consolidating his own political position. Many believed that the regime was becoming authoritarian. Gorbachev was clearly walking a fine line between Communist Party hard-liners and Western-oriented supporters. No one was happy—neither capitalists nor communists.

Boris Yeltsin in Power. In August 1991, the world watched in shock as a quasi-military council of communist hard-liners usurped power to restore communist rule and reverse democratic reforms. Tens of thousands of Muscovites poured into the streets to defy the tanks and troops of the rebel government. Three people were killed outside Russia's parliament building, which had become the rallying point for the demonstrators. Soviet citizens from the Baltic republics to Siberia protested the takeover and the resulting violence. Meanwhile, Gorbachev was held prisoner by the communist rebels in his vacation home in the Crimea. The timing of the coup was probably determined by the fact that the day after his house arrest Gorbachev was scheduled to sign a new union treaty with nine of the republics that had been part of the Soviet Union.

Boris Yeltsin emerged as spokesperson for the democratic movement, publicly defied the plotters, and rallied popular support behind him in a dramatic move that captured international attention. He helped to convince Soviet army troops to disobey orders and to attack the occupied White House, as the parliament building is called. After only two days, the coup d'état had failed. Gorbachev returned to Moscow and proceeded to ban the Communist Party. Although Gorbachev retained his title as Soviet president, his prestige was seriously damaged by the coup and by Yeltsin's new dominance as a popular hero. In the national elections for the Congress of People's Deputies that followed, Boris Yeltsin, who had been dismissed as the head of the Moscow party in 1987, garnered 89 percent of the popular vote. As Yeltsin's star was on the rise, the Soviet Union was now in full collapse.

Conclusion

THE DIVISION OF THE WORLD INTO TWO CAMPS framed the recovery of combatant nations dealing with the losses of World War II. The Cold War instilled fear and terror in the populations who lived on both sides of the divide. Yet the Cold War also created the terms for stability following the upheaval of war. It promoted prosperity that preserved the long-term policies of both the United States and the Soviet Union in the twentieth century. The Soviet Union had buffered itself from the West by creating a ring of friendly nations on its borders and had continued its race to industrialize. The belief that the Soviet Union had won the war for the Allies and the sense of betrayal that followed the war determined the outlook of grim distrust shared by postwar Soviet leaders who had survived the years from 1939 to 1945.

The United States, on the other hand, found itself playing the role of rich uncle in bankrolling the European recovery. Its long-term commitment to promote its own economic interests by helping future trading partners led it also into playing the role of policeman throughout the world. The escalating war in Vietnam made the United States vulnerable to growing world criticism and to growing domestic discontent.

The gains of economic recovery began to unravel in the mid-1960s. The protests of 1968 were a response to changing economic conditions. In the West, rising expectations of consumer societies came up against the harsh realities of slowed growth. In the East, frustrated nationalism, the lack of consumer goods, and repressive conditions resulted in low morale, demonstrations, and outright conflict. After Stalin's death, resources were diverted to consumer goods, but there was little measurable improvement in the quality of life.

By the end of the 1980s, the threat of nuclear annihilation had considerably diminished. If the rivalry between East and West no longer dominated the international arena, what lay ahead? In describing all the changes that accompanied the collapse of the Soviet Union, then U.S. President George Bush spoke of the emergence of a new world order. The world of 1989 was now a world dominated by one superpower, the United States, and characterized by the rise of new political entities and the search for integration and stability in Europe.

QUESTIONS FOR REVIEW

1. Why did western Europe's economy recover so rapidly, and how did that contribute to a gradual process of European economic integration?
2. What is the welfare state, and how did it transform the lives of ordinary Europeans?
3. What were some of the concerns that provoked protests from women, students, and others in the 1960s?
4. How did the ideas of *glasnost* and *perestroika* help bring about the end of the Soviet Union?

DISCOVERING WESTERN CIVILIZATION ONLINE

You can obtain more information about the postwar recovery and the new Europe at the websites listed below. See also the companion website that accompanies this text: www.ablongman.com/kishlansky, which contains an online study guide and additional resources.

Reconstructing Europe

www.fordham.edu/halsall/mod/modsbook49.html
www.fordham.edu/halsall/mod/modsbook50.html
Two collections of links to primary sources and other sites on postwar Western and Eastern Europe.

www.loc.gov/exhibits/marshall
A virtual museum exhibit with images and electronic primary and secondary texts on the Marshall Plan presented by the Library of Congress.

www.yale.edu/lawweb/avalon/un/unchart.htm
This site contains the electronic text of the Charter of the United Nations.

Creating the Welfare State

www.fordham.edu/halsall/mod/modsbook56.html
A collection of primary source documents and links to sites on modern social movements including feminism, black power, and gay and lesbian rights.

Youth Culture and the Generation Gap

lists.village.virginia.edu/sixties/
Website of The Sixties Project, which brings together discussion lists, primary documents, bibliographies, museum exhibits, and personal testimonies about the 1960s and the Vietnam War from an exclusively American perspective.

Toppling Communism in the Soviet Union

www.almaz.com/nobel/peace/1990a.html
A biography of Mikhail Gorbachev with electronic texts compiled by the Nobel Prize Internet Archive.

SUGGESTIONS FOR FURTHER READING

Reconstructing Europe

Eric Hobsbawm, *The Age of Extremes: A History of the World, 1914–1991* (New York: Vintage Books, 1996). This volume covers what the author calls "the short twentieth century" from the outbreak of World War I to the fall of the Soviet Union. Of particular interest is the section on the 30 years following World War II, which the author sees as a "golden age" of extraordinary economic growth and social transformation.

Michael J. Hogan, *The Marshall Plan: America, Britain, and the Reconstruction of Western Europe* (Cambridge: Cambridge University Press, 1987). A thoroughly researched argument on the continuity of U.S. economic policy in the twentieth century. Hogan counters the belief that the Marshall Plan was merely a response to the Cold War.

Creating the Welfare State

Jane Jenson, "Both Friend and Foe: Women and State Welfare," *Becoming Visible: Women in European History*, ed. Renate Bridenthal, Claudia Koonz, and Susan Stuard (Boston: Houghton Mifflin, 1987). This essay illuminates the mixed blessing of the welfare state for women after 1945 by focusing on the experiences of women in Great Britain and France.

Susan Pederson, *Family, Dependence, and the Origins of the Welfare State: Britain and France, 1914–1945* (Cambridge: Cambridge University Press: 1994). Although this work covers the earlier period, the comparative approach to differing attitudes and policies provides an essential background to understanding family policy in postwar Europe.

Mary Ruggie, *The State and Working Women: A Comparative Study of Britain and Sweden* (Princeton, N.J.: Princeton University Press, 1984). A sociological study comparing the economic status of women in two European welfare states.

Youth Culture and the Generation Gap

David Caute, *The Year of the Barricades: A Journey Through 1968* (New York: Harper & Row, 1988). More than its title suggests, this work is an overview of postwar youth culture on three continents. The politics of 1968 are featured, although other topics regarding the counterculture, lifestyles, and cultural ramifications are considered.

John R. Gillis, *Youth and History: Tradition and Change in European Age Relations, 1770–Present* (New York: Academic Press, 1981). Connects the history of European youth to broad trends in economic and demographic modernization over the last 200 years.

Toppling Communism in the Soviet Union

Archie Brown, *The Gorbachev Factor* (New York: Oxford University Press, 1996). Traces the career and examines in detail Gorbachev's attempts to convert the Soviet Union into a social democratic variant of socialism.

Patrick Cockburn, *Getting Russia Wrong: The End of Kremlinology* (London: Verso, 1989). A Moscow correspondent takes measure of the politics of the Gorbachev era while attempting to correct Western misconceptions about the Soviet Union.

Stephen F. Cohen, *Rethinking the Soviet Experience: Politics and History Since 1917* (New York: Oxford University Press, 1985). Offers a revisionist analysis of the historiographical debates in Soviet studies, with the intention of casting light on contemporary Soviet politics.

Geoffrey Hosking, *The Awakening of the Soviet Union* (Cambridge, Mass.: Harvard University Press, 1990). Published in the midst of the dramatic changes taking place in the Soviet Union, this study emphasizes the social bases of reform and the challenges to Soviet leadership.

Walter Laqueur, *The Dream That Failed: Reflections on the Soviet Union* (New York: Oxford University Press, 1994). This work recognizes the tenuous hold of capitalism in Russia and the possibility of a Communist party return.

Martin Malia, *The Soviet Tragedy: A History of Socialism in Russia, 1917–1991* (New York: Maxwell Macmillan International, 1994). A reevaluation of the failure of communism by a leading Russian historian.

Brian McNair, *Images of the Enemy: Reporting the New Cold War* (London: Routledge, 1988). Focuses on the importance of television in conveying the East-West debate to a mass audience in the 1980s. McNair demonstrates that the Soviets learned in the 1980s to manage communication techniques to their own advantage.

CHAPTER 30

THE WEST FACES THE NEW CENTURY, 1989 TO THE PRESENT

- THE VISUAL RECORD: Lost in Space
- RESHAPING EUROPE
- WAR IN THE BALKANS
- THE WEST IN THE GLOBAL COMMUNITY

THE VISUAL RECORD

LOST IN SPACE

"THE RACE TO SPACE" was a hallmark of the competition between East and West during the Cold War. In 1957, the Soviet Union gained the advantage early over the United States by launching two Soviet space satellites, *Sputnik I* and *Sputnik II*, thereby establishing the Soviet Union as a world force in science and technology. Adding further to its prestige, Yuri Gagarin, a Soviet citizen, became the first person launched into space in 1961.

The Age of Sputnik set high stakes for the United States as the other superpower undertaking costly space exploration. After 1957, space exploration and achievement became a measure of national prowess and a source of patriotic pride among the citizens of the two nations.

The competition for space was not merely about scientific dominance and prestige. From the very beginning, the exploration of outer space was measured in military terms, both offensive and defensive. The majority of satellites, for example, launched by both sides had military purposes of surveillance, intelligence gathering, and communications. Manned space missions became a cornerstone of space exploration and were embraced in terms similar to justifications of imperial conquest in the nineteenth century.

Space programs in the two nations fell on tough times with the winding down of the Cold War and economic hardships and recessions that affected East and West. Missions that laid claim to advancement of scientific knowledge persisted. In 1996, the examination of a rock from Mars that indicated the possibility that life existed on that planet billions of years ago fueled political arguments for the ongoing support for the National Aeronautics and Space Administration (NASA).

The Soviets launched one such science-based mission in 1991, apparently routine but with unforeseen consequences. Soviet cosmonaut Sergei Krikalev was sent into space for ten months. His comrade, Aleksandr Volkov, joined him for the last five months of the mission as commander of the Mir space outpost. While orbiting the earth, the two men learned of revolution at home and the collapse of their mother country. If the nation that sponsored the mission no longer existed, what country would bring them back? Workers on the ground assured the

cosmonauts that they would not be lost in space, even as the wages of ground workers were cut, some lost their jobs, and others went on strike in protest.

When brought back to earth, the cosmonauts returned to a vastly altered world. (The photo shows Sergei Krikalev returning to earth after 313 days in space.) The Soviet Union had ceased to exist. Communism, an ideology that had inspired followers around the globe, had been defeated in its country of origin, its leaders replaced, and its party disbanded.

The experience of the former Soviet cosmonauts provides a metaphor for what was happening to people throughout central and eastern Europe as well as in the territory of the former Soviet Union. Millions of Europeans from both East and West struggled to make sense of the new nationalism that motivated breakaway republics, ethnic minorities, and long-standing national communities to express their political aspirations and grievances in new and sometimes violent ways. The alien world was not the one that Krikalev and Volkov explored in outer space but the one they found when they returned to earth. While it might have looked the same from space, the map of Europe was being redrawn according to principles of ethnicity and a new nationalism.

LOOKING AHEAD

In this chapter, we shall see that people throughout the Western world entered the last decade of the twentieth century filled with hope, as symbols of Cold War antagonism gave way to signs of republicanism, democracy, and self-rule. Yet not all transformations were without violence. Most notably, a history of ethnic differences led to war in the Balkans. The place of the West in the global community continued to depend on social and gender inequalities. And a new kind of war based on the terrorism of civilian populations emerged as the weapon of choice of dispossessed groups around the globe.

RESHAPING EUROPE

The year 1989 marked a watershed in the history of European politics. The beginnings of transformation were first evident in the Soviet Union. But no less dramatic, transformations in central and eastern Europe among Warsaw Pact allies rivaled the democratization of Soviet political life in 1989. The democratic tide appeared to be irreversible as symbols of freedom and democratic cooperation proliferated throughout the region. One million people joined hands in a widely publicized event to form a 370-mile-long human chain that stretched across the Soviet Baltic republics of Estonia, Latvia, and Lithuania in protest against the 1940 Soviet annexation. Other bodies defied borders, as in September 1989, when East Germans began a mass exodus into West Germany, voting with their feet for economic prosperity and democracy. Poland and Hungary opted for democratic regimes, and Bulgarians ended the 35-year reign of the dictator Todor Zhivkov and endorsed parliamentary government. Tens of thousands of Czech demonstrators in the capital city of Prague typified the peaceful "Velvet Revolution" of the democratic movement that swept through eastern and central Europe as they poured into the streets to sing songs about freedom and cheer their new heroes, dissidents who had been persecuted and jailed under the former communist regime. One of these dissidents, the playwright Václav Havel, became president of the newly formed Czech Republic.

One of the most dramatic symbols of communism's fall came late in 1989. In November, bulldozers moved against the Berlin Wall, the tangible symbol of Cold War politics that had cut Berlin in two since 1961. As this most tangible of barriers came down, people spoke of the birth of a new democratic age of free markets and free expression. Yet freedom was not the only force unleashed with the collapse of communism. Ugly battles based on long-standing grievances erupted. Groups intent on autonomy and independence vied with each other over territories and borders. The Balkans, where borders had been imposed at the end of World War I, erupted into genocidal strife that shocked the world.

Nowhere was violence more pronounced than in the Balkans. In Bosnia, where a bloody war dragged on for years in the former Yugoslavia, the term "ethnic cleansing" laid bare the barbarity and genocide that were still very much a part of the Europe of the late twentieth century. In March 1999, the North Atlantic Treaty Organization (NATO) began bombing Kosovo to stop the Serb "cleansing" of Albanians. The international arena seemed bereft of solutions to the troubling problem of borders at the end of the twentieth century.

Russia and the New Republics

The failed coup of August 1991 effectively brought an end to the authority of Mikhail Gorbachev, although he retained the title of Soviet president. The tide of reform he unleashed could not, however, be turned back.

Economic Challenges. Following the events of August 1991, Russia embarked on a drive toward Westernization in playing catch-up with capitalist nations. Liberal reformers pressed for privatization of industry and the lifting of price controls. The long lines in front of stores disappeared, but inflation galloped to new heights, wiping out savings and pensions overnight. The black market, always in the shadows even in the most repressed of times, emerged boldly as a corrupt "mafia" became the new business leaders of Russia. New markets relied on dollars, and neither banks nor police had the power to stem illegal activities. In spite of official government policy, a visitor to St. Petersburg (the former Leningrad) could ride in taxis whose meters registered in dollars and could eat in restaurants in sections reserved for dollar-paying customers where the service and the food were better. The Russian ruble crashed in October 1994.

The Nationalities Problem. A crucial element in understanding the end of the Soviet Union is the nationalities problem within its borders—the claim to self-determination made by Soviet minorities. The Soviet Union had listed 102 separate nationalities in its 1979 census. Twenty-two of those nationalities had populations of one million or more. This very diversity contributed to the disintegration of the Soviet Union from within. As Gorbachev supported the demands for self-determination in eastern Europe, he faced similar claims to autonomy in a growing number of Soviet republics. The nationalities problem proved to be even more challenging to Gorbachev's regime than the freemarket economy was. In fact, the demands for more freedom in the marketplace went hand in hand with demands for greater cultural self-expression and political autonomy among minority nationalities.

The three major areas of nationalist conflict—Central Asia, Armenia, and the Baltic States—had been voicing grievances against the Soviet state since the 1920s. The protests of the 1980s differed from earlier outcries because claims were now being advanced by a new and educated urban elite, formed after World War II. Moscow relied on these groups of university-educated and upwardly mobile professionals to further economic reforms. These groups now became the driving force behind demands for nationalist reforms. Gorbachev failed to harness their protests for autonomy and thereby undermined the Communist Party. Ethnic minorities, especially in the Soviet Baltic republics of Latvia, Lithuania, and Estonia, threatened the dominance of Party rule in favor of immediate self-determination. Endorsing diversity of opinion, individual rights, and freedom as the bases of good government, Gorbachev now had to deal with vocal nationalities that took him at his word. Large-scale riots erupted in Lithuania over demands for nationalist rights. In 1988,

Estonians demanded the right of veto over any law passed in Moscow. The Russian minority in Estonia protested attacks and prejudicial treatment in the Estonian republic. In the same year, violence erupted in Azerbaijan as tens of thousands of Armenians took to the streets to demand the return of the Armenian enclave of Nagorno-Karabakh, incorporated into Azerbaijan in 1921. In the Azerbaijani capital of Baku, the center of Russia's oil-producing region, demonstrators demanded greater autonomy for their republic and the accountability of their deputies in Moscow. Violence between Azerbaijanis and Armenians resulted in 32 deaths and the displacement of tens of thousands of people. The state of upheaval climaxed in December 1988 when an earthquake in Armenia killed 25,000 people. Soviet troops were placed in the area, ostensibly to deal with the aftermath of the natural disaster.

In 1986, university students in the central Asian republic of Kazakhstan incited two days of demonstrations and rioting over the removal of a corrupt local leader who was replaced with a Russian Communist Party official. The Soviet government's attempts to clean up politics in the area betrayed a clumsy disregard for ethnic issues and seemed at odds with Gorbachev's commitment to decentralization. Crimean Tatars, who had been exiled in Islamic fundamentalist Kazakhstan since World War II, agitated for return home.

The Breakaway Republics Lead the Way. One by one, all 15 of the Soviet republics proclaimed their independence, following the lead of the breakaway Baltic republics of Estonia, Lithuania, and Latvia. Having failed to agree on a new plan for union, Gorbachev and the leaders of ten republics transferred authority to an emergency State Council in September 1991 until a plan could be devised. By the end of the year, the Soviet Union was faced with serious food shortages and was bankrupt, unable to pay its employees and dependent on the financial backing provided by Yeltsin as head of the Russian state. Rejecting all Soviet authority, Russia, Belarus, and Ukraine joined together in December 1991 to form the Commonwealth of Independent States (CIS). Eight other republics followed their lead. The Soviet Union thereby came to its end on 21 December 1991 with the resignation of Mikhail Gorbachev, who had become a man without a state to rule. Russian president Yeltsin moved into Gorbachev's Soviet presidential offices at the Kremlin.

Many issues remained unresolved. The new political organization did not address the endemic problems of economic hardship and left unanswered the questions of who would control the former Soviet Union's vast military machine, including its nuclear arsenal, and how trade networks and a stable monetary policy would be determined. The Soviet Union, which had ruled as a great power for over seven decades, no longer existed. Communism had been totally discredited.

The Chechen Challenge

In December 1994, Russia committed itself to a war with another of its ethnic minorities, the secessionist Chechens, who had declared themselves independent of Russia in 1991. The war was denounced in the international arena because of the Russian attacks against the civilian population. By the summer of 1996, Russia appeared to have lost the war and agreed to a truce, despite the fact that it possessed the largest army in Europe deployed against a much smaller opponent.

The development of a peace plan that would acknowledge Chechen autonomy within the Russian state was acceptable to the rebels, who saw the advantage of regrouping their forces and the need for a break in hostilities. But Kremlin officials expressed dismay that the move toward Chechen autonomy threatened "Russian territorial integrity."

In the summer of 1999, conflict again escalated into open warfare because of terrorist bombings in Moscow attributed to Chechen rebels. Affected by arguments of self-defense against terrorists, Russian popular opinion now turned in favor of repressing the Chechen bid for independence. Russia also had important economic motives for subduing the runaway republic, as Chechnya's location was central to the oil pipeline routes near the Caspian Sea. Several former Soviet states had begun building a new pipeline in the 1990s in order to circumvent the Russian supply and to sell directly to Western buyers.

In 2001, Russian president Vladimir Putin declared the war in Chechnya over. Yet violence continued. Following terrorist attacks in the United States on 11 September 2001, the Russians escalated their war against terrorism in Chechnya.

The Unification of Germany

The German Democratic Republic (East Germany) and the German Federal Republic (West Germany) continued to develop after 1968 as two separate countries with different social, economic, and political institutions. On the surface, these differences seemed insurmountable.

The Movement of Populations. The Berlin Wall, erected in 1961, divided the former German capital and served its intended purpose of keeping East Germans confined behind it. East Germany's chief problem in the 1950s was the exodus of skilled workers and professionals in search of a better life in the West. The flow of emigration throughout the 1950s turned into a torrent in the first eight months of 1961, when the number of refugees fleeing from East to West Germany reached 160,000 people. West German leaders continued to voice their long-term commitment to reunification. East German leaders insisted on the independence and autonomy of their state.

The two Germanys were linked economically, if not politically, throughout most of the postwar period. When

A WOMAN REPORTER BEHIND THE LINES OF THE WAR IN CHECHNYA

Anne Nivat was the Moscow correspondent for the French daily newspaper Libération *in October 2000 when she interviewed the rebel president of Chechnya. Fluent in Russian and holding a doctorate in political science, Nivat traveled to southern Russia disguised as a Chechen woman to cover the war from the Chechen side. Her newspaper reports led to antiwar protests in Paris.*

FOCUS QUESTIONS

What indications does the Chechen rebel leader give that he sees guerrilla warfare within Chechnya as the best means of defeating Russia? What are his motives for opposition to the presence of Russian troops in Chechnya?

I FINALLY FIND MASKHADOV. He is wearing a military uniform with a pistol in his belt and appears to be in perfect health. Seated on a comfortable sofa in a "safe house," he seems relaxed and eager to share his thoughts on the situation in Chechnya. Outside, Russian armored vehicles pass through the autumn mist. Since he left Grozny the previous winter, the rebel president hasn't spent more than two consecutive days in any one spot. He usually communicates with his men and with the outside world by means of audiotapes. Few journalists take the trouble to hunt him down and interview him. In any case, he's very suspicious of the press. We talk for several hours over a meal of soup.

"The Russian intervention in Chechnya is about one year old. Where are we now?" I ask Maskhadov.

The fugitive leader answers simply: "As far as we're concerned, it all began on September 5, 1999, when the Russians bombed our country for the first time, and not on October 1. This time we're not so naïve to throw ourselves into all-out combat with the Russians, as we did in the first war. We know that's not the way to make any headway against their army. All we can do is mount a series [of] diversionary actions," he explains. "Our goal is not to halt their army but to conserve our own forces. While they occupy our territory—that is, while they remain inactive—their forces grow weaker, while ours get stronger. Our men are everywhere. The Russians know it, and yet they never mount an offensive. Their army is demoralized." . . .

Maskhadov is silent for a moment. He lets out a deep sigh. The Chechens, he admits, are tired of this war. "I recognize that the situation is difficult for the civilian population, which has become the target of the Russian army. I also regret that thousands of my countrymen have had to leave for Ingushetia or elsewhere. But each time I send out my representatives, they come back with the same message: 'Continue the fight. We're with you.' We can't afford to lose face, and the population knows it as well as I do. One way or another, the Russians will be forced to come to the negotiating table. I am constantly reminding Putin that he will be better off negotiating with me, as long as I am alive. It will be worse without me. And the Russians will leave in the end. Last time they led us to believe that they would never leave and then they disappeared. The worse thing would be if they stayed and we had to defend their troops here in Chechnya!" . . .

Maskhadov is enjoying our discussion. It is rare that he has the full attention of a member of the foreign press. He has a hard time tearing himself away, but he finally gets up to leave, followed by his Minister of Defense and two bodyguards. His old car starts up crankily. It carries him away to the edge of the forest. From there he will go on horseback to his camp.

From Anne Nivat, *Chienne de Guerre: A Woman Reporter Behind the Lines of the War in Chechnya,* translated by Susan Darnton (New York: Public Affairs Press, 2001), pp. 251–255.

West Germany entered the European Community in 1957, it insisted that in matters related to trade, the two Germanys were to be treated as one country. As a result, East Germany benefited from its free-trade relationship with West Germany. This advantage provided an important part of East Germany's prosperity since the 1960s. West Germany, in turn, achieved much of its prosperity through export-led growth, and it found markets in East Germany.

In the 1980s, West Germany stood as an economic giant, second only to the United States in foreign trade and far ahead of Japan. With its economic opportunities and advanced social welfare programs, West Germany exerted considerable influence on East Germans. And although East Germany, too, established itself as an important trading nation—fifteenth in the world in 1975—citizens in East Germany were lured by the greater prosperity of the West.

The Berlin Wall Comes Down. Applications for authorized immigration increased in the 1980s, and in 1984 East Germany allowed 30,000 citizens to emigrate to the West. Throughout the late 1980s, the emigration rate remained high, with an average exodus of 20,000 a year. With Hungary's refusal to continue to block the passage of East

In a scene that symbolizes the end of the Cold War, people dance atop the Berlin Wall in November 1989. Pieces of the demolished wall soon were being sold as souvenirs.

Germans into West Germany, the floodgates were opened: 57,000 East Germans migrated within a matter of weeks. In the face of angry demonstrations, Erich Honecker, head of the East German state, was forced to resign. The new government opened the Berlin Wall on 9 November 1989, ending all restrictions on travel between East and West. An East Germany with open borders could no longer survive as its citizens poured into the promised land of the West in record numbers. The West German government intervened to assist East Germany in shoring up its badly faltering economy; the West German deutsche mark was substituted for the East German currency. Monetary union prefigured political unification. In October 1990, Germany became a single, united nation once again.

BALANCE SHEET: EAST AND WEST GERMANY ON THE EVE OF UNIFICATION

East Germany built the strongest economy in the Soviet bloc, but its standard of living lagged far behind that of West Germany, creating challenges for the unified German state after 1990.

	Federal Republic of Germany (West)	**German Democratic Republic (East)**
Population	61 million	17 million
Life Expectancy	Men, 71.2 years; women, 78.1 years	Men, 69.5 years; women, 75.4 years
Gross National Product	$1.12 trillion	$207.2 billion
Public Spending on Education	9.4% of all government expenditures	5.5% of all government expenditures
New Books Published	50,903 volumes	5,636 volumes

Source: *Statistical Yearbook*, UNESCO, 1988; *Demographic Yearbook*, United Nations; *CIA World Factbook*, 1988.

Germans represent the largest nationality in Europe west of Russia. Other Europeans feared the prospect of a united Germany, although publicly, European leaders endorsed the principle of the self-determination of peoples. In addition, western Europeans were troubled by the impact a united Germany might have on plans for European unification in the European Union. Not least of all, Germans themselves feared reunification. Former East Germans were wary about marginalization and second-class citizenship, while West Germans worried that their poor cousins from the east would act as a brake on West Germany's sustained economic expansion. Nevertheless, Germany committed itself to a course of action that promised to make of the German nation a unified people whose economy would continue to dominate European and world markets.

Eastern Europe: Nationalism and Ethnicity

The Soviet example of restructuring and Gorbachev's calls for reforms and openness gave the lead to eastern Europe. In 1988, Gorbachev, speaking before the United Nations, assured the West that he would not prevent eastern European satellites from going their own way: "Freedom of choice is a universal principle."

Poland and Grassroots Protest. Poland's first free elections in 40 years were part of a vast mosaic of protest from which a pattern began to emerge in 1989. Poland, the most populous country in eastern Europe, played an important role in the Soviet bloc because of its strategic location as a corridor for supplies to 380,000 Soviet troops in East Germany. Yet its economy was never robust, and it had a 20-year history of worker protest and resistance. Throughout the 1970s, one-party rule prevailed, while workers attempted to maintain forms of permanent organization. The Polish government obtained loans from abroad for investment in technology and industrial expansion. Resisting raising prices at home, Poland increased its foreign indebtedness. In 1976, however, price increases were again decreed. A new wave of spontaneous strikes erupted, forcing the government to rescind the increases.

Poland's indebtedness to the West rose from $2.5 billion in 1973 to $17 billion in 1980. Poland was sinking into the mire of ever higher interest payments that absorbed the country's export earnings. At the beginning of July 1980, the government was forced once again to raise food

▼ Events in Eastern Europe, 1989–1990. The events of 1989 and 1990 seemed to indicate that peaceful democratic change through free elections and liberal reforms would fill the void left by the collapse of communist rule.

1. **Albania.** Communist party still retains Leninist orientation, Jan. 1990. Parliament backs liberal reforms, May 1990.
2. **Yugoslavia.** Government decides to hold free elections, Dec. 1989.
3. **Bulgaria.** Government disavows "dominant role" for Communist party; pledges free elections and new constitution in 1990.
4. **Romania.** Communist dictator Ceauşescu overthrown and executed, Dec. 1989; Salvation Front led by dissident former Communists wins elections, May 1990.
5. **Hungary.** Free election sweeps non-Communists into power, April 1990.
6. **Czechoslovakia.** Communist leadership ousted, Nov. 1989; Václav Havel named president, Dec. 1989.
7. **Germany.** Berlin Wall breached, Nov. 1989. Reunification of East and West Germany, Oct. 1990.
8. **Poland.** Solidarity party sweeps elections, June 1989.
9. **Lithuania** declares independence, March 1990; Moscow calls move illegal.
10. **Latvia and Estonia** begin process of separation from Soviet Union, April 1990.

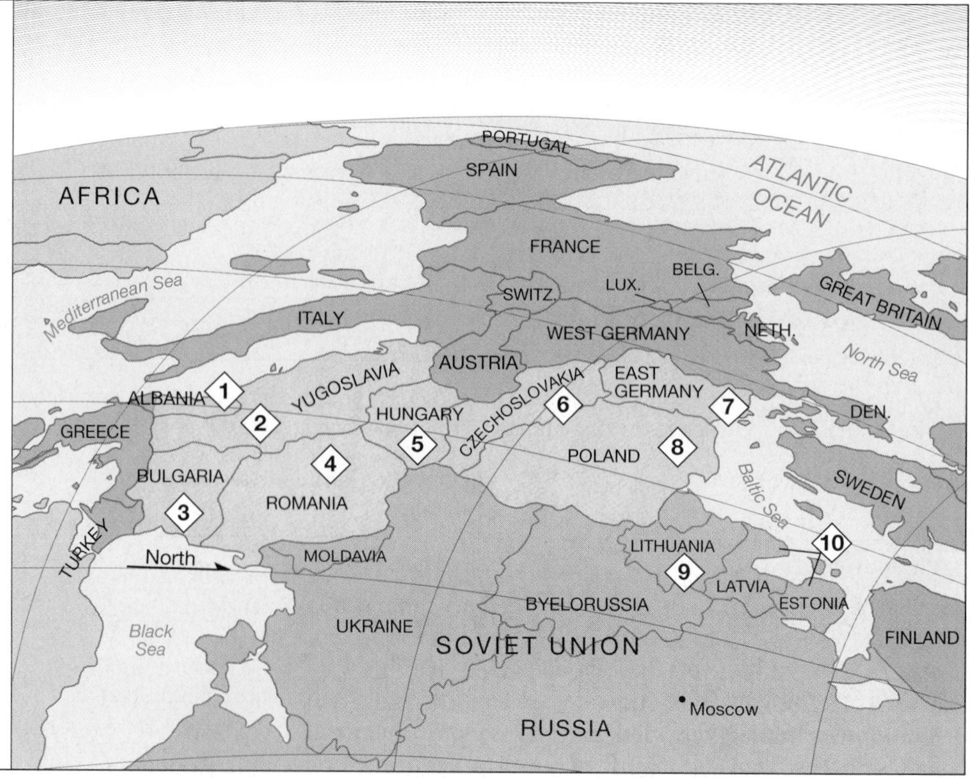

"Nothing Lasts Forever" reads the sign hanging from the battered bust of communist dictator Joseph Stalin being carried through the streets of Prague by Czech demonstrators celebrating the end of the communist regime in their country.

prices. Shipyard workers in Gdansk were ready, organized in a new non-communist labor union called Solidarity under the leadership of Lech Walesa, a politically astute electrician. The union staged a sit-down strike that paralyzed the shipyards. Union committees coordinated their activities from one factory to the next and succeeded in shutting down the entire economy. The government agreed to a series of union-backed reforms known as the Gdansk Accords, which, among other measures, increased civil liberties and acknowledged Solidarity's right to exist.

Within a year, Solidarity had an astounding 8 million members out of a population of 35 million. The Catholic Church lent important support to those who opposed communist rule. Dissident intellectuals also cast their lot with the organized workers in demanding reforms. General Wojciech Jaruzelski, who became prime minister in February 1981, was unable to change the situation of shortages appreciably. Jaruzelski attempted to curb the union's demands for democratic government and participation in management by harsh measures. He declared martial law on 13 December 1981 in an effort to save the Polish Communist Party and used the Polish military to crack down on dissidents. The Soviet response was to do nothing. Poland was left to Polish rule.

Martial law in Poland produced military repression. Solidarity was outlawed, and Walesa was jailed. The West did not lose sight of him: in 1983, the union leader was awarded the Nobel Peace Prize for his efforts. After years of negotiations and intermittent strikes, Solidarity was legalized again in 1989. Jaruzelski knew that he needed Solidarity's cooperation to address dire economic conditions. He therefore agreed to open elections. At the polls, Solidarity candidates soundly defeated the Communist Party. Poland was the first country in eastern Europe to turn a communist regime out of office peacefully.

The great challenge before the new Solidarity government, as had been the case for the communist regime that preceded it, was economic recovery. Inflation drove food prices up at the rate of 50 percent a month. Poland faced the task of earning enough foreign trade credits to alleviate its indebtedness and to justify foreign investment. In the mid-1990s, Poland continued its pursuit of a free market economy by attracting Western companies and corporations to open subsidiaries and do business within its borders, as inflation slowed to a still high 20 to 30 percent. A prosperous management class began emerging.

Hungary, Czechoslovakia, and Romania. In the same period as the Polish free elections, Hungary dismantled the barbed-wire fences on its borders, opening itself to the West in September 1989. People wanted freedom of movement and freedom of expression. Everywhere, east Europeans demanded democratic institutions modeled on those of Western nations. "People power" swept away communist leaders and ousted the Communist Party. The leader of the New Socialist party in Hungary, Imre Pozsgay,

CHRONOLOGY

THE VELVET REVOLUTIONS

1989	Free elections in Poland lead to the ouster of the communist regime
September 1989	Hungary opens its borders to the West
November 1989	German Democratic Republic lifts travel restrictions between East and West Germany; the Berlin Wall comes down
December 1989	Václav Havel elected president of Czechoslovakia
July 1990	Havel reelected as president of the Czech and Slovak Federated Republic
1990	Boris Yeltsin elected president of the Russian Republic
1990	Gorbachev ends the Communist Party's monopoly of power
1990	Lech Walesa elected president of Poland
October 1990	Federal Republic of Germany and German Democratic Republic reunited
December 1991	Eleven former Soviet republics form Commonwealth of Independent States (CIS); Mikhail Gorbachev resigns and the Soviet Union is dissolved

declared, "Communism does not work. We must start again at zero." Unlike other eastern European countries, Hungary had begun experimenting cautiously with free markets and private control as early as the 1970s. As a result, Hungary was best positioned to engage in a serious trade with western Europe and made the most prosperous adjustment to democratic autonomy.

Czechoslovakia's revolution began with angry university student protesters. The police responded by bludgeoning the protesters and that spark touched off a mass movement that within days drove out the Czech Communist party. Idealism and growing public sympathy were on the side of the protesters. The dissident playwright Václav Havel emerged as a new kind of leader of the democratic opposition and was elected president. He became a powerful spokesperson for democratic institutions and oversaw a relatively peaceful separation of the Czech Republic from Slovakia. All of the countries underwent what were considered "velvet revolutions," characterized by a lack of violence and an apparently smooth passage to new order and the achievement of independence.

The year 1989 did not end, however, without bloody upheaval. Romania, under communist dictator Nicolae Ceaucescu, appeared to be pursuing a peaceful path. It had evaded its military responsibilities as a signatory of the Warsaw Pact; it alone of the member states had refused to participate in the intervention in Czechoslovakia in 1968. Yet Romania was a state that could not tolerate internal protest. In December 1989, Ceaucescu ordered his troops to fire on demonstrators. Thousands of men, women, and children were killed and then buried unceremoniously in mass graves. The slaughter set off a revolution in which Ceaucescu and his wife and co-ruler, Elena, were captured, tried, and executed by a firing squad. They were charged with genocide—the slaughter of 64,000 people—and the mismanagement of the economy. In the days that followed, Romanians spoke in the international media of their newly won freedom, as videotaped images of the slain leaders were broadcast to the world.

WAR IN THE BALKANS

Hopes for social transformation and liberal economic reforms were highest for Yugoslavia in 1989 with the waning of Soviet power and the end of the Cold War. Yugoslavia, after all, was the success story of the Soviet bloc with open borders and its escape from the Stalinist grasp in 1948. Many Europeans believed it was moving toward a market economy with its liberal economic policies and trade agreements. Yet within two years the country had ceased to exist and by 1992 war tore apart the former Yugoslavia.

The most enduring and bloody of the ethnic crises came in Yugoslavia. In 1991, festering differences erupted in civil war between Serbs and Croats, as Serbian nationalists overran multi-ethnic Bosnia and Herzegovina in a bid for territorial aggrandizement of Serbia. Yugoslavia was a federation of six people's republics, with Serbia, Croatia, and Bosnia and Herzegovina the three largest in descending order. With the collapse of Yugoslavia, Serbs became an aggrieved minority in Croatia and Bosnia. Serbia and Croatia were more than long-standing rivals. They were enemies with a history of hostility that had been masked by their federated status in the Yugoslav state.

The History of Ethnic Differences

The divide between the Serbs and Croats was partly identified with religious differences—the Croats were historically Catholic, the Serbs Orthodox—but for the most part, their enmity was based on the competing claims over the south Slavic lands, Bosnia and Herzegovina, that were part of the former Ottoman and Austro-Hungarian empires.

These conflicting territorial claims of the Serbs and Croatians were exacerbated by two facts. First, a large number of Serbs lived in Croatia, and, of course, Croatians were present in the Serbian-claimed lands of Bosnia. Under Tito's rule, ethnic differences were held in check. After 1991, land claims were complicated by the mixed population of Bosnia and Herzegovina. Second, another

Balkans, 2000. New republics, federations, and sectors were carved out of the former Yugoslavia in the 1990s, with conflicts still unresolved at the turn of the new century.

group, neither Catholic nor Orthodox but Muslim, amounting to 9 percent of the population of the former Yugoslavia and a majority of the Bosnian population, got caught in the crossfire of the war between Serbs and Croats and became a target for massacre and atrocities by the Serbs.

The War for a "Greater Serbia"

In 1992, the Serbian army evicted 750,000 Muslim civilians from their homes. Serb forces also continued to bomb civilians in the Bosnian capital of Sarajevo. It later came to light that in 1992 Serb leaders had authorized a policy of *ethnic cleansing*, the term used to connote the genocide and atrocities—including concentration camps, rape, and starvation—used against Muslims.

With more than a quarter of a million lives lost and two million people displaced, the Bosnia conflict was recognized as the bloodiest ground war in Europe in 50 years. The United Nations placed peace-keeping forces in Bosnia. NATO intervened against the Serbian attempt to overrun Bosnia after the outbreak of hostilities, and in September 1995 NATO stepped up the bombing of Bosnian Serb military installations and Serbian-held positions in Bosnia with the policy of avoiding civilian targets. European leaders looked to the United States for intervention, but two U.S. presidents, George Bush and Bill Clinton, sought to avoid involvement in Bosnia.

The Dayton Peace Accords brokered by the United States brought Muslim, Croat, and Serb leaders together to Ohio in November and December 1995. The aim of the accord was to create a unified country in Bosnia while recognizing ethnic interests. As part of the commitment to the accord, the Clinton administration sent 20,000 U.S. troops to join the 60,000 NATO troops already present to help enforce the peace.

Kosovo and the Ongoing Balkans Conflict

Yet another arena of bloodshed opened up in 1998. Kosovo, one of the six former Yugoslav republics, had been known as the "autonomous province" of Serbia. With the break up of Yugoslavia, there had been movement toward an independent Kosovo, and even talk of a "Greater Albania," which would reunify Albanians in Kosovo, western Macedonia, and Albania. Checking attempts at Kosovo independence, Serbia proceeded to strip it of its autonomous status after 1990. In addition, there was overwhelming evidence that the Serb state intended to drive more than one million Kosovo Albanians from the province. The Kosovo Liberation Army responded by dedicating itself to guerrilla actions against the Serbs.

Civil rights abuses and atrocities against Kosovo Albanians by Kosovo Serbs shocked the world into action in 1998. The Western powers, meeting in France with leaders of both sides, attempted to negotiate a peace agreement and failed. Kosovo Albanians fled by the thousands toward the Albanian and Macedonian borders, driven out by Serbs. On the night of 24 March 1999, NATO forces began attacking Serbian targets in Kosovo in a massive military campaign of air strikes that lasted for almost 11 weeks. The war, a first in NATO's history, marked a failure in its policy of deterrence. As the lead partner, the United States justified an unpopular war at home by promising not to commit ground troops in battle. The air war succeeded, and United Nations peace-keeping forces, including U.S. troops, entered Kosovo in June 1999. The Serbs were probably responsible for the deaths of at least 10,000 and the expulsion of 800,000 Kosovo Albanians. With the defeat of Serb forces, Kosovo Albanians took the place of their Serb oppressors and committed new atrocities, now under the nose of peacekeeping forces, with the aim of driving non-Albanians out of the province. Intolerance and the desire for revenge boded ill for the future of peace in the region.

Serbia, and the Balkans in general, continued to be plagued by weak economies, low wages, and high unemployment. But Albania, a tiny nation of 3.5 million people, was in the worst economic shape of all at the end of the twentieth century, with the highest infant mortality rate and the lowest life expectancy rate in Europe, its industrial infrastructure in ruins, its government in shambles, and its environment polluted.

Other eastern European states also were riddled with ethnic troubles—including Czechs and Slovaks, the Hungarians and Romanians over the border region of Transylvania, and the Bulgarians and Turks in Bulgaria—but none of those disputes involved the extent of violence that had occurred in the Balkans.

THE WEST IN THE GLOBAL COMMUNITY

Western European nations had met the challenges of wartime devastation with miraculous economic recoveries in the 1950s and 1960s. Their economies were able to grow despite labor shortages, thanks to an available pool of workers from southern Europe and from former colonies in Asia and Africa. After the phenomenal growth and prosperity of the postwar years, western Europe experienced a new set of harsh realities in the 1970s with skyrocketing oil prices, inflation, and recession. The permanent presence of foreign workers, many of them unemployed or erratically employed because of the economic downturns of the 1970s and 1980s, came to be seen as a problem by welfare state leaders and politicians of the new Right, who played on xenophobic fears and racial hatred. Prosperity brought greater educational and career opportunities for women but also raised their expectations regarding their place in society.

Other large-scale changes were taking place in the very ways in which political arrangements were structured. With the goal of reviving the economy, in the 1980s 12 member states of the European Economic Community devoted themselves to making western Europe competitive as a bloc in world markets. At the same time as Russian satellites in eastern Europe were breaking free of Soviet control and attempting to strike out on their own, the nations of western Europe were negotiating a new unity based on a single market and centralized policy making.

The Founding of a European Union

In 1957, the founders of the European Economic Community, Robert Schuman and Jean Monnet, envisioned the idea of a United States of Europe, a continent where all nations worked together in a common cause. Both men perceived that Europe's best hope of competing in a new world system was through unity. The European Community (EC) was created in 1967 by merging three transnational European bodies: the European Coal and Steel Community, the European Economic Community or Common Market, and the European Atomic Energy Community or Euratom. It operated with its own commission, parliament, and council of ministers, although it had little real power over the operations of member states. In

1974, a European Council was created within the European Community, made up of heads of government who met three times a year for the purpose of furthering European integration.

The Politics of Oil. The oil crisis of the 1970s encouraged isolationism among the members of the EC and eroded foreign markets, with growing dependence on national suppliers. As the crisis abated, competition and efficiency reemerged as priorities within the European Community. Europeans were well aware that the United States and Japan had surged ahead after the 1973 crisis. Leaders also recognized that the Common Market had been successful in promoting European growth and integration since 1958. They now realized that integration was the only defense against the permanent loss of markets and dwindling profits.

Toward a Single Europe. In 1985, the EC negotiated the Single European Act, which by 1987 had been ratified by the parliamentary bodies of all the member nations. Final steps were taken to establish a fully integrated market beginning at midnight on 31 December 1992. The 12 members of the EC intended to eliminate internal barriers and to create a huge open market among the member states, with common external tariff policies. In addition, the elimination of internal frontier controls, with a single-format passport, was intended to make travel easier and to avoid shipping delays at frontiers, thereby lowering costs. An international labor market based on standardized requirements for certification and interchangeable job qualifications would result. The easier movement of capital into areas where profitability was greatest was encouraged. All aspects of trade and communication, down to electric plugs and sockets, were targeted for standardization. The goal behind the planning was to make the EC think and act as a single country. Supporters compared it to the 50 individual American states participating in the single U.S. nation.

In 1989, 320 million people lived in the 12 countries of the European Community: the original Common Market six of France, West Germany, Belgium, the Netherlands, Luxembourg, and Italy had been joined by Britain, Denmark, and Ireland in 1973, Greece in 1981, and Portugal and Spain in 1986. Plans for European economic integration moved dramatically forward in October 1991, when the 12-nation European Community and the 7 nations of the European Free Trade Association (EFTA) joined forces to form a new common market to be known as the European Economic Area. The EFTA countries that joined forces with the EC included Austria, Finland, Iceland, Liechtenstein, Norway, Sweden, and Switzerland. Several of the EFTA nations announced plans to join the EC as well. The European Economic Area constituted the world's largest trading bloc, stretching from the Arctic Circle to the Mediterranean and consisting of approximately 380 million consumers. The nations of the EFTA agreed to abide by the EC's plans for economic integration and adopted the vast array of laws that governed the European Community.

The European Union. Meeting in Maastricht, the Netherlands, in December 1991, the heads of the 12 EC countries ratified the Treaty on the European Union. They agreed that a common currency, the euro, would replace the national currencies of eligible nations, and that a single central banking system, known as the European Monetary Institute, would guide member nations in reducing inflation rates and budget deficits. Economic union would be reinforced by political union, with member states sharing a common European defense system and common social policies regulating immigration and labor practices. In that sense, the new European Union (EU) was intended as something more than the European Community (EC), which had been primarily an economic entity. Prior to the Maastricht Treaty, President François Mitterrand of France had endorsed the goals of the 1992 integration: "One currency, one culture, one social area, one environment."

On 1 January 2002, Europeans in 12 nations began using the new common currency, the euro. Since 1999, the euro had been a virtual currency, existing as a bookkeeping device. In 2002, the new hard currency replaced national monetary units including the French franc, the German mark, the Spanish peseta, the Greek drachma, and the Dutch guilder. Hailed as the European Union's boldest achievement, the new currency was intended to solidify the basis of integrated European markets and be competitive in international markets against the dollar. Within two months of the introduction of the euro, at the end of February 2002, the 15 member nations of the European Union convened a Convention for the purpose of considering the creation of a Europe-wide constitution.

Many worried, however, that the long histories, traditions, and national identifications of the individual member states would stand in the way of a fully integrated and politically united Europe. Britain was the most reluctant of the member states at the prospect of European integration. British negotiators strongly resisted plans for monetary union because of fear of losing national sovereignty rights. Nonetheless, Prime Minister Margaret Thatcher and her successor, John Major, solidly committed Great Britain to the EU. As Thatcher explained it: "Our destiny is in Europe." In addition to resisting monetary union, British public opinion polls reflected cynicism over the 1991 Maastricht negotiations and a social policy affecting working hours, minimum wages, and conditions of employment throughout Europe.

The plan for a single European market affected more than politics and economics. Education, too, faced standardization of curricula and requirements for degrees. There were proposals for a single common European

▲ Europe, 2000. The most stable and prosperous European nations formed the member states of the European Union in 2000. These 15 members agreed to share a common currency, economic and social policies, and planning.

history textbook that, in place of national perspectives, would emphasize the values of a single political entity in its discussion of battles, wars, social change, and culture.

Export-producing nations, including Japan and the United States, expressed concerns over "Fortress Europe," that is, Europe as a global trading bloc with a common external tariff policy that would exclude them. A united Europe would constitute a formidable presence in the world arena, with the world's largest volume of trade and highest productivity. The move might easily place Europe at the center of world politics, as the Cold War thawed and the bloc politics of East versus West no longer dominated the international system.

Originally intended to offset American dominance in European markets, in the 1990s the EU offered the opportunity of a closer economic relationship with the United States. The EU became the largest customer for American products. The possibility of the emergence of a truly global marketplace seemed, paradoxically, more likely with the creation of the EU and other regional associations throughout the world. By fostering economic competition as well as cooperation, the EU offered a counter-balance to the void filled by the end of the Cold War and the promise of peace based on productivity and trade.

A New Working Class: Foreign Workers

Foreign workers played an important role in the industrial growth of western Europe beginning in the 1950s. To expand production, western European nations needed cheap, unskilled laborers. Great Britain, France, and West Germany became the chief labor-importing countries, whose economic growth in the 1950s and 1960s was made possible by readily available pools of cheap foreign labor. The chief labor-exporting countries were Portugal, Turkey, Algeria, Italy, and Spain, whose sluggish economic performances spurred their workers to seek employment opportunities beyond national borders. Great Britain imported workers from the West Indies, Ireland, India, Pakistan, Africa, and southern Europe.

Migrant employment was by definition poorly paid, unskilled, or semiskilled manual work. Commonly, married men migrated without their families with the goal of earning cash to send home to those left behind. Most immigrants who came looking for jobs carried with them the "myth of return," the belief that they would someday go back home. For the most part, however, foreign workers stayed in the host country.

Working Conditions and Rights. The lot of foreign workers residing in European countries was difficult and sometimes dangerous. Foreign workers could be badly treated by employers and ostracized, or worse, by other workers. Onerous and demanding labor was common. Foreign workers were often herded together in crowded living quarters, socially marginalized, and identified with the degrading work they performed. Foreign workers were frequently denied the rights of citizenship and subjected to the vagaries of legislation. In economic downturns they were the first to be laid off. Third and fourth generations of foreign workers born on West German soil were refused the rights of citizenship and denied the possibility of naturalization. Yet the obligation of foreign workers to send money back home to aged parents, spouses, children, and siblings persisted.

Women endured special problems within the foreign workforce. Between 1964 and 1974, for example, the majority of Portuguese female immigrants who entered France to work as domestics brought their families with them, but there was little in the way of social services to support them on their arrival. Dependable child care was either too expensive or unavailable to female workers with children. Increasing numbers of single women began migrating to western Europe independently of households and male migrants. Like men, they often worked to send money back to their country of origin.

Opposition and Restrictions. Before 1973, most countries in western Europe, including Great Britain, actively encouraged foreign labor. After 1973, restrictions became the order of the day. It is no coincidence that restrictions against the presence of foreigner workers in western Europe followed fast on the heels of the 1973 oil crisis and accompanied economic downturns. Western governments began enforcing new conservative policies throughout the 1970s and 1980s that were intended to keep out third-world refugees. Opposition to the presence of foreign workers was often expressed in an ultranationalist rhetoric and usually flared up in periods of economic reversals.

In 1986, the xenophobic National Front in France campaigned on a platform of "France for the French" and captured 10 percent of the vote in national elections. In 1992, with the slogans "Immigration Equals Unemployment" and "Protect Our Frontiers," the same party garnered 16 percent of the vote in regional elections. Racism was out in the open in France and other western European countries that had depended on a foreign labor force for their prosperity. Race riots in Great Britain in 1980 and 1981, particularly in the London ghetto of Brixton, were ignited by racial discrimination against blacks, severe cuts in social welfare spending, and deteriorating working conditions.

On the whole, restrictions failed to achieve what they set out to do—remove foreign workers from Western countries by repatriation. Foreign workers learned how to get around the restrictions and sent for their families to join them. British laws also had the effect of converting temporary migrations by single men into permanent family migrations. In 1974, the French government halted new immigration altogether. In 1977, foreign workers were offered cash incentives to encourage them to return to their home countries, but to little avail. Governments refused to acknowledge the reality of the plight of foreign workers.

By the end of the 1970s, there were 10 million foreign workers settled in Europe. Their presence heightened racism and overt antagonism from a resurgent extreme Right. In the late 1980s, when movements for democratic freedom and human rights were being endorsed in eastern Europe, the problem of permanent resident "aliens" was without a solution in western Europe. Yet the need for cheap labor made the preservation of such a labor pool likely.

The issue of immigration became a prominent one in electoral campaigns throughout Europe in the 1990s. Opposition to the presence of foreign workers and concerns about protecting small business interests fueled ballot-box victories for the far right in Austria, the Netherlands, and France. In the first presidential election of the twenty-first century in France, the National Front candidate Jean-Marie Le Pen ran on the party's "France for the French" platform and garnered an unprecedented 18 percent of the electorate, giving pause to the democratic leadership of many European countries.

Women's Changing Lives

During the last quarter of the twentieth century, the lives of women in Western industrialized countries reflected dramatic social changes. With more education than ever before, women made careers in law, medicine, and business. Women had been active in the politics of liberation of the 1960s, including civil rights movements and worker and student protests. These activities served to heighten the collective awareness of disparities between their own situations and the position of men in Western societies. Women worked at home without pay; in the workplace, women received less than men for the same work.

In this period of increased educational and work opportunities, an international women's movement emerged. International conferences about issues of concern to women brought women from all over the world together in highly visible media events. For example, the U.N. Conference on the Decade for Women convened in Mexico City in 1975. On 8 March 1976—International Women's Day—the International Tribunal of Crimes Against Women was convened in Brussels. Issues of fertility, reproductive rights, and sexuality were at the center of the new politics of the women's movement, as justified in the slogan "The personal is political." Rape and abortion were defined as problems of international concern. In 1995, the U.N. conference on women, held in Beijing, declared that women were due equality and respect and had rights to autonomy and the control of their own bodies.

Reforms and Political Action. In some countries, women enjoyed only limited legal privileges. In Italy, women's political action resulted in a new law in 1970 that allowed divorce to women under very restricted circumstances. Italian feminists used the legal system as a public forum. In France, the sale of contraceptives was legalized in 1968, and French feminists worked through the courts until abortion was legalized in 1975.

With the increasing integration of Europe in the 1990s, differing national practices in child care, health care, and gender parity were reviewed by the deliberative bodies of the European Union. Yet national differences of women's social and family roles still prevailed across Europe, from outlawed abortions in Portugal to greater presence of women in the work force of eastern European countries at the beginning of the twenty-first century.

The feminist movement also created a new scholarship that incorporated women's experiences and perspectives into the disciplines of the humanities and social sciences. Women's studies courses, which emphasized the history and contributions of women, became part of university and college curricula in Europe and the United States. Reformers also promoted changes in language to avoid male-oriented usages, which, they argued, tended to make women invisible in history texts and other literature.

Issues of domestic violence, incest, and sexual orientation, which in the past had often been covered up and kept private, now also entered the political arena as women increasingly joined together and spoke out. In 1970, Western feminists were discovering that the liberal politics of the welfare state and socialism were not enough in addressing problems of gender discrimination.

At the turn of the new century, feminists, student activists, environmentalists, and internationalists found common ground in concerns of the exploitation of a global work force, sweatshops, ecological devastation, and the pollution and exploitation of the environment. The biggest of these demonstrations occurred in Seattle, Washington, in November and December 1999, when thousands of protesters, women and men from around the world, converged for a week to protest the actions of the World Trade Organization and international corporations, perceived as prime culprits in global exploitation and pollution.

Terrorism: The "New Kind of War"

A new kind of warfare emerged globally as disenfranchised groups rejected the avenues of cooperation and reform and instead chose violence as the sole means of achieving their political ends.

The history of contemporary terrorism began after World War II. The creation of the state of Israel in part of the land of Palestine in 1948 led to conflict between the Israelis and the Palestinian Arabs, who refused to accept the new Jewish state. Israel's Arab neighbors went to war to support the Palestinians but were defeated by Israel in late 1948. Hundreds of thousands of Palestinians became refugees in neighboring Arab states, and Palestinian guerrillas decided that the best way to attack Israel and its protectors was with a global strategy of terrorist violence. The first Palestinian hijacking took place in the summer of 1968. Ejected from Jordan, Palestinian guerrillas set up their headquarters in Syria and Lebanon in order to continue their terrorist activities.

Another influence figured prominently in terrorism of the late twentieth century: Islamic fundamentalism. Muslim militants intent on waging a "holy war" for the oppressed could be found throughout the world in areas as different as Algeria, Bosnia and Herzegovina, France, and the Philippines. Muslim radicals in those and other countries shared a truly global commitment and were often heavily influenced by their formative volunteer experiences in the Afghan war of the 1980s. Conceiving of their mission as a holy one, they were able to form a series of loose connections with Muslims from other countries for the purposes of recruitment, training, and deployment of dedicated fighters. A taxi driver from Egypt, for example, who fought in the Afghan war was convicted for the 1993 bombing of New York's World Trade Center. Conspirators led by the convicted Egyptian cleric Omar Abdel Rahman plotted to bomb the United Nations building, FBI headquarters in lower

Manhattan, and Lincoln and Holland tunnels linking Manhattan with New Jersey. The French blamed Afghan-trained Algerian Muslims for the 1994 Christmas Eve hijacking of an Air France airbus in which three passengers were killed in the initial shoot-out in Algiers.

Terrorists came from many nations and religious backgrounds. Peace-loving Muslims could be maligned because of fundamentalists' actions. Following the 1995 bombing of the federal building in Oklahoma City, Arabs and Muslims across the United States were singled out for reprisals and intimidation until it was discovered that the Oklahoma City bombing was the act of domestic terrorists protesting U.S. government policies. The Oklahoma City attack, which terrorized the nation, fit the essential definition of the new terrorism as a violent act against innocent civilians for the purpose of undermining the power of the government.

Terrorism in the Last Quarter of the Twentieth Century. By the late 1970s, a strategy of terrorist violence appealed to European revolutionaries intent on advancing a variety of political causes. Political killings became a tactic of choice for terrorists throughout the world. Victims were targeted by terrorists not because they merited any punishment themselves but as a means of attracting international attention to the terrorists' cause. Although motivated by different political agendas, terrorist groups often formed cooperative networks on an international basis, sharing training, weapons, and information. A small group of West German left-wing radicals known as the Red Army Faction executed key industrial, financial, and judicial leaders. The Red Army Faction was also responsible for a number of bombings, including that of the West German embassy in Stockholm. In Italy, a small group known as the Red Brigades was responsible for violent incidents, including the "kneecapping"—permanent crippling of people by shooting them in the knees—of leading Italian businessmen and the kidnapping and murder of the former Italian prime minister Aldo Moro. In 1981, the Red Brigades targeted the United States for their terrorist reprisals when they abducted an American general, James Dozier.

Western Europe served as an important arena for terrorist acts by non-European groups. To succeed—that is, to terrify mass populations—terrorists needed publicity. Terrorists relied on media exposure and claimed responsibility for acts only after they had been successfully completed. In September 1972, members of the Palestinian Black September movement kidnapped 11 Israeli athletes at the Olympic Games in Munich. An estimated 500 million people watched their televisions in horror as all 11 were slaughtered during an American sports broadcast. In a dramatic shoot-out, also televised, five of the terrorists died as well. Incidents such as the taking hostage of the OPEC oil ministers later in the decade in Vienna made urban populations aware of their vulnerability to gratuitous acts of violence. In 1979, 52 Americans were kidnapped from the American Embassy in Teheran and were held hostage for 444 days by a group of young Iranian revolutionaries, who claimed to be battling against the "great Satan."

A recurrent pattern of terrorism prevailed throughout the 1980s with Israel and the United States often the targets of attacks. Incidents highlighted by international media coverage included the attempted assassination of the pope in 1981 by a Turkish fascist; the blowing up of the U.S. Marine garrison in Beirut in 1983 by a Lebanese Shi'ite, whose act took the lives of 241 American soldiers as well as his own; the 1985 hijacking of a cruise ship, the *Achille Lauro*, by Palestinian ultranationalists, who killed one aged Jewish American passenger; and the bombing of TWA and El Al registration counters at two of Europe's busiest airports, in Rome and Vienna, in 1985. In December 1988, hundreds of people died when a Pan American plane on which a bomb had been planted exploded in flight over Lockerbie, Scotland. The bombing was probably in retaliation for the downing of an Iranian passenger airliner by the U.S. Navy in the Persian Gulf.

Terrorist activities against the United States escalated following the U.S. military action against Iraq in 1991 known as the Persian Gulf War. In February 1993, the explosion of a bomb planted in a small truck parked in the basement garage of the World Trade Center in New York killed six people, wounded 1,000, and did limited damage to the structure. Two terrorist attacks in Saudi Arabia in 1995 and 1996 killed 24 Americans. In August 1998, two major assaults against American embassies, one in Tanzania and the other in Kenya, killed 224 people and injured hundreds of others. In October 2000, a suicide attack against the USS Cole in the port of Aden took the lives of 17 sailors.

All of these attacks against the United States perpetrated after the Persian Gulf War were attributed to the network of a single man, Osama bin Laden, a Saudi Arabian millionaire who had been trained by the U.S. Central Intelligence Agency and who, between 1980 and 1989, had fought against the Russians in Afghanistan. In June 2001, bin Laden called on the Muslims of the world to mobilize themselves into a general *jihad*, or holy war, against its enemies. Three months after this call-to-arms, terrorists dealt their most extreme blow against the United States.

11 September 2001: A Turning Point. On 11 September 2001, four U.S. passenger planes were hijacked and used as flying bombs in a coordinated action that targeted the World Trade Center in New York City and the Pentagon just outside of Washington, D.C. Two of the four hijacked planes slammed into the twin towers of the World Trade Center, and a third plane hit its mark by diving into the Pentagon. The fourth plane crashed in a field in Pennsylvania, its suicide attack foiled by passengers who opposed their captors. Over 3,000 lives were lost, thousands more were wounded, and the loss of property was unprecedented in the worst terrorist attack in history. These events horrified people around the world who understood that two symbols of American global financial

This photograph captures the massive explosion caused when a second hijacked plane crashed into the World Trade Center in New York on 11 September 2001. The landmark twin towers were destroyed in the attack, and thousands of people were killed.

and military dominance had been singled out in a carefully planned and executed mission of destruction. President George W. Bush declared, in the wake of the terrorist attacks, that the United States was entering "a new kind of war," one not waged between nations but one whose stateless enemy would be sought out and hunted down. Terrorism had long plagued Europe and the Middle East, but these attacks marked the first time in history that an act of terrorist warfare by an external enemy took place on American soil. The event marked a turning point in the struggle against terrorism and a new focus on state security measures of Western governments.

When the European Union and the United States passed new laws and directives to combat terrorism, critics feared the curtailment of civil liberties. Racist incidents against Muslims and Arabs mounted, even as European and American leaders stressed that bin Laden and his network was a nonrepresentative and fanatical fringe within the Muslim world.

In October 2001, the United States and Britain undertook war in Afghanistan in an unsuccessful pursuit of bin Laden. Throughout the post-9/11 era, Iraq and its leader Saddam Hussein continued to be singled out by the U.S. government as sympathetic to the terrorist cause and as committed to developing "weapons of mass destruction." In pursuit of these weapons and with the intention of removing Hussein from power, President Bush ordered U.S. troops in coalition with British forces to lead an attack against Iraq in March 2003. U.S. action was widely opposed by its Allies and was inconclusive in its results. Both the Afghan and Iraqi military actions demonstrate the inability of conventional warfare to engage a terrorist enemy.

Terrorism and Counterterrorism. Terrorism in the last quarter of the twentieth century was not a single movement but a wide variety of groups and organizations on both the left and right. Some organizations were Marxist; some were nationalist; some were Islamic fundamentalists intent on waging a holy war. All defined the enemy as an imperialist and a colonizer. Western capitalist nations, especially the United States and Israel, were common targets of terrorist attacks. Terrorists all shared a vision of the world based on the commonly held belief that destruction of the existing order was the only way of bringing about a more equitable system. Palestinian terrorists, for example, were willing to sacrifice their lives to ensure the establishment of an independent Palestinian state. In the case of bin Laden's fundamentalist Muslim terrorists, holy war was perceived as the only way to create an Islamic state free of Western influence and the corruption of a U.S.-dominated global economy.

Terrorists justified their violent actions in terms of the legitimacy of their cause. The Provisional Wing of the Irish Republican Army, for example, explained that it bombed crowds of Christmas shoppers in London as a means of uniting Northern Ireland with the Independent Irish Republic. Terrorists argued that just as resistance fighters in World War II had used bombs and assassinations as their means of fighting a more powerful enemy, they themselves were engaged in wars of liberation, revolution, and resistance and were using the only weapons at their disposal to fight great imperialist powers. Plastic explosives in suitcases, nearly impossible to detect by available technology, became the weapon of choice. If all was fair in war—and in World War II both sides bombed innocent civilian victims in pursuit of victory—then, terrorists countered, they were fighting their war with the only weapons and in the only arena they had.

By the mid-1990s it was clear that terrorism was an effective challenge to the tranquillity of Western capitalist nations. Modern terrorists were often able to evade policing and detection. Surveillance had not prevented terrorists from striking at airplanes and cruise ships. Yet terrorists accomplished little in the way of bringing about political change or solutions to problems.

Western European governments often refused on principle to bargain with terrorists. Yet at times, European nations and the United States have been willing to negotiate for the release of kidnapped citizens. They have also been willing to use violence themselves against terrorists. Israel led the way in creating antiterror squads. In 1976, Israeli commandos succeeded in freeing captives held by pro-Palestinian hijackers of an Air France plane in Entebbe, Uganda. The following year, specially trained West German troops freed Lufthansa passengers and crew held hostage at Mogadishu, Somalia, on the east coast of Africa. The Arab kidnappers had hoped to bargain for the release of the imprisoned leaders of the Red Army Faction; the West German government refused. In 1986, the United States bombed Libya, long recognized as a training ground for international terrorist recruits, in retaliation for the bombing of a discotheque frequented by U.S. service personnel in West Germany. Israel bombed refugee camps to retaliate against Palestinian nationalists. The greatest mobilization in counterterrorist efforts came with U.S. leadership following the events of 11 September 2001. The goal of this "counterterrorism" was to undermine support for terrorists among their own people; its tactics and ends opened counterterrorism to the criticism that it was very similar to the terrorism it was opposing.

In spite of tactics of meeting violence with violence, the advanced industrial states of western Europe and the United States remained vulnerable to an invisible terrorist enemy. That elusive enemy could terrorize populations and incapacitate the smooth functioning of the modern industrial state. As Europeans entered the twenty-first century, terrorism continued to threaten peace and paralyze security, at the very moment when people all over the globe celebrated the birth of a better world. After the large-scale terrorist attacks of 2001, the promise of a new and better world in the twenty-first century seemed, for many, to move further out of reach.

Conclusion

THE WESTERN WORLD WAS UNDOUBTEDLY A DIFFERENT PLACE in the last quarter of the twentieth century from all that had gone before. But was the world really so transformed that one could speak of its being ordered in a different way? The iceberg of communism had melted. As democrats replaced dictators, some observers wondered if counterrevolution was waiting in the wings, should the new capitalist experiments fail. In other countries, the dictators did not leave; they only changed their political allegiances. Protofascist and anti-Semitic groups became more vocal in the early 1990s amid the economic chaos.

One potentially unifying force was the marketplace. Democratic institutions seemed most stable in those countries with developed market economies. In the former Yugoslavia, for example, little had changed for the better since the fall of the communist regime. Russia itself suffered from a similar problem of economic readjustment and restructuring. Even where political reforms had been accomplished, economic reforms lagged behind or were nonexistent.

Western Europe and the United States realized the devastation that industrialization had wrought in their own countries after a century and a half of development, and were taking steps to control pollution and to clean up the air and the environment. Yet in eastern Europe, ecological concerns were considered a luxury as industries struggled, uncontrolled, to establish footholds in competitive markets. In spite of the emergence of a new world order of democratic states, many Europeans, both in the East and in the West, saw an uncertain future of misery and repression fueled as long as virulent nationalism remained unchecked.

Problems that plagued Western states in the modern era persisted. The triumph of the nation-state in the nineteenth century had carried the seeds of violence and destruction, as two world wars and countless local conflicts had proven. Democracy, likewise viewed as the best hope for a new world order, struggled in new settings that lacked the institutions, the culture, and the experience of democratic values. Elected elites from Russia to Romania used positions of power for aggrandizement, both political and economic.

As the benefits of the welfare state in the West dwindled with slowed economic growth, the gap between the rich and the poor widened. The widening gulf characterized the new capitalist economies of the former Soviet bloc as well as those of the West. In the United States, the richest 1 percent of households controlled about 40 percent of the nation's wealth. In Germany, high wage-earning families earned about two and a half times as much as low-wage workers. And the gap between rich and poor on a global scale yawned even wider into a gulf.

At the end of the twentieth century, Western women and men faced the birth of a new century and a new millennium. Some did so apprehensively, just as inhabitants of Europe in medieval Europe at the end of the tenth century did, and perhaps with some of the same superstition about what the future held. Investing a date with such meaning is not new in the history of Western societies. At the end of the nineteenth century, Europeans defined a new sensibility of progress and advancement at the fin-de-siècle, aware that they were on the threshold of a new age. And they were right. But with that new age of the twentieth century, Europeans ushered in the bloodiest and most violent period in history. Talk of ethnic purity ominously echoed the despicable racial policies of Nazi Germany.

What lay ahead for Western societies? Would the third millennium be so different? Arthur Miller, the renowned American playwright, commented in the aftermath of the terrorist attacks of 11 September 2001, "It is so simple to destroy a city." Citizens of Western industrial societies had a new and shocking sense of their own vulnerability as they stood at the beginning of a new age of anxiety and fear. The symbols of civilization and economic achievement—skyscrapers and office buildings—could appear to melt in an instant, taking the lives of all those trapped inside. What is best in civilization at the beginning of the third millennium—selflessness, self-sacrifice, and willingness to help others in spite of personal cost—came face to face with mindless destruction and attacks on civilian populations, leaving only hope that the best values of civilization would prevail.

QUESTIONS FOR REVIEW

1. How did the collapse of communist regimes in Russia and Eastern Europe promote national and ethnic conflict?
2. What social, economic, and political forces contributed to German reunification?
3. How did the treaty signed by the nations of the European Community at Maastricht in 1991 create both hopes and fears of European unity?
4. In what ways have women's lives in eastern and western Europe been similar, and in what ways have their experiences differed since the 1960s?
5. What is the difference between the European Community and the European Union?
6. How have democracy and nationalism come into conflict since 1989?

DISCOVERING WESTERN CIVILIZATION ONLINE

You can obtain more information about the West facing the new century at the websites listed below. See also the companion website that accompanies this text: www.ablongman.com/kishlansky, which contains an online study guide and additional resources.

Reshaping Europe

www.departments.bucknell.edu/russian/chrono4.html
A chronology of Russian history since 1991 with links to additional resources.

www.cs.indiana.edu/hyplan/dmiguse/Russian/bybio.html
A chronology of Yeltsin's presidency with links to further materials on key events and personalities.

www.remote.org/frederik/culture/berlin
A photo tour of the fall of the Berlin Wall supplemented by text from several German newspapers (in English).

www.wall-berlin.org/gb/berlin.htm
A virtual exhibit to commemorate the tenth anniversary of the fall of the Berlin Wall with links to further readings.

www.libraries.wright.edu/libnet/subj/pol/pls460.html
A research guide to post-Soviet Russian library and Internet resources sponsored by the Wright State University libraries.

War in the Balkans

www.its.caltech.edu/~bosnia/
This site provides links to essays and documents on the history of the disintegration of Yugoslavia and subsequent developments in the region.

www.usip.org/library/regions/bosnia.html
The United States Institute of Peace provides links to Web resources on the Balkan conflict and its resolution.

The West in the Global Community

www.let.leidenuniv.nl/history/rtg/resl
This site provides primary source materials and bibliographies of the history of European integration. It also includes links to statistical data relating to the European Union and its organizations. It provides annotated links to the broader theme of Cold War history.

www.ihf-hr.org/
Official website of the International Helsinki Federation for Human Rights, a nonprofit organization. This site is useful as a resource for the latest developments in the Balkans and in Chechnya from a human rights activist perspective.

www.phrusa.org/research/chechnya/chech_resources.html
Part of the Physicians for Human Rights official Web page with links devoted to the conflict on Chechnya, including current newspaper and journal articles.

www.terrorism.com/index.shtml
The home page of the Terrorism Research Center. The site provides essays, documents, and links to additional materials on terrorism and political violence.

SUGGESTIONS FOR FURTHER READING

Reshaping Europe

Timothy Garton Ash, *In Europe's Name: Germany and the Divided Continent* (London: Jonathan Cape, 1993). An original and complex thesis that looks at German reunification from its origins in the 1970s.

Michael Ignatieff, *Blood and Belonging: Journeys into the New Nationalism* (Toronto: Viking Press, 1993). A companion to a BBC television series, the volume provides a sophisticated exploration of expressions of nationalism throughout Europe.

Adam Michnik, *Letters from Freedom: Post–Cold War Realities and Perspectives* (Berkeley: University of California Press, 1998). Michnik, a journalist, politician, and writer imprisoned for his political views in the 1980s, is widely regarded as a hero in Poland today. This volume includes his articles, speeches, and interviews with leading European political figures and addresses the political realities of Europe after the end of the Cold War.

Joseph Rothschild, *Return to Diversity: A Political History of East Central Europe* (New York: Oxford University Press, 1989). A historical and analytical survey of Poland, Czechoslovakia, Hungary, Yugoslavia, Romania, Bulgaria, and Albania that appeared just before the great changes that swept through eastern Europe in 1989. Rothschild highlights the tensions between nationalist aspirations and communist rule.

War in the Balkans

David Fromkin, *Kosovo Crossing: American Ideals Meet Reality on the Balkan Battlefields* (New York: The Free Press, 1999). This work raises important questions about the use of U.S. military power in the world today and the future of U.S. foreign policy within the context of the history of the Balkan conflict.

Richard Holbrooke, *To End a War* (New York: The Modern Library, 1998). The author offers a firsthand account of the intense diplomatic negotiations surrounding the Dayton Accords and a clear understanding of the problems plaguing Bosnia.

Tim Judah, *Kosovo: War and Revenge* (New Haven, Conn.: Yale University Press, 2000). Based on careful research, the author analyzes "the last great European war of the twentieth century."

Noel Malcolm, *Kosovo: A Short History* (New York: Harper Collins, 1999). The author is a historian who traces Kosovo's history to medieval times and challenges myths and debates about national origins.

Julie A. Mertus, *Kosovo: How Myths and Truths Started a War* (Berkeley: University of California Press, 1999). Having spent two years in Kosovo interviewing people affected by the conflict, the author is able to offer an understanding from the perspective of the victims of what has happened there.

Michael A. Sells, *The Bridge Betrayed* (Berkeley: University of California Press, 1996). The author stresses the role of religious nationalists, Serbian Orthodox and Croatian Roman Catholic, in waging a holy war resulting in genocide and destruction.

Susan L. Woodward, *Balkan Tragedy: Chaos and Dissolution After the Cold War* (Washington, D.C.: The Brookings Institution, 1995). This important study explains, in terms of the breakdown of political and civil order, why Yugoslavia disintegrated into ethnic hatreds so rapidly after 1989. Western actions and international developments contributed to the collapse which, she argues, cannot be reversed until root causes are addressed.

The West in the Global Community

Michael Emerson et al., *The Economics of 1992: The E.C. Commission's Assessment of the Economic Effects of Completing the Internal Market* (Oxford: Oxford University Press, 1988). A work replete with empirical data that give a comprehensive assessment of the potential impact of establishing a single internal market in the European Economic Community.

Mark Juergensmeyer, *The New Cold War? Religious Nationalism Confronts the Secular State* (Berkeley: University of California Press, 1994). The author examines the growing significance of religious nationalism from a global perspective.

Geir Lundestad, *"Empire" by Integration* (New York: Oxford University Press, 1998). This work provides a comprehensive overview of U.S. policy toward European integration.

Richard E. Rubinstein, *Alchemists of Revolution: Terrorism in the Modern World* (New York: Basic Books, 1987). The author examines the local root causes of terrorism in historical perspective and argues that terrorism is the social and moral crisis of a disaffected intelligentsia.

CREDITS

DOCUMENT CREDITS

Chapter 14

"War Is Hell": From Hans Jacob Christoph von Grimmelhausen, in *The Adventurous Simplicissmus,* translated by A. T. S. Goodrick, 1912.

Chapter 15

"The Devil's Due": From "Medieval Witchcraft," from *Translations and Reprints from the Original Sources of European History, Volume III,* published for the Department of History of the University of Pennsylvania, Phildelphia.

Chapter 16

"A Glimpse of a King": From *Memoirs of the Duke of Saint-Simon,* translated by Bayle St. John. (London: Swan Sonnonschein & Co., 1900).

Chapter 17

"Encountering Pirates": From Jean Doublet, *Encounter with a Barbary Pirate* (1682).

Chapter 18

"Childhood Traumas": From *The Memoirs of Catherine the Great,* edited by Dominique Maroger.

Chapter 19

"Love and Marriage": From *The Old Maid,* Number 1, by Frances Brooke, November 15, 1755.

Chapter 20

"The Civil Code of the *Code Napoléon* (1804)": From Henry Cachard, *The French Civil Code.* (London: Stevens and Son, 1895).

Chapter 21

"Exploiting the Young": From "Child Labor in the Coal Mines," Testimony to the Parliamentary Investigative Committee (1842).

Chapter 22

"Flora Tristan": From "Flora Tristan" in *L'Union Ouvriere,* 3rd ed., (Paris and Lyons, 1843) as translated by Giselle Pincetl in *Harvest Quarterly,* 7 (Fall 1977). Reprinted by permission of Giselle Pincetl.

Chapter 23

"Red Women in Paris": From *The Memoirs of Louis Michel, The Red Virgin,* edited and translated by Bullitt Lowry and Elizabeth Ellington Gunter. Copyright © 1981. Used by permission of the University of Alabama Press.

Chapter 24

"Constance Lytton": From *Constance Lytton, Prisons and Prisoners,* 1914.

Chapter 25

"Joseph Chamberlain's Speech to the Birmingham Relief Association"**:** From Joseph Chamberlain, M.P., *Foreign and Colonial Speeches* (1897).

Chapter 26

"All Quiet on the Western Front": From Erich Maria Remarque, *All Quiet on the Western Front* (1928).

Chapter 27

"Adolph Hitler on Racial Purity": from "Racial Purity: Hitler Reverts to the Dominant Theme of the National Socialist Program, January 30, 1937" in *Hitler's Third Reich,* edited by Louis L. Snyder. Copyright © 1981 by Louis L. Snyder. Reprinted by permission of Rowman & Littlefield Publishing Group.

Chapter 28

"President Franklin Roosevelt's Request for a Declaration of War on Japan, 8 December 1941": From *World War II: Policy and Strategy* by Hans Adolf Jacobsen and Arthur J. Smith, Jr.

Chapter 29

"The Marshall Plan": From Department of State Bulletin, 15 June 1947.

Chapter 30

"A Woman Reporter Behind the Lines of the War in Chechnya": From *Chienne de Guerre,* 1st edition (hard) by Anne Nivat. Copyright 2001 by Perseus Books Group. Reproduced with permission of Perseus Books Group in the format Textbook via Copyright Clearance Center.

PHOTO CREDITS

Unless otherwise acknowledged, all photographs are the property of Pearson Education, Inc. Page abbreviations are as follows: (T) top, (B) bottom, (L) left, (R) right.

Prints appearing on the following pages were hand-colored for Pearson Education, Inc., by Cheryl Kucharzak: 263, 265, 373, 467.

Chapter 14

281 Giraudon/Art Resource, NY; **282** Art Resource, NY; **283** François Dubois, Saint Bartholomew's Day, 1572–1584, oil on canvas, 94 cm x 154 cm, Musée Cantonal des Beaxu-Arts de Lausanne, Photo: J.-C. Ducret, Musée Cantonal des Beaxu-Arts de Lausanne; **287** Erich Lessing/Art Resource, NY; **293** Musée des Beaux-Arts de Strasbourg (2.86.12970)

Chapter 15

299 Roudnice Lobkowicz Collection/Bridgeman Art Library; **307** La Tour, Georges de (1593–1652) *The Fortune Teller.* Oil on canvas. J. 40 /8 in. W. 48 5/8 in. (101.9 x 123.5 cm.) Signed (upper right): G. de La Tour Fecit Luneuilla Lothar: Metropolitan Museum of Art, Rogers Fund, 1960 (60.30) Photograph © 1982 The Metropolitan Museum of Art; **309** Rijksmuseum Foundation, Amsterdam; **311** Scala/Art Resource, NY

Chapter 16

319 Réunion des Musées Nationaux/Art Resource, NY; **320** National Portrait Gallery, London; **328** The Granger Collection, New York; **334** Chateau de Versailles, France/Bridgeman Art Library; **335** Scala/Art Resource, NY

Chapter 17

339 Photograph © Maritshuis, The Hague; **341** By Permission of The British Library (Maps C6C3. between 22–23); **349** Rijksmuseum Foundation, Amsterdam

Chapter 18

359 Reproduced by courtesy of the Trustees, © The National Gallery, London (NG681); **365** Central Naval Museum, St. Petersburg; **371** Kunsthistorisches Museum, Vienna

Chapter 19

381 Sameul H. Kress Collection, © Board of Trustees, National Gallery of Art, Washington, D.C. (1946.7.7[772]/PA); **383** Giraudon/Art Resource, NY; **388** Sotheby's, London; **392** Scala/Art Resource, NY

Chapter 20

401 Spencer Collection, The NewYork Public Library, Astor, Lenox and Tilden Foundations; **403** Réunion Des Musées Nationaux/Art Resource, NY; **409** Bulloz/Photo © RMN/Art Resource, NY; **417** Musée de Beaux-Arts, Rouen

Chapter 21

421 The Tate Gallery, London/Art Resource, NY; **427** AKG London; **428** The Granger Collection, New York; **430** Daumier, Honore (1808–1879) *The Third Class Carriage.* Oil on canvas. H. 25 3/4 in. W. 35 1/2 in. (65.4 x 90.2 cm.) The Metropolitan Museum of Art, H. O. Havemeyer Collection, Bequest of Mrs. H. O. Havemeyer, 1929. (29.100.129) Photograph by Malcolm Varon. Photograph © 1984 The Metropolitan Museum of Art; **441** Gift of Quincy Adams Shaw through Quincy A. Shaw, Jr. and Mrs. Marian Shaw Haughton. Courtesy, Museum of Fine Arts, Boston (17.1505)

Chapter 22

448 Giraudon/Art Resource, NY

Chapter 23

465 © bpk, Berlin; **471** Bridgeman Art Library; **474** The Master and Fellows, Trinity College, Cambridge; **475** Giraudon/Art Resource, NY

Chapter 24

481 Bridgeman Art Library; **488** Mary Evans Picture Library; **490** Jewish Museum/Art Resource, NY

Chapter 25

497 Mansell Collection/Time Life Pictures/Getty Images

Chapter 26

519 (L) "Deutsche Frauen Arbeitet im Heimate-Heer! Kriegsamtstelle Magdeburg" ("German Women Work in the Home-Army! Magdeburg War Office", by George Kirchbach, Germany, 194-18. From copy in the Bowman Gray Collection, Rare Book Collection, University of North Carolina Library, Chapel Hill; **(R)** "Take Up the Sword of Justice" by Sir Bernard J. Partridge, England, 1915. From copy in Bowman Gray Collection, Rare Book Collection, University of North Carolina Library, Chapel Hill **524** Imperial War Museum, London; **528** Imperial War Museum, London; **532** Brown Brothers

Chapter 27

541 © bpk, Berlin/© Estate of George Grosz/Licensed by VAGA, New York, NY; **547** Michael Holford; **550** Liaison International/Getty Images; **555** Corbis

Chapter 28

565 Österreichische Nationalbibliothek, Vienna; **567** Corbis; **569** Imperial War Museum, London; **572** Roger-Viollet/Getty Images

Chapter 29

593 Bettmann/Corbis; **594** Corbis; **599** AP/Wide World Photos; **602** Don McCullin/Contact Press; **604** Los Alamos National Laboratory

Chapter 30

605; 611; 617 AP/Wide World Photos; **626** AFP/Corbis

INDEX

C

E

T

U

CONTEMPORARY EUROPE
Land Elevation
Feet
Meters
13,123
4,000
6,562
2,000
3,281
1,000
1,640
500
656
200
0
0
Below sea level
Below sea level
0
250
500 mi.
0
250
500 km
60°N
50°N
40°N
30°W
20°W
10°W
0°
70°N
10°E
Arctic Circle
N
S
E
W
ICELAND
Norwegian Sea
FAROE IS.
SHETLAND IS.
HEBRIDES IS.
ORKNEY IS.
KJØLEN MOUNTAINS
SCANDINAVIAN
NORWAY
SWEDEN
L. Vänern
L. Vättern
Scotland
Northern Ireland
UNITED KINGDOM
BRITISH ISLES
IRELAND
Wales
England
Celtic Sea
ATLANTIC OCEAN
North Sea
JUTLAND PENINSULA
DENMARK
Elbe R.
NORTH
Oder R.
NETHERLANDS
RUHR VALLEY
Thames R.
English Channel
BELGIUM
GERMANY
Rhine R.
BRITTANY PENINSULA
Seine R.
CZECH REPUBLIC
LUXEMBOURG
Loire R.
LIECHTENSTEIN
Danube R.
FRANCE
SWITZERLAND
L. Geneva
Bay of Biscay
AUSTRIA
CENTRAL MASSIF
ALPS
SLOVENIA
Drava
Garonne R.
Rhone R.
Po R.
Sava R.
CROATIA
PYRENEES
ITALY
SAN MARINO
BOSN
Duero R.
Ebro R.
APENNINES
DINA
MONACO
IBERIAN PENINSULA
ANDORRA
Adriatic Sea
CORSICA
PORTUGAL
Tagus R.
SPAIN
Guadiana R.
Tyrrhenian Sea
Guadalquiver R.
BALEARIC ISLANDS
SARDINIA
SIERRA NEVADA
Strait of Gibraltar
Mediterranean Sea
SICILY
AFRICA
MALTA

Barents Sea
70°E
KOLA
PENINSULA
Pechora R.
URAL MOUNTAINS
Ob R.
White
Sea
N. Dvina R.
FINLAND
L.
Onega
L.
Ladoga
RUSSIA
of Finland
Volga R.
STONIA
L.
Peipus
Ural R.
LATVIA
CENTRAL RUSSIAN UPLAND
VOLGA UPLAND
Oka R.
HUANIA
PEAN PLAIN
BELARUS
Volga R.
Dnieper R.
CASPIAN
DEPRESSION
UKRAINE
Don R.
Dniester R.
THIAN MTS.
Prut R.
Siret R.
MOLDOVA
Sea of
Azov
Caspian Sea
CAUCASUS
CRIMEA
ROMANIA
NSYLVANIAN ALPS
GEORGIA
Black Sea
Danube R.
BALKAN MTS.
ARMENIA
BULGARIA
Bosporus
PENINSULA
AZERBAIJAN
TURKEY
REECE
Dardanelles
Aegean
Sea
ASIA
CRETE

180°
160°W
140°W
120°W
100°W
80°W
60°W
40°W
20°W
0°
80°N
ARCTIC OCEAN
Beaufort Sea
Baffin Bay
GREENLAND
Arctic Circle
Yukon R.
ICELAND
ROCKY MOUNTAINS
NORTH AMERICA
Hudson Bay
Gulf of Alaska
GREAT PLAINS
Great Lakes
Missouri R.
Mississippi R.
APPALACHIAN MTS.
40°N
ATLAS MTS.
ATLANTIC OCEAN
Gulf of Mexico
Tropic of Cancer
WEST INDIES
20°N
Niger R.
Caribbean Sea
GUIANA HIGHLANDS
Equator
0°
Amazon R.
AMAZON BASIN
SOUTH AMERICA
ANDES
BRAZILIAN HIGHLANDS
20°S
ATACAMA DESERT
Tropic of Capricorn
Paraná R.
PACIFIC OCEAN
PAMPAS
40°S
PATAGONIA
N
W
S
Cape Horn
60°S
Antarctic Circle
Weddell Sea
Ross Sea

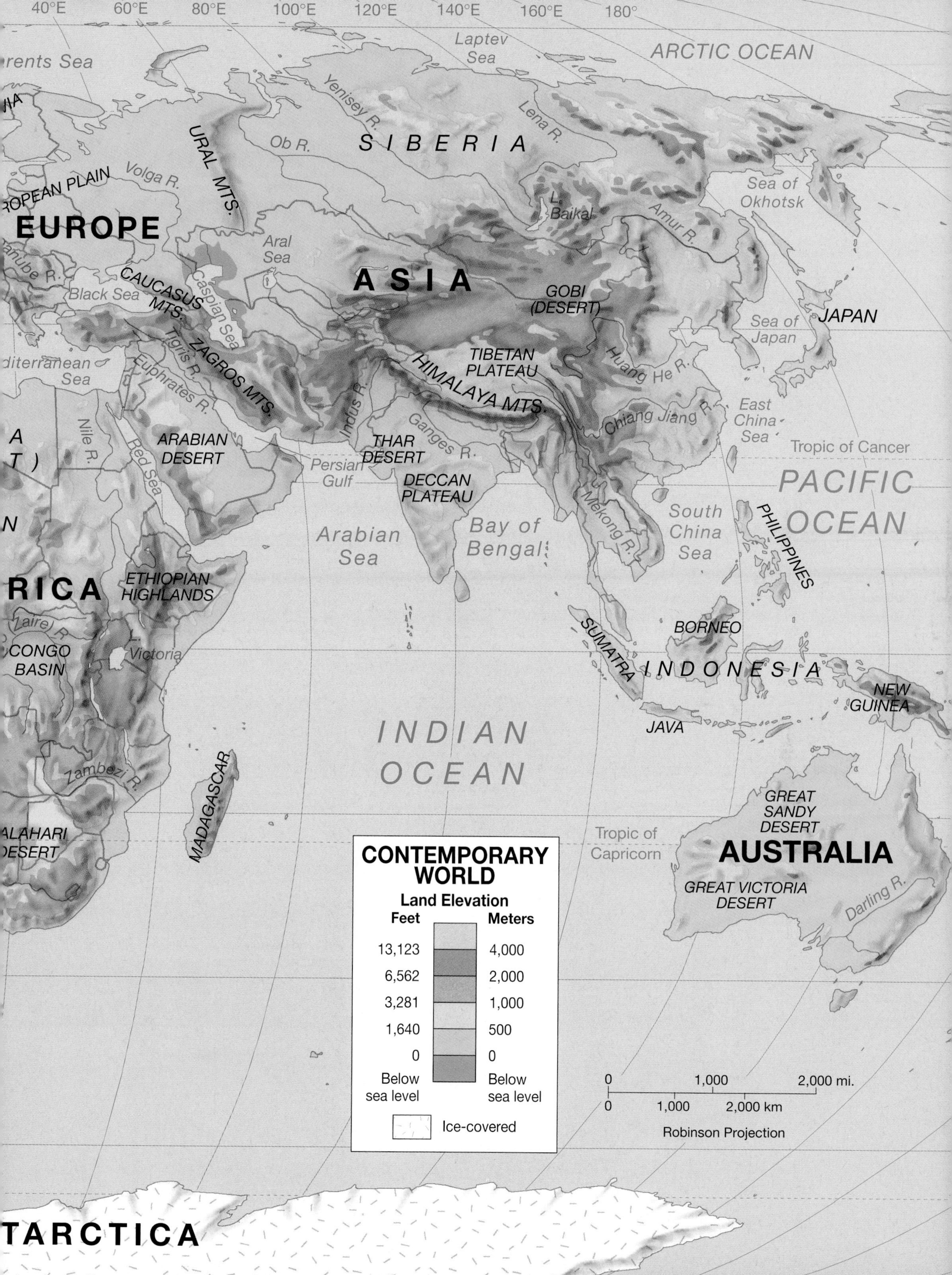

40°E
60°E
80°E
100°E
120°E
140°E
160°E
180°
Laptev Sea
ARCTIC OCEAN
rents Sea
Yenisey R.
Lena R.
URAL MTS.
Ob R.
SIBERIA
ROPEAN PLAIN
Volga R.
Sea of Okhotsk
L. Baikal
Amur R.
EUROPE
Aral Sea
anube R.
CAUCASUS MTS.
Caspian Sea
ASIA
GOBI (DESERT)
Black Sea
Sea of Japan
JAPAN
Tigris R.
ZAGROS MTS.
TIBETAN PLATEAU
HIMALAYA MTS.
Huang He R.
diterranean Sea
Euphrates R.
Indus R.
Chiang Jiang R.
East China Sea
Nile R.
ARABIAN DESERT
Ganges R.
THAR DESERT
Tropic of Cancer
Red Sea
Persian Gulf
DECCAN PLATEAU
PACIFIC OCEAN
Mekong R.
South China Sea
Arabian Sea
Bay of Bengal
PHILIPPINES
RICA
ETHIOPIAN HIGHLANDS
Zaire R.
BORNEO
CONGO BASIN
L. Victoria
SUMATRA
INDONESIA
NEW GUINEA
JAVA
INDIAN OCEAN
Zambezi R.
MADAGASCAR
GREAT SANDY DESERT
ALAHARI DESERT
Tropic of Capricorn
AUSTRALIA
CONTEMPORARY WORLD
Land Elevation
Feet
Meters
13,123
4,000
6,562
2,000
3,281
1,000
1,640
500
0
0
Below sea level
Below sea level
Ice-covered
GREAT VICTORIA DESERT
Darling R.
0
1,000
2,000 mi.
0
1,000
2,000 km
Robinson Projection
TARCTICA

A SAMPLER OF THE WIT AND WISDOM OF JOHN F. KENNEDY

ON POETRY—

"When power corrupts, poetry cleanses. For art establishes the basic human truths which must serve as the touchstone of our judgment."

ON SECRECY—

"We are as a people inherently and historically opposed to secret societies, to secret oaths and to secret proceedings."

ON BIG GOVERNMENT—

"The myth here is that big government is big and bad—and steadily getting bigger and worse. Obviously this myth has some excuse for existence."

ON BEING A HERO—

"It was absolutely involuntary. They sank my boat."

ON AMERICA'S FUTURE—

"I look forward to an America which commands respect throughout the world not only for its strength but for its civilization as well."

ALEX AYRES, former editor at *Running Times* and *Harvard Lampoon*, has edited five previous titles in the successful "Wit and Wisdom" series. He also has to his credit the screenplays *Marlowe* and *Search for Grace*. He lives in Canyon Country, California.

ALSO EDITED BY ALEX AYRES

The Wit and Wisdom of Eleanor Roosevelt
The Wit and Wisdom of Will Rogers
The Wisdom of Martin Luther King, Jr.
The Wit and Wisdom of Abraham Lincoln
The Wit and Wisdom of Mark Twain

The Wit and Wisdom of JOHN F. KENNEDY

EDITED BY
ALEX AYRES

A MERIDIAN BOOK

MERIDIAN
Published by the Penguin Group
Penguin Books USA Inc., 375 Hudson Street,
New York, New York 10014, U.S.A.
Penguin Books Ltd, 27 Wrights Lane, London W8 5TZ, England
Penguin Books Australia Ltd, Ringwood, Victoria, Australia
Penguin Books Canada Ltd, 10 Alcorn Avenue,
Toronto, Ontario, Canada M4V 3B2
Penguin Books (N.Z.) Ltd, 182–190 Wairau Road, Auckland 10, New Zealand

Penguin Books Ltd, Registered Offices: Harmondsworth, Middlesex, England

First published by Meridian, an imprint of Dutton Signet,
a division of Penguin Books USA Inc.

First Printing, November, 1996
10 9 8 7 6 5 4 3 2 1

REGISTERED TRADEMARK—MARCA REGISTRADA

LIBRARY OF CONGRESS CATALOGING-IN-PUBLICATION DATA
Kennedy, John F. (John Fitzgerald), 1917–1963.
The wit and wisdom of John F. Kennedy / edited by Alex Ayres.
p. cm.
ISBN 0-452-01139-6
1. Kennedy, John F. (John Fitzgerald), 1917–1963—Quotations.
2. Kennedy, John F. (John Fitzgerald), 1917–1963—Humor. I. Ayres, Alex. II. Title.
E838.5.K42 1996
973.922'092—dc20 96-17299
CIP

Printed in the United States of America
Set in Palatino
Designed by Julian Hamer

ACKNOWLEDGMENTS

Thanks to John F. Kennedy, to the Estate of John F. Kennedy, and HarperCollins Publishers, Inc., for making this book possible.

Thanks to Hy Cohen and Hugh Rawson for their continuing efforts to perpetuate "wit and wisdom" generally, and to Cassia Farkas and Jacqueline Kinghorn Brown of Penguin Reference Books, particularly; and to Janine Cooper, especially, for valuable research assistance; and to Josh Henson, for *Harvard Lampoon* quality assistance; and Vicky Charlton for help with rare books; and Pam Ayres for help with numbers.

And thanks to you, the reader, for taking an interest not only in what was said about JFK but in what JFK had to say.

—A.A.

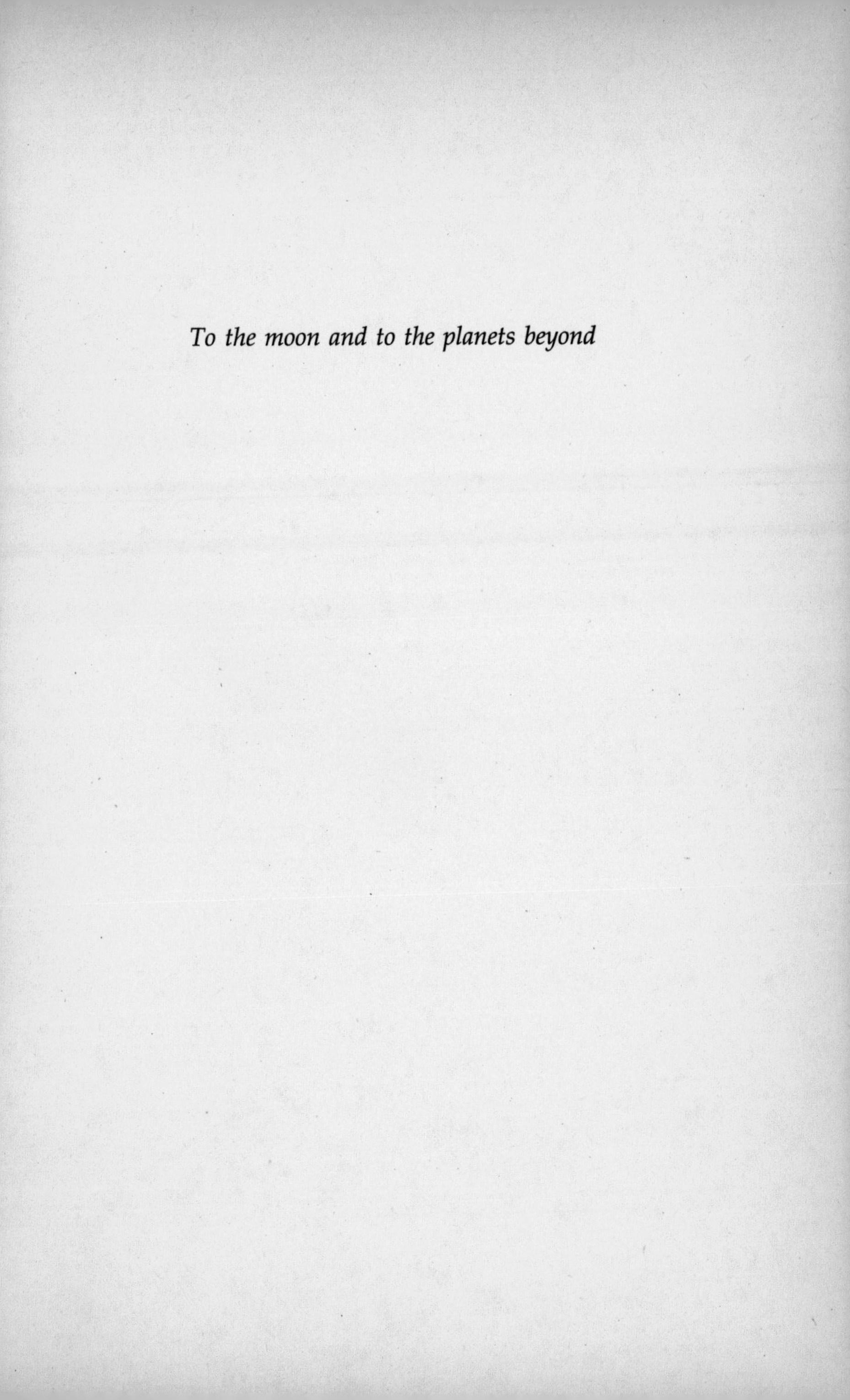

To the moon and to the planets beyond

WHY READ THIS BOOK?

"It has recently been suggested that whether I serve one or two terms in the Presidency," John F. Kennedy wrote in 1961, "I will find myself at the end of that period at what might be called the awkward age, too old to begin a new career and too young to write my memoirs."

John F. Kennedy did not live long enough to write his memoirs or to be "too old" for anything. At 43, the youngest man elected President—and tragically assassinated at 46—he did not live long enough to write his magnum opus, the masterpiece of which he was clearly capable. Yet, as one of the leading spokespersons of the twentieth century and one of history's most eloquent champions of the "freedom doctrine," John F. Kennedy left behind a legacy of *wit and wisdom*—in his passionate speeches and stylish writings, in his vision of a great future and his observations on a great past, and in the flashes of his famous wit.

Young and old in one, John F. Kennedy combined in his being the thinker and the man of action. He embodied the youthfulness and agelessness of the American spirit and the American dream. John F. Kennedy was like the growing-up nation he represented, which he called "this old but youthful union."

JFK's memoirs would have made a memorable book, for he was a writer of distinction. He made his literary debut young, only 23 when his Harvard honors thesis was published as *Why England Slept* in 1940 and became an acclaimed bestseller. His historical compilation, *Profiles in Courage,* was also a bestseller and was awarded the Pulitzer Prize for Biography in 1957. A few of JFK's word portraits are included in *The Wit and Wisdom of John F. Kennedy*.

What would John Kennedy have said if he had lived longer? Included in this book is the text of what President Kennedy was going to say in Dallas on November 22, 1963, released to the press minutes before the assassination.

The Kennedy inaugural address is included complete (see INAUGURAL ADDRESS). Other significant speeches are condensed and can be found alphabetically by topic, title, or name (see BERLIN ADDRESS, CIVIL RIGHTS ADDRESS, CUBAN MISSILE CRISIS, etc.).

You can find here not only what was said about JFK but also what JFK said. In *The Wit and Wisdom of John F. Kennedy* a voice that was silenced by assassination speaks for itself on a wide variety of topics. Not one word of John Kennedy's has been changed; however, text has been edited, paragraphs shortened, and speeches abbreviated. The name John F. Kennedy is also abbreviated as JFK to save space.

The wit and wisdom of John F. Kennedy are a part of our American national heritage. I hope you will pick a topic and look it up to see what JFK had to say—and what he is saying to us today.

—A.A.

ON JOHN F. KENNEDY

There are moments in the cause of human freedom when his words move with a measured passion.

—Carl Sandburg, 1962

John Fitzgerald Kennedy . . . a great and good President, the friend of all people of goodwill; a believer in the dignity and equality of human beings; a fighter for justice; an apostle of peace.

—Earl Warren, Chief Justice
of the Supreme Court, 1963

We, Kennedy's godchildren, the baby-boom generation that believed his stirring words and handsome image, are like Hamlet in the first act, children of a slain leader, unaware of why he was killed or even that a false father figure inhabits the throne.

—Oliver Stone, director, 1993

His wisdom and eloquence will undoubtedly rank with that of Jefferson, Lincoln, Wilson, and Roosevelt, men whom Kennedy himself enjoyed quoting. Future generations will surely be quoting our late President.

—T. S. Settle, editor, 1965

When Cicero finished an oration, the people would say, "How well he spoke." Ah, but when Demosthenes finished speaking, the people would say, "Let us march."

—Adlai Stevenson on John F. Kennedy

The thing about him was the extraordinary sense he gave to being alive: This makes his death so grotesque and unbelievable. No one had such vitality of personality. . . . He was life-affirming, life-enhancing. When he entered the room, the temperature changed; and he quickened the sensibilities of everyone around him.

—Arthur Schlesinger, Jr., *A Eulogy*, 1963

This is part of the fundamental dichotomy in Kennedy's character: half the "mick" politician, tough, earthy, bawdy, sentimental, and half the bright, graceful, intellectual *Playboy of the Western World* . . .

—Benjamin Bradlee, *Conversations with Kennedy*, 1975

He was, perhaps, a step or two ahead of the people at times. But as an American who understood America, who brought form to its amorphous yearnings, who gave direction to its efforts, John Kennedy walked with the people.

—Senator Hubert Humphrey, 1963

More than any President before him, he committed the Presidency to achieving full civil rights for every American. He opposed prejudice of every kind. There was no trace of meanness in this man. There was only compassion for the frailties of others. If there is a supreme lesson we can draw from the life of John Kennedy, it is a lesson of tolerance, a lesson of conscience, courage, and compassion.

—Senator Abraham Ribicoff, 1963

His last speech on race relations was the most earnest, human and profound appeal for understanding and justice that any President has uttered since the first days of the Republic. Uniting his flair for leadership with a program of social progress, he was at his death undergoing a transformation . . .

—Martin Luther King, Jr., 1963

So we are free to wonder, having been given not only the Presidential models over the last three decades of Johnson, Nixon, Ford, Carter, Reagan, and Bush, but also the secondary examples of Humphrey, McGovern, Mondale, and Dukakis, whether any protagonist as innovative, flexible, daring, ironic, witty, and as ready to grow as Jack Kennedy ever did have a chance to change the shape of our place.

—Norman Mailer, 1992

A man who can inspire intensely bitter enemies as well as intensely devoted followers is best judged after many years pass, enough years to permit the sediment of political and legislative battles to settle, so that we can assess our times more clearly.

—John F. Kennedy, *Profiles in Courage*

THE WIT AND WISDOM OF JOHN F. KENNEDY

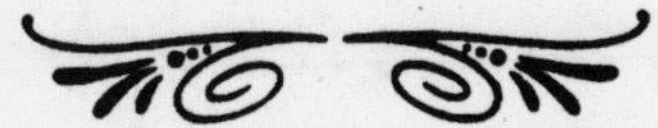

ACTION

"History and our own conscience will judge us more harshly if we do not make every effort to test our hopes by action," President Kennedy said in announcing the Nuclear Test Ban Treaty on July 26, 1963, "and this is the place to begin."

ADAMS, JOHN

John F. Kennedy concluded his Pulitzer Prize–winning book, *Profiles in Courage* (1956), with the story of John Adams.

> To close our stories of American political courage, we would do well to recall an act of courage which preceded the founding of this nation, and which set a standard for all to follow. On the night of March 5, 1770, when an abusive and disorderly mob on State Street in Boston was rashly fired upon by British sentries, *John Adams of Massa-*

chusetts was already a leader in the protests against British indifference to colonist grievances.

But this militant foe of the Crown was asked to serve as a counsel for the accused soldiers, and did not even hesitate to accept. The case, he later noted in his autobiography, was one of the "most exhausting and fatiguing cases I ever tried, hazarding a popularity very hardly earned, and incurring popular suspicions and prejudices which are not yet worn out." Yet the man who would later be a bold President—and father of an independent Senator and President—not only remained as counsel, but acquitted his clients of the murder charge, demonstrating to a packed courtroom that no evidence was at hand to show that the firing was malicious and without provocation:

> Gentlemen of the Jury—I am for the prisoners at the bar; and shall apologize for it only in the words of the Marquis Beccaria: "If I can but be the instrument of preserving one life, his blessings and tears shall be sufficient consolation to me for the contempt of mankind!"

Asked how he wanted to be remembered, President Kennedy cited John Adams: "All I want them to say about me is what they said about John Adams, 'He kept the peace.' "

ALASKA

John F. Kennedy campaigned hard in Alaska and lost there in 1960. He never visited Hawaii at all and won handily.

A thinker as well as a man of action, JFK remarked, "Just think what my margin might have been if I had never left home!"

ALL OR NOTHING

We have rejected any all-or-nothing posture which would leave no choice but inglorious retreat or unlimited retaliation.

—State of the Union message, January 11, 1962

ALLIES

We are not alone. We have friends and allies all over the world who share our devotion to freedom.

—message to Congress, May 25, 1961

AMERICA

For the first time we have the capacity to strike off the remaining bonds of poverty and ignorance, to free our people for the spiritual and intellectual fulfillment which has always been the goal of our civilization.

Yet at this very moment of maximum opportunity, we confront the same forces which have imperiled America throughout its history, the alien forces which once again seek to impose the despotisms of the old world on the people of the new.

—address to Latin-American diplomats, March 13, 1961

AMERICAN FUTURE

I look forward to a great future for America, a future in which our country will match its military strength with our moral restraint, its wealth with our wisdom, its power with our purpose.

I look forward to an America which will not be afraid of grace and beauty, which will protect the beauty of our natural environment, which will preserve the great old

American houses and squares and parks of our national past, and which will build handsome and balanced cities for our future.

I look forward to an America which will reward achievement in the arts as we reward achievement in business or statecraft.

And I look forward to an America which commands respect throughout the world not only for its strength but for its civilization as well.

—Amherst College, Massachusetts, October 26, 1963
(see ARTIST, FUTURE, UNITED STATES)

AMERICAN REVOLUTION

Let us once again awaken our American Revolution until it guides the struggles of peoples everywhere—not with an imperialism of force or fear, but through the rule of courage and freedom and hope for the future of man.

—address to Latin-American diplomats, March 13, 1961

AMERICANS

Americans have always believed in progress—Americans have always kept their eyes fixed on far horizons and new frontiers. If we are faithful to our past, we cannot be fearful of our future.

—remarks, Wheeling, West Virginia, September 27, 1962
(see NEW FRONTIER)

ANCHORS AWEIGH

"I want to thank that band," JFK cut in in Akron, Ohio. "One more chorus of 'Anchors Aweigh' and we will just float this building right out."

ANNOYMENT

Asked whether the books and recordings poking fun at the Kennedy family produced more enjoyment or annoyment, the President answered, "Annoyment. Yes, I have read them and listened to Mr. Meader's record, but I thought it sounded more like Teddy than it did me, so he's annoyed."

(see KENNEDY, TED)

ANTIQUES

At their tenth wedding anniversary celebration, Jack Kennedy's present to his wife was a letter from J. J. Klejman, the New York antiquities dealer, listing all the most unique antiques he had in stock, with a description and a price for each, none less than $1,000.

Jackie could have any one she wanted, he said. JFK read aloud to the crowd the descriptions, but not the prices. However, as JFK read the descriptions of the most expensive ones he would whisper aside, "Got to steer her away from that one."

Ultimately the First Lady chose a coiled serpent bracelet.

(see KENNEDY, JACQUELINE)

APPLAUSE

"I appreciate your welcome," JFK acknowledged the applause at a campaign stop in Los Angeles in 1960. "As the cow said to the Maine farmer, 'Thank you for a warm hand on a cold morning.' "

ARISTOCRACY

This country reserves its highest honors for only one kind of aristocracy—that which the Founding Fathers called "an aristocracy of achievement arising out of a democracy of opportunity."

—message to Congress, June 6, 1963
(see JEFFERSON, THOMAS)

ARMS

Our arms must be subject to ultimate civilian control and command at all times, in war as well as peace.

—message to Congress, March 28, 1961

Each increase in tension has produced an increase in arms; each increase of arms has produced an increase of tension.

—address to the American people, July 26, 1963

The primary purpose of our arms is peace, not war: to make certain that they will never have to be used; to deter all wars, general or limited, nuclear or conventional, large or small; to convince all potential aggressors that any attack would be futile. . . . The basic problems facing the world today are not susceptible to military solution.

—message to Congress, March 28, 1961
(see DEFENSE, NUCLEAR WEAPONS, WAR)

ARTIST

"You have to be a free man to be a great artist," declared President Kennedy at the dedication of the marker at the grave of Ignacy Jan Paderewski in Arlington National Cemetery.

"We must never forget that art is not a form of propaganda; it is a form of truth," affirmed JFK at Amherst College on October 26, 1963, a month before his assassination.

The President delivered a eulogy in memory of the poet Robert Frost, taking this occasion to stress the importance of art and the artist to the life and greatness of the nation.

> The artist, however faithful to his personal vision of reality, becomes the last champion of the individual mind and sensibility against an intrusive society and an officious state.
>
> I see little of more importance to the future of our country and our civilization than full recognition of the place of the artist.
>
> If art is to nourish the roots of our culture, society must set the artist free to follow his vision wherever it takes him. We must never forget that art is not a form of propaganda; it is a form of truth.
>
> In free society art is not a weapon and it does not belong to the sphere of polemics and ideology. Artists are not engineers of the soul. It may be different elsewhere. But democratic society—in it, the highest duty of the writer, the composer, the artist is to remain true to himself and let the chips fall where they may. In serving his vision of the truth, the artist best serves his nation. And the nation which disdains the mission of art invites the fate of Robert Frost's hired man, the fate of having "nothing to look backward to with pride, and nothing to look forward to with hope."
>
> I look forward to an America which will steadily raise the standards of artistic accomplishment and which will steadily enlarge cultural opportunities for all our citizens.
>
> And I look forward to a world which will be safe not only for democracy and diversity but also for personal distinction.

(see TRUTH)

ARTISTS

The Kennedy White House hosted many literary and artistic notables.

"It's becoming a sort of eating place for artists," JFK was heard to say. "But *they* never ask *us* out."

ASSET

We . . . have no greater asset than the willingness of a free and determined people . . . to face all problems frankly and meet all dangers free from panic or fear.

—State of the Union message, January 29, 1961

ASSUMPTIONS

Among the assumptions to be invalidated will be the following ten, which probably are most fundamental to our thinking of the twentieth century:

1. American arms and science are superior to any others in the world.
2. American efforts for world-wide disarmament are a selfless sacrifice for peace.
3. Our bargaining power at any international conference table is always more vast and flexible than that of our enemy.
4. Peace is a normal relation among states; and aggression is the exception—direct and unambiguous.
5. We should enter every military conflict as a moral crusade requiring the unconditional surrender of the enemy.
6. A free and peace-loving nation has nothing to fear in a world where right and justice inevitably prevail.

7. Americans live far behind the lines, protected by time, space and a host of allies from attack.
8. We shall have time to mobilize our superior economic resources after a war begins.
9. Our advanced weapons and continental defense systems, established at tremendous cost and effort, will protect us.
10. Victory ultimately goes to the nation with the highest national income, gross national product, and standard of living.

All of these concepts will be altered or questioned in but a few years.

—in the Senate, August 14, 1958

B

BABY

Shown a picture of a newborn nephew in August 1963, President Kennedy remarked laconically, "He looks like a fine baby—we'll know more later."

BAILEY, JOHN

"I am delighted that John Bailey's going to take over this job," JFK complimented John Bailey on becoming chairman of the Democratic National Committee. "He is more popular today than he will be any time again in his life. I will feel that he is doing a good job when you all say, 'Well, Kennedy is all right, but Bailey's the one who is really making the mistakes.' "

BALANCED BUDGET

An unbalanced economy does not produce a balanced budget. The Treasury's pocketbook suffers when the economy performs poorly. The Federal budget can and should be made an instrument of prosperity and stability, not a deterrent to recovery.

—message to Congress, February 2, 1961

BASEBALL

"Last year, more Americans went to symphonies than went to baseball games," JFK observed at a White House Youth Concert in 1962. "This may be viewed as an alarming statistic, but I think that both baseball and the country will endure."

BERLIN

"Once again Berlin and the Federal Republic have spoiled us for home," JFK acknowledged an enthusiastic reception at a city hall luncheon in Berlin on June 26, 1963. "Now, when we don't get a million people out for a political speech in Worcester, Massachusetts, or Danbury, Connecticut, everyone, especially the reporters, is going to write that there are signs of apathy in the United States. And when we have crowded dinners of fifty at the White House, I am afraid this dinner is going to throw a pall on the entire affair."

BERLIN ADDRESS

Two thousand years ago the proudest boast was "*Civis Romanus sum.*" Today, in the world of freedom, the proudest boast is "*Ich bin ein Berliner.*"

I appreciated my interpreter translating my German!

There are many people in the world who really don't understand, or say they don't, what is the great issue between the free world and the Communist world. Let them come to Berlin. There are some who say that communism is the wave of the future. Let them come to Berlin.

Freedom has many difficulties and democracy is not perfect, but we have never had to put a wall up to keep our people in, to prevent them from leaving us.

While the wall is the most obvious and vivid demonstration of the failures of the Communist system for all the world to see, we take no satisfaction, for it is, as your Mayor [Willy Brandt] has said, an offense not only against history but an offense against humanity, separating families, dividing husbands and wives and brothers and sisters, and dividing a people who wish to be joined together.

You live in a defended island of freedom, but your life is part of the main. So let me ask you, as I close, to lift your eyes beyond the dangers of today, to the hopes of tomorrow, beyond the freedom merely of this city of Berlin, or your country of Germany, to the advance of freedom everywhere, beyond this wall to the day of peace with justice, beyond yourselves and ourselves to all mankind.

Freedom is indivisible, and when one man is enslaved, all are not free. When all are free, then we can look forward to that day when this city will be joined as one and this country and this great Continent of Europe in a peaceful and hopeful globe. When that day finally comes, as it will, the people of West Berlin can take sober satisfaction in the fact that they were in the front lines for almost two decades.

All freemen, wherever they may live, are citizens of Berlin, and, therefore, as a free man, I take pride in the words *"Ich bin ein Berliner."*

—remarks in the Rudolf Wilde Platz, June 26, 1963

BERLIN WALL

All the world knows that no successful system builds a *wall* to keep its people in and freedom out—and that the wall of shame dividing Berlin is a symbol of Communist failure.

—State of the Union message, January 14, 1963

BIG BUSINESS

When a reporter told the President that a reputable columnist said the attitude of Big Business was, "Now we have you where we want you," President Kennedy shook his head and said, "I can't believe I'm where big business wants me."

BIG GOVERNMENT

The truth about big government is the truth about any other great activity: It is complex. Certainly it is true that size brings dangers, but it is also true that size also can bring benefits.

One great and little-noticed expansion of government which has brought strength to our whole society: the new role of our federal government as the major patron of research in science and in medicine.

The myth here is that government is big and bad—and steadily getting bigger and worse. Obviously this myth has some excuse for existence.

—commencement, Yale University, June 11, 1962

BIRTHDAY

"I got a telegram tonight," President Kennedy announced at a birthday party soon after his clash with steel executives over steel prices, "from Roger Blough [president of United States Steel]. The telegram said, 'In honor of your birthday, I believe that you should get a rise in pay.' Signed 'Roger.'

" 'P.S. *My* birthday is next month.' "

BLOW UP

"I never know when I press these whether I am going to blow up Massachusetts or start the project," remarked President Kennedy as he threw a switch in Salt Lake City to activate generators at the Green River 150 miles away. Fortunately, it did not blow up.

(see TECHNICAL DIFFICULTIES)

BOYLE, CONGRESSMAN CHARLES

At a press conference the President was asked, "What do you think, sir, of the rather harsh things that Congressman Boyle had to say about you . . . ?"

JFK answered this way: "I will say that I never read as much about a Congressman in the papers as I do about that Congressman and see less legislative results."

BRAINPOWER

It requires skilled manpower and brainpower to match the power of totalitarian discipline.

—message to Congress, January 29, 1963

This nation cannot afford to maintain its military power and neglect its brainpower.

—State of the Union message, January 14, 1963

(see GRADUATE EDUCATION, SCHOLARS)

BREAKFAST

Arriving late for a breakfast in Wyoming on the campaign trail in 1960, JFK cleared his throat: "I first of all want to express on behalf of my sister and myself our gratitude to all of you for being kind enough to have this breakfast and make it almost lunch."

BRIEFINGS

"Senator, you were promised a military intelligence briefing from the President. Have you received that?" asked a reporter at a press conference in Anchorage, where JFK was campaigning for the 1960 election.

"Yes. I talked on Thursday morning to General Wheeler from the Defense Department."

"What was his first name?" inquired the note-taking reporter.

"He didn't brief me on that."

BRISTOL, TENNESSEE

"Ladies and gentlemen, it is my understanding that the last candidate for the Presidency to visit this community in a Presidential year was Herbert Hoover in 1928," asserted JFK in Bristol, Tennessee, during a 1960 campaign stop. "President Hoover initiated on the occasion of his visit the slogan 'Two chickens for every pot,' and it is no accident that no Presidential candidate has ever dared to come back to this community since."

BRONX

"I have been, in the last three days, in eight states," announced JFK on arrival in the Bronx, November 5, 1960, "among them California, New Mexico, Arizona, Ohio, Illinois, Virginia, and the Bronx, the ninth state."

BUFFET

During his trip to Ireland, President Kennedy visited his third cousin Mary Ryan, who prepared a sumptuous buffet in his honor.

"I want to thank all of those who prepared this," said JFK. "It was a great effort on their part. We can promise we will come only once every ten years."

BUNDY, McGEORGE

"Nothing beats brains," replied President Kennedy when asked his opinion of McGeorge Bundy, his Special Assistant for National Security Affairs.

JFK liked to tell the story of Charles R. Cherington, a Harvard professor critical of Bundy when "Mac" was dean of the faculty of arts and sciences at Harvard and Cherington was teaching government. The government professor, in one of his classes, referred to Bundy as a "son of a bitch." In his next lecture, Cherington informed his students that one of them had apparently reported his remark to Bundy, who had then summoned Cherington to his office. There, Cherington said, he apologized to Bundy for calling him a son of a bitch, and Bundy apologized to him for being one.

BUSINESS

"Many businessmen who are prospering as never before during this administration are convinced, nevertheless, that we must be anti-business," President Kennedy told the Tampa Chamber of Commerce. "When our bill to grant a tax credit for business investment was before the

Congress, Secretary of the Treasury Dillon was on a plane to this state, and he found himself talking to one of the leading Florida businessmen about the investment tax credit. He spent some time, he later told me, explaining how the bill would help this man's corporate outlook and income and the businessman was most impressed. Finally, as the plane landed at Miami, he turned to Secretary Dillon and said, 'I am very grateful to you for explaining the bill. Now tell me just once more why is it I am against it?' "

BUSINESS AND GOVERNMENT

"A dilemma, it seems to me, is posed by the occasion of a Presidential address to a business group on business conditions less than four weeks after entering the White House," the President said while addressing a National Industrial Conference in February 1961, "for it is too early to be claiming credit for the new administration and too late to be blaming the old one."

Attacking the myth that business and government are adversarial, JFK declared, "Far from being natural enemies, government and business are necessary allies."

If those of you who are in the world of business and we who are in the world of government are necessarily partners, what kind of partnership is this going to be? Will it be marked by mutual suspicion and recrimination or by mutual understanding and fruitful collaboration?

—address to the National Industrial Conference, February 13, 1961 (see GOVERNMENT AND BUSINESS)

BUSINESSMEN'S LUNCHEON

"It would be premature to ask your support in the next election, and it would be inaccurate to thank you for it in the past," President Kennedy teased the businessmen at a luncheon in his first year in office.

"In the last campaign most of the members of this luncheon group today supported my opponent—except for a very few who were under the impression that I was my father's son."

(see KENNEDY, JOSEPH; SMILES)

CALHOUN, JOHN C.

The second and probably the most extraordinary of the triumvirate [the other members were Senators Daniel Webster and Henry Clay] was John C. Calhoun of South Carolina, with bristling hair and eyes that burned like heavy coals, "the cast-iron man," according to the English spinster Harriet Martineau, "who looks as if he had never been born, and never could be extinguished." Calhoun, in spite of this appearance, had been born in 1782, the same year as Webster and five years after Clay. He was six feet two inches tall, a graduate of Yale University, a member of Congress at the age of twenty-nine, a War Hawk who joined Henry Clay in driving the United States into the War of 1812, and a nationalist who turned sectionalist in the 1820s as the economic pressures of the tariff began to tell on the agricultural economy of South Carolina. Calhoun had a mind that was cold, narrow, concentrated, and powerful. Webster considered him "much the ablest man in the Senate," the greatest in fact that he had met in his entire public life. "He could have," he declared, "demolished Newton, Calvin or even John Locke as a logician."

His speeches, stripped of all excess verbiage, marched across the Senate floor in even columns, measured, disciplined, carrying all before them. Strangely enough, although he had the appearance, especially in his later days, of a fanatic, he was a man of infinite charm and personality. He was reputed to be the best conversationalist in South Carolina, and he won to him through their emotions men who failed to comprehend his closely reasoned arguments. His hold upon the imagination and affection of the entire South steadily grew, and at his death in the midst of the great debate of 1850 he was universally mourned.

—*Profiles in Courage*, 1956
(see CLAY, HENRY; WEBSTER, DANIEL)

CALIFORNIA

Today we celebrate the one hundred and tenth anniversary of the admission of the State of California into the Union. It seems to me that the great story of California has come about because people were not satisfied with things as they were. They liked Massachusetts and they liked Ohio and they liked Oklahoma, but they thought they could do better when they came to California. I don't know why they felt that way about Massachusetts.

—Modesto, California, September 9, 1960
(see MASSACHUSETTS)

CAPITAL PUNISHMENT

President Kennedy was not opposed to capital punishment. He was confronted with a mercy plea soon after he took office. The case involved an American GI in Germany convicted of raping an eleven-year-old girl twice and killing her.

The President declined the mercy plea and allowed the execution to proceed.

CAPITALISM

In regard to capitalism, we observe first that it was obedience to its principles that contributed so largely to England's failure. It has been estimated in authoritative circles that Hitler has spent anywhere from $50,000,000,000 to $100,000,000,000 in building up Germany's armaments. He ran Germany's debt to skyrocket heights and saved Germany from suffering violent inflation only by rigid state control.

—*Why England Slept,* 1940, "Conclusion"
(see DEMOCRACY)

CAPOTE, TRUMAN

President Kennedy was proud of the White House operators and boasted that they could find anyone, anywhere, any hour of the day or night. Once JFK dared Jackie and some friends to come up with the name of someone the operators couldn't find.

Jackie suggested Truman Capote because he had an unlisted number.

The President picked up the telephone and said only, "Yes, this is the President. Would you please get me Truman Capote?" No further identification was given or requested.

Thirty minutes later Truman Capote was on the line. He was not located at his own number in Brooklyn, but at the home of a friend in Palm Springs, California, another unlisted number.

CATHOLIC

John F. Kennedy, the first and only Roman Catholic to be elected President, did not completely accept all the teachings of the Catholic Church. He supported the use of birth control and opposed federal aid to parochial schools.

When the "religious issue" was raised during the 1960 Presidential race, the candidate confronted it in a speech before the Greater Houston Ministerial Association.

"I believe in an America where the separation of Church and State is absolute," JFK said, "where no Catholic prelate would tell the President (should he be a Catholic) how to act and no Protestant minister would tell his parishioners for whom to vote."

JFK added passionately: "But if this election is decided on the basis that 40 million Americans lost their chance of being President on the day they were baptized, then it is the whole nation that will be the loser in the eyes of the Catholics and non-Catholics around the world, in the eyes of history, and in the eyes of our own people."

Once elected, President Kennedy sometimes attended Protestant services and declined to raise relations with the Vatican to the ambassadorial level.

(see RELIGIOUS ISSUE)

CERTAINTY

Every apparent blessing contains the seeds of danger; every area of trouble gives out a ray of hope; and the one unchangeable certainty is that nothing is certain or unchangeable.

—State of the Union message, January 11, 1962

CHANGE

Goethe tells us in his greatest poem that Faust lost the liberty of his soul when he said to the passing moment, "Stay, thou art so fair." And our liberty, too, is endangered if we pause for the passing moment, if we rest on our achievements, if we resist the pace of progress. For time and the world do not stand still. Change is the law of life. And those who look only to the past are certain to miss the future.

—remarks in Frankfurt, Germany, June 25, 1963
(see WINDS OF CHANGE)

CHICAGO

President-elect Kennedy acknowledged his debt to Chicago Democrats after a narrow victory in the 1960 Presidential race. "Some years ago, in the city of Fall River, Massachusetts, the mayor was elected by one vote, and every time he went down the street, everyone would come up to him and say, 'Say, Dan, I put you in office.' And I feel a little like that in Chicago tonight. If all of you had voted the other way—there's about fifty-five hundred of you here tonight—I wouldn't be President of the United States."

CHIEF EXECUTIVE

Impressed by Robert Kennedy's racket-busting style, a prominent lawyer wrote to President Kennedy that Bobby would make a better Chief Executive.

"I have consulted Bobby about it," JFK wrote back, "and, to my dismay, the idea appeals to him."

(see KENNEDY, ROBERT)

CHILD EDUCATION

A good education is the most valuable resource that you pass on to your children.

—Carpentersville, Illinois, October 25, 1950

A child miseducated is a child lost.

—State of the Union message, January 11, 1962

An uneducated American child makes an uneducated parent who produces, in many cases, another uneducated American child.

—commencement, San Diego State College, June 6, 1963

(see EDUCATION, HIGH SCHOOL DROPOUTS)

CHILDREN

At a campaign stop in 1960, Jack Kennedy tried to elicit a kiss from the shy four-year-old daughter of his friend Paul Fay. Unimpressed by JFK's charm, the little girl resisted, squirming and wriggling in his arms, until he laughed and handed her back to her father, saying: "I don't think she quite caught that strong quality of love of children so much a part of the candidate's make-up which has made him dear to the hearts of all mothers."

The nation's children, now 40 percent of our population, have urgent needs which must be met.

—message to Congress, February 9, 1961

CHIMPANZEE IN SPACE

The President interrupted a press conference on November 29, 1961, to announce to the assembled reporters that the United States had successfully sent a chimpanzee into space.

"This chimpanzee who is flying in space took off at 10:08. He reports that everything is going perfectly and working well."

(see DOGS IN SPACE, SPACE)

CHINESE

During a negotiation with Premier Khrushchev on the nuclear test ban treaty, President Kennedy quoted a Chinese proverb: "The journey of a thousand miles begins with one step."

"You seem to know the Chinese very well," Chairman Khrushchev commented.

JFK smiled and said prophetically, "We may both get to know them better."

CHOICES

The choices we make, for good or ill, will affect the welfare of generations yet unborn.

—State of the Union message, January 14, 1963

CHRISTIAN CHARITY

John Quincy Adams placed the national interest, as he saw it, above the regional interests of his constituents and supported President Jefferson's Embargo in 1807, as JFK writes in *Profiles in Courage*, "in a fight where he stood with the President who had defeated his father!—John Quincy maintained the unflinching and inflexible bearing which became his Puritan ancestry. When he was accosted in Boston by a politically minded preacher who assailed his views 'in a rude and indecent manner, I told him that in consideration of his age I should only remark that he had one lesson yet to learn—*Christian charity.*' "

(see ADAMS, JOHN)

CITIES

The good life is still just a dream for too many of the people who live in cities.

—Pittsburgh, Pennsylvania, October 10, 1960

We will neglect our cities at our peril, for in neglecting them we neglect the nation.

—message to Congress, January 30, 1962

CIVIL RIGHTS

Every American ought to have the right to be treated as he would wish to be treated, as one would wish his children to be treated. This is not the case.

—television address to the nation, June 11, 1963
(see CIVIL RIGHTS ADDRESS, EMANCIPATION PROCLAMATION CENTENNIAL, HUMAN RIGHTS)

CIVIL RIGHTS ADDRESS

This afternoon, following a series of threats and defiant statements, the presence of Alabama National Guardsmen was required at the University of Alabama to carry out the final and unequivocal order of the United States District Court of the Northern District of Alabama. That order called for the admission of two clearly qualified young Alabama residents who happened to have been born Negro.

I hope that every American, regardless of where he lives, will stop and examine his conscience about this and other related incidents. This nation was founded by men of many nations and backgrounds. It was founded on the principle that all men are created equal, and that the rights of every man are diminished when the rights of one man are threatened.

We are confronted primarily with a moral issue. It is as old as the Scriptures and is as clear as the American Constitution. The heart of the question is whether all Americans are to be afforded equal rights and equal opportunities, whether we are going to treat our fellow Americans as we want to be treated.

One hundred years of delay have passed since President Lincoln freed the slaves, yet their heirs, their grandsons, are not fully free. They are not yet freed from the bonds of injustice. They are not yet freed from social and economic oppression, and this nation, for all its hopes and all its boasts, will not be fully free until all its citizens are free.

Next week I shall ask the Congress of the United States to act, to make a commitment it has not fully made in this century to the proposition that race has no place in American life or law.

The old code of equity law under which we live commands for every wrong a remedy, but in too many communities, in too many parts of the country, wrongs are inflicted on Negro citizens for which there are no remedies at law. Unless the Congress acts, their only remedy is in the street.

I am, therefore, asking the Congress to enact legislation giving all Americans the right to be served in facilities which are open to the public—hotels, restaurants, theaters, retail stores and similar establishments.

This seems to me to be an elementary right. Its denial is an arbitrary indignity that no American in 1963 should have to endure, but many do.

My fellow Americans, this is a problem which faces us all, in every city of the North as well as the South.

Therefore, I am asking for your help in making it easier for us to move ahead and to provide the kind of equality of treatment which we would want ourselves.

—television address to the nation, June 11, 1963
(see MEREDITH, JAMES)

CLAY, HENRY

Henry Clay of Kentucky—bold, autocratic and magnetic; fiery in manner with a charm so compelling that an opponent once declined a meeting which would subject him to the appeal of Harry of the West. To Abraham Lincoln, "He was my beau ideal"; to the half-mad, half-genius John Randolph of Roanoke, he was, in what is perhaps the most memorable and malignant sentence in the history of personal abuse, "a being, so brilliant yet so corrupt, which, like a rotten mackerel by moonlight, shines and stinks." Not even John Calhoun, who had fought him for years, was impervious to his fascination: "I don't like Henry Clay. He is a bad man, an impostor, a creator of wicked schemes. I wouldn't speak to him, but, by God, I love him."

Others besides John Calhoun loved him. Like Charles James Fox, he reveled in a love for life, and had a matchless gift for winning and holding the hearts of his fellow-countrymen—and women. Elected to the Senate when still below the constitutional age of thirty, he was subsequently sent to the House, where in a move never duplicated before or since he was immediately elected Speaker at the age of thirty-five.

Though he lacked the intellectual resources of Webster and Calhoun, Henry Clay nevertheless had visions of a greater America beyond those held by either of his famous colleagues. And so, in 1820, 1833 and 1850 he initiated, hammered and charmed through reluctant Congresses the three great compromises that preserved the

Union until 1861, by which time the strength of the North was such that secession was doomed to failure.

—*Profiles in Courage*, 1956

(see CALHOUN, JOHN C.; WEBSTER, DANIEL)

CLIFFORD, CLARK

"Clark is a wonderful fellow," President Kennedy testified after Washington lawyer Clark Clifford, his representative to the Eisenhower Administration, completed the transition to the Kennedy White House.

"In a day when so many are seeking a reward to what they contributed to the return of the Democrats to the White House, you don't hear Clark clamoring. He was invaluable to us and all he asked in return was that we advertise his law firm on the backs of one dollar bills."

CLOTHES

John F. Kennedy, the fashion-plate President, had a penchant for expensive clothes, usually conservative and neat. He changed frequently and was intimately familiar with his large wardrobe.

One night Ted Sorenson needed a necktie, and Dave Powers swiped one from the Senator's closet that he was sure JFK never wore.

The Senator's first words as he stepped into the room were, "Is that my tie you're wearing?"

(see SHIRTS)

COLD WAR

Today we may have reached a pause in the Cold War, but that is not a lasting peace. A test ban treaty is a milestone, but it is not the millennium.

—United Nations address, September 20, 1963

COLLEGE GRADUATES

Addressing students at the University of North Carolina, President Kennedy said he did not plan to adopt "from the Belgian constitution a provision giving three votes instead of one to college graduates—at least not until more Democrats go to college."

Unemployment rates among college graduates are much lower than among those graduated from high school. But unfortunately, only one out of every ten finish college.

—remarks in Chicago, March 23, 1963
(see LABOR DEMAND, UNEMPLOYMENT)

COLLEGE STUDENTS

The welfare and security of the nation require that we increase our investment in financial assistance for college students both at undergraduate and graduate levels.

—remarks at Rice University, September 12, 1962

COLONIALISM

My nation was once a colony, and we know what colonialism means: the exploitation and subjugation of the weak by the powerful, of the many by the few, of the governed who have given no consent to be governed, whatever their continent, their class or their color.

Let us debate colonialism in full, and apply the principle of free choice and the practice of free plebiscites in every corner of the globe.

—United Nations address, September 25, 1961

COLUMBUS, OHIO

"There is no city in the United States," President Kennedy told a crowd in Columbus, Ohio, "in which I get a warmer welcome and less votes than Columbus, Ohio."

(see OHIO)

COMMON MARKET

If the Common Market should now move toward protectionism and restrictionism, it would undermine its own basic principles.

—State of the Union message, January 14, 1963

(see EUROPEAN COMMON MARKET)

COMMUNISM

Across the face of the globe freedom and Communism are locked in a deadly embrace.

—Zembo Mosque Temple,
Harrisburg, Pennsylvania, September 16, 1960

Communism has sometimes succeeded as a scavenger, but never as a leader. It has never come to power in any country that was not disrupted by war or internal repression or both.

—remarks at NATO headquarters, Naples, Italy, July 2, 1963

COMMUNIST EMPIRE

There is no ignoring the fact that the tide of self-determination has not yet reached the Communist empire, where a population far larger than that officially termed "dependent" lives under governments installed by foreign troops instead of free institutions, under a system which knows only one party and one belief, which suppresses free debate, free elections, free newspapers, free books and free trade unions, and which builds a wall to keep truth a stranger and its own citizens prisoners.

—United Nations address, September 25, 1961

(see FREE EXPRESSION, SELF-DETERMINATION)

COMMUNIST SOCIETIES

Marx is proven wrong once again, for it is the closed Communist societies, not the free and open societies, which carry within themselves the seeds of internal disintegration.

This disarray of the Communist empire has been heightened by two other formidable forces. One is the historic force of nationalism and the yearning of all men to be free. The other is the gross inefficiencies of their economies. For a closed society is not open to ideas of progress, and a police state finds it cannot command the grain to grow.

—State of the Union message, January 14, 1963

COMPLIMENTS

Jack Kennedy enjoyed neutralizing insults by accepting them as compliments.

"Just before you met," JFK told a convention in New York in September 1960, "a weekly news magazine with a wide circulation featured a section, 'Kennedy's Liberal Promises,' and described me, and I quote, as 'the farthest-out Liberal Democrat around,' unquote. While I am not certain of the beatnik definition of 'farthest-out,' I am certain that it was not intended as a compliment."

John Kennedy accepted a barb from his rival Richard Nixon as a compliment in the heat of the 1960 campaign.

"Someone was kind enough, though I don't know whether he meant it kindly, to say the other night that in my campaign in California I sounded like a Truman with a Harvard accent."

(see TRUMAN, HARRY)

COMPROMISE

We can compromise our political positions, but not ourselves. We can resolve the clash of interests without conceding our ideals.

—*Profiles in Courage*, 1956

CONFORMITY

We cannot expect that all nations will adopt like systems, for conformity is the jailer of freedom and the enemy of growth.

—United Nations address, September 25, 1961

CONGRESS

"I know there are some Americans and some Democrats who say that they have now developed a wonderful arrangement in Washington," JFK remarked during the 1960 Presidential campaign. "The Congress is Democratic and the President is Republican and nothing happens and isn't it wonderful?"

Members of the Congress, the Constitution makes us not rivals for power but partners for progress. We are all trustees for the American people, custodians of the American heritage. It is my task to report the state of the Union; to improve it is the task of us all.

—State of the Union message, January 11, 1962

CONGRESSMAN

Will Rogers once said it is not the original investment in a Congressman that counts; it is the upkeep.

—Alton, Illinois, October 3, 1960

CONSERVATIVE REVIVAL

"For all that I have been reading in the last three, four, or five months about the great conservative revival sweeping the United States," JFK commented to a Miami Beach crowd in December 1961, "I thought perhaps no one was going to show up today."

CONSTITUTION

If we are to give the leadership the world requires of us, we must be true to the great principles of our Constitution, the very principles which distinguish us from our adversaries in the world.

—telegram, February 2, 1961

The Constitution of the United States . . . stressed not independence but interdependence, not the individual liberty of one but the indivisible liberty of all.

—Independence Day address, July 4, 1962
(see INTERDEPENDENCE)

COOPER, GORDON

Peace has her victories as well as war, and this was one of the victories for the human spirit today.

—radio-television address after flight of astronaut L. Gordon Cooper, May 16, 1963
(see SPACE)

CORUSCATINGLY

When one of his White House aides was described in newspapers as "coruscatingly" brilliant, the President noted, "Those guys should never forget, 50,000 votes the other way and we'd all be coruscatingly stupid."

(see SARDONIC)

COURAGE

In the final chapter of *Profiles in Courage*, Kennedy concludes: "The stories of past courage can define that ingredient—they can teach, they can offer hope, they can provide inspiration. But they cannot supply courage itself. For this each man must look into his own soul."

Courage, the universal virtue, is comprehended by us all. For without belittling the courage with which men have died, we should not forget those acts of courage with which men have *lived*.

The courage of life is often a less dramatic spectacle than the courage of a final moment; but it is no less a magnificent mixture of triumph and tragedy.

—*Profiles in Courage*, 1956

COURAGEOUS

In the days ahead, only the very courageous will be able to take the hard and unpopular decisions necessary for our survival in the struggle with a powerful enemy—an enemy with leaders who need give little thought to the popularity of their cause, who need pay little tribute to the public opinion they themselves manipulate, and who may force, without fear of retaliation at the polls, their citizens to sacrifice present laughter for future glory. And only the very courageous will be able to keep alive the spirit of individualism and dissent which gave birth to this nation, nourished it as an infant and carried it through its severest tests upon the attainment of its maturity.

—*Profiles in Courage*, 1956

CUBAN MISSILE CRISIS

In October 1962 the Cuban Missile Crisis brought the world to the brink of nuclear war. The United States confronted the Soviet Union over its installation of ballistic missiles in Cuba. President Kennedy demonstrated his determination to have the missiles removed. After days of tension and anxiety, Soviet premier Nikita Khrushchev ordered their withdrawal.

At the height of the Cuban Missile Crisis President Kennedy remarked, "I guess this is the week I earn my salary."

CUBAN MISSILE CRISIS ADDRESS

Facing the greatest crisis of the Cold War, President Kennedy informed the American people of the danger in a televised address on October 22, 1962.

> This government, as promised, has maintained the closest surveillance of the Soviet military build-up on the island of Cuba. Within the past week, unmistakable evidence has established the fact that a series of offensive missile sites is now in preparation on that imprisoned island. The purpose of these bases can be none other than to provide a nuclear strike capability against the Western Hemisphere.
>
> Each of these missiles, in short, is capable of striking Washington, D.C., the Panama Canal, Cape Canaveral,

Mexico City or any other city in the Southeastern part of the United States, in Central America or in the Caribbean area.

This urgent transformation of Cuba into an important strategic base, by the presence of these large, long-range and clearly offensive weapons of sudden mass destruction, constitutes an explicit threat to the peace and security of all the Americas, in flagrant and deliberate defiance of the Rio pact of 1947, the traditions of this nation and hemisphere, the Joint Resolution of the Eighty-seventh Congress, the Charter of the United Nations and my own public warnings to the Soviets on September 4 and 13.

Neither the United States of America nor the world community of nations can tolerate deliberate deception and offensive threats on the part of any nation, large or small. We no longer live in a world where only the actual firing of weapons represents a sufficient challenge to a nation's security to constitute maximum peril. Nuclear weapons are so destructive and ballistic missiles are so swift that any substantially increased possibility of their use or any sudden change in their deployment may well be regarded as a definite threat to peace.

But this secret, swift and extraordinary build-up of Communist missiles, in an area well known to have a special and historical relationship to the United States and the nations of the Western hemisphere, in violation of Soviet assurances and in defiance of American and hemispheric policy—this sudden, clandestine decision to station strategic weapons for the first time outside of Soviet soil is a deliberately provocative and unjustified change in the status quo which cannot be accepted by this country, if our courage and our commitments are ever to be trusted again by either friend or foe.

The 1930s taught us a clear lesson: aggressive conduct, if allowed to grow unchecked and unchallenged, ultimately leads to war. This nation is opposed to war. We are also true to our word. Our unswerving objective, therefore, must be to prevent the use of these missiles against this or any other country, and to secure their withdrawal or elimination from the Western Hemisphere.

I have directed that the following initial steps be taken immediately:

First, to halt this offensive build-up, a strict quarantine on all offensive military equipment under shipment to Cuba is being initiated. All ships of any kind bound for Cuba from whatever nation or port will, if found to contain cargoes of offensive weapons, be turned back.

Second, I have directed the continued and increased close surveillance of Cuba and its military build-up.

Third, it shall be the policy of this Nation to regard any nuclear missile launched from Cuba against any nation in the Western Hemisphere as an attack by the Soviet Union on the United States, requiring a full retaliatory response upon the Soviet Union.

I call upon Chairman Khrushchev to halt and eliminate this clandestine, reckless and provocative threat to world peace and to stable relations between our two nations. I call upon him further to abandon this course of world domination, and to join in an historic effort to end the perilous arms race and transform the history of man.

My fellow citizens: Let no one doubt that this is a difficult and dangerous effort on which we have set out.

But the greatest danger of all would be to do nothing.

The path we have chosen for the present is full of hazards, as all paths are, but it is the one most consistent with our character and courage as a nation and our commitments around the world. The cost of freedom is always high, but Americans have always paid it. And one path we shall never choose, and that is the path of surrender or submission.

Our goal is not the victory of might, but the vindication of right; not peace at the expense of freedom, but both peace *and* freedom, here in this hemisphere, and, we hope, around the world. God willing, that goal will be achieved.

CUBAN MISSILE QUARANTINE LIFTED

I have today been informed by Chairman Khrushchev that all of the Il-28 bombers now in Cuba will be withdrawn in thirty days. He also agrees that these planes can be observed and counted as they leave. Inasmuch as this goes a long way toward reducing the danger which faced this hemisphere four weeks ago, I have this afternoon instructed the Secretary of Defense to lift our naval quarantine.

—news conference, November 20, 1962

DADDY

After the assassination of President Kennedy, his young son, John Jr., asked William Haddad, an associate of JFK's, "Are you a daddy?"

Haddad admitted that he was.

Little John Jr. said, "Then will you throw me up in the air?"

DALLAS ADDRESS

If President Kennedy had not been assassinated, he would have made the following remarks. The speech was released to the press at noon, on November 22, 1963, an hour before the assassination:

> This nation's strength and security are not easily or cheaply obtained—nor are they quickly and simply explained. There are many kinds of strength, and no one kind will

suffice. Overwhelming nuclear strength cannot stop a guerilla war. Formal pacts of alliance cannot stop internal subversion.

It should be clear by now that a nation can be no stronger abroad than she is at home. Only an America which practices what it preaches about equal rights and social justice will be respected by those whose choice affects our future. Only an America which has fully educated its citizens is fully capable of tackling the complex problems and perceiving the hidden dangers of the world in which we live.

Leadership and learning are indispensable to each other. . . . This link between leadership and learning is not only essential at the community level. It is even more indispensable in world affairs. Ignorance and misinformation can handicap the progress of a city or a company—but they can, if allowed to prevail in foreign policy, handicap this country's security.

There is no longer any fear in the free world that a Communist lead in space will become a permanent assertion of supremacy and the basis of military superiority. There is no longer any doubt about the strength and skill of American science, American industry, American education and the American free enterprise system. In short, our national space effort represents a great gain in, and a great resource of, our national strength.

America today is stronger than ever before. Our adversaries have not abandoned their ambitions; our dangers have not diminished; our vigilance cannot be relaxed. But now we have the military, the scientific and the economic strength to do whatever must be done for the preservation and promotion of freedom.

We in this country, in this generation, are—by destiny rather than choice—the watchmen on the walls of world freedom. We ask, therefore, that we may be worthy of our power and responsibility—that we may exercise our strength with wisdom and restraint—and that we may achieve in our time and for all time the ancient vision of peace on earth, goodwill toward men. That must always be our goal—and the righteousness of our cause must always underlie our strength. For as was written long ago: "Except the Lord keep the city, the watchmen waketh but in vain."

(see LEADERSHIP AND LEARNING)

DAUGHTERS

Asked if he hoped the expectant Mrs. Kennedy would have a baby boy in 1960, JFK smiled. "I have a daughter, and I know it sounds terrible and treasonous, but I really don't mind having another daughter again if that is the way it goes."

DAY

One day the First Lady asked the President what kind of day it was. JFK shook his head and named ten things that had gone wrong throughout the morning. He flashed a grin: "And the day is only half over."

DEBT

Debts, public and private, are neither good nor bad, in and of themselves. Borrowing can lead to overextension and collapse, but it can also lead to expansion and strength. There is no single, simple slogan in this field that we can trust.

—commencement, Yale University, June 11, 1962

DECISION

Our responsibility is one of decision, for to govern is to choose.

—Independence Day address, Philadelphia, July 4, 1962

DEFENSE

In the conclusion of his Harvard honors thesis (published as *Why England Slept*), the hawkish young JFK wrote: "We must always keep our armaments equal to our commitments. Munich should teach us that; we must realize that any bluff will be called. We cannot tell anyone to keep out of our hemisphere unless our armaments *and the people behind those armaments* are prepared to back up the command, even to the ultimate point of going to war."

Our arms will never be used to strike the first blow in any attack. This is not a confession of weakness but a statement of strength. It is our national tradition.

—message to Congress, March 28, 1961
(see CUBAN MISSILE CRISIS, ENGLAND, GUERILLA WARFARE, WAR)

DEFENSE POSTURE

Our defense posture must be both flexible and determined. Any potential aggressor contemplating an attack on any part of the free world with any kind of weapons, conventional or nuclear, must know that our response will be suitable, selective, swift and effective.

—message to Congress, March 28, 1961

DEFENSE SPENDING

You will be involved in economic judgments which most economists would hesitate to make. At what point, for example, does military aid become burdensome to a country and endanger freedom rather than help to secure it? To what extent can the gold and the dollar cost of our overseas deployments be offset by foreign procurement?

Or at what stage can a new weapons system be considered sufficiently advanced to justify large dollar appropriations?

—address at West Point, June 6, 1962

DE GAULLE, CHARLES

Soon after the inauguration President Kennedy greeted Madame Herve Alphand, wife of the French ambassador, at a White House dinner:

"*Comment allez-vous?* . . . My wife speaks good French. I understand only one out of every five words, but always *'de Gaulle.'* "

President Kennedy, as the guest of French president Charles de Gaulle, attended a Paris ballet on the evening of June 1, 1961.

At one point during intermission de Gaulle admitted a group of French photographers briefly for a historic photograph with JFK, then dismissed them with a flick of his finger.

"Don't you wish you could control your photographers like that?" one reporter asked JFK.

The American President replied, "You must remember that I wasn't recalled to office as my country's savior."

DELAWARE COUNTY, PENNSYLVANIA

I was informed when I started out this morning that we were going to travel in Delaware County, which voted 8 to 1 for Alf Landon. We are going to wipe that record out. No county in the United States should have that reputation.

—Norristown, Pennsylvania, October 29, 1960

DEMOCRACY

Freedom of the individual is in essence democracy.

—*Why England Slept*, 1940, "Conclusion"

We can proudly say that no secular idea has taken such a powerful hold on man's imagination as the idea of democracy which has gone forth from this hemisphere.

—San José, Costa Rica, March 19, 1963

For democracy means much more than popular government and majority rule, much more than a system of political techniques to flatter or deceive powerful blocks of voters. A democracy that has no George Norris [a Republican Senator from Nebraska (1912–1942) whose disregard for the limitations of party politics ultimately cost him his Senate seat] to point to—no monument of individual conscience in a sea of popular rule—is not worthy to bear the name.

—*Profiles in Courage*, 1956

Democracy and capitalism are institutions which are geared for a world at peace. It is our problem to find a method of protecting them in a world at war.

—*Why England Slept*, 1940, "Conclusion"

I believe it is one of democracy's failings that it seeks to make scapegoats for its own weaknesses.

—*Why England Slept*, 1940, "Conclusion"

Imported democracy is never as meaningful or viable as the domestic brand.

—San Juan, Puerto Rico, December 15, 1958

DEMOCRACY AND FREEDOM

No area of the world has ever had an overabundance of democracy and freedom.

—Zionists' convention, New York City, August 26, 1960

DEMOCRACY'S WEAKNESSES

JFK concluded his Harvard honors thesis (published as *Why England Slept*, 1940) with a perceptive critique of democracy:

> We must be prepared to recognize democracy's weaknesses and capitalism's weaknesses in competition with a totalitarian form of government. We must realize that one is a system geared for peace, the other for war. We must recognize that while one may have greater endurance, it is not immune to swift destruction by the other.
>
> I say, therefore, that democracy's weaknesses are great in competing with a totalitarian system. Democracy is a superior form of government, because it is based on a respect for man as a reasonable being. *For the long run*, then, democracy is superior. But for the short run, democracy has great weaknesses.
>
> When it competes with a system of government which cares nothing for permanency, a system built primarily for war, democracy, which is built primarily for peace, is at a disadvantage. And democracy must recognize its weaknesses; it must learn to safeguard its institutions if it hopes to survive.

(see DICTATORSHIP)

DICTATORSHIP

We concede that a dictatorship does have great advantages. We concede that the regimentation and the unification achieved by force and propaganda will give a dictator an initial jump on his opponents. However, we believe that a democracy can, by voluntary action, equal this effort when the emergency comes and sustain it over a longer period of time. We believe that groups will co-ordinate their private interests with national interest, thus giving a greater force and vigor than could have been attained by totalitarian methods.

—*Why England Slept*, 1940, "Conclusion"

DIFFERENCES

If we cannot end now our differences, at least we can help make the world safe for diversity.

—commencement, American University, June 10, 1963

DINNER SPEECHES

"I recognize tonight that I bear a heavy responsibility of having kept a distinguished group of Americans who paid $125 for this dinner," Jack Kennedy apologized to the swank crowd at the Eleanor Roosevelt Cancer Foundation Dinner in New York.

"But, I wish to say that—if I may quote an old East Side expression—what you have lost on bananas, you are going to make up on the apples, because this could have been one of the longest dinners in the history of these occasions.

"Lyndon [Johnson] is good for forty-five minutes, when he is given a chance; Ambassador Stevenson has been known to go for a very long time; Frank Pace has a very long story to tell; and Bob Hope will, if called upon. So this might have gone to one or two in the morning but, because of my imminent journey to Paris, you'll be out—hungry, rather unhappy—but you will be home tonight.

"I also want to commend this idea of the $250 dinner.

This is like that story of the award of prizes by the Moscow Cultural Center, the first prize being one week in Kiev and the second prize being two weeks. For $100 you get speeches, for $250 you don't get any speeches. You can't get bargains like that anymore."

(see DINNER TICKET PRICES)

DINNER TICKET PRICES

"I have a few opening announcements," the President addressed a White House correspondents' dinner in 1962, shortly after his dramatic clash with the steel industry over the increase in steel prices. Demonstrating a talent for self-parody, JFK railed against the rise in dinner ticket prices.

"First, the sudden and arbitrary action of the officers of this organization in increasing the price of dinner tickets by two dollars and fifty cents over last year constitutes a wholly unjustifiable defiance of the public interest. If this increase is not rescinded but is imitated by the Gridiron, Radio-TV, and other dinners, it will have a serious impact on the entire economy of this city. In this serious hour in our nation's history, when newsmen are awakened in the middle of the night to be given a front page story, when expense accounts are being scrutinized by the Congress, when correspondents are required to leave their families for long and lonely weekends at Palm Beach, the American people will find it hard to accept this ruthless decision made by a tiny handful of executives whose only interest is the pursuit of pleasure. I am hopeful that the Women's Press Club will not join this price rise and will thereby force a rescission."

DIPLOMACY

Diplomacy and defense are no longer distinct alternatives, one to be used where the other fails; each must complement the other.

—message to Congress, March 28, 1961
(see DEFENSE)

DISARMAMENT

Men may no longer pretend that the quest for disarmament is a sign of weakness—for in a spiraling arms race, a nation's security may well be shrinking even as its arms increase.

—address to the United Nations General Assembly, September 25, 1961
(see ARMS, PEACE, UNITED NATIONS, WAR)

DISCRIMINATION

I know that some of you have experienced discrimination in this country. But I ask you to believe me when I tell you that this is not the wish of most Americans, that we share your regret and resentment, and that we intend to end such practices for all time to come, not only for our visitors but for our own citizens as well.

—United Nations address, September 20, 1963

DIVERSITY

We can welcome diversity; the Communists cannot. For we offer a world of choice; they offer the world of coercion.

—State of the Union message, January 11, 1962

DOGS IN SPACE

"It is, I think, a source of concern to us all that the first dogs carried around in outer space were not named Rover and Fido but instead were named Belka and Strelka," JFK commented at a campaign stop in Muskegon, Michigan, on September 5, 1960, adding, with a reference to Vice President Nixon's dog: "It was not named Checkers, either."

(see SPACE RACE)

DOMESTIC AFFAIRS

Today the safety of all the world—the very future of freedom—depends as never before upon the sensible and clear-headed management of the domestic affairs of the United States.

—commencement, Yale University, June 11, 1962

DONKEY

"I have been presented with this donkey by two young ladies down there for my daughter." JFK held up a toy donkey at a West Virginia fair. "My daughter has the greatest collection of donkeys. She doesn't even know what an elephant looks like. We are going to protect her from that knowledge."

(see ELEPHANTS)

DREAM

In 1958 there were three leading Democratic front-runners for the 1960 presidential nomination: John F. Kennedy, Stuart Symington, and Lyndon Baines Johnson.

JFK liked to tell this story of a dream he had about the

three of them: "Several nights ago I dreamed that the good Lord touched me on the shoulder and said, 'Don't worry, you'll be the Democratic Presidential nominee in 1960. What's more, you'll be elected.' I told Stu Symington about my dream. 'Funny thing,' said Stu, 'I had exactly the same dream about myself.' We both told our dreams to Lyndon Johnson, and Johnson said, 'That's funny. For the life of me, I can't remember tapping either of you two boys for the job.' "

DUCK

A friend, comparing common backgrounds with Jack Kennedy, including Choate prep school, concluded that the two of them were very much alike and said so.

"You're not at all like me," replied JFK. "You walk like a duck."

EARTH

The earth can be an abundant mother to all of the people that will be born in the coming years if we learn how to use her with skill and wisdom to heal her wounds, replenish her vitality, and utilize her potentialities. And the necessity is now urgent and worldwide.

—National Academy of Sciences, October 22, 1963

EASTER

President Kennedy's personal secretary, Evelyn Lincoln, recalled first meeting JFK in 1952, when Senator Kennedy was preparing to leave town for Easter recess. He dictated dozens of instructions to another secretary, then added, "Oh yes, one last thing. Easter Sunday." He hesitated as the woman's face sank. "Yes, Easter Sunday." He laughed and added, "You can take Easter Sunday off."

EATING WORDS

A reporter seized upon an apparent change in President Kennedy's position at a press conference on March 7, 1962, and asked if the president was going to "eat" his words.

"Well," said JFK, "I'm going to have a dinner for all the people who've written it [that he would make a retraction] and we'll see who eats what."

ECONOMIC DECLINE

The nation cannot, and will not, be satisfied with economic decline and slack.

—message on Economic Recovery and Growth, February 2, 1961

ECONOMIC GROWTH

The United States cannot afford, in this time of national need and world crisis, to dissipate its opportunities for *economic growth.*

Our rate of growth has slowed down disturbingly.

Our potential growth rate can and should be increased. To do so, we propose to expand the nation's investments in physical and human resources, and in science and technology.

—message on Economic Recovery and Growth, February 2, 1961

The processes of growth are gradual, bearing fruit in a decade, not a day.

—State of the Union message, January 14, 1963

(see BALANCED BUDGET, SCIENCE, TECHNOLOGICAL CHANGE)

ECONOMIC SECURITY

I say that economic security is the No. 1 issue today.

—remarks at AFL-CIO convention, November 15, 1963

ECONOMY

Soon after President Kennedy blocked the steel price hike in 1961, as he liked to tell the story, he was visited by a prominent businessman who was gloomy about the economy.

"Things look great," JFK reassured the businessman. "Why, if I weren't President, I'd be buying stock myself."

"If you weren't President," replied the businessman, "so would I."

The history of our economy has been one of rising productivity, based on improvement in skills, advances in technology and a growing supply of more efficient tools and equipment.

—message to Congress, April 20, 1961

We shall be judged more by what we do at home than by what we preach abroad. . . . Nothing our opponents could do to encourage their own ambitions would encourage them half so much as a chronic lagging United States economy.

—State of the Union message, January 14, 1963

On the strength of our free economy rests the hope of all free nations. We shall not fail that hope, for free men and free nations must prosper and they must prevail.

—at the Economic Club of New York, December 14, 1962

(see BUSINESS, ECONOMIC GROWTH, MODERNIZATION)

EDUCATION

Urging passage of his education bill, President Kennedy, in his second State of the Union address on January 11, 1962, quoted H. G. Wells. " 'Civilization,' said H. G. Wells, 'is a race between education and catastrophe.' It is up to you in this Congress to determine the winner of that race."

Upon education rests the fate of the nation.

—*NEA Journal*, January 1958

There is no greater asset in this country than an educated man or woman.

—commencement, San Diego State College, June 6, 1963

No country can possibly move ahead, no free society can possibly be sustained, unless it has an educated citizenry.

—commencement, San Diego State College, June 6, 1963

Our progress as a nation can be no swifter than our progress in education. Our requirements for world leadership, our hopes for economic growth, and the demands of citizenship itself in an area such as this all require the maximum development of every young American's capacity.

The human mind is our fundamental resource.

—message to Congress, February 20, 1961

The first question, and the most important is: does every American boy and girl have an opportunity to develop whatever talents he or she has? All of us do not have equal talent, but all of us should have an equal opportunity to develop our talents.

—commencement, San Diego State College, June 6, 1963

American children today do not yet enjoy equal educational opportunities for two primary reasons: One is economic and the other is racial. If our nation is to meet the goal of giving every American child a fair chance—because an uneducated child makes an uneducated parent, who in another day produces another uneducated child—we must move ahead swiftly in both areas.

—commencement, San Diego State College, June 6, 1963

It does no good . . . to say that that is the business of another state. It is the business of our country. These young, uneducated boys and girls know no state boundaries and they come West as well as North and East. They are your citizens as well as citizens of this country.

—commencement, San Diego State College, June 6, 1963

EDUCATION AND GOVERNMENT

Education must remain a matter of state and local control, and higher education a matter of individual choice. But education is increasingly expensive. Too many state and local governments lack the resources to assure an adequate education for every child. Too many classrooms are overcrowded. Too many teachers are underpaid. Too many talented individuals cannot afford the benefits of higher education.

Our twin goals must be: a new standard of excellence in education, and the availability of such excellence to all who are willing and able to pursue it.

—message to Congress on education, February 20, 1961

Crucial questions confront America today: Will we provide world leadership or display fatal weakness? Will we succeed or fail in the struggle for survival during the years to come?

The answers, I sincerely believe, depend on whether our educational system is capable of meeting the challenge of today or whether a shortage of teachers, classrooms, and money—with a consequent lack of high-quality *education*—will prove in the long run to be the undoing of our nation.

—*NEA Journal*, January 1958

(see GRADUATE EDUCATION, LEADERSHIP AND LEARNING)

EISENHOWER, DWIGHT D.

JFK joked that the worse Eisenhower did as President, the more popular he became with the public. When a Gallup Poll taken after the ill-fated Bay of Pigs invasion revealed that President Kennedy's own popularity was higher than ever—with an 83 percent approval rating—he shook his head and said, "My God, it's as bad as Eisenhower!"

ELEPHANTS

"While we meet here tonight in the Golden Gate of California, the rescue squad has been completing its operation in the city of New York," JFK said at the Cow Palace in San Francisco a week before the election in 1960, and commented on the Republican leadership meeting in New York.

"Governor Rockefeller, Henry Cabot Lodge, Vice-President Nixon, and President Eisenhower all rode together. I thought it was very unfair not to have Barry Goldwater along.

"We have all seen those circus elephants, complete with tusks, ivory in their heads and thick skins, who move around the circus ring and grab the tail of the elephant ahead of them."

(see DONKEY)

EMANCIPATION PROCLAMATION CENTENNIAL

One hundred years ago the Emancipation Proclamation was signed by a President who believed in the equal worth and opportunity of every human being. That Proclamation was only a first step—a step which its author unhappily did not live to follow up, a step which some of its critics dismissed as an action which "frees the slave but ignores the Negro."

Through these long one hundred years, while slavery has vanished, progress for the Negro has been too often blocked and delayed. Equality before the law has not always meant equal treatment and opportunity. And the harmful, wasteful and wrongful results of racial discrimination and segregation still appear in virtually every aspect of national life, in virtually every part of the nation.

The Negro baby born in America today—regardless of the section or state in which he is born—has about one-half as much chance of completing high school as a white baby born in the same place on the same day—one-third as much chance of becoming a professional man—twice as much chance of becoming unemployed. . . .

No American who believes in the basic truth that "all men are created equal, that they are endowed by their Creator with certain unalienable Rights," can fully excuse, explain or defend the picture these statistics portray.

Race discrimination hampers our economic growth by preventing the maximum development and utilization of our manpower. It hampers our world leadership by contradicting at home the message we preach abroad. It mars the atmosphere of a united and classless society in which this Nation rose to greatness.

It increases the costs of public welfare, crime, delinquency and disorder. Above all, it is wrong.

Therefore, let it be clear, in our own hearts and minds,

that it is not merely because of the Cold War, and not merely because of the economic waste of discrimination, that we are committed to achieving true equality of opportunity. The basic reason is because it is right.

—message to Congress, February 28, 1963

EMPLOYMENT GROWTH

There will be new employment in our growth industries —and this will come mostly in our high-wage industries, which are our most competitive abroad.

—at Conference on Trade Policy, May 17, 1962

(see ECONOMIC GROWTH)

ENDORSEMENT

"This district was the first district to endorse me as a candidate for President, nearly a year ago," Jack Kennedy gratefully acknowledged an enthusiastic reception in Brooklyn on October 27, 1960. "My family had not even endorsed me when you endorsed me."

ENEMIES

The common enemies of man [are] tyranny, poverty, disease and war itself.

—inaugural address, January 20, 1961

We must remember that there are no permanent enemies. Hostility today is a fact, but it is not a ruling law.

—address to Irish parliament, June 28, 1963

ENERGY

Observing a small boy crawling restlessly back and forth, President Kennedy nodded approval. "Well, I suppose if you could have only one thing, it would be that—energy. Without it, you haven't got a thing."

ENGLAND

John Kennedy's Harvard thesis (published in 1940 as *Why England Slept*) begins with a single question: "Why was England so poorly prepared for the war?" The remainder of the book is the author's answer to this question:

"Thus, bearing in mind the strangely similar condition America may be called on to face, let us study the story of British rearmament. England made many mistakes; she is paying heavily for them now. In studying the reasons why England slept, let us try to profit by them and save ourselves her anguish."

JFK concludes the book with a warning of American military unpreparedness, prophetic words published the year before the surprise attack on Pearl Harbor:

> We should profit by the lesson of England and make our democracy work. We must make it work right now.
>
> For England has been a testing ground. It has been a case of a democratic form of government, with a capitalistic economy, trying to compete with the new totalitarian system, based on an economy of rigid state control. For a country whose government and economic structure is similar to England's and which may some day be similarly in competition with a dictatorship, there should be a valuable lesson.
>
> Like England, we will be a democracy competing with a dictatorship. Like England, our capitalist economy will be competing with the rigid totalitarianism of the dictatorships. Like England, our armaments will have to be paid for out of our national budget. Like England, a towering national debt may appear to us more dangerous than any external menace. Like England, we have general commitments that we may not be able to fill. . . . And, like England, we have always considered ourselves invulnerable

from invasion. But the airplane changed this position for England and may change it for us.

—*Why England Slept*, 1940
(see DEFENSE)

EQUAL RIGHTS

We are confronted primarily with a moral issue. It is as old as the Scriptures and is as clear as the American Constitution. The heart of the question is whether all Americans are to be afforded equal rights and equal opportunities, whether we are going to treat our fellow Americans as we want to be treated.

—address to the nation, June 11, 1963

This is one country. It has become one country because all of us and all the people who came here had an equal chance to develop their talents. We cannot say to 10 percent of the population that they can't have that right; that their children can't have the chance to develop whatever talents they have; that the only way that they are going to get their rights is to go into the streets and demonstrate. I think we owe them and we owe ourselves a better country than that.

—television address to the nation, June 11, 1963

EQUALITY

Equality in America has never meant literal equality of condition or capacity; there will always be inequalities of condition or capacity; there will always be inequalities in character and ability in any society. Equality has meant . . . that in a democratic society there should be no inequalities in opportunities or in freedoms.

—*The Immigrant Contribution*, Chapter 5

This nation was founded by men of many nations and backgrounds. It was founded on the principle that all men are created equal, and that the rights of every man are diminished when the rights of one man are threatened.

—television address to the nation, June 11, 1963
(see CIVIL RIGHTS)

EUROPE

The United States cannot withdraw from *Europe,* unless and until Europe should wish us gone. We cannot distinguish its defenses from our own.

—remarks at trade conference, May 17, 1962

War in Europe, as we learned twice in forty years, destroys peace in America. A threat to the freedom of Europe is a threat to the freedom of America.

—remarks in Frankfurt, Germany, June 25, 1963

Our policies in Europe today are founded on one deep conviction: that the threat to Western Europe and freedom is basically indivisible, as is the Western deterrent to that threat. The United States, therefore, is committed to the defense of Europe, by history as well as by choice.

—remarks at trade conference, May 17, 1962

Free Europe is entering into a new phase in its long and brilliant history. The era of colonial expansion has passed; the era of national rivalries is fading; and a new era of interdependence and unity is taking shape. Defying the old prophecies of Marx, consenting to what no conqueror could ever compel, the free nations of Europe are moving toward a unity of purpose and power and policy in every sphere of activity.

—State of the Union message, January 14, 1963

EUROPEAN COMMON MARKET

But the greatest challenge of all is posed by the growth of the European Common Market. . . . There will arise across the Atlantic a trading partner behind a single external tariff similar to ours with an economy which nearly equals our own. Will we in this country adapt our thinking to these new prospects and patterns, or will we wait until events have passed us by?

—State of the Union message, January 11, 1962

EVIL

No government or social system is so evil that its people must be considered lacking in virtue.

—commencement, American University, June 10, 1963

EXCELLENCE

I have tried to make the whole tone and thrust of this office and this administration one that will demand a higher standard of excellence from every individual.

—letter to *Newsday*, May 11, 1961

EXERCISE

The Greeks sought excellence not only in philosophy and drama and sculpture and architecture, but in athletics. The same people who produced the poetry of Homer and the wisdom of Plato and Aristotle—they also produced the Olympic Games. The Greeks understood that mind and body must develop in harmonious proportion to produce a creative intelligence. And so did the most brilliant intelligence of our earliest days, Thomas Jefferson, when he said, "Not less than two hours a day should be devoted to exercise." If a man who wrote the Declaration of Independence, was Secretary of State, and twice President could give it two hours, our children can give it ten or fifteen minutes.

We are under-exercised as a nation. We look, instead of play. We ride, instead of walk. Our existence deprives us of the minimum of physical activity essential for healthy living. And the remedy, in my judgment, lies in one direction; that is, in developing programs for broad participation in exercise by all our young men and women—all of our boys and girls.

—National Football Foundation, Hall of Fame banquet, December 5, 1961
(see JEFFERSON, THOMAS; PHYSICAL FITNESS)

EXPERIENCE

He was too young, he lacked "experience"—that is what the opposition had to say about John Kennedy running for President. He addressed the experience issue in Minneapolis in October 1960:

"Ladies and gentlemen, the outstanding news story of this week was not the events of the United Nations or even the Presidential campaign. It was a story coming out of my city of Boston that Ted Williams of the Boston Red Sox had retired from baseball. It seems that at forty-two he was too old. It shows that perhaps experience isn't enough."

Kennedy shrugged off Nixon's supposed "experience" advantage.

"Mr. Nixon may be very experienced in his kitchen debates. So are a great many other married men I know."

Jack Kennedy kidded with reporters about the "experience" issue at a Gridiron dinner later that year: "On this matter of experience, I had announced earlier this year that if successful I would not consider campaign contributions as a substitute for experience in appointing Ambassadors. Ever since I made that statement I have not received one single cent from my father."

FAILURE

"The Republican National Committee recently adopted a resolution saying you were pretty much of a failure," stated an aggressive reporter at a press conference on July 17, 1963. "How do you feel about that?"

President Kennedy, instead of defending himself against the charge of failure, shrugged and said, smiling, "I assume it passed unanimously."

(see COMPLIMENTS)

FAIR RETURN

A fair return is a necessity for labor, capital and management in industry.

—message to Congress, March 16, 1961

FAMILY OF MAN

Just as the Family of Man is not limited to a single race or religion, neither can it be limited to a single city or country. The Family of Man is more than three billion strong. It lives in more than one hundred nations. Most of its members are not white. Most of them are not Christians. Most of them know nothing about free enterprise or due process of law.

If our society is to promote the Family of Man, let us realize the magnitude of our task. This is a sobering assignment, for the Family of Man in the world of today is not faring well.

Even little wars are dangerous in this nuclear world. The long labor of peace is an undertaking for every nation, large and small, for every member of the Family of Man. "In this effort none of us can remain unaligned. To this goal none can be uncommitted." If the Family of Man cannot achieve greater unity and harmony, the very planet which serves as its home may find its future in peril.

But there are other troubles besetting the human family. Many of its members live in poverty and misery and despair.

For the blessings of life have not been distributed evenly to the Family of Man. Life expectancy in this most fortunate of nations has reached the Biblical three score years and ten; but in the less developed nations of Africa, Asia and Latin America, the overwhelming majority of infants cannot expect to live even two score years and five. In those vast continents, more than half the children of primary school age are not in school. More than half the families live in substandard dwellings. More than half the people live on less than $100 a year. Two out of every three adults are illiterate.

The Family of Man can survive the differences of race

and religion. Contrary to the assertions of Mr. Khrushchev, it can accept differences of ideology, politics and economics. But it cannot survive in the form in which we know it a nuclear war—and neither can it long endure the growing gulf between the rich and the poor.

—remarks to Protestant Council, November 8, 1963

FANATICISM

So long as fanaticism and fear brood over the affairs of men, we must arm to deter others from aggression.

—State of the Union message, January 11, 1962

FARMER

"I understand near here there was a farmer who planted some corn. He said to his neighbor, 'I hope I break even this year. I really need the money.' "

Kennedy's voice rose.

"The farmer is the only man in our economy who buys everything at retail, sells everything he sells at wholesale, and pays the freight both ways."

Kennedy's voice rose higher.

"What's wrong with the American fah-mah today?" JFK, with his Cape Cod accent, was passionately addressing a group of farmers in Sioux City, Iowa, about the agricultural depression.

As he paused dramatically for a moment, one of the farmers yelled out: "He's stah-ving!"

The audience laughed, and so did JFK.

Automation has hit the farmers much harder than it has hit any other element in our community, and their production is growing faster than our consumption.

—news conference, Washington, D.C., May 22, 1963

Our farmers deserve praise, not condemnation; and their efficiency should be a cause for gratitude, not something for which they are penalized. For their very efficiency and productivity lies at the heart of the distress in American agriculture.

—message to Congress, March 16, 1961

Abundant production has filled our bins and warehouses, but one out of ten American households has a diet so inadequate that it falls below two-thirds of the standard nutrition requirements. These paradoxes are of concern to all of us: the farmer, the taxpayer and the consumer.

—message to Congress, March 16, 1961

FATHER

"Caroline's very bright," Joseph Kennedy once commented on his granddaughter to Jack Kennedy, "smarter than you were, Jack, at that age."

"Yes, she is," Jack agreed. "But look who *she* has for a father."

(see KENNEDY entries)

FEDERAL GOVERNMENT

The Federal Government is not a stranger or an enemy. It is the people of 50 states joining in a national effort to seek progress in every state.

—Muscle Shoals, Alabama, May 18, 1963

(see BIG GOVERNMENT)

FINGER PAINTING

As a joke, Jackie Kennedy framed a group of gaudy finger paintings featuring blobs of red, yellow, and blue. She presented it to the President as the latest effort by their painter friend, Bill Walton.

Jackie said shyly that she had paid $600 for it.

President Kennedy did not flinch at the price, but he nevertheless appeared quite perplexed by the far-out "abstract" turn Walton seemed to have taken.

When Jackie confessed that the artist was their daughter Caroline, JFK shrugged and said, "Pretty good color."

(see KENNEDY, CAROLINE; WYETH, ANDREW)

FLORIDA

"I come here to Florida today where my family has lived for thirty years," John Kennedy said with some confidence at a campaign stop in Miami a month before the Presidential election, "and I feel it looks pretty good to get at least two votes in Florida."

JFK went on to say a few words about the Florida economy. "Those of you who live in this State of Florida depend upon a moving and expanding country. I know something about the economy of this state. When the rest of the country catches cold, Florida gets pneumonia and Miami is very sick."

FOOTBALL

"I want to express my thanks to you for this award." President Kennedy accepted an award as an honorary member of the Football Hall of Fame at the National Football Foundation and Hall of Fame Banquet.

"Politics is an astonishing profession—it has permitted me to go from being an obscure lieutenant serving under General MacArthur to Commander in Chief in 14 years, without any technical competence whatsoever; and it's also enabled me to go from being an obscure member of the junior varsity at Harvard to being an honorary member of the Football Hall of Fame."

Football is far too much a sport for the few who can play it well. The rest of us—and too many of our children—get our exercise from climbing up to the seats in stadiums, or from walking across the room to turn on our television sets. And this is true for one sport after another, all across the board.

—National Football Foundation, Hall of Fame banquet, December 5, 1961
(see EXERCISE, PARTICIPATION)

FOREIGN AID

The fundamental task of our foreign aid program . . . is to help make an historical demonstration that in the twentieth century as in the nineteenth, in the southern half of the globe as in the north, economic growth and political democracy can develop hand in hand.

—message to Congress, March 22, 1961

FOREIGN POLICY

Americans have come a long way to accepting in a short time the necessity of world involvement, but the strain of this involvement remains and we find it all over the country.

We find ourselves entangled with apparently unanswerable problems in unpronounceable places. We discover that our enemy in one decade is our ally the next. We find ourselves committed to governments whose actions we cannot often approve, assisting societies with principles very different from our own.

It is little wonder that there is a desire in the country to go back to the time when our nation lived alone. . . .

This is an understandable effort to recover an old feeling of simplicity, yet in world affairs, as in all other aspects of our lives, the days of the quiet past are gone forever. Science and technology are irreversible.

—remarks at the Mormon Tabernacle, September 26, 1963

There is no single simple policy which meets this challenge. Experience has taught us that no one nation has the power or the wisdom to solve all the problems of the world or manage its revolutionary tides; that extending our commitments does not always increase our security; that any initiative carries with it the risk of a temporary defeat; that nuclear weapons cannot prevent subversion; that no free peoples can be kept free without will and energy of their own; and that no two nations or situations are exactly alike.

—message to Congress, May 25, 1961

Our task is to pursue a policy of patiently encouraging freedom and carefully pressuring tyranny—a policy that looks toward evolution, not revolution—a policy that depends on peace, not war.

—Polish-American Congress, Chicago, October 1, 1960
(see DIPLOMACY, NEGOTIATIONS)

FRANCE

French President de Gaulle announced that France had developed her own nuclear force to be independent of the United States. Soon afterward, President Kennedy accepted a loan of the *Mona Lisa* from the French Minister of Culture.

"We in the United States are grateful for this loan from the leading artistic power in the world, France. I must note further that this painting has been kept under careful French control. And I want to make it clear that, grateful as we are for this painting, we will continue to press ahead with the effort to develop an independent artistic force and power of our own."

During his visit to Paris, on June 1, 1961, President Kennedy addressed his hosts in Paris. "A few years ago it was said that the optimists learned Russian and the pessimists learned Chinese. I prefer to think that those with vision studied French and English."

(see GOLD)

FREE

If the self-discipline of the free cannot match the iron discipline of the mailed fist—in economic, political, scientific and all the other kinds of struggles as well as the military—then the peril to freedom will continue to rise.

—American Society of Newspaper Editors, April 20, 1961

FREE CHOICE

The issue in the world struggle is not Communism versus capitalism, but coercion versus a free choice.

—State of the Union message, January 14, 1963

FREE ECONOMY

We can show the whole world that a free economy need not be an unstable economy, that a free system need not leave men unemployed, and that a free society is not only the most productive but the most stable form of organization yet fashioned by men.

—State of the Union message, January 11, 1962

On the strength of our free economy rests the hope of all free nations. We shall not fail that hope, for free men and free nations must prosper and they must prevail.

—Economic Club of New York, December 14, 1962

FREE EXPRESSION

New means should be found for promoting the free expression and trade of ideas, through travel and communication, and through increased exchanges of people and books and broadcasts. For as the world renounces the competition of weapons, competition in ideas must flourish, and that competition must be as full and as fair as possible.

—United Nations address, September 20, 1963

FREE PEOPLE

For a city or a people to be truly free, they must have the secure right, without economic, political, or police pressure, to make their own choice and to live their own lives.

—United Nations address, September 25, 1961

FREE WORLD

We in the free world are moving steadily toward unity and cooperation, in the teeth of the old Bolshevik prophecy, and at the very time when extraordinary rumbles of discord can be heard across the Iron Curtain. It is not free societies which bear within them the seeds of inevitable disunity.

—State of the Union Message, January 11, 1962

FREEDOM

I am here to promote the freedom doctrine.

—message to Congress, May 25, 1961

The way of the past shows clearly that freedom, not coercion, is the wave of the future.

—State of the Union message, January 11, 1962

Freedom is not merely a word or an abstract theory, but the most effective instrument for advancing the welfare of man.

—Punta del Este, Uruguay, August 5, 1961

What freedom alone can bring is the liberation of the human mind and spirit which finds its greatest flowering in the free society.

—on the National Cultural Center, November 29, 1962

We stand for freedom. That is our conviction for ourselves; that is our only commitment to others. No friend, no neutral and no adversary should think otherwise. We are not against any man, or any nation, or any system, except as it is hostile to freedom.

—message to Congress, May 25, 1961

The central issue of freedom, however, is between those who believe in self-determination and those in the East who would impose on others the harsh and oppressive Communist system.

—address to Irish parliament, June 28, 1963

Freedom of local governments from centralized control is one of the cornerstones upon which we have erected our democracy.

—*Why England Slept*, 1940, "Conclusion"

While we shall negotiate freely, we shall not negotiate *freedom*.

—University of Washington, November 16, 1961

It is increasingly clear that nations united in freedom are better able to build their economies than those that are repressed by tyranny.

—remarks at NATO headquarters, Naples, Italy, July 2, 1963

We possess weapons of tremendous power, but they are least effective in combating the weapons most often used by freedom's foes: subversion, infiltration and civil disorder.

—University of Washington, Seattle, November 16, 1961

In today's world, freedom can be lost without a shot being fired, by ballots as well as bullets.

—from undelivered speech, Dallas, November 22, 1963
(see FREEDOM'S ADVERSARIES, LIBERTY, UNITED STATES)

FREEDOM OF INFORMATION

We seek a free flow of information across national boundaries and oceans, across iron curtains and stone walls. We are not afraid to entrust the American people with unpleasant facts, foreign ideas, alien philosophies and competitive values. For a nation that is afraid to let its people judge the truth and falsehood in an open market is a nation that is afraid of its people.

—to employees of Voice of America on its 20th anniversary, Washington, D.C., February 26, 1962

FREEDOM'S ADVERSARIES

The adversaries of freedom . . . their aggression is more often concealed than open. They have fired no missiles, and their troops are seldom seen. . . . But where fighting is required, it is usually done by others, by guerillas striking at night, by assassins striking alone—by subversives and saboteurs and insurrectionists, who in some cases control whole areas inside of independent nations. With these formidable weapons, the adversaries of freedom plan to consolidate their territory, to exploit, to control, and finally to destroy . . .

—message to Congress, May 25, 1961

FROST, ROBERT

John Kennedy liked to quote well-known poets. One of his favorites was Robert Frost. JFK once concluded a speech at New York University: "But I have promises to keep . . . And miles to go before I sleep . . . And miles to go before I sleep." He paused and added: "And now I go to Brooklyn."

"Great idea!" JFK responded enthusiastically when it was suggested he invite Robert Frost to speak at the Inauguration. "But with Frost's skill with words, people will remember his speech instead of mine. I think we'd better have him read a poem."

He was supremely two things: an artist and an American. A nation reveals itself not only by the men it produces but also by the men it honors, the men it remembers.

—Amherst College, Massachusetts, October 26, 1963

FUND-RAISING

President Kennedy spoke at many $100-a-plate fund-raising dinners. "I am deeply touched," he said at one such fund-raiser on September 23, 1960, in Salt Lake City, "not as deeply touched as you have been by coming to this dinner, but nevertheless, it is a sentimental occasion."

JFK went on to say: "I don't know whether you realize that this is an historic occasion. We have paid off nearly $4,000,000 that the Kennedy-Johnson ticket ran up in November of 1960. It is now gone forever, which is sad, and all we have left is the Federal deficit."

(see DINNER TICKET PRICES)

FUTURE

The wave of the future is not the conquest of the world by a single dogmatic creed but the liberation of the diverse energies of free nations and free men.

—address at the University of California, Berkeley, March 23, 1962

Change is the law of life. And those who look only to the past or the present are certain to miss the future.

—remarks in Frankfurt, Germany, June 25, 1963

Hold fast to the best of the past and move fast to the best of the future.

—address at Vanderbilt University, May 18, 1963

G

GENERATION

John F. Kennedy saw himself as a spokesman for a generation as well as a nation. "The events and decisions of the next ten months may well decide the fate of man for the next ten thousand years," JFK told the United Nations on September 25, 1961. "There will be no avoiding these events. There will be no appeal from these decisions. And we shall be remembered either as the generation that turned this planet into a flaming funeral pyre or the generation that met its vow 'to save succeeding generations from the scourge of war.' "

The generation which I speak for has seen enough of warmongers. Let our great role in history be that of peacemakers.

—Cow Palace, San Francisco, November 2, 1960

I do not want it said of our generation what T. S. Eliot wrote in his poem "The Rock"—"and the wind shall say:

'these were decent people, their only monument the asphalt road and a thousand lost golf balls.' " We can do better than that.

—Columbus, Ohio, October 17, 1960

Never before has man had such capacity to control his own environment—to end thirst and hunger, to conquer poverty and disease, to banish illiteracy and massive human misery. We have the power to make this the best generation of mankind in the history of the world or to make it the last.

—United Nations address, September 20, 1963

GENIUS

"Genius can speak at any time, and the entire world will hear it and listen." President Kennedy spoke at a fundraiser for the National Cultural Center on November 29, 1962. "Behind the storm of daily conflict and crisis, the dramatic confrontations, the tumult of political struggle, the poet, the artist, the musician, continues the quiet work of centuries, building bridges of experience between peoples, reminding man of the universality of his feelings and desires and despairs, and reminding him that the forces that unite are deeper than those that divide."

In 1964 the National Cultural Center was renamed the John F. Kennedy Center for the Performing Arts.

GERMAN

Today there are no exclusively German problems, or American problems, or even European problems. There are world problems, and our two countries and continents are inextricably bound together in the tasks of peace as well as war.

—remarks in Frankfurt, Germany, June 25, 1963

GERMANY

What does liberty require? The answer is clear: a united Berlin in a united Germany, united by self-determination and living in peace. This right of free choice is no special privilege claimed by the Germans alone. It is an elemental requirement of human justice.

—address at the Free University, West Berlin, June 26, 1963

GOALS

Our goal is not the victory of might, but the vindication of right; not peace at the expense of freedom, but both peace *and* freedom, here in this hemisphere, and, we hope, around the world. God willing, that goal will be achieved.

—television address to the nation, October 22, 1962

Yet our basic goal remains the same: a peaceful world community of free and independent states, free to choose their own future and their own system, so long as it does not threaten the freedom of others.

—State of the Union message, January 11, 1962

We will not reach that goal today, or tomorrow. We may not reach it in our lifetime. But the quest is the greatest adventure of our century.

—State of the Union message, January 11, 1962

GOD

The supreme reality of our time is our indivisibility as children of God and our common vulnerability on this planet.

—address to Irish parliament, June 28, 1963
(see PRAY)

GOLD

During their 1961 visit to France, President Kennedy and Mrs. Kennedy stayed in a Quai d'Orsay suite with a gold bathtub. Noting the extravagance, JFK remarked, "It may seem funny to us, but maybe it's a better use for gold than locking it up in Fort Knox."

GOLDBERG, ARTHUR

Addressing the AFL-CIO Convention, President Kennedy teased his Secretary of Labor.

> I am delighted to be here with you and with the Secretary of Labor, Arthur Goldberg. I was up in New York, stressing physical fitness, and in line with that, Arthur went over with a group to Switzerland to climb some of the mountains there. They got up about five and he was in bed. He got up to join them later and when they all came back at four o'clock in the afternoon he didn't come back with them.
>
> So they sent out search parties and there was not a sign that afternoon and night. The next day the Red Cross went out and around, calling: "Goldberg, Goldberg! It's the Red Cross!" Then this voice came down from the mountain: "I gave at the office!"

GOLDWATER, BARRY

Barry Goldwater, a good photographer, snapped a photograph of President Kennedy and sent it to him for an autograph.

It came back to Senator Goldwater with this inscription:

> "For Barry Goldwater, whom I urge to follow the career for which he has shown so much talent—photography. From his friend, John Kennedy."

GOLF

"You're yelling for that damn ball to go in the hole and I'm watching a promising political career coming to an end!" Jack Kennedy spoke calmly to his excited golf partner in a game played late in the 1960 Presidential campaign.

On a short hole Jack hit a nearly perfect shot; it landed on the green and rolled straight for the flag—almost a hole-in-one.

"If that ball had gone into that hole," JFK said with a sigh of mock relief, "in less than an hour the word would be out to the nation that another golfer was trying to get in the White House."

He glanced up at a small crowd of onlookers. "If that group of people hadn't been watching from the road, I wonder what it would have cost me to have our two trusted caddies keep quiet till after the convention?"

GOVERNMENT

"My experience in government," stated President Kennedy, "is that when things are non-controversial, beautifully coordinated, and all the rest, it must be that there is not much going on."

Any system of government will work when everything is going well. It's the system that functions in the pinches that survives.

—*Why England Slept*, 1940, "Conclusion"

GOVERNMENT AND BUSINESS

There is no inevitable clash between the public and private sectors, or between investment and consumption, nor . . . between government and business. All elements in our national economic growth are interdependent. Each must play its proper role.

—to the National Industrial Conference Board, February 13, 1961
(see BUSINESS AND GOVERNMENT)

GOVERNMENT AND JOBS

Anyone who honestly is seeking a job and can't find it deserves the attention of the United States government and the people.

—news conference, Washington, D.C., April 12, 1961

GOVERNMENT GROWTH

Is the federal government growing so large that our private economy is endangered? My answer to that is no. The federal government has been growing for 175 years. Our population has grown even faster. Our territory and economy have grown and become more closely linked. The real growth in government has been at the state and local level.

—remarks in Tampa, Florida, November 18, 1963
(see BIG GOVERNMENT)

GRADUATE EDUCATION

Expansion of high-quality graduate education and research in all fields is essential to national security and economic growth.

One of our most serious manpower shortages is the lack of Ph.D.'s . . . only about one-half of 1 percent of our school-age generation is achieving Ph.D. degrees in all fields.

—message to Congress, January 29, 1963
(see LEADERSHIP AND LEARNING, RESEARCH AND DEVELOPMENT, SCHOLARS)

GREEN BAY PACKERS

"Ladies and gentlemen, I was warned to be out here in plenty of time to permit those who are going to the Green Bay Packers game to leave," JFK confessed to the carnivorous crowd at a 1960 campaign appearance in Green Bay. "I don't mind running against Mr. Nixon but I have the good sense not to run against the Green Bay Packers."

GUERILLA WARFARE

This is another type of war, new in its intensity, ancient in its origin—war by guerillas, subversives, insurgents, assassins; war by ambush instead of by combat, by infiltration instead of aggression, seeking victory by eroding and exhausting the enemy instead of engaging him. It is a form of warfare uniquely adapted to what have been strangely called "wars of liberation," to undermine the efforts of new and poor countries to maintain the freedom they have finally achieved. It preys on economic and ethnic conflict. It requires . . . a wholly new kind of strategy, a wholly different kind of force, and therefore a wholly different kind of military training.

—remarks at West Point, June 6, 1962
(see ARMS, DEFENSE)

H

HANDSHAKING

John Kennedy suffered painful abrasions on his right hand from excessive handshaking during the 1960 Presidential campaign, which left his hand bruised, callused, and swollen. He raised his sore hand and remarked, "With all that handshaking, this is probably the greatest right hand in America today!"

HAPPEN

Things do not happen. They are made to happen.

—at San Luis Dam, Los Banos, California, August 18, 1961

HARD WAY

When he was a candidate for Congress, Jack Kennedy appeared one night at a rally with dozens of other candidates. The chairman kept Kennedy waiting until late in the evening while he introduced one speaker after another as "a young fellow who came up the hard way."

Finally, sometime after midnight, Jack Kennedy arrived at the podium. He began his speech with the observation, "I seem to be the only person here tonight who didn't come up the hard way."

HARRISON, BENJAMIN

What are we going to do with the Republicans? They can point to Benjamin Harrison, who according to legend saw a man forced by the depression to eat grass on the White House lawn and had only one suggestion for him—that he go around to the back where the grass was longer.

—Springfield, Illinois, October 3, 1960

HATS

The "fashion-plate President" was reported to have an aversion to hats. However, one day President Kennedy was spotted carrying a felt hat in Newport in 1963—not wearing it, carrying it.

"I've got to carry one for a while," JFK explained sheepishly; "they tell me I'm killing the industry."

(see CLOTHES)

HEALTH

The health of our nation is a key to its future—to its economic vitality, to the morale and efficiency of its citizens, to our success in achieving our own goals and demonstrating to others the benefits of a free society.

—message to Congress, February 9, 1961

The basic resource of a nation is its people. Its strength can be no greater than the health and vitality of its population.

—message to Congress, February 17, 1962

HELLER, WALTER

Under fire from critics of his economic policies, President Kennedy turned to his economic adviser, Walter Heller, and said, "Walter, I want to make it perfectly clear that I resent these attacks on you."

HEREAFTER

Asked whether he thought he would lose any votes because of his Catholic religion, John Kennedy answered: "I feel as a Catholic that I'll get my reward in my life hereafter, although I may not get it here."

(see GOD, RELIGIOUS ISSUE)

HERO

"Mr. President, how did you become a war hero?" a little boy asked President Kennedy on a West Coast trip.

"It was absolutely involuntary," the President replied. "They sank my boat."

(see *PT-109*, "A Brief Biography" at end of book—1943)

HEROES

In the concluding chapter of *Profiles in Courage*, John F. Kennedy names qualities these American heroes had in common:

These men were not all on one side. They were not all right or all conservatives or all liberals. . . . Some of them may have been pure and generous and kind and noble throughout their careers, in the best traditions of the American hero; but most of them were not. Norris, the unyielding bitter-ender; Adams, the irritating upstart; Webster, the businessmen's beneficiary; Benton, the bombastic bully—of such stuff are our real-life political heroes made.

Most of them, despite their differences, held much in common—the breath-taking talents of the orator, the brilliance of the scholar, the breadth of the man above party and section, and, above all, a deep-seated belief in themselves, their integrity and the rightness of their cause.

(see ADAMS, JOHN; CALHOUN, JOHN C.; CLAY, HENRY; WEBSTER, DANIEL)

HIGH SCHOOL DROPOUTS

Today one out of every three students in the fifth grade will drop out of high school and only two out of ten will graduate from college. In the meantime, we need more educated men and women and we need less and less unskilled labor.

—commencement, San Diego State College, June 6, 1963

HIGH SCHOOL GRADUATES

At the turn of the century, only 10 percent of our adults had a high school or college education. Today such an education has become a requirement for an increasing number of jobs.

—message to Congress, January 29, 1963

In our modern society, even high school graduates find that their skills are inadequate.

—remarks in Chicago, March 23, 1963

If this nation is to grow in wisdom and strength, then every able high school graduate should have the opportunity to develop his talents. Yet nearly half lack either the funds or the facilities to attend college.

—State of the Union message, January 11, 1962
(see COLLEGE GRADUATES, SCHOOL DROPOUTS)

HISTORY

"Some of us think it wise to associate with historians and cultivate their goodwill," President Kennedy said to a historical society in Washington, D.C., "though we always have the remedy which Winston Churchill once suggested when he prophesied during World War II that history would deal gently with him. 'Because,' Mr. Churchill said, 'I intend to write it!' "

If . . . history . . . teaches us anything, it is that man, in his quest for knowledge and progress, is determined and cannot be deterred.

—address at Rice University, Houston, September 12, 1962

Let us resolve to be the masters, not the victims, of our history, controlling our own destiny without giving way to blind suspicion and emotion.

—remarks at University of Maine, October 19, 1963

HOBAN, JAMES

"The White House was designed by James Hoban, a noted Irish-American architect," President Kennedy addressed the Irish parliament in Dublin, June 28, 1963, "and I have no doubt that he believed by incorporating several features of the Dublin style he would make it more homelike for any President of Irish descent. It was a long wait, but I appreciate his efforts. There is also an unconfirmed rumor that Hoban was never fully paid for his work on the White House. If this proves to be true, I will speak to our Secretary of State about it."

(see WHITE HOUSE)

HOPE, BOB

When Bob Hope was honored in Hollywood on March 4, 1962, for his outstanding work entertaining American servicemen, President Kennedy sent a tape-recorded message.

The President asked Mr. Hope to consider a Road-to-Washington film. "From my own experience, I can tell him it's not the easiest road to travel, but it will give him a chance to visit his money—at least what's left of it."

HORSE

On one of his last weekends, in November 1963, the President and First Lady visited their newly constructed home in Virginia.

JFK was photographed by the visiting White House reporter feeding lumps of sugar to his pet pony. When the sugar lumps were all gone, the pony began nibbling on the President.

"Keep shooting," JFK instructed the photographer. "You're about to watch a President being eaten by a horse."

HUMAN ADVENTURES

For we know now that freedom is more than the rejection of tyranny, that prosperity is more than an escape from want, that partnership is more than a sharing of power. These are all, above all, great human adventures.

—address in Frankfurt, Germany, June 25, 1963

HUMAN FAMILY

No nation, large or small, can be indifferent to the fate of others, near or far. Modern economics, weaponry and communications have made us realize more than ever that we are one human family and this one planet is our home.

—address to Irish parliament, June 28, 1963

The United States and other free countries are committed to this great end: the development of the human family. In time, the unity of the West can lead to the unity of East and West, until the human family is truly a single sheepfold under God.

—remarks at NATO headquarters, Naples, Italy, July 2, 1963
(see FAMILY OF MAN)

HUMAN RIGHTS

The cause of human rights and dignity, some two centuries after its birth in Europe and the United States, is still moving men and nations with ever-increasing momentum. The Negro citizens of my own country have strengthened their demand for equality of opportunity. And the American people and the American Government are going to respond. The pace of decolonization has quickened in Africa. The people of the developing nations have intensified their pursuit of economic and social justice. The people of Eastern Europe, even after eighteen years of oppression, are not immune to change. The truth does not die. The desire for liberty cannot be fully suppressed.

—address at the Free University, West Berlin, June 26, 1963

INAUGURAL ADDRESS

John F. Kennedy's inaugural address was one of the most inspiring speeches of the twentieth century, although he was modest about it. After reading over Thomas Jefferson's inaugural address the night before, he remarked, "Better than mine."

On his first day in the White House, President Kennedy noticed that his personal secretary, Evelyn Lincoln, had his reading copy of his inaugural address on her desk. "I read the other day that one of the former Presidents was offered $75,000 for his inaugural address," he said. "Mrs. Lincoln, give me a pen so I can sign mine."

JFK signed his inaugural address and said, "Here—Mrs. Lincoln, keep this $75,000 for me!"

INAUGURAL ADDRESS TEXT

Fellow citizens:

We observe today not a victory of party but a celebration of freedom—symbolizing an end as well as a beginning

—signifying renewal as well as change. For I have sworn before you and Almighty God the same solemn oath our forebears prescribed nearly a century and three quarters ago.

The world is very different now. For man holds in his mortal hands the power to abolish all forms of human poverty and all forms of human life. And yet the same revolutionary beliefs for which our forebears fought are still at issue around the globe—the belief that the rights of man come not from the generosity of the state but from the hand of God.

We dare not forget today that we are the heirs of that first revolution. Let the word go forth from this time and place, to friend and foe alike, that the torch has been passed to a new generation of Americans—born in this century, tempered by war, disciplined by a hard and bitter peace, proud of our ancient heritage—and unwilling to witness or permit the slow undoing of those human rights to which this nation has always been committed, and to which we are committed today at home and around the world.

Let every nation know, whether it wishes us well or ill, that we shall pay any price, bear any burden, meet any hardship, support any friend, oppose any foe to assure the survival and the success of liberty.

This much we pledge—and more.

To those old allies whose cultural and spiritual origins we share, we pledge the loyalty of faithful hands. United, there is little we cannot do in a host of cooperative ventures. Divided, there is little we can do—for we dare not meet a powerful challenge at odds and split asunder.

To those new states whom we welcome to the ranks of the free, we pledge our word that one form of colonial control shall not have passed away merely to be replaced by a far more iron tyranny. We shall not always expect to find them supporting our view. But we shall always hope to find them strongly supporting their own freedom—and to remember that, in the past, those who foolishly sought power by riding the back of the tiger ended up inside.

To those peoples in the huts and villages of half the globe struggling to break the bonds of mass misery, we pledge our best efforts to help them help themselves, for whatever period is required—not because the Communists may be doing it, not because we seek their votes, but because it is right. If a free society cannot help the many who are poor, it cannot save the few who are rich.

To our sister republics south of the border, we offer a special pledge—to convert our good words into good deeds—in a new alliance for progress—to assist free men and free governments in casting off the chains of poverty. But this peaceful revolution of hope cannot become the prey of hostile powers. Let all our neighbors know that we shall join with them to oppose aggression or subversion anywhere in the Americas. And let every other power know that this Hemisphere intends to remain the master of its own house.

To that world assembly of sovereign states, the United Nations, our last hope in an age where the instruments of war have far outpaced the instruments of peace, we renew our pledge of support—to prevent it from becoming merely a forum for invective—to strengthen its shield of the new and the weak—and to enlarge the area in which its writ may be run.

Finally, to those nations who would make themselves our adversary, we offer not a pledge but a request: that both sides begin anew the quest for peace, before the dark powers of destruction unleashed by science engulf all humanity in planned or accidental self-destruction.

We dare not tempt them with weakness. For only when

our arms are sufficient beyond doubt can we be certain that they will never be employed.

But neither can two great and powerful groups of nations take comfort from our present course—both sides overburdened by the cost of modern weapons, both rightly alarmed by the steady spread of the deadly atom, yet both racing to alter that uncertain balance of terror that stays the hand of mankind's final war.

So let us begin anew—remembering on both sides that civility is not a sign of weakness, and sincerity is always subject to proof. Let us never negotiate out of fear. But let us never fear to negotiate.

Let both sides explore what problems unite us instead of belaboring those problems which divide us.

Let both sides, for the first time, formulate serious and precise proposals for the inspection and control of arms—and bring the absolute power to destroy other nations under absolute control of all nations.

Let both sides seek to invoke the wonders of science instead of its terrors. Together let us explore the stars, conquer the deserts, eradicate disease, tap the ocean depths and encourage the arts and commerce.

Let both sides unite to heed in all corners of the earth the command of Isaiah—to "undo the heavy burdens . . . [and] let the oppressed go free."

And if a beachhead of cooperation may push back the jungle of suspicion, let both sides join in creating a new endeavor; not a new balance of power, but a new world of law, where the strong are just and the weak secure and the peace preserved.

All this will not be finished in the first one hundred days. Nor will it be finished in the first one thousand days, nor in the life of this Administration, nor even perhaps in our lifetime on this planet. But let us begin.

In your hands, my fellow citizens, more than mine, will rest the final success or failure of our course. Since this country was founded, each generation of Americans has been summoned to give testimony to its national loyalty. The graves of young Americans who answered the call to service surround the globe.

Now the trumpet summons us again—not as a call to bear arms, though arms we need—not as a call to battle, though embattled we are—but a call to bear the burden of a long twilight struggle, year in and year out, "rejoicing in hope, patient in tribulation"—a struggle against the common enemies of man: tyranny, poverty, disease and war itself.

Can we forge against these enemies a grand and global alliance, North and South, East and West, that can assure a more fruitful life for all mankind? Will you join in that historic effort?

In the long history of the world, only a few generations have been granted the role of defending freedom in its hour of maximum danger. I do not shrink from this responsibility—I welcome it. I do not believe that any of us would exchange places with any other people or any other generation. The energy, the faith, the devotion which we bring to this endeavor will light our country and all who serve it—and the glow from that fire can truly light the world.

And so, my fellow Americans: ask not what your country can do for you—ask what you can do for your country.

My fellow citizens of the world: ask not what America will do for you, but what together we can do for the freedom of man.

Finally, whether you are citizens of America or citizens of the world, ask of us here the same high standards of strength and sacrifice which we ask of you. With a good conscience our only sure reward, with history the final judge of our deeds, let us go forth to lead the land we love, but knowing that here on earth God's work must truly be our own.

INAUGURAL BALLS

"I think this is an ideal way to spend an evening," said President Kennedy at an inaugural ball, "and I hope that we can all meet here again tomorrow at one A.M. to do it all over again.

"I don't know a better way to spend an evening—you looking at us and we looking at you.

"The Johnsons and I have been to five balls tonight, and we still have one unfulfilled ambition—and that is to see somebody dance."

INDEPENDENCE

On Independence Day 1962, at Independence Hall in Philadelphia, President Kennedy spoke on independence.

> It is a high honor for any citizen of the great Republic to speak at this Hall of Independence on this day of Independence.
>
> In a very real sense you and I are the executors of the testament handed down by those who gathered in this historic hall 186 years ago today.
>
> Today, 186 years later, that Declaration, whose yellowing parchment and fading, almost illegible lines I saw in the past week in the National Archives in Washington, is still a revolutionary document. To read it today is to hear a trumpet call. For that Declaration unleashed not merely a revolution against the British, but a revolution in human affairs.
>
> Its authors were highly conscious of its world-wide implications, and George Washington declared that liberty and self-government were, in his words, "finally staked on

the experiment entrusted to the hands of the American people."

This prophecy has been borne out for 186 years. This doctrine of national independence has shaken the globe, and it remains the most powerful force in the world today.

The theory of independence, as old as man himself, was not invented in this hall, but it was in this hall that the theory became a practice, that the word went out to all the world that "the God who gave us life gave us liberty at the same time."

And today this nation, conceived in revolution, nurtured in liberty, matured in independence, has no intention of abdicating its leadership in that world-wide movement for independence to any nation or society committed to systematic human suppression.

With the passing of ancient empires, today less than 2 percent of the world's population lives in territories officially termed "dependent." As this effort for independence, inspired by the spirit of the American Declaration of Independence, now approaches a successful close, a great new effort for independence is transforming the world around us.

Since the close of World War II, a world-wide declaration of independence has transformed nearly one billion people and nine million square miles into forty-two free and independent states.

—United Nations address, September 25, 1961

The longing for independence is the same the world over, whether it is the independence of West Berlin or Vietnam.

—State of the Union message, January 14, 1963

(see COLONIALISM, NATIONAL INDEPENDENCE)

INDIA

President Kennedy wrote a letter to Peter Galbraith, the young son of his nominee as United States Ambassador to India, John Galbraith.

April 1, 1961

Dear Peter:

I learned from your father that you are not anxious to give up your school and friends for India.

I think I know a little bit about how you feel.

More than 20 years ago, our family was similarly uprooted when we went to London where my father was Ambassador.

My younger brother and sisters were about your age. They had, like you, to exchange new friends for old.

For anyone interested, as your father says you are, in animals, India has the most fascinating possibilities. The range is from elephants to cobras, although I gather the cobras have to be handled professionally.

P.S. I wish a little I were going also.

INDIANA

"I want to express my great appreciation to all of you for your kindness in coming out and giving us a warm Hoosier welcome," Jack Kennedy greeted a gathering at a campaign stop in Anderson, Indiana. "I understand that this town suffered a misfortune this morning, when the bank was robbed. I am confident that the *Indianapolis Star* will say, 'Democrats Arrive and Bank Robbed.' "

INDIVIDUAL

The dynamic of democracy is the power and the purpose of the individual.

—State of the Union message, January 11, 1962

Our program is . . . to make society the servant of the individual and the individual the source of progress, and thus to realize for all the full promise of American life.

—State of the Union message, January 11, 1962

INFLATION

Always a cruel tax upon the weak, inflation is now the certain road to a balance of payments crisis and the disruption of the international economy of the Western world.

—message to Congress, February 2, 1961

(see TAX RATES)

INTELLIGENCE

Both legitimate and necessary as a means of self-defense in an age of hidden perils, our whole intelligence effort must be reviewed, and its coordination with other elements of policy assured.

—message to Congress, May 25, 1961

(see SECRECY, SECURITY)

INTERDEPENDENCE

I will say here and now on this day of Independence that the United States will be ready for a Declaration of Interdependence, that will be prepared to discuss with a United Europe the ways and means of forming a concrete

Atlantic Partnership, a mutually beneficial partnership between the new union now emerging in Europe and the old American union founded here 175 years ago.

—Independence Day address, July 4, 1962

INTEREST RATES

"First, we will not rely on a monetary policy that puts its emphasis on tight money and tight interest rates," the candidate stated at a campaign stop in Saginaw, Michigan. "The fact of the matter is," said JFK, "if Rip Van Winkle went to sleep and he woke up and he wanted to know whether the Republicans or the Democrats were in office, he would just say 'How high are the interest rates?' "

INTERESTING

JFK referred to his harrowing brush with death in the Pacific during World War II as "an interesting experience" during a television interview with Edward R. Murrow.

"Interesting," repeated Murrow. "I should think that would be one of the great understatements."

(see *PT-109*)

INTERNATIONALISM

For we live in an age of interdependence as well as independence, an age of internationalism as well as nationalism.

—remarks in Frankfurt, Germany, June 25, 1963

IRELAND

"It is my pleasure to be back from whence I came," announced President Kennedy on arrival in Wexford, Ireland, on June 28, 1963. "Many people are under the impression that all the Kennedys are in Washington, but I am happy to see so many present who have missed the boat."

In Cork the American President quipped, "I don't want to give the impression that every member of this administration in Washington is Irish. It just seems that way."

The visiting President fondly recalled his Irish ancestors. "When my great-grandfather left here to become a cooper in East Boston, he carried nothing with him except two things, a strong religious faith and a strong desire for liberty. And I'm glad to say that all of his great-grandchildren have valued that inheritance. If he hadn't left, I'd be working over at the Albatross Company."

President Kennedy addressed the Irish parliament on June 28, 1963:

> I am deeply honored to be your guest in the free Parliament of a free Ireland. If this nation had achieved its present political and economic stature a century or so ago, my great-grandfather might never have left New Ross, and I might, if fortunate, be sitting down there with you. Of course, if your own President had never left Brooklyn, he might be standing up here instead of me.
>
> The Ireland of 1963, one of the youngest of nations and the oldest of civilizations, has discovered that the achievement of nationhood is not an end, but a beginning.
>
> Ireland's role is unique. For every new nation knows that Ireland was the first of the small nations in the twentieth century to win its struggle for independence.
>
> Ireland pursues an independent course in foreign policy, but it is not neutral between liberty and tyranny and never will be.

IRISH WIDOW

When campaigning for the Senate in Irish wards of Massachusetts, Jack Kennedy liked to tell the story of the little old Irish widow. "She came to the ward leader with a complaint that the officials wouldn't accept the answer she gave to a question they asked her about her late husband, which was 'What did he die of?' When the ward leader asked her what her answer was, the little old Irish lady answered, 'He died of a Tuesday, I remember it well.' "

IVORY COAST

President Kennedy made the most of an Ivory Coast toast. "I do not think that any visitor to our country has had a more constructive career than our distinguished guest of honor," said the American President, toasting President Houphouet-Boigny of the Ivory Coast, "and I am not alone referring to the fact that in a free election he was elected by 98 percent of the voters of his country—a record which has not been equalled recently in the United States—and from all I read, will not be."

IVORY TOWER

President Kennedy asked Professor James Tobin of Yale University to come to Washington as a member of his Council of Economic Advisors.

"I'm just an Ivory Tower economist," Tobin told the President.

"That's the best kind," replied JFK. "As a matter of fact, I'm an Ivory Tower President."

JEFFERSON, THOMAS

At a White House dinner honoring a group of Nobel Prize winners in April 1962, President Kennedy welcomed the distinguished guests:

"I think this is the most extraordinary collection of talent, of human knowledge, that has ever been gathered together at the White House, with the possible exception of when Thomas Jefferson dined here alone."

Kennedy admired Jefferson as one of his heroes, like himself a passionate intellectual, a great American aristocrat, who could have had an easy life and chose a difficult one.

(see ARISTOCRACY, EXERCISE)

JOHNSON, LYNDON ("LANDSLIDE")

Jack Kennedy liked to play the humorous nickname game with close friends. JFK's humorous nickname for Lyndon

Baines Johnson was "Landslide." It was a teasing reference to the fact that LBJ was first elected to the Senate in the primary by a scant margin of eighty-seven votes.

President Kennedy addressed his vice president as "Lyndon," however. He knew Johnson would be sensitive about the nickname. LBJ was so sensitive that JFK said writing a birthday telegram to him was like "drafting a state document."

In April 1961 President Kennedy decided to send Vice President Johnson to visit a number of Asian countries, including Vietnam.

Johnson was not enthusiastic about going to Saigon and said so.

"Don't worry, Lyndon," JFK reassured him, "if anything happens to you, Sam Rayburn and I will give you the biggest funeral Austin, Texas, ever saw."

Ironically, it was John Kennedy whose funeral was next, and it was the biggest the world has seen.

The margin of victory for the Kennedy-Johnson ticket in 1960 was slim, but in 1964 Lyndon Johnson won the Presidential election by a landslide, fulfilling John Kennedy's ironic nickname, "Landslide."

(see RUNNING MATE)

JUSTICE

What does justice require? In the end, it requires liberty.

—address at the Free University, West Berlin, June 26, 1963

KENNEDY, CAROLINE

The Kennedy parents did not realize Caroline could read until one night when Jack Kennedy, still a senator campaigning for the Presidency, was soaking in the tub of their Georgetown house. Caroline burst in and threw a copy of *Newsweek* with her father on the cover into the tub, shouting gleefully, "Daddy!"

After his nomination in the summer of 1960, the famous father made his nightly call to his young daughter Caroline, only to be told by her nurse, Maud Shaw, one night that Caroline had not yet returned from a friend's birthday party.

JFK sighed and said to Miss Shaw, "She's got to start staying home at night."

Caroline Kennedy became a favorite of the White House press corps. She frequently engaged in repartee with reporters.

When a congressman told her father Caroline had informed him she didn't want to live in the White House, the President was skeptical. "That's not my problem with Caroline," said her father. "My problem is to keep her from holding press conferences."

(see FATHER)

KENNEDY, JACQUELINE

When President Kennedy and the First Lady visited Paris in 1962, Jacqueline, speaking fluent French, charmed everyone, including President de Gaulle.

At a press conference in Paris before departing, President Kennedy bid farewell to his French hosts:

"I do not think it entirely inappropriate to introduce myself to this audience. I am the man who accompanied Jacqueline Kennedy to Paris, and I have enjoyed it."

Jack Kennedy first met Jacqueline Bouvier at a dinner party at the home of the Charles Bartletts ("who had been shamelessly matchmaking for a year," she said). He did not hesitate. "I leaned across the asparagus and asked her for a date."

On his last trip with Jacqueline, in Fort Worth, President Kennedy paid Mrs. Kennedy one of his last compliments. "I appreciate you being here this morning," he told a Fort Worth audience. "Mrs. Kennedy is organizing herself. It takes her longer, but, of course, she looks better than we do when she does it."

KENNEDY, JOSEPH

One night Joseph Kennedy presided over a Kennedy family gathering. He held forth about the family finances. "I don't know what is going to happen to this family when I die . . ." he remonstrated. "No one appears to have the slightest concern for how much they spend. I don't know what is going to happen to you after I am gone."

He turned to one of his daughters and reprimanded her so severely that she rushed out of the room in tears. When she returned, Jack Kennedy glanced up and said, "Well, don't worry. We've come to the conclusion that the only solution is to have Dad work harder."

They all laughed at that, even Joseph Kennedy.

KENNEDY, JR., JOHN

A photograph of two-year-old John Kennedy, Jr., racing toward his father, reaching up to be caught and tossed in his arms, captured the imagination of the nation at the height of "Camelot." Taken as the President deplaned from Air Force One and walked toward his waiting family, the photograph was widely reproduced. When the President saw the picture on a front page he smiled and said, "Every mother in the United States is saying, 'Isn't it wonderful to see that love between a son and his father, the way that John races to be with his father.' Little do they know that that son would have raced right by his father to get to that helicopter, but his dad stepped into his path and grabbed him."

KENNEDY, JR., ROBERT

"Speaking of jobs for relatives," President Kennedy remarked while they were still buzzing about his appointment of his brother as Attorney General. "Master Robert Kennedy, who is four, came to see me today, but I told him we already had an Attorney General."

KENNEDY, ROBERT

Asked by his friend Ben Bradlee how he intended to make the sensitive announcement of nominating his brother Robert for Attorney General, the President smiled. "Well, I think I'll open the front door of the Georgetown house some morning about 2:00 A.M., look up and down the street, and if there's no one there, I'll whisper 'It's Bobby.' "

There were some cries of nepotism after John Kennedy announced his brother as his choice for Attorney General. When critics said Bobby at thirty-four was too young and inexperienced to head the Justice Department, President Kennedy refused to apologize and/or be put on the defensive and retorted:

"I see nothing wrong with giving Robert some legal experience as Attorney General before he goes out to practice law."

Just before the formal announcement to the press, John Kennedy turned to Robert Kennedy and said, "Damn it, Bobby, comb your hair and don't smile so much. They'll think we are happy about the announcement."

Robert Kennedy turned out to be one of the most dynamic Attorney Generals in American history. A few days after a national magazine called Robert Kennedy "the man with the greatest influence at the White House," the President received a call from his Attorney General.

JFK turned to a guest as he put his hand over the phone mouthpiece and said, "This is the second most powerful man in the nation calling."

KENNEDY, TED

John Kennedy's youngest brother, Edward, called Ted, campaigned hard in 1960. At a West Virginia primary Ted was concluding an enthusiastic speech, saying, "Do you want a man who will give the country leadership? Do you want a man who has vigor and vision?"

When Ted handed the microphone to the candidate, JFK began his remarks this way: "I would like to tell my brother that you cannot be elected President until you are thirty-five years of age."

In the 1962 Massachusetts Senate race Ted Kennedy defeated House Speaker John McCormack's nephew Eddie, and JFK's only comment was this: "All I can say is: I'd rather be Ted than Ed."

When Edward Kennedy was elected Senator from Massachusetts in 1962, the President told a gathering of Democrats in Harrisburg, Pennsylvania: "I should introduce myself. I am Ted Kennedy's brother."

(see SARDONIC)

KHRUSHCHEV, NIKITA

When President Kennedy first met with Soviet leader Nikita Khrushchev in Vienna for foreign policy talks, Khrushchev tried to claim some credit for Kennedy's victory over Nixon.

Khrushchev explained if he had released Francis Gary Powers (the American U-2 pilot shot down over Russia in May 1960) just before the election, Kennedy would have lost by at least 200,000 votes.

"Don't spread the story around," JFK said, smiling. "If you tell everybody that you like me better than Nixon, I'll be ruined at home."

I know something about Mr. Khrushchev, whom I met a year ago in the Senate Foreign Relations Committee, and I know something about the nature and history of his country, which I visited in 1939.

Mr. Khrushchev himself, it is said, told the story a few years ago about the Russian who begun to run through the Kremlin shouting, "Khrushchev is a fool. Khrushchev is a fool."

He was sentenced, the Premier said, to twenty-three years in prison, "three for insulting the party secretary, and twenty for revealing a state secret."

—Pikesville, Maryland, September 16, 1960
(see LENIN PEACE PRIZE; MISTAKES; RUSK, DEAN)

KNOWLEDGE

Knowledge, not hate, is the passkey to the future—that knowledge transcends national antagonisms—that it is the possession, not of a single class or of a single nation or a single ideology, but of all mankind.

—commencement, University of California, Berkeley, March 23, 1962

KNOWLEDGE AND IGNORANCE

We meet in an hour of change and challenge, in a decade of hope and fear, in an age of both knowledge and ignorance. The greater our knowledge increases, the greater our ignorance unfolds.

—remarks at Rice University, September 12, 1962

KNOWLEDGE PURSUIT

The pursuit of knowledge itself implies a world where men are free to follow out the logic of their own ideas. It implies a world where nations are free to solve their own problems and to realize their own ideals. It implies, in short, a world where collaboration emerges from the voluntary decisions of nations strong in their own independence and their own self-respect.

It is in the interests of the pursuit of knowledge, and it is in our own national interest, that this revolution of national independence succeed. For the Communists rest everything on the idea of a monolithic world—a world where all knowledge has a single pattern, all societies move toward a single model, all problems and roads have a single solution and a single destination.

The pursuit of knowledge, on the other hand, rests everything on the opposite idea—on the idea of a world based on diversity, self-determination and freedom. And that is the kind of world to which we Americans, as a nation, are committed by the principles upon which the great Republic was founded.

As men conduct the pursuit of knowledge, they create a world which freely unites national diversity and international partnership.

—commencement, University of California, Berkeley, March 23, 1962

(see NATIONAL INDEPENDENCE, SCIENCE)

LABOR DEMAND

The greatest growth in labor demand today is for highly trained professional workers with sixteen or more years of education . . . while jobs for those with no secondary education decreased 25 percent in the last decade.

—news conference, August 1, 1963
(see EDUCATION, GRADUATE EDUCATION, SCHOLARS)

LADY

"I come to ask your help in doing it," Jack Kennedy appealed at a Democratic women's luncheon in Queens. "There's an old saying, 'Never send a boy to do a man's job, send a lady.' "

LAND

Every time an acre of land disappears into private development or exploitation, an acre of land which could be used for the people, we have lost a chance. We will never get it back.

—University of North Dakota, September 25, 1963

LAND'S

At the Inauguration, Robert Frost read a poem that began, "The land was ours before we were the land's," meaning, in part, that this new land of ours sustained us before we were a nation. And although we are now the land's, a nation of people matched to a continent, we still draw our strength and sustenance in this city and in every other city across the country from the earth.

—message to Congress on natural resources, February 23, 1961

LASKY, VICTOR

"I haven't read all of Mr. Lasky. I've just gotten the flavor of it," the President replied, asked to comment on a book by Victor Lasky highly critical of him. "I see it's been highly praised by Mr. Drummond, Mr. Krock, and others. I'm looking forward to reading it, because the part that I read was not as brilliant as I gather the rest of it is from what they say about it."

LATIN

Eight girls at the Dalton School in New York, inspired by Kennedy's inaugural address and a teacher's comparison of the Kennedy oratorial style to the great Roman orator Cicero, collaborated on a translation. They sent it to the

White House and were astonished to receive a reply, entirely in Latin, beginning "Johannes Filiugeraldi Kennediensis, Respublicae Preaesidens, puellis Scholae Daltoni salutem pluraimam dicit."

The President, with some scholarly assistance from a White House aide, responded with a letter written in Latin. The English translation follows:

> President John Fitzgerald Kennedy sends heartiest greetings to the girls of Dalton School.
>
> Distinguished young ladies, I have received your letter, in which you mention the translation of my speech, and I have read over that translation. I am pleased and delighted with many features of it. I strongly admire your knowledge of the Latin language and your skillful eloquence in writing. The style of your translation seems to me praiseworthy and admirable; the fact is it has both richness and variety.
>
> What is there which could be done by you which would not deserve approval? I thank you not only for your kindness but also because through your efforts you have made it possible for me to read my own speech speaking the Latin language.
>
> Best wishes to you! From the city of Washington on the twenty-seventh of May in the year of Our Lord 1961.

In his letter to the Dalton girls, JFK named (in Latin) virtues he admired, including "skillful eloquence in writing," "praiseworthy and admirable" style, "both richness and variety" in composition, and "kindness."

LATIN AMERICA

Latin America is the fastest-growing continent in the world.

—remarks to Inter-American Press Association, November 18, 1963

As a result of poverty, illiteracy, hopelessness and a sense of injustice, the conditions which breed political and social unrest, are almost universal in the Latin-American.

—message to Congress, March 14, 1961

We propose to complete a revolution of the Americas, to build a hemisphere where all men can hope for a suitable standard of living, and all can live out their lives in dignity and in freedom.

To achieve this goal political freedom must accompany material progress.

—address to Latin-American diplomats, March 13, 1961

Our motto is what it has always been: "Progress yes, tyranny no—*Progreso sí, tirania no!*"

—address to Latin-American diplomats, March 13, 1961
(see FOREIGN AID, WESTERN HEMISPHERE)

LATIN-AMERICAN EDUCATION

Perhaps the greatest stimulus to our own development was the establishment of universal basic education. But for most of the children of Latin America education is a remote and unattainable dream.

—message to Congress, March 14, 1961

LAUGHTER

Laughter was important to John Kennedy. To a friend he gave the gift of a silver beer mug with this inscription:

> There are three things which are real:
> God, human folly and laughter.
> The first two are beyond our comprehension
> So we must do what we can with the third.

LAW

If this country should ever reach the point where any man or group of men, by force or threat of force, could long defy the commands of our court and our Constitution, then no law would stand free from doubt, no judge would be sure of his writ, and no citizen would be safe from his neighbors.

—message to Congress, February 28, 1963

LAWFORD, PAT

I want you to meet my sister, Pat Lawford, from California. Somebody asked her last week if I was her kid brother, so she knew it was time this campaign came to an end.

—Manchester, New Hampshire, November 7, 1960

LEAD

We cannot lead for long the cause of peace and freedom, if we ever cease to set the pace at home.

—State of the Union message, January 14, 1963

LEADER

We don't want to be like the leader in the French Revolution who said, "There go my people. I must find out where they are going so I can lead them."

—Sioux Falls, South Dakota, September 12, 1960

LEADERS

For a free society to survive, to successfully compete, the leaders have to tell the truth. They have to be informed. They have to share their information with the people.

—University of Southern California, November 1, 1960

LEADERS AND SCHOLARS

Our nation's first great leaders were also our first great scholars.

—University of North Carolina, Chapel Hill, October 12, 1962
(see LEADERSHIP AND LEARNING, LIBERTY AND LEARNING, SCHOLARS)

LEADERSHIP

It is time for a new generation of leadership, to cope with new problems and new opportunities. For there is a new world to be won.

—television address, July 4, 1960

The great advantage a democracy is presumed to have over a dictatorship is that ability and not brute force is the qualification for leadership. Therefore, if a democracy cannot produce able leaders, its chance for survival is slight.

—*Why England Slept*, 1940, "Conclusion"

The success of our leadership is dependent upon respect for our mission in the world as well as our missiles—on a clearer recognition of the virtues of freedom as well as the evils of tyranny.

—from undelivered speech, Dallas, November 22, 1963

LEADERSHIP AND LEARNING

The "link between leadership and learning" was a main theme of John F. Kennedy's undelivered Dallas address, released to the press at noon, November 22, 1963:

> Leadership and learning are indispensable to each other.
>
> The advancement of learning depends on community leadership for financial and political support, and the products of that learning, in turn, are essential to the leadership's hopes for continued progress and prosperity.
>
> This link between leadership and learning is not only essential at the community level. It is even more indispensable in world affairs. Ignorance and misinformation can handicap the progress of a city or a company—but they can, if allowed to prevail in foreign policy, handicap this country's security. In a world of complex and continuing problems, in a world full of frustrations and irritations, America's leadership must be guided by the lights of learning and reason.

LEARNING

We must stimulate interest in learning in order to reduce the alarming number of students who now drop out of school or who do not continue into higher levels of education.

—message to Congress, January 29, 1963

A free society today demands that we keep on learning or face the threat of national deterioration.

—to the Adult Education Association, October 14, 1960
(see LIBERTY AND LEARNING)

LENIN PEACE PRIZE

During the Vienna talks, at a lunch given by the Soviets, President Kennedy asked Premier Nikita Khrushchev about the two medals he was wearing.

Khrushchev lowered his pudgy chin to his chest and explained: "This one is the Lenin Peace Price," and before he could describe the second one, Kennedy turned to the translator and said, "Tell him I hope they never take it away from him."

The two leaders had a good laugh over this one.

(see KHRUSHCHEV, NIKITA)

LEVELING UP

The difference in living standards will have to be reduced by leveling up, not down.

—address at the Free University, West Berlin, June 26, 1963

LIBERTY

We are on the side of liberty, and since the beginning of history, and particularly since the Second World War, liberty has been winning out all over the globe.

—message to Congress, May 25, 1961

Unless liberty flourishes in all lands, it cannot flourish in one.

—remarks in Frankfurt, Germany, June 25, 1963

It is well to love liberty, for it demands much of those who live by it. Liberty is not content to share mankind.

—St. Patrick's Day speech, March 17, 1962

It is one of the ironies of our time that the techniques of a harsh and repressive system should be able to instill discipline and ardor in its servants, while the blessings of liberty have too often stood for privilege, materialism and a life of ease.

—State of the Union address, January 29, 1961

LIBERTY AND LEARNING

Liberty without learning is always in peril and learning without liberty is always in vain.

—address at Vanderbilt University, May 18, 1963
(see LEADERSHIP AND LEARNING, SCHOLARS)

LIFE

Life is never easy. There is work to be done and obligations to be met—obligations to truth, to justice and to liberty.

—address at University of Berlin, June 26, 1963

LIGHT

What more can be said today, regarding all the dark and tangled problems we face than: Let there be light.

—University of Washington's 100th anniversary, November 16, 1961

LOOK

Being interviewed by a *Look* magazine reporter, John Kennedy was asked about a particularly vicious rumor in private circulation. "You print that story," he said, "and I just might wind up owning *Look* magazine."

M

MACARONI

"I would like to recall a speech Franklin Roosevelt made in regard to his dog," said President Kennedy in response to attacks. "He said, 'These Republicans have not been content with attacks on me, or my wife or my brother. No, not content with that, they now include my little girl's dog, Macaroni. Well, I don't resent such attacks but Macaroni does.' "

McNAMARA, ROBERT

President Kennedy, asked for his assessment of Secretary of Defense Robert McNamara, had this to say: "He's one of the few guys around this town who, when you ask him if he has anything to say and he hasn't, says, 'No.' That's rare these days, I'm telling you."

Another reporter asked the President about McNamara. "There have been published reports that some high-placed Republican people have been making overtures to your Secretary of Defense for him to be their 1968 candidate for President. If you thought that Mr. McNamara were seriously considering these overtures, would you continue him in your cabinet?"

President Kennedy replied: "I have too high a regard for him to launch his candidacy yet."

MAINE POTATO

What can you say when you have seen everything, including the potato?

"Ladies and gentlemen, I have been informed that the object in front of me is a model of a small potato grown in this county last year," JFK remarked at a campaign stop in Presque Isle, Maine. "I have been under the impression that it was a new Snark missile which was about to go in the state, but I am going to take everybody's word for it."

MARX, KARL

Marx is proven wrong once again, for it is the closed Communist societies, not the free and open societies, which carry within themselves the seeds of internal disintegration.

—State of the Union message, January 11, 1962

(see NEWSPAPER PUBLISHERS)

MASSACHUSETTS

This has been my home; and God willing, wherever I serve, this shall remain my home. It was here my grandparents were born—it is here I hope my grandchildren will be born.

—speech to Massachusetts legislature, January 9, 1961

MAYBE

During the Cuban missile crisis, the President noticed his daughter, Caroline, sprinting across the White House lawn.

"Caroline," JFK shouted, "have you been eating candy?"

Caroline did not answer.

"Caroline," repeated the President, "have you been eating candy? Answer yes, no, or maybe."

MEREDITH, JAMES

The governor of Mississippi, Ross Barnett, appeared in person at Oxford, seat of the state university, to deny James H. Meredith admission to the institution on September 25, 1962. Meredith, a Korean War veteran, satisfied all the admissions requirements except one—his skin color was not white.

President Kennedy explained the actions he took in response to Barnett's defiance of a Supreme Court order in a televised address from the White House:

> The orders of the court in the case of Meredith versus Fair are going to be carried out. Mr. James Meredith is now in residence on the campus of the University of Mississippi.
>
> This has been accomplished thus far without the use of National Guard or other troops.
>
> This is as it should be, for our nation is founded on the principle that observance of the law is the eternal safeguard of liberty and defiance of the law is the surest road to tyranny. The law which we obey includes the final rulings of the courts, as well as the enactments of our legislative bodies.
>
> In this case . . . Mr. Meredith brought a private suit in federal court against those who were excluding him from the university. A series of federal courts all the way to the

Supreme Court repeatedly ordered Mr. Meredith's admission to the university. When those orders were defied, and those who sought to implement them threatened with arrest and violence, the United States Court of Appeals . . . made clear the fact that the enforcement of its order had become an obligation of the United States Government.

My responsibility as President was therefore inescapable.

It was for this reason that I federalized the Mississippi National Guard as the most appropriate instrument should any be needed to preserve law and order while United States marshals carried out the orders of the court and prepared to back them up with whatever other civil or military enforcement might have been required.

I deeply regret the fact that any action by the Executive Branch was necessary in this case, but all other avenues and alternatives, including persuasion and conciliation, had been tried and exhausted.

Let us preserve both the law and the peace, and then, healing those wounds that are within, we can turn to the greater crises that are without, and stand united as one people in our pledge to man's freedom.

METROPOLITAN CLUB

President Kennedy resigned his Metropolitan Club membership as a gesture of disapproval of the exclusive Washington club's refusal to admit African-Americans. However, the President refused Moise Tshombe, the rebel Congolese leader, a U.S. entry visa.

Arthur Krock of the *New York Times*, who remained a member of the Metropolitan Club, took up Tshombe's cause with President Kennedy.

JFK cut off Krock with this: "Arthur, I'll give Tshombe a visa if you'll take him to lunch at the Metropolitan Club."

MILITARY FORCES

The strength and deployment of our forces in combination with those of our allies should be sufficiently powerful and mobile to prevent the steady erosion of the free world through limited wars; and it is this role that should constitute the primary mission of our overseas forces. Nonnuclear wars, and sublimited or guerilla warfare, have since 1945 constituted the most active and constant threat to free world security.

—message to Congress, March 28, 1961
(see ARMS, DEFENSE, GUERILLA WARFARE)

MILITARY SOLUTION

The basic problems facing the world today are not susceptible to a military solution.

—message to Congress, March 28, 1961

MILK

President Kennedy was pro-milk. As part of his fitness campaign in 1962, the President urged Americans to drink more milk. "I am certainly enjoying being with you newsmen this evening," he began a press conference in Washington. "None of you know how tough it is to have to drink milk three times a day."

MIND

The human mind is our fundamental resource.

—message to Congress on education, February 20, 1961
(see EDUCATION)

MINERS

Campaigning to win the West Virginia primary, Jack Kennedy visited a mine and mingled with the miners.

"Is it true you're the son of one of our wealthiest men?" asked one of the miners.

JFK admitted it was true.

"Is it true that you've never wanted for anything and had everything you wanted?"

JFK hesitated. "I guess so."

"Is it true you've never done a day's work with your hands all your life?"

JFK nodded.

"Well, let me tell you this," said the miner. "You haven't missed a thing."

(see WEST VIRGINIA)

MISSION

We are called to a great new mission. The mission is to create a new social order, founded on liberty and justice, in which men are the masters of their fate, in which states are the servants of their citizens and in which all men and women can share a better life.

—remarks in Frankfurt, Germany, June 25, 1963

MISTAKES

During the talks between President Kennedy and Premier Khrushchev at Vienna, the discussion became heated.

"Do you ever admit a mistake?" Kennedy exclaimed.

"Certainly," said Khrushchev. "In a speech before the Twentieth Party Congress, I admitted all of Stalin's mistakes."

"Those were Stalin's mistakes," replied President Kennedy. "Not your mistakes."

(see KHRUSHCHEV, NIKITA; RUSSIA)

MODERNIZATION

We must give special attention to the modernization of our plant and equipment. Forced to reconstruct after wartime devastation, our friends abroad now possess a modern industrial system helping to make them formidable competitors in world markets.

—message to Congress, April 20, 1961

MOON

But why, some say, the moon? Why choose this as our goal? And they may well ask, why climb the highest mountain?

We choose to go to the moon in this decade, and do the other things, not because they are easy but because they are hard; because that goal will serve to organize and measure the best of our energies and skills.

—remarks at Rice University, September 12, 1962

(see NEW FRONTIER, SPACE)

MORALITY

A man does what he must—in spite of personal consequences, in spite of obstacles and dangers and pressures —and that is the basis of all human morality.

—*Profiles in Courage*, 1956

NATIONAL INDEPENDENCE

This doctrine of national independence has shaken the globe, and it remains the most powerful force anywhere in the world today. There are those struggling to eke out a bare existence in a barren land who have never heard of free enterprise, but who cherish the idea of independence.

—Independence Day address, July 4, 1962

Wisdom requires the long view. And the long view shows us that the revolution of national independence is a fundamental fact of our era. This revolution will not be stopped. As new nations emerge from the oblivion of centuries, their first aspiration is to affirm their national identity. Their deepest hope is for a world where, within a framework of international cooperation, every country can solve its own problems according to its own traditions and ideals.

—commencement, University of California, Berkeley, March 23, 1962
(see INDEPENDENCE, KNOWLEDGE)

NATIONAL PARKS

Our already overcrowded National Parks and recreation areas will have twice as many visitors ten years from now as they do today. If we do not plan today for the future growth of these and other great natural assets—not only parks and forests, but wildlife and wilderness preserves and water projects of all kinds—our children and their children will be poorer in every sense of the word.

—State of the Union message, January 14, 1963

NATIONAL SECURITY

It means, finally, that government at all levels must meet its obligation to provide you with the fullest possible information outside the narrowest limits of national security—and we intend to do it.

—address to newspaper publishers, April 27, 1961
(see DALLAS ADDRESS, FREEDOM OF INFORMATION, SECURITY)

NATIONAL SPORT

I will not enter into a debate about whether football or baseball is our national sport. The sad fact is that it looks more and more as if our national sport is not playing at all—but watching. We have become more and more a nation of *spectators*.

—National Football Foundation, Hall of Fame banquet, December 5, 1961
(see PARTICIPATION)

NATURAL RESOURCES

The ocean, the atmosphere and outer space belong not to one nation or to one ideology but to all mankind.

—address, National Academy of Sciences, October 22, 1963

From the beginning of civilization, every nation's basic wealth and progress has stemmed in large measure from its natural resources. This nation has been, and is now, especially fortunate in the blessings we have inherited. Our entire society rests upon, and is dependent upon, our water, our land, our forests and our minerals. How we use these resources influences our health, security, economy, and well-being.

But if we fail to chart a proper course of conservation and development, if we fail to use these blessings prudently, we will be in trouble within a short time. In the resource field, predictions of future use have been consistently understated. But even under conservative projections, we face a future of critical shortages and handicaps.

By the year 2000, a United States population of 300 million, nearly doubled in forty years, will need far greater supplies of farm products, timber, water, minerals, fuels, energy and opportunities for outdoor recreation. Present projections tell us that our water use will double in the next twenty years; that we are harvesting our supply of high-grade timber more rapidly than the development of new growth; that too much of our fertile topsoil is being washed away; that our minerals are being exhausted at increasing rates; and that the nation's remaining undeveloped areas of great natural beauty are being rapidly pre-empted for other uses.

Problems of immediacy always have the advantage of attracting notice—those that lie in the future fare poorly in the competition for attention and money. . . . We cannot, however, delude ourselves—we must understand our resources problems, and we must face up to them now.

—message to Congress on natural resources, February 23, 1961
(see LAND, WATER)

NATURAL WEALTH

It is our task in our time and in our generation to hand down undiminished to those who come after us . . . the natural wealth and beauty which is ours.

—dedication, National Wildlife Federation building, March 3, 1961

NEGOTIATIONS

If vital interests under duress can be preserved by peaceful means, negotiations will find that out. If our adversary will accept nothing less than a concession of our rights, negotiations will find that out. . . . But it is a test of our national maturity to accept the fact that negotiations are not a contest spelling victory or defeat.

—remarks at the University of Washington, November 16, 1961
(see FOREIGN POLICY, UNITED NATIONS)

NEHRU, JAWAHARLAL

When Indian Prime Minister Jawaharlal Nehru visited the White House, President Kennedy was uncomfortable with Nehru's sudden sullen silences. Later it was remarked that Nehru seemed to be interested and vivacious only when conversing with the First Lady. The President nodded knowingly and smiled. "A lot of our visiting statesmen have the same trouble."

NEW FRONTIER

President Kennedy sought a "New Frontier" involving "invention, innovation, imagination, decision . . . science, commerce and cooperation."

The New Frontier of which I speak is not a set of promises—it is a set of challenges. It sums up not what I intend to offer the American people, but what I intend to ask of them.

—acceptance speech for the Democratic Presidential nomination, Los Angeles, July 15, 1960

We have undertaken . . . a great new effort in outer space. Our aim is not simply to be first on the moon, any more than Charles Lindbergh's real aim was to be the first to Paris. His aim was to develop the techniques of our own country and other countries in the field of air and the atmosphere, and our objective in making this effort, which we hope will place one of our citizens on the moon, is to develop in a new frontier of science, commerce and cooperation, the position of the United States and the free world.

—State of the Union message, January 11, 1962
(see SCIENCE, SPACE)

NEW IDEAS

What we need most of all is a constant flow of new ideas—a government and a nation and a press and a public opinion which respect new ideas and respect the people who have them.

—*Strategy of Peace*, 1960

NEW NATIONS

More energy is released by the awakening of new nations than by the fission of the atom itself.

—acceptance speech for the Democratic Presidential nomination, Los Angeles, July 15, 1960

NEW YORK TIMES

John Kennedy was surprised to receive the endorsement of the *New York Times,* which usually supported Republicans. Once elected, the President testified: "In part, at least, I am one person who can truthfully say, 'I got my job through the *New York Times.*' "

NEWPORT, RHODE ISLAND

President Kennedy took Prime Minister Nehru of India on a boat trip aboard his boat, the *Honey Fitz,* sailing past the plush mansions of Newport, Rhode Island.

The President turned to the Prime Minister and said, "I wanted you to see how the average American family lives."

NEWSPAPER PUBLISHERS

"Karl Marx used to write for the *Herald Tribune,* but that isn't why I canceled my subscription." President Kennedy, addressing the American Newspaper Publishers Association, November 18, 1962, placed Marxism in historical perspective, and blamed the publishers for inspiring Marx's monumental hatred of capitalism.

> You bear heavy responsibilities these days and an article I read some time ago reminded me of how particularly heavily the burdens of present-day events bear upon your profession.
>
> You may remember that in 1851, the New York *Herald Tribune,* under the sponsorship and publishing of Horace Greeley, employed as its London correspondent an obscure journalist by the name of Karl Marx.
>
> We are told that foreign correspondent Marx, stone

broke, and with a family ill and undernourished, constantly appealed to Greeley and Managing Editor Charles Dana for an increase in his munificent salary of $5 per installment, a salary which he and Engels ungratefully labeled as the "lousiest petty bourgeois cheating."

But when all his financial appeals were refused, Marx looked around for other means of livelihood and fame, eventually terminating his relationship with the *Tribune* and devoting his talents full time to the cause that would bequeath to the world the seeds of Leninism, Stalinism, revolution and the cold war.

If only this capitalistic New York newspaper had treated him more kindly; if only Marx had remained a foreign correspondent, history might have been different. And I hope all publishers will bear this lesson in mind the next time they receive a poverty-stricken appeal for a small increase in the expense account from an obscure newspaper man.

NIXON, RICHARD

"Senator, when does the moratorium end on Nixon's hospitalization and your ability to attack him?" asked a reporter during the 1960 Presidential campaign.

"Well, I said I would not mention him unless I could praise him until he got out of the hospital," answered John Kennedy diplomatically, "and I have not mentioned him."

After Nixon emerged from the hospital, Kennedy mentioned him occasionally and debated with him four times on television.

Once when Nixon was ahead in the polls and things looked bad for the Kennedy camp, JFK was heard to say, "Do you realize the responsibility I carry? I'm the only person standing between Nixon and the White House."

Only once did both candidates appear together at the same dinner. It was the occasion of the Alfred Smith Memorial Dinner at the Waldorf-Astoria Hotel in New York City. Kennedy did not mention Nixon except in the following remarks:

> I am glad to be here at this notable dinner once again, and I am glad that Mr. Nixon is here, also. Now that Cardinal Spellman has demonstrated the proper spirit, I assume that shortly I will be invited to a Quaker dinner honoring Herbert Hoover.
>
> Cardinal Spellman is the only man so widely respected in American politics that he could bring together, amicably, at the same banquet table, for the first time in this campaign, two political leaders who are increasingly apprehensive about the November election, who have long eyed each other suspiciously, and who have disagreed so strongly, both publicly and privately—Vice President Nixon and Governor Rockefeller.
>
> Mr. Nixon, like the rest of us, has had his troubles in this campaign. At one point even the *Wall Street Journal* was criticizing his tactics. That is like the *Osservatore Romano* criticizing the Pope.
>
> One of the inspiring notes that was struck in the last debate was struck by the Vice President in his very moving warning to the candidates against the use of profanity by Presidents and ex-Presidents when they are on the stump. And I know after fourteen years in the Congress with the Vice President, that he was very sincere in his views about the use of profanity. But I am told that a prominent Republican said to him yesterday in Jacksonville, Florida, "Mr. Vice President, that was a damn fine speech." And the Vice President said, "I appreciate the compliment but not the language." And the Republican went on, "Yes, sir, I liked it so much that I contributed a thousand dollars to your campaign." And Mr. Nixon replied, "The hell you say."

Mr. Nixon, in the last seven days, has called me an economic ignoramus, a Pied Piper, and all the rest. I've just confined myself to calling him a Republican, but he says that is getting low.

—New York City, November 5, 1960

Mr. Nixon trots out the same old program. He has given it new names, Operation Consume and Operation Safeguard. But the words are the same, the melody is the same. Only the lighting and make-up are different.

—La Crosse, Wisconsin, October 23, 1960

NUCLEAR AGE

Nuclear powers must avert those confrontations which bring an adversary to a choice of either a humiliating retreat or a nuclear war. To adopt that kind of course in the nuclear age would be evidence only of the bankruptcy of our policy or of a collective death wish for the world.

—commencement, American University, June 10, 1963

(see ALL OR NOTHING)

NUCLEAR TEST BAN TREATY

Yesterday a shaft of light cut into the darkness. Negotiations were concluded in Moscow on a treaty to ban all nuclear tests in the atmosphere, in outer space, and under water. For the first time, an agreement has been reached on bringing the forces of nuclear destruction under international control. This treaty is not the millennium. It will not resolve all conflicts, or cause the Communists to forgo their ambitions, or eliminate the dangers of war. It will not reduce our need for arms or allies or programs of assistance to others. But it is an important first step—a step toward peace—a step toward reason—a step away from war.

—announcing the Nuclear Test Ban Treaty, July 26, 1963

NUCLEAR TESTS

When all nuclear powers refrain from testing, the nuclear arms race is held in check. That is why this nation has long urged an effective worldwide end to nuclear tests.

—television address to the nation, March 2, 1962

NUCLEAR WAR

A war today or tomorrow, if it led to nuclear war, would not be like any war in history. A full-scale nuclear exchange, lasting less than sixty minutes, with the weapons now in existence, could wipe out more than 300 million Americans, Europeans and Russians, as well as untold numbers elsewhere. And the survivors, as Chairman Khrushchev warned the Communist Chinese, "The survivors would envy the dead." For they would inherit a world so devastated by explosions and poisons and fire that today we cannot even conceive of its horrors. So let us try to turn the world from war.

—announcing the Nuclear Test Ban Treaty, July 26, 1963

NUCLEAR WEAPONS

But until mankind has banished both war and its instruments of destruction, the United States must maintain an effective quantity and quality of nuclear weapons, so deployed and protected as to be capable of surviving any surprise attack and devastating the attacker.

—television address to the nation, March 2, 1962

NUCLEAR WEAPONS PROLIFERATION

I ask you to stop and think for a moment what it would mean to have nuclear weapons in so many hands, in the hands of countries large and small, stable and unstable, responsible and irresponsible, scattered throughout the world. There would be no rest for anyone then, no stability, no real security and no chance of effective disarmament. There would only be the increased chance of accidental war and an increased necessity for the great powers to involve themselves in what otherwise would be local conflicts.

—announcing the Nuclear Test Ban Treaty, July 26, 1963

OHIO

At a birthday dinner for Ohio Governor DiSalle in Columbus, Ohio, on January 6, 1962, President Kennedy began his remarks with a historical footnote.

"A hundred years ago, Abraham Lincoln stayed up all night in a telegraph office, watching the results of an essential gubernatorial contest in this state, in the darkest days of the Civil War. And at the end of the night when the Unionist candidate who supported Lincoln's policies had finally emerged as the victor, Lincoln wired, 'Glory to God in the highest, Ohio has saved the nation.'

"Two years ago yesterday, when Governor DiSalle was kind enough to endorse my candidacy, I had somewhat similar sentiments about Ohio."

(see COLUMBUS, OHIO)

OIL

President Kennedy was vitally interested in the renovation of the White House. When the Rose Garden was being torn up and replanted, he would periodically call out the White House window to the men digging in the garden, "Struck oil yet?"

ON-THE-JOB TRAINING

"I want to say that I have been in on-the-job training for about eleven months," President Kennedy said in a speech to the AFL-CIO convention after nearly a year in office, "and feel that I have some seniority rights."

OPINION

The unity of freedom has never relied on uniformity of opinion.

—State of the Union message, January 14, 1963

OUTER SPACE

As we extend the rule of law on earth, so must we also extend it to man's new domain—outer space.

The new horizons of outer space must not be driven by the old bitter concepts of imperialism and sovereign claims. The cold reaches of the universe must not become the new arena of an even colder war.

To this end we shall urge proposals extending the United Nations Charter to the limits of man's exploration in the universe, reserving outer space for peaceful use, prohibiting weapons of mass destruction in space or on celestial bodies, and opening the mysteries and benefits of space to every nation.

—United Nations address, September 25, 1961
(see MOON, NEW FRONTIER, SPACE)

PALM BEACH

After a holiday in Palm Beach, the President returned to Washington chastened. "Like members of Congress, I have been, during the last few days over the Easter holiday, back in touch with my constituents and seeing how they felt," he said, "and, frankly, I have come back to Washington from Palm Beach and I'm against my entire program."

PALM BEACH FLOCK

On his visit to Cork, Ireland, President Kennedy introduced a friend to the crowd: "And now I would like to introduce to you the pastor at the church which I go to, who comes from Cork—Monsignor O'Mohoney. He is the pastor of a poor, humble flock in Palm Beach, Florida."

PARTICIPATION

The result of this shift from participation to, if I may use the word, "spectation," is all too visible in the physical condition of our population.

—National Football Foundation, Hall of Fame banquet, December 5, 1961

We do not want in the United States a nation of spectators. We want a nation of participants in the vigorous life.

—Youth Fitness Conference, February 21, 1961
(see EXERCISE)

PAST

The only significance of analyzing the past is that it does give us some key to the future.

—Pocatello, Idaho, September 6, 1960
(see FUTURE)

PEACE

In the speech he was scheduled to give in Dallas on November 22, 1963, President Kennedy would have spoken of humanity's ancient vision of peace: "We ask . . . that we may be worthy of our power and responsibility, that we may exercise our strength with wisdom and restraint, and that we may achieve in our time and for all time the ancient vision of 'peace on earth, goodwill toward men.' "

America's enduring concern is for both peace *and* freedom.

—message to Congress, May 25, 1961

And is not peace, in the last analysis, basically a matter of human rights—the right to live out our lives without fear of devastation—the right to breathe air as nature provided it—the right of future generations to a healthy existence?

—commencement, American University, June 10, 1963

What kind of peace do we seek? . . . Not the peace of the grave or the security of the slave. I am talking about genuine peace, the kind of peace that makes life on earth worth living, the kind that enables men and nations to grow and to build a better life for their children—not merely peace for Americans, but peace for all men and women; not merely peace in our time, but peace for all time.

—commencement, American University, June 10, 1963

I speak of peace, therefore, as the necessary rational end of rational men. I realize that the pursuit of peace is not as dramatic as the pursuit of war, and frequently the words of the pursuer fall on deaf ears. But we have no more urgent task.

—commencement, American University, June 10, 1963

First, let us examine our attitude toward peace itself. Too many of us think it is impossible. Too many think it unreal. But that is a dangerous, defeatist belief. It leads to the conclusion that war is inevitable, that mankind is doomed, that we are gripped by forces we cannot control.

We need not accept that view. Our problems are man-made; therefore they can be solved by man.

—commencement, American University, June 10, 1963

Peace is a daily, a weekly, a monthly process, gradually changing opinions, slowly eroding old barriers, quietly building new structures. And however undramatic the pursuit of peace, that pursuit must go on.

—United Nations address, September 20, 1963

In a world of danger and trial, peace is our deepest aspiration, and when peace comes, we will gladly convert not our swords into plowshares, but our bombs into peaceful reactors, and our planes into space vehicles.

—campaign address, Seattle, September 6, 1960

PEACE AND FREEDOM

Peace and freedom do not come cheap, and we are destined—all of us here today—to live out most if not all of our lives in uncertainty and challenge and peril.

—University of North Carolina, October 12, 1961

PEACEFUL COOPERATION

To be fully secure, we need a much better weapon than the H-bomb, a weapon better than ballistic missiles or nuclear submarines, and that better weapon is peaceful cooperation.

—United Nations address, September 20, 1963

PERSONALITIES

In this country, of course, great emphasis has always been placed on the individual. Personalities have always been more interesting to us than facts.

—*Why England Slept*, 1940, "Conclusion"

PHYSICAL FITNESS

Good physical fitness is essential to good physical and mental health.

—message to Congress on the nation's youth, February 14, 1963

Despite our much publicized emphasis on school athletics, our own children lag behind European children in physical fitness. . . . In short, what we must do is literally change the physical habits of millions of Americans; and that is far more difficult than changing their tastes, their fashions or even their politics.

—National Football Foundation, Hall of Fame banquet, December 5, 1961
(see EXERCISE, PARTICIPATION)

POETRY

When power leads man toward arrogance, poetry reminds him of his limitations. When power narrows the areas of man's concern, poetry reminds him of the rightness and diversity of his existence. When power corrupts, poetry cleanses. For art establishes the basic human truth which must serve as the touchstone of our judgment.

—Amherst College, Massachusetts, October 26, 1963
(see ARTIST; FROST, ROBERT)

POLITICAL

Of course, it would be much easier if we could all continue to think in traditional political patterns—of liberalism and conservatism, as Republicans and Democrats, from the viewpoint of North and South, management and labor, business and consumer or some equally narrow framework. It would be more comfortable to continue to move and vote in platoons, joining whomever of our colleagues are equally enslaved by some current fashion, raging prejudice or popular movement. But today this nation cannot tolerate the luxury of such lazy political habits. Only the strength and progress and peaceful change that come from independent judgment and individual ideas—and even from the unorthodox and the eccentric—can enable us to surpass that foreign ideology that fears free thought more than it fears hydrogen bombs.

—*Profiles in Courage,* 1956

POPE

President Kennedy was criticized by Catholic Church officials for opposing federal aid to parochial schools. After proposing his education bill to the Congress, JFK quipped, "As all of you know, some circles invented the myth that after Al Smith's defeat in 1928, he sent a one-word telegram to the Pope: 'Unpack.' After my press conference on the school bill, I received a one-word wire from the Pope: 'Pack.' "

POPULATION

Our population is growing each decade by a figure equal to the total population of this country at the time of Abraham Lincoln.

—commencement, San Diego State College, June 6, 1963

POSTMASTER GENERAL

President Kennedy could not resist the temptation to tease the Postmaster General.

Unable to attend a testimonial luncheon in honor of Postmaster General J. Edward Day, the Chief Executive sent his regrets and added: "I am sending this message by wire, since I want to be certain that this message reaches you in the right place at the right time."

Later a reporter asked: "Mr. President, have you narrowed your search for a new Postmaster General? And are you seeking a man with a business background or a political background?"

The President replied: "The search is narrowing, but we haven't—there are other fields that are still to be considered, including even a postal background."

POVERTY

The conquest of poverty is as difficult as the conquest of outer space.

—reception, Washington, D.C., March 13, 1962

There is inherited wealth in this country and also inherited poverty.

—Amherst College, Massachusetts, October 26, 1963

Poverty weakens individuals and nations.

—message to Congress on welfare, February 1, 1962

It is hard for any nation to focus on an external or subversive threat to its independence when its energies are drained in daily combat with the forces of poverty and despair.

—State of the Union message, January 14, 1963

The war against poverty and degradation is not yet over.

—FDR memorial program on the 25th anniversary of signing Social Security Act, Hyde Park, New York, August 14, 1960

POWER

The men who create power make an indispensable contribution to the nation's greatness, but the men who question power make a contribution just as indispensable, especially when that questioning is disinterested. For they determine whether we use power or power uses us.

—Amherst College, Massachusetts, October 26, 1963

We cannot diminish our contributions to Western security or abdicate the responsibilities of power. And it is a fact of history that responsibility and influence—in all areas, political, military and economic—ultimately rise and fall together.

—remarks at trade conference, May 17, 1962

In a time of turbulence and change, it is more true than ever that knowledge is power.

—commencement, University of California, Berkeley, March 23, 1962
(see KNOWLEDGE, LEADERSHIP AND LEARNING)

POWERS, DAVE

President Kennedy sent Dave Powers (his special assistant and close friend, with whom he swam daily in the White House pool) a scroll in recognition of his fiftieth birthday:

"President's Special Award, Physical Fitness Program. Walking fifty miles per month from TV to refrigerator and back. Presented to Dave Powers on his fiftieth birthday. In recognition of your athletic ability in hiking to my icebox to drink my Heineken's."

PRAY

"Do not pray for easy lives," urged President Kennedy at a prayer breakfast in Washington. "Pray to be stronger men."

PRESIDENCY

Asked how he liked being President, Jack Kennedy shrugged and said simply, "I have a nice home, the office is close by and the pay is good."

After losing the vice presidential nomination to Estes Kefauver in 1956, Jack Kennedy went on a vacation at his father's rented Riviera home. Michael Canfield, the former husband of Jackie's sister, asked Jack why he wanted to be President.

Basking in the sun, his eyes still closed, JFK said, "I guess it's the only thing I can do."

That turned out to be true—for him. In Georgetown just before his inauguration the President-elect said: "It's a big job. It isn't going to be so bad. You've got time to think. You don't have all those people bothering you that you had in the Senate—besides, the pay is pretty good."

President Kennedy donated his Presidential salary to charity, so he may have been joking about the pay.

After a few months in office he said, "The only thing that really surprised us when we got into office was that things were just as bad as we had been saying they were; otherwise we have been enjoying it very much."

At the end of his first year in office, President Kennedy commented: "The job is interesting, but the possibilities for trouble are unlimited. It's been a tough year, but then, they're all going to be tough."

Later President Kennedy was asked: "If you had to do it over again would you work for the Presidency and would you recommend the job to others?"

"Well, the answer to the first is yes and the answer to the second is no. I don't recommend it to others, at least not for a while."

PRESIDENT

Jack Kennedy received a very flattering introduction from a fellow Democrat during the 1960 Presidential campaign.

"I want to express my appreciation to the Governor," JFK began his speech at a campaign rally in Muskegon, Michigan. "Every time he introduces me as the potentially greatest President in the history of the United States, I always think perhaps he is overstating it one or two degrees. George Washington wasn't a bad President and I do want to say a word for Thomas Jefferson. But, otherwise, I will accept the compliment."

—Muskegon, Michigan, September 5, 1960
(see JEFFERSON, THOMAS; WASHINGTON, GEORGE)

PRESS

President Kennedy was asked at a press conference on May 9, 1962, to comment on the press treatment of his administration so far. His answer: "Well, I'm reading more and enjoying it less."

PROBLEMS

"Let's see," President Kennedy liked to say of the latest problems. "Did we inherit these, or are they our own?"

I believe the problems of human destiny are not beyond the reach of human beings.

—United Nations address, September 20, 1963

PROBLEM-SOLVING

"We are committed to no rigid formula," President Kennedy told the United Nations in 1961. "We seek no perfect solution."

Our problems are man-made; therefore they can be solved by man.

—commencement, American University, June 10, 1963

No problem of human destiny is beyond human beings. Man's reason and spirit have often solved the seemingly unsolvable, and we believe they can do it again.

—commencement, American University, June 10, 1963

PROFILES IN COURAGE

Recovering from back surgery in 1955, Jack Kennedy could not sleep more than an hour or two at a stretch at first. He worked on his book *Profiles in Courage* day and night, doggedly, distracting himself from his physical pain with a heroic mental task.

When he was too tired to write or read, Jack asked Jackie or his friend Dave Powers to read to him.

"I would be reading to him from a book about Texas in Sam Houston's time, and he would be stretched out flat on his back with his eyes closed for a couple of hours, listening to every word I said," Powers recalled. "I would think he had fallen asleep, and I'd stop reading. He would open his eyes and tell me to keep going. When I came to a line that he liked, he would stop me and tell me to read it again."

The stories of men who accomplished good in the face of cruel calumnies from the public are not final proof that we should at all times ignore the feelings of the voters on national issues. For, as Winston Churchill has said, "Democracy is the worst form of government—except all those other forms that have been tried from time to time." We can improve our democratic processes, we can enlighten our understanding of its problems, and we can increase our respect for those men of integrity who find it necessary, from time to time, to act contrary to public opinion.

—*Profiles in Courage*, 1956

PROFIT

We want prosperity, and in a free enterprise system there can be no prosperity without profit. We want a growing economy, and there can be no growth without the investment that is inspired and financed by profit.

—remarks to Chamber of Commerce, April 30, 1962

PROGRESS

It is impossible to have real progress as long as millions are shut out from opportunity and others forgiven obligations.

—remarks to Inter-American Press Association, November 18, 1963

PROSPERITY

As they say on my own Cape Cod, a rising tide lifts all the boats.

—remarks in Frankfurt, Germany, June 25, 1963

Together we have been partners in adversity; let us also be partners in prosperity.

—remarks in Frankfurt, Germany, June 25, 1963

PROTESTANT

During the 1960 campaign a reporter in Los Angeles asked facetiously, "Do you think a Protestant can be elected President in 1960?"

JFK answered: "If he's prepared to answer how he stands on the issue of separation of church and state, I see no reason why we should discriminate against him."

PT-109

During World War II Jack Kennedy served in the Pacific as a commissioned naval officer. In August 1943 in Blackett Strait in the Solomon Islands, a Japanese destroyer rammed the *PT-109* torpedo boat he commanded and sank it.

Jack Kennedy saved the life of one wounded man by seizing the end of his life jacket in his teeth and towing him to an island three miles away.

Lt. Kennedy, with some others, reached a nearby island but found it held by the Japanese.

Kennedy and another officer then swam to another island, where they persuaded the inhabitants to send a message to other U.S. forces, who rescued them. It was several days before Jack Kennedy and his crew were rescued. They suffered severely from lack of food and water during that period, and Lt. Kennedy kept up the spirits of the survivors with his sense of humor.

When he finally heard the voice of a rescuer crying, "Hey, Jack!" from a distance, Jack yelled back, "Where the hell have you been?"

"We've got some food for you!" called out the rescuer.

"No, thanks," quipped Lt. Kennedy, who kept his sense of humor throughout all crises. "I just had a coconut."

Shortly thereafter JFK had a run-in with a doctor. "I went in to see the Doc about some coral infections I got," he recalled. "He asked me how I got them—I said, 'Swimming.' He then burst out with, 'Kennedy, you know swimming is forbidden in this area. Stay out of the goddamned water!' So now it's an official order."

(see "A Brief Biography" at end of book—1943)

PUBLIC ADDRESS

When a public address system failed during a campaign stop in St. Paul, Minnesota, JFK remarked:

"I understand that Daniel Webster used to address a hundred thousand people without any trouble at all, and without a mike, so it should be easy for us. However, we are a little softer than they used to be."

(see WEBSTER, DANIEL)

PUBLIC CONFIDENCE

The basis of effective government is public confidence, and that confidence is endangered when ethical standards falter or appear to falter.

—message to Congress, April 27, 1961

PUBLIC OFFICE

When he was a young Congressman, Jack Kennedy was once seen parking his car flagrantly in front of a "NO PARKING" sign in downtown Washington.

"This is what Hamlet means," he explained, "by 'the insolence of office.' "

PUBLIC OFFICIALS

Public officials are not a group apart. They inevitably reflect the moral tone of the society in which they live.

—message to Congress, April 27, 1961

PUBLIC SCHOOL

Our public school system must be preserved and improved. Our very survival as a free nation depends upon it.

—telegram, February 2, 1961

RACE

No one has been barred on account of his race from fighting or dying for America—there are no "white" or "colored" signs on the foxholes or graveyards of battle.

—message to Congress on proposed civil rights bill, June 19, 1963 (see CIVIL RIGHTS)

RADZIWILL, PRINCESS

"It is not true that we're going to change the name of Lafayette Square to Radziwill Square," President Kennedy reassured a Gridiron dinner crowd, referring to his sister-in-law Princess Radziwill, "at least, not during the first term."

RAINS

I regret the rain, but it rains, as the Bible tells us, on the just and the unjust alike, on the Republicans as well as Democrats.

—Sioux Falls, South Dakota, September 22, 1960

READING

One of the best ways for one to expand his horizons is through a regular reading program.

—White House memorandum, November 7, 1963

RECESSIONS

Recessions are not inevitable. . . . I believe that someday in this country we can wipe them out . . . and this tax cut is the single most important weapon that we can now add.

—television address to the nation, September 18, 1963
(see TAX CUT)

RELIGION

I do not regard religion as a weapon in the cold war. I regard it as the essence of the differences which separate those on the other side of the Iron Curtain and ourselves.

—to International Christian Leadership, February 9, 1961

RELIGIOUS ISSUE

The "religious issue" was Kennedy's Catholicism in a country which had never elected a Catholic president. Hearing that he was criticized by the Vatican for his statements that he would not be influenced by the Vatican,

Senator Kennedy smiled sadly and said, "Now I understand why Henry the Eighth set up his own church."

(see POPE)

REPUBLIC

President Kennedy referred to the United States as a republic; he called it "the great Republic."

You and I are privileged to serve the great Republic in what could be the most decisive decade in its long history.

—State of the Union message, January 11, 1962

RESEARCH AND DEVELOPMENT

A basic source of knowledge is research. Industry has long realized this truth. Health and agriculture have established the worth of systematic research and development.

—message to Congress, January 29, 1963

RESPONSIBILITY

In a democracy, every citizen, regardless of his interest in politics, "holds office"; every one of us is in a position of responsibility and, in the final analysis, the kind of government we get depends upon how we fulfill these responsibilities. We, the people, are the boss, and we will get the kind of political leadership, be it good or bad, that we demand and deserve.

—*Profiles in Courage*, 1956

REVOLUTION

Those who make peaceful revolution impossible will make violent revolution inevitable.

—address to Latin-American diplomats, March 12, 1962

History has removed for governments the margin of safety between the peaceful revolution and the violent revolution. The luxury of a leisurely interval is no longer available.

—message to Congress, March 12, 1962
(see AMERICAN REVOLUTION)

RIGHTS

We need to strengthen our nation by protecting the basic rights of its citizens. The right to competent counsel must be assured to every man accused of crime in federal court, regardless of his means. And the most precious and powerful right in the world, the right to vote in a free American election, must not be denied to any citizens on grounds of their race or their color.

—State of the Union message, January 14, 1963
(see CIVIL RIGHTS, HUMAN RIGHTS)

ROCKING CHAIR

A reporter asked President-elect Kennedy if he planned to take his rocking chair with him to the White House.

"Whither I goest," answered JFK, "it goes."

He added: "You will recall what Senator Dirksen said about the rocking chair—it gives you a sense of motion without any sense of danger."

ROOSEVELT, FRANKLIN DELANO

JFK campaigned very hard to become President by a narrow margin in 1960. Campaigning in Dayton, Ohio, he spoke with admiration of FDR's brilliant campaign strategy leading to victory in 1932:

"Franklin Roosevelt started his campaign here in Ohio. I don't know what has happened in politics. . . . Franklin Roosevelt stayed in Albany all winter, spring, summer, didn't go to the convention until he was nominated. He then took a boating trip up the coast of Maine with his son, started his campaign late in September, made some speeches, and was elected by a tremendous majority."

(see MACARONI)

ROOSEVELT, JR., FRANKLIN

JFK loved to tell stories to children. His daughter, Caroline, was his most attentive listener. One day, while they were sitting on the stern of their boat, *Honey Fitz*, JFK began to tell a story about a huge white whale that lived in the ocean.

Sitting on the stern next to the President, sunning, was a shoeless Franklin Roosevelt, Jr., wearing an old, dirty pair of sweat socks.

The President continued telling his whale story to Caroline, explaining that one of the favorite delicacies for this whale was "old, dirty sweat socks."

Suddenly he reached over and snatched a sock off Roosevelt Jr.'s foot and threw it in the Atlantic.

Franklin Roosevelt, Jr., was slightly shocked and stared at the President, who went on to say that the only thing this strange whale liked better was a second sock—whereupon JFK reached over, grabbed the second sock and threw it overboard.

RUNNER

President Kennedy, as a national spokesman, offered this rebuttal to Khrushchev's statement in the summer of 1961 that the United States was like a worn-out "runner."

"Chairman Khrushchev has compared the United States to a worn-out runner living on its past performance and stated that the Soviet Union would out-produce the United States by 1970. Without wishing to trade hyperbole with the Chairman, I do suggest that he reminds me of the tiger hunter who had picked a place on the wall to hang the tiger's skin long before he caught the tiger. The tiger has other ideas. . . . In short, the United States is not such an aged runner and, to paraphrase Mr. Coolidge, 'We *do* choose to run.' "

RUNNING MATE

On election night in 1960 Jack Kennedy received a long-distance call from his running mate, Lyndon Johnson. Grinning, JFK reported to his staff what LBJ had said to him: "I hear *you're* losing in Ohio, but *we're* doing fine in Pennsylvania."

(see JOHNSON, LYNDON)

RUSK, DEAN

Secretary of State Dean Rusk played an important role in the Vienna talks between President Kennedy and Premier Khrushchev.

One day at lunch, Secretary of State Rusk boasted to Khrushchev about a new kind of experimental American corn that grew three feet from seed in sixty days.

Khrushchev interrupted Rusk: "I know what's what—you told Gromyko in Geneva and he told me, but I wrote a friend of mine in America [Roswell Garst, whose Iowa farm Khrushchev had visited during his trip to the United States] and he told me it wasn't true."

Later Khrushchev was boasting to Kennedy about Soviet technological feats, not only in space but on earth, including a newly developed process of making vodka out of natural gas.

President Kennedy interrupted Khrushchev: "That sounds like some of Dean Rusk's sixty-day corn to me."

(see KHRUSHCHEV, NIKITA)

RUSSIA

Mr. Khrushchev says with confidence that our children and grandchildren will be Communists. I think we should say with the same confidence that his children will be free.

—at the Michigan State Fair, Detroit, October 26, 1960

RUSSIAN PEOPLE

As Americans we find Communism profoundly repugnant as a negation of personal freedom and dignity. But we can still hail the Russian people for their many achievements—in science and space, in economic and industrial growth, in culture and in acts of courage.

—commencement, American University, June 10, 1963

S

SALINGER, PIERRE

Pierre Salinger, the President's press secretary, was one of the few who had a relationship with the President that allowed him to burst into the Oval Office unannounced.

"Plucky," as JFK called him, took pride in being able to trace leaks to their sources.

One time the President was furious when there was a leak on the Cuban embargo. He asked Salinger to spare no effort in finding out who leaked it.

Salinger, a former investigative reporter, worked for two days and then reported back to the President that he was pleased to be able to announce he had traced the leak.

"Who was it?" the President asked intently.

"You," said Salinger.

"What do you mean?" asked JFK.

"Didn't you tell George Smathers?"

JFK nodded. He had told the Florida senator.

"Well, George told a friend of his on the *Tampa Tribune* and that was that," declared Salinger.

JFK stared at Salinger, grinned, and said, "Plucky . . ."

(see SMATHERS, GEORGE)

SAND TRAP

Getting out of a sand trap can be humbling even for the rich and famous. Jack Kennedy was playing golf with Jackie at the seventeenth hole on the Hyannis Port golf course. She was having difficulty blasting out of the sand trap. The ball kept trickling back down into the trap.

"Open the face of the club," Jack called commandingly from his golf cart. "Follow through."

Jackie remained stuck in the sand trap after many swings. Finally Jack Kennedy lost patience. Taking the club from Jackie he said firmly, "Let me show you."

After a few fluid practice swings, he brought the club back gracefully and swung mightily. The ball rose a couple of inches and trickled back into the sand.

A lesser man might have lost his poise, but Jack Kennedy handed the golf club back to Jackie and said, "See, that's how you do it."

SANTA CLAUS

An eight-year-old girl, Michelle Rochon of Marine City, Michigan, was upset that nuclear tests were being conducted close to the North Pole. Her letter to the President received a reply from the Chief Executive:

> Dear Michelle,
>
> I was glad to get your letter about trying to stop the Russians from bombing the North Pole and risking the life of Santa Claus.

I share your concern about the atmospheric testing by the Soviet Union, not only for the North Pole, but for countries throughout the world.

However, you must not worry about Santa Claus. I talked with him yesterday and he is fine. He will be making his rounds this Christmas.

[signed] John F. Kennedy

SARDONIC

President Kennedy took exception to a June 1962 article in *Time* about his brother Ted's nomination for the Senate. JFK especially objected to a description of Ted as smiling "sardonically."

"Bobby and I smile sardonically," declared the President, smiling. "Ted will learn how to smile sardonically in two or three years, but he doesn't know how yet."

(see KENNEDY, TED)

SCHOLARS

"Prince Bismarck once said that one third of the students of German universities broke down from overwork, another third broke down from dissipation, and the other third ruled Germany," President Kennedy addressed the students of West Berlin's Free University on June 26, 1963. "I do not know which third of the student body is here today, but I am confident that I am talking to the future rulers of this country."

President Kennedy stressed the important role of the scholar in modern society. "The scholar, the teacher, the intellectual have a higher duty than any of the others, for society has trained you to think as well as do."

He went on to emphasize the link between scholarship and leadership throughout history.

It is a fact that in my own country the American Revolution and the society developed thereafter were built by some of the most distinguished scholars in the history of the United States, who were, at the same time, among our foremost politicians. They did not believe that knowledge was merely for the study, but they thought it was for the marketplace as well; and Madison and Jefferson and Franklin and all the others who built the United States, who built our Constitution and built it on a sound framework, I believe set an example for us all. And what was true of my country has been true of your country, and the countries of Western Europe.

(see SCHOLARSHIP AND LEADERSHIP)

SCHOLARSHIP AND LEADERSHIP

A great and laudable tradition . . . combined American scholarship and American leadership in political affairs. It is an extraordinary fact of history, I think, unmatched since the days of early Greece, that this country should have produced during its founding days, in a population of a handful of men, such an extraordinary range of scholars and creative thinkers—Jefferson, Franklin, Morris, Wilson and all the rest. This is a great tradition which we must maintain with increasing strength and increasing vigor.

—commencement, San Diego State College, June 6, 1963

(see KNOWLEDGE, LEADERSHIP AND LEARNING, LIBERTY AND LEARNING)

SCHOOL DROPOUTS

This is a serious national problem. A boy or girl has only a limited time in life in which to get an education, and yet it will shape their whole lives and the lives of their children. So I am asking all American parents to urge their children to go back to school in September, to assist them in every way to stay in school.

—news conference, August 1, 1963
(see HIGH SCHOOL DROPOUTS)

SCHOOL PRAYER

"Speaking of the religious issue," JFK jested with White House correspondents, "I asked the Chief Justice tonight whether he thought our new education bill was constitutional and he said: 'It's clearly constitutional—it hasn't got a prayer.' "

(see RELIGIOUS ISSUE)

SCIENCE

Stressing the increasing "importance of pure science" in the twentieth century, President Kennedy addressed the National Academy of Sciences one month before his death.

"We realize now that progress in technology depends on progress in theory; that the most abstract investigations can lead to the most concrete results; and that the vitality of a scientific community springs from its passion to answer science's most fundamental questions."

President Kennedy also emphasized the growing role of government in scientific research: "In the last hundred years, science has thus emerged from a peripheral concern of government to an active partner."

Science is the most powerful means we have for the unification of knowledge, and a main obligation of its future must be to deal with problems which cut across boundaries.

—National Academy of Sciences, October 22, 1963

The greatest challenge to science in our times [is] to use the world's resources to expand life and hope for the world's inhabitants.

—National Academy of Sciences, October 22, 1963

Science remains universal, and the fruits of science, if wisely chosen, provide a means by which humanity can realize a full and abundant life. Yet the vitality of science, its ability to enrich our culture and our understanding, and the material benefits it promises all depend in large measure upon international pooling of knowledge and effort.

—conference on science, Stowe, Vermont, September 4, 1961

We are bound to grope for a time as we grapple with problems without precedent in human history. But wisdom is the child of experience. . . . As we begin to master the destructive potentialities of modern science we move toward a new era in which science can fulfill its creative promise.

—letter to the Senate on oceanography, March 29, 1961

SCIENCE AND TECHNOLOGY

Science and technology are irreversible. We cannot return to the day of the sailing schooner or the covered wagon, even if wished.

—remarks at Mormon Tabernacle, September 26, 1963

SCIENTISTS

American scientists remain second to none in their independence and in their individualism.

—commencement, Yale University, June 11, 1962

SECRECY

The very word "secrecy" is repugnant in a free and open society; and we are as a people inherently and historically opposed to secret societies, to secret oaths and to secret proceedings. We decided long ago that the dangers of excessive and unwarranted concealment of pertinent facts far outweighed the dangers which are cited to justify it.

—address to newspaper publishers, April 27, 1961

(see NATIONAL SECURITY, SECURITY)

SECURITY

There is little value in insuring the survival of our nation if our traditions do not survive with it. And there is very grave danger that an announced need for increased security will be seized upon by those anxious to expand its meaning to the very limits of official censorship and concealment.

—address to newspaper publishers, April 27, 1961

(see FREEDOM OF INFORMATION, NATIONAL SECURITY)

SELF-DETERMINATION

Political sovereignty is but a mockery without the means to meet poverty and illiteracy and disease. Self-determination is but a slogan if the future holds no hope.

—United Nations address, September 25, 1961

SELF-EXTINCTION

Seventeen years ago man unleashed the power of the atom. He thereby took into his mortal hands the power of self-extinction.

—television address to the nation, March 2, 1962

SELF-RESPECT

In the final chapter of *Profiles in Courage*, JFK concludes that self-love or self-respect is a characteristic that courageous people have in common. The courageous senators profiled in the book all exemplified it:

> It was not because they "loved the public better than themselves." On the contrary it was precisely because they did *love themselves*—because each one's need to maintain his own respect for himself was more important to him than his popularity with others—because his desire to win or maintain a reputation for integrity and courage was stronger than his desire to maintain his office—because his conscience, his personal standard of ethics, his integrity or morality, call it what you will—was stronger than the pressure of public disapproval—because his faith that *his* course was the best one, and would ultimately be vindicated, outweighed his fear of public reprisal.

(see ADAMS, JOHN; CALHOUN, JOHN C.; CLAY, HENRY; WEBSTER, DANIEL)

SENATE

I am convinced that the complication of public business and the competition for the public's attention have obscured innumerable acts of political courage—large and small—performed almost daily in the Senate Chamber.

—*Profiles in Courage*, 1956

SENATOR

By retelling *some* of the most outstanding and dramatic stories of political courage in the Senate, I have attempted to indicate that this is a quality which may be found in any Senator, in any political party and in any era.

—*Profiles in Courage*, 1956

SENIOR CITIZENS

"This state knows the issues of this campaign—Senior Citizens," stated JFK at a stop in Warren, Michigan, October 26, 1960. "Senator McNamara is chairman of the Senate Committee on Senior Citizens. I am the vice chairman. We are both aging rapidly."

SEX APPEAL

"I gave everything a good deal of thought," Jack Kennedy wrote to his friend Paul Fay, Jr., in July 1953, "so am getting married this fall. This means the end of a promising political career as it has been based up to now almost completely on the old sex appeal."

(see WOMEN VOTERS)

SHEPARD, ALAN

President Kennedy introduced astronaut Alan Shepard, Jr., on May 8, 1961, after a successful space flight.

"We have with us the nation's number one television performer, who I think on last Friday morning secured the largest rating of any morning in recent history . . .

"And I think it does credit to him that he is associated with such a distinguished group of Americans whom we are all glad to honor today—his companions in the flight to outer space . . ."

The President proceeded to name some unsung heroes of the space program.

"Most of these names are unfamiliar. If the flight had not been an overwhelming success, these names would be very familiar to everyone."

SHIRTS

John F. Kennedy, the most fashion-conscious and fashionable of Presidents, was rumored to change his shirt six times a day. One day a bold journalist asked the President how many times he had changed his shirt that day.

"Four."

Pressed for details, the President explained he had started off with a clean shirt, put on another after his swim before his lunch honoring the Bolivian president, donned a third shirt after the lunch because it had been so hot during the lunch, and his fourth clean shirt after a bath before dinner.

(see CLOTHES)

SHORTCUTS

We must recognize there are no shortcuts, no easy way . . .

—campaign remarks, Providence, November 7, 1960

SHRIVER, EUNICE

"I would like to introduce my sister, Eunice Shriver, who lives in Chicago," said John Kennedy to a crowd in Libertyville, Illinois. "I have sisters living in all the key electoral states in preparation for this campaign."

(see SISTERS)

SIGNATURES

Leonard Lyons informed President Kennedy of the going rates for signed portrait photos of Presidents, past and present: George Washington—$175; Franklin D.

Roosevelt—$75; U.S. Grant—$55; John F. Kennedy—$65. JFK wrote back:

> Dear Leonard:
> I appreciate your letter about the market on Kennedy signatures. It is hard to believe that the going price is so high now. In order not to depress the market any further, I will not sign this letter.

SISTERS

"And my sister, Eunice, Mrs. Sargent Shriver, who lives in Illinois," said Senator Kennedy, introducing his sister to a crowd at a campaign stop in Elgin, Illinois. "One of my sisters is married to someone who lives in New York, one in California. We realized long ago we have to carry New York, Illinois, and California."

SKEPTICS

The problems of the world cannot possibly be solved by skeptics or cynics whose horizons are limited by obvious realities. We need men who can dream of things that never were and ask, "Why not?"

—address to Irish parliament, June 28, 1963
(see VISIONARIES)

SMATHERS, GEORGE

At a fund-raiser in Miami for Florida senator George Smathers, President Kennedy spoke fondly of Senator Smathers.

> Senator Smathers has been one of my most valuable counselors at crucial moments. In 1952 when I was thinking of

running for the United States Senate, I went to Senator Smathers and said, "George, what do you think?"

He said, "Don't do it, can't win, bad year."

[JFK ran and won.]

In 1956, I didn't know whether I should run for vice president or not so I said, "George, what do you think?" And Senator Smathers replied, "It's your choice!" So I ran and lost.

In 1960 I was wondering whether I ought to run in the West Virginia primary, but the Senator said, "Don't do it. That state you can't possibly carry."

[JFK ran and won.]

And actually, the only time I really got nervous about the whole matter of Los Angeles was just before the balloting and George came up and said, "I think it looks pretty good for you."

(see SALINGER, PIERRE)

SMILES

Jack Kennedy liked to tell stories about what a tough businessman his father was. When one of his sisters was married, a newspaper reported that someone in Joseph Kennedy's office had acknowledged "with a smile" that the cost of the wedding was in the six-figure category.

"Now I know that story is a phony," scoffed JFK. "No one in my father's office ever smiles."

(see SARDONIC)

S.O.B.

An international incident was barely averted when Canadian Prime Minister Diefenbaker angrily charged that President Kennedy had written "S.O.B." on some official State Department document concerning Diefenbaker and Canada.

The Canadian prime minister refused to release the controversial document, even after President Kennedy denied having written "S.O.B." on it.

JFK shrugged it off and said he wondered why the Canadian prime minister "didn't do what any normal, friendly government would do . . . make a photostatic copy, and return the original."

SOFT SOCIETIES

The complacent, the self-indulgent, the soft societies are about to be swept away with the debris of history. Only the strong, only the industrious, only the determined, only the courageous, only the visionary who determine the real nature of our struggle can possibly survive.

—address to newspaper editors, Washington, D.C., April 20, 1961

SOVIET UNION

The people of the Soviet Union, even after forty-five years of party dictatorship, feel the forces of historical evolution. The harsh precepts of Stalinism are officially recognized as bankrupt. Economic and political variation and dissent are appearing, for example, in Poland, Rumania and the Soviet Union itself. So history itself runs against the Marxist dogma, not toward it.

—address at the Free University, West Berlin, June 26, 1963

SPACE

The day before his assassination, President Kennedy spoke at the dedication of the Aero-Space Medical Health Center at Brooks Air Force Base in Texas. The President quoted Frank O'Connor's statement that he and his boyhood friends would trudge across the country until they came to a seemingly insurmountable wall. Then they would toss their hats over the wall so that they had to follow.

"This nation has tossed its cap across the wall of space," avowed President Kennedy, "and we have no choice but to follow it."

It is time . . . for this nation to take a clearly leading role in space achievement, which in many ways may hold the key to our future on earth.

—message to Congress on urgent national needs, May 25, 1961

If we are to win the battle that is now going on around the world between freedom and tyranny, the dramatic achievements in space which occurred in recent weeks should have made clear to us all, as did the Sputnik in 1957, the impact of this adventure on the minds of men everywhere, who are attempting to make a determination of which road they should take.

—special message to Congress, May 25, 1961

First, I believe that this nation should commit itself to achieving the goal, before this decade is out, of landing a man on the moon and returning him safely to the earth. No single space project in this period will be more impressive to mankind, or more important for the long-range exploration of space; and none will be so difficult or expensive to accomplish.

—special message to Congress, May 25, 1961

It is a most important decision that we make as a nation. But all of you have lived through the last four years and have seen the significance of space and the adventures in space, and no one can predict with certainty what the ultimate meaning will be of mastery of space.

—special message to Congress, May 25, 1961

We believe that when men reach beyond this planet, they should leave their national differences behind them.

—news conference, Washington, D.C., February 21, 1962
(see MOON, OUTER SPACE, SPACE RACE)

SPACE RACE

John Kennedy criticized the Republican administration for losing ground to the Russians in the space race.

"I wonder when he [Mr. Nixon] put his finger under Mr. Khrushchev's nose whether he was saying, 'I know you are ahead of us in rockets, Mr. Khrushchev, but we are ahead of you in color television.' I would just as soon look at black and white television and be ahead of them in rockets!" JFK spoke out on the space race in Pittsburgh, October 10, 1960.

President Kennedy placed a higher priority on space exploration than any President before or since; the Kennedy Space Center was renamed in his honor. During John F. Kennedy's "thousand days" in office the U.S. caught up with and surpassed the U.S.S.R. in the space race.

"We have a long way to go in this space race," affirmed President Kennedy after congratulating Col. John H. Glenn for his orbital space flight on February 20, 1962. "But this is the new ocean, and I believe the United States must sail on it and be in a position second to none."

To be sure, we are behind, and will be behind for some time in manned flight. But we do not intend to stay behind, and in this decade we shall make up and move ahead.

The exploration of space will go ahead, whether we join in it or not. And it is one of the great adventures of all time, and no nation which expects to be the leader of other nations can expect to stay behind in this race for space. We mean to lead it, for the eyes of the world now look into space, to the moon and to the planets beyond; and we have vowed that we shall not see it governed by a hostile flag of conquest, but by a banner of freedom and peace.

In short, our leadership in science and in industry, our hopes for peace and security, our obligations to ourselves as well as others, all require us to make this effort, to solve these mysteries, to solve them for the good of all men, and to become the world's leading space-faring nation.

Those who came before us made certain that this country rode the first waves of the industrial revolution, the first waves of modern invention and the first wave of nuclear power. And this generation does not intend to founder in the backwash of the coming age of space. We mean to be a part of it—we mean to lead it.

—address at Rice University, September 12, 1962

SPACE SCIENCE

Space science, like nuclear science and all technology, has no conscience of its own. Whether it will become a force for good or ill depends on man, and only if the United States occupies a position of pre-eminence can we help decide whether this new ocean will be a sea of peace or a new, terrifying theater of war.

—address at Rice University, September 12, 1962

SPACE SOVEREIGNTY

Space offers no problems of sovereignty. By resolution of this Assembly, the members of the United Nations have forsworn any claim to territorial rights in outer space or on celestial bodies, and declared that international law and the United Nations Charter will apply.

—address to the United Nations, September 20, 1963

SPENDERS ANONYMOUS

Jack and Jacqueline Kennedy sometimes quarrelled, and as with many married couples, money quarrels topped the list of domestic disputes.

Once, furious about discovering that his wife had spent nearly $150,000 in a year at department stores, JFK exclaimed, "She thinks she can go on spending forever. I don't understand what the hell she's doing with all those things. God, she's driving me crazy!"

He turned to an aide and asked, "Is there a Spenders Anonymous?"

SPIRIT

Our national strength matters, but the spirit which informs and controls our strength matters just as much.

—Amherst College, Massachusetts, October 26, 1963

STASSEN, HAROLD

"Mr. Stassen announces he will run for governor of Pennsylvania," JFK, asked at a press conference about the Stassen candidacy, said. "He has already been governor of Minnesota. That leaves only forty-six states still in jeopardy."

STATE

It is not our military might or our higher standard of living that has most distinguished us from our adversaries. It is our belief that the state is the servant of the citizen and not its master.

—State of the Union message, January 11, 1962

We face an adversary who mobilizes all of the resources of the state for the service of the state.

—remarks, Norristown, Pennsylvania, October 29, 1960

STATES

My country favors a world of free and equal states.

—United Nations address, September 25, 1961

STRENGTH

Neither smiles nor frowns, neither good intentions nor harsh words, are a substitute for strength.

—campaign address, Alexandria, Virginia, August 24, 1960

STYLE

The Kennedy White House was known for its style. John Kennedy could appreciate style, grace, and eloquence anywhere, anytime.

French President de Gaulle sent President Kennedy a letter urging him not to negotiate. The President read the letter excitedly to several colleagues, praising its style. "Isn't that beautiful?"

"You agree with it?" asked one of his astonished listeners, knowing the President had different ideas from de Gaulle.

"Oh no!" exclaimed JFK. "But what a marvellous style!"

TAX CUT

The support in this country for a tax cut crosses political lines. . . . A tax cut means new strength around the world for the American dollar and for freedom.

—television address to the nation, September 18, 1963

TAX LAWS

President Kennedy, at a dinner party in 1963, told friends the tax laws favored the wealthy. He pointed out that J. Paul Getty, reputedly the richest man in the world, had paid exactly $500 in taxes the previous year, and H. L. Hunt, the Texas oil tycoon, had paid only $22,000.

When Benjamin Bradlee pointed out that that was what he and his wife had paid in 1962, JFK shook his head and said, "The tax laws really screw people in your bracket, buddy boy."

TAX RATES

The fact is that the high wartime and postwar tax rates we are now paying are no longer necessary. They are, in fact, harmful. These high rates do not leave enough money in private hands to keep this country's economy growing and healthy. They have helped cause recessions. Our tax rates are so high today that the growth of profits and paychecks in this country has been stunted.

—television address to the American people, September 18, 1963
(see FAIR RETURN, PROFIT)

TEACHER

The quality of education is determined primarily by the quality of the teacher.

—message to Congress, January 29, 1963

TEACHERS

We must find better means for providing better rewards for our better teachers, we must make actual use of probationary periods to retain only those with satisfactory performance records, and we must demonstrate concretely to young beginners in the field that real opportunities for advancement await those whose contribution is of the highest caliber.

—*NEA Journal*, January, 1958

TEACHING

"Knowledge is power," said Francis Bacon. It is also light. In the dark and despairing days ahead, our youth shall need all the light the teaching profession can bring to bear upon the future. . . .

No profession of such importance in the United States

today is so poorly paid. No other occupational group in the country is asked to do so much for so little.

—*NEA Journal*, January, 1958

(see KNOWLEDGE, LEADERSHIP AND LEARNING, SCHOLARS)

TECHNICAL DIFFICULTIES

After pulling the switch in Salt Lake City to reactivate generators at the Green River, 150 miles away, the President listened intently to the speaker for the voice that was supposed to announce the successful starting of the generators.

There was a long, ponderous silence.

"If we don't hear from him," said JFK, "it's back to the drawing boards."

TECHNOLOGICAL CHANGE

Rapid technological change is resulting in serious employment dislocations, which deny us the full stimulus to growth which advancing technology makes possible.

—message to Congress, February 2, 1961

TECHNOLOGY

Occupationally, the new technology has been altering manpower requirements in favor of occupations requiring more education and training.

—manpower report to Congress, March 11, 1963

TERM LIMITS

A reporter asked President Kennedy how he felt about former President Eisenhower's suggestion that the number of terms of congressmen be limited.

"It's the sort of proposal which I may advance in a post-presidential period," JFK replied, "but not right now."

TERROR

Terror is not a new weapon. Throughout history it has been used by those who could not prevail, either by persuasion or example. But inevitably they fail, either because men are not afraid to die for a life worth living, or because the terrorists themselves came to realize that free men cannot be frightened by threats, and that aggression would meet its own response.

—United Nations address, September 25, 1961

TEXAN STORIES

Jack Kennedy had two favorite Texas stories, and he told them both in El Paso on September 12, 1960. One story concerned a Texan and a Bostonian.

"You remember the very old story about a citizen of Boston who heard a Texan talking about the glories of Bowie, Davy Crockett, and all the rest, and finally said, 'Haven't you heard of Paul Revere?' To which the Texan answered, 'Well, he is the man who ran for help.' "

The other story concerned a Texan and a New Yorker.

"There is a story about a Texan who went to New York and told a New Yorker that he could jump off the Empire State Building and live. The Easterner said, 'Well, that would be an accident.' He said, 'Suppose I did it twice?' The Easterner said, 'That would be an accident, too.'

" 'Suppose I did it three times?'

"And the Easterner said, 'That would be a habit.' "

TEXAS

Texas has sent twenty-one Democratic congressmen to Congress and one Republican—a fair proportion, a good average.

—El Paso, Texas, September 12, 1960

THURMOND, STROM

At a press conference the President was asked by a reporter: "This being Valentine's Day, sir, do you think it might be a good idea if you would call Senator Strom Thurmond of South Carolina down to the White House for a heart-to-heart talk over what he calls your defeatist foreign policy?"

"Well," replied President Kennedy, "I think that that meeting should probably be prepared at a lower level."

TOLERANCE

Tolerance implies no lack of commitment to one's own beliefs. Rather, it condemns the oppression or persecution of others.

—letter to the National Conference of Christians and Jews, October 10, 1960

TOUCHÉ

Reading a CIA report, Presidential aide Major General Chester Clifton came across the word *draconian*. Puzzled by its meaning, he looked it up and wrote the definition in the margin: "Cruel, inhuman!"

When President Kennedy read the report, he noticed the marginalia. "Who put this in here?" he asked.

"I did," Clifton answered.

"That's the trouble with you military," said JFK. "Now

if you'd had a classic Harvard education, you would have known what the word meant."

A few days later, JFK was reading another CIA report and stumbled across a technical military term, *permissive link*. Kennedy asked Clifton, "What's this mean?"

Clifton explained it, adding, "Mr. President, if you'd had a classic military education at West Point, you would have known what the word was."

The President laughed and said to Clifton, "Touché."

TRADE

We stand at a great divide: we must either trade or fade.

—New Orleans, May 4, 1962

The trade of a nation expresses in a very concrete way its aims and its aspirations. When the people of Boston in 1773 threw cargoes of tea into the harbor, the American Revolution was in effect under way, symbolized by this revolution against a tariff—a tariff which meant taxation without representation.

—at a conference on trade policy, May 17, 1962

Most Americans were largely unaware of the benefits of foreign trade. Many can "see" an import, but very few could "see" an export.

—at a conference on trade policy, May 17, 1962

TRANSPORTATION

I believe the way to a more modern economical choice of national transportation service is through increased competition and decreased regulation.

—State of the Union message, January 14, 1963

TREES

"Many thanks for your gracious message," President Kennedy replied to Prime Minister Diefenbaker of Canada after a tree-planting ceremony aggravated his back during a Presidential visit to Canada. "The tree will be there long after the discomfort is gone."

(see S.O.B.)

TROUBLE

" 'If there is going to be trouble, let it come in my time, so that my children may live in peace.' " President Kennedy concluded a speech in Seattle with a quote from Thomas Paine. "We live in a troublesome time, but let it come in our time, so that in this country and around the world our children and their children may live in peace and security."

TRUMAN, HARRY

Congressman Kennedy made a name for himself criticizing President Truman's foreign policy. Not surprisingly, Harry Truman was initially unsupportive of Kennedy's Presidential candidacy. "It's not the Pope I'm afraid of," said Harry Truman in his inimitable style. "It's the pop!" (referring to Joseph Kennedy).

Before John Kennedy was nominated at the 1960 convention, Harry Truman said that Senator Kennedy was not his first choice for the nomination.

Asked to comment on Truman's remark, Senator Kennedy replied: "He said we must all join together to secure the best man. I did not feel that on that occasion he was asking me to step aside."

After the nomination, Truman supported Kennedy.

President Kennedy welcomed the former President when Truman revisited the White House in November 1961, and favored the dinner guests with a few selections on the piano.

After the piano recital was over, President Kennedy was heard to remark: "Don't say there is no justice in the world. Stalin has been kicked out of Lenin's tomb and President Truman is back in the White House."

On May 8, 1963, Truman's 79th birthday, President Kennedy called the former President and said:

"I must say that I share the view of the country that you can't be 79 when you can out-walk Bobby and out-talk Hubert. I think we can look forward to a lot more good years."

As fate would have it, Harry Truman outlived John Kennedy by nine years.

TRUTH

The truth does not die. The desire for liberty cannot be fully suppressed.

—address at the Free University, West Berlin, June 26, 1963

What does truth require? It requires us to face the facts as they are, not to involve ourselves in self-deception; to refuse to think merely in slogans.

—address at the Free University, West Berlin, June 26, 1963

For the great enemy of the truth is very often not the lie —deliberate, contrived, and dishonest—but the myth— persistent, persuasive, and unrealistic. Too often we hold fast to the clichés of our forebears. We subject all facts to a prefabricated set of interpretations. We enjoy the comfort of opinion without the discomfort of thought.

—commencement, Yale University, June 11, 1962

There are few if any issues where all the truth and all the right and all the angels are on one side.

—*Profiles in Courage*, 1956

TWO-PARTY SYSTEM

The two-party system remains not because both are rigid but because both are flexible.

—*Profiles in Courage*, 1956

U

UDALL, STEWART

Secretary of the Interior Stewart Udall was chatting with the daughter of President Ayub Khan of Pakistan at a Mount Vernon reception hosted by President Kennedy.

Secretary Udall told her he once climbed a mountain in Pakistan. He was mistaken; the mountain he was referring to was in neighboring Afghanistan.

President Kennedy, overhearing, interceded.

"Madam, that is why I named Mr. Udall Secretary of the *Interior*."

UNEMPLOYMENT

They say there is waste in government. There may be, and we are working to get rid of it, but let us not forget the waste in four million unemployed men and women.

—television address to the nation, September 18, 1963

Youth unemployment poses one of the most expensive and explosive social and economic problems now facing this country. We urgently need to improve our schools and colleges, to reduce the number of dropouts, to reduce the number of unskilled workers, to keep young people out of the labor market until they are ready for the jobs which automation creates, instead of those it is sure to replace.

—remarks in Chicago, March 23, 1963
(see EDUCATION, HIGH SCHOOL DROPOUTS)

UNIONS

"I must say I hope I have normal courage as a politician and candidate for office," Jack Kennedy confessed to a union convention in Portland, "but I don't have quite enough courage to settle the dispute as to whether we should have craft unions or industrial unions. I will let you gentlemen settle that."

UNITED

United, there is little we cannot do. . . . Divided, there is little we can do.

—inaugural address, January 20, 1961

UNITED NATIONS

For in the development of this organization rests the only true alternative to war—and war appeals no longer as a rational alternative.

—United Nations address, September 25, 1961

Disarmament without checks is but a shadow—and a community without law is but a shell. Already the United

Nations has become both the measure and the vehicle of man's most generous impulses—a means of holding man's violence within bounds.

—United Nations address, September 25, 1961

But the great question which confronted this body in 1945 is still before us: whether man's cherished hopes for progress and peace are to be destroyed by terror and disruption, whether the "foul winds of war" can be tamed in time to free the cooling winds of reason, and whether the pledges of our Charter are to be fulfilled or defied—pledges to secure peace, progress, human rights and world law.

—United Nations address, September 25, 1961

Today the United Nations is primarily the protector of the small and the weak and a safety valve for the strong. Tomorrow it can form the framework for a world of law, a world in which no nation dictates the destiny of another, and in which the vast resources now devoted to destructive means will serve constructive ends.

—State of the Union message, January 14, 1963

UNITED STATES

The United States did not rise to greatness by waiting for others to lead.

—State of the Union message, January 11, 1962

Our nation is commissioned by history to be either an observer of freedom's failure or the cause of its success.

—State of the Union message, January 11, 1962

The United States is becoming increasingly identified in the minds of the people with the goal they move toward: a better life with freedom.

—message to Congress, March 12, 1962

These are extraordinary times. And we face an extraordinary challenge. Our strength as well as our convictions have imposed upon this nation the role of leader in freedom's cause. No role in history could be more difficult or more important. We stand for freedom. That is our conviction for ourselves; that is our only commitment to others. No friend, no neutral and no adversary should think otherwise. We are not against any man, or any nation, or any system, except as it is hostile to freedom.

—message to Congress, May 25, 1961

Speaking for the United States of America, I welcome such a contest. For we believe that truth is stronger than error—and that freedom is more enduring than coercion. And in the contest for a better life, all the world can be a winner.

—United Nations address, September 20, 1963
(see AMERICA, FREEDOM)

UNITED STRENGTH

We live in a world in which our own united strength and will must be our first reliance.

—remarks in Frankfurt, Germany, June 25, 1963

UNIVERSITY

"I feel honored to join you at this distinguished university," President Kennedy greeted his audience at the University of Maine. "In the year 1717, King George I of

England donated a very valuable library to Cambridge University and at very nearly the same time, had occasion to dispatch a regiment to Oxford. The King, remarked one famous wit, had judiciously observed the condition of both universities—one was a learned body in need of loyalty and the other was a loyal body in need of learning."

JFK smiled graciously. "I am deeply honored by the degree which you awarded me today and I think it is appropriate to speak at this university known for both loyalty and learning."

(see LEADERSHIP AND LEARNING, SCHOLARS)

URBAN COMPLEXES

In less than twenty years we can expect well over half of our expanded population to be living in forty great urban complexes. Many smaller places will also experience phenomenal growth.

—message to Congress, April 4, 1962

VAT 69

"I have a very grave announcement," President Kennedy said in mock solemnity to a Gridiron Club crowd in Washington, D.C. "The Soviet Union has once again recklessly embarked upon a provocative and extraordinary change in the status quo in an area which they know full well I regard as having a special and historic relationship. I refer to the deliberate and sudden deployment of Mr. Adhzubei to the Vatican."

The President was alluding to the fact that Mr. Adzhubei, Premier Khrushchev's son-in-law, had made an unprecedented visit to Rome.

"I am told that this plot was worked out by a group of Khrushchev's advisers who have all been excommunicated from the Church. It is known as Ex-Com.

"Reliable refugee reports have also informed us that hundreds of Marxist bibles have been unloaded and are being hidden in caves throughout the Vatican.

"We will now pursue the contingency plan for protecting the Vatican City which was previously prepared by the National Security Council. The plan is known as Vat 69."

VICE PRESIDENT

When a well-meaning friend told Jack Kennedy that he would have no trouble getting the vice presidential nomination in 1960, he just shook his head.

"Let's not talk so much about vice," he said. "I'm against vice in any form."

VIETNAM

President Kennedy once told Arthur Schlesinger that if troops were sent to Vietnam they would be greeted with an ovation but "in four days" few would remember.

"Then we will be told we have to send in more troops," JFK spoke prophetically. "It's like taking a drink. The effect wears off, and you have to take another."

VISION

This is our guide for the present and our vision for the future: a free community of nations, independent but interdependent, uniting north and south, east and west, in one great family of man, outgrowing and transcending the hates and fears that rend our age.

—State of the Union message, January 11, 1962
(see GOALS)

VISIONARIES

So we are all idealists. We are all visionaries. Let it not be said of this Atlantic generation that we left ideals and visions to the past, nor purpose and determination to our adversaries.

—remarks in Frankfurt, Germany, June 25, 1963

VOTE

In a free society, those with the power to govern are necessarily responsive to those with the right to vote.

—message to Congress, February 28, 1963

The right to vote in a free American election is the most powerful and precious right in the world—and it must not be denied on the grounds of race or color. It is a potent key to achieving other rights of citizenship.

—message to Congress, February 28, 1963

VOTE-BUYING

During the 1960 election campaign, Jack Kennedy was sometimes accused of trying to buy the election with his daddy's money. He acknowledged it humorously at a Gridiron dinner in Washington:

"I have just received the following telegram from my generous Daddy. It says, 'Dear Jack: Don't buy a single vote more than is necessary. I'll be damned if I'm going to pay for a landslide.' "

VOTE-SELLING

Campaigning in Wisconsin, Jack Kennedy was annoyed when a heckler called out, "Kennedy, I hear that your dad offered only two dollars a vote. With all your dough, can't you do better than that?"

"You know that statement is false," JFK retorted. "It's

sad that the only thing you have to offer is your vote, and you're willing to sell that."

VOTING PUBLIC

One of the hazards of political courage is that it often costs the leader the support and confidence of the voting public. The courageous politician, however, is ever hopeful that the voters will change their views in time. JFK wrote in *Profiles in Courage*:

> If their careers are temporarily or even permanently buried under an avalanche of abusive editorials, poison-pen letters, and opposition votes at the polls—as they sometimes are, for that is the risk they take—they await the future with hope and confidence, aware of the fact that the voting public frequently suffers from what ex-Congressman T. V. Smith called the lag "between our way of thought and our way of life." Smith compared it to the subject of an anonymous poem:
>
> There was a dachshund once, so long
> He hadn't any notion
> How long it took to notify
> His tail of his emotion;
> And so it happened, while his eyes
> Were filled with woe and sadness,
> His little tail went wagging on
> Because of previous gladness.

WAR

Historians report that in 1914, with most of the world already plunged in war, Prince von Bülow, the former German chancellor, said to the then–Chancellor Bethmann-Hollweg, "How did it all happen?" And Bethmann-Hollweg replied, "Ah, if only one knew." My fellow Americans, if this planet is ever ravaged by nuclear war, if 300 million Americans, Russians and Europeans are wiped out by a sixty-minute nuclear exchange, if the pitiable survivors of that devastation can then endure the ensuing fire, poison, chaos and catastrophe, I do not want one of those survivors to ask another, "How did it all happen?" and to receive the incredible reply, "Ah, if only one knew."

Therefore, while maintaining our readiness for war, let us exhaust every avenue for peace. Let us always make clear our willingness to talk, if talk will help, and our readiness to fight, if fight we must.

—remarks at the University of Maine, October 19, 1963

Unconditional war can no longer lead to unconditional victory. It can no longer serve to settle disputes. It can no longer concern the great powers alone. For a nuclear disaster, spread by wind and water and fear, could well engulf the great and the small, the rich and the poor, the committed and the uncommitted alike. Man must put an end to war—or war will put an end to mankind.

—United Nations address, September 25, 1961

The 1930s taught us a clear lesson: aggressive conduct, if allowed to go unchecked and unchallenged, ultimately leads to war.

—Cuban Missile Crisis address, October 22, 1962

This generation learned from bitter experience that either brandishing or yielding to threats can only lead to war. But firmness and reason can lead to the kind of peaceful solution in which my country profoundly believes.

—United Nations address, September 25, 1961

Today no war has been declared—and however fierce the struggle may be, it may never be declared in the traditional fashion. Our way of life is under attack. Those who make themselves our enemy are advancing around the globe. The survival of our friends is in danger. And yet no war has been declared, no borders have been crossed by marching troops, no missiles have been fired.

—address to newspaper publishers, April 27, 1961

WAR AND PEACE

The science of weapons and war has made us all . . . one world and one human race, with one common destiny. In such a world absolute sovereignty no longer assures us of absolute security. The conventions of peace must pull abreast and then ahead of the inventions of war. The United Nations, building on its successes and learning from its failures, must be developed into a genuine world security system.

—United Nations address, September 20, 1963

WASHINGTON, D.C.

Washington is a city of Southern efficiency and Northern charm.

WASHINGTON, GEORGE

President George Washington stood by the Jay Treaty with Great Britain to save our young nation from a war it could not survive, despite his knowledge that it would be immensely unpopular among a people ready to fight. Tom Paine told the President that he was "treacherous in private friendship and a hypocrite in public. . . . The world will be puzzled to decide whether you are an apostate or imposter; whether you have abandoned good principles, or whether you ever had any."

With bitter exasperation, Washington exclaimed: "I would rather be in my grave than in the Presidency"; and to Jefferson he wrote:

> I am accused of being the enemy of America, and subject to the influence of a foreign country . . . and every act of

my administration is tortured, in such exaggerated and indecent terms, as could scarcely be applied to Nero, to a notorious defaulter, or even to a common pickpocket.

But he stood firm.

—*Profiles in Courage*, 1956

WATCHDOG COMMITTEES

A reporter asked for Kennedy's reaction to Senator Margaret Chase Smith's ambitious proposal to create a Senate "Watchdog Committee."

"To watch Congressmen and Senators?" JFK shrugged, and smiled. "Well, that will be fine if they feel they should be watched."

WATER

Our nation has been blessed with a bountiful supply of water; but it is not a blessing we can regard with complacency. We now use over 300 billion gallons of water a day, much of it wastefully.

—message to Congress on natural resources, February 23, 1961

WATER POLLUTION

Pollution of our country's rivers and streams has, as a result of our rapid population and industrial growth and change, reached alarming proportions. To meet all needs—domestic, agricultural, industrial, recreational—we shall have to use and reuse the same water, maintaining quality as well as quantity. In many areas of the country we need new sources of supply, but in all areas we must protect the supplies we have.

—message to Congress on natural resources, February 23, 1961

WATER RESOURCES

No water resources program is of greater long-range importance, for relief not only of our shortages, but for arid nations the world over, than our efforts to find an effective and economical way to convert water from the world's greatest, cheapest natural resources, our oceans, into water fit for consumption in the home and by industry. Such a breakthrough would end bitter struggles between neighbors, states and nations, and bring new hope for millions who live out their lives in dire shortage of usable water and all its physical and economic blessings.

—message to Congress on natural resources, February 23, 1961
(see NATURAL RESOURCES)

WEALTH

We are not developing the nation's wealth for its own sake. Wealth is the means, and people are the ends. All our material riches will avail us little if we do not use them to expand the opportunities of our people.

—State of the Union message, January 11, 1962

WEBSTER, DANIEL

Daniel Webster is familiar to many of us today as the battler for Jabez Stone's soul against the devil in Stephen Vincent Benet's story. But in his own lifetime, he had many battles against the devil for his own soul—and some he lost. Webster, wrote one of his intimate friends, was "a compound of strength and weakness, dust and divinity," or in Emerson's words "a great man with a small ambition."

There could be no mistaking he was a great man—he looked like one, talked like one, was treated like one and insisted he was one. With all his faults and failings, Daniel

Webster was undoubtedly the most talented figure in our Congressional history: not in his ability to win men to a cause—he was no match in that with Henry Clay; not in his ability to hammer out a philosophy of government—Calhoun outshone him there; but in his ability to make alive and supreme the latent sense of oneness, of Union, that all Americans felt but which few could express.

But how Daniel Webster could express it!

The peroration of his reply to Senator Hayne of South Carolina, when secession had threatened twenty years earlier, was a national rallying cry memorized by every schoolboy—"Liberty and Union, now and forever, one and inseparable!"

Such was the perilous state of the nation in the early months of 1850.

And so came the 7th of March, 1850, the only day in history which would become the title of a speech delivered on the Senate floor. No one recalls today—no one even recalled in 1851—the formal title Webster gave his address, for it had become the "Seventh of March" speech as much as Independence Day is known as the Fourth of July.

For three hours and eleven minutes, with only a few references to his extensive notes, Daniel Webster pleaded the Union's cause. Relating the grievances of each side, he asked for conciliation and understanding in the name of patriotism. The Senate's main concern, he insisted, was neither to promote slavery nor to abolish it, but to preserve the United States of America.

"Let us make our generation one of the strongest and brightest links in that golden chain which is destined, I fondly believe, to grapple the people of all states to this Constitution for ages to come."

There was no applause. Buzzing and astonished whispering, yes, but no applause.

—*Profiles in Courage*, 1956

(see CALHOUN, JOHN C.; CLAY, HENRY)

WEIGHT

Not unlike many other Americans, President Kennedy was preoccupied with his weight and weighed himself frequently.

One night, as the President was undressing for a swim, Ben Bradlee observed that he had put on a little weight.

JFK nodded. "Friday I weighed 171, and everyone told me I was looking great. Four days later, I weigh 177 and I had two helpings of that dessert tonight," JFK sighed, referring to whipped cream, meringue and chocolate sauce.

Bradley bet him he weighed more than 177 right now. The President rushed to the scale: it was 177 on the nose.

JFK shook his head. "But I weighed 175 after swimming!"

WELL WRITTEN

President Kennedy admired "well written" memos, as he admired any good writing. One of JFK's favorite literary devices was the reverse cliché (e.g., "Washington is a city of Southern efficiency and Northern charm") and he admired this style in writing of any kind, even governmental memos.

As an example of excellence in memo-writing, JFK cited a "well written" memo he received from CBS Washington bureau chief David Schoenbrun about King Hassad of Morocco. JFK said he was fascinated to read all the usual phrases, like "amusing, but not fun," "brave, but not courageous," reversed in Schoenbrun's memo. Schoenbrun's memo, according to JFK, described King Hassad as "courageous, but not brave," and "funny, but not amusing," and so it was a "damn good, well written memo."

WEST

We in the West will make it clear that we are not hostile to any people or system, providing they choose their own destiny without interfering with the free choice of others.

—address at the Free University, West Berlin, June 26, 1963

WEST VIRGINIA

After a hard-fought West Virginia campaign, Kennedy wrote to a friend: "Thank you for the cognac. I would like to say that I am planning to keep it to sip during the warm spring nights. Unfortunately last night I began to think about West Virginia and drank the whole bottle."

(see MINERS)

WESTERN HEMISPHERE

On the success of the Alliance, on our success in this hemisphere, depends the future of that human dignity and national independence for which our forebears in every country of the hemisphere struggled.

—remarks at Bogotá, Colombia, December 17, 1961

WHITE HOUSE

"About fifty years ago, an Irishman from New Ross traveled down to Washington with his family," President Kennedy told an Irish crowd in New Ross, Ireland, June 28, 1963, "and in order to tell his neighbors how well he was doing, he had his picture taken in front of the White House and said, 'This is our summer home. Come and see it.' "

WHITE HOUSE GARDENS

Strolling through the replanted White House gardens, President Kennedy gazed admiringly at the petunias and ageratum, sighed, and said, "This may go down as the real achievement of this administration."

WHITE HOUSE PRESS CORPS

Soon after taking office, President Kennedy spoke to a group of newspaper publishers. "If in the last few months, your White House reporters and photographers have been attending church services with regularity, that has surely done them no harm."

Alluding to the golf practices of his predecessor, the President continued, "On the other hand, I realize that your staff and wire service photographers may be complaining that they do not enjoy the same green privileges at the local golf courses which they once did. It is true that my predecessor did not object as I do to pictures of one's golfing skill in action. But neither, on the other hand, did he ever bean a Secret Service man."

(see GOLF, SAND TRAP)

WHITE HOUSE TOURISTS

Informed that the millionth tourist during his term of office was about to walk through the White House, President Kennedy asked:

"Will he be a Cuban or a freedom fighter or a woman in shorts?"

WHITES

Do you know the greatest minority in the world today? The greatest minority in the world today is whites. The whole world, Africa, Asia, the Middle East—people who are colored, yellow, brown, black, they look to us, they look to the Communists, and they want to decide which road they will take.

—remarks, Los Angeles, November 1, 1960

WINDS OF CHANGE

Now the winds of change appear to be blowing more strongly than ever, in the world of Communism as well as our own. For 175 years we have sailed with those winds at our back, and with the tides of human freedom in our favor. We steer our ship with hope, as Thomas Jefferson said, "leaving fear astern." Today we still welcome those winds of change, and we have every reason to believe that our tide is running strong.

—State of the Union message, January 14, 1963

WINTER

There is an old saying that only in the winter can you tell which trees are evergreens.

—remarks to Peace Corps volunteers, June 22, 1962

WISCONSIN

"I can make one boast that no other Presidential candidate in history can make," Jack Kennedy announced on the campaign trail at La Crosse, Wisconsin. "I have spent more time in the Third District than any candidate for the

Presidency since George Washington. I chased Hubert Humphrey all over this district and never caught him."

WISDOM

Wisdom requires the long view.

—commencement, University of California, Berkeley, March 23, 1962

WOMEN

"Looking at all you ladies and seeing what you have done with some of your distinguished officeholders," Jack Kennedy observed at a Democratic Women's breakfast, "I recall an experience of the suffragettes who picketed the White House back during the First World War. The leader of the suffragettes was arrested. And as she was taken away in a truck, she turned to her girls and said, 'Don't worry, girls. Pray to the Lord. *She* will protect you.' "

WOMEN VOTERS

John Kennedy attributed much of his success in politics to women voters. When running for the Senate in 1952, the "tea party" was a favorite Kennedy campaign practice.

"In the first place, for some strange reason there are more women than men in Massachusetts, and they live longer. Secondly, my grandfather, the late John F. Fitzgerald, ran for the United States Senate thirty-six years ago against my opponent's grandfather, Henry Cabot Lodge, and he lost by only 30,000 votes in an election where women were not allowed to vote. I hope that by impressing the female electorate I can more than take up the slack."

(see SEX APPEAL)

WOMEN'S STATUS

"I want to express my thanks to all of you for an important assignment," President Kennedy addressed the newly appointed President's Commission on the Status of Women. "We have established the Commission for two reasons. One is for my own self-protection: every two or three weeks Mrs. May Craig asks me what I am doing for women!"

WORK

Benjamin Bradlee, a friend of the President's, was laid up at home in bed with the flu. It was the first day of work Bradlee had missed in about twenty-five years.

President Kennedy called him at home at 2:30 in the afternoon. When Bradlee answered, the President said, "Don't you ever work anymore?"

WORLD

Never have the nations of the world had so much to lose, or so much to gain. Together we shall save our planet, or together we shall perish in its flames. Save it we can—and save it we must—and then shall we earn the eternal thanks of mankind and, as peacemakers, the eternal blessing of God.

—United Nations address, September 25, 1961

WORLD ECONOMY

Our job, in its largest sense, is to create a new partnership between the northern and southern halves of the world, to which all free nations can contribute, in which each free nation must assume a responsibility proportional to its means.

—message to Congress, March 22, 1961

WORLD FUTURE

In short, we believe that in all the world—in Eastern Europe as well as Western, in Southern Africa as well as Northern, in old nations as well as new—people must be free to choose their own future, without discrimination or dictation, without coercion or subversion.

—United Nations address, September 20, 1963

WORLD LAW

We far prefer world law, in the age of self-determination, to world war, in the age of mass extermination.

—United Nations address, September 25, 1961
(see LAW, SELF-DETERMINATION)

WORLD ORDER

We must be prepared to take our part in setting up a world order that will prevent the rise of a military dictatorship.

—*Why England Slept*, 1940, "Conclusion"

WORLD PEACE

It is the most important topic on earth: world peace.

We shall . . . do our part to build a world of peace where the weak are safe and the strong are just. We are not helpless before that task or hopeless of its success. Confident and unafraid, we labor on.

—commencement, American University, June 10, 1963

WORLDWIDE VICTORY

For we seek not the worldwide victory of one nation or system, but a worldwide victory of men. The modern globe is too small, its weapons are too destructive, they multiply too fast, and its disorders are too contagious to permit any other kind of victory.

—State of the Union message, January 14, 1963

WYETH, ANDREW

President and Mrs. Kennedy instituted the awards called the Medal of Freedom. JFK favored the artist Ben Shahn in the early selection, but eventually Andrew Wyeth was selected. The President resolved: "Next year, we'll have to go abstract."

YALE

"Let me begin by expressing my appreciation for the very deep honor you have conferred upon me," President Kennedy accepted an honorary degree from Yale as he began the 1962 commencement address.

"As General de Gaulle occasionally acknowledges America to be the daughter of Europe, so I am pleased to come to Yale, the daughter of Harvard.

"It might be said now that I have the best of both worlds—a Harvard education and a Yale degree.

"I am particularly glad to become a Yale man because as I think about my troubles, I find that a lot of them have come from other Yale men. Among businessmen, I have had a minor disagreement with Roger Blough [steel executive] of the Law School class of 1931 and I have had some complaints too from my friend, Henry Luce, of the class of 1920, not to mention, always, William F. Buckley, Jr., of the class of 1950."

YOUNG

"There are always some people who feel that Americans are always young and inexperienced and foreigners are always able and tough and great negotiators," President Kennedy proclaimed at a press conference. "But I don't think the United States would have acquired its present position of leadership in the free world if that view were correct."

John F. Kennedy, the youngest man ever elected President of the United States, always looked younger than his years.

He enjoyed telling how he was mistaken once for an elevator boy and several times for a page boy when he first entered the House of Representatives. Even when he was a senator in his thirties, a guard once tried to stop him from using a special telephone in the Capitol.

"Sorry, Mister," said the guard to the younger man, "these are reserved for the senators."

(see YOUTH)

YOUNG COUNTRY

"You're an old country," Premier Khrushchev told President Kennedy at their Vienna meeting on June 3, 1961. "We're a young country."

"If you'll look across the table," replied the forty-four-year-old American President, "you'll see that we're not so old."

YOUNG PEOPLE

John Kennedy always seemed to attract large numbers of very young people to hear his speeches. At Girard, Ohio, he commented on an especially young crowd:

"If we can lower the voting age to nine, we are going to sweep the state."

The future of these young people and the nation rests in large part on their access to college and graduate education.

—message to Congress, January 29, 1963

This combination of a tremendously increasing population among our young people, of less need for unskilled labor, of increasingly unskilled labor available, combines to form one of the most serious domestic problems that this country will face.

—commencement, San Diego State College, June 6, 1963
(see EMPLOYMENT GROWTH, LABOR DEMAND)

YOUTH

John F. Kennedy at age 43 became the youngest man elected President. He represented the potential of American youth.

"We dare not forget today that we are the heirs of that first revolution," affirmed President Kennedy in his inaugural address in 1961. "Let the word go forth from this time and place, to friend and foe alike, that the torch has been passed to a new generation of Americans . . ."

President Kennedy embodied both the youthfulness and agelessness of the American spirit and the American dream. JFK embodied in himself the union of old and young, "this old but youthful Union." As he described the country he loved he described himself, always growing older yet always youthful.

First, we need to strengthen our nation by investing in our youth. The future of any country which is dependent upon the will and wisdom of its citizens is damaged, and irreparably damaged, whenever any of its children are not educated to the full extent of their talents, from grade school through graduate school. Today an estimated four out of every ten students in the fifth grade will never finish high school, and that is a waste that we cannot afford.

—State of the Union message, January 14, 1963

A BRIEF BIOGRAPHY OF JOHN F. KENNEDY

~1917~

John Fitzgerald Kennedy is born on May 29, 1917, at home, 83 Beals Street, Brookline, Massachusetts, the second of nine children of financier Joseph Patrick Kennedy and Rose Fitzgerald Kennedy.

~1917–1926~

JFK lives at 83 Beals Street, Brookline, and attends Dexter School.

JFK, called "Jack," spends much of his childhood recuperating from ailments including scarlet fever, whooping cough, measles, chicken pox, bronchitis, tonsillitis, appendicitis, jaundice, and a bad back.

~1925~

Brother Robert Kennedy is born November 20.

~1926–1930~

JFK attends fourth, fifth, and sixth grades at Riverdale Country Day School, in the Bronx.

~1930~

JFK spends one year in Catholic preparatory school, Canterbury, in New Milford, Massachusetts.

~1931~

JFK enrolls in Choate, a private school in Wallingford, Connecticut.

~1932~

Brother Edward M. Kennedy born February 22.

~1931–1935~

JFK attends Choate prep school, where he is nicknamed "Rat Face" for his scrawny appearance.

JFK graduates only 64th of 112 students, but is voted "most likely to succeed."

~1935~

JFK studies at the London School of Economics during the summer and contracts jaundice.

JFK enrolls at Princeton University. A recurrence of jaundice forces his withdrawal.

~ 1936–1940 ~

JFK attends Harvard University, majoring in political science with an emphasis on international relations. He participates in sailing and holds a place on a champion sailing crew.

~ 1937 ~

Joseph P. Kennedy appointed Ambassador to Great Britain by President Roosevelt. JFK tours Europe with a friend from Choate, visiting France, Spain, and Italy, where he has an audience with the Pope.

~ 1938 ~

At age 21, John F. Kennedy receives a $1 million trust fund established by his father.

~ 1939 ~

JFK spends the second semester of his junior year working as secretary to his father, the Ambassador to Great Britain, and touring Europe. He visits Poland, Russia, Turkey, Germany, France, and his father's embassy in London.

~ 1940 ~

JFK graduates from Harvard *cum laude* with a Bachelor of Science degree. His senior honors thesis (entitled *Appeasement at Munich: The Inevitable Result of the Slowness of the British Democracy to Change from a Disarmament Policy*") is published as *Why England Slept* (New York, Wilfred Funk,

Inc.). The book is well received and becomes a bestseller; it earns JFK $40,000, the English royalties of which he donates to the bombed town of Plymouth, England.

JFK enrolls at Stanford Business School in the fall for graduate study in business but withdraws after six months.

~ 1941 ~

JFK tours South America. In September he enlists in the Navy.

~ 1941–1945 ~

JFK serves in the Navy from September 1941 to April 1945, rising from ensign to lieutenant.

~ 1943 ~

Through his father's influence, JFK gets a sea command as skipper of the *PT-109*. He holds the rank of lieutenant (j.g.).

On August 2, 1943, his torpedo boat is rammed in two by the Japanese destroyer *Amagiri* in the South Pacific. Two U.S. sailors are killed, the rest thrown into water aflame with burning gasoline.

JFK swims four hours to safety, towing an injured crewman by the life jacket strap with his teeth.

Days later they are discovered on Olasana Island by two natives. JFK scratches a message on a coconut shell with his knife: "Native knows posit. He can pilot. 11 alive need small boat."

The natives deliver the coconut shell to the Allies, who rescue Lt. Kennedy and the crew on August 8.

JFK earns a Purple Heart and the Navy Marine Corps medal. The citation signed by Admiral W. F. Halsey reads, in part, "His courage, endurance, and excellent leadership contributed to the saving of several lives and was in keeping with the highest traditions of the United States Naval Service."

JFK's back trouble is aggravated; he is rotated home in December and hospitalized.

~ 1944 ~

JFK's brother Joseph Kennedy, Jr., is killed piloting an airplane over Europe on August 12.

~ 1945 ~

JFK is honorably discharged from the Navy in April.

JFK works briefly as a journalist-correspondent for the New York *Journal American*, covering the United Nations Conference in San Francisco, founding the United Nations.

~ 1946 ~

JFK launches his political career, entering the congressional race in Massachusetts' Eleventh District.

JFK is elected to Congress November 5.

~ 1947 ~

JFK at age 29 takes a seat in the House of Representatives, where he serves three terms.

~1949~

JFK makes a speech in Congress on January 25 attacking Truman's foreign policy for letting China "fall" to the Communists.

~1952~

JFK announces his decision to seek a Senate seat and receives full support from the Kennedy family—parents, brothers, and sisters.

JFK defeats Henry Cabot Lodge, Jr., on November 4 to become a U.S. senator from Massachusetts.

~1953~

Senator John Kennedy, 36, marries Jacqueline Lee Bouvier, 24, on September 12, 1953, at St. Mary's Church in Newport, Rhode Island. The wedding is performed by Archbishop Richard Cushing, who reads a special blessing on the marriage from Pope Pius XII. Following a honeymoon in Acapulco, the couple settles in McLean, Virginia.

~1954~

Senator John Kennedy enters the Hospital for Special Surgery in New York and undergoes a difficult operation on October 21. Infection sets in. Twice in the next month he is given the last rites of his church. He rallies in December and is able to be flown on a stretcher to the Kennedy home in Palm Beach for the Christmas holidays.

~1955~

JFK returns in January to the Hospital for Special Surgery for a second operation, which is more successful. During the long months of convalescence, he works on a book, a collective biography of courageous senators who took unpopular stands on principle.

~1956–1957~

JFK's book *Profiles in Courage* (Harper, 1956) is a critical and commercial success, and wins the Pulitzer Prize for biography.

JFK is a candidate in August for the vice presidential nomination, but loses to Senator Estes Kefauver of Tennessee.

~1957~

Daughter Caroline Bouvier Kennedy born November 27.

~1958~

JFK is reelected to a second term in Senate by more than a million votes.

~1960~

JFK calls a press conference on January 2: "I am announcing today my candidacy for the Presidency of the United States."

JFK wins each of the seven primaries he enters.

On July 13 in Los Angeles John F. Kennedy is nominated on the first ballot with 806 votes to 409 votes for Lyndon Johnson. He chooses Johnson as his running mate.

JFK debates Richard M. Nixon in the first of four televised debates on September 26.

JFK wins the election on November 8 narrowly, 34,227,096 votes to 34,108,546 for Nixon. JFK is the youngest man and the first Catholic to be elected President.

Son John F. Kennedy, Jr., is born November 25.

~ 1961 ~

John F. Kennedy is sworn in January 20 as the first President born in the twentieth century and delivers a memorable inaugural address, announcing a "new generation" of leadership. (See INAUGURAL ADDRESS.)

JFK delivers his first State of the Union message January 29, stressing dangers abroad and economic problems at home.

JFK asks Congress on February 7 to raise the minimum wage from $1 to $1.25 an hour and extend coverage to over 4 million more workers.

JFK's Special Message to Congress on February 20 asks for a package of $5.6 billion for federal aid for education.

JFK's executive order of March 1 creates the Peace Corps.

JFK's Alliance for Progress announced March 13 at a White House reception.

JFK announces on March 28 the initiation of a program to rapidly build U.S. military strength.

The first man in space, Soviet Major Yuri Gagarin, orbits Earth on April 12.

The Bay of Pigs invasion of Cuba happens on April 17.

JFK confers with ex–President Eisenhower on Cuba at

Camp David, Maryland, holding a joint press conference on April 22.

The first U.S. man in space, Alan Shepard, completes his flight on May 5.

JFK proposes on May 25 a national effort by the U.S. to put an American space team on the moon "in this decade."

JFK and Mrs. Kennedy fly to Paris to confer with French President Charles de Gaulle on May 31.

JFK signs a bill doubling the federal effort to halt water pollution on July 20.

JFK signs the $1.25 Minimum Wage Bill on September 3.

JFK renews the American commitment to preserve the independence of the Republic of Vietnam and pledges assistance to its defense on December 15.

~ 1962 ~

JFK's State of the Union message on January 11 asks for authority to reduce tariffs and to reduce income taxes.

> A year ago, in assuming the tasks of the Presidency, I said that few generations in all history had been granted the role of being the great defender of freedom in its hour of maximum danger. This is our good fortune; and I welcome it now as I did a year ago. For it is the fate of this generation . . . to live with a struggle we did not start, in a world we did not make. But the pressures of life are not always distributed by choice. And while no nation has ever faced such a challenge, no nation has ever been so ready to seize the burden and the glory of freedom.

JFK establishes a United States Military Command in South Vietnam on February 8 with about 4,000 Americans acting as "advisers" and air support.

First U.S. orbital flight by John H. Glenn on February 20.

JFK's message to Premier Khrushchev on March 18 proposes a joint action in the exploration of outer space.

JFK denounces U.S. Steel's raising of steel prices on April 11 as unjustifiable and an irresponsible defiance of the public interest.

Steel price rises are rescinded on April 13.

JFK signs a bill on July 26 providing for a revision of public welfare laws, emphasizing family rehabilitation and training instead of dependency.

JFK orders federal troops and marshals on September 30 to ensure James Meredith's admission to the University of Mississippi and preserve order.

JFK signs on October 10 the first major improvement in the Food and Drug laws since 1938, protecting families against untested and ineffective drugs.

JFK signs the Trade Expansion Act on October 11, granting the President unprecedented authority to reduce or eliminate tariffs.

President Kennedy makes a television address on October 22 condemning the Soviet Union for lying about the "defensive" nature of the missile buildup in Cuba and orders a quarantine of Cuba.

Soviet Premier Khrushchev agrees on October 28 to halt construction of missile bases in Cuba and remove Soviet rockets under United Nations supervision. By the end of the year U.S. intelligence confirms removal of the missiles from Cuba.

~1963~

In his third State of the Union address on January 14, President Kennedy points to his achievements, including 22 months of uninterrupted economic recovery.

> Little more than one hundred weeks ago, I assumed the office of the President of the United States. In seeking the help of the Congress and our countrymen, I pledged no easy answers. I pledged, and asked, only toil and dedication. These the Congress and the people have given in good measure. And today, having witnessed in recent months a heightened respect for our national purpose and power, having seen the courageous calm of a united people in a perilous hour, and having observed a steady improvement in the opportunities and well-being of our citizens, I can report to you that the state of this old but youthful Union is good.

JFK sends Congress on January 17 the biggest budget ever, $98 billion, with a planned deficit of $10 billion.

JFK sends a Civil Rights message to Congress on February 28 with emphasis on African-American voting rights.

President Kennedy dispatches federal troops on May 12 to bases near Birmingham, Alabama, when race riots break out in Birmingham.

JFK makes an impassioned Civil Rights television address to the people on June 11.

JFK sends a strong Civil Rights message to Congress on June 19 urging legislation to give all Americans equal opportunity in education, employment, public accommodations, and access to federal programs.

JFK travels to Germany, Ireland, England, and Italy June 23–July 2.

President Kennedy makes an emotional speech at the Berlin Wall on June 26, stirring an audience of West Germans.

> All free men, wherever they may live, are citizens of Berlin, and, therefore, as a free man, I take pride in the words *"Ich bin ein Berliner."*

JFK's message to Congress on July 23 calls for modifying the nation's immigration laws, replacing the national origins system with a policy recognizing skills of the immigrant regardless of place of birth.

JFK addresses the nation on July 26 on the signing of the nuclear test ban treaty, banning tests in the atmosphere and space and under water.

A son, Patrick Bouvier Kennedy, is born on August 7, and dies two days later.

JFK stresses the need of a tax reduction bill to stimulate the economy on August 21.

JFK makes a statement in support of the March on Washington on August 28: "The cause of 20 million Negroes has been advanced by the program conducted so appropriately before the Nation's shrine to the Great Emancipator, but even more significant is the contribution to all mankind."

President Kennedy makes a statement on Vietnam on September 2: "In the final analysis it is their war. They are the ones who have to win it or lose it. We can help them . . . but they have to win it, the people of Vietnam, against the Communists."

JFK speaks of the role of the artist in society at the dedication of the Robert Frost Library in Amherst, Massachusetts, on October 26: "When power leads man toward arrogance, poetry reminds him of his limitations. . . . When power corrupts, poetry cleanses."

JFK calls on economic advisers on November 21 to prepare the "War on Poverty Program for 1964" and declares that almost all United States tariffs are subject to reduction.

President Kennedy is assassinated on November 22 in Dallas, Texas, and pronounced dead at 1:00 P.M. at Parkland Memorial Hospital.

Vice President Johnson is sworn in as the 36th President on the Presidential plane in Dallas.

Lee Harvey Oswald, accused assassin of President Kennedy, is shot and killed by Jack Ruby on November 24 while in custody of the Dallas police.

State funeral of John Fitzgerald Kennedy and burial on November 25 with full military honors in Washington in the Arlington National Cemetery.

~ 1964 ~

Much of the Kennedy civil rights legislative program is enacted in the 1964 Civil Rights Bill signed by President Johnson.

~ 1969 ~

The U.S. space program achieves President Kennedy's stated national goal of landing a man on the moon before the end of the decade as Neil Armstrong, commander of Apollo 11, becomes the first man to set foot on the moon on July 21.

~ 1979 ~

The House Select Committee on Assassinations, called to reinvestigate the deaths of JFK and civil rights leader Martin Luther King, Jr., completes a two-year investigation and concludes that a conspiracy was "likely" and that organized crime figures were "probably" involved.

ADDITIONAL SUBJECT REFERENCES

ADAMS, JOHN: *Profiles in Courage*, Ch. X, p. 207; ARTIST: Arlington, Virginia, May 9, 1963; BASEBALL: White House Youth Concert, August 6, 1962; BREAKFAST: September 23, 1960; BUSINESSMEN'S LUNCHEON: National Association of Manufacturers, December 6, 1961; COLUMBUS, OHIO: January 6, 1962; DAUGHTERS: Syracuse, New York, September 29, 1960; DEMOCRACY: Remarks to Inter-American Press Association; DINNER SPEECHES: May 30, 1961; EXPERIENCE: Alfred E. Smith Memorial Dinner, New York City, October 19, 1960; FARMER: Grand View, Missouri, October 22, 1960; FOOTBALL: December 5, 1961; IVORY COAST: May 22, 1962; KENNEDY, JACQUELINE: SHAPE Headquarters, Paris, France, June 2, 1961; KENNEDY, ROBERT: Alfalfa Club, Washington, D.C., January 21, 1961; KENNEDY, TED: September 20, 1962; LADY: New York City, November 5, 1960; McNAMARA: press conference, January 25, 1963; MAINE POTATO: Presque Isle, Maine, September 12, 1960; PRAY: prayer breakfast, Washington, D.C., February 7, 1963; ROCKING CHAIR: note to Arthur Sulzberger, May 1, 1961; ROOSEVELT, FRANKLIN D.: October 17, 1960; SHRIVER, EUNICE: Libertyville, Illinois, October 25, 1960; TROUBLE: Seattle, November 16, 1961; UNIONS: Portland,

Oregon, September 7, 1960; WATCHDOG COMMITTEES: March 21, 1963; WHITE HOUSE PRESS CORPS: American Newspaper Publishers Association, April 27, 1961; WISCONSIN: October 23, 1960; YALE: Yale Commencement Address, June 11, 1962; YOUNG PEOPLE: October 9, 1960.

BIBLIOGRAPHY

Adler, Bill. *The Kennedy Wit.* Citadel Press, 1964.

Bishop, Jim. *A Day in the Life of President Kennedy.* Random House, 1964.

Bradlee, Benjamin C. *Conversations with Kennedy.* W. W. Norton, 1975.

Chase, Harold William. *Kennedy and the Press: The News Conference.* Crowell, 1965.

David, Lester, and David, Irene. *JFK: The Wit, the Charm, the Tears: Remembrances from Camelot.* PaperJacks, 1988.

Donald, Aida DiPace. *John F. Kennedy and the New Frontier.* Hill, 1966.

Donovan, Robert. *PT-109: John F. Kennedy in World War II.* Fawcett Crest, 1961.

Fairlie, Henry. *The Kennedy Promise: The Politics of Expectation.* Doubleday, 1973.

FitzSimmons, Louise. *The Kennedy Doctrine.* Random House, 1972.

Gadney, Reg. *Kennedy.* Holt, Rinehart, and Winston, 1983.

Hamilton, Nigel. *JFK: Reckless Youth.* Random House, 1992.

Kennedy, John F. *Why England Slept.* Wilfred Funk, 1940.

———. *Profiles in Courage.* Harper & Brothers, 1956.

———. *The Strategy of Peace.* Harper & Brothers, 1960.

———. *To Turn the Tide*. Harper & Brothers, 1962.

———. *A Nation of Immigrants*. Anti-Defamation League of B'Nai B'Rith, reprinted by permission of Harper & Row, 1964.

———. *The Cumulated Indexes to the Public Papers of the Presidents of the United States: John F. Kennedy, 1961–1963*. KTO Press, 1977.

Kennedy, Rose Fitzgerald. *Times to Remember*. Doubleday, 1974.

Lasky, Victor. *J.F.K.: The Man and the Myth*. Macmillan, 1963.

Lincoln, Evelyn. *My Twelve Years with John F. Kennedy*. David McKay Co., 1965.

Lowe, Jacques. *The Kennedy Legacy: A Generation Later*. Viking Studio Books, 1988.

Manchester, William. *Portrait of a President: JFK in Profile*. Little, Brown, 1967.

———. *One Brief Shining Moment: Remembering Kennedy*. Little, Brown, 1983.

Martin, Ralph G. *A Hero for Our Time*. Macmillan, 1983.

Mills, Judie. *John F. Kennedy*. Franklin Watts, 1988.

Newcomb, Joan I. *John F. Kennedy: An Annotated Bibliography*. Scarecrow Press, 1977.

O'Donnell, Kenneth P., Powers, David F., et al. *Johnny, We Hardly Knew Ye: Memories of John F. Kennedy*. Little, Brown, 1970.

Schlesinger, Arthur M. *A Thousand Days: John F. Kennedy in the White House*. Houghton Mifflin, 1965.

Shaw, Mark. *John F. Kennedys: A Family Album*. Farrar, 1964.

Sidey, Hugh. *John F. Kennedy, President*. Atheneum, 1964.

Sorenson, Theodore. *Kennedy*. Harper & Row, 1965.

———. *The Kennedy Legacy*. Macmillan, 1969.

White, Theodore H. *The Making of the President: 1960*. Atheneum, 1961.

Wills, Garry. *The Kennedy Imprisonment: A Meditation in Power*, Little, Brown, 1982.